PASSCHENDAELE

Peter Barton

PASSCHENDAELE

Peter Barton

In association with the Imperial War Museum

With research by Jeremy Banning

CONSTABLE · LONDON

For Irene Smith

Constable & Robinson Ltd
3 The Lanchesters
162 Fulham Palace Road
London W6 9ER
www.constablerobinson.com

First published in the UK in 2007 by Constable, an imprint of Constable & Robinson Ltd

A copy of the British Library Cataloguing in Publication data is available from the British Library

ISBN: 978-1-84529-422-9

Designed by Les Dominey
Cartography by William Smuts
Line drawings by Andy Gammon
Printed and bound in Italy

Title page
The portico of St Martin's Cathedral,
Ypres as seen through the central
archway of the Cloth Hall. September
1917.

CONTENTS

PROLOGUE
BY CAPTAIN MATTHEW ROACH MC

23RD JANUARY 1916

Sunday night in the trenches. A great big, peaceful placid moon is climbing majestically up from the dim shadowy east flooding the sleeping earth with her pure white light. There is a suspicion of frost in the air. The sky is cloudless and clear and the stars hang like suspended arc-lamps in the shimmering heavens. It is a perfect night, nature is tranquil and calm.

And somewhere up behind those wondrous systems, galaxies and clusters of mighty worlds, circling in majestic unity through eternity's of time and space there is, we are told, a Being, a God, a force that directs and controls, creates and destroys as suits His purpose or His whim. He brought these mighty orbs into being … He sees the cooling of the whirling spheres, the crusting and the shaping. He sees at last the beginnings of life, He watches as the senseless protoplasms gradually fashion into organisms, and organisms, though subject and submissive to His great eternal laws, grow into many various and wonderful shapes. And then as he watches, immutable and unseen, the fires of the planets cool, and the life that thrilled and throbbed on their verdant faces wither and die, the splendid forests and the grassy plains bleach naked and sear until only jagged rocks remain. And then, as the ages roll on, the great central sun that bred these ancient worlds also grows cold and lifeless and as its power wanes so the lesser worlds stray farther and farther from their dying parent until one by one, drawn by some force more powerful, some sun more virile, they leave the orbit in which they have circled since the beginning and leap off into the measureless infinities of space, to collide perhaps with other worlds and form a new nebula, and Matter commences the Great Circle all over again.

And so the Almighty Force works out his inscrutable will from the Beginning to the end.

So say the scholars and the seers. The priests and prophets do not quite concur. Their vision is hardly as comprehensive or as clear. They are more concerned with inspiration than with logical and rational thought. They profess an intimate and comradely acquaintance with the All Highest, but these other worlds exist only, for them, "to give light unto the earth". And so they maintain that the Great Force with whom they are in daily communion is mainly concerned with this little pin-head planet on which we microscopic maggots live and love, and breed and fight and die. They claim that we are the supreme creations of the Great Potter who, when He fashioned us, did so "in his own image", made us the culmination of and the masterpiece of His omnipotent handicraft (How God must laugh), … Why some of our priests and prophets, those we pay to expound to us the will and wishes of the almighty, profess to be on terms of the closest intimacy with Him, knowing His wishes, interpreting His desires, stating positively His likings and aversions, His intentions and plans. Unhappily there is no unanimity amongst them but each warring sect has a large following who have implicit faith in their leader's perfect understanding of the Great Omnipotence. Lacking unanimity they even sometimes enter into acrimonious controversy concerning the attributes and purposes of the Divine and waste much bitter invective on each other.

So much for the Priests and Prophets.

About a year and a half ago the nations of the earth declared war on each other. Not for many years had the cannon of contending armies been heard in Western Europe and the people's rulers, with the arrogant ambition which comes of full bellies, accumulated power, and much wealth were eagerly anxious to draw the long white swords which they were wont to rattle so threateningly when dealing with the humble and meek, and which were rusting in their scabbards. And so they went to war. They, the people, proceeded to kill each other wholesale with the terrible engines and machines which they had been busily perfecting during the long years of peace. The best brains of civilisation had been engaged on the invention and manufacture of these machines, for great wealth and honour accrued to him who could devise and construct improvements in the man killing equipment of the armies, and each nation jealously competed with the other in the provision of these things. The success of these marvellous engines of war has been astounding and the numbers of lives lost, and the amount of blood shed, far transcending anything in history, has provided ample testimony of the cleverness of the human race in devising means for the extermination of humanity.

Each nation, of course, invoked the aid and sympathy of the Almighty in this horrible business and the priests and prophets of the various peoples interpreted the intentions and purposes of the Almighty to their credulous flocks. And to each side he was, for the time being, a very real God who would surely intervene and smite the Assyrians, their enemies. Nevertheless, not being quite sure in their innermost hearts they continued to pile up a colossal plenitude of the engines of war so that, if it eventually happened that God should definitely favour the other side, they would still have the comforting consciousness of the power and omnipotence of their Big batteries. Up to now the Almighty certainly seems to have favoured the "big gun" side, but the others are fast making up their deficiencies in this respect and will soon be able to claim a decided advantage. Perhaps the Almighty, perceiving the trend of affairs, will soon transfer his favours, and the great victories which are expected this year will be attributed by the priests and prophets of what has hitherto been the losing side, to His divine intervention and proclaim exultingly to a watching world as conclusive proof of the righteousness of their cause.

I don't know what has impelled me to write the foregoing. Most people will consider it blasphemous and irreverent. But I make no apology. I have simply recorded the unbidden thoughts that have flitted through my mind this Sabbath night. As written they are a satire on the attitude of Christianity towards the war. It is surely no worse to write than to think, and I do not believe that Christianity today is expressive of the teachings and precepts of its founder.

Very unmartial and unsoldierly thoughts too, some may think. Perhaps so, but I think every man in the trenches is, more or less, a dual personality, a sort of Dr. Jekyll and Mr. Hyde. He will go over the top with a red film over his eyes and the lust of killing in his heart, but in the cold calm hours of his sentry duty at night he realises the wanton futility, the savage, senseless wickedness of it all. The "common soldier" (a rotten expression) thinks deeper thoughts than he is ever credited with, he is no "dumb driven cattle", he is a philosopher, but he is inarticulate, he cannot express his profoundest convictions and perhaps would not if he could, but his brain is quietly active and when this war is over I am looking for a revolt against all that makes war possible such as has never been seen before.

Coming in from the mine just now I passed the stretcher-bearers carrying a limp and bloodstained form to the dressing station – or the burial ground, I do not know which. Probably the latter for he had been hit in the head. His face was covered with blood save where patches of white skin gleamed ghastly in the moonlight. His arms swung limp over the side of the stretcher and his head lolled from side to side in horribly suggestive fashion. No uncommon occurrence but it set me thinking and explains the mood which prompted me to write the foregoing.

The attitude of Christianity toward the war is, to me, entirely out of keeping with the teachings and admonitions of the meek and lowly Jesus. God has no chosen race. I would not want a God that had. God has, I believe, a great love and pity for all this seething and writhing world of maggot-like humanity, pitying most those who have erred most, concerned most with those who have strayed farthest. And I believe that He looks down on this welter of universal hate and carnage with eyes of infinite compassion. That He has planned or pre-ordained the conflict, I refuse to believe. That He soils His omnipotent Majesty by descending to aid or abet either side, I refuse to believe. That the war is anything but man's reversion to his baser instincts and passions, I refuse to believe. War is the capital crime of nations. War is the Great Sin of Communities. And just as God looks down on individual sin so He looks down on the great collective sin of war, with pity and commiseration I believe, but with no power to intervene. Man must work out his own salvation for he has been endowed with the gifts of conscience and free-will which make him the arbiter of his own destiny. And so he climbs a little in a century of peace only to drop back again into the mire of his primitive state in a year or two of war, and the net gain of his progress is pitifully small. Almost hopeless it seems to talk of progress when all the most progressive nations are clawing and hacking at each others throats. I have before me an old newspaper with reports of the Intercession Day Services throughout England. And the leaders of Christianity throughout the land have offered up long and eloquent prayers for the favour and assistance of the Almighty in the breaking and exterminating of the German nation. To me it is nauseating that Christianity can give us nothing greater than this. I believe that, according to our circumscribed understanding our cause is just, but for pity's sake let us keep God out of it. Let us retain something that is not steeped in blood. Let us keep our conceptions of Divinity above the carnage. The slaughter, and the wickedness of it all. Let us keep our Great Ideal unbesmirched.

I cannot claim to have the faith that will move mountains. I do not claim to be one of the elect on the highway to Heaven. But I would rather denounce the little faith I have and become an atheist, heretic, anything, than have a God whose hands were dripping with the blood of my fellow-creatures, however vile they may be. It may occur to some that I am doing what I accused the orthodox of – making God in *my* own image, according my own ideals. Perhaps so, but at least I am convinced that my God is a greater, higher, grander God than theirs.

Just one more thought as the preachers say. I have heard of the spread of religious thought and feeling among our fighting men in the trenches. I have looked for it in vain. I do not believe that it exists. Men here live hard, curse hard, and die hard. I have seen many going out on the Long Trail, torn and bleeding by bullet or shell but they spoke no word of religion. Some of the things they say are unwritable. Yet they are splendid fellows, men who have been for months face to face with the dark realism of war, men free from hypocrisy and cant, and if they die cursing they die game, game to the last. I must confess that I like the cursing sorts, the virile, devil-may-care type best.

Occasionally among the scores of letters I have to censor every day, I come across one from the praying type. They are generally unpleasant reading with their selfish, cowardly egotism and fear of death. I trust the dear Lord will bring *me* safely through, preserve *my* life, guard *me* against danger, etc. is the burden of their supplications. Their one obsession seems to be the safety of their own paltry skins. If Christianity can do no more than this for men then Christianity has failed.

24TH JANUARY 1916

All quiet on this part of the Front. Placed order with Barclay & Co. for 200 Daggafonteins.

CAPTAIN MATTHEW ROACH SERVED WITH THE DUKE OF CORNWALL'S LIGHT INFANTRY, THEN 180 AND 255 TUNNELLING COMPANIES, ROYAL ENGINEERS. HE WAS KILLED IN ACTION ON 2 JULY 1916 AND HAS NO KNOWN GRAVE. HIS NAME CAN BE FOUND ON BAY 1 OF THE FAUBOURG D'AMIENS CEMETERY (MEMORIAL TO THE MISSING), ARRAS.

INTRODUCTION

In the confusion of wartime in which we are caught up, relying as we must on one-sided information, standing too close to the great changes that have already taken place or are beginning to, and without a glimmering of the future that is being shaped, we ourselves are at a loss as to the significance of the impressions which press in upon us and as to the value of the judgments which we form. We cannot but feel that no event has ever destroyed so much that is precious in the common possessions of humanity, confused so many of the clearest intelligences, or so thoroughly debased what is highest. Science herself has lost her passionless impartiality; her deeply embittered servants seek for weapons from her with which to contribute towards the struggle with the enemy. Anthropologists feel driven to declare him inferior and degenerate, psychiatrists issue a diagnosis of his disease of mind and spirit. Probably, however, our sense of these immediate evils is disproportionately strong, and we are not entitled to compare them with the evils of other times which we have not experienced.

SIGMUND FREUD, *THOUGHTS FOR THE TIMES ON WAR AND DEATH*, 1915

Certain events climb to the front of our minds when the subject of the Great War is raised. By reason of frequent exposure in the media, more often than not it is the grand battles, the battles that defined the war that defined the twentieth century, and the blueprints by which we construct our perceptions of the conflict as a whole. There was a time long ago when my heartbeat quickened if a veteran uttered the mesmeric words Somme or Passchendaele. The richest of cultural land-scapes, these were the holy grails for 'collectors of memories' such as I, haunting my imagination and pressing the correct reactionary buttons of someone brought up on a diet of John Mills, Richard Attenborough, Jack Hawkins, Dirk Bogarde and co. The greater the ill-fame of a battle, the better. But, as is almost always the case, my own perceptions had been imperfectly shaped by others, and the more veterans I met (from a variety of conflicts) and the more I understood the critical amalgamation of the vast range and style of service that combined to make up the whole, the more the sensational reaction dissipated. And the more I looked to the wings – to those who made the 'show' possible, and the kind of work they did. Other than for their extreme old age, these men (and women) seldom attracted leading media attention, for the required sound-bites – two minutes of tears and emotion quite deliberately induced – were deemed absent. Judging by today's repeated evidence our sophisticated twenty-first century sensibilities can still only be satisfied in this contemptible and immature fashion. An abhorrent modern disease, and indeed a serious error of judgement.

Yet at the same time it cannot be denied that the great offensives form the milestones along the temporal path of the First World War. Research into the 1917 battles is especially profitable, for it is in this year above all others that we see the greatest ingenuity, deliberation, planning, and colossal communal and personal effort that made up the writhing serpent of a modern military machine at the beginning of the 20th century. The year 1917 saw the apogee of the efforts of a forgotten army whose task was to make possible the continuing prosecution of the war under the most challenging circumstances. Many were the soldiers who had to lay aside their rifles to carry out this work, men whose sole offensive tools were skills learned in civilian life: railwaymen, miners, carpenters, blacksmiths, farriers, veterinarians, bakers, surveyors. Hundreds of thousands served for years never to fire a shot even in self-preservation, for the tail of the army dog was long and grew longer every month after August 1914. So, in the same way as I have tried to do with my *Somme* volume, this book will not only attempt to relate the narrative of battle through the words of those who served in the trenches and at the guns, but celebrate the often surprising labours of a wider spectrum of troops whose efforts were, though far less celebrated, just as critical, whose experiences just as formative, inventiveness just as marvellous, memories just as harrowing, and sacrifice just as significant.

The Ypres Salient is not a landscape like the Somme where for decades vistas have remained relatively unchanged. The battlefields of Belgian Flanders have been greatly transformed, with the most recent transformations taking place within the last twenty-five years or so. Motorway embankments, bridges, ribbon housing development and especially factories now both obscure and occupy places of huge symbolic import. There is an irony here, for in 1914 the ground itself was industrialized in its own way, metamorphosing from quiet productive agricultural husbandry to a man-made monoculture with one aspiration: the annihilation of its residents. As always, nature had no respect for the pro-

ceedings and began healing, occupying, adjusting at the very moment each of the tens of millions of shells tore and re-tore the pastures. From the human point of view, however, those who came to know the Salient were to develop a profound intimacy, respect and reverence with this land. Contemporary maps and plans do not simply register who occupied a certain portion of terrain at a given time, they chart profoundly personal, and supremely idiosyncratic memories and experiences of four years of anguish, comradeship and longing. I make no differentiation between nationalities. That landscape is expressed in marvellous clarity through the medium of the British and German panoramic photographs in this book, many of which have never before been published. Through their use on the battlefield today one is better able to pass on to visitors old and new a fresh awareness of the Salient's strange and timeless connection to so many individuals. Often intimate and deeply emotive, they always induce awe, veneration even, a response that is clearly manifested in the eyes and voice of the viewer. The Salient, therefore, is a landscape drenched in memory and meaning; two simple words, but imbued with such profound and apparently perpetual historic and symbolic weight that this small portion of West Flanders can rightly be considered an integral part of the entity once known as the British Empire, and by extension integral to the disparate band of countries that today make up the Commonwealth. In turn, through letters, memoirs and more recently recorded testimony, the endurance, humour, courage and ultimate forfeit of those who served in the cauldron of Passchendaele, the greatest of the four battles of Ypres, pass unerringly from generation to generation. Judging by the permanent swell of what can still justly be called pilgrimage, it seems it always shall. The real memory of course speaks only to those who carry it within themselves as a strange half-life lived during an age with no equal. Just a handful remain. I wish this man did:

I don't ever remember thinking how I am I going to cope with this lot later in life. There was no later. You were either trying to stay alive, or you had momentarily lost all sense of danger or fear, and then you were just doing what everyone else was doing or not caring if you were killed. I was the fittest I had ever been, but I spent a lot of the time exhausted, not through fighting but lumping stuff around at night. You didn't look into the future at all, didn't look into what you were feeling because you had to block that out. We all did. You have to remember what kind of world it was then. The kind of society we had. I worked in an outfitters and pawnshop before war came. When I got home afterwards I went back for my old job. I won't say his name, but I was told I had let him down by joining up, and anyhow he had two women working now for the same money as I had got. I never said anything – you didn't. Like in the army, it's the way it worked. I feel more angry about that now than I did then. But that's the kind of world we lived in then. It was a sight worse for a lot of others. So it's never been a surprise to me that so many wanted to sign up. I know – at least in our lot, the LF's – we weren't thinking about death, or glory, or medals and that; we just didn't want to be left out of this great thing. You had the white feather brigade – the women, you know, socialites mainly. A disgrace, they were. But I think for lads like me it was just the chance to escape from having no prospects at home; you know - army service might lead somewhere beyond the mill or the mine or the shop. I was naïve, still a boy even at 18, we all were. Like I say, it was a different world: an 18-year old in 1915 was the same as a 12 or 13-year old today. We knew nothing, we'd been nowhere, and the chance to go to France – even to fight a war – was like going to the Moon or Mars. It was. People always say, 'Weren't you afraid of being killed?' They don't know the world in those days. If something broke, you mended it, you darned your socks (or your mother did!), you wore clothes till they were ragged, then used them for something else. There was no waste, we couldn't afford waste then. And the world was full of death, *from tuberculosis and other diseases. Life in the mines, at sea, in factories and in the mills where most folk in Lancashire worked, was terrible. We had poverty, overwork, poor food – and the slums; no one today knows what a slum is. Look what the flu did at the end of the war – we had no protection, no education. Child mortality was awful; but it wasn't to us at the time – that was just how it was for everyone. Big family or small, rich or poor, you expected death. If you were illegitimate, you know, they could lock you up! There was no state support like today, you relied on your family and friends to look after you. When you were poorly, no money meant no hope. Only charity was left. Life was always fragile and always cheap. War holds no special threat to people like that. Anyhow, nobody believed we would ever lose it. This was England!*
Private Bert Fearns, 2/6th Lancashire Fusiliers

It is impossible to offer more than a flavour of Third Ypres in any book. A grandiose turmoil of hope, misery, abuse of power, human frailty, sacrifice, tragedy and romance, 'Passchendaele' can never be comfortably placed between covers. I have not, for example, focused upon the many extraordinary deeds of gallantry witnessed in the Salient – these can be found in matchless detail elsewhere. Nor, sadly, have I been able to include as much German testimony as was originally intended; the omission will be rectified at a later date in subsequent volumes. This, therefore, like every other appreciation of the battle, is just as incomplete and selective. I know readers will find many things fresh within these pages, but the customary qualification must still apply: the book should be read in conjunction with others. My anticipation is that it will carry sufficient value to eyes perhaps jaded by over-exploitation, and not prove like the battle itself: promising much but achieving little.

Peter Barton
February 2007

'They say we shall not go back to Ypres,' somebody said to me.

'I hope to God we never do,' I returned, and never uttered a

more fervent prayer.

PRIVATE ARTHUR LAMBERT, 2ND HONOURABLE ARTILLERY COMPANY

CHAPTER ONE
Primary Moves

What a tightening of the heart-strings there is when you see the boat that is to take you away, rolling and hissing gently like an implacable monster! Of course it took hours to get the men on board, and the crush there was terrific – but of this more anon. There was a room for the Officers: being on a ship it was of course called a saloon, and the thing by which you went down to it was called not a staircase but a companion way. We started off at last at about 6.00 p.m. It was rather misty weather, and the English coast came and went as we approached or receded from it. George and I went down below for a bit, and when we came up again after having arranged our kits on the floor of the saloon, all we could see was cold, grey water, a white wake, and a destroyer and a couple of other boats going over with us.

That was the only time I felt down in the dumps at all – that first moment that I realised we were out of sight of England. Half the Tommies began catting when we met the swell in the Channel, and there were a fat lot of men on board, crammed between decks, on the deck, up the stairs, every mortal place – so the frig was perfectly awful, and the stink deadly.
SECOND LIEUTENANT J.T. GODFREY, 104TH FIELD COMPANY, ROYAL ENGINEERS

Since the dawn of European military history Flanders has been a 'popular' and regular battleground choice. In its most ancient manifestation the region stretched from Picardy in northern France to today's Belgian coast. At the beginning of the twentieth century, however, the redefined modern locality incorporated part of France's Pas de Calais region running north and west from Vimy Ridge, and the rich agricultural country from Armentières to the dune-fields of the North Sea – Belgian Flanders. The district offered a flat and direct pathway to and from the key strategic (and wealthy) ports of Calais, Dunkirk, Ostend and Boulogne, all primary embarkation points for the British Isles.

The entire region is one of gentle ridges, shallow valleys and wide plains, with the odd hill here and there. At its seaward edge is a kilometre-wide belt of sand dunes, integral to events on the Ypres and Messines battlefields from the early days of the war and throughout its duration. They protect the polders, a flat, fertile, low-lying belt of largely arable land running from northern France through Belgium into Holland. The polders' 'capital', Nieuport, an anchorage since mediaeval times, sits astride the short tidal stretch of the River Yser at a point exactly on the interface between dune and polder. From the town radiated (and still do) a filament of large canals, each one a critical arterial trade and transport route to inland cities in Belgium and far beyond. As a strategic objective for invaders down the centuries, Nieuport was repeatedly and successfully defended by inundation – the deliberate flooding of surrounding land to baulk an attack. The town held out in this way five times between 1488 and 1677, on one occasion surviving a five-year siege by Louis XIV of France. In autumn 1914 the same ancient ploy was destined to play a key role, not only in the creation of the Ypres Salient and all that that entailed for so many nations, but the formation of the Western Front itself. For being the seat of the problem, during the war Nieuport was to suffer the same fate as Ypres: almost total obliteration.

Eastwards, and some 16 kilometres inland, the billiard-table smoothness of the polders almost imperceptibly begins to give way to the next geological feature, the gentle swell of the Flanders plain. Here, we find a significant change in surface soil from a light loam to a dense, more impervious material, slow to drain, quick to bake and always

Left
Passchendaele village, 1907. The old timber-framed church seen here was replaced by a stone-built edifice shortly before the war arrived in Flanders.

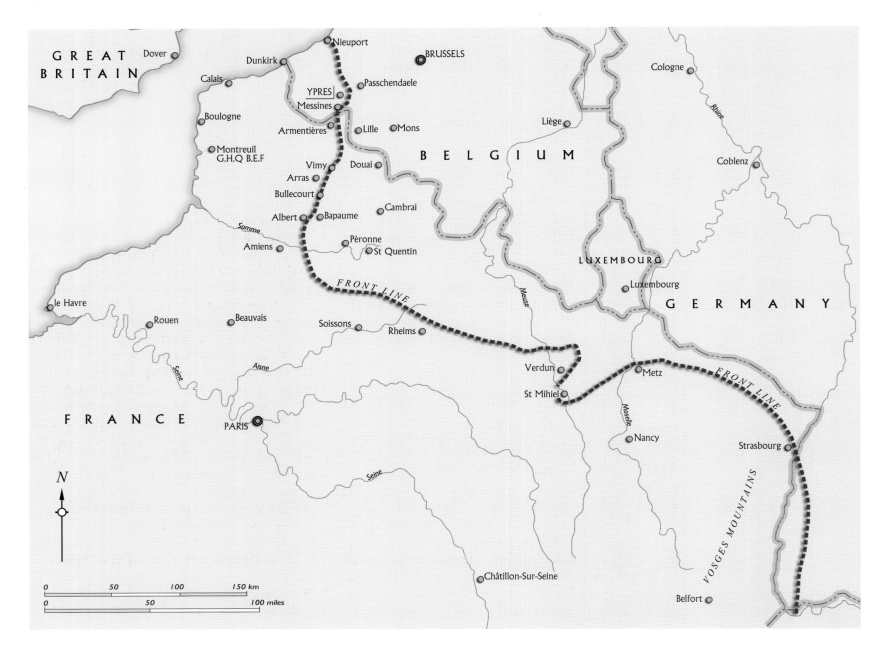

heavy to work. The landscape now becomes as much pastoral as arable and is dotted with countless ponds and moated farms. The patchworks of small fields are interlaced with ditches, each feeding a further labyrinth of *bekes* – small streams, the humble tributaries of the few large rivers that run sluggishly and often muddily seawards. Water is unquestionably the predominant landscape feature, for after rain it is everywhere held in place on or close to the surface by the geological sub-stratum, a bed of largely impervious clay up to 100 metres in thickness. The existence of the clay means that except on the low ridges the general water table everywhere sits around a metre beneath the surface, fluctuating little from winter to summer. Natural drainage is tediously slow. Curiously, a vast reservoir of pure water also exists deep *beneath* the great clay bed, trapped by the same impervious geological barrier that blocks surface percolation downwards.

Sited upon the Flanders plain, and also close to the River Yser, lies the town of Ypres, today known by its Flemish title, Ieper. Created in mediaeval times as a result of agricultural prosperity especially in wool, like Nieuport and many other Flemish towns, it had been looked upon as a desirable acquisition for many centuries. As a result Ypres was subjected to regular invasion, occupation and siege by forces both from within Europe and far beyond, with France being the most determined invader.

The British, ever anxious to expand their commercial and military power, had long been highly influential visitors. One of their more curious early visitations was by the Bishop of Norwich who in the fourteenth century besieged the town and almost starved the inhabitants to extinction. A more beneficial action, the defeat of the Armada in 1588, served to release Flanders from Spanish shackles – but at the same time opened the door to further French ambitions. Later, in 1658, Oliver Cromwell captured Ypres whilst fighting *alongside* the French, once more against Spain. In 1701 Louis XIV of France occupied all of the Spanish Netherlands, including Flanders, until the decisive Battle of Ramillies in 1706, when John Churchill, the 1st Duke of Marlborough, destroyed the French army and occupied the region. The prevailing politics meant that the region then became Austrian territory! In 1793, as part of the Revolutionary Wars, the 'Grand Old' Duke of York thwarted another French ambition to finally annexe the country, at the same time making nursery-rhyme history by marching his '10,000 men' up and down a famous nearby 'hill' – Mont Kemmel, a key First World War location. The final British military visitation before 1914 was during the Napoleon's Hundred Days War. As part of the campaign that culminated at Waterloo on 18 June 1815, the Duke of Wellington's engineers were detailed to survey and bolster dozens of fortifications throughout the Low Countries. Ypres, a town whose defences had been designed and put in place in the seventeenth century by the illustrious French siege-master and tactician Marshal Sebastien le Prestre de Vauban, benefited from a partial reconstruction of its ramparts.

THE LANDSCAPE OF BATTLE

The plain to the north-east and south of Ypres is broken by a series of low-lying, wooded hills. These are the ridges that would play *the* critical role in the nature and outcome of the First World

War in Belgian Flanders, and in the life and death of millions of men who served here for more than four years. The ridges' geology – different again – was vitally significant, in warfare both on and under the surface.

Over many millennia, the ridges have been moulded into today's gently rounded hills by the action of streams – the famous *bekes* – draining into the major waterways of the region, the Yser and the Lys rivers. They left behind a low, snaking, interconnected ridge chain, with few crests exceeding 50 metres above sea level, known

geologically and somewhat euphemistically as the *Alpes de Flandres*. A series of distinctive appendages from their main spine formed minor 'spurs': the Messines, Pilckem, Westhoek and Broodseinde ridges – names which by the end of 1915 would already have become indelibly engraved into the bloody history of not only Flanders but almost the entire world. Each was a component of the single main geological feature that long before the war geologists had named the Passchendaele Ridge after the small village of the same name. For those who commanded them, these 'heights' provided

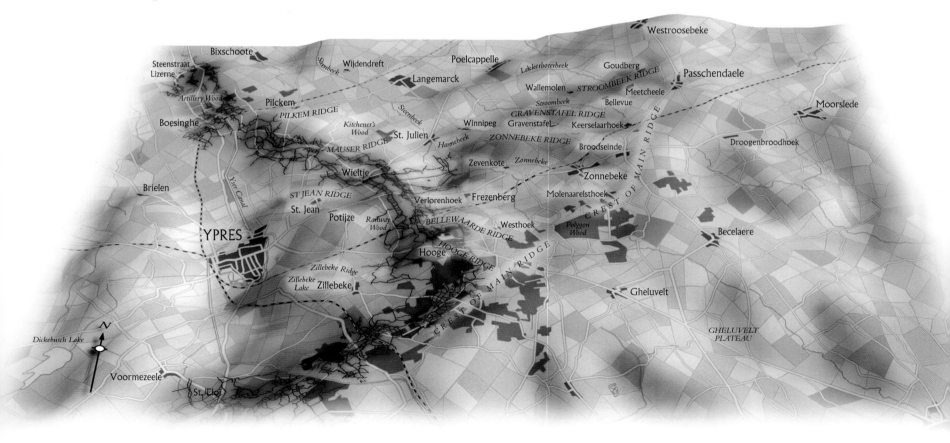

multiple panoramic viewpoints far across the landscape below – and perfect tactical locations for positional warfare.

Most importantly for the soldiers of 1914–1918, the geological structure of the ridges was based not only upon clay, but sand – a multiple strata of various colours and densities, each with distinct 'personalities'. Critically, the sands were more free-draining than the heavy soils of the valleys and plains. Underlying the ridges and in every one of the myriad valleys separating each spur, however, still lay the ubiquitous Ypresian clay, and it was this clay/sand combination that was to become *the* critical aspect of the conflict.

THE PATH FROM PEACE TO WAR

In August 1914, when hostilities broke out, the Belgian nation had not yet celebrated its centenary. After centuries of being shuffled between various external rulers, the peoples of west Flanders were no strangers to forced change. Although peace had reigned since the nation had become an independent entity on 20 January 1831, they had no reason to believe that this new European war would be any different from others that had ebbed and flowed across their pastures down the centuries. In the end, as they always did, the Flemish peoples and cultures would adapt, survive and retain many aspects of their culture. One thing was sure: France, Britain, Belgium, Germany, Austria-Hungary, indeed every nation on earth which took an interest, agreed that any war fought between wealthy industrialized countries at this stage of military technological development was certain to be a mobile affair. As for Flanders, her lengthy narra-

tive of conflict indicated that fighting would either soon come to grief in the mud of the plains, as it had done for the Goths, Romans and others down the centuries, or pass swiftly through.

The background to war was one of complex alliances. On the one hand lay the Entente Powers – France, Russia and Great Britain – each tied in agreement by a series of treaties in the early 1900s, designed to protect them against the growth of the Imperial German Navy. On the other were the Central Powers – Germany , Austro-Hungary and Italy. This 'Triple Alliance' was a long-standing affair, later to grow by bond with Turkey and Bulgaria. This political partition endured throughout the war.

On 31 July 1914 the Belgians, well aware of the growing threat of war, mobilized their 150,000-strong army. In just thirteen days the Germans had assembled no less than 1.6 million troops, whilst their Central Alliance allies, Austria-Hungary, who had declared war on Serbia on 28 July, mustered eight corps on the Russian frontier. Concentrating four formidable armies in the Flanders theatre, the Germans began to advance on 3 August 1914, initially crossing the Belgian border at Gemmenich with two cavalry divisions. The move not only signalled the commencement of direct hostilities against France, it also guaranteed British imperial involvement. Within thirty-six hours she had declared war on Germany.

In following the northern route via Belgium towards the channel ports and Paris, the Germans were enacting a variation of the Schlieffen Plan, a scheme devised in the early years of the century by the then Chief of the

Left
Relief map showing the town of Ypres with its semi-encircling ridges, valleys and spurs, all intersected by the bekes and traversed by the trench lines of the Salient.

General Staff, Count Alfred von Schlieffen. Utilizing tactics which had been so successful in the Franco-Prussian War of 1870-71, the aim was to subdue two main rivals, France in the west and Russia in the east, with a view to subsequent expansion of the German empire to rival that of the world's greatest power, Britain. In 1906 Schlieffen's successor, General Helmuth von Moltke, re-examined the terrain and defences of the proposed western battlefront and adapted the plan. By selecting a route through Belgium he sought to avoid the difficult Ardennes woodlands, a beaded string of powerful French fortresses either side of Verdun, the Vosges mountains and, near the Swiss border, the great bastion city of Belfort, all of which had been reinforced by the French following their ignominious defeat of 1870 and the loss of the territory known as Alsace-Lorraine. In the well-defended southern region a considerable German force was, however, to be deployed as security in case of a French advance. But it was action in the north that held the key to triumph. Here, an army six times greater than that deployed in the south would seek a lightning victory. The strategy charted a vast anti-clockwise strike, using Metz as the pivot, that would rapidly annexe Paris and force swift French submission. Afterwards the Austro-Hungarian/German hammer would fall hard and fast upon Russia, a nation, it was calculated, that although powerful and dangerous would take fully six weeks to mobilize. By then, France should be under German rule. Belgium, far less Flanders, was not even envisaged as even a short-term battleground: the tide of invasion would sweep through in moments. As a result, when Belgium

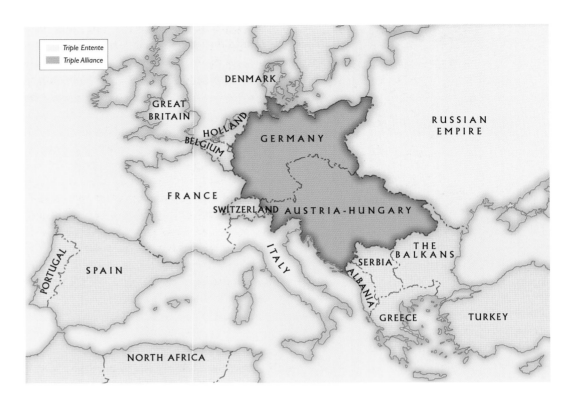

protested her neutrality and refused German access across her territories, she was simply ignored.

In 1839, Britain had signed the Treaty of London, a promise to defend Belgium in the event of hostile military threat. Warned by the Germans to disregard the document, the British government saw the potentially serious consequences of a forced occupation of Belgian and French ports. They therefore followed the 75-year-old agreement to the letter, mobilizing the British Expeditionary Force (BEF) on 3 August. It was a very different organization to those of France or Germany. Being an island, Britain had

Above

The Great War – Alliances and Ententes.

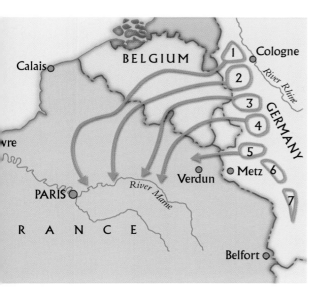

Above
The German attack plan showing the five invading armies and their projected movements.

no borders to defend and therefore required no permanent large-scale protective garrison; at this time the Royal Navy 'ruled the international waves' absolutely, holding the key not only to home defence, but the security of many territories in a vast and far-flung empire. Dispersed across the world from the Far East to the West Indies, for almost 100 years British troops had seldom been called upon to enter into any conflict greater than a skirmish; there was therefore no conscription, no national service, simply a relatively small, very highly trained, and very proud regular army. At the outbreak of war the entire British Army numbered just one-fifteenth of its French counterpart.

ADVANCE

Like the French in the south, Belgium too felt it was able to depend upon its impressive complex of well-placed, well-developed, nineteenth-century fortifications. These should certainly arrest enemy incursions long enough for Triple Entente assistance to turn up. Like many other European powers, Belgium's old stone and brick-built fortresses had been upgraded in recent decades by the augmentation of ferroconcrete. They were indeed a tough nut for nineteenth-century ordnance – but artillery technology had already far outstripped that of fortress construction, and the defences formed no barrier to modern German weaponry. On 17 August the bastion of Liège was the first of many to crumble. The following day King Albert of Belgium ordered his army to retire. It

was the first of many pull-backs. In less than three weeks the capital Brussels was occupied and half of Belgium lay under German rule. During the afternoon of the 24th the invader crossed the French border for the first time, pushing into Champagne, and on the same day the Belgians were forced to retire again, this time falling back on Antwerp, their government now rueing the 3 August decision to decline the support of five French Army corps. As for the Belgian people, when the first troops were mobilized on 31 July 1914 – a month before fear of impending war escalated in Flanders – the initial exodus of civilians began. As German boots fell upon French soil, British troops were already in Belgium and optimistically looking to stem the tide.

MONS
SUNDAY 23.8.14
Paraded at 3.15 a.m. and our first work was to put the village in a state of defence. The German force has been sighted by our cavalry patrol about 10 miles out. The Glosters and S.W. Borderers have also been entrenching. An artillery duel is now taking place. The Germans are advancing fast and in great numbers. Later. We are retiring from this position back towards the French frontier. It is a pitiable sight to see the women and children and other villagers packing up chattels and fleeing from the village. The village is bound to be burnt from shellfire. We start retiring at 7 p.m. till 10 p.m. when we halt for the night. We slept on the roadside for 2 hours in full kit.

MONDAY 24.8.14
Off again at 5 a.m., again a further retirement, the Germans are following us fast, shells bursting over camp but doing no harm. We have had very few casualties indeed. The Glosters and S.W. Borderers were in the trenches all last night but retirement is part of a great plan which will certainly envelop the whole German

divisions operating in this area and eventually destroying or capturing the whole force.
CORPORAL A.A. WILKINSON, 26TH FIELD COMPANY,
ROYAL ENGINEERS

Under the command of Field Marshal Sir John French, the BEF first saw action on Sunday, 23 August near the Belgian town of Mons, advancing to protect the French left flank. Encouraged by their arrival, the Belgians ordered localized assaults near Antwerp. It was a welcome but short-lived respite from retirement, but when the news of the British retreat from Mons arrived – inevitable after a reckless and ineffective French offensive in Alsace that yielded more than 140,000 casualties – they were once more forced to slip back behind the city walls. The Germans then increased pressure everywhere on all northern battlefronts. By the end of August the French had been driven from Lille, Soissons, Laon, Craonne, Maubeuge and Reims, and on 3 September German mounted scouts were spotted a bare 13 kilometres from Paris.

With British, French and Belgian forces all falling back fast, the situation looked bleak, but a spectacular reversal of fortune was about to take place. Between 6 and 10 September, at the Battle of the Marne, the Germans were themselves forced into retreat, with fighting eventually coming to a standstill along the trace of the River Aisne. To great celebration and anticipation of further gains, Reims was retaken. Repairing bridges they had blown just days before, the BEF also began pushing forward. Then the conflict gridlocked – and trench warfare took root. As both sides began extending their attacks northwards in a series of unsuccessful attempts to outflank each other, the seed of the Western Front was sown. The line inexorably lengthened in what came to be called the 'Race for the Sea', and as each German and Allied flank attack failed, windows of strategic opportunity closed. There were a strictly limited number of such windows: should the fight be carried all the way to the Belgian coast no enemy flank would be left to turn – for either side.

On the northern battlegrounds, by 17 September the entire Belgian Army and the newly arrived British Naval Brigade lay within Antwerp's ring of forts. After crushing victories at Namur and Liège, the Germans now knew full well the power of their guns – perhaps the Belgian Army could be eliminated here from the equation altogether. The giant 17-inch howitzers began the demolishment of Antwerp on 27 September. Inside the ramparts civilian and military authorities were left with little choice: if the city and its population were not to be wiped out, and even a remnant of the mixed defence force saved, Antwerp must first, if possible, be abandoned by the troops then surrendered to the enemy. As the shelling continued, the military crept away by night, until by 10 October the city was left undefended, whereupon the Mayor capitulated. Not all the military managed to escape, however – over 900 British troops were stranded. Antwerp had been lost to a force one-third the size of its defending garrison.

As the war entered its tenth week, three-quarters of Belgium was already occupied and its military establishment was reduced almost by half. Ostend was the next potential refuge. Here, it was hoped that with fresh Allied assistance a stand could be made, possibly to secure western

Above
A German mounted Uhlan patrol moves into Flanders.

Below
The streets of Antwerp throng with invading troops.

Flanders, but at that time British supports were only just mustering at St Omer, and the French were still fighting over 90 kilometres away at Arras. Lacking immediate aid, Ostend too was seen to be untenable, so the Belgians pulled back again, to the banks of the River Yser. As they awaited their fate, General Erich von Falkenhayn, Chief of the German General Staff, issued orders to his Fourth Army to cut off the ports of Dunkirk and Calais.

By 15 October, fighting in the southern sectors had largely subsided and the northern French army was nearing La Bassée, not far from the Belgian border. In addition, the British 7th Division and 3rd Cavalry Division had at last arrived, taking up positions in front of Ypres on the immediate Belgian right, and making probing patrols towards Menin and Roulers. Ostensibly, the battle line now stretched from Switzerland to the North Sea, but nowhere was it considered strong enough to withstand concerted hostile action. This was a supremely critical time. All the signs were that a massive German effort would shortly be made to crash through the coastal sector where the depleted Belgians still remained unsupported.

Above
German troops stride into Antwerp on 11 October 1914.

Right
Townspeople look on unconcerned as the first British troops arrive in Ypres on 14 October 1914.

THE YSER

The new Belgian line, just 35 kilometres long, followed the trace of the River Yser and the Yperlee Canal that linked Nieuport and its great system of waterways with Boesinghe, a small village near Ypres, passing through Dixmude in the centre of the polder plain. The river, 20 metres wide with embankments on both sides, formed a substantial obstacle. Between Nieuport and Dixmude, where the land was barely 2 metres above sea level, it ran sluggishly through the polders. There were also other landscape features, all man-made: a canalized tributary of the Yser constructed for water-borne traffic to and from Ypres; and a 2-metre-high railway embankment carrying the single line linking Ypres with Dixmuide, Nieuport and its small satellite seaside resort, Nieuport-Bains.

The Germans approached the Yser in strength. By 26 October, after a week of battering by heavy artillery, the remnants of the Belgian Army had already been forced from its banks, retiring to the final potentially defendable position in west Flanders, the Nieuport-Dixmude railway embankment. It offered 2 metres of cover, but little else. The Belgian artillery had been reduced to a total of 100 rounds per field gun, there was no hope of extra supplies and the little embankment appeared to be the flimsiest of barriers. As for Allied infantry support, the main British force, now massing alongside the French for a joint counter-offensive astride the Lys near Armentières, was unable to assist; and there were too few troops deployed in the meagre defence of Ypres to send any men northwards. The Belgians were on their own.

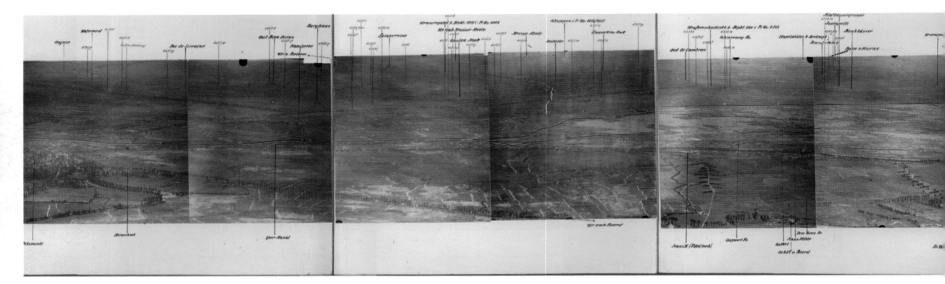

The situation was reaching breaking point. As a final resort to slow the German advance on the coast, the Belgians had had no choice but to place their dwindling hope in an ancient military stratagem: inundation. They would flood as much of the potential battlefield as possible. On 22 October 1914, at Nieuport, the town that had seen it all before, a 4-square-kilometre inundation created by opening the sluices of sea locks stemmed, albeit temporarily, a strong enemy assault. This success, and the timely arrival of a division of French Marne veterans, the 42nd, encouraged Belgian military engineers to seek ways to flood more land.

FLOOD

Apart from the River Yser, the polders were incised by many kinds of waterways, from large navigable canals and 'evacuation canals', to the extraordinarily complex network of drainage ditches that over many centuries had been painstakingly installed both to displace excess rainwater (evacuate) in winter and irrigate the land in summer. The key to the entire system was a complex of locks and sluices in and around Nieuport. It was from here that the balance of water levels over tens of thousands of hectares of flatland was controlled, and therefore also from here that any inundation must originate. However, it was not just a case of releasing every stopcock, lock-gate and sluice at the same time: opening certain waterways would have no effect at all; opening the wrong ones at the wrong time would be deleterious and wasteful. And whilst seeking to halt the Germans by inundating the greatest area in the shortest time, it was equally imperative that the Belgians did not flood themselves out. The decision to inundate, therefore, may have been made, but it soon became clear

Above
The family Geeraerts. Henri the lock-keeper stands on the left, prominently displaying his medals.

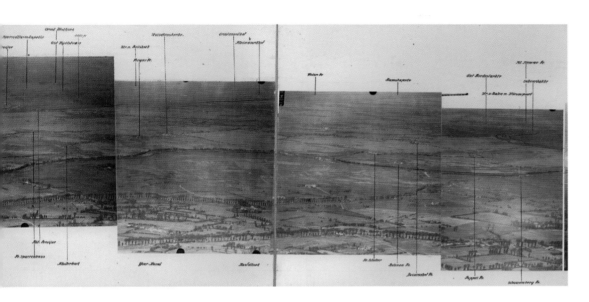

Above
3 July 1917. Dixmuide (left of frame) and the inundations as seen from a German observation balloon at a height of 630 metres. Note the screened roads.

Above right
Belgian troops gaze out across the man-made sea from the cover of the Nieuport–Dixmuide railway embankment – and dam. 11 September 1917.

Left
Karel Cogge of the Waterings company, who identified the culverts beneath the railway.

that there was a problem: even experienced Belgian military engineers were unable to decipher the mass of controls in and around Nieuport – they had no idea which devices controlled what system. Would this sluice be good for evacuation, and that for inundation? Or vice-versa? How were the myriad of waterways interconnected, and where did one system pass above or beneath another? What was needed was local knowledge – but the civilian population had already fled. With absurd good fortune a single Nieuport lock-keeper, Henri Geeraerts, was found; he advised the Army which gates and sluices to open and close, and when. At almost the same time a second water specialist, this time a man who understood intimately the polder 'waterings', i.e. the inland drainage system, was located. Karel Cogge had worked on drainage all his life; amongst other things he was able to point out twenty-two critical culverts beneath the

Nieuport–Dixmude railway embankment that must be firmly sealed before inundation commenced – otherwise the Belgians would flood their own positions. On 29 October, when the defence was hanging on by the thinnest of threads, the sluices of the old Furnes Canal were opened wide. The rising North Sea tide surged through, flowing around the canal to the south of town and out across the polder plain. With Karel Cogge's blocked culverts creating a dam of the railway embankment, over a period of three nights and under enemy shellfire, the sluices were opened before high tide and closed as the ebb took hold. The unchecked sea seethed over the lowlands, but was unable to return. And the Belgian positions west of the railway stayed dry.

Realizing the implications, as the waters rose the Germans strove desperately to break through before the route of advance was irreversibly blocked, but they were beaten by the

Ölmühle.

power of the tide. Against all odds the Belgians had triumphed: the coastal route to the Channel ports had been decisively and, as it turned out, permanently sealed.

The inundations left a waist-deep, watery impasse covering many thousands of hectares and stretching 15 kilometres inland. The Germans, dismayed but by necessity undeterred, had no choice but to shift their attacks yet further towards the drier ground beyond the polder plain — back inland. Tremendous German onslaughts at the last real bridgehead, Dixmude, were again held off by the Belgians, once more at shocking cost in life. With every river and canal crossing destroyed and traversal of the inundations out of the question, the Germans, still resolute in their quest for victory before winter, pushed yet further inland towards higher and dryer ground. Accordingly, the Belgians further extended their watery barricade by flooding parts of the sector between Dixmude and Ypres, enhancing the serious defensive barrier of the canalized River Yser that connected the two towns. The man-made sea had now reached Steenstraat, almost lapping against the walls of Ypres itself.

Above
German view of the town of Dixmuide in ruins showing the Belgian lines in the middle distance.

Right
The great five-lock system at Nieuport with the Yser river running away to the sea beyond. These great sea locks had to be kept sealed throughout the war to keep the inundations in place.

ick

g in Dixmude.

weinghen.

Gehöft 0,7 km südl. Caeskerke

Gehöft 0,0 km südl. Caeskerke

In front of Ypres the Germans knew that large-scale inundation was unachievable: time was now the key factor. The French were moving northwards with fresh British troops augmenting their numbers, so with each passing day the window of opportunity for a decisive victory was narrowing. As the first frosts of winter glistened on the Flemish pastures, the sole remaining arena for battle now lay pincered between Armentières, 14 kilometres south of Ypres, and Boesinghe, 3 kilometres north. Thus was born the small piece of Flanders that would soon become the feared Salient.

CHAPTER TWO

First Battle, First Winter

By the end of August 1914 refugees were spilling from cities, towns and villages across Belgium towards France and Holland. It was during the third week of the month that the first German scouts were reported drawing close to the Westhoek – the Ypres area. On the 24th of that month, the same day the British Expeditionary Force began its weary retreat from Mons, the first parties of Uhlan cavalry were spotted scouting between Poelcappelle and Westroosebeke. Two weeks later a clash between German troops and Belgian volunteers resulted in the first Flemish casualties – on the Menin Road at Hooge, just 4 kilometres from Ypres. As more uhlans arrived and skirmishes became increasingly likely the stream of refugees became a torrent. Further clashes followed, at Passchendaele, Becelaere and at Zwarteleen.

On 3 October, three German cavalry divisions entered Voormezele, Ypres, and on the Messines Ridge, Wytschaete. In Ypres they looted food, money, clothing and jewellery, and 'encouraged' the *Burgermeister* to pay a security levy of 75,000 francs. The invaders then settled in and despatched reconnaissance parties towards nearby Poperinghe. Twenty-four hours later the scouts returned with a report that British troops – the 7th Division – were approaching. The Germans chose to vacate. On the following day the force headed south towards the French border. En route they were greeted with news of Lieutenant General Sir Douglas Haig's I Corps moving northwards fast to join the Cavalry Corps, IV Corps and several French and Belgian units.

On their arrival both British and French troops took up positions in and around Ypres and its satellite villages, and awaited orders; on 15 October 1914 the Household Cavalry were actually billeted in houses in the village of Passchendaele. Considering the gathered coalition force had sufficient offensive potential, plans were made to advance: the 7th Division in conjunction with French and Belgian cavalry were to secure the towns of Menin and Roulers.

Three days later Roulers fell to the French, with Menin expected to follow suit the next day. At this time the roads of West Flanders were thronged with refugees moving southwards towards the Franco-Belgian border. As Allied commanders pushed more troops and guns forward, cursing every delay, the alarming cause of the civilian tide was revealed when French air reconnaissance identified a hostile force of no less than two armies advancing towards Ypres from the east.

It was far too robust. The Germans quickly reoccupied Roulers, thus wrecking Allied plans to occupy Menin. The date, 19 October, signalled the

Above
Belgian civilians on the Ypres ramparts await developments.

opening day of the First Battle of Ypres. Even though the whole of Belgium was now under German rule, apart from a tiny corner of western Flanders, and despite the very real and clearly imminent danger of serious large-scale conflict, many locals still chose to remain, guarding their homes and farms, possessions, businesses and livestock, and hoping against hope that regardless of the outcome the period of danger would be short and temporary. But a certain event on this day, later known as 'Black Monday', was to have repercussions that would dash everyone's hopes. In Roulers a German unit was ambushed by a small section of French troops who, having killed a number of soldiers, managed to slip away unseen. Suspecting the attack to have been the act of Belgian civilians, the German authorities responded by burning houses and ordering summary executions. When the news reached Ypres it created a flood of terrified refugees. The following day German troops occupied the Passchendaele Ridge.

SATURDAY, 24 OCTOBER

My first job this morning was with another man escorting 5 Belgian refugees (2 men, 3 women) who wanted to return home, back to a village 4 miles away and handed them over to the French police. We afterwards paraded to go out making entanglements, but the shellfire of the enemy was so heavy we could not proceed to our destination so returned to our bivvy. At 7 p.m. we got orders to parade ready to march off. We marched due south for about 3 hours and bivouacked for the night just outside a place called Ypres. Another great move.

TUESDAY 27 OCTOBER.

No movement today, battle still in progress, too heavy for us to go to work. Where we slept last night we are making dugouts, in case we have to stay here a day or two.
CORPORAL A.A. WILKINSON, 26TH FIELD COMPANY, ROYAL ENGINEERS

Despite the setbacks on the Aisne and those continuing on the Yser, and the less than lightning speed of progress originally envisaged, the Germans were still confident of victory before winter. They were fully aware of how pummelled and bruised the French, British and Belgians had been during these first few months of fighting, equally how meagre were the numbers of Allied supports arriving in the Ypres sector. British reinforcements from the now quiet Somme and Aisne sectors were known to be entraining daily en route for Flanders, but German numerical superiority still looked overwhelming. A better opportunity for victory was unlikely to present itself, while to fail at this juncture would mean waiting until the spring of the following year to launch another offensive; by then fresh troops from the United Kingdom and British colonies across the world would have arrived at the front. There was also another German anxiety: without decisive victory here and now in Flanders they might also be faced with the possibility of fighting on two fronts – against Russia to the east and France and Belgium to the west; such a complication had to be avoided at all costs. Belgium and France *must* fall.

Drawing upon reserves from other parts of the Western Front the Germans doubled their fighting strength to make sure of the annexation of the Channel ports and the Pas de Calais – and if all went well, perhaps Paris itself – in time for Christmas.

THURSDAY, OCTOBER 20TH

Moved off to Bathenel [Bailleul] across the frontier into Belgium into a place called Ypres. Here the language is a mixture of Flemish, Dutch and English. When they speak slowly, one can understand them. Hundreds of refugees. People very good. Will be a 'Professor of languages' soon. Plenty of firing a good distance away. Our fellows are doing fine. Tobacco cheap, but not like the English.

Lance Corporal G. Dickenson, 2nd Signal Company, Royal Engineers

On 19 October, the German Fourth Army had moved from the ridge tops towards Ypres. Opposite, two British corps commanders, Sir Douglas Haig (I Corps) and Sir Henry Rawlinson (IV Corps), were about to play their part in the 'Battle for Calais'. With the help of an overwhelming artillery advantage and beneath the expectant eye of Kaiser Wilhelm himself, seven German divisions were gathering, ready to sweep Ypres aside, opening the path to Paris and the Channel ports. For days the fighting was hand-to-hand with much bayonet work. In the forefront was Sir Douglas Haig's I Corps. His diary offers a flavour of the chaos of the era.

MONDAY, 26 OCTOBER

By 4 p.m. the bulk of the 7th Division had retired from the Salient about Kruiseik [Kruiseeke], most units in disorder. One brigade came back to the vicinity of Hooge Chateau where I had my reporting centre. I rode out at about 3 p.m. to see what was going on, and was astounded at the terror-stricken men coming back. Still there were some units in the division which stuck to their trenches. I arranged for the necessary number of units from the 1st Division to support the latter, and hold a line from Poezelhoek to the left of the Cavalry Corps near Zandvoorde. It was sad to see fine troops like 7th Division reduced to inefficiency through ignorance of their leaders in having placed them in trenches on forward slopes where Enemy could see and so effectively shell them.

It was a period of 'dash', with cavalry encounters, hedge-to-hedge and house-to-house skirmishes, and patrols venturing out in search of the enemy. Allied counter-attacks were as desperate as they were furious, but each one slowly drained more and more German energy and confidence.

HOOGE
SUNDAY, NOVEMBER 1ST 1914

Still holding trenches in support this morning; a hellish battle is still raging. It has now lasted in all seven days. It is terrible. At 10 am the G.O.C. immediately ordered us up to the trenches. Our O.C. led us there at once and when we arrived found not even enough room for a section, let alone a company. We were at once subjected to a terrible enfilade shellfire (high explosive shrapnel). It was so great that after remaining half an hour we were ordered to retire. During that short time we lost 42 killed and wounded in our company. I and four sappers were the remains of our section. How I escaped I do not know, five men immediately on my right were either killed or wounded. A bullet struck my rifle and a splinter struck my thumb. My chum, Lance Corporal Trigg was killed, the last words he spoke were 'Wilkie, Wilkie, turn me over', he had been blown on to his stomach. I left my trench and turned him over, every moment expecting to receive the same fate, but I couldn't do anything myself with him. As I left the trench he was, poor fellow, breathing his last and I was helpless with him. It was a terrible half hour. In our section we lost one sergeant, two corporals, one lance corporal, and seven sappers, the Company in all losing 42 NCO's and men and one officer.

Corporal A.A. Wilkinson, 26th Field Company, Royal Engineers. Gideon Trigg's name can be found on the Menin Gate Memorial to the Missing, Ypres.

The fighting ebbed and flowed in and around the woods of the Gheluvelt Plateau. Heavily outnumbered, every available man was thrown into the fight: cooks, blacksmiths, officers' servants, signallers, all took part in the chaotic and frantic defence. Alongside the French, the British brawled by day and dug and wired by night, all the time

Left

A mounted patrol of British lancers heads off towards Passchendaele in search of the enemy.

Below

German troops remove the last of the aged populace from a shattered Flemish village.

being pushed back ever closer to the ramparts of the old town.

IN A HOT QUARTER
6.11.14

My Dear Dad

Parcel number 5 has been received, also the four previous which have been consumed. Matches, like tobacco, are permitted. Underclothing was excellent, and I am now enjoying the comfortable feeling of clean clothes. My desire for cotton vest was not prompted from a wish to avoid irritation; I hoped that being a cooler material it would not be so encouraging to my 'pests'. My complaint in this respect is not individual. We ALL suffer, excepting, perhaps, the officers who are allowed baggage and can obtain a change. Our circumstances are such as render cleanliness an impossibility. For three or more weeks at a time we are not allowed to take boots or puttees off, likewise equipment. Occasionally we can shave and wash hands and faces, but that does not clean the body. None of us, since we have been on Active Service, have had a bath; moreover we sleep and lie about in trenches on straw, or else in cowsheds, stables, and such like palaces of cleanliness. I estimate that half a dozen Turkish Baths, two changes into clean clothing (from head to foot, cap and boots included) might get me clean again, but even so, perhaps sandpaper, paraffin oil and brickdust might be necessary.

War is, as you remark, far from the interesting nature that a Henty would lead one to expect. Here is a day's experience:

4.30 pm. Wet through, standing up in trenches, covered in mud, peering into twilight, expecting Germans to attempt a surprise attack. Darkness approaches and arrangements are made for every alternate man to snatch two hours rest. I struggle down to the bottom of the trench, the equipment making one uncomfortably broad and awkward. My head is propped against my comrade's knee; my legs are drawn up and twisted so as to take up as little room as possible. Cramp attacks me now and again and I have to jump up in order to stretch my legs. The two hours rest is up. My turn to do two hours watching, or 'Standing to

arms'. See! There's one! No, it's only a bush which tired eyes imagine to be moving. A shot cracks out, here and there. An occasional Whiz! goes by one's head. Boom, boom! goes a gun. Never silence, never peace. Presently, Swish! A German scout is cutting the barb wire. Two rounds, Fire!!! All is noise. The German trenches reply, probably thinking we are attacking. It is some time before the firing can be stopped. Meanwhile, the boom of the guns still goes on. The lightning flashes of bursting shells still illuminate the sky. Again I struggle down for 2 hours rest, or rather change of posture. One cannot rest in the firing line at night. Early hours of morning approach. It gets colder and colder. One gives up lying down and gets up to stamp some feeling into frozen feet! An hour before dawn. All 'Stand to arms'. Strange light, anxious moment. Have the Germans advanced at all during the night? Sun rises. Can see German trenches. Relief, they are still there. One or two dead Germans near barb wire. Our firing during night paid result.

Rations have been issued under cover of darkness, and we munch our breakfast when we like, and how we like. 'Duck your nuts!' The bang, rattle, whiz and whiz of shrapnel. 'They have started.' We get well under cover, in front of, and very occasionally on top of our trenches. Our artillery reply. After a while things quieten down a little. Some of us are eating dinner. Others tell of incidents relating to the humorous events of some Sergeant Major, Corporal, Private or anyone . . . 'You remember old "Porky", well . . . I say, "Emma," how about when you . . .'; so the day passes. Laughter, joking, yarns, experience, munching, keeping under cover, and so on.

Presently, the lookout announces that the Germans are making a move. Up we all get. Yes, they are advancing. Crowds of them. We take no notice. Let them get nearer. Crash! Bang! etc., etc. Our artillery have peppered them with shrapnel. They go down in a heap. They begin to dig fresh trenches. We open fire! They reply! 'Jones is hit.' 'Is he?' Bang, bang. Oh! A low cry, my comrade slips to the bottom of the trench. Blood on my trousers. 'Is he dead or is he wounded?' Do not know, will see presently. Meanwhile, Bang! Bang!!! Bullet hits ground in front of me,

knocks dirt in my face. Wipe dirt out of my eyes, and carry on with snapping. Firing getting thin, shrapnel is doing much damage. Reinforcements come up. 'Mind that man down there,' I say as someone pushes himself by my side. Twilight approaches. Firing dies down. Darkness, Firing ceases. Every alternate man 'Stand to arms', remainder, two hours rest. Another day gone! Stretcher bearers clear trenches of dead and wounded. Tomorrow? It may be quieter, it may be worse. Do not worry.
Love, Con.
SERGEANT CONRAD BARDEN, 1ST QUEEN'S OWN (ROYAL WEST KENT REGIMENT). KILLED IN ACTION ON 4 OCTOBER 1917 AND COMMEMORATED ON THE TYNE COT MEMORIAL.

The First Battle of Ypres was a sprawling, confused, exhausting and desperate mêlée – but within it the great German offensive withered and wasted away. Their forces had been numerically vastly superior, but too many troops had been trained in haste – an inadequate six weeks – before being cast into battle. They were faced with a potent combination: a small but highly professional force of British and Indian regulars, well led, and even in defence inculcated with the spirit of the offensive; a force fighting not only for their own lives, but that of an empire. Alongside, the French were struggling to save their nation from occupation and ignominious defeat.

15 NOVEMBER 1914

Awoke this morning to find it snowing and a very cold wind blowing, about 11 o'clock it turned to sleet and then to rain. It is simply wretched, wet boots to put on, wet puttees and clothes, and only living in a hole in the ground on bully beef and biscuits, with one of the heaviest cannonades and shell fire, both shrapnel and Jack Johnsons that we have experienced during the whole campaign. The Kaiser has been with his army this last week and they are making every endeavour to capture this town. They have been reinforced by the thousands, but our men have kept them back, they

attack our trenches time after time and our men simply mow them down, their losses must be enormous as their dead lie in heaps in front of our trenches. I don't know what our job is tonight, but it is simply terrible this lot, it is not war, but simply murder and butchery. I'm nearly deaf from gunfire and everybody is suffering from the very severe cold. We have many sick. We have lost thousands of men killed and wounded. Heaven only knows what the Germans have lost. It is shocking, how my nerves stand it I don't know. We parade at 6 p.m. for work . . .
CORPORAL A.A. WILKINSON, 26TH FIELD COMPANY, ROYAL ENGINEERS

In the southern sectors the situation had been similar. On 31 October seven fresh German divisions went into the attack between Gheluvelt on the Menin Road and Armentières. The London Scottish, a pre-war territorial battalion, were holding a part of the Messines Ridge and as the German juggernaut attacked became one of the first territorial units to see combat.

31ST OCTOBER 1914

Get into a wood and lie down for a bit but have to go across fields with shells bursting all round. Get out into open again and approach the firing line. Advance in open order in dead ground. Up a small hill and are under fire. Orders to silence a Maxim that had enfiladed our trenches. Go off to do so under Grant but lose the direction and get into a field behind a barn where coal boxes bursting just behind us. Retire again and get down under a hedge which was practically no cover at all really, but was the most welcome hedge I have ever seen. The guns were about 400 yds in our rear so we got the benefit of all the coal boxes and shrapnel as they had not found the range. We had had many casualties by now and it was about two o'clock in afternoon. We lay under that hedge in a fearful funk with a perfect inferno of shell fire and stray bullets till long after sunset, which was by the way very beautiful. Made a little head cover in the afternoon and

Above
A long captivity lies ahead of this early group of British prisoners being marched back through a Belgian village under mounted Uhlan guard.
Below
Souvenir-toting remnants of the London Scottish after the abortive final 1914 attempt to retake Messines.

Above
Sir Hubert Gough in a peaceful Messines in October 1914.

about sunset the fire slackened and we dug trenches. We smoked quite a lot while all the fun was going on just to give us something to do. Later we ate biscuits and jam which was about the first food we had had since morning. About 8 o'clock were told to move out and dig trenches the other side of the hedge in open field. Had some difficulty in finding a 'five' but got shoved into one at length. Dug trenches about 3ft 6in deep and got in. Had some bully and jam, but was still thirsty. Get to sleep in terrible discomfort and wake to find that the Germans were making a night attack. Told off to go as stretcher bearer. Leave equipment and rifle and go and carry a poor chap about 500 yards on a door to the field hospital. Bullets began whistling round but we got him safely down a very steep incline and were then attacked with rifle fire. Get into a wood and then have to come out and make a line in a small valley. Many of our chaps still in trenches in front so can't fire. Get into a big trench and are told we can go to sleep which most of us did. Woken again soon, as things were getting serious. However, no shots fired and we have to retire round a wood. There was a bright moon during that night but it had gone down by now. Many barns and villages and a church on fire. Get into field just as it was beginning to get light, and lie down as we were all exhausted. Was a most mixed crowd having some of every company. Presently Germans began to fire on us from a wood about 500 yards away. We had to retreat again and they followed us for about ¼ mile. Out into open country we thought we were captured but got away somehow just as it was dawning. Had to fight a 'rearguard action' as it was called, but we had to advance over open fields to some farm houses. Then coal boxes began falling and after lying under hedge had to fall back and back till we came to a small ditch with willows along it. There we waited most of the day while the Carbiniers and 18th Hussars drove them back. Coal boxes and shrapnel was falling all day about 300 yds to our right. They put in about 20 coal boxes one after another all in exactly the same place. So hungry that our chaps were eating turnips out of the fields. About 4 o'clock in afternoon we fell back to a village about 3 miles back. Rest on way at farm house to get water. Another rest in road fur-ther on in mud. Many Frenchmen past us. And staff officer gave three cheers for Scottish from a car. Got to village where we found some more Scottish and there was great enthusiasm when we arrived with Colonel. About 450 left out of nearly 1000. All wounded lost we think. Got billet in cafe never more thankful to lie down. Had some food and praised Heaven that I was alive. Slept on stone floor and very comfortable it was.

PRIVATE LAURENCE SYMINGTON, 14TH LONDON REGIMENT (LONDON SCOTTISH)

Despite heroic resistance the overwhelming German force took the Wytschaete-Messines Ridge and began another ferocious onslaught against British, Indian (the Lahore Division had arrived in Flanders in summer kit on 22 October) and French troops. The ridge and the two crest villages were lost by 2 November, and despite a sequence of occasionally successful British and French counter-attacks, would remain firmly in German possession.

The third and final phase of the battle began on 11 November: a last gasp attempt to gain the Channel ports before allied reinforcements arrived – and before winter set in. The assault followed the axis of the already notorious Menin Road, driving through Gheluvelt, Nonne Boschen and Polygon Wood. It was brought to another bloody standstill within a whisker of success at Hooge, just 3 kilometres outside Ypres.

At the end of proceedings, any further advance of the enemy line from the high ground which they now held was both unnecessary and unwise, so there they dug in. As the intensity of attacks subsided across the Salient, the Allies recognized that their main aim must be to put the present positions into a state of organized defence for the coming unpleasant wintry months of waiting, wondering and quite possibly, more enemy hostility. Just

one final attempt to dislodge the Germans took place on 19 December, this time from 'The Kink', a small salient facing Ploegsteert Wood on the extreme right wing of what was now quickly becoming the Ypres Salient. The enterprise was doomed from the start, not only by enemy action but by an element over which, outside their own trenches, the British were to exert no control for almost four years – mud – an aspect of fighting in Flanders that Sir Douglas Haig's diary mentions several times during First Ypres.

The attack was the last major British foray of 1914, and as the survivors crept back homeward, the pecked line of the nascent Salient was complete. When the battle officially ended on 22 November 1914, the BEF had been almost destroyed. Half its establishment were dead or wounded, and Britain's French allies had suffered similar losses. As for Germany, an entire army had been wiped from the establishment. As the grip of a Flemish winter closed upon the land, time was no longer on anyone's side, and the first stabilization and definition of trench lines began. Although piecemeal actions continued, most men were obliged to put aside their rifles, take up a fresh defensive tool – the spade – and dig for all they were worth. The war of movement was over, and the foundations for the greatest siege in military history had been laid.

The Germans were probably oblivious of just how close they had come to routing the British and French – but Sir Douglas Haig was certainly fully aware of the hair's breadth escape. He came to the alarming personal conclusion that just one single concerted final attack might well have broken the British defences, and burst the Ypres door wide open. Towards the end of the battle the British had

been deadbeat, unable to counter-attack, and with some units, in the words of their own commanders, 'thoroughly broken'. The firm belief that the Germans had wasted a golden opportunity for the want of a single final push was to influence Haig's future actions profoundly throughout the war.

Perhaps out of a sense of bitter frustration the German artillery then began the process of annihilating Ypres. They were clear in their future intentions: the struggle was far from over. Until they could regroup and plan the next great offensive, the hold on the amphitheatre of ridges semi-encircling the town was to remain vice-like. By Christmas 1914, the initial manifestation of the Salient, an 18-kilometre, sickle-shaped, double arc running from Het Saas in the north to Ploegsteert in the south, was in place. However, there was as yet no real trench line, just a series of disconnected ditches protected here and there by a few flimsy strands of gleaned barbed wire. By later standards the fieldworks were more than feeble, but now the real defensive effort was about to begin.

THURSDAY, 26TH/FRIDAY, 27TH NOVEMBER
Pontoon drill etc. Sir John French's despatch read on parade this morning. Reading between the lines I believe the hardest part of the British Army's work is finished.
CORPORAL A.A. WILKINSON, 26TH FIELD COMPANY, ROYAL ENGINEERS (AS A RESULT OF HIS ACTIONS AT FIRST YPRES, CORPORAL WILKINSON WAS PROMOTED TO SERGEANT AND WAS AWARDED THE DCM)

FIRST WINTER

Logically, the line around Ypres should have been abandoned by the British in favour of a new straight defensive position to the east. It was not,

Right
Highland troops in an early entrenchment. There are as yet no duckboards, but a low, home-made hurdle revetment helps to form a fire-step on the right. Note also the lack of protective headgear – steel helmets were only introduced in 1916.

and the winter ground conditions and lack of suitable equipment was to make life desolate for the troops. The situation was both brought about by Commander-in-Chief, Sir John French's almost universal intransigent denial of permission for any kind of withdrawal – even a few metres – to drier and tactically or topographically superior ground. He forbade almost all movement, leaving many positions quite inappropriate for even a moderate period of occupation. In the few places where it was simply not possible to live, the troops were allowed to withdraw – but come spring they had once more to take up the abandoned positions. Pleadings of infantry commanders fell upon deaf ears at GHQ.

The intrinsic prevailing psychology – a Victorian legacy – of the British Army decreed that this forced period of stasis was no more than a temporary inconvenience. Breakthrough in spring was a formality and until then a distinctly 'stiff-upper-lip' impression must be made upon the enemy. The troops must show no signs of weakness, and in addition the Commander-in-Chief required 'as much pressure as possible' to be brought, meaning that harassing operations were to be carried out throughout the winter. The German attitude was somewhat different. Having advanced thus far they saw no shame in digging in and waiting in safer – and drier – ridge-top abodes.

Dearest Family,

We spent the most extraordinary Xmas Day I expect it will ever be our lot to see. I was down in Chapelle d'Armentières all day on Xmas Eve on a Field General Court Martial and when I got back to our trenches after dark I found the 'Boschers' trenches looking like the Thames on Henley Regatta night! They had got little Xmas trees burning all along the parapet of their trench. No truce had been proclaimed and I was all for not allowing the blighters to enjoy themselves, especially as they had killed one of the men that afternoon, but my long captain (6' 6") who hadn't seen our wounded going mad and slowly dying outside the German trenches on the Aisne, wouldn't let me shoot – however, I soon had an excuse as one of the Germans fired at us, I quickly lined up my platoon and had those Xmas trees down and out. Meanwhile, unknown to us, two officers of D Coy on our right, without saying a word to anybody, got out of their trench and were met by two German officers and talked away quite civilly and actually shook hands! It was an awful stupid thing to do as it might easily have had different results – but all our Captains are new, and not having seen the Germans in their true light yet won't apparently believe the stories of their treachery and brutality; two men of B Coy actually walked over to the German trenches to talk and were immediately hauled in and taken prisoner! A lot of men of D Coy also walked over halfway and talked to the Germans who met them and smoked together – meanwhile I was shooting away quite merrily at the trenches in front of us, and the Leinsters on our left sang to them, and they rendered in return 'Der Vaterland', 'Der wacht am Rhein' etc.!

On Xmas Day we had a sort of mutual truce, nothing on paper or even in words, but a sort of mutual understanding. Bligh and self after breakfast walked halfway to the trenches in front of us and shouted for an officer as we wanted to see what regiment was in front of us. That did it! The Germans came out, as soon as we saw they were Saxons I knew it was all right – because they are good fellows on the whole and play the game as far as they know it.

LIEUTENANT C.T.F. SWAN, 3RD RIFLE BRIGADE

The truce varied in duration along the line, dependent upon local attitudes. But it was an unexpected opportunity to relax from the strain of trench warfare. For many though, the hiatus was too short lived.

The German trenches were roughly 200 yds from ours. Our Company Officer's name was Captain Unwin. The Saxons were beckoning with their hands for us to go over to their trench but we shouted over that we would meet them half way so Captain Unwin asked for a volunteer. I happened to be standing by the side of him at the time and it fell my lot to go over and meet one of the Saxons and a nice fellow he was. We shook hands and his first words to me was there any Scotch Territorials out yet as he was himself a waiter in Glasgow. After that I cannot remember what was passed between us as there was quite a crowd of us, but we were the best of friends for the next seven days. We used to walk about on top of the trench or in front of it without anything happening. I remember one day during the truce they accidentally killed one of our H.Q. Signallers and they sent over and apologized and the last day of the truce one of their fellows brought over a message to say they had orders to open fire with their automatic machines but their first shots would be fired high. Captain Unwin in return gave him a box of chocolates. And they certainly acted according to message. Then we were at war again.

PRIVATE B. HUTCHINGS, 1ST HAMPSHIRE REGIMENT

As the first Christmas and New Year passed by relatively peacefully, true trench warfare began. On 15 November British troops had moved out of much of the territory in front of Ypres, leaving it in French hands until early February 1915 when they returned to take over 8 kilometres of line from Poelcappelle to the Menin Road. By the beginning of April, two-thirds of the Salient had devolved to their care, and from 7th of that month the first imperial troops to arrive in France, the Indians,

Above
Home coastal breastwork defences at Scrapsgate on the Isle of Sheppey.

were joined by a second force, the Canadians. During the winter the front lines remained relatively static and although not yet fully connected to form the continuous ribbon we recognize today, certain permanently turbulent sub-sectors such as Hooge, Hill 60 and The Bluff, were already keenly developed for defence because of the proximity of the opposing lines. Here, patrols and trench raids were frequent and mine warfare, albeit on a limited scale, had been started by French engineers the moment movement had ceased.

The BEF, now installed at Ypres for the duration, were short of everything throughout this early period: wire, pumps, material for shelters, even spades. Britain was combed for any kind of lightweight machinery that would help keep water levels down, and new RE contracts went out to manufacturers nationwide for urgent supplies. Suitable weapons of war were also scarce. There were no trench mortars or grenades for this unexpected, static, close-range conflict; and no periscopes, fixed rifles, or steel loopholes for observation and sniping. However, improvization and experimentation was a long British military tradition, and 'unofficial' products, mostly devised and manufactured in several workshops employing local people but run by the Royal Engineers, appeared everywhere. With stasis

came challenge, and the British sapper was about to come into his own, gradually conceiving every aspect of the fabric, and by extension, nature of the battlegrounds of the First World War. The texture of trench warfare war was indeed largely engraved upon the Western Front by the sappers. Here was an almost blank canvas for the imaginative and inventive. Ever since the Peninsular War in the early nineteenth century, there had been no shortage of enquiring minds – in 1820 almost 50 per cent of Britain's qualified engineers were RE officers. A century later they were to scrutinize everything from huge machines for digging trenches or tunnels, to a veritable multiplicity of designs for something as apparently mundane as the humble sandbag. To the infantryman, it meant nothing more than heavy, repetitive and dull labouring work as fatigue parties put the sappers' designs into practice.

The task was gargantuan, and was of course not restricted to France and Belgium. To guard against a potential enemy breakthrough, parallel sets of auxiliary defensive positions were ultimately installed all the way back to the Channel ports. And indeed beyond – across the sea in Kent identical defences to those on the Western Front were installed, whilst London was entirely encircled by an unbroken ring of trenches.

CHAPTER THREE

The Second Battle and the Shrinking of the Salient

Within the grim struggle of First Ypres, the earliest of the four battles to which the town would lend its name, the mould for the character of the First World War in Belgian Flanders was cast. From the ashes of the BEF in December 1914, the British created two armies, the First under Haig (promoted to full General on the 20th) and the Second under General Sir Herbert Plumer. The First Army tried their offensive hand at Neuve Chapelle in March 1915, the first substantial British offensive of the war. The result was disappointing to say the least, but Haig met it head on with a composed scrutiny of events. From his reaction, we can already see the future pattern forming as he demanded more guns, bigger guns, more machine guns and an enhanced system of aerial reconnaissance. On 22 April, across the same Flemish fields as the previous autumn, the expected fresh German thrust once more took place. And at Second Ypres, it came just as close to victory. A month of punishing and costly attacks was heralded by the first use of poison gas on the Western Front. Although entirely experimental the effort was a great success; fortunately for the British, French, Belgian and Canadian troops holding the Salient at the time, the Germans had not considered bringing up support units to take advantage of it simply because only a minor advance towards Ypres

Left
German troops prepare to release cloud gas. The cylinders are protected within the trench parapet with dispersal hoses reaching out into no man's land.

Below
Second Army pan 8, 13 July 1915. The Pilckem Ridge sector. Part of the area across which chlorine gas was employed by the Germans on 22 April 1915. The cloud would have come directly towards the camera.

was envisaged – enough to make the town indefensible and force an Allied withdrawal. Also, and more importantly, they remained unaware of the terrific coup created by the use of gas until it was too late. It was, however, just the beginning of more than three years of chemical warfare in the Salient.

German *Pioniers* had already waited patiently to test their new weapon for several weeks, but the wind had remained stubbornly unfavourable. When it did blow, it came out of the south and west, rather than the east from where it would carry the gas towards the Allies' front lines. On the morning of Thursday, 22 April a gentle north-easterly breathed across the fields, but it was considered too light for a safe release and the Germans were forced to wait until the evening before conditions altered in their favour. As the valves of 5,700 cylinders were opened releasing almost 170 tons of chlorine gas across a front of almost 8 kilometres, querulous Allied eyes peered from trench loopholes to see an unseasonal evening mist drifting towards them. When it reached the French Algerian lines in front of Langemarck there was a brief moment of confusion before panic set in.

On April 15th we were told that Langemark had to be conquered. A special system was to be tried out for the first time which promised to be a great success. We were lying in our trench at Poelcappelle when our days of rest ended (on April 15th) because, as the wind turned to the east, the alarm went. Twice we got into position but each time in vain. On the 23rd [sic – the attack was actually on 22 April] it appeared to be the right time at last. At 3 o'clock in the afternoon, I received the order to put the enemy's trench, about one hundred metres in front of ours, under fire in order to divert their attention. Then both sides started firing, but with little consequence. Suddenly, one of my men called, 'Sir, look to your right towards Langemark.' And there it was! A giant cloud crept over the enemy's trenches and rolled slowly on to the East leaving behind only the dead and the suffocating. The enemy commands were very clear. 'Everyone who wanted to avoid the cloud should abandon the trenches.' But those who did only fell very quickly under our gunfire. I was only an onlooker. The sun sent its rays into this red-brown cloud which crawled slowly on its way. That which had seemed impossible despite our great numbers, i.e. the conquest of the heavily armed and fortified French trench, was achieved with a relatively small German sacrifice. In short, this is the method: at a depth of one metre, large bottles similar to oxygen cylinders are secured in the trench; each is attached to a [hose] that is fed over the parapet of the trench. The bottles are filled with poison gas which is heavier than air. On the command the valves of all the bottles are opened and the concentrated

Canadian
Farm

Kitchener's   Wood

Hampshire Farm

gases escape. The men attending to this wear masks. During the development of the gas cloud, heavy firing is continued. Then the infantry follow directly behind the cloud. Those who were alive were picked up; those who were not in the line of the gas cloud lost their courage and surrendered. This was the way the ring around Langemark was shattered.

LEUTNANT FRITZ ROMBERG, IMPERIAL GERMAN ARMY

Men not dead or dying from the effects – the gas caused men to drown in their own mucus – bolted. A huge breach appeared in the Allied line.

I saw the first green cloud of poison gas come over our front line troops, and in a short time we felt the effects of it. But the worst poison had gone to the ground before it reached our trench. Even so, we had to protect our mouths and breathing with body belts that we carried with us. Unfortunately, the men in the front line had no time to consider what to do before the poison gas had done its deadly work. Many fell on the way back, and those that I witnessed left this world in agony. The gas caused the tongue to swell to the full extent of the mouth, and then a gradual choking took place, until the life was squeezed out of the person affected.

COMPANY SERGEANT MAJOR CORNELIUS LOVE DCM,
2ND MONMOUTHSHIRE REGIMENT

But the combination of late timing, unexpected results, restricted expectation and a daunting defence by the recently arrived 1st Canadian Division who swarmed across to partly fill the breach, meant that there was simply not enough time for the Germans to bring up supports and exploit the surprise before night fell. As dusk turned to darkness, Belgian troops had already responded swiftly to augment the Canadian defences, and more Allied reserves were being rushed forward. Fighting continued all that night. By morning the enemy line had

been held on the crest of Pilckem Ridge.

It is generally believed that had the assault taken place earlier in the day, leaving plenty of light for German commanders to recognize and react to the success, Ypres may well have been lost, with serious consequences for the Channel ports, Paris, France as a nation, and ultimately Britain and her Empire.

I received the order to make a recce of the English trench to find out whether it was still occupied. The trench was empty. The English had left everything behind and got out. My Company took possession of everything there was to eat out of their packs, and within an hour everybody was smoking English cigarettes; there was tobacco, corned beef and marmalade. It really was comical. I couldn't allow my men a long rest as I had to see to the [trench]. All eatables were carefully put away and the work commenced. The communication trench dug at right angles was finished, and at 5 o'clock in the morning my Battalion-commandant, Captain Licht, and his adjutant appeared – both were later wounded and they led the march of the III Battalion through my newly-dug trench which enables us to get to our old positions. At daybreak the enemy began to open fire and in this mighty onslaught we had our first losses. The battle then developed. Our artillery literally poured 'iron' into the enemy position and, having made contact with Regiment 234 the front was ready. Totally shaken by the terrible artillery fire, the enemy stopped firing and the command came 'Auf Marsch' – March! It was a wonderful sight to see our Battalions advance in one great line. The English had ceased firing. The artillery attack had forced them to give in and draw back. Their trenches were in a terrible state but the war has blunted our feelings. They were Canadian soldiers: tall, beautiful people. There they lay, torn to pieces by German shells or killed by our rifles. Those who were able to raise their hands did so and were marched off. One sight I shall never forget. It was a young man who had saved himself and was

Above and below
These two images illustrate the aftermath of the 22 April gas attack. The top one is captioned 'an English trench', the other states that a French position is pictured. Both, however, show exactly the same scene, with the casualties (which appear to be French) moved a little.

Below
British casualties (possibly Scottish troops) in positions adjacent to the St Julien road.

Below
British and probably Canadian prisoners captured during Second Ypres are marched back to captivity.

hauled up from a deep hole. I approached him, trying to make him talk, but all in vain. The youngster had lost his mind.
LEUTNANT FRITZ ROMBERG, IMPERIAL GERMAN ARMY

Just over 2,000 Allied troops were taken prisoner during the initial assaults. As the battle ground on, a series of more German gas attacks, localized Allied defeats and tactical withdrawals pushed the defence further back towards Ypres. The contracting salient was witness to countless scenes of horror.

Going up to the Batt one night saw the worst sight of the war, a man of our Regt was crying 'shoot me'; when I looked he had his two legs and right hand blown off, he said 'shoot me out of it, shoot you coward' he said. My God, I ran from him to the Battalion, I told the regimental Sergeant Major Noble about him but at present they were all away, worked to death. Going back the same way the man was still alive, when I got near he said 'I know what I got, shoot me out of the way', once daylight comes he is here for a day for sure, he cries 'shoot me' and swears at me, at last I get behind him but my courage fails me, but I look again at him, he is dead, I drop my rifle and ran to Irish Farm. Sgt. Shaw is there. 'Hello Taff, saw a ghost?' I tell him of it, I am trembling and sweating.
PRIVATE CHARLES HEARE, 1/2ND MONMOUTHSHIRE REGIMENT

The arc of the Salient contracted three times during the battle, first from trenches at the foot of the Passchendaele Ridge just before the battle started, and then from the Pilckem, Frezenberg, Wieltje and Bellewaerde ridges, positions from which it was hoped successful stands might have been be made. Both north and south of the Menin Road the German assault came to rest upon a line that ran through all the most effective topographical sites for observation and bombardment. The positions occupied on 25 May 1915, the final day of battle, were to remain largely fixed for the next two years. The Salient had completed it contractions.

24TH APRIL

The effects of the successful gas attack were horrible. I am not pleased with the idea of poisoning men. Of course, the entire world will rage about it first and then imitate us. All the dead lie on their backs, with clenched fists; the whole field is yellow. They say that Ypres must fall now. One can see it burning – not without a pang for the beautiful city. Langemarck is a heap of rubbish, and all rubbish-heaps look alike; there is no sense in describing one. All that remains of the church is the doorway with the date '1620'.

27TH APRIL

After fresh attacks a sleeping army lies in front of one of our brigades; they rest in good order, man by man, and will never wake again – Canadian divisions. The enemy's losses are enormous. The battlefield is fearful. One is overcome by a peculiar sour, heavy and penetrating smell of corpses.
RUDOLPH BINDING, IMPERIAL GERMAN ARMY

Almost 5,000 men died as a result of the several gas attacks at Second Ypres, with a total of more than 100,000 casualties sustained by both sides during the entire battle. Sir John French described the employment of gas as 'a cynical and barbarous disregard of the well-known usages of civilized war and a flagrant defiance of the Hague Convention'. However, the potential of chemical weaponry was swiftly recognized by the British High Command and on 3 May 1915 Lord Kitchener himself began the process that would sanction British retaliatory action in kind on 25 September at Loos – prosecuted unsuccess-

fully by Sir Douglas Haig's First Army. Unknown to all, the northern battlefront was now definitely fixed and the war of movement was over. Ypres was a smoking shambles and the great mutual siege was settling like a shroud over Flanders.

31st May 1915. As it was such a quiet morning we came back right through Ypres which was indeed a scene of desolation. I don't suppose in the whole town of well on to 20,000 inhabitants there is one single house unharmed. Most have one or two holes, even in the suburbs; round the Place practically all are levelled to the ground. The famous Cloth Hall where William II was to have been crowned king of Belgium last November is a roofless shattered ruin. The barrel organ cylinder which used to work the famous Carillon was lying at the foot of the clock tower. Half a dozen houses were burning briskly as we passed and in fact the only live Belgian we saw belonging to Ypres was a half-starved cat. No words or even photos can express the havoc caused in what was once the show place in western Flanders.

MAJOR S.H. COWAN, 175TH TUNNELLING COMPANY, ROYAL ENGINEERS

Above
Left-hand section of a German panorama taken from Passchendaele Church before the Second Battle.

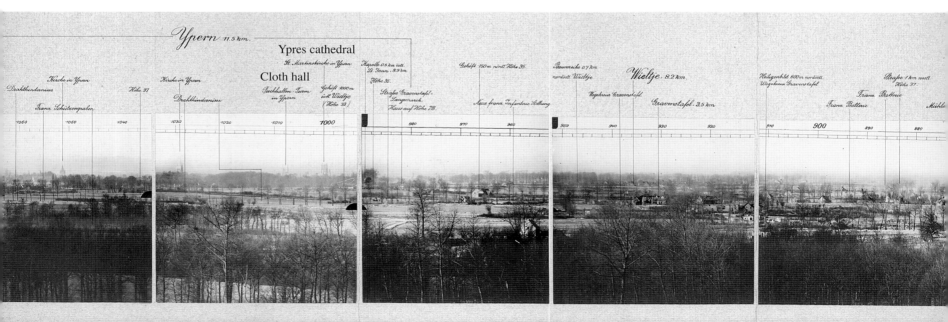

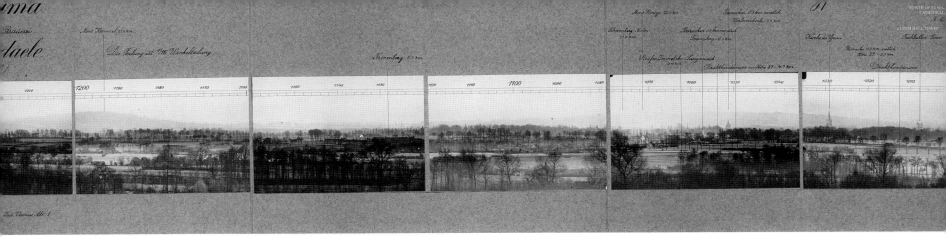

Below
The foreground of the right-hand (rechter teil) section of the same panorama shows the sector which was to become hallowed ground during the latter stages of the Third Battle some two and a half years later. See also British pan on page 48.

Once again, Sir Douglas Haig noted how little extra German force would have been required to break Plumer's line. When the German attacks at last relented, the Allies, whilst still acknowledging that the next operation order was more than likely to be of the offensive variety, began the process of again shielding themselves from enemy fire. The British attitude to the war is amply illustrated in the fortifications installed at this time: simple structures, waterproof if possible, but still built purely as platforms for the next attack. None were to know that

that attack was to be a full two years away. With the inundations forming an impassable barrier to the north, and an equally immobile situation in the south, the Salient, unsatisfactory from almost every tactical, topographical and strategic perspective, would be maintained at all costs.

At First Ypres Germany had launched colossal multiple assaults against a far weaker force of regular troops installed in the most primitive of fieldworks – and failed catastrophically. During the second battle it happened

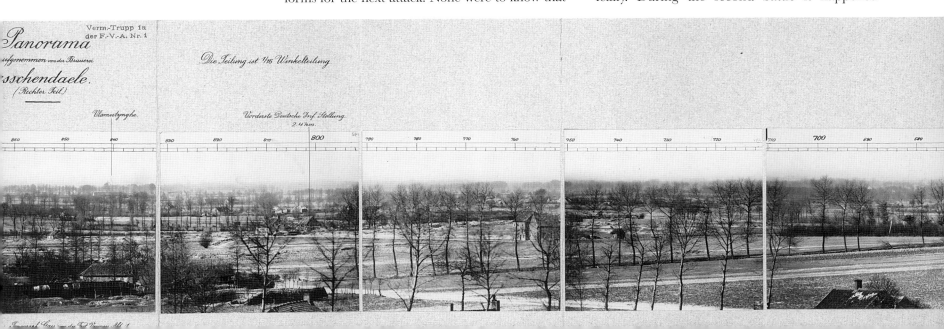

again. The failures reinforced an uncomfortable suspicion that even an apparently overwhelming force was incapable of penetrating the most rudimentary of positions defended by accomplished gunners, riflemen and machine gunners. The critical aspect of this first period of true positional warfare was therefore to create an impenetrable line by the extension and completion of the Salient's defensive fieldwork system. By the end of July 1915, a set of continuous trench lines faced each other across a 'no man's land' of varying widths. As an unbroken pair of fortress walls with no vulnerable flanks, all future attacks now had to be frontal. It was at this point that troops began to develop a curious familiarity with their new home, a familiarity more profound than any other sector of the Western Front. Every farm, road, trench and natural feature was christened with names that continue to ring symbolic bells almost nine decades later: Hellfire Corner, Mousetrap Farm, Sanctuary Wood, the Menin Road, Hooge, to name but a small handful. As the troops bonded with the landscape, it was to become a longer, more intimate and more painful relationship than any could have imagined.

AFTER THE BATTLE

After Second Ypres limited assaults and trench raids became commonplace. In those places where the opposing lines had settled in close proximity and where observation potential was greatest, small cauldrons of conflict developed – some of it brief and bloody on the surface, but much unseen, unseeable and secret, far beneath. It was on the low ridges at Hooge, Hill 60, St Eloi, and The Bluff, that engineers resorted to ancient siege warfare techniques – the underground war that would culminate more than two years later at the Battle of Messines Ridge. Ultimately this strange, primitive and invisible struggle would encompass almost every sub-sector, not only in the Salient but along the entire Western Front, and it was to play a key role at the beginning of the Third Battle of Ypres.

Each of the Allied offensives of 1915 promoted a profound scrutiny and adjustment of fieldworks by the engineers of both sides. Losses at subsequent British offensive endeavours – Neuve Chapelle, Aubers Ridge, Festubert and especially Loos – were progressively more shocking, and it was only following profound disappointment at the latter battle in September 1915 that a concerted effort was made to create a state of impenetrability. In Britain criticism had long been pungent, for shell shortages and blatantly faulty ordnance were cited as primary causes of the repeated failures. However, German tactics, particularly the idea of defending a deep band of territory – defence-in-depth – were beginning to make Allied strategists sit up. The defence-in-depth policy worked like a rubber band, allowing hostile penetration up to a point where with initial impetus drained and assaulting force weakened, the defence could counter-attack strongly, flinging the enemy back and inflicting serious loss. The answer? In the absence of bulletproof troops, there was only one: more artillery, more heavy guns that could obliterate a wide ribbon of enemy territory, thereby neutralizing the entire garrison within it.

At Second Ypres the great pre-attack artillery bombardment was not yet established as a staple, but by Christmas 1915 it was obligatory, and with it the age-old battle winner, surprise, was abandoned in favour of total destruction. There were hugely increased numbers of guns, howitzers, mortars and heavy ordnance in 1916. To those who witnessed them, the British bombardments of this era appeared devastating. The spectacle, however, turned out to be illusory: first, because enemy fieldworks were to advance faster in the form of ferro-concrete emplacements and deep protective dugouts; and second, because a week's bombardment gave defenders all the warning they required of impending attack. Gas was proving to be a strictly curate's-eggish weapon, and far from the battle-winner that had been anticipated, a form of mutual nullification appeared once both sides were able to employ it. Nevertheless, the use of gas increased. Once various forms could be delivered in shell form it became a weapon of supreme harassment, disruption and irritation. Now, neither wind direction nor strength were relevant, and it could be deployed at any time, day or night, forcing men to wear uncomfortable and debilitating masks for long periods, depriving them of food, sleep and clear vision.

Underground warfare, although in progress along the full length of the front by mid-1916, was developing into a strictly private conflict with strictly localized effects upon surface strategy. As for tanks and aircraft, each were still in their infancy. Lead and steel in the form of bullet, shell and wire held absolute rule over the primary offensive hurdle – no man's land.

THE PRIMACY OF THE GUN

Artillery came to be looked upon as the key to the deadlock: both the objective and its garrison could be obliterated before one's infantry made a move. By comparison to the battles of the final eighteen months of the war, including Third Ypres, the effect of shellfire on fieldworks was relatively unconvincing throughout 1914, 1915 and indeed much of 1916: there were simply too few available heavy guns to pulverize adequately the wide and deep battlefronts selected for each offensive. It took the Somme debacle of 1 July 1916 to convince British commanders that a combination of truly overwhelming concentrations plus fresh tactics were required if the enemy were ever to be in any way subdued. Indeed, a handful of unorthodox but successful artillery-led assaults during the Somme campaign appeared to point to good progress being made, especially with regard to the creeping barrage.

Historically, artillery was a siege-breaking weapon, used to break down castle walls or bludgeon positions; guns were also used to destroy man and beast, with grapeshot or shrapnel spraying infantry and cavalry advances over open ground. With the stasis of trench warfare guns began to fight guns – counter-battery fire with high-explosive shells. With increased need came increased development and increased precision, tailored to fit specific circumstances. For trench raids, for instance, box barrages were employed. Here the enemy defence was trapped within a framework of bursting shells, a framework that also kept support troops out. And there were area shoots, intense bombardments designed to obliterate a farm, a suspected mining scheme, a trench, a road or rail junction, or a wider locale and everything that lay within. The barrages preceding each stage of the major offensives of 1917 were the ultimate incarnation of this latter device: successive ribbons of ground were literally torn to shreds before the infantry went over. As the attack got underway the finely tuned co-operation of man and gun, known as the creeping barrage, was deployed. Then there was wire – as crucial a feature of trench warfare as the trench itself. Every attack was obliged to expend huge amounts of preliminary explosive effort, not only in pounding enemy positions, but in cutting paths through entanglements. If continual augmentation and repair could be achieved the barrier was usually capable of delaying an assault long enough for it to be completely neutralized by defensive fire. The more wire there was, the more guns were required to cut it. At the same time the cohesively defended forward areas (on both sides of no man's land) broadened, covering an average depth of around a kilometre from front line to reserve trench, with subsequent lines of resistance behind. The Somme saw the advent of German long-range machine-gun barrages posing yet

more dispersed and difficult-to-subdue targets which, being out of effective range of small-arms fire, only artillery could deal with. Neutralization demanded more powerful guns and more accurate shooting. The widespread application of the delayed-action shell, which burrowed deep into the ground before exploding, made sure that even the deepest dugouts were death traps. For the British this development came too late for the 1915 battles and especially the Somme, where the tactic could have been highly influential. In the summer and autumn of 1917 the fighting was to take place in a theatre where it would have an extremely limited application, for in the Salient the enemy defences were almost entirely surface-based.

That's the worst of the Ypres Salient. He has perfect Artillery Observation from Wytschaete, St Eloi, Hill 60 and Bellewarde Ridge. And we are downhill everywhere – even at Hooge there is rising ground in front of us so we have to depend upon observing from our own trenches for the close work and from Aeroplanes and Balloons when we shell further back. How we all curse the SALIENT.

Major S.H. Cowan, 175th Tunnelling Company, Royal Engineers

Goudberg Spur   Bellevue   Marsh Bottom

Left
A magnificent German observation tower situated several kilometres behind the front lines in the Staden area.

Below
This British view from the Gravenstafel crossroads just before the British retirement of April 1915 illustrates the foreshortened horizon of those holding the lower contours. The spurs seen here were the scene of some of the bitterest fighting during the Third Battle. Panorama 58, 17 April 1915.

The key to artillery success is observation. From their high vantage points on the ridges around Ypres, German observers were able to scan the British front, support and reserve lines, their communication trenches, and tracks, roads and railways – by day. Selecting a target and ranging the guns could hardly have been more straightforward. When the nightly round of British activity began in the cul de sac of the Salient, German gunners could happily blaze away in the knowledge that every round was probably finding a target. By contrast, the British gazed everywhere uphill. At no point, except from a short stretch of line astride Tor Top above Sanctuary Wood, could they observe any enemy movements from ground level. Even from here, however, the view was completely blocked by dense woodland. The key observation position was Kemmel Hill. From here the entire Salient could be viewed – up to the ridges. To see beyond, balloons or aircraft – both dependent upon good weather – were necessary. And the difficulties did not end there. The British were also forced to use military personnel only for supply and construction work in

the forward areas. By contrast, on the outside of the Salient's arc, their enemy enjoyed excellent road and rail communication, and frequent invisibility. When British balloons and aircraft were grounded, enemy supplies could be brought up by day as well as night and secreted close to the places where they were required. Soon after Second Ypres, Belgian forced labour began helping not only with German supply but field defences, often appearing in the front lines themselves: 175 Tunnelling Company personnel working at Hooge in July 1915 regularly saw – and shot at – the bobbing top hats of civilian contractors. Later, they would be joined across the region by Russian and Rumanian prisoners.

After two years of uninterrupted labour the Germans had taken the concept of defence-in-depth to new heights; likewise across no man's land. In the belief that the Ypres sector was likely to be central in Sir Douglas Haig's 1916 plans, the British also determined that German spoiling attacks must be fruitless, so they too fortified more strongly than anywhere else on the Western Front.

Passchendaele   Church (behind tree)   Tree lined road along Passchendaele Ridge

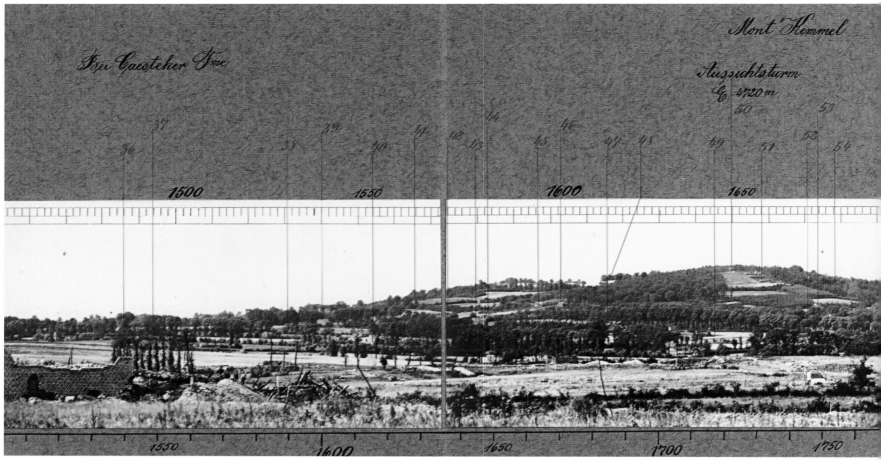

Bei Caesteker Fme

Mont Kemmel

Aussichtsturm
4720 m

50

53

37

39

44

46

50

53

36

38

40

41 42 43

45

47 48

49 51

52

54

1500   1550   1600   1650

1550   1600   1650   1700   1750

Above
This German panorama taken during the summer of 1916 from positions in front of Wytschaete on the Messines Ridge shows the dominant British-held Kemmel Hill. Their sole elevated vantage point in the region, it nevertheless enjoyed limited tactical utility.

Right
The present-day view taken from a position close to the original.

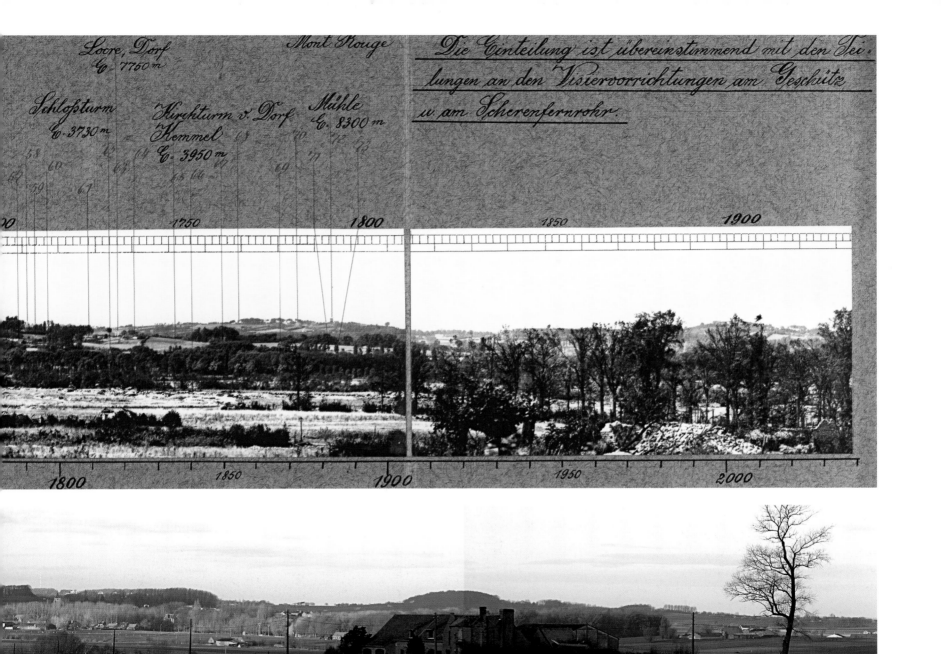

Locre, Dorf
€ 7750 m

Mont Rouge

Schloßturm
€ 3730 m

Kirchturm v. Dorf
Kemmel
€ 3950 m

Mühle
€ 8300 m

Die Einteilung ist übereinstimmend mit den Teilungen an den Visiervorrichtungen am Geschütz
u. am Scherenfernrohr.

1750   1800   1850   1900

1800   1850   1900   1950   2000

CHAPTER FOUR
Consolidation, Clay and Concrete

Above
The Salient's northern boundary: a
listening post in no man's land opposite
Boesinghe.

Below
The southern boundary: the blockade at
Le Gheer crossroads.

Right
Hand-annotated 1915 British map. The
panorama on page 41 was taken near La
Belle Alliance (bottom) looking towards
Turco Farm.

The lessons that could have been learned from the siege and defence of Port Arthur in 1904 were ignored, and no attention was paid to the German siege manoeuvres of 1908, of which a full account was published in English. The infantry also had very scanty training in field entrenching. They were indeed discouraged from practising it at manoeuvres by the rule that units who dug trenches must return afterwards and fill them in. It is not surprising that the Expeditionary Force arrived in France very ill prepared for the conditions which faced it after a few months of the opening phase of the war, conditions that, after the flanking movement to the north had reached the sea, soon became those of siege warfare.

HISTORY OF THE CORPS OF ROYAL ENGINEERS, VOLUME V

HOMEMAKING

Since the British Expeditionary Force first arrived in the Ypres region in the autumn of 1914, they had been more or less in constant conflict – not with the Germans, for apart from the first two battles of Ypres the fighting was intermittent and often highly localized – but with Mother Nature. The primary irritant was water. Ironically, although it had been an Allied lifeline in the form of the great inundations, possibly even a nation and empire saver, once definite trench lines had been installed, connected and expanded, water

became far more foe than friend. It mattered not whether one was in static defence or in mobile attack, the nature of the Flemish climate and geology was the source of a permanent heavy workload, not only for the engineers, the natural wardens for all things environmental, but everyone. Indeed, the same had been true in peacetime: in Flanders it was a fineable offence not to keep one's waterways clean and most important of all, flowing.

The challenge to create a trench infrastructure that could master just this one element was tremendous. Yet the goal was largely achieved, given that trenches were just glorified holes in the ground, and other than during times of deluge, by mid-1916 the troops occupying positions in the forward areas were able to live in relative comfort. As for defence against enemy action, the Germans held most of the best cards as regards field position; so security, like comfort, was down to respecting the ever-progressing basic but rigid rules of trench construction laid down by the engineers, and common sense in exercising caution in one's own movements. All knew and accepted the truism 'it has your name on it'.

Like sniping, the incidence and intensity of

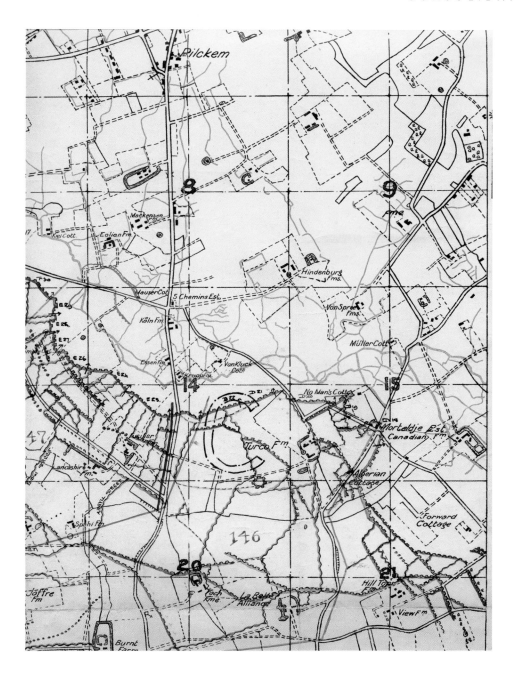

shellfire was extremely variable; some days might see practically incessant fire, others none at all. Work, heavy work, however, was ubiquitous, a round-the-clock occupation, installing wire, draining and resurrecting old trenches to the latest patterns, organizing water supply and telephonic communication, siting machine-gun posts, dugouts, observation posts and dressing stations, and delivering the eternal material wherewithal to conduct a troglodyte war by boat, barge, road, rail, track and by hand. Most duties outside battle itself were engineer related and sapper officer led – but with the infantry supplying the muscle. Entrenchment, wiring and other front-line work all fell traditionally within the RE domain, but the Corps had been instantly overextended as soon as static warfare set in. It was a situation that endured for the entire war.

Behind the lines the engineering burden was no less heavy: apart from permanent attention required on bridges, roads and billets, there was very soon a need for workshops, hospitals, laundries, camps, water treatment centres, sewage treatment works, canals, veterinary units, factories, dumps, forestry, printing, survey, trench maps, sawmills, postal services, airfields, docks, railways and tramways, water transport, carrier pigeons, camouflage, meteorology, dogs, cinemas, water-boring units, searchlights, training schools for all purposes including mining and gas, a host of research and experimental bodies, and the administration and repair of devastated zones, as well as salvage, during and after battle. Later, in 1916, vast dugout schemes were instigated. All these works had the single ultimate function of better serving the individual soldier in the line.

THE TEXTURE OF THE SALIENT

It is a mistake to believe the oft-peddled myth that British troops lived in squalor in primitive, filthy holes, whilst the Germans enjoyed a comfortable existence in better-built, better-designed, better-placed trenches. Certainly, British field positions were universally inferior, a far from ideal situation, but the best had to be made of a bad job and the RE constantly strove to improve the trench infrastructure. In the early period the greatest challenge had been the education of often recalcitrant regular and territorial troops whose rigorous training had understandably not included skulking in trenches and digging for salvation. The arrival of the first New Army units in the spring of 1915 immensely boosted fieldwork resources, in both numbers and skills, and indeed permitted the 'art' of trench warfare to flourish. Deploying expertise derived from largely manual-labour based civilian occupations, these fresh troops were better able to create a remarkably safe and dry trench environment of the highest quality. Indeed, this was what GHQ demanded, for a sick soldier was of no use

Above
May 1916. German 'before and after' showing the results of an artillery and mortar attack on the British breastworks near Ploegsteert Wood.

Right
Primitive German communication trench near St Julien, flooded out after torrential rains during the winter of 1915/16. No trench system could cope with such weather.

either in defence or attack, and if trenches were waterlogged and fitted with poor shelters, as they universally were during the first winter, widespread maladies of all kinds, including the highly debilitating and sometimes fatal trench foot, were to be expected. Unlike the regulars, every New Army battalion, however, incorporated large numbers of manually skilled and often supremely versatile men. By the autumn of 1915 British positions in the Ypres and Messines Salients were already unrecognizable from the simple scrapes of early spring, and soon all fieldworks were as minutely conceived, drawn and constructed as the most meticulously designed civilian engineering project at home in Britain. A year later they were models of efficiency, with every aspect of trench life receiving the engineers' attention. Although differing from sector to sector, the basic specifications for a trench were as follows:

1. Offer sufficient cover as to make one's movements invisible to the enemy.

2. Withstand, as far as possible, shellfire by the most common enemy ordnance, the

5.9-inch field howitzer.

3. Be deep and robust enough to offer total protection from surface rifle and machine-gun fire, with sufficient splinter-proof shelters for the garrison (it was only in 1916 that deep dugouts, proof against all but delayed-action shells, became commonplace).

4. Keep the troops' feet above the water level *at all times*.

5. Offer adequate waterproof shelter from the elements.

6. Allow maximum but safe mobility in both fire and communication trenches.

7. Incorporate sufficient space for all forms of 'trench store'.

8. Include positions for all required forms of defensive weaponry.

Putting this infrastructure in place was one thing, maintaining it once installed was another. Each section of trench was built to suit local topographical circumstances. Varying ground conditions – geology and contour – required different treatment. Whereas excavations on the slopes of the sandy ridges could be deep and secure at around 2 metres, others might be half-trench, half-breastwork affairs, whilst those in the wettest valley bottom positions, where the water table precluded almost any digging, were constructed as full breastworks – literally a trench created by building its two side walls on the ground surface utilizing material 'won' nearby. According to research, the (present) record for a party of infantry attached to an RE Field Company was just under 18,000 filled sandbags in a single night. Ultimately, every metre of every trench (almost 2,200 miles are believed to have been installed by both sides in the Salient during the war) was graded, drained and bled of water, usually into sumps (literally reservoir pits sited at varying intervals within a trench system) from whence it was pumped away. Without this work trenches would very quickly degrade; indeed, in their post-war histories the RE repeatedly stated that far more trenches were destroyed by simple neglect assisted by the action of weather, than by enemy action.

Development in materials and methods can clearly be distinguished as the war progressed, but the best appreciation of the careful investment of thought is always to be found in the effort made to supply that most basic of human requirements, drinking water. To the troops, Flanders was a land of little else but ponds, pools, streams, moats, wells, rivers and canals, all of which claimed their nightly number of unwary victims, but there was no guarantee that water from any of these sources was safe to drink.

Widespread sickness through water-borne bacteria was a serious hazard, potentially affecting thousands of men, so contamination had to be avoided at all costs. Purification was therefore a major endeavour. The Salient was mainly supplied by water taken from the River Yser at two points, Haringhe and Rousbrugge. Here it was de-poisoned, filtered, sterilized and carried via 180 miles of 4-inch piping to

Above
Controlling water in the half-trench, half-breastwork positions in the Ploegsteert sector.

Below
German drainage methods on sloping ground (above) and flat terrain. On the ridges, any pumped or drained water happily flowed towards their enemy.

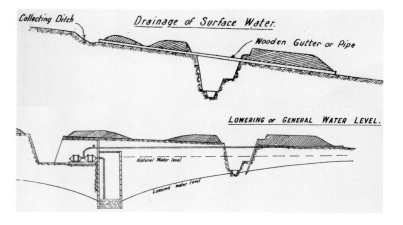

A whistle-stop evolution of British trench construction in the Salient. *Above left* shows the squalor of winter 1914. Above centre: early simple breastworks in Sanctuary Wood in spring 1915 show duckboards but no other structural elements. *Above right*: trench/breastwork amalgamation in the same sector in 1916, but now much more developed with suspended duckboards and timber, wire and corrugated-iron revetment. *Right*: full breastwork with built-in shelters, Hill 60, September 1916. *Left*: a strong and well-built trench/breastwork construction with corrugated-iron and expanded metal revetments, easy to maintain, dry and quick to repair. *Below left*: the proof of the quality and durability of British trench design and workmanship can be found in modern excavations, Pilckem Ridge, 2005. *Below right*: Yorkshire Trench. An interesting but seriously misleading reconstruction near Boesinghe.

various delivery points along and behind the battlefront. Haringhe alone supplied 120,000 gallons daily. In addition, on the canals radiating from Nieuport 32 million extra gallons were provided by barges equipped with specialized filtration units. Ultimately, due to the intensity of shelling at Third Ypres, it would only be possible to pipe water to about 5 kilometres from the front lines. Beyond that, muscle-power – man, mule and horse – was the most reliable and indeed sole alternative. Just as in civilian life, the system then demanded constant upkeep.

Having designed the environment, finding the necessary manpower to install and maintain it was of course seldom a problem, especially in the relatively quiet two-year period between the Second and Third battles of Ypres. Obtaining the raw materials to fortify in depth the entire Flanders region, however, often was. With the high water table the British required vast amounts of timber for trench A-frames, dugouts and duckboards; revetting material (the structure used to stabilize trench walls) was employed in many guises according to availability: in the same length of trench one might therefore see a mixture of corrugated iron, timber boards or sheets, rough-sawn forest planks, expanded metal, the traditional woven hurdle, and a variety of 'won' material such as house doors and window frames. Eventually, to feed the First World War hydra, the military were forced to import timber from Britain and the Empire, the Baltic and the USA.

For the critical bullet-proof upper section of the trench, where were situated the berm and fire-step, snipers' and observation loopholes etc., sandbags were the primary element.

Commander Royal Engineers (CRE) instructions stated that unless absolutely necessary (in the case of full or half-breastworks) sandbags were not to be employed to form trench walls simply because of their strictly limited lifespan: they both rotted quickly and were subject to rapid wear in a busy trench, lasting little more than a fortnight in busy operational lines. Once worn or decayed, a bag split and shed its load, so wherever sandbags were an integral part of the construction, working parties were permanently detailed on replacement *before* they had 'gone too far', as the sappers put it. Dull work, it very often simply entailed putting the old bag and its contents inside a new one. In typical fashion, the engineers attempted to design and procure a rot-proof bag, but could find no suitable material to withstand rigorous tests at the School of Military Engineering at Chatham. A distinct evolution in the design of certain structures, especially dugouts, trench elements (A-frames), revetting frames, drains and sumps, even latrines, is readily discernible throughout the war, but once the basic tenets of construction had been established and adhered to, it mainly required unceasing and tedious work to maintain a safe, dry and indeed hygienic environment. The troops called it 'housekeeping', and the more one did, the fewer awkward repairs one could expect and the more comfortable life became.

Neither battles nor wars are won by sitting in a trench, however, no matter how well designed and constructed it may be. The true battleground lay beyond the front line, beyond one's parapet. The critical interface between control and lack of control, both of the built environment and military direction, lay exactly at this point. It was a

Top
Early (1915) German trench in the Salient. Deep, unrevetted, but already with tunnelled shelters.
Above
Screened German communication walkway across the inundations near Dixmuide.

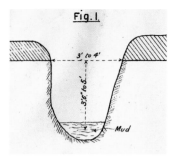

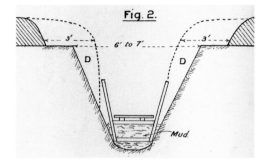

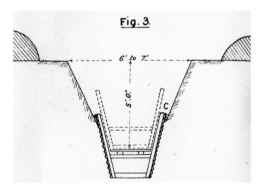

Above

Rules for the conversion of early 'ditch trenches' into dry and durable positions by the use of 'A-Frames' were simple but effective, and were strictly adhered to.

boundary that every man must cross in order to attack, and in so doing troops effectively abandoned a habitat which they knew more than intimately, to move into an alien world with no infrastructure whatsoever, except, should they gain the opposing trenches, an unfamiliar one created by their enemy. The process of reinstalling a manageable environment suiting one's own requirements then restarted afresh. Captured trenches had first to be reversed so that the fire-step was facing the correct way, then consolidated, laundered and camouflaged if necessary. They needed rechristening, routes signposting, and the whole system connected to one's original lines by trench (sap), track, road or rail (but preferably all four), whilst all the time being surveyed, drawn and photographed, and added to trench maps. Dependent upon the ebb and flow of battle, one's stay in the enemy lines might be brief or lengthy, but such work had always at least to be commenced. Above all, this was an area with scant communication with those commanding the battle; indeed crossing the critical parapet interface more often than not entirely truncated all influence beyond Brigade level, and completely severed links with higher authority. Once the troops left their front-line trench, those at Army, Corps and Division could make no impression on events, no matter how they were unfolding – for they were not on the spot.

The Germans had been more industrious and indeed prescient before the war, arriving on the Western Front with functional and practical weaponry for the campaign, before putting in place carefully considered and constructed field-work defences in the most effective topographical locations. Critically, and unlike

the British, they made certain to protect the prime battle-winning branch of the Army, the infantry. In the dry chalk areas south of the La Bassée Canal in northern France, defences were based upon deep underground cover – deep dugouts – the principal curse of Allied troops at Aubers, Festubert and Loos, and in particular on the Somme. On the first day of the Somme offensive, German troops emerging unscathed from such dugouts demolished attacks on two-thirds of the battlefront, in the process producing the bloodiest day in British military history. The same chalk geology pertained northwards to Arras and beyond into the Gohelle battlefields of Vimy, Lens and Loos. North of the La Bassée Canal, however, the ground conditions begin to shift from chalk-based to clay, and so therefore did the nature of German defences. Positions in the wet, low-lying plains of French and Belgian Flanders (from Cuinchy to Ypres) depended primarily although not entirely upon a deep belt of mutually supporting, steel-reinforced concrete blockhouses and pillboxes. The further north one travelled, the more widespread the rash of concrete on the landscape. In front of Ypres this belt was almost 10 kilometres deep. Here, tens of thousands of emplacements, some visible but most not, formed a malignant and forbidding obstacle for attacking troops. In this way, the German defence infrastructure was almost entirely surface based, whereas the British chose to go underground. Why did the British not follow the German example in Flanders? As is so often the case, the reason lies in the geology, and the best way to explain is by looking at the most secret and bitter conflict of all, military mining.

A SUBTERRANEAN CHRONOLOGY

Until the First World War the objectives of military miners had traditionally been forts and castles, individual 'islands' of resistance with the besieger often better equipped and outnumbering the besieged. Not so on the Western Front. By 1915 both sides faced an enemy with comparable resources. It was a grand mutual linear siege, and the nature of the static battle lines produced not a lone castle-like target, but in the form of strongpoints, outposts, pillboxes, dugouts, redoubts, saps, gun and mortar emplacements etc. – tens of thousands of potential targets.

It was soon clear that successful mining, even on this vast, flankless battlefield, demanded precisely the same preconditions as Egyptian, Roman, Mediaeval, Renaissance and Victorian miners required: that the objective was immobile and would remain so, that it was within reach and that there was enough time to carry out the work. Finally, the most fundamental requisite of all had to be satisfied: was the subsurface geology mineable? The answer on the Western Front was: yes – everywhere. From La Bassée to the Swiss border the ground was variously composed of dry and malleable geologies, each suitable for subterranean warfare. In Flanders, however, there were serious complications.

Underground warfare in the Ypres Salient can be circumscribed by the events of five key dates between 1914 and 1917. The first is 21 December 1914, when ten small German mines planted beneath Indian troops of the Lahore Division at Givenchy in northern France, roused the British from their ambivalence towards min-

ing. The first underground attack of the war, unexpected and leaving the British undefended, caused serious panic as the news spread up and down the lines. The military authorities called early in the new year upon the services of civilian engineer, entrepreneur and MP for Wednesbury, John Norton-Griffiths. Given the rank of Major he swiftly set the mining ball in motion. Griffiths' first 'moles' (his favoured term for tunnellers, but one unacceptable to the authorities) began work in Flanders on 13 February 1915. Although earlier mining had been undertaken by small groups of

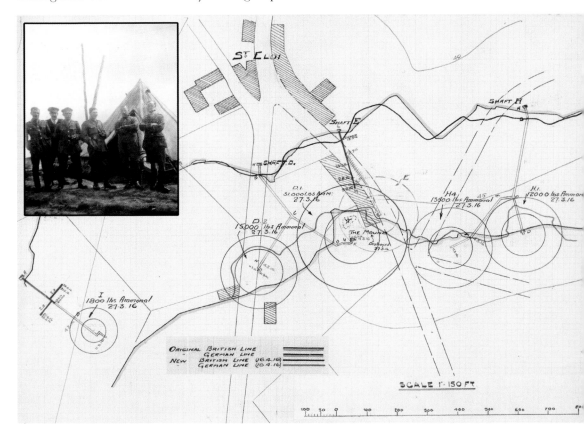

Below

The geology of the Wytschaete–Messines Ridge. The stratum marked as number 4, Ypresien Fine Sand, was the troublesome running sand or schwimmsand layer, the defining element separating British and German troops topographically, and largely determining subterranean success and failure. The presence of the stratum reversed the tactical and topographical advantage enjoyed by the Germans on the surface.

qualified men already in uniform (known as Brigade Mining Sections), there was no overall structure to the activity, but this date effectively saw the beginning of the gestation of an organized, comprehensive and deliberate British tunnelling endeavour. However, *the* crucial moment for underground warfare in all of Flanders was 6 May 1915. On this day, also at Givenchy, Lieutenant J.A. Leeming of 170th Tunnelling Company sank a timber shaft that pierced the wet surface geology, known as the running sand layer, and reached the dry clay bed beneath – the perfect mining environment. Givenchy and the Ypres Salient possessed the same awkward geological feature that Leeming had managed to overcome: it was a feature that would control underground success and failure. Running sand, known to the Germans as *Schwimmsand,* was simply a layer of quicksand trapped and under immense pressure between the underlying clay bed and the surface geologies. As the plan shows, although present in many places in

the Salient, the problem was ubiquitous on all the ridges, varying in thickness from place to place. Those who held the higher ground therefore could not avoid it. Sinking a shaft through quicksand is daunting even in peacetime, armed with the finest equipment; in war it is infinitely more difficult. Through the experience and determination of J.A. Leeming, Norton-Griffiths and Lieutenant Horace Hickling of 172nd Tunnelling Company in particular, working at St Eloi, the British met and conquered the challenge, whilst German engineers repeatedly tried and repeatedly failed. By the middle of 1915 they had practically given up the effort in the belief that their British counterparts faced similarly impossible geological difficulties. Because the British had succeeded almost immediately, however, they gained a huge advantage, one so unassailable that it guaranteed German underground defeat. That defeat was embodied in the monumental events that opened Sir Douglas Haig's Flanders campaign, the Battle of Messines Ridge on 7 June 1917.

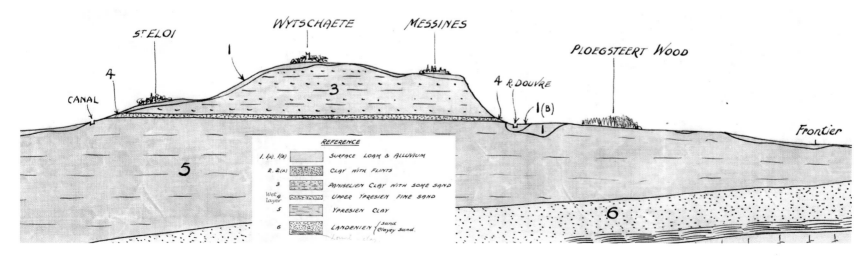

REFERENCE

1. 1(a). 1(b)	SURFACE LOAM & ALLUVIUM
2. 2(A)	CLAY WITH FLINTS
3	PANISELIEN CLAY WITH SOME SAND
Wet 4 layer	UPPER YPRESIEN FINE SAND
5	YPRESIEN CLAY
6	LANDENIEN { sand / clayey sand.

Put simply, as long as the Germans continued to fail to master the *Schwimmsands*, British tunnel systems could be secretly established at will deep in the dry clay, out of sight and sound of enemy miners. Over two years before the Messines attacks, therefore, John Norton-Griffiths had grasped the potential of deep mining, told every tunnelling company commander in the Salient to 'get into the clay' – and showed them how to do it. A second critical aspect of British success was in the digging process employed by the tunnellers. Clay-kicking was a north-country method used by canal workers and sewer drivers for digging small tunnels. It was not a case of swinging a pick or mattock, but 'kicking' a 'grafting tool' – a razor-sharp, spade-like implement that was worked with the legs and feet, not the arms. The method, was quick – almost three times more productive than digging with a mattock – far less tiring, but most important of all, almost silent. It was not employed anywhere in Germany. The *Pioniere*, on the other hand, universally used mattocks. Clay-kicking therefore furnished the British with the two ultimate advantages for mine warfare in clay ground – speed and silence.

Sourcing and ordering all the necessary equipment both in France and Britain, Norton-Griffiths paved the way for almost complete British underground dominance within a year of his appointment. The next date in the sequence, 27 March 1916, saw the first five deep, clay-based, British mine blows at St Eloi. Planned by Horace Hickling and colleagues almost a year before, the mines, planted between 12 and 15 metres beneath the surface, not only caused serious German casualties, but horror within their

mining establishment: now they *knew* that British sappers were so far ahead in the game that catching up was very likely a forlorn hope. What they did not and could not know was how many other schemes were already underway beneath their feet in the clay geology – the entire Salient and northern France – and it was this thought that caused the most profound concern. All the *Pionier-Mineurs* could do was try to find and destroy them – almost an impossibility with the British working silently. They failed and the Battle of Messines Ridge marked the culmination of one of the most extraordinary examples of British military engineering in history.

THE SILENT MENACE

The 3rd East Yorkshire Regiment were the first infantry in the Salient to be 'lifted' by a German blow. Although diminutive by later standards, the sense of shock and fear created by the blast on 3 February 1915, also near St Eloi, caused havoc; the demand for protection was immediate. Two weeks later at Hill 60, completing a scheme started by the French, Lieutenant White's miners

Above
A German tunneller in a close-timbered gallery. The sandy geology suggests this may be a shallow working in a sector between The Bluff and Mount Sorrel sectors.

Right
How clay-kicking worked. During their six to eight-hour shift, the kicker, bagger and trammer would alternate between jobs. Also illustrated here is a rum jar (for water), an air hose connected to pumps near the surface, a light source in the form of a single candle to preserve oxygen, and a caged canary to warn of any potential breakthrough into carbon-monoxide saturated ground, a residue from previous underground action.

Below left
The thrusting and insightful Major John Norton-Griffiths in a communication trench in the Salient.

of 28th Divisional engineers retaliated with the first British mine. From these two actions grew a widespread psychology of fear amongst the infantry on both sides, as mine warfare became unavoidably and firmly integrated into trench warfare. Tunnelling was begun in every sub-sector where the opposing trenches were sufficiently close to warrant the effort. If one side started a scheme, the other had no choice but to respond, for the infantry could not be left undefended. Although the prime intention of a military miner was to destroy surface features and their garrisons with offensive mines, in practice his primary activity came to be defensive, and it was the installation of hundreds of miles of galleries serving thousands of listening posts that created the extraordinary multi-levelled tunnel labyrinths that still hibernate today beneath the old battlefields.

Listening was the key to success, for prior to planting a mine the only weapon a tunneller had in his armoury was that of his hearing. One's enemy was of course seldom if ever seen; his whereabouts could only be determined by listeners sitting alone in tiny, cramped and stuffy posts at various levels beneath the surface. Each was equipped with devices that magnified sound through earpieces, a compass and a notebook. Any audible warning of hostile mining would thus be picked up by several pairs of ears, and if each listener took and recorded a bearing, the place where several bearings intersected indicated – very accurately – the position of an enemy tunnel. Judgment of distance came through experience. By 1916, with armies of listeners installed underground on both sides, it became difficult for anyone to pierce what came to be a sort of submarine net of posts beneath no man's land, and plant an offensive mine. The British, however, were by this time already working on schemes far beyond the earshot of German listeners, and indeed far beyond German capabilities at the time – in the blue Flanders clay beneath the *Schwimmsands*. The longer their work remained undetected, the more schemes could be completed. If the tunnellers were able to prepare a mine for blowing without being discovered, it was to all intents and purposes permanently safe for use at any time, for once charged and tamped there would no longer be any sounds for enemy listeners to pick up. This is precisely what happened with the Messines scheme.

It was not offensive mining that caused most casualties, however, but defensive – stopping one's enemy reaching a point where he could cause surface damage. This style of warfare was the most primitive, barbaric and calculated on the Western Front. It entailed killing one's enemy underground whilst he was at work by planting small charges called '*camouflets*' either within a tunnel closest to his activity, or by boring a hole and using a device resembling a torpedo. Both kinds of explosive charges, seldom more than 200 pounds, were carefully calculated to destroy a strictly limited underground area, i.e. not to blow through and crater the surface. In this way, not only would the enemy threat be neutralized, but one's own tunnels left as little affected as possible, and the location of the action would not be given away by cratering. Depending upon the proximity, a *camouflet* killed by instant obliteration, gassing (from lethal carbon monoxide given off by the explosion – the primary cause of casualties in mine warfare), or by entombment in the collapsed gallery.

No quarter was ever given in this grim struggle, for if one did not kill one's enemy, he would surely kill you. No sound, therefore, was ever left uninvestigated; each and every one was plotted, followed and reacted to. In this way one was able not only able to plan the demise of an enemy tunnelling team, but with careful forethought and preparation, to 'bag' the obligatory rescue party as well. However, the system was somewhat more insidious than it might appear: just because no sounds of hostile intent could be detected did not mean the enemy was not present. He might be 50 metres away – or 5 centimetres. Silence, therefore, did not always disqualify presence, and the constant stress and tension of underground warfare, a conflict where every moment spent below ground might be one's last – combined with the most intense mental strain, extreme physical effort, cramped conditions and oxygen-deprived air – burned out many a tunneller. As a rule, affected men were quickly transferred, customarily spending a period with Inland Water Transport (canals) to recover. Serious cases, however, were sent home

permanently. There were considerable numbers of 'blighty ones', for the RE sought experience and steadiness for this grim conflict, so tunnellers from a tough civilian mining background tended to be older than the average infantryman. It need hardly be said that tunnelling was necessarily a 24-hours-a-day, 365-days-a-year activity, so much so that by June 1915 the underground war had already become a sprawling and sizeable conflict. In Flanders its key characteristic compared to the surface war was that by virtue of the geology and hydrology, the topographical advantage held by the Germans on the surface was reversed underground: it was those who held not the higher but the lower ground – the blue Ypresian clay – who claimed the benefits, and this came to be the sole province of British, Canadian and Australian tunnellers.

Until the end of July 1917, all the major British offensive surface actions following the Second Battle of Ypres took place south of the Salient: at Loos in September 1915, the Somme during the second half of the following year, and at Vimy and Arras in April and May 1917. The cumulative effect of their failure was to extend the gestation of Norton-Griffiths' original deep-mining scheme at Messines by almost a year. The delay encouraged GHQ to order as many more schemes to be prepared as was feasible with the available skilled manpower, and within the projected time frame. Present research shows an extraordinary forty-nine separate mines were considered.

Above
A group photo of fully-equipped tunnellers pose together after passing their mine- rescue course in England.

Right
A typical German 'blind' pillbox near Gheluvelt. A vent/periscope aperture is just visible in the roof, and a built-in fire-step has been installed above the entrances.

Above
MEBU pit fully prepared and ready for the installation of a timber and steel framework prior to pouring the concrete.

THE SURFACE BATTLE ZONE DEFINED

The Germans started construction of a comprehensive defensive trench system the moment Second Ypres was brought to a close and the Salient completed its final 1915 contraction. Each line covered a broad swathe of territory and consisted of interconnected, well-revetted trench systems situated on the forward slopes, crests and reverse slopes of every ridge. Ultimately, they were to serve thousands of concrete *Mannschafts Eisenbeton Understände* (*MEBU*), quickly labelled 'pillboxes' by British Tommies. Stretching across the fields of Flanders in rows, clusters, echelons

and as single isolated fortresses, the system was served by a network of trench tramways. On the Messines Ridge three such lines formed the defensive backbone, whilst in front of Ypres no less than six were installed. Presenting mutual crossfire protection, the pillbox patterns formed the key components. Seeking total impregnability, after the Somme battles of 1916 the Germans brought to Flanders their prime defence specialist. A demanding man, feared for his rough treatment of senior officers who failed to do their jobs, Colonel Fritz von Lossberg relied almost entirely upon concrete for protection against shelling, for accommodation, and machine-gun, mortar and field-gun emplacements. His brief was to make the Salient impregnable. Deep dugouts as seen on such a grand scale in the chalk regions – proven on the Somme to be the safest and most desirable protective option – were indeed installed wherever Flemish geological conditions permitted; however they were few, for the presence of the troublesome *Schwimmsands* again obviated widespread use. German tunnelled dugouts in the Salient therefore tended to be shallow, sitting above the wet geology just a few metres below the surface, and offering inadequate head cover against heavy shells. Throughout 1915 and 1916, however, such workings were quite sufficient to cope with the constrained British artillery presence. However, the Germans were well aware that any major offensive in Flanders, which would surely come one day, and be preceded and prosecuted primarily by heavy artillery fire, would render them perilous. Concrete was the only option.

MEBU came in a variety of guises. Whereas most German pillboxes were 'monolithic' (i.e.

built from poured concrete with steel rod rein-
forcing), in certain locations structures were
'block-built'. Concrete was mixed and poured
into moulds at central *Mischplatze*, with the finished blocks later transported forward by night
via trench tramways. Fixed with rods and ties
located in holes through each block, they were no
less 'thick' than the monolithic type, but much
less resilient to the effects of shellfire. British
experiments with 5.9-inch shells, the most common German gun (a field howitzer), showed that
in monolithic examples the average penetration
of a direct hit was less than 10 centimetres. Not
so with the block-built variety: in the words of
one British CRE after Messines, all the examples
surveyed were found to be 'done in'. All were
constructed beneath camouflage, the majority
being built within existing buildings, farmhouses,
outhouses etc. Wherever the water-table permitted, those sited in 'open country' were installed
entirely below ground level and covered with
earth and turf. This sunken type were for accom-
modation/protection only, and built 'blind', i.e.
without loopholes to fire through, but equipped
with a vent/periscope aperture in the roof.
Defensive arrangements consisted of a fire-step
to the rear from which riflemen and machine
gunners used their weapons in the open. In the
event of close combat, cubby holes built into the
rear wall contained substantial caches of
grenades. It may be surprising to many that
British post-battle RE reports state that *every* concrete emplacement in the old German front line
system was of this 'blind' variety.

In wetter localities pillboxes sat slightly above
ground level but were still earth-covered, and
therefore almost as difficult to distinguish in the

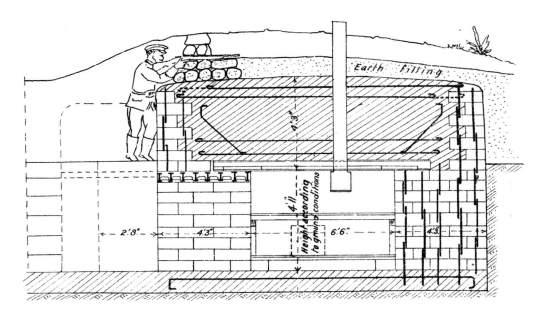

landscape. Examples in German support and
reserve lines occasionally but rarely included aper-
tures in the front and/or side wall for machine
guns and riflemen, plus the rear fire-step. The
most evident form of *MEBU* was the blockhouse,
an imposing, immensely strong fortress, standing
'in' rather than under the surface, sunken to the
prevailing trench level. Often large by comparison
to pillboxes, they were used as
HQs, signal or medical centres as well as for defence.
Probably the most famous
examples in the Salient today
are to be found inside Tyne
Cot Cemetery on the
Passchendaele Ridge. The
present rather squat look of
the two examples nearest the

Above and below
How a 'blind' pillbox was defended.

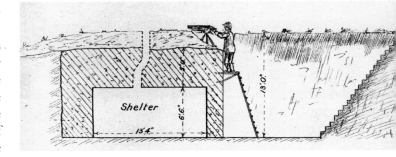

road is deceptive: the ground level of the cemetery was raised after the war to make the structures – which originally stood a full 2 metres above ground level – appear less intrusive amongst the British graves. On a post-war visit to Flanders, King George V commented upon their dominance and advocated their removal, but so great and strong was the ferro-concrete mass that destruction by explosive was out of the question – it might destroy much of the cemetery itself; hence the cemetery being raised instead. Tyne Cot's Cross of Sacrifice also stands upon a smaller example. As they cast such a clear shadow, blockhouses were easy to spot from the air. If fully or semi-interred, however, pillboxes did not; they became practically invisible. It caused many a problem when the British advance through the Salient's concrete jungle began on the last day of July 1917, for many emplacements had not been identified and noted by aerial observers, and in turn were left unmarked on British trench maps. Some were providentially discovered by shellfire blowing away the earth cover, as was the case in examples placed within buildings, but considerable numbers of these lethal carbuncles were overlooked, and could not therefore be taken into consideration in the battle plan.

Why, then, did the British not widely employ concrete in the Salient as well? The Royal Engineers certainly understood the many advantages: fast, easy access and especially egress, guaranteed weatherproofing, and less 'depth of protection' required against heavy shells (i.e. against an 8-inch shell a metre or so of steel-reinforced concrete provided a similar degree of protection to around 7 metres of soil). Pillboxes were not widely employed by the British mainly because, compared to the Germans, the construction logistics on the inside arc of the Salient were many times multiplied. Trapped in this observed pocket, and reliant upon few transport routes, all of which were well known and well targetted by enemy guns, the troops were in an invidious position regarding *all* activities. In addition, construction materials required for pillboxes – timber, steel, sand, cement and gravel – were costly, bulky and heavy, while concealing the necessary dumps was extremely problematic. Then there was the time required to excavate the site, 'shutter' the structure with a timber 'mould', and mix and pour the concrete without being detected, plus the lengthy period for it to 'cure' and become strong enough for use. Combine this with the problems of camouflage against ground and aerial observation both during and after construction, and one can see that in the Salient's goldfish bowl the prospect was an unappetizing one. Finally, of course, the legacy of Sir John French and his 'offensive spirit' must be considered; pillboxes smacked of those undesirable characteristics: lack of aggression and permanence. However, the survey of German works following the 1917 offensives, revived British interest in concrete, and led to considerable numbers of pillboxes appearing along the front.

Examining aspects of German fieldwork during the period leading up to Third Ypres, one is left with a single overriding impression: no matter how great an attacking force and how strong its artillery presence, the advantages lay very firmly with the defenders. On the ridges that partly encircled Ypres that impression is enhanced, for the German concrete-protected zone extended back not just the 7 kilometres over the rolling battlefields to the Passchendaele Ridge, but far beyond, and, importantly, each of the several lines of defence judiciously used the sluggish *bekes* that traversed the prospective battlefield. The Germans well knew that not only many a low-lying area could be deliberately and easily inundated – a miniature version of what the Belgians had done using the Nieuport sluices – but that the moment their *Pioniere* stopped nursing the drainage and the British artillery began its inevitable onslaught, given poor weather the ground would swiftly deteriorate into a quagmire. The grim winter of 1914 had provided proof of this – and there had been no fighting to aggravate the experience. Only surface-based defensive fieldworks were viable.

Right
The forward trench systems of the Ypres Salient as they existed just before the Battle of Messines Ridge in June 1917.

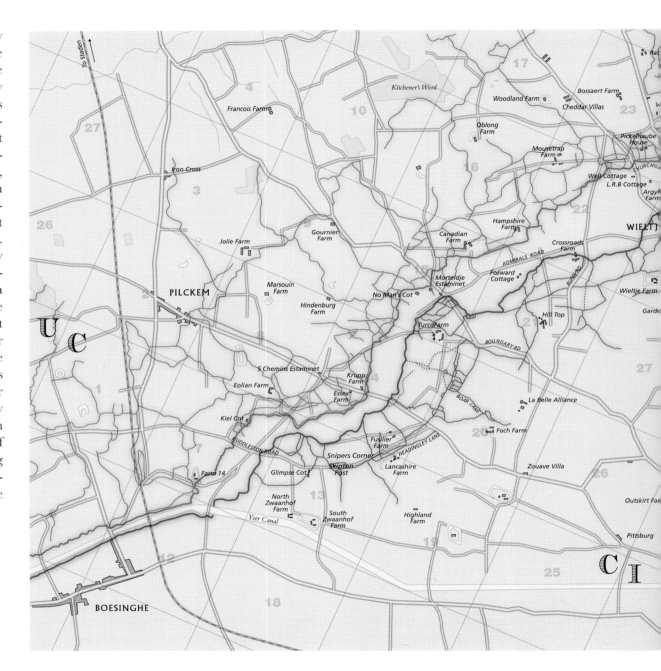

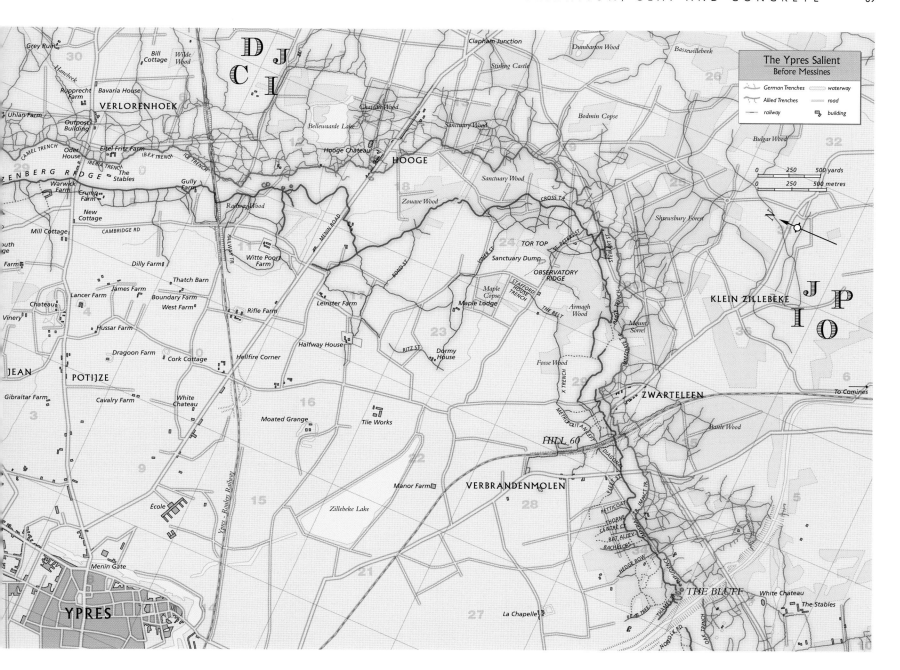

CHAPTER FIVE
Preparing the Push

The Somme knocked all the glamour out of the war for most peo-ple. It was partly the utter waste of life, and the sense that the leadership comprised many for whom hundreds of thousands of lives were of no interest, which produced the change of mood. Another factor was the necessity for recruiting extensively from the ranks of those who – often for very good reason – would have preferred to be excused. But one outstanding cause was the apparent inability of the High Command to treat soldiers as men, with a need for ordinary human fellowship and the sense of 'belonging'. Although at the beginning of the war much empha-sis was laid on the need to build up esprit de corps, this became a sheer impossibility after 1916, because nobody could expect to remain attached to any corps for any length of time. Every sig-nificant promotion meant a change of unit. A wound implied movement via one or more hospitals to different training camps, with a return to any unit that happened to be in need of rein-forcement and able to stake a claim.

CAPTAIN J.R. BELLERBY, 8TH WEST YORKSHIRE REGIMENT

With the injection of further reservists, territorials and the arrival of the first batches of Lord Kitchener's volunteers, in 1915 the British Army grew substantially, yet in every offensive still acted largely as a diversionary tool for greater French endeavours elsewhere. During the summer and autumn the BEF acceded to French requests to take over the Vimy and Arras sectors, extending their battlefront to incorporate all the ground between Ypres and the River Somme. In Picardy

the following year they were to feel for the first time the burden of playing the lead role in a major offensive. The unexpected promotion came about as a result of a massive German assault upon Verdun beginning in February 1916. The crisis occupied the French to such an extent that their planned contribution at the Battle of the Somme was effectively halved, leaving the British to make up numbers where possible. The venture in Picardy began poorly, had many more lows than highs, dragged on far longer than had been envis-aged, claimed more lives than any previous battle in British or German military history, and threw into mourning countless communities across the world. After four months of bitter fighting the fact that the Germans were still more adaptable, better equipped, better prepared and better led had, as in 1915, been once more forcefully accentuated. Both sides ended the year severely depleted in numbers and especially experienced soldiers. In spring 1917 the Germans then threw another spanner in the works by withdrawing to the formid-able Hindenburg Line defences, a move that in shortening their territorial tenure on the Western Front strengthened their general position. It was, however, as a result of events during that long summer and autumn of 1916 that the activities, tactics and equipment of the BEF were forced to undergo a profound transformation.

Above
Old and young of an occupied Flemish village gathered to be photographed for new identification papers.

Left
German troops punting at Zonnebeke. The Second Battle of Ypres left the village two kilometres behind the front line.

Right
Sir Douglas Haig, British Commander-in-Chief, at his desk.

POLITICAL MEANDERINGS

The management of British war strategy was originally the domain of the Committee of Imperial Defence. In November 1914 it first metamorphosed into the War Council, then the Dardanelles Committee, and ultimately in October 1915, the War Committee of the Cabinet. Composed of a mixture of military advisers and politicians, its role was largely advisory, the Allies' strategic direction on the Western Front being steered, as the principal military force, by France. In May 1915, partly as a result of the sequence of failed British endeavours and the resulting scandals surrounding shell-shortages and defects, Herbert Asquith's Liberal government fell, to be replaced by a fully-fledged Coalition. Soon afterwards, in July, the first Inter-Allied Conference took place at Chantilly. As a result of the search for alternative strategies, and indeed theatres of war, in December 1915 the second such meeting included military representatives from Serbia, Russia and Italy. Within this complex mélange the critical link between the British government and the British military was the Chief of the Imperial General Staff (CIGS), a post held from 1915 to 1918 by General Sir William Robertson. A close ally of Sir Douglas Haig, Robertson achieved the unique career distinction of rising from a private soldier to the highest rank in the British Army, Field Marshal. Alongside Haig's long-time Chief Intelligence Officer, Brigadier General John Charteris, Robertson's influence played a major role in the preamble and prosecution of the 1917 offensives, whilst both men helped steer Haig through the political minefield of coalition warfare.

In 1916 the Somme and Verdun forced the Allies to accept that the war was going to be a longer struggle than anticipated. BEF and Dominion forces were obliged to experiment with more complex battle plans. As always, certain agreements had to be made beforehand. The hydra-like nature of coalition warfare meant that this was by no means solely a military exercise; indeed it was governments who held the 'whip-hand' rather than Army GHQ, for they controlled the purse strings. The political and personal consequences of failure were often far more profound and lasting than those suffered by commanders falling from military favour. In Britain a whirlpool of political debate came to surround expectations and desires for 1917. Having served Asquith as Chancellor of the Exchequer, Minister of Munitions and then Secretary of State for War, just before Christmas 1916 another Liberal politician, David Lloyd George, took up residence in 10 Downing Street. Although the new Prime Minister had long held personal reservations about Sir Douglas Haig as Commander-in-Chief, indeed favouring French talent over British for the highest military positions on the Western Front, at least governmental and military parties on both sides of the channel were unanimous on the most desirable ultimate resolution for the war: that it should be ended not through diplomatic means, but with Germany's absolute defeat on the field of battle. Despite his misgivings, Lloyd George, and many others, had to accept that none other than Haig and Robertson could truly be pictured in the frame as C-in-C and CIGS. An accommodation must

therefore be arrived at. However, after the carnage of the Somme he was at the same time determined to use the influence of high office to try to avoid the huge casualty lists which their tactics appeared repeatedly to promote.

In January 1917, Lloyd George sought partly to resolve the Haig problem by largely cutting him out of the strategic equation. He attempted this by suggesting an amplification of offensives on the Italian Front: letting the Italians, with British and French support, continue the ongoing drain on Austro-Hungarian and, by extension, German resources – the attritional strategy activated at Verdun, expanded on the Somme, and indeed still deliberately being pursued there at considerable cost in British lives. In Lloyd George's view the Western Front could be left 'dormant' for a while. Haig could continue as C-in-C but remain responsible solely for France and Belgium – he need not be directly involved at all in Italian proceedings. Not unnaturally British GHQ scorned the idea, as did the entire French military and government. The Italians, who on the Isonzo had already battered away at the Austro-Hungarians time after time (ten attacks) without any success, read between Lloyd George's lines and pictured battlefields carpeted with their dead troops, not British Tommies. No thank you, was their response. The plan perished. What else was on the table at this time? The prime alternative was a scheme proposed by General Robert Nivelle, now Commander-in-Chief of French forces after the forced resignation of Joseph Joffre, and a man whom Lloyd George admired. Brimming with confidence after

turning near defeat to repulse, then repulse to victory at Verdun, Nivelle had his own grand designs for 1917.

In these, the British would again play a diversionary role, albeit a large and important one, at an offensive around Arras and Vimy to be delivered in the spring. Haig, of course, should be in control, but there was a key difference in Lloyd George's approach to the proposals: behind the scenes he had devised more skulduggery, agreeing that the British would serve under *French* military leadership – effectively under a supreme Allied commander: Nivelle. Strategically emasculated, Haig was 'thoroughly disgusted', as was the entire establishment of British GHQ, but such was Lloyd George's faith in his own judgment and Nivelle's plans that he stood firm. Ultimately, after further objections, discussions and adjustments, Haig was actually left with almost exactly the same powers as before the pronouncement, being subordinated in name only. It left a nasty taste in many a mouth, however. Apart from the cutting personal insult, and the plummeting of military trust in the Prime Minister, the key potential consequence should Nivelle's offensive succeed would be hugely diminished British credit. Yet in his diary Sir Douglas Haig appears remarkably phlegmatic about Lloyd George's interference and deviousness, simply noting: 'It is indeed a calamity for the Country to have such a man at the head of affairs in this time of great crisis. We can only try and make the best of him!' Similar forbearance is evident on several future occasions.

As for Nivelle, he promised the Allies – as Haig himself had done on the Somme – breakthrough within two days.

Background: Panorama across the rooftops to the country east of Arras, one of the stages for the great Franco-British offensive that immediately preceded Messines and Third Ypres.

Right
David Lloyd George, British Prime Minister throughout the Third Ypres campaign.

ARRAS AND VIMY

9TH APRIL

The great attack began early in the morning. We calmly slept through the greatest barrage the world has ever known and woke about 10 to find the attack over.
PRIVATE H.L. CHASE MM, 2/1ST LONDON FIELD
AMBULANCE, RAMC

Nivelle's main offensive thrust for his own French Army was planned for 16 April. The earlier launch of the British attack, 9 April, was devised partly with the aim of diverting German reserves from his chosen battlefront on the Aisne northwards to Arras. Here, the Germans occupied one of the most heavily fortified defensive positions on the Western Front – the northernmost section of the Hindenburg Line, or *Siegfried Stellung*, to which they had recently withdrawn.

The first few days of battle on the ground east of Arras saw substantial territorial gains, whilst on the northern flank at Vimy Ridge, a limited-objective, Anglo-Canadian endeavour resembling a giant 'bite-and-hold' exercise also provided almost complete victory. These were great days, great events, great triumphs, and the grim slaughter of the Somme suddenly appeared to be a distant and never-to-be-repeated memory. Before the initial attacks troops had been kept secure and hidden until the last moment, assembled in specially dug underground subways at Vimy, and at Arras in the extensive system of *boves*, large chalk caverns on the eastern outskirts from which the stone to build the mediaeval town had been excavated. The *boves* had been connected and extended by the engineers, and linked with the sewer and cellar system to create a labyrinth of safe if somewhat malodorous accommodation and communication. But from these grand shelters – the *boves* alone could house almost 13,000 men – more tunnels were driven to form a radial pattern of 'Russian saps' east of the town. The shallow tunnels linked not only with the forward British trenches, but in the same way as those installed on the Somme for the July and November 1916 attacks, continued beneath no man's land to positions hard up against the German line. It was from here that attacking troops, invisible from enemy view and shielded from shellfire before battle, emerged, moving forward to swarm into the enemy trenches soon after zero. The critical and all-too-rare elements of speed and surprise were brilliantly effected, overwhelming opposition in the front lines and delivering the required springboard into the enemy hinterland beyond. Almost 3,000 guns and howitzers, and more than 2,000 Livens projectors had prepared the ground with a crushing three-week bombardment before lifting their barrels at zero to support eighteen Third Army and Canadian Corps divisions with carefully planned creeping barrages and counter-battery fire. The Canadians under Byng (part of the British First Army) seized most of Vimy Ridge in a matter of hours, whilst in the central sectors east of Arras, Horne's Third Army annexed a swathe of German territory to a depth of almost 4 miles – the greatest advance since the advent of static warfare in autumn 1914. To the south of the River Scarpe, however, little progress was made. The northern gains were increased on 12 April, but then the apparently inevitable happened: the artillery were unable to maintain precision and concentration, and offensive unity degenerated.

German resistance grew stronger by the day. The Royal Flying Corps lost control of the skies to Baron Manfred von Richtofen's Fighter Wing One, equipped with fewer but faster and more agile machines, and as a result intermittent contact with ever-harried artillery spotting aircraft caused problems for British gunners. Even with the contribution of sixty tanks and several cavalry attacks, the advances faltered and stopped. This permanent change in British fortunes was mainly due to the talent of one German officer, the aforementioned Colonel Fritz von Lossberg, legendary specialist 'fire-fighter' who had reshaped German defensive tactics on the Somme and assisted in the planning of the Hindenburg Line. Lossberg had been called in to stop the rot. In the few months between the end of the Somme and Arras, he had already managed to completely retrain, re-equip and reorganize much of the German Army. Now, by the application of an 'elastic defence-in-depth' system, the principles of which he had also co-authored, every British move following the initial few days of progress suffered from depleting counter-attacks, sapping energy and interrupting momentum.

The basic tenet of the system was to dispense entirely with the old German diktat of retention of territory. Four other straightforward rules were also applied: the defence must never allow its attacker to gain the initiative; it should trust in organized and suitable firepower as opposed to heavy garrisons; no position was to be held 'at all costs'; and defensive arrangements must be established in great depth. The arrangement was quickly and vividly applied at Arras. We will later be examining in greater detail both how it worked, and how it was further adapted in

June 1917 when von Lossberg transferred to the Ypres sector as Fourth Army Chief of Staff.

After the first arrest of progress, Sir Douglas Haig's desire for immediate further attacks east of Arras was temporarily shelved by the arrival of substantial numbers of German reserves – exactly what Nivelle had wished to assist his own endeavours. On 11 April, on the southern flank of the battlefront, Sir Hubert Gough's Fifth Army, later to play a very prominent role at Ypres, went into action in a snowstorm at Bullecourt. Poorly supported by British tanks, and forced to lie two nights in the snow before the attack, the troops made no progress against the formidable Hindenburg Line. On 16 April, as the Aisne offensive was launched, the British were consolidating their ever more meagre gains and preparing for another phase. On 23 and 24 April another mile of ground was captured. To assist the French Haig ordered yet more assaults on 3 May, but they only succeeded in capturing the small village of Fresnoy. During the latter stages of the battle, largely due to the same kind of obstinate organized German defence that von Lossberg had produced on the Somme, British territorial gains withered whilst the casualty count crept ever higher. In Gough's final act, a second crack at Bullecourt, both infantry and tank attacks again failed miserably, and at a terrible cost in Australian lives. The offensive became a shambles. Ultimately, *average* daily losses at Arras exceeded all other battles of the war – and the breach that would open up a route to Cambrai, which the cavalry had been again detailed to exploit, remained firmly locked and bolted. The final statistics were 6 miles of Hindenburg Line captured, 150,000 British losses and more than 100,000 German casualties.

Although the early British performance at Arras had been more than encouraging, the total of 187,000 French casualties (40,000 on the first day) in their attacks along the Chemin des Dames, a crest running between the Aillette and Aisne rivers north-east of Soissons, was disastrous. Nivelle's tactics, actions and attitude led to mutiny in more than thirty divisions within the French Army. This was no case of lack of courage – the offensive had not resulted in greater losses than earlier ventures – it was more a situation of the troops needing to believe that their lives were being exploited with care, that they had a definite value in the great scheme. Nivelle's often haughty manner only served to aggravate their feelings of worthlessness. The 'mutineers' declared that they were prepared to defend but not attack. The dangerous combination of failure and rebellion could lead to only one end: Nivelle was sacked. Whilst the mutiny problem was being attended to (somewhat brutally) by his replacement, General Henri-Philippe Pétain, it became necessary for British and Dominion forces to act as a strategic pressure release valve and buy the French time to repair the damage. This was achieved by assuming the full offensive mantle, and attracting and holding German attention until the crisis was resolved. Pétain himself was all for staying on the defensive until the Americans arrived. Not so Sir Douglas Haig.

With Nivelle gone, a chastened and discomfited Lloyd George and an emboldened Haig came together to consider summer plans. With the Prime Minister now publicly if not privately deferring to the C-in-C, nobody 'in the know' had any doubt what form the forthcoming offensives were likely to take: Haig's hands had been freed by the Nivelle fiasco. After much inconclusive and confusing discussion over whether the summer campaign would take place in Italy, France, Belgium, the Balkans or even Mesopotamia, the coalition settled firmly upon Belgian Flanders.

The spring offensives were not the only complicating upheavals Germany faced during the first half of 1917. In March the Liberal Revolution in Russia briefly enhanced her fighting powers on the Eastern Front causing fresh headaches (nine months later following the Bolshevik Revolution, Russia began the process of bowing out completely), and in April the Americans, albeit in passive mode, entered the fray; a move that seriously focused German minds. As a result, by the end of April Germany had not only shortened and strengthened her position on the Western Front by retiring to the Hindenburg Line, but also begun unrestricted submarine warfare from bases at Bruges, Zeebrugge and Ostend. Although making American intervention almost certain, the latter step was seen by some to promise potentially shocking consequences for Britain's war effort, and indeed her very survival.

THE GRAND DESIGN

'I think the time has nearly come for me to take up our "alternative plan" in earnest.'
SIR DOUGLAS HAIG

It was in early 1917 that the establishment of the BEF reached its wartime peak of eighty-two divisions. With the arrival of hosts of new drafts the

MONITOR

MONITOR

PONTOON → DIRECTION OF MOVEMENT.

1⅜" Cable

1⅜" Cable

1⅜" Cable

1⅜" Cable

1½" S.W. Rope

Capstan

Capstan

Existing fairlead to be so fitted as to prevent Wire Slipping out

6" Rope

WOOD RUBBING STRAKE

WOOD RUBBING STRAKE

CENTRE GANGWAY

| SPACE FOR MEN | AMBULANCE CAR | BOX CAR | SPACE FOR MEN | GUNS AND WAGONS 12 AXLES | 25 HAND CARTS | 4 STOKES CARTS | SPACE |
| To Be Clear of Troops when required by Navy | | | | | | | |

SPACE FOR BICYCLES

SPACE FOR 24 TONS OF STORES STACKED 3 WIDE AND 2-6⅞

| SPACE FOR MEN | AMBULANCE CAR | BOX CAR | MOTOR CAR CENTRE COLUMN ONLY | SPACE FOR MEN | GUNS AND WAGONS 12 AXLES | 25 HAND CARTS | 4 STOKES CARTS | 7 S |
| REQUIRED BY NAVY AT ALL TIMES | | | | | | | | |

MEN WILL BE ACCOMMODATED IN CENTRE GANGWAY, BUT GANGWAY OF 4-0 CLEAR WILL BE LEFT

SPACE FOR BICYCLES

first changes in purpose, activity and equipment were revealed at Arras and Vimy in April. Here, infantry had still shouldered the burden, but heavier artillery was becoming so much more numerous and shells so much more reliable that target areas, their occupants and weapons could ostensibly be entirely obliterated before occupation unless encased within a metre of concrete or concealed well below ground. The failure to neutralize enemy batteries that had done so much additional damage to British infantry assaults on the Somme had been corrected to a degree, greatly enhancing prospects once the infantry had left the safety of their trenches. The creeping barrage too was coming ever closer to being mastered. At Arras the guns had been able to deploy simultaneously half a dozen parallel curtains of

Below left
Aerial view of the coastline at Lombartzyde which was to be attacked amphibiously. The shadow cast by the sea wall can clearly be seen.

Below
German seaward defences in the dunes manned by troops of the Naval Corps. Apart from machine guns, there were scores of both light and heavy artillery positions.

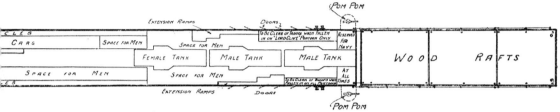

covering and suppressing fire on a band of territory up to almost 2 kilometres beyond the leading wave of infantry, a feat that had been unachievable just six months before. With more guns, more could surely be achieved. Tanks too were more numerous and more dependable, and although generally less successful than had been envisaged during the major forays of 1917, by the end of that year, with Haig's strong support, they were very nearly a battle-winner at Cambrai. Machine guns too had multiplied, both light (Lewis) and heavy (Vickers), the former making the infantry company a more independent and powerful force in attack, and the latter now employed to fire long-range unsighted barrages, harassing enemy supply routes by night and forming-up positions of potential counter-attacks by day. As for gas warfare, Captain W.H. Livens of the Royal Engineers' Special Brigade, had perfected his projector, a weapon that permitted the mass delivery of both gas and flame (Thermit) projectiles. By mid-1917 thousands were available.

So if the early period of combat at Arras had demonstrated the efficacy of new British infantry tactics and hugely enhanced gunnery practices, would the accumulated experience of twelve months of fighting be sufficient to conjure a decisive victory in the next 'round'? Briefly, Sir Douglas Haig's plan for Flanders was as follows. The troublesome Wytschaete-Messines salient south of Ypres must first be sliced off, causing sufficient enemy confusion to assist the central mission: a massive offensive that would punch through German defences at the core of the Ypres Salient, centred upon the ridges either side of Passchendaele village. Then, driving hard into the hinterland beyond, the capture of major road and rail links at Roulers and Thourout would sever arteries of German supply. At the same time enemy reserves would be sucked into this Flemish cauldron, further assisting the French. As soon as the advance beyond Passchendaele had gained momentum, the extreme left flank of the Western Front, the Belgian coast, was to be cleared with attacks both overland along the dune fields and through an ambitious and imaginative plan for the first mechanized sea-borne landings in history at Lombartzyde, a small seaside village just north of Nieuport. These twin attacks would create more defensive confusion for the Germans *and* deliver into British hands the troublesome German submarine bases that were creating havoc with Allied shipping in the North Sea, the English Channel and the Atlantic.

Haig's passionate repetition of his mantra (espoused also by Robertson and Charteris) that the Germans were weak and becoming ever weaker, convinced soldier and civilian alike of the potential of the plans. If all three endeavours went well, the British, French and Belgians would drive the Germans north over the border into Holland *and* potentially wheel southwards to 'roll down' the weakened enemy line. With luck and good weather, the scale and speed of defeat might well produce conditions for a total Allied victory on the Western Front before the end of 1917. If nothing else, it would sufficiently cripple the Germans in time for the Americans to assist with the coup de grâce.

But who was going to command the mortal demise of the German Army in Flanders, and how would the plans be timed and co-ordinated? Having held the Salient since the earliest days, the Second Army were a natural choice, but they would need much help. Sir Douglas Haig approached Plumer for a scheme. He received a beautifully detailed plan, but one that covered only the Messines Ridge, not the entire Ypres-Messines Salient. With action in Flanders having been postponed from 1916 until 1917, Plumer and his MGGS (Major General General Staff), Sir Charles 'Tim' Harington, had had plenty of time for deliberation. Expand the scheme and give it more thought, said Haig. Surprisingly, he at the same time sought the opinion of a man whom he had constantly countermanded and undermined during the Somme campaign, General Sir Henry Rawlinson. In typical fashion, Haig also charged another member of his headquarters staff, Lieutenant Colonel C.N. Macmullen, with the same task. Nothing materialized from Rawlinson, but Plumer and

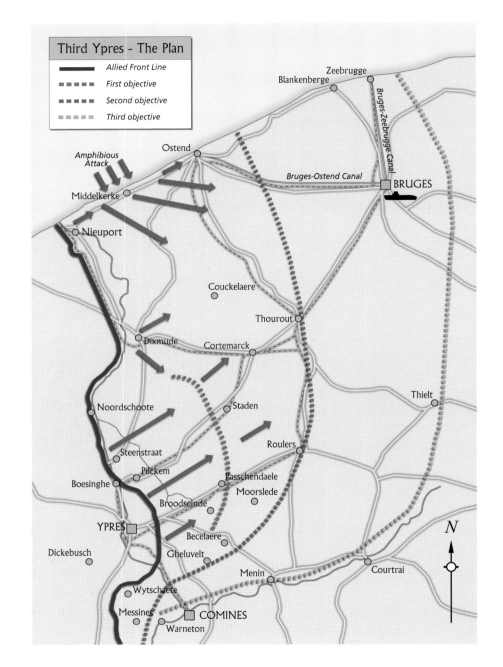

Harington quickly obliged with a fresh proposal, enlarging their original Messines scheme to include an attack on the Pilckem Ridge and the Gheluvelt Plateau, all to be launched simultaneously. Haig indicated that even with all the new ordnance arriving daily in France, there would still be insufficient artillery firepower to subdue the enemy on such a wide battlefront. What did Macmullen have to offer? A similar plan to Plumer's but with a key difference – a difference that strongly appealed to Haig. Macmullen suggested dividing the artillery between Messines and Pilckem, leaving the Gheluvelt Plateau, bisected by the Menin Road in the 'centre' of the proposed battleground, to the tanks: a massed attack – the heaviest the British could muster. Haig put the proposal to Major General Hugh Elles and Brigadier J.F.C. Fuller of the Heavy Section Machine-Gun Corps, precursor to the Tank Corps. They were stunned: it was as if no one had learned anything from the Somme and Arras offensives. Not only was the Flanders geology a serious concern (a shower made shelled ground almost impossible to negotiate), but any tank attack would be forced to pass over several marshy valleys and through narrow avenues separating the many woodland plantations covering the approach to the plateau and ridges (see map). Knowing the likely strength of resistance, the task was more than unappealing. And since tanks had been on the scene for almost a year the Germans would almost certainly have installed countermeasures. It was quite out of the question to rely so heavily upon tanks. Exit the Macmullen plan.

Meanwhile Plumer and Harington had devoted more thought to the problem. Why not, they suggested, make the attacks a rolling sequence? Start at Messines, but extend the left flank of the assault to snatch a foothold on the Gheluvelt Plateau north of Observatory Ridge, *then* attack at Pilckem, Frezenberg and either side of the Menin Road, finally concluding the initial phase with the total capture of the ridge flanking Passchendaele, including the high ground around Gheluvelt? Surprisingly, Haig again approached Rawlinson for an appraisal. He approved fully, but with an ardent proviso that as soon as the guns had done their work at Messines they needed to be rushed north in no more than three days to assure continued British momentum and German turmoil for the subsequent phases. Each attack, he warned, *must* follow closely on the heels of its predecessor. 'Go all out' on day one, he said.

In a rerun of the build-up to the Somme, Sir Douglas Haig, as was his prerogative, proceeded to cherry-pick pleasing aspects of all the suggestions to produce his own plan. At a meeting of British and French politicians and military commanders in early May 1917 he outlined his intention to assault the Messines Ridge on 7 June – a date that had been absolutely guaranteed by Plumer. To allow the firmest of consolidation here, and enough time to move the artillery northwards, including those employed in the offensive now drawing to a close at Arras, the main attack in front of Ypres would take place on an unspecified date: not a few days after Messines, nor even a week or two, but in late July, a full six weeks later. The decision was baffling, for Haig was fully aware of the treacherous nature of the Flanders geology and the criticality of using the prime dry campaigning months. Early June may have been earmarked for Messines, but that still left the second half of that month and more than half of July before restart. The British had at their disposal eighty years' worth of Belgian meteorological records, all of which pointed to June and July as being the most settled, with August at best a curate's egg, at worst a monsoon. Choosing to delay the Ypres assaults was a serious gamble.

Regardless of the reason for this decision, there still remained the question of who would direct the all-important second phase. Haig's choice was the man whose command, the Fifth Army, had just failed so wretchedly in the closing action of the Arras offensive, Sir Hubert Gough. Gough's qualifications for this profoundly significant undertaking were nebulous: he was emerging from fresh failure, had had an average record on the Somme (where he had come to be known by the Canadians to have a flagrant disregard for human life, an accusation that he later very vehemently refuted), and was relatively inexperienced, but – and it was a big but – he was of like mind to the C-in-C: ambitious, impulsive, optimistic, forceful, instilled with the spirit of the offensive – a true cavalryman. One of Gough's first contributions was a request to delay the attacks for a further five days on top of the six weeks. Haig was disappointed but still not unduly worried. Royal Flying Corps supremo General Trenchard expressed confidence in having 'complete command of the air' by that time, infantry practices were going well, artillery was transferring as arranged, shell supply was plentiful, manpower 'wastage' was low, materiel and troop numbers were being constantly augmented, and Charteris' Intelligence staff continued to indicate confidently an ever-weakening enemy, both militarily on the various fronts and in civilian

Germany, where shortages were causing serious unrest, discomfort and even hunger. Time was evidently not seen to be that critical, so Gough's request was granted and another critical window of potentially dry weather vanished.

The command scene for the offensive was set: Plumer's Second Army would take the first phase at Messines; for the second phase, Gough's Fifth Army would look after the northern and central sectors in front of Ypres. Rawlinson's Fourth Army, with the significant assistance of six French divisions, would deal with the Belgian coast. For the assault upon the Passchendaele Ridge, although limited, the French contribution was substantial and important: elements of General Francois Anthoine's First Army were charged with securing the left flank of the battle-front north of Boesinghe. On Gough's right flank, Sir Herbert Plumer's troops, having hopefully prevailed at Messines, would later launch a further diversionary push from the eastern slopes of the ridge to attract attention and draw in enemy reserves. Gough pleaded for far heavier Second Army co-operation on this flank, saying that unless the Gheluvelt Plateau was taken, his troops were likely to drive forward and bury themselves in an exposed and dangerous salient. The warning was ignored. The whole scheme was a colossal enterprise requiring vast organization. It was also hugely optimistic, for in front of Ypres the British faced not just defence in depth, but defence in the greatest depth on the Western Front.

In August 1916 German Commander-in-Chief Erich von Falkenhayn had been replaced by the Hindenburg-Ludendorff team. It was a powerful pairing. From 1904 to 1913 Erich Ludendorff was a German Army staff officer.

Above
Concrete blocks for pillboxes being transported on a light railway for use in defences being built behind the Passchendaele Ridge.

Left
Russian and Rumanian prisoners labouring on German defences at Hollebeke in the early spring of 1917.

On the outbreak of the First World War he was appointed Chief of Staff in East Prussia. Working with Paul von Hindenburg, commander of the German Eighth Army, Ludendorff won decisive victories over the Russians at Tannenberg (1914) and the Masurian Lakes (1915). By 1917 Ludendorff and Hindenburg led the military-industrial dictatorship known as the Third Supreme Command.

One of their first acts was to abandon offensives in the west to concentrate on defence. In September the German Fourth Army began work on no less than six fresh protective lines in the already well-fortified Salient: powerful positions to fall back upon in case of attack. Their system of defence – the *Flandern Linie* – combined with Haig and Gough's projected speed of advance presented the British artillery with a host of problems. First, it was deep; second, there would be a vast number of pillbox targets; third, there was a mass of wire to contend with; fourth, the terrain/geology mix might be problematic; and fifth, the entire attacking front was crisscrossed by waterways. Experience at Messines was to show that pillboxes, the key challenge, were only susceptible to blows by the heaviest ordnance. To drive the enemy into the open, they *had* to be neutralized; the problem was that although the artillery was now reaching heights of power, intensity, accuracy – and quantity – undreamed of in 1915 and 1916, the infantry who were going to take the ground still had to remain within range of supporting gunfire in order to succeed. Unless all the basic artillery requirements could be substantially met, and met without break as the attack progressed (i.e. reposition light and medium artillery at the same rate

of advance as the infantry), troops moving over the exposed Flanders terrain would become dreadfully vulnerable, for they were leaving their own zone and limit of control, and advancing into that of the enemy. And this was without taking into account the effect of bad weather on ground that at the best of times was loathe to recover, or the possibility of hampered or even impossible aerial observation of German batteries secreted in folds in the landscape, behind ridges, and in the woods. But the performance of the British guns in the Artois spring offensive had given GHQ confidence. If, they felt, the Third Ypres artillery programme could be made as efficient as it had been at the beginning of Arras, and produce a series of obliterating barrages every few days, fresh infantry moving in unison and maintaining momentum should smash German resistance.

ESTABLISHING THE OPPOSITION

In addition to aerial and ground-based reconnaissance, before launching a major endeavour it was important to gain as accurate an idea of how heavily manned the enemy positions were, and the type and number of weapons concealed within. Aside from information from ground observation, aerial photography, prisoner interrogation and night-time patrols, all of which often rendered few specifics, there was another more profitable form of intelligence gathering: the 'flying matinee' – the trench raid.

Troops not unnaturally disliked raids, for in most cases they yielded poor returns for the loss of life incurred; it was often felt they had been devised simply to perpetuate Sir John French's offensive spirit. Most frightening of all – deliberately so – were the 'stunts' handed to newly arrived troops.

It felt like we'd hardly been there long enough to catch our breath [it was actually four and half months after their arrival at the front] when we heard there was going to be a raid, and we were in it. This was at Festubert and the idea was for the R.E. to find out something about German mines or gas or something, and blow whatever they found to kingdom come. We went over as protection. I was given a bag of bombs and told with another bloke not to enter the Jerry front trench but stay just out in no man's land and guard the left flank with the bombs. If anyone came down the trench, I should chuck a bomb in. I didn't like it at all, because we were told we had to stand in the open to do it; if you got into a shellhole you couldn't see if anyone was coming. A 'responsible task upon which success and failure balanced', they said, or something like that. Anyhow, we lined up, two companies I think, with the R.E. and signals behind – and got gas shelled. I was trembling like a leaf, but I got into my mask quickly, and it worked alright. The gas slowed us down, I don't know what it was, but it didn't stop the raid. Off we went and there were men being sick as we crossed over, probably too slow with their masks. The lads who got into the German trenches then just disappeared; I couldn't see a soul, and I felt very alone stood there in the open, but there was so much noise, what with the shelling and firing and bombing – our gunners had dropped what was called a box barrage that was supposed to seal off that bit of his trench and stop German support getting in – and I was having to keep my eyes peeled for Jerries. It felt like a lifetime we were there – I believe it was only actually about 45 minutes – and I threw all my bombs. There were bullets flying about all over the place and I never expected to come out unhurt. The journey back home across no man's land was hell on earth – or so I thought then because it was my first action. I got to know different later. But how I wasn't hit I'll never know. We lost about a dozen killed I think, but had a lot of men wounded, mostly coming back. So that was my first real action. We didn't know what was achieved – they don't tell you that unless you really do achieve something, so I thought we couldn't have done so much. Then not long after Haig himself came to look us over and say well done and a heap of medals were given out – none to me. So we must have done alright after all.

PRIVATE BERT FEARNS, 2/6TH LANCASHIRE FUSILIERS

Right
Map of the sector where the British raid of 20 February 1917 took place. The targeted German trenches are those with a 'flat face' lying directly opposite the word Ravine.

Below
German panorama of summer 1916 taken from Rondellwald (Oostaverne Wood) north-east of Wytschaete looking westwards towards Ypres (right of frame) and Vlamertinghe (left). The British needed to capture this high ground on 7 June to obviate such expansive views.

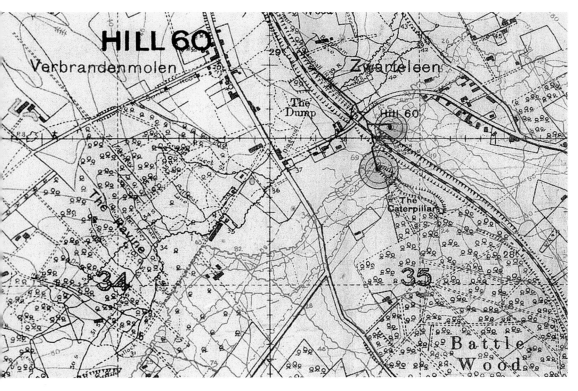

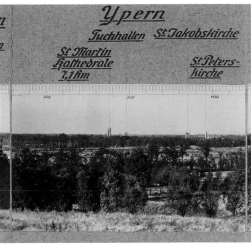

In 1932 the Kirke Report on the Lessons of the Great War dismissed the majority of raids as largely ineffective for that which was gained, and unnecessarily costly, but this referred to piecemeal ventures for the purposes of harassment; raids as a part of preparations for a major offensive were often essential, for many lives might be saved if one was pre-warned of the enemy's potential garrison and weapon strengths, and could develop neutralizing tactics. Assaults of this special nature were complex and carefully prepared, and the best of them go some way to dispelling the impression that lives were needlessly thrown away on futile and ill-planned jaunts. An excellent example can be found in a raid carried out on 20 February 1917 by 1/6th London Regiment. The target was a small German salient in the Ravine sub-sector between Hill 60 and The Bluff. Tunnelling Company proposals to plant a heavy mine here had been scotched by Sir Douglas Haig who saw the scheme as unnecessary, and so it was of especial importance to obtain on-the-spot intelligence to minimize the risk on zero day.

The entire 1/6th Battalion of the London Regiment was to take part, all 4 companies, plus 6 Lewis gun teams, an officer and 20 sappers of 520 (Field) Company RE, and one officer and 4 men of a tunnelling company. The party totalled 20 officers and 640 other ranks. Each company was equipped with 102 pairs of wire-cutters, eight 15-foot lengths of rope, four traversing mats (coir matting for throwing over and negotiating dense wire entanglements) and several ladders. Rifle bombers and carriers each clutched canvas bags of sixteen bombs, whilst every man involved in the attack tucked a further brace of Mills grenades into tunic pockets. As usual, the RE (tunnellers) carried heavier mobile charges for the destruction of dugouts and mine shafts. Zero hour was 5.00 p.m., offering daylight for the action, and therefore more efficient control, but dusk to screen the withdrawal. For two weeks the attack was practised twice daily (as were watches synchronised) in a camp marked out with tapes simulating the two trench systems. At the same time reconnoitring parties visited the line each day to acquaint themselves with the actual terrain. The parapets of their trenches having been heightened to cover the assembly, the men moved into position on the night of 19/20 February.

Immediately before the attack a bogus raid

was made at Hill 60, where a mine was blown five minutes before zero hour to distract the enemy; a second followed at zero minus two. As it blew a diversionary barrage by field guns and trench mortars fell upon the craters; this was lifted at zero hour to form a ten-minute box barrage in the immediate area, the plan being to convince the Germans an attack was about to take place there. At the same time rockets of all colours were sent up from many points behind the British line, and all significant trench junctions and strong points behind the German line were bombarded by howitzers.

When we were at Hill 60 the battalion on our right raided the trenches opposite them, and the task given to us was to draw as much fire away from their area as we possibly could. An hour before the attack was timed to start, we withdrew all our men into the tunnels and at zero hour two mines were blown under the enemy trenches opposite us. My own task was to fire correct light signals to indicate the German S.O.S., and this I did and fled below. All hell seemed to break loose and for over an hour the ground overhead was subjected to immense shell-fire. It was like being in a wooden railway carriage travelling through an interminable tunnel. Then when the German guns located where the real attack was, the firing on our area began to lessen and about two hours later it had practically died away. At 9 p.m. we cautiously re-occupied our trenches to find that beyond a tremendous lot of loose earth thrown into them, there was little repair work to be done.
LIEUTENANT G.A. BRETT, 1/23RD LONDON REGIMENT
(COUNTY OF LONDON BATTALION)

Because both Hill 60 and the Caterpillar overlooked the real area of attack, each was also doused with smoke by trench mortars. To the immediate south 41st Division artillery drenched The Bluff (also a key enemy observation point)

with heavy shells, deployed more smoke and sent up salvos of confusing rockets, whilst Corps heavy artillery attended to counter-battery work. On the raid front itself the opposing trenches were too close for safe artillery work, so eighteen Stokes mortars and the machine guns of the 47th and 23rd Divisions laid down covering fire on all enemy positions in and behind the sector.

Assembly began at 4.45 p.m. and at zero hour the first wave went over covered by the trench mortar barrage, soon followed by three further waves. Two double telephone lines were taken across for use on either flank, and a power buzzer (code-based rather than direct-speech telephony) for the central attacking company. The objectives were three lines of trenches on a 350-metre front. With the wire well cut by mortar fire, and the advantage of total surprise, the Germans were 'at once demoralized'. Their first line fell immediately, the second within 30 seconds of the British barrage lifting. These two positions were found to contain considerable numbers of troops, many of whom were killed; at the same time six Lewis gun teams and parties of rifle bombers caused havoc amongst groups of men trying to escape over the top. Meanwhile, on either flank the bombing teams kept enemy lateral incursions at bay. The German trenches were found to contain large numbers of concrete emplacements sunk 2 metres into the ground, many of which were strongly garrisoned; they were blown up by the RE who also severed signal wires and created much destruction with mobile charges. The withdrawal, guided homewards by one red rocket per minute launched from a point 750 metres behind the British line, commenced at 6.00 p.m. One German officer and 117 other ranks had been

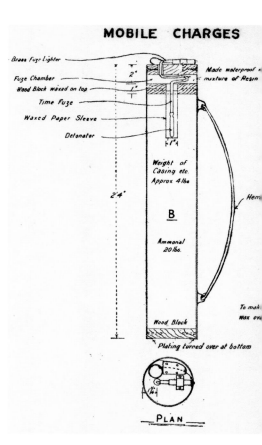

Left

A disgruntled German officer surveys the front-line damage after the Londons' successful raid of 20 February.

Below

Types of mobile charge used by the RE to destroy pillboxes, shafts and dugouts.

Right

German concrete mine shaft, also destroyed by the RE on the 20 February raid.

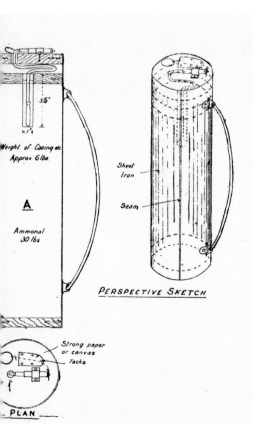

captured, plus five machine guns and a heap of valuable maps, plans and papers. The nature of the enemy defence had been clearly ascertained and with additional recent information could be confidently extrapolated for other sectors. British losses were 11 killed, 2 missing, one shell-shocked and 62 wounded – a favourable 'rate of exchange', it was thought. The relieving battalion began occupation of the line at 7.15 p.m.

There was also a cunning alternative. Unlike the fast, furious and often brutal raid, a Chinese attack was usually a bloodless affair – on the part of the perpetrators. It did not employ Chinese troops, indeed such 'attacks' were carried out not by flesh and blood at all but millboard cut-outs shaped and painted to simulate British Tommies in aggressive postures. Several were employed before and during Third Ypres; an actual event will be described in detail in a later chapter. Such were the preambles for the great offensive. What was clear, despite the delays, was that after the rigours and depletions of the previous twelve months the British Army was no longer feeling especially belligerent.

Ten months had made deep changes in the battalion. It was like an ancient garment which had been darned and redarned until, though it hangs in the same shape, few fragments of the original cloth remain. Here and there were patches of the first fabric. The transport, the stores, the orderly room still showed familiar faces. The R.S.M. still roared, though in a voice hoarser than of old. There was the calm and capable C.S.M., with his quiet persistent cheerfulness. The quartermaster-sergeants were the same, but they had shed all their militarism. In the ranks appeared now and then a face one remembered . . . But the change was more definite than the loss of familiar landmarks. The spring, which had driven the battalion, was worn. The last flickers of our early

credulous idealism had died in the Arras battles. The men, though docile, willing, and biddable, were tired beyond hope. Indeed, they knew now too well to hope, though despair had not overthrown them. They lived from hand to mouth, expecting nothing, and so disappointed nowhere. They were no longer decoyed by the vociferous patriotism of the newspapers. They no longer believed in the purity of politicians or the sacrifice of profiteers. They were as fed up with England as they were with France and Belgium: 'fed up, f----- up, and far from home'. The best they could count on was a blighty good for a year; the next, a little breathing space to stretch their legs and fill their lungs with sweet air in some back area, a village with good estaminets. The worst – they knew so much now that they dare not envisage worse than they knew: yet they felt worse did exist and might even now be ripening for them. The officers in degree were as the men. Very few of the pre-Somme vintage remained . . . Many were as worn as the men, suffering in turn irritation, fear, and cafard. Our speech has grown coarser; our humour threadbare, at best cruel, met by sardonic laughter . . . and we have learned to appreciate that grim jape, 'The first seven years will be the worst'.

LIEUTENANT GUY CHAPMAN, 13TH ROYAL FUSILIERS

CHAPTER SIX
Earthquakes and Aftershocks

Right
Sir Herbert Plumer en route to another meeting.

I suppose I may say that my dugout is not a dugout at all. It is a commodious modern residence on the reverse slope of a great earthwork or artificial bank. It is built of iron arches covered with sandbags, bricks and earth to the depth of six feet all round. It is large enough to stand up in, which is a great blessing. It is lit with electric light. It has a stove and a chimney. The only luxury that is wanting is a window, and as you will gather that the view is not a very cheerful one you will see that this is easily dispensed with.

As for the site, the front is towards the town that is no town and the back is shoved into the earthwork I mentioned.

This is, in reality, the ancient rampart of the town on the east, an immense mound about half a mile long, faced on the outside with brick many feet deep and forming a steep wall that slopes down into a broad moat. Once upon a time the favourite Sunday evening walk must have been along the top where the trees grow thick and you could sit down near the edge above the cold moat thirty feet below. Now unfortunately it is not always safe to ramble there and the place has gone out of fashion. I regret to say also that the sole remaining fragment of the Cathedral tower, which stood high as a landmark in all the country round, came

Below
The expansive German prospect from Wytschaete Church in spring 1917.

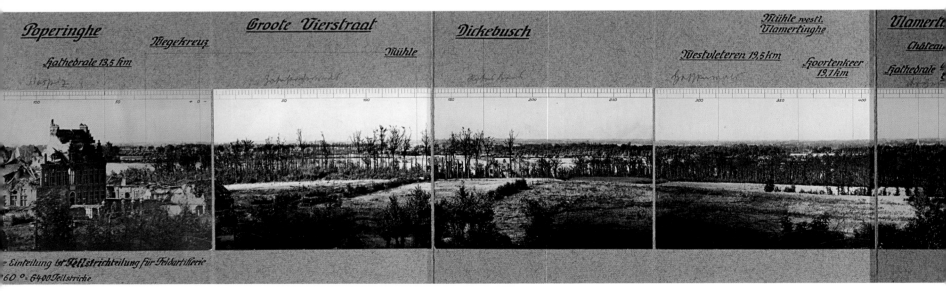

down the other day and now only the least bit of a stump rises above that particular heap of bricks. Something must have hit it.
CAPTAIN WILLIAM FERRIE, 196TH MACHINE GUN COMPANY

The crucial first act in Sir Douglas Haig's summer plans, the Battle of Messines, was at once a distinctly separate operation to the Ypres scheme, yet at the same time integral to its prospects. General Sir Herbert Plumer viewed it purely as a colossal siege. No breakthrough was sought, the objective being strictly limited to excising the heights around Wytschaete and Messines, for from this ridge since late 1914 the Germans had exploited a splendidly unhindered 'lateral' view of British positions in front of Ypres, and of course the opportunity to shell those positions from the rear. Remove that view, and much of the preparations for Ypres could be made invisible. Although front-line German troop concentrations were believed to be below average on the gently-sloping western face of the ridge, it was still a bastion. Plumer's preparations were more careful, rehearsed and painstaking than any battle of the war to date, for he was fully aware that further success depended upon the results of his Messines 'stunt'. The ridge *had* to fall.

Equally, the Germans recognized its strategic importance to their enemy. Field defences were long-established, concentrated, deep, and, as elsewhere, based largely upon pillboxes. Everywhere, concrete studded the slopes. Throughout 1915 and 1916 the spread had been weekly augmented until every metre of no man's land was covered by cross-fire from at least three strong points, a considerable number being secreted within farm ruins.

Plumer's original proposal was simply to take and consolidate the ridge crest. Too timid, said Sir Douglas Haig in early April 1917, adding that ideally he would like to see plans laid to

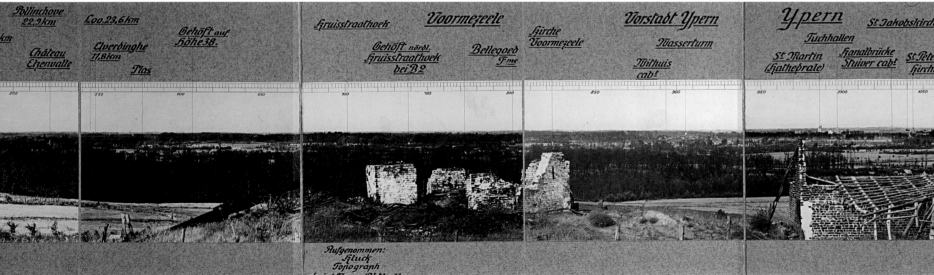

Delbeque 9me   Wegehreuz le Gheer   Kirche   Entenschnabe.
Au Gheer cabt   Le Gheer   Ploegsteert   Au Cerf cabt

Die Einteilung ist ½° Teilung für
Fußartillerie 360° = 5760 °.

sweep over the hill and on to Courtrai and Roulers, some 40 kilometres distant. Plumer, perhaps recalling his C-in-C's similarly ambitious and unfulfilled aspiration to seize Cambrai towards the end of the Somme offensive, chose not to respond. The offensive at Arras and Vimy then engaged all Haig's attentions. To Plumer's relief the subject was not raised again. The next time the two men met a month later, Haig was able to offer the Second Army more guns in exchange for the promise of a greater advance – up to and including a position on the eastern face of the ridge known as the Oostaverne Line, a projected advance of some 4 kilometres. When consolidated, British occupation of this new line should obviate any chance of German counter-attacks regaining the heights and upsetting arrangements for the Ypres stage. Harbouring certain reservations – it was a greater advance than he thought necessary – Plumer complied.

The Second Army's enhanced artillery presence was impressive: more than 1,500 field pieces and around 750 medium and heavy guns. They would also benefit from a splendid array of aircraft (almost 300) for artillery spotting, combat and harassing ground attack. In addition Plumer's troops, having been established in the Ypres/Messines sector for over two years, knew the ground intimately, were pretty fresh, well trained, knowledgeable about their task and could count on the support of more than seventy tanks, many of them the faster, more robust and reliable Mark IV model. And then there were the mines. As for these, well, they were an entirely unknown quantity. No one in history had ever exploded such huge charges before, and certainly not such a great clutch of them. As June 1917 approached a few had been hibernating for over a year, whilst others were being finished in a rush. Ultimately no one could say how many of the

Below
Australian troops gather in the sunshine to examine a model of the terrain which they were to attack on 7 June. During the forthcoming offensive several such models were made by the RE on behalf of corps and divisions.

Fabrik gelände *Tonnenwall* *Haubourdin Höhe* *Château Yves* *Tonnenweg*

Gut einzelne Weide" *St Yves*

Above
The southern hinge of the Messines salient. This German panorama taken fron La Grand Haie Farm shows the village of Le Gheer and the famous Ploegsteert Wood. The central part of the image includes Le Pelerin where the four heavy mines unused on 7 June were positioned. One blew in March 1955; the other three remain.

Following pages
Two British views from Kemmel Hill. The upper image (Second Army pan 62, 29 April) was taken in spring 1915, the lower (Second Army pan 106) on 24 March 1917. The thin ribbon of enhanced destruction astride the front lines after two years of war is clearly evident.

twenty-five mines completed by zero day would blow, how many would fail, or what their likely effect might be on the terrain – and the enemy. Perhaps some chambers had been lost to the swelling clay geology, perhaps they were flooded and would not explode, perhaps the Germans had devised a way of locating and neutralizing them. Bizarrely, the RE were equally unsure precisely how hazardous the blows might be to their own troops – how far away they might need to be to avoid the fallout! Certainly fairly heavy charges had been blown several times during the previous year, but these were an unsatisfactory guide as they had been planted in chalk, a geology that reacted entirely differently to Flanders clay. So it was a matter of educated guesswork, extrapolating effects from earlier and smaller blows. The unusual situation was probably best summed up by Major General Sir Charles 'Tim' Harington who, on the eve of battle, was simply to declare,

'I don't know if we are going to make history tomorrow, but at any rate we'll change the geography.' What concerned everybody, however, was whether the Germans were sufficiently concerned about warnings of British mining to retire to support lines before zero day.

THE MESSINES TERRAIN

INTELLIGENCE SUMMARY. EXTRACT FROM CAPTURED DOCUMENTS. A MAN OF 413 INFANTRY REGIMENT WROTE ON 30 MAY 1917:
We have been in the trenches since last Friday. We have already five dead and eight wounded in the company. The trench is absolutely blown in. I don't know what plans the villains are hatching.

Although described as a ridge, the ground at Messines could by no means be classed as precipitous. As usual, the British held the lower ground; above them the German positions

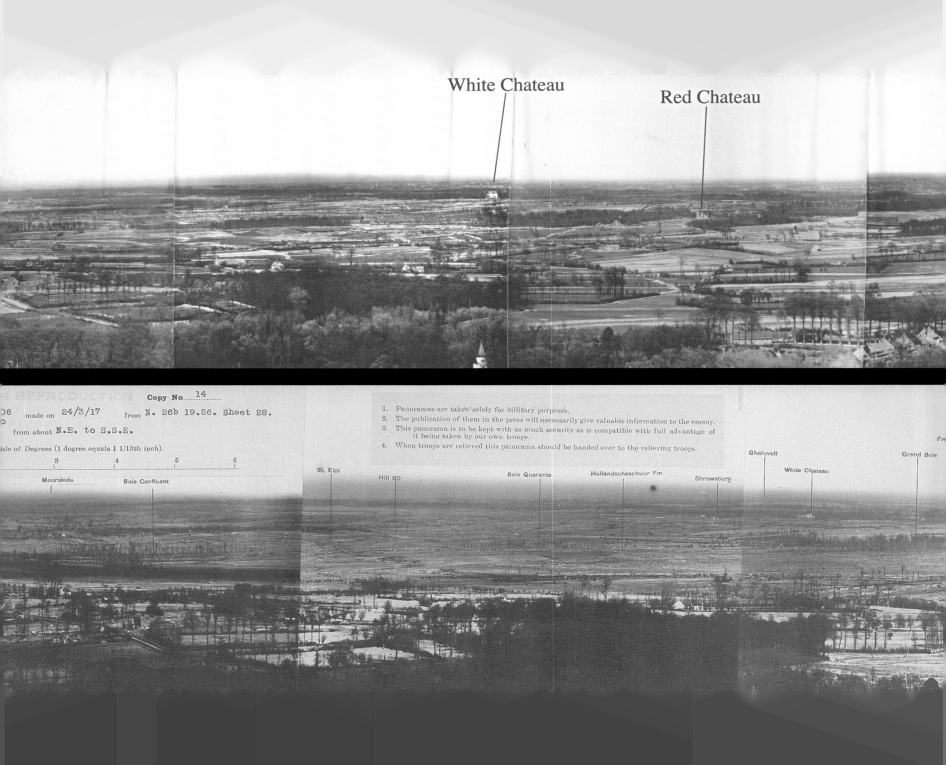

White Chateau

Red Chateau

Copy No. 14

06 made on 24/3/17 from N. 26b 19.56. Sheet 28.

from about N.E. to S.S.E.

ale of Degrees (1 degree equals 1 1/13th inch).

3   4   5   6

1. Panoramas are taken solely for military purposes.
2. The publication of them in the press will necessarily give valuable information to the enemy.
3. This panorama is to be kept with as much security as is compatible with full advantage of it being taken by our own troops.
4. When troops are relieved this panorama should be handed over to the relieving troops.

Moorslede   Bois Confluent   St Eloi   Hill 60   Bois Quarante   Hollandscheschuur Fm.   Shrewsbury   Gheluvelt   White Chateau   Grand Bois

Wytschaete

Red Chateau

Unnamed Wood

Zandvoorde

Onraet Wood

Petit Bois.

Brickstack

Hospice

Oosttaverne Wood

Bois de Wytschaete

WYTSCHAETE

Church

Lagache Farm

Houthem

Messines

A simplified representation of a mine scheme beneath the Messines Ridge. *Inset top*: a steel-built gallery in the Salient and (*below*) a timber example showing the blue Ypresien clay.

MESSINES

SWAYNES FARM

MIDDLE FARM

LUMM FARM

WYTSCHAETE

MESSINES RIDGE

GERMAN FRONT LINE

BIRTHDAY FARM

4 HUNS FARM

SLOPING ROOF FARM

L'ENFER WOOD

HELL FARM

BELL FA

ANDY GAMMON 20..

GERMAN TUNNEL

RUNNING SAN

No.1

MINE CHAMBER

BRITISH TUNNEL UNDER THE

CLAY

No.1

No.2

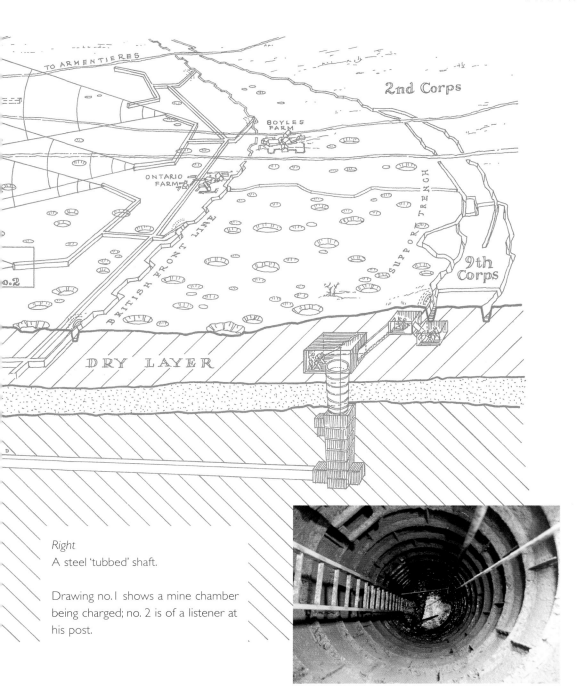

TO ARMENTIERES

2nd Corps

BOYLES FARM

ONTARIO FARM

SUPPORT TRENCH

BRITISH FRONT LINE

9th Corps

DRY LAYER

Right
A steel 'tubbed' shaft.

Drawing no. 1 shows a mine chamber being charged; no. 2 is of a listener at his post.

appeared to wander aimlessly along the 9 kilometres of battlefront, but this is deceiving for they had been carefully sited to utilise each advantageous contour and incorporate every spur and wood on the central and upper slopes. A glance at either British or German panoramas reveals how dominating the positions were. The entire potential battleground was heavily speckled with strong points (note the numerous farm buildings), with the typical interspersal of mini-salients and re-entrants to offer enfilade fire along no man's land. Like the Somme, it was these mini-salients, all made into commanding redoubts by the enemy, which formed Plumer's key targets. It was they which, again like the Somme, were capable of entirely wiping out an attack, so it was they too that the tunnellers targetted.

In no other place on the Western Front – indeed at any previous time or place in military history – did the topography, geology, technology and timing all coincide to favour the British in such a lengthy tunnelling endeavour. The importance of conquering the running sands in early 1915 cannot here be overstated: it bestowed so great an advantage that in all the many British schemes beneath the ridge only one charge was lost to enemy action, and that down to luck rather than judgment. The tunnellers' main challenge therefore was not the Germans but the geology – they had conquered the running sands, but now faced the immense power of clay. When pierced by a gallery and opened to the air for the first time in millions of years, the geology swelled, crushing mine timbers and breaking cables. The tunnellers doubled then tripled timber thicknesses in an effort to make galleries and chambers stable. Sometimes these measures were successful, but in the worst geology – pure clay – timber was actually dispensed with in favour of steel: entire galleries built of cut-to-size railway lines or heavy I-beams. It was a lengthy, dangerous, immensely arduous task, and some men had toiled on nothing else for eighteen months. Their moment of glory was just that: a moment – the single split-second when their mine blew. Or not. After such an immense endeavour, failure would be crushing. But there were no guarantees.

THE OFFENSIVE OPENS

As the calendar flipped onto 7 June 1917, zero day, twenty-five charges had been completed. Had Sir Douglas Haig assaulted the ridge a year earlier as he had originally contemplated, just four might have been ready for use; the added time bestowed by enhanced British participation in the lengthy Somme offensive proved crucial. So too was the dismissal of warnings of serious British mine schemes by German Fourth Army HQ. Despite months of ever more pressing recommendations for evacuation by *Kommandeur de Mineur* Colonel Otto Fusslein – just a 200-metre withdrawal would have wrecked every British mine scheme – his suggestions were persistently scorned. Blame was later laid quite unashamedly at Fusslein's door. His own son was to die during the Messines fighting, whilst in a mocking twist of fate Fusslein himself survived the war only to lose his life in a civilian mining accident in 1921.

6TH JUNE 1917.
FROM A SHELL HOLE IN HELL.
You have no idea what it is like; fourteen days spent under hellish fire night and day. In this beautiful weather we crouch in shell holes and await our doom. Here the dead are piled in heaps from the effect of their artillery alone, which is far superior to ours. All night long we lie ready for action, with our gas masks on, for 'Tommy' shoots all night with gas shell and aerial torpedoes weighing three to four hundred-weights. We cannot think of doing any work on the trenches with the shrapnel fire that goes on at night. The wounded and gassed cases are carried off in batches, and also many killed by gas. So far our Division (only three infantry regiments) has suffered 3,400 casualties in barely three months. We are quite powerless against the English. We all look forward with joy to being taken prisoner.
LETTER FOUND ON A SOLDIER CASUALTY OF THE GERMAN 2ND DIVISION, WYTSCHAETE SECTOR

The British pre-attack bombardment, which concentrated on cutting wire and targetting German batteries, opened up on 21 May. It increased daily in intensity and from the 31st deliberately sought out MEBU with the heavier guns. Opposed by a total of six German divisions, Plumer's infantry attack comprised II Anzac Corps assaulting the southern battlefront, consisting of the 3rd Australian Division and the New Zealand Division plus the British 25th Division, with the 4th Australian Division in reserve; IX Corps was responsible for the central sectors with the 36th (Ulster), 16th (Irish) and 19th (Western) Divisions, plus the 11th in reserve; whilst X Corps was in the north, with the 47th (London), 41st, 23rd and 24th (in reserve) Divisions. Supported by 2,266 guns, the infantry were presented with three objectives: the key 'Black Line' that ran along the ridge top; the 'Observation Line' on the upper eastern slope; and the final Oostaverne Line that should, if all went well, eventually form the chord of the newly excised salient. Excepting prisoners, the view from these

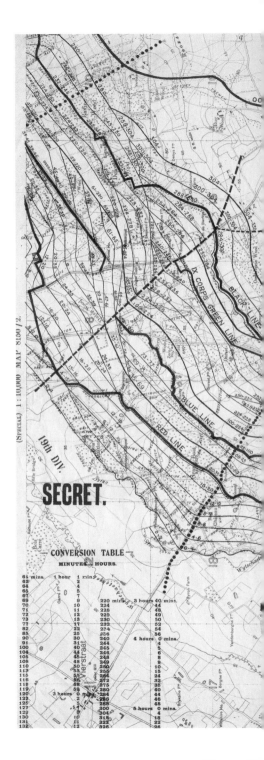

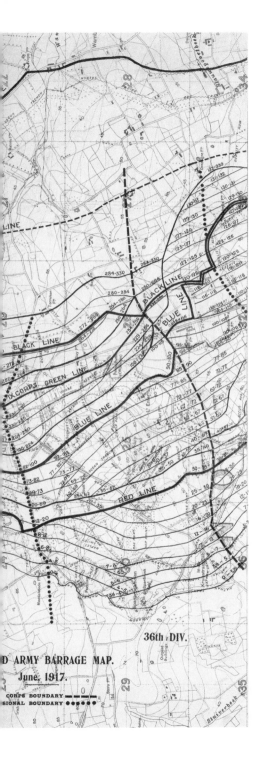

D ARMY BARRAGE MAP.
June, 1917.

CORPS BOUNDARY ━ ━ ━
SIONAL BOUNDARY ● ● ● ● ●

eastern slopes had not been seen by a British infantryman since the autumn of 1914.

Whereas new 'fire-and movement' procedures had been devised to neutralize pillboxes, the mines still posed that knotty problem of how the blows should be combined with infantry, tank and artillery. The office of the Inspector of Mines came up with the following instructions:

1. No man to be within 200 yards of the charge until 20 seconds after the mine is sprung.
2. All trenches and surface dugouts within 300 yards of the charge to be vacated at the moment of firing, and all men to be well down behind the parados, and well clear of any parapets which might collapse.
3. All tunnelled dugouts and subways within a radius of 400 yards to be vacated at the moment of firing.
4. All old brick buildings, walls and damaged trees within 500 yards to be avoided at the moment of firing.
5. The bottom of craters to be avoided by the assaulting troops. Any work of consolidation to be confined to the top 10 feet of the lip to avoid poisoning from mine gas [carbon monoxide was produced in such huge quantities that lethal concentrations often 'sat' at the bottom of large craters for some considerable time before dispersing into the atmosphere].

Left
Part of the creeping barrage plan for 7 June attacks. The table at left shows the varying rates of 'creep'.

Zero hour was set at 3.10 a.m. – just before dawn – and at this moment, to the immense relief of the tunnellers, the mines began to explode.

6.6.17

In the shelter of some trees were a number of tanks in readiness for the attack. It was 9 p.m. before we were in our allotted positions in the support trenches. It was a wretched night – the strain of waiting was great. Our guns were going continually. Fritz was 'nervy', and in addition to throwing over trench mortars, 'flying pigs' and the like, kept his guns traversing our trench all the time. He had got it taped to a nicety and as the trench was so crowded there were a good many casualties.

7.6.17

The night wore on with a miserable slowness but towards dawn the fire on both sides slackened and just before 3 a.m. we were ordered to leave the trench and lie out in the open. It was an impressive time – the gun-fire ceased altogether with the exception of an occasional shell here and there. A thick mist was over the land and we had to lie full length, partly because of the shock that would result from the explosion of the mines and partly to prevent Fritz seeing us in the growing dawn . . . Out of the silence came the song of blackbirds from a clump of battered trees a little way back only to be rudely silenced at 3.10 a.m. by the simultaneous explosion of nineteen mines. For several minutes the earth rocked to and fro and oscillating quite twelve inches. It was an experience I shall remember very vividly for the rest of my life. It was stupendous beyond the imagination of even an Edgar Allan Poe. The blowing of the mines was the signal for all the guns to open out. The noise rendered talking or shouting impossible. Every type of gun was in action, from immense howitzers to machine-guns which were arrayed some little distance behind us. As daylight increased I looked directly on to the line that was being battered and the sight was so awfully impressive that the real horror of it all was temporarily quite obliterated. The prisoners came over in dozens and scores, and passed behind us into safety. About five o'clock

'Hookey' Walker took us out of the trench and we advanced to the Damstrasse. Ordinarily he has a languid sort of bearing that would give one the impression that he was rather dull and unobservant, but he led us across that open, shell-holed country that only two hours before had been held by the Germans since 1914 as if he knew every inch of the ground.
SAPPER ALBERT MARTIN, 41ST SIGNAL COMPANY,
ROYAL ENGINEERS

Albert Martin's position lay towards the northern flank of the battle. The mines' effect was identical on the southern extremity.

On the night of 31 May we moved into our trenches and relieved a Yorkshire regiment. Our artillery barrage was timed to commence at 3.10 a.m. on June 7th and directly it commenced our infantry were to advance. At 3.00 a.m. our Adjutant visited me to synchronise my wrist watch with his and told me that the mines were being blown one minute before the barrage began. He had seen all the company commanders and told them. As we had to stay put until further notice [they were in reserve], we just tried to find a decent spot to sit on. I was standing up in the trench looking down on my wrist watch by the shaded light from the torch on my belt and saw 3.09 come up. The next thing I remember was finding myself lying on the bottom of the trench and the earth was quivering like a shaken jelly. An awful vertigo gripped me and all sense of balance and being on solid earth left me. This state must have lasted over a minute because when I managed to get back on my feet our barrage had started and you had to shout as loud as you could to make yourself heard.
LIEUTENANT E.C.P. THOMAS, 33RD INFANTRY BATTALION,
AUSTRALIAN IMPERIAL FORCE.

At the same moment that the earth had begun to crack and heave with the first mine, the greatest concentration of British artillery of the war opened fire, saturating the entire ridge with high

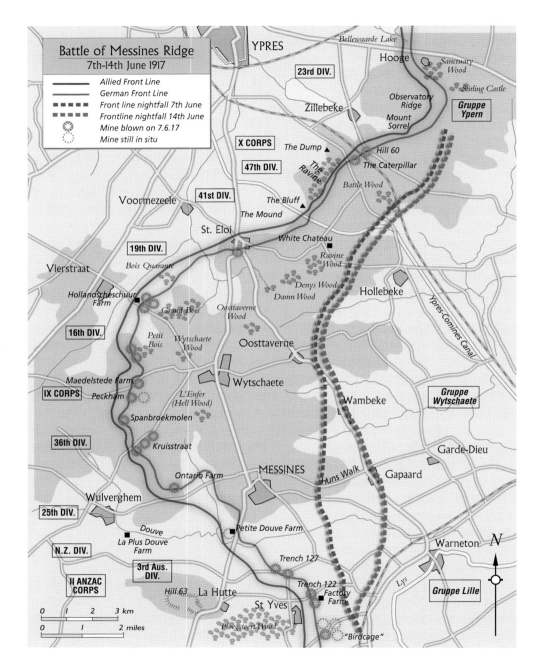

Above
German lines and the village of Messines endure the British pre-attack bombardment.

Left
The mines of 7 June 1917, and subsequent British gains to 14 June. The high ground is in British hands, with the troublesome salient successfully removed ready for the next great and decisive blow in front of Ypres.

explosive. Extra guns, silent until this point, then laid down a perfect creeping barrage for the infantry to follow. Mines, shells and dust caused the battlefield to be covered by an almost impenetrable storm of fumes.

The darkness cleared gradually and I saw that there were no infantry waves at all, every one seemed to be going ahead on his own and all the units seemed to be mixed up. It was slow and heavy going for all the ground had been chewed up by shells and mortars. There were many large deep holes from the shelling and these we had to go around or down them and then up again – one as bad as the other. We knew there was a stream called the Wytschaetebeek but this was almost non-existent. If I had not

sunk in mud up to my knees I would never have known it was there. With the heavy load I was carrying I was unable to get out by myself. All around there were dead Bosche and of course many wounded. The odd thing is that this did not disturb me in the least. I noticed that we had many first aid men and our wounded were taken care of quickly. All this time I was hoping to find my men but everyone lost direction in the murk. Anyway I knew they would know what to do when it became clear enough to see, so did not worry unduly. A group of twenty Bosche prisoners came by with their hands on their heads in charge of one small Tommy. This chap walked nonchalantly behind them, rifle slung, smoking a cigarette, apparently the most unconcerned individual. The prisoners were indeed poor specimens, either very young or old. They appeared to be half starved and green with fright – as well they might be. Some of them carried bits of dry bread in their hands, perhaps they thought we had been starved out by their U boats. The big concrete strong points and dugouts we saw had been blown to bits. From the remains of one of these I saw a miserable little Bosche run out. Here was my chance to shoot a Bosche personally but he raised his hands when he saw me so of course I could not. I judged him to be about fifteen years old, weak and about half my size. He looked at me like a dog that knows he has done something wrong and croaked 'Kamerade'. By shouting and gesticulating I made him understand that if he wished to live he was to carry some of my load. The agility with which he picked up two boxes of ammunition was astounding considering his physical condition. Now I had only three to carry and that was a big relief. We progressed slowly.
LIEUTENANT ALAN MAY, 49TH MACHINE GUN COMPANY

Despite a defence-in-depth of more than two and half kilometres, dense belts of wire, and myriad pillboxes and strong points, the heights were British property by 9.00 a.m. The fiercest resistance came in the places where mines had been unfinished – near The Bluff, for instance, where four key schemes had been forcibly abandoned as a result of difficult geology. Here the 47th (2nd London) and 41st Divisions suffered heavily. But they were unhappy exceptions to the rule. Counter-attacks by the feared *Eingreif* units were easily beaten off, and even that most painful of carbuncles, Hill 60, fell in a matter of moments. In fact the hill ceased to exist – one of the pair of massive charges planted either side of the Ypres–Comines railway (the two totalled 123,500 pounds of explosive) had blown it away. As almost 80,000 troops gazed over the welcome sight of green and unblemished countryside east of the ridge, a hiatus of five hours allowed a firm line to be consolidated ready for the next stage. Meanwhile tanks and patrols, even cavalry, pushed out to harass German posts and deter resistance. And over good, dry ground the guns were brought forward.

In mid-afternoon the second stage began, supported yet again by a beautifully delivered creeping barrage. This phase was not quite as plain sailing as the morning's actions and British casualties mounted with stiffening German resistance, particularly by artillery, but before the sun set on 7 June the Oostaverne Line objective had been reached, taken and held. The following day more hostile counter-attacks were driven off and the engineers had already set about creating their own fortress along the ridge crest. The Second Army continued to grind away with minor actions, continually consolidating the eastern slopes until battle ceased on 14 June, by which time Plumer's men had achieved everything necessary to allow and assist the Fifth Army to pursue its goals in front of Ypres. Over 7,000 field-grey clad troops now languished in British cages, and almost fifty guns had been captured.

Just over 3,500 British soldiers from a total of 25,000 casualties had lost their lives – a remarkably meagre number compared to earlier battles, and indeed in stark contrast to the sombre expectations of many.

For the meticulous planning, the credit for victory was mainly Plumer's. But his desire to maintain momentum by quickly bringing up the guns (as Haig had wished and suggested before the battle) to attack the stronghold of Gheluvelt Plateau with two Reserve Corps (II and VIII) were set aside by the C-in-C after consultations with Gough resulted in a request for more time to consider options. On 8 June British patrols made several informative incursions onto the plateau from the Mount Sorrel sector on the extreme left flank of the recent battlefront. They found it heavily defended but far from unapproachable at that time, especially in the mêlée created by Messines. This was important data. The following day Haig transferred both II and VIII Corps to Fifth Army, directing Gough to use them immediately *against the plateau* to begin the wearing down of enemy forces. The order was not carried out because Gough continued to ponder and as he did so the Germans proceeded to buttress the sector. With each passing day the benefits of Plumer's triumph slowly dissipated. On the very day Messines closed, 14 June, Gough made it plain that he was no longer in favour of attacking the Gheluvelt Plateau at all, concluding that if won it would be too exposed a position to hold. Instead, he said, he would wait until his guns and troops were fully ready to press a concerted simultaneous attack across the entire Ypres battlefront from the Menin Road to Boesinghe. Had they been given a choice in the

Above and right
Two forms of German shelter employed on the Messines Ridge. *Above*, a tunnelled dugout, *right* a concrete MEBU. Dugouts in the mines' 'sphere of destruction' were crushed. The pillbox has been tossed into the air by the mine blast.

matter, this was precisely the outcome the Germans would have voted for.

A key characteristic of the Messines push, and one which was to haunt British GHQ later, was the fine settled weather in the period leading up to and during the battle. Without rain the going was good for man, beast and machine, and clear skies meant Royal Flying Corps observers were able to accurately and continuously direct British counter-battery fire onto German gun positions. With one or two exceptions, the creeping barrage, SOS and protective barrages had worked very well, dissipating counter-attacks, shielding assaults and aiding consolidation. There is, however, also a curious but critical qualification regarding the events of zero hour on 7 June. It involved what one might call 'accidental genius'. Contrary to the long-established plans (and many histories of the battle), the nineteen great mines *did not* explode simultaneously. The cause was simple human error: faulty synchronization of watches supplied to the Tunnelling Companies. It was an inadvertently fractured detonation sequence that created the utter terror, disorientation, weeping and shattered spirit of the German troops – it may well have been the major influence on their awesome defeat on that first morning. Almost every enemy report had been the same, that of the 204th Reserve Infantry Division being typical:

The ground trembled as in a natural earthquake, heavy concrete shelters rocked, a hurricane of hot air from the explosions swept back for many kilometres, dropping fragments of wood, iron and earth; and gigantic black clouds of smoke and dust spread over the country. The effect on the troops was overpowering and crushing.
ANONYMOUS REPORT, 204TH RESERVE INFANTRY DIVISION

In the half-light of dawn, blast succeeded blast around the curve of the salient. Because of this curve, the mines appeared to blow in front, behind, and to the left and right of defenders. The 'jumping' here and there of the vast eruptions disorientated the traumatized troops, leading many to believe that mines were blowing behind them as far away as the ridge crest itself, a kilometre behind the front line (such schemes had actually been planned). Then there was the fact that no one had ever before blown so many mines on such a narrow battlefront: after a few blasts the sequence was naturally expected to cease, but it continued, and continued, and continued. There was no telling how many more might exist, or indeed where they might be planted. And there was nowhere to run, neither forward nor backwards. As five blows turned to ten, ten to fifteen, and fifteen to nineteen, German morale was demolished and replaced by abject terror. Prisoners later stated that the supreme overriding effect of the mines had been their apparently endless succession – a period of about eighteen seconds from first to last – a view later supported by Quartermaster General Erich Ludendorff, who in his memoirs stated that but for the mines the ridge would have remained in German hands. In actual fact it could all have gone horribly wrong for the British as the watches nearly failed to reach their destinations at all in time for the battle.

6.6.17

6 p.m. Went to 171 Coy. H.Q. and picked up Major Hudspeth, proceeding to H.Q. 36th Div. Kemmel Dugouts, to arrange about synchronising watches. Were stopped at IX Corps boundary by sentry. My pass satisfactory, but sentry stated it would not cover

Major Hudspeth (who knew nothing of the matter and had no pass). I pointed out urgency of Major H. proceeding – road control firm – Major H. could not proceed. Orders were definite. Found out in course of discussion that anyone could walk in. Hudspeth alighted, walked past the post, and got into car again 20 yards further along. The restrictions related simply and solely to vehicles and not persons, who could walk in anywhere.
WAR DIARY, MAJOR R.S.G. STOKES, ASSISTANT INSPECTOR OF MINES, ROYAL ENGINEERS

Major Stokes's first report on operations was delivered on the evening of 7 June. Not yet knowing of the devastating effect that the disjointed synchronization had had on the enemy, he noted, 'Timing arrangements poor'. Which, in truth, they had been. Several British units, having taken RE advice about the potential radius of fallout, formed up in no man's land. They were close, many too close to the colossal blasts: when the

Inset
British officers occupying a comfortable German dugout after the successful advance.

Above
German aerial of 7 June mine craters. Left to right: Petit Bois (two mines), Maedelstede Farm (one), Peckham (one), Spanbroekmolen (one), and (right) the triple charges known as Kruisstraat one, two and three. Note how the pre-battle no man's land has remained relatively undamaged.

seconds. Going on slowly with the men it was hard to see because of the dust and debris. Suddenly I noticed that some of the infantry were running back, presumably terror stricken by the mines. Naturally I did my best to stop them, shouting at them, brandishing my revolver, and succeeded in stopping a few. Must say they appeared a bit ashamed. One of them told me he thought he would be crushed by the debris. Shouting of course was futile for no one could possibly hear though those close enough to see in the near dark could understand gesticulations. There was confusion on all sides, many men were lost to sight.
LIEUTENANT ALAN MAY, 49TH MACHINE GUN COMPANY

MESSINES AFTERMATH

The number of German casualties caused by the mines has never been calculated with any degree of accuracy and probably never will. Of the total of around 20,000 at the end of the first day, 689 men perished in the Hill 60 (53,500 lb) and Caterpillar (70,000 lb) blasts, with a further 400 at St Eloi – at almost 96,000 pounds the largest single charge in the assemblage. Other sites require further research. Even an approximate final number cannot at present be estimated for different sectors were manned in differing densities. In contrast to the two examples stated above, for instance, the positions obliterated by five mines at Petit Bois (2) and Hollandscheschuur (3) were known to have been lightly held, whilst farther south opposite Trench 121, Haig and Plumer's greatest fear for the whole mining scheme, a limited withdrawal had been independently effected by the German sector commander, so that casualties here were light. Whatever the statistics, the mines gave the battle an extraordinary and unique foundation.

Awarding Plumer the highest of accolades,

mines blew, they felt the sight, sound and shock just as keenly as the enemy.

Silhouetted against the flame I saw huge blocks of earth that seemed to be as big as houses falling back to the ground. Small chunks and dirt fell all around. I saw a man flung out from behind a huge block of debris silhouetted against the sheet of flame. Presumably some poor devil of a Boche. It was awful, a sort of inferno. All this of course was noticed in the first few

Haig noted in his diary that, 'The operations undertaken today are probably the most successful I have yet undertaken. Our losses are reported to be very small. Under 11,000 for the nine divisions which attacked.' For two reasons, however, they could have been considerably less. The first was directly connected with the swiftness of the initial success: so many British and Dominion troops were crowded upon the ridge crest around midday that German guns were presented with unexpectedly profitable targets. The second involved friendly fire. As 7 June drew to a close, confusion by artillery observers erroneously called down a series of heavy barrages, not against German counter-attacks, but upon Australian troops consolidating the Oostaverne Line. Nevertheless, at Messines the Second Army bit hard and held firm. The victory was complete and comprehensive, by far the most successful venture of the war to date, and a tremendous shot in the arm for all the Allies.

So swift and accomplished was the victory that German defensive tactics had not been allowed to properly emerge in order to be observed. The most important practical study with direct relevance to the next stage of the offensive was carried out by 105 Field Company and 4th Australian Pioneers. It was entitled *German Concrete Structures on the Messines Ridge and the Effect of Shellfire on them*. Today we can see that the results, which were made available almost immediately, foretold the likely unfolding of Third Ypres. The tunnellers were, as usual, involved in similar surveys.

I had to make a plan of all the undamaged pillboxes and concrete machine-gun emplacements on the slope of the ridge, and by the time I had finished there was room for little else on the plan and very few of these had been even slightly damaged, in spite of the intensity of our bombardment. These had been sites chosen with great care and it is inconceivable that any troops could have advanced up that slope, had there not been a complete panic on the part of the enemy.

ANONYMOUS OFFICER, 250TH TUNNELLING COMPANY, ROYAL ENGINEERS, 1927

Useful and informative though these studies undoubtedly were, the key word in this piece is 'panic': without the stultifying effect of the mines and their triggering of the colossal bombardment, the Messines story might have been very different. On two counts, therefore, the battle was no useful object lesson unless the same tactics could be employed again. They could not – because there were no mines elsewhere on the Ypres battlefront, a fact unknown to the Germans, as we shall see. Now, the crucial component was time, and it was stealing by. Whilst some had always advocated waiting until the arrival of overwhelming numbers of American troops before launching a 'breakthrough' offensive, as the fighting at Messines concluded, Sir Douglas Haig was, not surprisingly, all for pressing the Germans 'now, as vigorously as possible' along the entire Western Front, and continuing to strike at unexpected places in order to continue the attritional wearing down that had begun a year earlier on the Somme. Ypres was still the heart of his hopes, but every day squandered after Messines allowed the enemy time to reorganize, reinforce, reflect and revise tactics, and make his next step more and more of a gamble. Yet Haig still elected to entertain Gough's slowly forming opinions over Plumer's desire to push on.

German defensive policy after the 'black day'

Below
Engineers installing water pipes through Wytschaete Wood as soon as the ground was consolidated.

Background
Plan of the three charges intended for the Peckham mine scheme. The 15,000-lb mine (top) was unfinished. The 20,000-lb charge at centre was completed but lost to swelling geology (and is still there). On 7 June only the single charge of 76,000 lb beneath the mini-salient occupied by the original farm buildings was blown. See also previous page.

of Messines was thus offered space to be radically rethought. It had been the first major Allied assault in the Salient for over two years, and was therefore the first test of the system of continuous lines of trenches with integral pillboxes and strong points. Despite the mines, results had fallen far short of expectations. The Germans were aware that only limited British ambitions had prevented a potentially catastrophic breakthrough – from noon onwards they could have swept down the eastern ridge flank almost unopposed. In the knowledge that hostilities were far from over in the Salient, the first few hours of battle on 7 June triggered serious discussion at German Fourth Army HQ. Curiously, it was the defensive core – pillboxes – that caused the greatest anxiety: they had not performed according to plan.

The dugouts [pillboxes] situated in old trenches, principally in the first and second lines, were man-traps and often led to the loss of a large number of prisoners. These circumstances prove the weakness of the rigid methods of defence practised hitherto.
GENERAL SIXT VON ARMIN, COMMANDER,
GERMAN FOURTH ARMY

British reports also noted that many German dead found inside pillboxes were killed by the concussion of heavy shells striking the rigid structures – the men were unmarked but had died from brain haemorrhage. For the Germans, the battle dictated that a new approach to defence had to be found – integrating but superseding the immense amount of defensive development completed since June 1916. Recognizing that although the shock of the mines had created the chief milieu for British success, it was gunfire that propagated it, von Armin and von Lossberg, the latter now

arrived in the theatre, radically revised orders to their troops in the Salient. First, they were to concentrate on concealment of all field positions to escape the eyes of British airmen and the wrath of the guns they directed: trenches, dugouts, pillboxes and battery positions were all to be immediately camouflaged. The repair of damaged trenches was outlawed: under a high-explosive deluge such as that experienced at Messines the troops were unable to keep up with the sheer scale and speed of destruction anyway – now, they should largely ignore it, saving all their energy for fighting. It was also decided to drastically adapt the existing defence-in-depth initiative forward of the Passchendaele Ridge, establishing well-concealed zones of defence to allow for counter-attacks, with lightly garrisoned forward positions and progressively stronger resistance to the rear. All old positions were to be dispensed with, and conspicuous works still under construction such as new pillboxes and blockhouses, discontinued. Instead, complementing the pillboxes and arranged in a chequerboard pattern to give crossfire support, countless small shell-hole-based garrisons with single machine guns would replace trench strong points, each position being camouflaged and made undetectable from the air. Close behind this line strong points were to be created. They should contain several machine guns, parties of *Eingreif* troops for counter-attack, and supports who could be brought forward at the first threat of an enemy advance. Behind these, more shell-hole posts, lightly wired, each containing a *gruppe* of nine men, were to be built. Finally, all 'unused' shell holes were be filled with dense thickets of barbed wire to obviate their use for cover by an enemy attack.

The most radical revision was the order to construct *minierte unterstand* (mined, i.e. deep, dugouts) in preference to concrete emplacements in the second and third positions. Driven from shell holes, they must accommodate one-sixth of the forward garrison; in the second line the figure rose to one-third, and further to the rear, a half. If a concrete emplacement was deemed absolutely necessary it was not to be of the tall blockhouse type but kept low with a flat roof, buried completely wherever the water table allowed, and earth-covered where not. Comfortable headroom was of no consequence. The mined dugouts should be deep enough to be shellproof, but if sufficient head cover was unattainable by depth due to the water table or unfavourable geology, then extra surface protection – burster, cushion and deflection courses – were to be added using concrete slabs, logs, bricks or steel beams. Again, everything was to be invisible from the air. Dugout exits were to be sufficiently wide and high to allow rapid egress in an emergency, whilst close by splinter-proof lookout posts were to be built. And dispersed across the entire Salient scores of dummy posts were to be installed to confuse attacking troops. One feature of the tunnelled dugouts was to have been the building of a rear exit for the use of troops still underground when front entrances were overrun. These were not to enable troops to retire, but to come back over the top and retake lost positions. At the front entrance specially built niches were to be manned by sentries who would engage

the enemy directly he entered the trench, and by keeping the entrance free for a period permit the full garrison to turn out and resist instead of being entrapped underground as had happened so often in the pillboxes and dugouts at Messines.

Von Armin commanded that the new work was to be started immediately and with all speed. Despite the catastrophic seven-week British delay between Messines and Third Ypres, it was too short a period to effect all the directives, but enough work was done to create serious unexpected difficulties when one of the bloodiest battles in world history began on 31 July 1917. And the adjustments would continue as the battle slogged on. The Salient was to become the ultimate elastic defence-in-depth. It was broken up into three distinct zones: the forward outpost zone, the battle zone, and a rear zone. Up to a kilometre deep, the outpost zone was designed to be 'brittle', dealing with hostile raids and sending out patrols, but not heavily manned, relatively easy to breach, the troops prepared to retire in an organized fashion. Behind this and arranged upon the most auspicious contours, lay the forward boundary of the battle zone – a defined trench system where true resistance began. Depth varied according to the topography, but was generally between 1 and 3 kilometres. On its rear boundary lay another comprehensive trench line plus the most forward of the artillery, located in positions offering excellent observation of the battle zone. In the rear zone lay further major lines of resistance, as

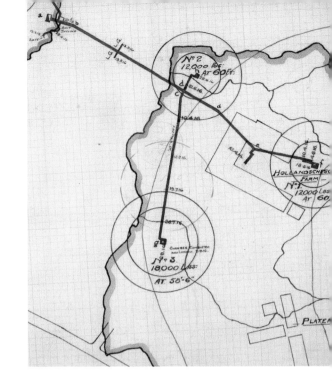

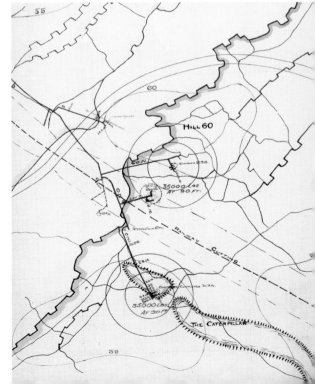

Left above
The three charges planted around Hollandscheschuur Farm by 250 Tunnelling Company RE.

Left below
The multi-national Hill 60 and Caterpillar mines, started by British tunnellers, planted by Canadians and blown by Australians.

Below
One of the fresh tactical ideas hatched by the Germans to replace MEBU-based defences: dugouts with front and rear entrances.

many as were deemed to be required, and with some linked by a switch trench. And heavier guns. Wherever the terrain permitted all these principal lines were located on the *rear* slopes of ridges. Although range was restricted, it had been found that not only were such positions hidden from enemy sight, but the effect of surprise fire – machine guns (even a single one) opening up unexpectedly – was far more debilitating than longer-range barrages. Pillboxes and blockhouses were not tied to the main lines but interspersed amongst the entire battle area like miniature fortress outworks. Von Armin and von Lossberg's ultimate ambition for their *Abwehrschlacht* was to fight the British in an area of their own choosing, an area that had been carefully pre-prepared with selected weaponry and garrisoned with specialist troops to inflict the greatest loss. Thus an attack entering their battle zone might be allowed to make a relatively deep incursion before being flung violently back by the elastic defence-in-depth.

STAGE FRIGHT

After Messines more than two and half years of venomous tunnelling was now more or less over. But only the British knew this. The tremors from the mines of 7 June rippled on through German GHQ and twitchy commanders suspected with an uncomfortable degree of certainty that the Royal Engineers must surely have similar schemes in place for the Ypres attacks.

The mining activity of the enemy has decreased considerably, and there has been practically no increase in the size of the spoil heaps. No new galleries have been observed. On the 22 July, for a period of two hours in the middle of the day, smoke, which issued slowly out of the ground in puffs, was observed about 80 yards in front of the enemy's foremost trench, half-way between 201 and 200. Presumably it came from a gallery which has been driven well out in front.
REPORT OF THE 392ND INFANTRY REGIMENT DATED 28 JULY 1917. THE UNIT WAS HOLDING POSITIONS ON THE PILCKEM RIDGE.

There was no gallery and there was no mine, but it was the very lack of activity and non-growth of spoil heaps that was so worrisome: the only conclusion was that, as at Messines, the British must surely have completed their schemes. The concern was so profound that the Germans panicked and blew a substantial series of heavy, medium-depth charges in known tunnelling sectors in the hoping of destroying any 'hibernating' deep British mines. There were none – there had been insufficient skilled manpower to effect such a scheme.

That fear, however, became a very useful ally for the British. Such was the state of German

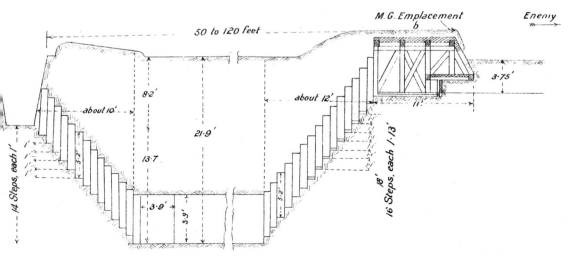

OOSTAVERNE Village   GHELUWE   TENBRIELEN

nervousness that any sign of blue clay spotted from the ground or the air, be it in the British front, reserve or support lines, or even farther back, triggered a heavy hostile response. In the northernmost sector of the Salient near Boesinghe, the miners of 173 Tunnelling Company had dug eighteen galleries into the canal bank, as storehouses for bridging material for extra crossings on the opening day of battle. An enemy trench raid supposed the newly dug earth to be spoil from mine shafts; on the basis of their report German GHQ entirely evacuated the opposing trenches, pulling back almost 500 metres. At nearby Lancashire Farm a similar event took place. Here, a deep British communication subway connected reserve and front lines to allow troops to move unmolested into position (it also incorporated an underground dressing station). German airmen again spotted blue clay near the shaft – and another withdrawal was made. As the RE later noted, it had long proved

difficult and costly to drive the Germans from their trenches, but being able to *frighten* them out was a real bonus.

WHITEHALL

It is important to look now at the political machinations that tracked and followed Messines. One would struggle to find a more inauspicious lead-in to a major offensive and again it was based upon the worries and consequent antics of Lloyd George. The very day after the mines had shaken the Germans from the Messines Ridge, a new assembly met for the first time. The War Committee, headed by Lloyd George, then called Haig and Robertson before them to scrutinize future British strategies, including that of the impending second stage. The two

Above

The green fields beyond. The British view from the Oostaverne lines after the Battle of Messines. Second Army pan 115 taken on 14 June 1917, the final day of the battle.

Right:

German underground heavy minenwerfer (trench mortar) position and (*below*) a cross-section of the workings.

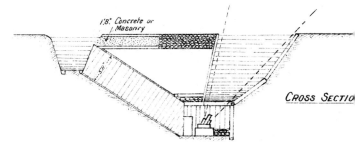

1'8" Concrete or Masonry

CROSS SECTION

MENIN HALLUIN Ch. WERVICQ Ch. BOUSBECQUE Ch. WERVICQ - Sud Church in COMINES

commanders gleaned what was in store and in private agreed to give no ground whatsoever. However, unknown to them, the Prime Minister had received notification of concern from another senior officer. Major General Sir George Macdonogh, the War Office's Director of Military Intelligence, had let it be known that he was hostile to Haig's offensive plans for 1917, suggesting it best for the British to remain on the defensive and wait for American assistance. After six days of tortuous discussion and indeed harsh attack, especially by Lloyd George who showed himself happy to do more than just bend the truth to sway his colleagues, Haig and Robertson emerged shocked and depressed. In the belief that Germany was within 'six months of the total exhaustion of her manpower', Haig despised what he saw as almost universal pessimism regarding his plans. He stood firm, saying that there must be no relaxation in belligerence, adding that after Messines he and his troops

were capable of delivering a second and far greater victory – but only if the plans were undiluted by distractions.

Lloyd George, however, was deeply and genuinely concerned that another Somme might emerge. He did his level best to undermine Haig and in the process astonished him by again advocating an offensive on Italian soil. It was probably only a compelling interjection by Sir John Jellicoe, the First Sea Lord, that swayed the committee to think again. Jellicoe revealed his personal perceptions of the true threat of Germany's submarine offensive, shocking the assembly by stating that unless something was done about the problem, i.e. annexe its sources at Bruges and Ostend – as Haig's Flanders plan included and advocated – Britain might have insufficient resources to continue the fight at all into 1918. The U-boats were truly a potentially fatal menace, he said. It was a decisive interjection, for the Committee were aware that at that

very time convalescent camps in France were
being enlarged and multiplied because so many
hospital ships carrying wounded were being sunk
in the Channel. Coming from the highest-rank-
ing officer in the senior service, the interjection
effectively halted proceedings. Yet Jellicoe's
wholehearted support for Haig's proposals still
led to the Committee being split, and no decision
was made. So, although planning for Ypres was
allowed to continue, GHQ's problems were not
over. It was only a full month later on 20 July that
the same committee informed Haig that the
offensive had been fully authorized – but with a
piquant proviso: should it develop into another
Somme, they would have no compunction in
pulling the plug. In effect, it was now Lloyd
George who was demanding – Nivelle-like –
instant success. When the news arrived at GHQ,
Gough's guns had already been shelling German
batteries for a fortnight and the main pre-attack
bombardment had been bellowing for a full
week. And yet the politicking was still unfinished.
On 25 July, almost on the eve of the greatest
British military offensive in history, Lloyd George
recommended that troops and guns should *immediately* be sent to Italy – an astounding
announcement to make at such a time, for should
Haig and Robertson refuse to comply it would
leave the British government only one course of
action – the dismissal of their Commander-in-
Chief and Chief of the Imperial General Staff.
In no uncertain terms, Robertson told the
Committee exactly what was felt at GHQ at this
most critical time, his stern words temporarily
bringing the dialogue to an end. The result was
passed to Sir Douglas Haig via telegram – now,
Robertson wired, he could apparently depend on

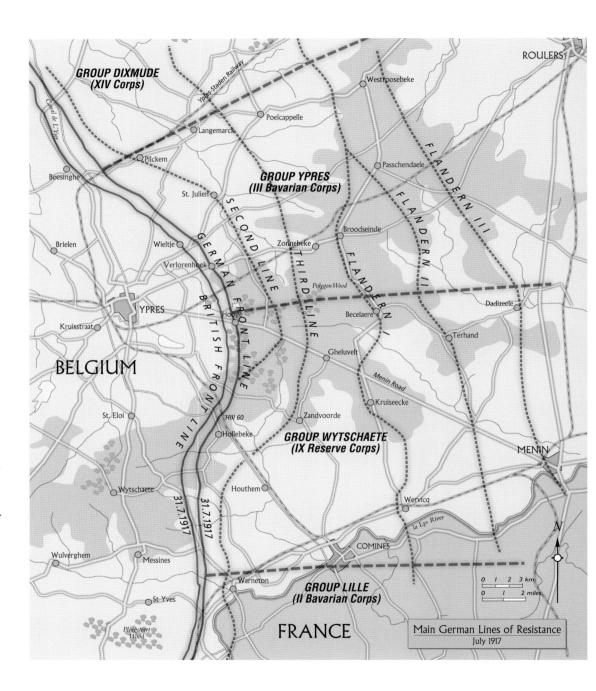

Main German Lines of Resistance
July 1917

Left

The front lines after the Battle of Messines and before 31 July, showing the ranks of German defences facing the Allies.

Following pages

The view from Wytschaete after German reoccupation in July 1918. Compare with the image on pages 86-7 taken from almost the same location in 1916.

the Committee's 'wholehearted support'.

The greatest aftershock of the period occurred whilst these political deliberations were in motion. As a result of appalling breaches in security, the Germans gleaned British plans for the coastal assault. On 10 July they launched a spoiling attack, the *Strandfest*, against trenches in the dunes on the northernmost extremity of the Western Front, the Belgian coast. The British positions were isolated on the east bank of the River Yser, connected to the rest of the heavily fortified coastal strip only by barrel bridges. They formed the sole critical bridgehead for the attack planned to run in tandem with the Passchendaele breakthrough, an attack that the entire 1st Division of Rawlinson's Fourth Army were already training hard for. Lose the bridgehead and the scheme was more than seriously compromised. But lost it was, plus 1,250 infantry and tunnellers and forty machine guns. British counter-attacks were out of the question, for there was no bridgehead: the two sides now faced each other across the River Yser. Still, it was early days and there was time for the British to think again subject to events at Ypres. The dunes were also the scene of a troubling new irritant for the Allies for it was on this same day that the Germans tested a new form of poison gas: Yperite. Its correct chemical term was dichlorethyl sulphide, but the troops came to know it as mustard gas. Two days later it was first

encountered at Ypres where life was noisy and frantic with preparation, roaring guns and no little hostile shelling. Yet there were still strangely peaceful interludes:

We read in the open room, our balcony we called it. Sometimes we took our chairs or substitute empty ammunition boxes outside and sat in the garden, enjoying afternoon sunshine. Though so much had been destroyed, yet much was left still, some of the willows and poplars still had life in them, and roses were as beautiful and smelled as sweetly here as in an Oxford garden. My servant picked a bunch for me and put them in a jar in my room, and when he saw that I was pleased he found other flowers for me as well. I had almost more than I wanted. Sometimes the concussion of a near shell outside, or my own clumsiness, knocked over one of the jars and water was spilled over my letters or books. My servant took me to see where a pair of swallows had made their nest on a rafter of one of the shelters. No one disturbed them, everyone used the other entrance. The five young birds had just hatched and we watched the parents feeding them. There seemed as many birds here as there were at home. I had not expected the war to be like this, and I never found it like this again. At Ypres, even in the summer of 1917, before the great battle began, there was still something of the old world left, something at variance with the war, a sense of homes that had once been lived in and gardens where children had played. At the wagon lines, which were in some fields by a farm, life still went on more or less as usual for the Flemish farmer and his family, and they all smiled when they saw us.

SECOND LIEUTENANT P.J. CAMPBELL, 150 BRIGADE, ROYAL FIELD ARTILLERY

Rundbild v. d. Höhe Wytschate

7 m nördl. d. Truppen Beob. Stelle, 15 m nördl.
des hohen einräumigen Unterstandes i. d. Mitte d. Dorfes

Haus nördl. d. Dickebusch Sees

Die Einteilungen sind übereinstimmen
mit den Teilungen an den Visiervorrich-
gen am Geschütz u. a. Scherenfernrohr

Südwestlicher
Hausgiebel

Hausreste a. d. Straße

Unterstände a. Wegekreuz

Hausruine

Vlamertingen Kirchenruine

Heckenecke

Ruine d. Küche in
Dickebusch

Baum b. Straßenkreuz

Schloss Vlamertingen

Heckenecke

Gehöft. Südwestgiebel

1200   1300   1400   1500   1600

69 50   66 52   68 49   65 50   70 47   69 48
28 67 52   69 50   67 50   70 48   64 51   69 48   26   27
26   27   26   27   26   26

200   300   400   500   600   700

Die Bezeichnung $\frac{6947}{26}$ besagt daß der Punkt
der Karte im Quadrat $\frac{6400}{47}$ liegt u.
lfde Nummer 26 im Quadrat hat

Unterstand

Kathedrale i. Yperen, T.P. 894

Hierzu eine Karte mit den photogrammetrisch fes-
gelegten Punkten.

Hausgiebel
a. Kanal

Tuchhallen-Turm in
Yperen, T.P. 895

Jacobskirche, T.P. 896

Wohltätigkeitsschule
östl. Yperen

Schornstein a. d. Bahn

Peterskirche, T.P. 898

1700   1800   1900   2000   2100

$\frac{47}{26}$ $\frac{66}{27}\frac{47}{}$ $\frac{66}{29}\frac{46}{}$ $\frac{65}{26}\frac{46}{}$ $\frac{6646}{28}$ $\frac{6646}{26}$ $\frac{66}{32}\frac{45}{}$
                                        $\frac{65}{27}\frac{46}{}$

800   900   1000   1100   1200

CHAPTER SEVEN
Towards the Third Battle

On arrival at Le Havre, we were marched for a very long distance to an enormous base camp, where reinforcements of all branches of the service were collected and sent up the line to join units as required. At these base camps the men were generally very badly treated. The officers who ran them of course did not know the men, and the whole thing was impersonal – in fact, the Army at its worst. I was made Orderly Officer of the Day, and had to go to the cookhouse to inspect the meal. I reported that it was virtually uneatable, and got myself immediately sent up the line, which was exactly what I had wanted. On my way there I met an older subaltern of considerable experience who told me that I was very lucky to be coming out to the front at this time, because the whole of the British front was unbelievably quiet, with the sole exception of the Ypres Salient which he said was simply hell on earth. Almost immediately afterwards an orderly put a note into my hand telling me to report to a railhead at a place called Poperinghe which was a few miles west of Ypres. So I realised I was in for the Salient with all its well-earned reputation for mud, blood and horror.

Lieutenant Douglas Wimberley,
232nd Machine Gun Company

Sir Hubert Gough began installing his staff at La Lovie Chateau near Proven on 10 June. Here, planning for the great Ypres breakthrough commenced in earnest. Gough and his Fifth Army Chief of Staff, Major General Neill Malcolm,

fully appreciated that a repeat of Messines was not on the agenda. There were no mines to stultify the enemy, their men would potentially face German defence over a depth of almost 9 kilometres, the Commander-in-Chief's ambition at Passchendaele was far greater than Plumer's restricted brief, and no one had any idea how the Germans would react tactically to the Messines disaster. What lessons, then, could be transferred from 7 June? With British artillery firepower further increased, any trench-based enemy was seriously threatened with complete eradication. But the Germans were not trench based. Subsequent to Messines reports of the effects of British shellfire on concrete had been noted; more and heavier guns were all that could assist here, and they were arriving daily. Certainly, the artillery performance in early June had been by far the finest of the war to date. Firing by map reference rather than direct observation was becoming ever more efficient, so there was no reason to believe improvements would not be more enhanced by zero day at Ypres. Tanks had been effective at Messines. Weather and terrain conditions had both been good on the day, but the victory had been so decisive and swift that they had not really been called upon; the battle, however, again revealed their role as morale boosters and a very useful 'fire-drawing' function. With decent going and disciplined artillery preparation tanks could be a powerful tool to help the infantry negotiate the Salient's concrete jungle, and arrest Lloyd George's fear, the dreadful haemorrhage of life that had come to characterize so many offensives. But – and this was universally agreed – their effectiveness could only be localized until swarms of machines with fully trained crews were made available. The Heavy Section Machine Gun Corps (as the tanks were still called until 27 July 1917) were notified of their participation at Ypres in mid-May. The entire establishment of 216 machines was required. Those not already in theatre were loaded onto trains and shunted to the Salient where they went into shrouded hibernation in woods near Oosthoek and Ouderdom. What of the cavalry? Known by all through long experience to be an unlikely asset in the forthcoming battle, they were therefore stationed behind the lines (on Haig's, not Gough's orders), but were still available in case of a comprehensive rout. Air support? At Messines, the British aerial presence was getting stronger and more effective. Plumer had employed no less than 280 ground-based wireless stations receiving information for counter-battery work. By July the British held an almost two-to-one advantage in the skies over Flanders. The reconnaissance aircraft's role in directing counter-battery fire and photographing enemy positions was critical to the fortunes of the infantry; but they were deadly slow, and horribly vulnerable. Aerial photographs, of which tens of thousands were taken, were quickly developed and 'advertised' as lists, the target area of each

picture being identified by map reference. Corps and divisions would then indent for relevant copies. Reconnaissance aircraft took to the air with protective flights of fighters and scouts, including the SE5A and recently introduced Sopwith Camel, which roved the skies protecting their own observers from hostile raptors. When conditions allowed, these nippy planes were also found to be valuable adjuncts to ground attack, flying low and appearing suddenly to strafe along trench lines and scatter engineers and gunners at work. As the battle unfolded, so ground attack took on an ever more important and expanded role. But it was by no means a cakewalk, with rifle and machine-gun fire being not the only risks. The following German report advocated an unusual form of anti-aircraft activity. It was sent by First Army to Crown Prince Rupprecht on 31 July 1917, and later captured by British troops.

In the 1st Guard Reserve Division and the 4th Guards Division, by the employment of light Minenwerfer [mortar – literally, mine-thrower], it has been possible to engage the enemy's aeroplanes effectively when flying near our front lines or over them at a height of 200-600 metres. In every case the aeroplanes were forced to turn back; in one case, it appeared for a moment as though the aeroplane was about to crash. Charges 3, 4 and 5 were used. Fuzes were set at 7 seconds (the lowest graduation). Aim was taken at the point the aeroplane would reach in about 7 seconds (i.e. about 200-500 metres ahead of it). The time of flight being 7 seconds, the shell burst almost at the highest point of its trajectory. As the shell is usually visible in flight, a rough correction can be made even before the shell has burst. Minenwerfer units have received instructions to carry out experimental shoots on a large scale against aerial targets. Experiments are also being made behind the front with the object of devising a practical system of open sights for use with light Minenwerfer.

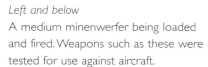

Left and below
A medium minenwerfer being loaded and fired. Weapons such as these were tested for use against aircraft.

For vitally important aerial photography the most stable platform was required. Bristol Fighters were a good multi-purpose machine, but it was the RE8, a fragile, string-and-card-board affair, that best fitted the bill. The plane was slow but reliable and very easy to manage; in good conditions it flew smoothly and straight for the camera, and was sufficiently spacious for the installation of a wireless for sending air-to-ground Morse-coded information for British guns. Awareness of the multiple role that aircraft could play led to them sometimes being rather overloaded. A pilot's biggest challenge was often simply getting airborne.

In those early days of flying, with such heavy loads to get off the ground, it was very difficult to get the old kites off the ground in time with the engine losing power if it was overheated on the ground. We would get off the ground as quickly as possible using full throttle and hoping the old engine would develop enough power to pull us over the trees and hop poles surrounding the air-field, and that the prop would keep working hard. Besides full tanks, heavy photographic equipment, we carried a twin Lewis machine gun, mounted round the observer's seat for the observer's use, and a Vickers gun mounted to fire through the propeller for the pilot's use in emergency, and the ammunition for these guns, also our bombs. The RE8's were capable of carrying a 260lb bomb load. We certainly were well loaded, which was a constant hazard in our minds, adding to the difficulties in getting the machine off the ground, anyway in battle conditions. This was a colossal task for such youngsters.
LIEUTENANT J.T.P. JEYES, NO. 21 SQUADRON,
ROYAL FLYING CORPS

In the lead-up to zero hour every metre of the prospective battlefield was photographed and re-mapped several times over. The rule was simple:

if the weather was favourable, the planes flew. Once in the air, the task was an all-consuming one. For the observer, there was the question of pinpointing targets for photography (and some-times bombing), spotting for artillery, signalling to the ground and receiving responses, keeping a sharp lookout for hostile aircraft, and fighting them off if necessary. In front, his pilot was sur-rounded by distractions and uncertainties: how best to avoid anti-aircraft shells bursting around, gauging from which direction enemy planes might attack, how he might make his escape, avoiding clouds (for photography) and being aware of every other machine in the air at that time, hostile or friendly, of which there were often large numbers. Then there was the mental and aural preoccupation with the mechanics of his machine, listening for subtle but potentially dangerous changes in engine noise, keeping it flying well. Effectively, each plane was on its own, contact with the ground dependent upon the vagaries of the nascent technology of wire-less signalling. The aerial was a long wire that was unwound from the plane as it took off, and rewound before landing. Not unsurprisingly, it had unexpected idiosyncracies.

Fortunately, not every day was fit for flying, and we would rest and play games, but we also had to go up to the lines near Ypres and the Menin Gate and contact the 4.5" and 6" and 12" guns which we had been spotting for. We only found by experience that if we were flying away from the battery they could not receive our signals. We would fly towards the Hun lines hoping to see the burst, and then turn to see if the ground signals were put out right. I had a whole shoot one time and never did find the correc-tion on a 12" gun shoot. There were three flights doing shoots and we each had our own problems which we had to go and dis-

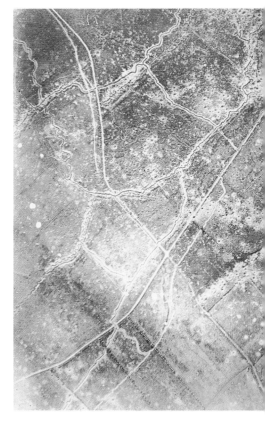

Left and below

The distinctive zig-zagging German trenches (Calf and Caliban) at La Brique. Top: June 1915; bottom, taken two years later, illustrates changes in the landscape including extensive development of British lines. Note Admiral's Road in no man's land. The British trench cutting through it then running parallel with the front line is the jumping-off trench dug for the 31 July attack.

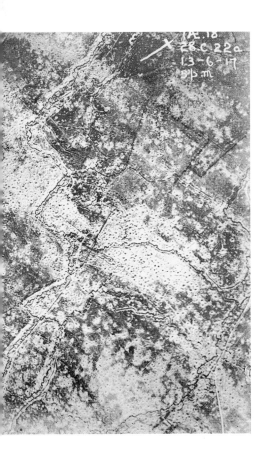

cuss with the batteries. The pilots and observers were able to visit battery commanders and to discuss their own methods of co-operation. This worked quite well as there was only a small number of batteries which worked with aeroplane observation. It permitted one observer in the squadron to work with one battery permanently. It would not have been possible for an observer to work with more than one, since between themselves, they evolved their own systems. It would have been considered a good flight when twenty or so rounds had been fired and observed. Consequently, the observers and battery commanders, who were expert with their co-operation, were very few, and as the work increased it became necessary to establish a system of simple standards to which other observers could be trained.

Lieutenant J.T.P. Jeyes, No. 21 Squadron, Royal Flying Corps

AT GHQ

As preparations at Ypres got into their stride and information daily streamed in, spirits rose further. The coastal offensive scheme was revisited and rescheduled, with new projected dates of 7 or 8 August. Sir Douglas Haig's optimism about the brittleness of the German war machine and waning enthusiasm in the ranks was bolstered and nurtured by Charteris' intelligence reports. The following extracts from captured letters were included in Intelligence summaries. They are typical of those that Haig was receiving every day.

WRITTEN BY A MAN OF THE 450TH INFANTRY REGIMENT, 233RD DIVISION, TO HIS BROTHER, A PILOT IN THE 211TH ARTILLERY FLIGHT.

6 June. One day we had a nice bombardment. All the dug-outs were blown in, although they had concrete head-cover a metre thick. One gun was smashed up too, and the artillerymen had to clear out. This was mainly the work of the English airmen; they

were so bold and impudent that they came down to a height of 100 metres and fired on us with machine guns. None of our aeroplanes could show themselves, they were driven off at once. The English airmen did what they liked, and this was why the bombardment was so good. A pursuit flight with red machines arrived the other day, but they did nothing.

FROM A MAN OF AN UNNAMED UNIT.

22/6/17. You are longing for the end of the war as no doubt everybody is. I too am heartily sick of the business. It is incredible that there will be no change. With our third of a loaf we shall soon get hunger-typhus.

LETTER FROM A SOLDIER OF THE 10TH COMPANY, 455TH REGIMENT, DATED 29 JULY 1917.

The situation is melancholy. Our Company has suffered heavy losses during the one day we have been here. At the present moment we are in the support trench, a few hundred metres behind the front line. The English shell the entire area incessantly with the heaviest guns, and the ground is one mass of shell holes, some of them large enough to build houses in. Tomorrow night we go into the front line. It is battered to pieces and consists merely of shell holes, in which we have to hold out for seven consecutive days . . . Our water supply consists of one water-bottle full, and we must make that suffice for a week, for no one can get back from the front line in consequence of the heavy shelling . . . Death lies in wait for us, like a fox for its prey.

The combination of such reports (many hundreds of them) and the lengthy afterglow of Messines made a potent mixture for optimism. Finely detailed intelligence was also available on the nature of German defences and their physical organization and dispositions. Gough was aware of the lightly held and supple front lines – the *Vorfeld* – and the fact that the strongest resistance would be encountered from support positions. The key to success was to maintain an even speed of progress on an even line of attack behind an even creeping barrage; irregularity would play into German hands. Surprisingly, Gough and Malcolm came up with a hugely ambitious scheme similar to that pursued on 1 July 1916. They took the step-by-step steady approach advocated by Plumer and Rawlinson as a model but modified it radically, increasing artillery intensity and demanding a much faster and *deeper* advance. Instead of securing the Pilckem Ridge and part of the Gheluvelt Plateau, consolidating and pausing for two days to bring up the guns, then repeating the crushing bombardment ahead of the next 'bite', and so on, Gough felt he could press much further onto the plateau *and* annexe the entire German second line in one bound: the guns would be given just four hours to move up. If all went according to plan the original projected depth of advance would be multiplied by five, on Day One taking the British to Gheluvelt on the right, Broodseinde in the centre, and beyond Langemarck on the left. Only at this point would the guns get a few days respite to move up. The breakout could then be completed by taking the rest of the northern Passchendaele Ridge including the Houthulst and Westroosebeke sectors. Thus Roulers and

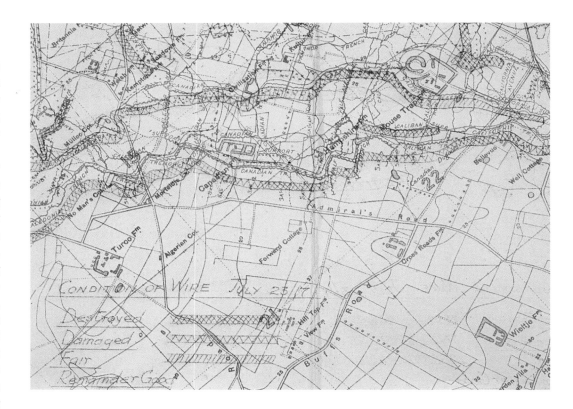

Thourout would be exposed. Several senior officers were worried that the bombardment would be over-diluted by so greatly deepening the target area, and that troops might run the risk of breaking the golden rule and straying beyond the range of their guns. Even with the best of conditions on the day there was almost no chance of the still

Above
XVIII Corps study of enemy wire on 23 July 1917 (see aerials on previous page).

Below
The view from Crossroads Farm (see map above) in June 1915.

Army Panorama 4
m Crossroads Farm
C 22 c 3.8
ne 1915

Kitchener's   Wood

Admiral's Road

Mousetrap Farm

Trees along Admiral's Road

be colossal, profoundly injuring their defensive prospects in any subsequent actions. If this was the case the British would drive right over the Passchendaele Ridge on Day One. Haig, albeit with his own expressions of concern, particularly about the hostile potential of the Gheluvelt Plateau, endorsed the plans but specifically asked Gough to bolster his assault here. Artillery intensity seemed to concern Haig less than infantry numbers. Despite the Fifth Army attacking a front of almost 25 kilometres, he appears to have believed that the concentration of heavy guns would be sufficient, even for a deep penetration. At the final decisive pre-battle conference Gough's approach was supported by several other highly respected commanders – curiously including Plumer – each of whom appeared to share Haig and Charteris' conviction that the enemy was practically on his last legs. Wider support for the enterprise was largely based on this erroneous belief. Gough was therefore given his head and began final preparations.

Meanwhile Rawlinson's Fourth Army continued their sojourn on the coast, waiting and secretly training in the dunes, whilst Plumer's men further consolidated their positions on the right flank and began arrangements for diversionary action. On the left, General Anthoine's French

Above

XVIII Corps appreciation of the effectiveness of the British pre-attack bombardment, also showing the Crossroads Farm sector, 23 July 1917.

mechanically unreliable tanks being able to support such a rate of advance. Any malfunction in the scheme was therefore likely to present the *Eingreifdivisionen* with tailor-made opportunities. If it worked, however, von Armin and von Lossberg's entire main battle zone would be overrun and German casualties would undoubtedly

Crossroads Farm

First Army continued bringing up heavy guns. Across no man's land, it was soon after 7 June that the Germans had become aware of a second British offensive phase, as they observed all kinds of feverish activity: new camps, new batteries, new roads, dumps and bridges, increased raids and an upsurge of hostile counter-battery fire. Excising the Messines salient had been essential, but it had only slightly dented German observational capability. As Gough himself said, unless preparations could be made covertly, each day allowed the enemy a day to prepare also. The Salient, spread out like an amphitheatre beneath German eyes and cameras, was in no way conducive to secrecy.

FIFTH ARMY

Sir Hubert Gough's Fifth Army was composed of five corps, XIV, XVIII and XIX, with in reserve V and VIII Corps, a total of eighteen divisions. As the men flooded into the Salient they had to be accommodated. Like the artillery and their battery positions and gun pits, the engineers had toiled to put in place an astonishing array of observation posts and tunnelled command and accommodation dugouts for Brigade and Divisional use. To install positions of control as close as possible to the forthcoming action, the majority were located close behind the front line. Each was interconnected by telephone, many electrically lit and ventilated, and some joined by underground subways. The dugouts were especially necessary because continuous heavy hostile shelling had made all shallow forward cover precarious. It was a trying time for those whose work was necessarily exposed: the Royal Artillery, Royal Engineers and personnel of the Army Service Corps. As the Germans were fully aware, gas was always likely to be especially problematic.

Strain started the night the enemy killed over one thousand transport animals with their phosgene gas. Dead transport animals had to be got off the road urgently so that the next night's transport could get through. After being dragged off they lay around unburied until someone could be spared to shovel earth over them. For hour after hour, mile after mile, night after night it meant getting round the job in a gas mask. The donning of a gas mask seemed to take away a third of a soldier's efficiency. If the design of gas masks had evolved with the care given say to the design of machine-guns, it could have been a contribution to the winning of the war. Phosgene affected breathing and pulse. Fritz varied the diet with mustard oil gas, a skin blisterer affecting the lungs fatally, and thermit shells which were meant to burn holes in our steel helmets but didn't. It was dinned into us that gas casualties were unsoldierly slobs who had not used their gas masks.
CAPTAIN BRIAN FRAYLING, 171ST TUNNELLING COMPANY, ROYAL ENGINEERS

On 12 July, the Germans showered an estimated 50,000 rounds of HE and gas shells on key British positions and transport routes, gassing (with the recently introduced mustard gas) more than 2,500 troops, the first of nearly 15,000 men and over 3,000 animals to succumb before the offensive began. The arrival of this new threat, shells that 'plopped' rather than roared, caused curiosity as well as concern.

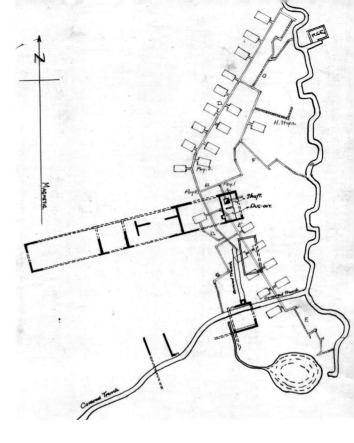

Above
Plan of Hilltop Farm dugout, one of many British underground headquarters systems installed prior to the battle. Scores more were constructed during the winter of 1917/18.

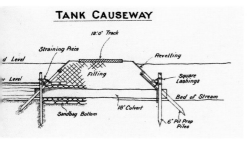

TANK CAUSEWAY

Above

A tank causeway designed to help the monsters negotiate patches of bad ground.

Right

Some of the bridge and dugout work carried out in preparation for battle by the RE.

Below

A 'jump crossing' designed to allow tanks to cross small waterways without building a bridge. The tracks straddled both banks.

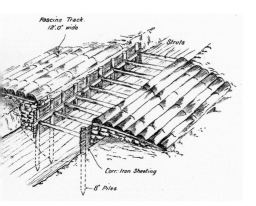

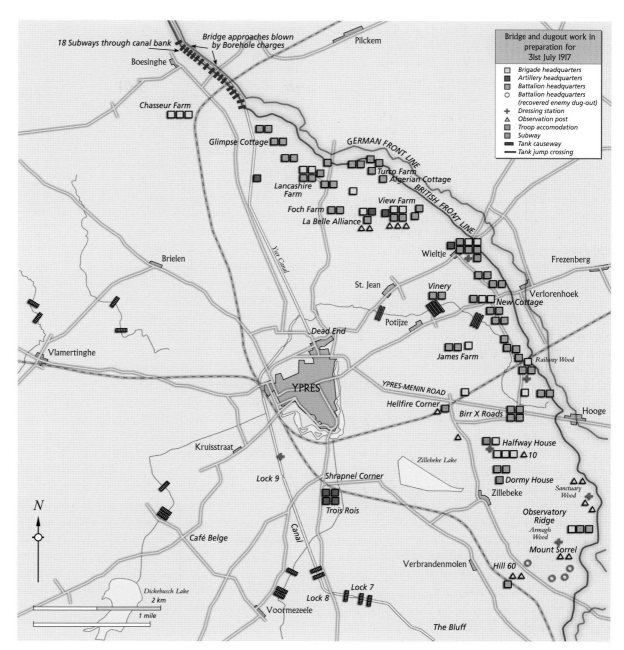

Bridge and dugout work in preparation for 31st July 1917

▫ Brigade headquarters
◼ Artillery headquarters
▣ Battalion headquarters
○ Battalion headquarters (recovered enemy dug-out)
✛ Dressing station
△ Observation post
▨ Troop accomodation
▦ Subway
▥ Tank causeway
— Tank jump crossing

JULY 17TH

My turn for O.P. – I started off with two telephonists about 6 a.m., and arrived shortly before 7 a.m. Had a fairly quiet day there. There was one continuous and unceasing whistle of our shells passing over the whole day. I counted 150 large shells pass almost immediately over the O.P. in five minutes; that is 1,800 in an hour. The same thing was going on all along this front, all day and every day for a fortnight before the attack! The expenditure of shells in connection with this operation must have been colossal. A certain number of Boche shells were bursting behind me. But the number coming our way was not to be compared with the number we were sending over. My telephone wire got cut with shell fire, and I had to send the linesman out to repair it. It was some time before I could get through to the battery again. I then learnt that the battery was again being heavily shelled. The road on my way back was being shelled, so we had to make a bit of a detour to avoid it. I got back at 7.30 p.m. and found the shelling had ceased. But it began again just as we were sitting down to dinner, and we had to clear, and were kept from our dinner for two hours. We then returned to the mess and had dinner. I was hungry after my day at O.P., with only a light lunch and no tea. The shelling shortly started again, but we stayed in the mess, as we came to the conclusion that we were not the actual target. The shells were falling very near our sleeping huts, however, – too near to make our beds very enticing, so we all stayed in the mess till about 1 a.m. The gas alarm came through on the phone, and soon the gas got pretty thick, necessitating the wearing of gas masks. Cripps sent and warned the men, and gave orders that they were to wear their gas masks. This gas was rather mysterious, as we could not hear the familiar sound of gas shells bursting, and there was not a breath of wind to bring the 'cloud' of gas over from the Hun lines. We came to the conclusion that the Hun now puts gas into some of his High Explosive shells, such as were bursting in the vicinity of our sleeping quarters. If so, this was new.

LIEUTENANT E.C. ALLFREE, 111TH SIEGE BATTERY, ROYAL GARRISON ARTILLERY

As the days passed, so use of the new weapon spread across the entire Salient.

24.7.17

Continued the march through Dickebusch and then across broken country to our old tunnels at E.S.O.9. (Spoil Bank). There has been a lot of shelling here since we left. Close to the Brick Stack a dump of 9.2 shells had been blown up and the hole was almost the size of a small mine crater. We took our old patch by the side of the canal and noticed a peculiar smell in the air and incidentally we were all seized with fits of sneezing. We learned that this was due to a new kind of gas which Fritz has been putting over during the last day or two. We call it 'Mustard gas'. It is very poisonous. One fellow who touched a piece of one of the gas shells had his arms and hands break out in most painful eruptions and had to be taken to hospital quickly. Fritz had an observation balloon looking straight down the canal and this spot is not the comparative home of rest that it was a month ago. The outgoing Brigade look rather haggard as if they have had a very rough time. The weather is bad and we wonder whenever the attack is to be made. Each day we expect to receive the order but it doesn't come, and nobody cares for this suspense. We know we have come to make the attack and we would prefer to get it over quickly, for we know that the sooner it is over the sooner we shall

Above left
Secure accommodation inside the ramparts of Ypres. Hundreds of thousands of troops sheltered here and in the town's cellars throughout the war. These men are from the 22nd Australian Infantry Battalion.

Above right
Entrances to the ramparts dugouts north of the Menin Gate. These are 177 Tunnelling Company RE men.

The Dean and Chapter of Rochester Cathedral have approved a woman organist and a woman verger.

SECOND ARMY INTELLIGENCE SUMMARY, TUESDAY, 17 JULY 1917.

Above and background
The canal bank north of Ypres, the site of scores of dugouts of all kinds from HQs to dressing stations such as Essex Farm, which can still be visited today. The far (north) bank was similarly undermined.

get back out of this hell of mud and shells and gas. We know that there will be a lot of casualties, but hope springs eternal, and each man reckons that he will get back safely.
SAPPER ALBERT MARTIN, 41ST SIGNAL COMPANY, ROYAL ENGINEERS

The threat spread beyond the battlefield itself, for medical teams in dressing stations, and even nurses in casualty clearing stations some 10 to 15 miles behind the lines were susceptible to gas lingering on soldiers' uniforms. Those removing uniforms to treat gas burns and other wounds inhaled the latent gases, thereby suffering lung and eye problems, sickness and dizziness, even yellowing of the hair. As an illustration of how swiftly men could be evacuated from the battlefield, this same problem was also recorded in hospitals in England and Scotland. The British response to 'this hell of mud and gas' was to create one of their own through a massive pre-battle bombardment. This included their own new liquid gas, chloropicrin, a weapon that was hoped would confound German masks through its smaller molecular structure infiltrating the chemical protection. It was a severe irritant, causing weeping eyes, vomiting and bronchitis. Traces in the air caused a burning sensation in the eyes, often the first warning of its presence. Not as lethal or insidious as mustard but still potentially fatal through lung damage and several other associated complications, the gas was known as PS after the Port Sunlight works where it was first developed by Lever Brothers.

In conjunction with the day and night artillery outbursts there were trench raids in all sectors, plus long-range machine-gun barrages. The RE Special Companies also played a key role. In the six days before zero day, 4,000 Livens projectors made daily attacks on a range of targets from the enemy front line to positions more than a kilometre distant. Fired electrically, rank on rank of projectors had been dug into the ground and camouflaged over a period of weeks. This time the cylinders were filled with gas – chloropicrin – which was found to be especially effective when used in conjunction with a barrage as it was difficult for defenders to differentiate between shell and cylinder.

As for engineer-based preparations for attacking troops, the most important task was to acquaint the men with the ground and enemy positions they were likely to encounter. In traditional and effective fashion this was achieved by outdoor models fashioned by Pioneer and Army Troops companies. They transformed prospective target areas into exact miniature replicas, complete with trenches, wire, pillboxes, rivers, woods, contours etc.

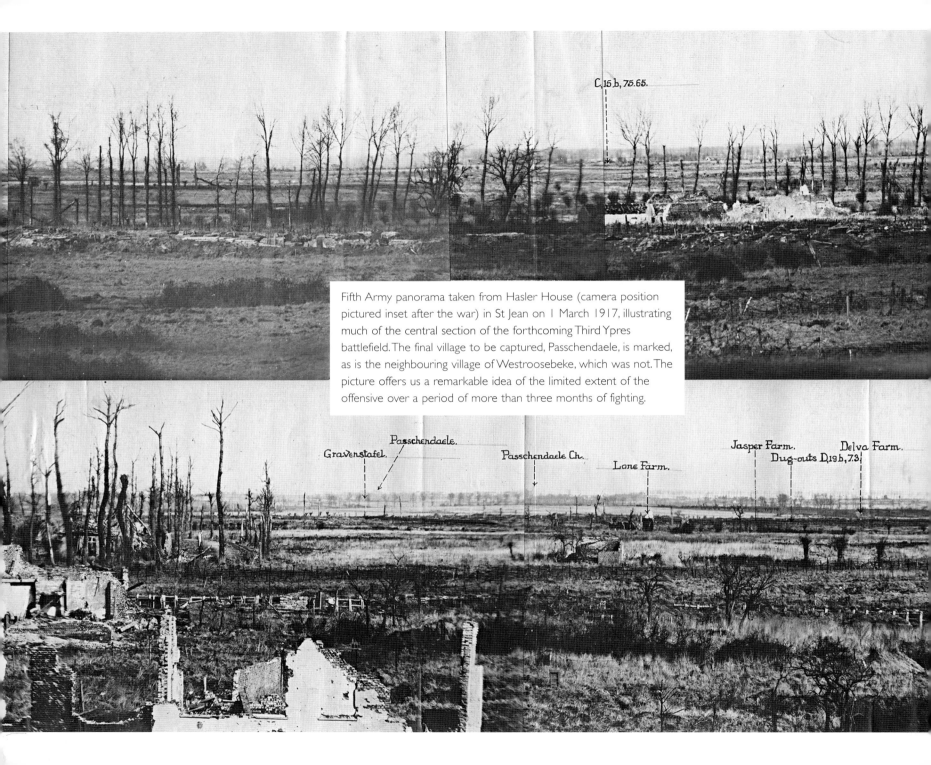

C.15 b, 75.65.

Fifth Army panorama taken from Hasler House (camera position pictured inset after the war) in St Jean on 1 March 1917, illustrating much of the central section of the forthcoming Third Ypres battlefield. The final village to be captured, Passchendaele, is marked, as is the neighbouring village of Westroosebeke, which was not. The picture offers us a remarkable idea of the limited extent of the offensive over a period of more than three months of fighting.

Gravenstafel.   Passchendaele.   Passchendaele Ch.   Lane Farm.   Jasper Farm.   Delva Farm.
Dug-outs D.19 b, 7.3.

Fifth Army Panorama No. 102. made on 1:3:17. from Hasler House.

Copy No...............

including a field of view of 130° from about N.N.W. to E.S.E. C. 27d. 6.4.

Hilltop Ridge

Approximate Scale of Degrees (1 degree equals 1 1/24 inch).

0   1   2   3   4   5   6   7

Mill.   Pilckem Cross Roads   Marsouin Farm.   Crab Apple Tree.   Stray Farm.   View Farm.

West Roosebeke Ch.

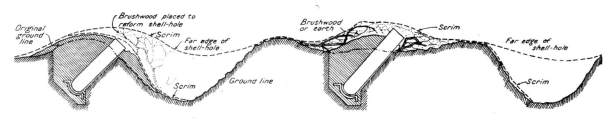

Original ground line — *Brushwood placed to reform shell-hole* — *Scrim* — *Far edge of shell-hole* — *Scrim* — *Ground line* — *Brushwood or earth* — *Scrim* — *Far edge of shell-hole* — *Scrim*

Left

The highly effective Livens gas projector, also used for firing Thermit and oil-filled liquid-fire cylinders. Large numbers of projectors were installed in parallel ranks and fired simultaneously or in salvoes.

We are moving up into line again soon in preparation for the 'Do'. West Kents are attached to 54th Brigade as 'Moppers Up', Queens are on 53rd Brigade strength for consolidation purposes, East Surreys are on road fatigue under the C.R.E. 18th Div: and Buffs are 'Stretcher Bearing' to whole of Division, so whole of Brigade is allotted to their various tasks. One very good plan of the staff, and one that is put into execution here, has more of wisdom about it than we believed the said staff possessed, that is, two ground plans of the actual ground over which the attack covers are laid out in scale, showing all Jerry's trenches and fortifications, wire, etc, in fact, everything necessary for officer and man. It is laid out like a large allotment, and each Battalion is taken in turn, has the attack, also peculiarities of the ground explained to them. This is something extremely brainy, yet so vitally necessary, that one wonders why it was not tried before. Every contour is shown, and his Machine-Gun posts, also likely places to expect them, on the whole it is very realistic, and the officers are very frequently viewing it and marking their maps accordingly. They know what part of the line they will be interested in, and so, each to his own degree of intelligence, marks his map where he thinks he will meet trouble, etc. What a smash this will be? For we have 'Tanks', Cavalry and R[oyal] H[orse] Artillery waiting for the breakthrough. Fritz is assured of a warm time soon, all is in readiness.

PRIVATE ROBERT CUDE MM, 7TH EAST KENT REGIMENT (THE BUFFS)

Every man involved in the attack would study the model and attend lectures on his Division's allotted ground and chosen tactics. In certain corps,

Maxse's XVIII for example, larger areas were kitted out with a section of mock battlefield over which the infantry practised.

In the knowledge that the Germans would employ their machine guns not through pillbox loopholes but from shell holes, trench parapets

Below

The Pilckem Ridge sector under British fire on 21 July 1917. Note Calabash Trench, and see picture opposite.

CALABASH TR. C 14

CALEDONIA TR.

P7F 90 SHEET 28 21-7-17

Above
XVIII Corps model of their attacking front for 31 July 1917, including a representation of Calabash Trench.

and pillbox roofs, it was speed of advance across no man's land that would reduce casualties, allowing the enemy the least possible time to set up their weapons. A wave system similar to the Somme was to be employed, preceded by a mixed artillery barrage to pound forward trenches and outposts and cut wire. Again in traditional manner, at the moment of zero hour the big guns would lift to the next target; in their place would fall a mixed deluge of high explosive and shrapnel – the creeping barrage – to keep hostile heads low. The British were instructed to move fast – no more going into the attack as if on parade – as soon as the protective barrage was seen to be in place. They should then follow the curtain of shells 'as closely as a horse will follow a nosebag filled with corn' and, crucially, all arrive in successive enemy lines at the same time. The rate selected was 100 metres per four minutes. As subsequent waves moved forward to leapfrog their predecessors, moppers-up would hunt close behind, resolving, often brutally, any

problems of lingering enemy resistance.

Meanwhile, as the attack advanced the artillery guided by forward observation officers (FOOs) and aerial observers were to direct dedicated heavier guns to more distant points in the battle zone: enemy troop concentrations, pre-selected pillboxes, machine-gun and mortar positions and counter-attack formations.

Before all this could take place, however, much work was needed on the battlefront itself, at the deadly parapet interface. In places where no man's land was deemed too wide for men to negotiate swiftly, jumping-off trenches were pushed out ahead of the front lines and the British wire. These were no more than simple ditches about a metre and a half deep, dug almost straight, i.e. lacking the firebays of a traditional fire-trench. They were built for a moment's use, no more. Of course, unless installed as a bluff, their appearance offered the enemy the penultimate piece in his intelligence jigsaw. What the Germans really needed to know was the date and time the onslaught would begin. About this timing there was much heated British discussion. Not knowing the hour and date of one's potential fate was a deep cause of anxiety for the troops – they were keen to end the waiting and get cracking.

WEDNESDAY 25TH JULY
Rumours that tomorrow is Y Day. Very wet today. Thunderstorms.

26TH JULY.
Relief of 57th Brigade postponed, also date. Everyone getting very irritable and fed up – too long in the line – nothing but rumours.

JULY 27TH.
Still no news: it is getting a real strain waiting all this time

of Mousetrap Farm

Juliet Farm.

Buidings of Potijze Chateau

Warwick Fm.

Rupprecht Fm.

Prowse Farm

Pagoda Corner.

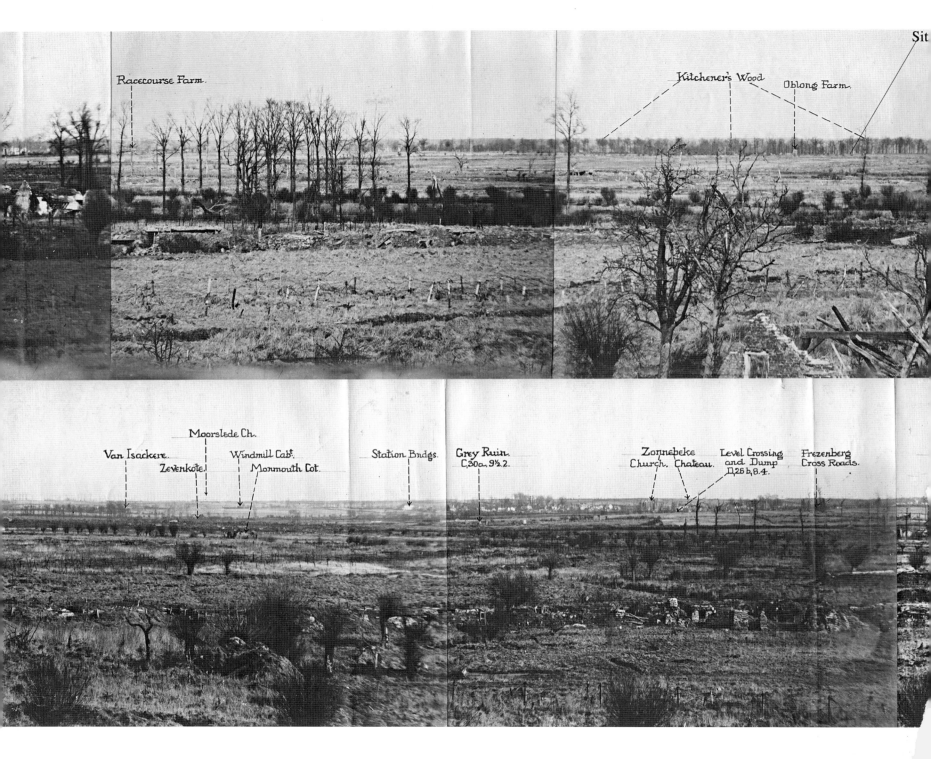

Racecourse Farm.

Kitchener's Wood   Oblong Farm.

Van Isackere   Moorslede Ch.   Windmill Caḇ̣.   Station Brdgs.   Grey Ruin.   Zonnebeke   Level Crossing   Frezenberg
Zevenkote!   Monmouth Cot.   C.30a, 9½.2.   Church. Chateau.   and Dump   Cross Roads.
D.26 b.8.4.

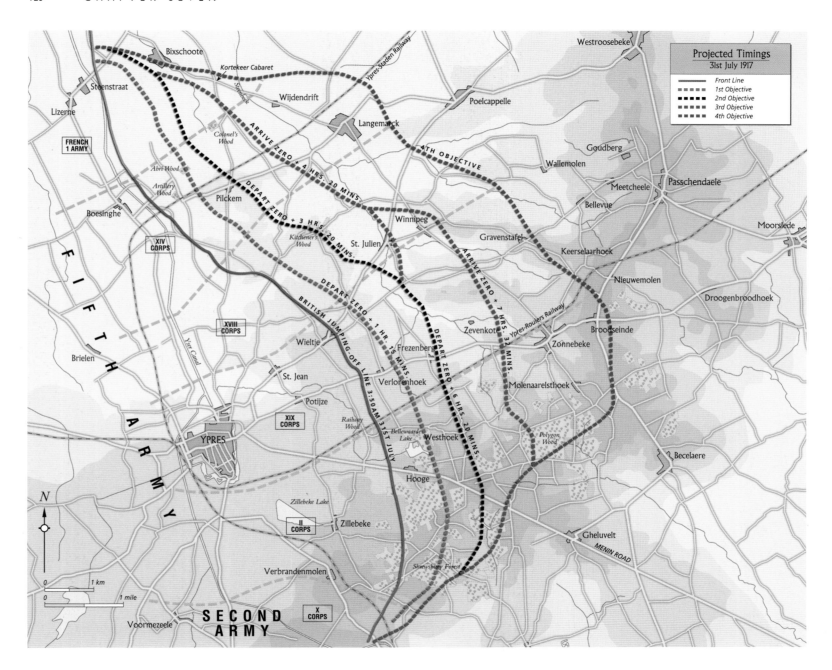

Above
A typical advanced observation position with two forward observation officers (FOOs) guiding guns onto targets by telephone.

Below
German observation post in trees near Langemarck.

Right
27 June 1917. Oblique view of the British front lines and jumping-off trench in the Crossroads Farm sector. *See also page 115.*

and everyone in the Division is feeling it. The Gloucesters had a very bad time of it this evening as the Boche sent a very heavy barrage over by Tool Farm and then their storm troopers came over. Our barrage was very slow in getting on to the S.O.S. signal.

SUNDAY 29TH.

An appalling wet day and everything very quiet and so it does not seem probable that it is Y Day. Spent the day going round to see the M.O.'s of the 56th Battalion who are going in tonight and fixed up with them how many squads they would have and how I proposed to clear their aid post etc. etc. Rumours that the attack will take place on 31st and that we shall all be relieved within 48 hours – so that sounds all right.

MAJOR A.G.P. HARDWICK MC, 59TH FIELD AMBULANCE, 19TH (WESTERN) DIVISION

The original date for Z (Zero) day had been set at 25 July, but subject to requests by both Gough and Anthoine, Sir Douglas Haig happily shifted it to the 31st. The adjustment was significant, because the weather remained fair, but not as critical as the 46-day gap since the close of

Messines. Charteris himself had urged Haig to attack earlier despite the incomplete preparations, for with such a long bombardment period the enemy would be bringing supports rapidly to the battlefront.

27 JULY 1917

The weather just now is glorious – too hot to move. Just by our tent there is a military railway constantly carrying things and men up to the front line. The engines and trucks are quaint little things. They have a bell which sounds like the trams running from Blackpool to Bispham and beyond. One expects to see the sea when one hears the tinkle, but one merely sees . . . well! One sees life at the Front; one hears the roar of the guns; and if one cares to lift one's eyes to the sky one sees copious observation balloons and aeroplanes. The day is very near now. This will probably be my last letter before going into action, so do not worry if you do not hear again for a week.

Cheer up . . . all's well that ends well!
SECOND LIEUTENANT THOMAS HOPE FLOYD,
2/5TH LANCASHIRE FUSILIERS

By 31 July Gough had at his disposal no less than 1,164 heavy and 1,872 field guns, and an abundant supply of now reliable shells. It was a fantastic array of firepower, but still somewhat thin on a wide battlefront where the commander had ordered an average advance of more than 4.5 kilometres. Additional guns could have been made available, for Sir Henry Rawlinson's Fourth Army were not yet in need of all those deployed on the coast, and Plumer's diversionary stunt at Messines could also have spared some. The guns held the key, for success was going to depend more than ever upon the neutralization of German artillery before *and during* battle by British counter-battery fire. At Messines it was exemplary, but the depth of advance had been severely limited, and with the ridge crest taken within hours of zero hour, British observational capability was abnormally advantageous. The topography of the Ypres battlefield offered neither potential, the benefits lying strongly on the German side. Gazing down from Observatory Ridge in the south to Stadenberg in the north, their tactics were to halt enemy attacks in the succession of wet valleys between the ridge spurs, restricting British observation to aerial, by plane or balloon, both of which were dependent upon weather.

For the moment, excellent British counter-battery work continued. German records show that in the sector astride the Menin Road occupied by *Gruppe Wytschaete*, almost 50 per cent of their heavy guns had been destroyed by 25 July, with other lighter weaponry suffering serious losses. But of course the battle proper had not yet begun and British guns were enjoying a certain liberty. Once it was underway the situation would be very different. Critically, unknown to the

Left
British heavy howitzer in action near Wieltje.

Below
18-pounder ammunition stockpiled ready for delivery to field guns as the advance progresses.

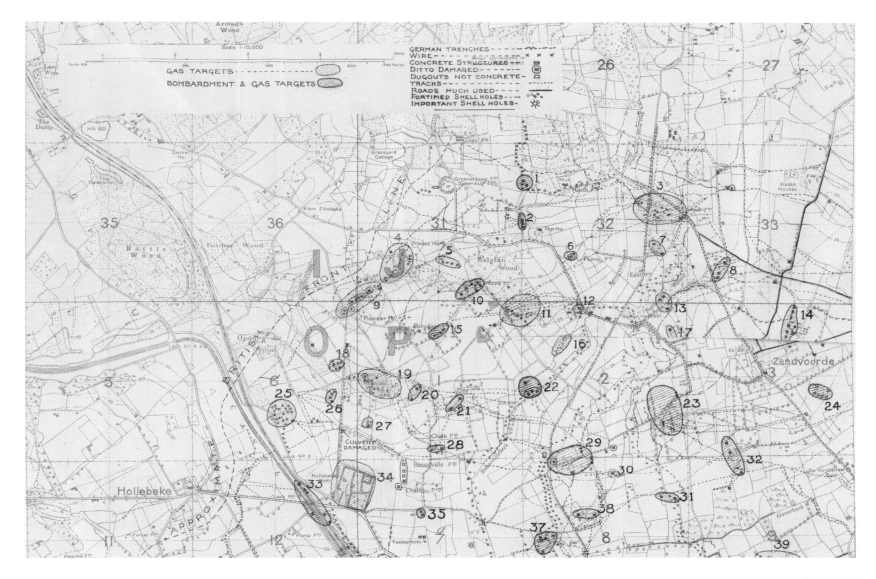

British, most German guns had been replaced by 31 July, reaching a total establishment of 3,091, of which 999 were heavy or medium. Unless Sir Douglas Haig's artillery could maintain the pre-battle rate of destruction, the infantry's task was going to be a tough one.

The Tail of the Dog

The offensive not only depended upon the closest of infantry, tank, air and artillery co-operation, but in creating an infrastructure of supply that would allow the advance to a) take place, and b) be pursued if initially successful. This included

Item	Divisional Advanced Dump	Brigade Dump
Shovels	1,000	250
Picks	400	100
Sandbags	40,000	10,000
Pit props	80	20
Steel rails	80	20
Corrugated-iron sheets	400	100
Nails, 4in. and 5in., lbs	200	50
Barbed wire, coils	200	50
Screw pickets, long	400	100
Screw pickets, short	1,200	300
Coils, French wire, with staples	24	6
Infantry foot bridges	40	10
Trench ladders	40	10

Above

A stockpile of rolled barbed wire ready for dispersal.

the provision of roads, railways and tramways up to the existing front lines, with facilities for immediate extension as battle was joined, plus dumps for everything from bags of nails to complete bridges. The scale of preparation is illustrated by the contents of a 'typical' RE dump in the forward area (see table above). Scores of dumps were located along the battlefront, always adjacent to roads and tramways. The offensive would eventually demand the use of no less than fifty-six infantry divisions (each comprising three brigades), including five Australian, four Canadian and one New Zealand. As the battle extended into captured enemy territory, more and more materiel would be required, and for this reason instruction before battle included study of the location of *enemy* dumps as potential sources of materiel. Engineering preparations were necessarily gargantuan, for it was known through bitter experience that unless new roads, railways, tramways and tracks were put in place, artillery could not support the advance. This was known

as 'forward communication'. Apart from improving and carrying forward all existing routes almost into the front line itself, new roads were built in rear areas, many of which were necessary simply in order to form the huge stockpiles of timber (beech wood for slab roads) and road 'metal' (stone) for extensions over captured ground. New quarries in France and on the Channel Islands were opened to supply the latter. Slab roads (also known as plank or corduroy) were constructed of heavy 10- to 12-foot planks placed side by side upon a wooden framework which itself sat on a levelled and drained earth base. Laid by Pioneers, Army Troops Companies, Tunnelling Companies and occasionally Field Company personnel, the timbers were 'dogged' together with heavy steel staples, then fitted with a wooden curb to help keep vehicles on the track. They consumed colossal amounts of wood, but the building process was far quicker and required much less labour than either creating or even repairing metalled roads. The initial laying, how-

Right

The Calais depot showing the wide range of facilities, including those for the Special Brigade (gas). Warehouses on this site included many similar to the inset photographs, each of which contain (left to right) cheese, jam and onions.

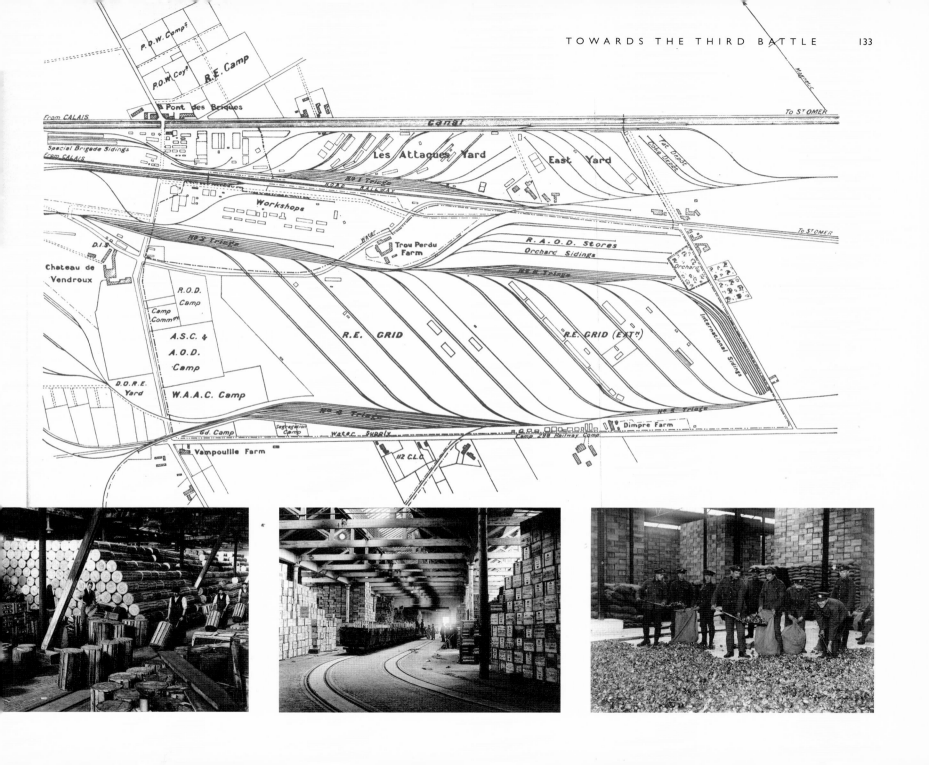

ever, did not signal the end of the task. Permanent maintenance, more often than not under shellfire, was essential to allow an uninterrupted flow of traffic to infantry and guns. The record length of slab road laid during the war was 1,820 yards (2 kilometres) in three and a half days. It is impossible to overestimate the importance of these arteries during an offensive. Not only did they serve the guns, but they were often the origin of the networks of duckboard pathways used by infantry and mule trains. Such hazardous routes across the battlefield were unavoidable, for the blend of artillery and geology in the Salient created a landscape where communication trenches could seldom be installed.

A comprehensive programme for a tramway and light railway network, again revealed to be fundamental requisites in every battle of the previous twelve months, was also drawn up prior to Third Ypres, but although many miles of light Decauville and 60-lb railway lines were laid, the envisaged plan was never fulfilled because of the appalling state of the ground in the latter stages of the struggle – it is almost impossible to lay a stable line across a swamp. It may be a truism that the more shells one fires, the greater the chance of infantry success; however, the equation has a serious corollary: the more shells one fires also increases the effort required to repair a landscape to allow an advance to continue. This logistical effort soon came to engage greater numbers of men than were actually deployed in the firing lines.

The aspect of ordering, stockpiling, care and issue of military stores is often overlooked, yet it was an equally critical part of the campaign. By July 1917 all supplies had for some time

been centrally controlled. Resources for the Salient came via the RE Base Depot at Les Attaques near Calais. Here, materials landed at Calais, Dunkirk and to a lesser extent, Boulogne, were stockpiled before being dispersed upon request – by indent or chit. The Les Attaques depot covered an area of 65 acres, with an adjacent timber yard of a further 150 acres. Run by the office of the Director of Works, a Royal Engineer body, and staffed by three RE officers, 132 Sappers, 18 skilled French civilians, 272 prisoner-of-war artisans, and assisted by almost 400 PoW labourers, it dealt with every conceivable requirement for trench warfare. Here, a division could order anything from sandbags to an entire girder bridge. The southern battlefields were served by a similar but smaller base at Abancourt. These depots were not only giant 'dumps', but also major manufacturing centres, both for timber and metal products. The following lists just part of their output for the year 1917:

Cement, barrels	302,400
Corrugated iron, bundles	709,800
Screwposts (wire pickets)	3,698,900
Elephant shelters	45,170
Trench boards (duckboards)	2,200,100
Trench frames (A-frames)	193,200
Picks	751,200
Shovels	1,560,600
Sandbags	308,763,900
Barbed wire, tons	17,120
Nails, lbs	17,087,800
Expanded metal sheets (for revetments)	1,254,400
Pumps	15,210
6in. and 4in. piping, miles	750
Revetting hurdles	166,500

Right
A study of the potential hazards posed by the major waterway, the Steenbeek. It was just one of many awkward streams that traversed the prospective battlefield.

Below
The Steenbeek today with the village of Langemarck beyond. It was very near this point that Private Harry Patch crossed the stream on a rather unstable pontoon bridge on 16 August 1917. See page 205.

As the offensive drew close the weight of military materiel crossing the Channel averaged a weekly 240,000 tonnes. To disperse the stores once they arrived in France 59,000 new railway trucks were imported, single-line railways doubled and new rail routes laid. During the war the engineers installed 2,689 miles of additional track, necessitating the building of an extra 536 bridges with a total span of 37,917 feet. The system employed almost 14,000 engineers and 27,000 unskilled labourers. The Western Front was quite simply the greatest engineering exercise in world history.

On the Somme and at Vimy and Arras, battles fought in areas which were exclusively chalk-based geology, the need for bridging rivers, streams and wet ditches was minimal; in Flanders however, the reverse was the case: when unmanaged the entire landscape was one of water. The patchwork of drains and *bekes* was already partially disrupted, and it was known that many more would necessarily be destroyed during the coming struggle. Those which once had flowed between banks a metre apart turned into 50-metre-wide morasses. Each had to be made negotiable by man, machine, horse, mule, gun and even tank. In the prospective battle zone, major and minor roads and the simplest of tracks would soon require colossal quantities of individually designed crossings.

At the same time prodigious numbers of sappers, pioneers, army troops personnel and attached infantry were employed in the construction of enlarged camps behind the lines, hundreds of battery positions and gun platforms, strengthening cellar dumps for food, water, fuel and small arms ammunition, constructing shell-proof dressing stations, fitting water pipelines,

devising camouflage schemes, and in the forward areas digging the new assembly and communication trenches. Each and every aspect was essential in order to facilitate what was now recognized by all to be the most important feature of the battle – the maintenance of a steady and unbroken advance.

A quarter of a million men marched toward the Salient, dispersing to batteries, dugouts, camps, horse lines, dumps and trenches. Few arrived with any illusions about the future.

As on my way up to the line one morning I rode slowly alongside a marching battalion, I heard the regular sound of an engine, and saw puffs of smoke shooting up from a house on the road. A steam saw was cutting rhythmically through wood, working at high pressure with a tearing sound. Seeing the yard in front of the house piled high with wooden crosses and thinking to spare the men this ominous sight, I hurried in to have them removed. The Belgians engaged in the work threw up their arms in despair and pointed through the window at the back, where there was a still bigger pile. Nothing could be done; I watched the men

as they passed by – some smiled, others passed a joke, some wouldn't look. But I knew they all saw and understood.
PAUL LUCIEN MAZE, DCM, MM, CROIX DE GUERRE,
FRENCH LIAISON OFFICER TO GENERAL SIR HUBERT GOUGH

Every day the bombardment continued and fresh details for the battle arrived, new orders, altered orders, and essential information about tanks, signals, artillery and machine-gun barrages. Men had to be prepared for all eventualities. The mass of activity and teeming troops not unnaturally provoked a belief in the most likely outcome: the great victory that Sir Douglas Haig and his staff desired. The men must therefore be ready with the correct responses. A brief guide was issued:

GLOSSARY OF USEFUL TERMS FOR THE OFFENSIVE.
Ergeteuch schnell, sonst keinen pardon – Surrender at once or you receive no quarter.
Hande Hoch – Hands Up.
Ergieb Dich (one man), *Ergebt Euch* – Surrender.
Alle, die sich jetzt ergeben, werden gut behandelt – We shall treat well all those who surrender now.
Nicht schiessen, streckt die waffen – Do not shoot, put down your arms.
Wert sich ruhrt, wird tot geschossen – Whoever moves will be shot.
Warter hier. Andere werden euch zuruckfuhren – Wait here. Others will take you back.
Behandlung ist gut – You will be well treated.

Although the thousands of man-hours spent in rehearsal were of enormous value, no amount of preparation could prepare men for the unknown, which is what Third Ypres, like all other battles, turned out to be.

> THE KING HAS RENOUNCED THE NAME OF GOTHA SAXE-COBURG AND ADOPTED WINDSOR AS THE FAMILY NAME OF THE ROYAL HOUSE.
>
> SECOND ARMY INTELLIGENCE SUMMARY, 18 JULY 1917.

Baum an d. Straße
Kamin
Kirchturm Poelcappelle
Scherpenbergmühle Signal Nr. 3057
Haus B 39/26
A 39/26
D 35/29
Trappis
Kamin
Haus C 37/37
Haus D 35/37
Kirchturm Locre
Baum C 36/41
Haus C 37/30
Kamin Haus C 36/33
Kemmelberg
Haus D 35/32
Straße von Staden nach Stadendreef
Haus C 36/40
Gehöft D 30/27
Haus C 36/36
Haus C 36/29
Haus C 36/31
Haus C 36/26
Ondank Windmühle
Haus C 36/39
Haus B 37/26
Haus C 36/34
Gehöft D 30/27
Haus Haus C 37/32
Baum C 37/26
Haus Flandern Stellung
Haus B 37/30
Haus C 36/27
Haus C 37/27
Haus B 37/30
Haus C 39/28
Haus C 37/27
Haus C 36/38
100
Haus C 37/27
Haus B 39/28
Haus B 39/27
Schornstein
5600
Haus D 35/30
Haus B 37/29
5700
5760
Baum C 36/42
Haus C 36/29
Haus C 36/37
5500
Haus B 38/27
Haus B 38/28
Haus D 35/29
Haus D 35/28
Baum

Bartl. Teilung
360° = 5760/16

dartl. Teilung
360° = 6400/16

6100   6200   6300   6400   100

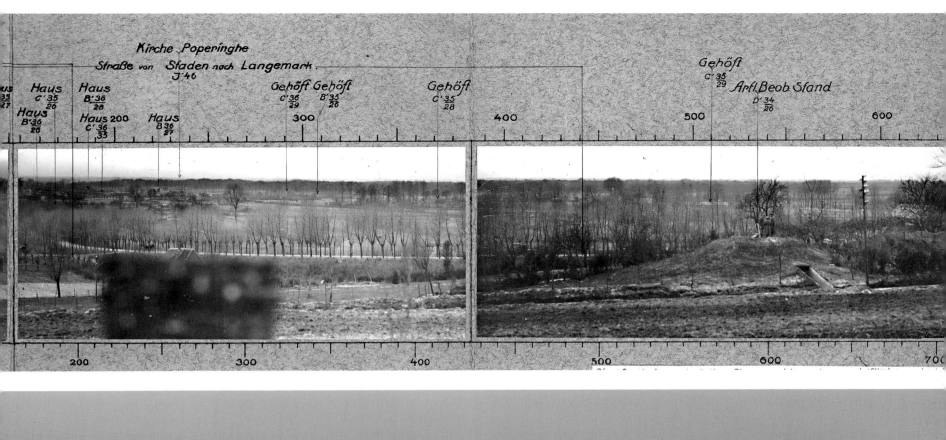

Kirche Poperinghe

Straße von Staden nach Langemark.
J 46

Gehöft
C 35/29

Haus
C 35/27

Haus
B 36/26

Gehöft Gehöft
C 36/29   B 35/26

Gehöft
C 35/28

Artl.Beob.Stand
D 34/26

Haus
B 36/26

Haus 200
C 36/33

Haus
B 36/27

200   300   400   500   600

200   300   400   500   600   700

CROSS-ROADS FARM.   RACECOURSE FARM.   BOENCASTEL EST   OBLONG FM   CANADIAN DUGOUTS   Bri

CHAPTER EIGHT

Flandernschlacht – The Battle of Pilckem Ridge

The boat leave train left Victoria at 7.35 am that Sunday morning, and on Monday 30th July I was back with No. 3 Section. They were not too happy – under canvas, near DICKE-BUSCH, about a mile south-west of YPRES, the ominous. We soon realised the truth of its reputation for ceaseless shelling. Carter and I shared a tent in a field off the cobbled road. One night a long range gun started firing right into our field – we soon had a shell in our tent – mercifully it must have been a dud, for no explosion followed, but it 'burrowed' deep and heaved up the ground under us – we moved the tent! We were lucky, but sadly many of our mules, and a few horses, out in the open were badly wounded – Carter had to shoot them beside a huge 'mass grave' – we'd begun well.

LIEUTENANT J.T. CAPRON, DIVISIONAL AMMUNITION COLUMN, 56TH (LONDON) DIVISION

The great pre-assault bombardment was heard in southern England. Lieutenant Robin Skeggs of 3rd Rifle Brigade, on leave at Godstone in Surrey noted, 'a benign reverberation that I told my fiancée bore no resemblance to the hurricane of sound and steel I knew from experience it must be. How I pitied my fellow countrymen, knowing that when the thunder again increased they would be going over; yet how I wished I was with them.' Before the guns were unleashed, the prospective battlefield was in pretty good order for combat. With only localized conflicts since the summer of 1915, the hand of nature had passed over the land making it green and lush, even jungle like in

places. Crops had self-seeded, trees coppiced by high-explosive regenerated, and trenches and pill-boxes lay masked by profusions of wild flowers, grasses, bramble thickets, nettle-beds – and of course, wire. Ribbon by ribbon, the illusion was about to disappear.

The O.P. [observation post] was in one of our support trenches, only a few hundred yards behind the front line. I had not been so close to the line before. Each gun at the battery fired in turn, and after the bursting shell had been observed Edward spoke over the telephone, changing its range or angle and fired it again until it was accurately on the target. I stood beside him in the trench, watching the shell bursts. He told me to keep my head down, and I tilted my helmet over my fore-head, as he had done, so that only my eyes were exposed over the top of the trench. There was not much to see. Only trenches in the foreground. I could not tell where ours ended and the enemy's began. Nothing was to be seen in any of them, just a succession of trenches. But in the distance, about a mile away, country began again, and colour. I could see grass and trees on the top of a low ridge, red-brick houses and the tower of a church looking almost undamaged. It was a pleasure as well as a surprise to see these ordinary things: the low green hill, the houses, a church. They contrasted so happily with the

trench scars immediately in front of us. The village was Passchendaele. Edward told me, but the name meant nothing to either of us. It was just one of the villages on their side of the line. Zonnebeke and St Julien, Langemarck and Poelkappelle were others whose names I had noticed on our map board.

SECOND LIEUTENANT P.J. CAMPBELL, 150 BRIGADE, ROYAL FIELD ARTILLERY

After the fighting of 1914 and 1915, the peace-time field drainage system had, entirely pragmatically, been extensively repaired and carefully maintained by the troops of both sides, the Royal Engineer Land Drainage Companies playing a major role for the more disadvantaged British. Its total re-destruction also commenced when the British guns opened up on 7 July. This pre-battle period heralded an era of mutual anni-hilation that before the campaign closed would turn the Salient into a desert, first of mud, then dust, then mud again. The number of *British* shells fired before 31 July (discounting German action) was four and a half million. The cost in 1917 was £22,000,000, today's equivalent of £1,282,770,000. Between 15 and 21 July the

Special Companies RE launched 5,100 gas projector drums and 14,000 thermit-filled Stokes mortar bombs.* Every night machine-gun battalions loosed off an average 30,000 rounds in harassing fire.

It is 'a la Somme'. We are to the left of Ypres and are equipped with steel helmets, body armour, daggers, hand grenades, luminous sights, etc., and also S and K ammunition.** We are expecting a great attack. Barrage fire is all the heavier – an annihilating fire; we have no positions, and lie in shell-holes. It was not for nothing that they gave us chocolate, tins of condensed milk, double allowance money, etc., and the band plays us only inspiriting airs. I have been in the line since 27th June, 4 days support, 4 days in readiness and 4 days in the front line, and so it goes on all the time. We are waiting anxiously for relief. From what I hear, this is a punishment position because we did not shout Hurrah! when the Kaiser passed through Pfurl [Vosges]. One needs good nerves in this place . . . Our regimental staff has been cut up, 30 dead and wounded, you can easily imagine from that what things look like. I would not like to write this to my wife.
LETTER FROM A SOLDIER OF 16TH BAVARIAN INFANTRY REGIMENT, DATED 30 JULY 1917

Although the British had been resident in the Salient since late 1914, many units and individuals had never served in this, the most symbolic of sectors. Diarists were keen to record initial impressions.

*Thermit. A weapon consisting of a mixture of powdered aluminium in a mortar bomb which when ignited by a suitable catalyst reaches temperatures of 5,000 degrees centigrade. Timed to air-burst about 25 metres above the enemy trench, the bomb showered occupants with cascades of molten metal. Whether wet or dry, anything combustible was set alight.
** Armour piercing: *Spitzgeschoss mit Kern (SmK)*, a steel-cored bullet designed for the standard Mauser infantry rifle for use against tanks.

The country was, on the whole, very flat, but it fell away in a slight decline in front of us, and was then dead flat till you came to the village (or what had been a village) of Boesinghe, about three miles off. This village consisted of one main street of ruined houses, which ran along near to, and parallel with the canal, and at this time was just within our front line. Over the canal the ground gradually rose again, forming a low ridge, which was occupied by the Boche, giving him considerable facilities for observation. There were trees along some of the roads between us and Boesinghe, which afforded a certain amount of cover from observation. In some of these trees the French had constructed observation posts. Along the roads were erected screens of canvas camouflage, to shut off from the Boche the view of what might be passing along.

Through this flat country had been cut numerous communication trenches along which one could travel for miles, and it was safer to use these rather than pass over the open. With regard to the battery position itself, the guns were in a small copse. In front of this there was a clear space of about a hundred yards in width, and then came the officers' mess and cookhouse, office and telephone exchange. The mess was a nice roomy compartment, and it was used also as B.C. [Battery Command] Post, and as sleeping accommodation for at least one officer. The officer on duty for the night slept here to be near the telephone, and on the spot in the event of S.O.S. calls. The other officers' sleeping accommodation was provided by one or two huts or shanties erected under some trees, along a hedge a short distance off. It was not a very snug battery position as there was absolutely no shell cover of any sort. The land here was too low and wet to dig dugouts in the ground; they would soon have filled with water. And to erect a shell proof structure above the ground was a task requiring time and a very large amount of material. The men slept in slightly excavated dugouts or pits to the right flank of the battery at first, but they were soon shelled out, and then used to seek cover for the night in communication trenches behind the battery using ground sheets and trench covers, but these trenches also used to be shelled at night, and often their nights were spent in

moving from one place to another to avoid shelling. It was soon apparent that they were getting knocked up from want of sleep, and something had to be done for them. So a small dugout was constructed in the basement of an old house on the main road a short way behind the guns by means of elephant iron and concrete for the gun detachments on duty when not actually engaged on night firing. It is very doubtful if this would have stopped a shell of any size, but they gained a sense of security from it, and were able to sleep, and so long as it did not get a direct hit on it, which it never did, they were all right. The rest of the men other than the bare gun detachments on duty were taken back to near Group Headquarters where they were safe, and the detachments were relieved from time to time. But unfortunately, several men had been wounded before these arrangements could be effected, and at least one man (a signaller named Britton) was killed here. The total casualties here were quite considerable.

LIEUTENANT E.C. ALLFREE, 111TH SIEGE BATTERY,
ROYAL GARRISON ARTILLERY

Because surprise was neither sought nor possible, the effectiveness of the guns and kindness of the weather held the two main keys to British success. Tank commanders, now working in close co-operation with the infantry divisions to whom they had been allotted, probably kept the closest eye on the skies and the barometer. Prior to battle they had recorded changing ground conditions, each day logging new information from specially commissioned aerial photographs onto special map sheets supplied by British military geologists. The maps showed surface and subsoils, suitability of ground for dugouts etc.: exactly the kind of data required for planning the actions of 28-ton landships. They aptly came to be called 'swamp maps', for with even little or no rainfall the disruption of drainage by the British bombardment was resulting in the rapid expansion of wet areas – areas that were clearly being further enhanced by judicious damming by an uneasy enemy. Re-annotated and sent daily to headquarters, the maps elicited no response except after a few days a curt request to cease the practice. The message was clear: the tanks were going into action no matter how many adverse reports they continued to send. In the forty-eight hours prior to Z-day, and as the British bombardment built to a crescendo, rain fell, not enough to cause serious concern, but making the ground rather heavy. The long preparation had been dull, wearying and worrisome.

27 JULY 1917

I hope and believe we are coming to the end of a pretty strenuous term up the line. By gum, I shall be as jolly as a sandboy if I get out of the place. I am simply living for the approaching change of work: it is the everlasting sameness of the job that gets on my nerves. I had an infantry party tonight, about 150 strong, connecting up between our left post and the 19th Division right post with a decent bit of trench. All went well, though it would have been a bad lookout if a Bosche machine gun had started up. While they were doing that, I had to crawl out with Wall and lay a tape for another trench in front of that – revolver in one hand, tape in the other, quite in the best style. I got that job done all right: there was a Bosche sniper at the bottom of a tree who annoyed me, but I reported the matter on getting back to the trench: and they sent a Lewis gunner after him and turfed him out: he was too far off to pot at with a mere peashooter. We have been up the line rather overlong and it is beginning to tell on the men and everybody. However, a change should come soon. Dear me, it is an animal life. Work a bit, sleep a bit, eat a bit; possibly read a bit, write a letter or two – and there is your day gone. How glad I should be to find a job that required a little brains. However, my present job does require a good deal of solid patient sticking to, so it must be doing me an enormous

amount of good. How far the man at home is from realising what a loathsome business war is. It would take a Gustav Doré to paint, or rather draw the weird effects you see in the front line at night as the Very lights flicker and sail up and down. Great long black shadows swaying and jumping over the pitted brown earth: white skeletons of trees showing up against a background of dead black stumps, through which the red gun flashes flicker: everything is a wild unearthly desolation, over which the shells shriek or whisper, moan or hiss according to their size and nearness: and of course there is always a medley of booms and detonations. To my mind, it is exactly Danté's Inferno, and the very setting of the piece inspires horrid forebodings. How one longs for a sane rational fireside. But it all teaches one to hang on: one gets accustomed to the scenery, and it only remains to carry on with the good work. But that picture, which will be deeply impressed on the mind of everyone who emerges from this war, would be a picture well worth drawing and preserving for all time to show what a hell on earth the blighters who start a war can make. Dear me, I wax rhetorical: but truth to tell, everyone now is a bit strung up. We have had a month in this place and even Arras was a beauty spot compared to it. Never mind: rest comes soon for the weary warrior.
SECOND LIEUTENANT J.T. GODFREY, 104TH FIELD COMPANY, ROYAL ENGINEERS

At this time many a unit would also have received the conventional visitation from Divisional and Brigade commanders, buoyantly doing the rounds, wishing men luck and boosting spirits and expectations with rousing words.

25 JULY 1917

Just a line to let you know that I have received all your letters up to July 20 and the parcel for which I thank you very much. I have been simply awfully busy – chiefly with maps and operation orders re. coming offensive – and have not been able to write home during the last few days as a result. We are supposed to be resting, but I

have hardly a moment to spare. General Stockwell lectured all officers and N.C.O.'s of this Battalion here in the field on Monday afternoon. He said that he was going to tell us everything that he knew himself about the coming battle, but did not tell us anything we did not already know! I do not think he told us all: if he did tell us all then I don't think much of the idea. The General had a cigarette in his mouth and his hands in his pockets the whole time he was speaking; he was quite jovial, cracking jokes all the time. He impressed upon us the importance of sending messages back when we reach our objectives; he said that if we do not do so it will mean his coming up to the front line himself for information, 'and I don't want to have to do that,' he laughed, 'but it will come to that if necessary,' he went on in a more serious tone, 'and it will be woe betide the platoon commander whose negligence has brought his Brigadier-General's life into danger!' At the conclusion of his speech the General asked whether any of us had any questions to ask. I could have asked one, but I know he would not have answered it; so I remained silent!
SECOND LIEUTENANT THOMAS HOPE FLOYD, 2/5TH LANCASHIRE FUSILIERS

Paschendaele 5

The following day Passchendaele church tower was finally brought down by British guns. It had actually not long been built, the old woodworm-ridden eighteenth-century timber-framed church having been demolished only in 1903. As Army, Corps and Divisional commanders took up residence in their own bishopric-like headquarters in Ypres, Proven and Cassel, brigadiers and battalion commanders, expected to follow the attack much more closely, made their own preparations.

Two nights prior to the attack I had slept in the trenches, where I still had some work to do. I was out early. The morning of July 30 broke in brilliant sunshine. Already at 7 o'clock it felt warm. No Man's Land was brown and the hills beyond it were casting long, soft shadows before them. I was thinking what I

Passchendaele Church
Sheet 28 D. 6d 3.5.

Above

Passchendaele village in early 1917 – a German view. The British sketches below were just two of scores of drawings produced and circulated to assist recognition of landmarks when the advance was underway. Other examples circulated to officers included farm ruins, distinctive tree groups and pillboxes.

Passchendaele Church Distant View.

would be doing on a day like this in peace-time, when I had to realize that we were making our big attack that night. I had slept badly thinking all the time about it.

For the attack I had arranged to be with a brigade placed in the centre of the battle. I had been in battle with the Brigadier on several occasions on the Somme. He always said that I brought him good luck. I received his instructions for zero day, which, though couched in nebulous terms, guided me admirably.

25 JULY 1917

Dear Maze, Will you join me on the afternoon of Y day at what used to be the Gloucester Pioneer Batt. Bd. Qrs. about 300x [yards] north of where you met me last on the west bank of the Canal. If you have any difficulty in finding it ask at my old Bd. Qrs. and they will know where. Only bring just what is necessary. I will arrange about food.

Yours ever,

G.A. Armitage

PAUL LUCIEN MAZE, DCM, MM, CROIX DE GUERRE,
FRENCH LIAISON OFFICER TO GENERAL SIR HUBERT GOUGH

Paul Maze also witnessed the final pre-battle task of the Royal Flying Corps: an attempt to clear the skies of enemy observation balloons. This they did as the sun was setting on 30 July with a massed lightning attack. Above Polygon Wood alone ninety-four aircraft clashed in one of the greatest dogfights of the war. Beneath, the salient swarmed with troops moving forward towards their various fates.

I wended my way through trenches towards its reserve battle station, feeling more absorbed in the beauty of the evening than in the coming offensive. Enemy balloons were still peering into our line, facing the fading sunlight. Suddenly one balloon, then another, and then others went up in flames and collapsed towards the ground. Our flying machines had cleared the sky of all enemy balloons with the exception of one, which was being hurriedly

hauled down. A line of parachutes had unfurled from the little black parcel I had seen drop like a stone from every balloon. They now formed a line of bubbles drifting gracefully to the ground. It was like a conjuring trick. I had now some difficulty in getting along, as every trench was crammed with troops waiting for the dark to move up to their assembly positions. It was vital that every unit should start at its proper scheduled time – the least deviation from the plan would have brought about delay and confusion. As soon as it was dark every communication trench became a moving platform. I found my Brigadier sharing a dug-out with another Brigadier of our division. As we had time, we looked again at the objectives on the map. It all seemed simple enough; every yard we had to take had now been studied both on the ground and from aerial photographs; every battalion had rehearsed the attack on ground models made to scale – everyone knew by heart what he had to do.

PAUL LUCIEN MAZE, DCM, MM, CROIX DE GUERRE,
FRENCH LIAISON OFFICER TO GENERAL SIR HUBERT GOUGH

It was now down to the performance of the guns, for the infantry could only follow their lead: if the barrage stopped, so too did the advance, if it failed, so too might the attack, if it moved too fast...

But there was also the German response to consider. At Messines Sir Herbert Plumer had largely conquered enemy gun batteries. Before the battle he had made it plain to Sir Douglas Haig that mastery *must* be complete before the whistles blew, receiving a promise that the attack would not be allowed to take place unless this goal was achieved – and that same promise had also embraced the Ypres phase. On 11 July, Haig notes British artillery losses as being 'wonderfully small'. On the 27th his Royal Artillery chief, Brigadier General Noel Birch, informed the C-in-C, 'counter-battery work proceeding satisfactorily'. The following day Haig's diary notes, 'My

nd Army Panorama No. 10 made on 29/7/15 from O.P. C 19a 2·3
including a field of view of 54° from about N.E. to E.N.E.
Approximate Scale of Degrees (1 degree equals 1 1/18th inch).

artillery adviser is of the opinion that we have already cowed the enemy's artillery', and on the 29th, 'All the enemy's artillery except a few scattered batteries have been withdrawn east of the Steenbeek.' But the German artillery response throughout the pre-battle period remained persistent. Although British troops could clearly see enemy field positions being apparently blown to kingdom come, day by day the intensity of hostile shelling seemed undiminished. Gas especially was

a severe burden, with attacks around the clock hindering preparations and tiring already tired men. Certainly, a sequence of overcast days with poor observation did not help Haig's gunners and strong winds upset the calculations of sound-ranging units,* but excuses were no panacea: the Germans were hitting their targets, why were the

* Determining the position of an enemy battery by trigonometry, cross-referencing sound recordings of guns' reports noted from a number of different locations.

Above

Before the industrial estate was extended here the land was left fallow for several years and archaeological test pits dug. The disturbance and subsequent natural regeneration allows us to glimpse a colour representation of the 1915-18 battlefields. The predominant species at this time of year (June) is ox-eye daisy.

Top
Second Army pan 10, 29 July 1915. The view from the canal bank. It was not greatly changed in July 1917.

Above
The view from the same spot today – blocked by a sewage treatment plant in the foreground and an industrial estate beyond.

British not? It was a serious and unexpected problem at a very late stage in proceedings. Charteris' supplications were the perfect solace – the resistance simply couldn't and wouldn't last. Only on the eve of battle itself does Haig make serious note of German artillery activity, and this by choosing to record the excellent performance (and heavy casualties) of lorry drivers delivering their nightly loads through Ypres and beyond into the Salient: 'These men have shown that they have the same spirit as the fighting soldiers.'

All that the British batteries could do was approach their final preparations with the care of master watchmakers.

I took my turn at O.P., and on other days acted as Section Commander on the guns, occasionally working out the targets for the guns, and finding 'the error of the day'. The error of the day always had to be ascertained several times during the day. This consisted of taking the calculations necessary to correct the effect

of the weather, and climatic conditions on shooting. The temperature of the air, the temperature of the charge or cartridge, the state
of the barometer and the strength and direction of the wind, all
had an effect on the distance the shell would carry, or rather on
the elevation to be given to the gun, to get a particular range; and
the wind would also necessitate a correction for line. Every battery received what was known as a 'meteor message' six times in
every twenty-four hours, which gave this information, including
the strength and direction of the wind and the temperature of the
air at varying heights. It, of course, depended on the range you
were firing at, how high the shell would have to go, and you
therefore wanted to know what the wind and temperature were
like up there.

LIEUTENANT E.C. ALLFREE, 111TH SIEGE BATTERY,
ROYAL GARRISON ARTILLERY

By now every battery was prepared. Each had
followed a similar routine of observation, ranging
and fire.

*The O.P. was in the remains of a house in Boesinghe. It was a
good three miles walk; after walking some way we turned into a
communication trench, which after about another quarter of an
hour's walk, with many windings and turns, brought us out into
the main street in Boesinghe. It was a street along which no traffic ever passed – it was strewn with bricks and debris from the
shelled buildings which bordered it. There were gaps between the
buildings, across some of which were stretched canvas screens,
but others were open, giving a clear view across the canal to
Bocheland, which was not more than a few hundred yards away.
The place wore a deserted, forbidding appearance, and seemed to
speak eloquently of desolation, destruction and death. No one
dared be seen moving about here. We made our way stealthily
along, crouching and hurrying past the open gaps, till we came to
the ruined house in which our O.P. had been established. The
ceiling of the ground floor room, into which we entered, had been
shored up with timber struts by R.E.s, who had also constructed*

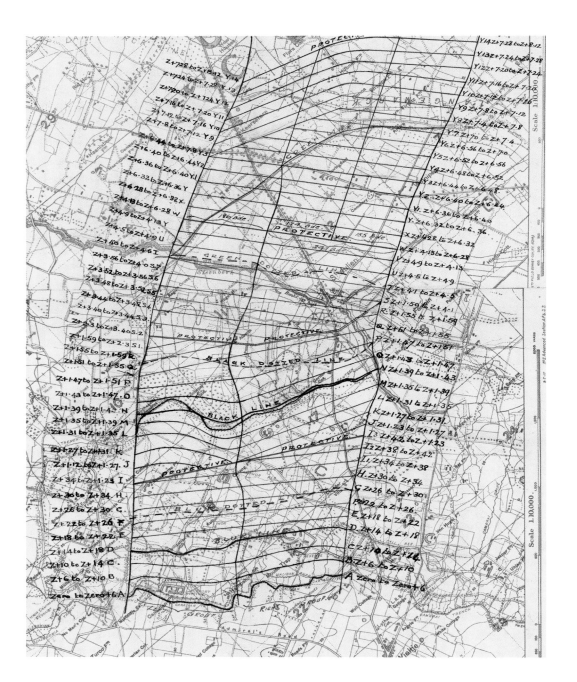

Left

XVIII Corps' creeping barrage plan showing stepped objectives and the standing protective barrages planned to deter exit and ingress of German troops.

in an upper storey (access to which was gained by clambering up a heap of brick, rubbish and timbers) a small chamber of iron girders and concrete, which was the O.P., from which one observed by means of a periscope. Having disguised the top of the periscope by tying a sand bag round it, you poked it over the concrete structure that faced you. Through the eyepiece of the periscope, I now saw for the first time the face of the ridge the other side of the canal. There were visible a few woods, a ruined house or two, perhaps a farm, a road here and there and systems of Boche trenches. The top of the ridge was the limit of our view. The first thing to do on arriving at a new O.P. was to pick up the country as soon as possible, so as to be able readily to pick up through your glass, the smallest detail marked on the map – and of course to know where our own and the Enemy's front line trenches ran. This was always harder when you could not obtain a general view of the country before you, but could only see it in small patches at a time, just so much as could be encompassed in the small field of view of your periscope lens. The best method was to pick up a few outstanding features that were clearly marked on the map, – such as the corner of a wood, a cross roads, a farm house etc. This I now proceeded to do. Soon I heard the telephonist, who is sitting on the debris below me, taking a message from the battery and repeating back some map reference. This he now repeats to me: 'The Captain wants to range the battery on trench junction at Y.15.b, 25.30; will you let him know if you can see it all right, Sir.' I look at the map: find the point referred to: yes, there is a trench junction there: now how many degrees is that from those cross roads I picked up just now? I get my protractor and measure off the degrees on the map, and find it is 12 degrees right of the cross roads, and about 500 yards further off. I now poke the periscope up, and find those cross roads again, then count off 12 degs. to the right by means of the graticules marked on the eyepiece. Yes, there is a trench junction just about there. I then have another look at the map to see if there is anything to check it by, and measure off 20 degs. left of the corner of that wood, – find the corner of the wood through the periscope, and count off 20 degs. left. This brings me to just

about the same spot as before. Good enough, – that is the trench junction all right. I shout down to the telephonist:-

'Let them know I can see that target all right, and ask them how soon they will be ready, and what is the time of flight.' He repeats my message, and receives the answer:

'Captain Cripps says he will be ready in five minutes. Time of flight 35 seconds, Sir.'

About ten minutes pass, and telephonist shouts up:-

'Look in, Sir.'

'Right.'

'No. 1 fired, Sir.'

I look at the second hand on my wrist watch, and count 25 seconds, then get the periscope on the target, counting off the remaining seconds of the total time of flight; allowing for the time of receiving the message, it ought to be there in 8 seconds. Yes, there it is, just up to time, so it must be our shell – a bit to the right and over.

'45 minutes right and plus.'

The telephonist repeats this to the battery. Then:-

'No. 2 fired, Sir.'

You go through the same performance.

'30 minutes left and plus.'

'No. 3 fired, Sir.'

You hear the shell coming and look in.

'1 degree right and minus.'

'No. 4 fired, Sir.'

'Line and plus.'

'No. 1 fired, Sir.'

'15 minutes left and minus.'

'No. 2 fired, Sir.'

'20 minutes right and minus.'

'No.3 fired, Sir.'

'30 minutes left and plus.'

'No. 4 fired, Sir.'

Here she comes.

'Line and minus.'

After from six to ten rounds per gun, the battery is probably

satisfactorily ranged, and the B.C. may now switch off to another target.
LIEUTENANT E. C. ALLFREE, 111TH SIEGE BATTERY,
ROYAL GARRISON ARTILLERY

All that now remained were four coloured lines – blue, black, green and red – marked upon trench maps.

The infantry had vanished, packed together in the trenches that led to the front line and No Man's Land. Now and then a solitary gun fired. At that moment nobody could have foretold the intensity of the impending bombardment, where along eight miles of front sixteen divisions – about one hundred thousand infantry – stood ready for assault. I went back to the dug-out, where everyone waited in suspense. A bottle of white wine stood uncorked on the table. We constantly asked each other the time. Soon the hour for the barrage would strike – we had nothing to do now but wait for the gong. We became hysterically nervous and made silly jokes and remarks to cloak our thoughts. When the barrage finally opened, its violence was such that we looked at one another aghast. I climbed up the stairs into the night. The wind caused by the displacement of air was terrific – I might have been standing on the bridge of a ship during a typhoon and held on to the side of the trench like a weather rail. Gun-flashes were holing the sky as though thousands of signal-lamp shutters were flashing messages. Field batteries placed in position immediately above our dug-out opened fire and rent the air with a deafening row.

At every report I felt as though my scalp were being removed. An uninterrupted succession of shells of every calibre was whirling through the air. This bombardment exceeded anything I had ever witnessed before. The enemy retaliation was hardly noticeable. Suddenly I imagined I was seeing things when the top of our parapet seemed to move. But it was only the terrified rats fleeing in an army.
PAUL LUCIEN MAZE, DCM, MM, CROIX DE GUERRE,
FRENCH LIAISON OFFICER TO GENERAL SIR HUBERT GOUGH

The night before battle was still drizzly and generally uncomfortable. Unceasingly, the bombardment howled and machine-guns chattered. Z-day, Tuesday, 31 July, dawned overcast with the odd shower here and there. Now targets and bayonets were fixed and creeping barrage patterns and timings set. No more alterations could be made. Dumps had been completed, cellars prepared in forward positions for petrol, oil and ammunition, and routes marked back to dressing stations behind the start line, from where motor ambulances and tramway trucks were mustered to evacuate wounded. Engineering troops waited, ready to move forward and reinstate communication infrastructure in captured territory the moment orders arrived. The forward trenches seethed with eager and edgy

Above
An officer watches shells bursting on a distant Pilckem Ridge.

Right
The objectives for the Pilckem Ridge attack on 31 July, and the gains made on the day.

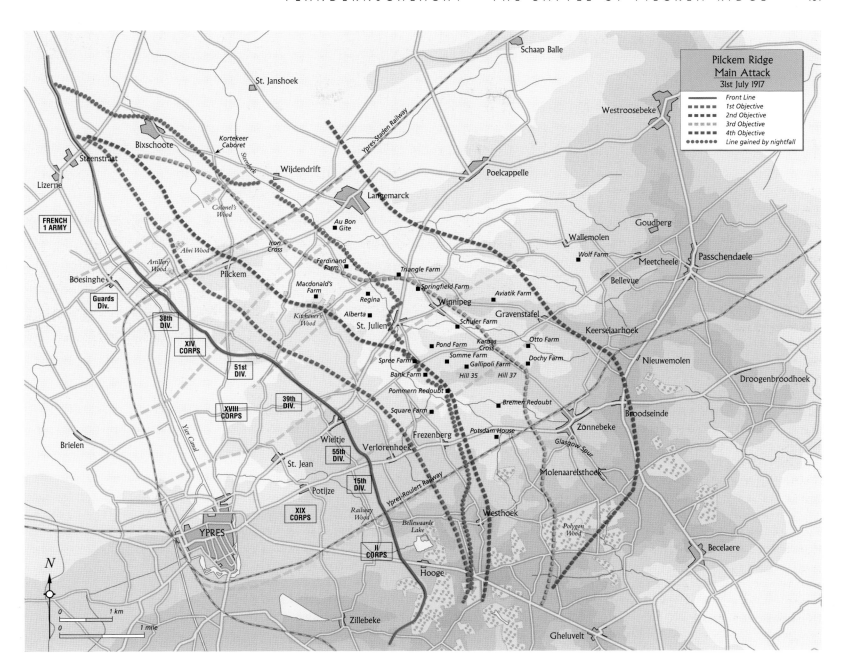

Pilckem Ridge
Main Attack
31st July 1917

Front Line
1st Objective
2nd Objective
3rd Objective
4th Objective
Line gained by nightfall

Schaap Balle
St. Janshoek
Westroosebeke
Bixschoote
Kortekeer Caboret
Steenstraat
Wijdendrift
Lizerne
Poelcappelle
Langemarck
FRENCH 1 ARMY
Colonel's Wood
Goudberg
Au Bon Gite
Wallemolen
Passchendaele
Abri Wood
Wolf Farm
Meetcheele
Iron Cross
Ferdinand Farm
Boesinghe
Artillery Wood
Triangle Farm
Bellevue
Pilckem
Springfield Farm
Guards Div.
Macdonald's Farm
Aviatik Farm
38th DIV.
Regina
Winnipeg
Gravenstafel
Alberta
Keerselaarhoek
XIV CORPS
Kitchener's Wood
St. Julien
Schuler Farm
Otto Farm
Nieuwemolen
51st DIV.
Pond Farm
Kansas Cross
Droogenbroodhoek
Somme Farm
Dochy Farm
Spree Farm
Gallipoli Farm
XVIII CORPS
39th DIV.
Bank Farm
Hill 35
Hill 37
Pommern Redoubt
Broodseinde
Yser Canal
Square Farm
Bremen Redoubt
Zonnebeke
Brielen
Frezenberg
Potsdam House
Wieltje
Glasgow Spur
55th DIV.
Verlorenhoek
Molenaarelsthoek
St. Jean
Potijze
15th DIV.
Ypres-Roulers Railway
Westhoek
XIX CORPS
Railway Wood
Bellewaarde Lake
Polygon Wood
YPRES
Becelaere
II CORPS
Hooge
N
Zillebeke
Gheluvelt

0   1 km
0   1 mile

Tommies. Before them, locations of gaps in British entanglements through which they should pass had been painted upon parapets, and everyone had memorized routes to their respective objectives. Fed and watered, they stood to and awaited the whistle.

31 JULY

All the evening it drizzled with rain and the men got soaked while forming up into their assembly positions. A few hours before zero we heard the throb, throb of engines, and presently we could see the dim shapes of many tanks, crossing by the canal bridges. Soon after my harassing fire [machine] guns returned and reported all correct, and then I dozed off for an hour or two, and was next awakened by the thunder of the zero hour. Stewart and I climbed up to the top of our canal bank to see what we could. It was still dark, but as far as we could see in front of us was one vivid red of the oildrums [Livens projectors firing incendiary canisters of Thermit] mixing with the whiter flash of the bursting H.E. The noise was so terrific that we could only make each other heard by shouting down our ears. The field guns in front of us were no doubt responsible for a part of it, as were the explosions themselves, but it was the roar of the series of guns, 6″ and 9.2″ howitzers dug into the bank behind us as they fired salvo after salvo of battery fire.

After watching for an hour or more, in which time we hardly had a shell near us, the Germans guns all firing on their S.O.S. lines in front, we went down and had an excellent breakfast of fried sausages and café au lait.

LIEUTENANT DOUGLAS WIMBERLEY,
232ND MACHINE GUN COMPANY

Lieutenant Wimberley's sixteen machine guns had fired harassing barrages throughout the night to within two hours of zero. Along the canal to his left, the western flank of the battle-front at Steenstraat and Bixschoote was held by

General Anthoine's I French Army. Their task was to advance almost three kilometres and form a lateral defensive barrier – a wall to block German counter-attacks as British territorial gains increased in the central sectors. The French were well equipped with heavy guns; all were now ready to belch forth a torrent of red-hot steel.

On their immediate right, straddling and paralleling the line of the Ypres–Staden railway, lay General Cavan's XIV Corps. The prospects for these two most northerly units had been enhanced by a mixture of the aforementioned mine-motivated anxiety and the fact that German intelligence anticipated attacks on 28 July. The day before, British patrols crossing the

Above
Aerial view of the Boesinghe sector and canal. The dividing line between British and French forces was a few hundred metres beyond the railway running across the top third of the picture. It was over this section of canal that elements of the Guards Division, crossing before the battle, found the opposing trenches unoccupied.

water on special floating mats made and installed by 76 Field Company RE, found the enemy trenches on the northern bank of the Yser Canal deserted. Why the Germans had gone or whether they planned to return or not was academic: the positions were immediately occupied and consolidated by Anthoine's men and elements of the Guards and 38th (Welsh) Divisions.

28 JULY

We did not go out today as they found out the Bosch had evacuated his front line so we followed up and occupied a new line 500 yards across the canal, rounding up one officer and forty ranks as prisoners. In the early morning the Bosch counter-attacked with disastrous results. The Bosch barrage must have been very heavy as he almost blotted out Hunter Street and badly knocked about our old front line.

29 JULY

Out at dawn putting a good bridge for infantry across canal and taping a line up to the new front line. We had to cut through the old German wire, to bridge two trenches and dig steps across the canal bank. 13 prisoners were taken. Hunter Street was very gruesome after last night.

Lieutenant Harold Ridsdale, 76th Field Company, Royal Engineers (Guards Division)

The timely bridging of the canal and repositioning of the line here was of huge import for it had eliminated probably the most hazardous action on the entire battlefront on zero day – crossing the canal – a perennial barrier since June 1915. For their cheek, the British were bludgeoned by German guns.

Spirit was what both Haig and Gough sought for their offensive. Gough was especially known for requiring a display of mettle, especially from officers, verbally flaying those who failed to reach his standards. Only the results would prove the success or failure of his approach, and the clocks had started ticking towards resolution.

31 JULY 1917

Shortly before 4 a.m. we were woken up by a terrific bombardment which told us that the stunt had begun. This increased in magnitude to a perfect tornado, immediately preceding the infantry attacking which was evidently launched at an early hour. We stood to go up and commence our construction work and after breakfast had orders to parade at East Spur siding at noon in fighting order.

After some hanging about we were dispatched up the line by train, I, as usual, travelling on the engine – this time a steam Baldwin Loco. At Mission Junction we exchanged for a petrol-electric and here saw the first Bosch prisoners being marched back in gangs from the corps prisoner 'Cages' guarded by cavalry with drawn sabres. They looked a fairly young lot but very clean considering the beastly time they must have had. On our way up we saw more of them in a 'cage' (barbed wire enclosure) near the Chateau des Trois Tours. Near Leipzig Farm we detrained and marched across the Yser canal by the railway causeway.

The guns are all moving up and heavy howitzers both on rails and ordinary 7" and 9.2" fellows are ready in the vicinity. The place is thronged with infantry going and coming, gunners and transport sweating away at their teams, R.E.'s and constructional troops at work; wounded and small batches of prisoners coming down the line. We hear that the push had been most successful all along the line and that we have advanced in some places up to 4 miles in depth, taking Pilckem, the ridge and St Julien, but everything is stories only.

We start work just across the canal, striking away to the left of the broad gauge line but owing to a most objectionable Naval high velocity railway gun firing consistently we had to move most of the company a bit more forward. All went well and pretty quietly till later in the afternoon when the Hun evidently

Below
A lantern is fitted inside a converted ammunition box. The light shining through the slit assisted machine gunners to gauge the correct firing lines for night-time barrages.

got his heavies into position and began biffing the canal with big stuff, making the crossing most objectionable. The 13th Glosters (Pioneers), working behind us widening the causeway across the canal, got it heavily; two shells pitching right in among the crowded workers. In all they had 24 casualties, many dead and blown about and the sight was horrible to see, a regular path of death. In addition to the discomfort, it started to rain later in the afternoon and continued all night without ceasing.
LIEUTENANT GERALD BRUNSKILL, 5TH ROYAL SUSSEX REGIMENT (CINQUE PORTS BATTALION), ATTACHED TO XVIII CORPS RAILWAY CONSTRUCTION

Because of the overcast conditions dawn was late in breaking on the 31st. It was somewhat darker than expected, and many commanders wished that zero hour, 3.50 a.m., had been set thirty to forty-five minutes later so that the direction of attack might have been easier to distinguish. In most places, however, courses had been taped out the previous night or marked with white discs, and every officer had taken compass bearings. On the stroke of zero the offensive began. Under cover of their crushing bombardment the two French divisions streamed forward from Steenstraat. On their right shoulder XIV Corps surged from the newly-annexed German trenches north of the canal, and echoed every move of Anthoine's advance, staying in close touch and following close behind an almost perfect creeping barrage.

TUESDAY 31ST
At 4 a.m. a most terrific bombardment started by our people. The whole ground shook, and the sky was like a sheet of flame

Above
Part of the ground captured by the Guards Division on 31 July. The pillboxes seen here are near a position known as Colonel's Farm. Fifth Army pan 111, undated.

Right
German troops at Bixschoote, facing a French onslaught when the battle began.

waving backwards and forwards. The lights going up only showed feebly through the dense smoke. At 5 a.m. our Corps went over (Guards and 38th Division). They took Pilckem Ridge after hard fighting. By 8 a.m. our battalion was up there, filling in the holes to make a track over the ridge. The Yser was dammed, and a road for heavies made over it. At midday the heavies were all moving forward, and balloons, ammunition, dumps and everything moving up, and prisoners coming down. 9.2", 12" and 15" guns were massed in dozens. 6" and 8" howitzers were standing in rows, wheel to wheel, with occasional gaps for infantry to get through. After the first hour Fritz didn't shell much. Fresh Brigades kept pushing up and advancing. By 4 p.m. they had crossed the Steenbeek near Langemarck and were in touch with the 1st French Corps on the left. Fritz started a barrage about 4.15 p.m., but his counter was smashed by our barrage fire. He tried again at 10 p.m. without success. Our guns were putting up 6 stationary barrages and 1 creeping barrage. The last one was a 12" and 15" barrage, about 5 or 6 miles behind his lines. The prisoners were the 73rd Fusiliers, the same mob that got wiped up by us at Guillemont [Somme]. About 5 p.m. it started raining, and kept on all night.

Private Frank Pope, 10th King's Royal Rifle Corps

Anthoine and Cavan's men attacked in exemplary fashion, summarily brushing aside both resistance and counter-attacks, and causing panic in the German ranks; several eyewitnesses spoke of their inability to progress as fast as the enemy were retiring. Here too, the guns effectively neutralized their opposite numbers, leaving the troops largely unmolested by hostile artillery. At the precise appointed moment supporting units leapfrogged, creating an unstoppable momentum that carried the men to, and in places beyond

their objectives. At the end of the day rain may
have been teeming down, but Bixschoote lay in
French hands and most of the Pilckem Ridge was
under British ownership. Prospects looked good,
for from here the British gazed upon two key targets for the next stage: first, the village of
Langemarck, now at their mercy; and second, the
valley of the Steenbeek, an awkward, deeply
sunken brook. This latter was the foremost tacti-
al landscape feature at this time, for every unit
operating on the left of the battlefield had to
cross it. Cavan's neighbours were XVIII Corps
(51st Highland and 39th Divisions) commanded
by the meticulous and mercurial General Sir Ivor
Maxse. Maxse's men faced a tougher challenge
for their patch not only had the Steenbeek barrier
traversing the entire sector, but the sector was
slightly hillier and more heavily defended than
the northern flank. Unlike Cavan and Anthoine,
however, XVIII Corps had the benefit of mechanized support. A true test for the freshly-named
Tank Corps, the attacks turned out to be something of a curate's egg, the performance and fate
of each machine and its crew depending upon
localized ground conditions – often a matter of a
few square metres of wet or dry earth making the
difference between success and failure, life and
death. Crews were warned that the best going,
the existing roads, might have been mined.
Ostensibly working their own 'wave and leapfrog'
system and working in pairs, it was therefore a

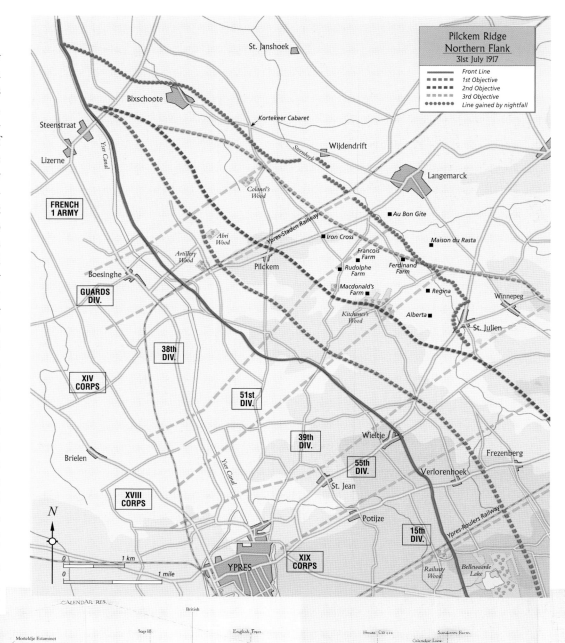

Above
Part of the German line known as the Wilhelm Stellung that passed behind Langemarck. The positions here were not trenches but breastworks with integral concrete shelters. See also pages 206 and 220.

Left
Targets for 31 July on the battlefield's northern flank.

Below
The Ypres battlefield in mid-summer 1917, five days before the offensive was launched at Messines. Fifth Army pan 111, 2 June.

case of picking one's way slowly and carefully across the battlefield whilst at the same time searching for targets.

REPORT FROM TANK G1, ATTACKING FROM BILGE TRENCH, LA BRIQUE:

At 3.56 a.m. the infantry advanced and I proceeded behind them, crossing no man's land, Canadian Trench and Canadian Support in the dark without much difficulty. As it got lighter I found myself to the left of my proposed route. At 4.30 another tank drew ahead of me and got ditched directly in front of me, and I had to draw to the right to avoid and in so doing got badly ditched at 4.50 a.m. in very marshy ground. I got my crew out and the unditching gear fitted and started digging the mud from in front of the sponsons. At this time the enemy started shelling his own front line, just behind us, and a machine-gun barrage seemed to be passing over us. About 6.20 a.m., after a severe struggle, my tank drew out onto a piece of firm ground. At 6.50 a.m. I proceeded on my route. I passed Oblong Farm and made for Canopus Trench. Saw two tanks ditched north-east of Juliet Farm. Pushed on across Canopus towards Steenbeek. After crossing Canopus appeared to come under direct observation of shells from heavy guns, landing alternately a few yards in front and behind, and making it very difficult to observe from the driver's seat. Ground one mass of shell holes. Engine started giving trouble. Exhaust red hot. Engine not pulling, and back-firing. Decided not to cross Steenbeek as infantry could be seen already across and advancing on Green line. Pushed on to St Julien and arrived about 10.10 a.m. Infantry in possession of St Julien. Sent off pigeon message.
SECOND LIEUTENANT GEORGE MCCHLERY, G BATTALION, TANK CORPS

McChlery's machine had not been able to fire a shot in anger to assist the infantry. By contrast, tanks with better local ground conditions such as G4, which was working in close proximity to G1, had more luck and 'sport'.

REPORT OF TANK G4, ALSO ATTACKING FROM BILGE TRENCH, LA BRIQUE:

Left starting point at zero and reached Juliet Farm at zero plus 2.15, when we received news that infantry were held up by machine-guns at Canopus and south-east of Kitchener Wood. Became ditched just beyond Juliet and got going again in less than ten minutes. We followed Canopus and did some firing into the redoubt. Result was 20 to 30 enemy surrendered and machine-guns silenced. Our infantry were then able to advance. Here, enemy surrendered between Canopus and Canteen Trenches. Became ditched just beyond Corner Cot and got out almost at once. Waited under cover for barrage to lift on Black Dotted Line, during which time we filled up with water. On barrage lifting we advanced towards St Julien, firing six-pounder over heads of infantry into the village. About 100 prisoners came out of St Julien during this fight. Ditched for a third time and while unditching Lewis gun was played on to Winnipeg; unditched in about 20 minutes. On proceeding to cross Steenbeek engaged with six-pounder enemy batteries firing from left and right. These batteries were silenced.
LIEUTENANT GARDNER, G BATTALION, TANK CORPS

The report goes on to explain how G4 managed to negotiate the ground: its commander, Lieutenant Gardner, guided the machine on foot

The view from a position near Cannabis Support trench in late August. Hosts of pillboxes have been revealed by gunfire and the ground annexed is now swathed in parallel screens to shield activity. Those pillboxes used by British troops have had entrances reversed. The battle area, already swept clean of many of its landmarks, is now difficult for men to get their bearings, so signs indicating position and direction have been erected everywhere. Inset left: Engineers erecting screens.

across the battlefield, being wounded in the process by a ground-strafing German aircraft. Eventually, the tank's unditching gear broke and it was forced to return to base. Tanks were a bizarre weapon from which to fight for the deafening roar of the battle outside was totally drowned by the mechanical din inside the machine, augmented of course, by machine guns and 6-pounders. Speech was out of the question, the crew communicating through signals. It was hot and fume-laden, and the only connection a commander had with his task was a visual one.

Above all, unless protected by smoke or counter-battery fire, they were tasty targets for German field guns and field howitzers, dug in and invisible until it was too late.

Like the tanks, XVIII Corps' attack resulted in mixed success. They had a terrific start, the German front lines instantly falling with the assistance of a pre-attack spot of 'frightfulness' by RE Special Companies. At this late stage gas would have been as much a hazard for the attacking British as the defending Germans, so now the cylinders, known as 'flaming oil drums', were

Below

Fifth Army pan 119. The prospect from Canopus Trench near St Julien during the battle. The trench from which the photograph was taken was captured on 31 July by 39th Division troops. In the right-hand half of the image the Passchendaele Ridge can clearly be seen in the distance. One of many ditched or knocked-out tanks is also visible (see inset).

filled with Thermit. Salvos of hundreds at a time were flung across no man's land.

At first, then, Maxses' 39th and 51st (Highland) Divisions faced little opposition, cruising over the ridge in front of Kitchener's Wood, astride Mousetrap Farm and before Wieltje. Wire was well cut in most places, but during the advance it was noted with surprise that many concrete emplacements had been 'practically undamaged' by British shellfire. Machine-gun nests based here and in fortified shell holes were cleared by the 'employment of rifle grenades and Lewis guns under the cover of which the infantry were enabled to work around the flanks and then rush the emplacement'. Momentum was good and the tanks were momentarily left behind until the first planned stoppage. Halts of varying periods had been written into the battle plans of every attacking division to allow mopping up of pockets of resistance, consolidation of the captured ground, and for support troops to arrive and leapfrog previous waves. As soon as progress was seen to be made, the field artillery relocated into more advanced positions, a manoeuvre on XVIII

Bottom
The same view today. The tree-lined route running through the entire photograph is the St Julien–Poelcappelle road along which the tanks advanced several times.

Corps front that took just two hours from orders being received to reopening fire – given the conditions, a remarkable achievement by the gunners. Despite the forced break during relocation and several already ditched and damaged tanks, everything was still progressing more than satisfactorily.

Before the battle had been raging half an hour German prisoners were streaming down, only too glad to get out of range of their own guns! I saw half a dozen at the corner of Liverpool Trench and Garden Street. They seemed very happy trying to converse with us. One of them – a boy about twenty – asked me the way to the nearest station; he wanted to get to England as soon as possible!
SECOND LIEUTENANT THOMAS HOPE FLOYD,
2/5TH LANCASHIRE FUSILIERS

In the morning drizzle St Julien fell, the Steenbeek was crossed and fresh troops surged forward towards the Langemarck line. Many Germans appeared exhausted and demoralized, readily surrendering, but by noon it became clear that the advance was beginning to lose shape. The British had now entered the heart of von Armin and von Lossberg's battle zone. Resistance grew with every metre of advance, ranks thinned and soon concerted action broke up into small piecemeal clashes over a pillbox here, a machine-gun nest there, a strongpoint, a sniper's post. The organized line disintegrated leaving a dog-toothed mess with several parties isolated in advanced positions. These men were doomed, for when the German *Eingreif* troops, held out of range of British field guns, were sent in, the momentum was reversed. By 1.00 p.m. those at the very apex of XVIII Corps' attack had reached almost the point near Gravenstafel from

which the British had withdrawn before Second Ypres in April 1915. There they would remain. In the meantime, the remnants of a dozen different units dribbled back towards St Julien and the Steenbeek. Without an organized line and no visual or physical contact with units on the flank, all control vanished. One either stayed where one was and awaited the enemy, or retired to fight again. In the chaos of battle the change in fortune seemed to take place so suddenly there was nothing any commander could do about the subsequent disarray.

Well, sir, you ask me where I got to when we went over the top. I think you will remember halting and lying down in no man's land. Well, as I lay there the time seemed to be long; then I got up and went to the front of the platoon to see what had gone wrong. When I got there I found you had gone on and the remainder of the men had not the sense to follow you. So I led on with the remainder, taking my direction from the compass. I reached the hill and passed Schuler Farm on the right. We started to climb the hill and then a funny thing happened: those already at the top came running back again shouting 'Get back and dig in; they are outflanking us.' I took the warning and retired to a suitable position and got the men digging themselves in. We could see the Boches coming over the ridge like a swarm of bees. When they got nearer we opened machine gun and rifle fire. All the time this was going on the artillery had ceased firing, and I began to feel a bit downhearted. Then things quietened down a bit; so I told the lads to make a drink of tea for themselves, which they did gladly enough. All the time we could see Fritz preparing for a counter-attack and we knew it had to come. I waited patiently keeping a look-out for them coming. The men were getting knocked out one by one, until I had only five; and the Lewis Gun had got a bullet through its pinion which rendered it useless. Nothing happened until the evening, and then the bombardment started and we knew we had

Below
A 1919 photograph of a British Mark IV tank which had come to grief on the banks of the Steenbeek two years before.

Above
Summer 1918 – the pre-31 July 1917 positions have now been reoccupied by the Germans. An officer inspects a British tank that appears to have suffered several direct hits. Note signboard.

Following pages
Opposing views of the Frezenberg battlefield. Both from 1915, the top one (Second Army pan 6) is the British perspective looking towards Passchendaele and Zonnebeke. Below: the Germans overlooked all the British trenches and the town of Ypres, accentuating how important just a few metres of elevation could be. The ridge was taken by 55th and 15th Divisions on 31 July. On the nearside of the railway seen bisecting the German picture, the British 8th Division advanced to take the site from where this picture was taken.

something to put up with. I sent up an S.O.S. rocket and our artillery opened out, but the shells were dropping short and hitting our men. Then we retired for about fifty yards and took up some shell-holes. I looked round and found all my men had vanished. I was amongst some of the Cambridgeshires. and Hertfordshires. I really did not know what to do. The artillery became more intense and still our shells were dropping short. There was another sergeant out of the Cambridgeshires in this shell-hole with a few men; so I told him I would go back and try and get in touch with the artillery. On my way back I got wounded in the leg, so I rolled into a shell-hole. It began to rain and rained heavily all the night. When day broke I found myself covered with clay and mud, and wet through to the skin. I crawled out and looked about me. It was a quiet morning except for a shell bursting now and again, and I could see some men through my glasses, about a mile away, working on a road. I made my way towards them. How I got there I do not know, for I was more dead than alive. I inquired for the dressing-station, which I found after a long walk. I was sent down to the Base to hospital and was sent to England on August 6.
Sᴇʀɢᴇᴀɴᴛ Rᴏʙᴇʀᴛ Bᴀʟᴅᴡɪɴ, 2/5ᴛʜ Lᴀɴᴄᴀsʜɪʀᴇ Fᴜsɪʟɪᴇʀs, ᴡʀɪᴛɪɴɢ ᴛᴏ ʜɪs ᴘʟᴀᴛᴏᴏɴ ᴄᴏᴍᴍᴀɴᴅᴇʀ, Sᴇᴄᴏɴᴅ Lɪᴇᴜᴛᴇɴᴀɴᴛ Tʜᴏᴍᴀs Hᴏᴘᴇ Fʟᴏʏᴅ, ꜰʀᴏᴍ ʜᴏsᴘɪᴛᴀʟ ɪɴ Oʀᴘɪɴɢᴛᴏɴ, Aᴜɢᴜsᴛ 1917

Behind the attack ancillary work had got underway the moment it was acknowledged the advance had potential. At 5.45 a.m. the order was given for engineer troops to leave the canal bank and start constructing tracks, bury communication cables, establish dumps, build strong points and repair roads. They immediately walked into a German counter-barrage falling on the old front lines and no man's land, a ploy designed precisely to target and hinder such work. Elsewhere on the central battlefront between Wieltje and the Ypres–Roulers railway a similar story unfolded. Excellent initial progress, rapid advance, but ever-increasing resistance as penetration deepened.

After a very anxious time, during which Fritz had his wind up severely, and he began bombing his own wire, whilst our boys were cutting passages in our own. Half a dozen tanks appeared just behind us and everything was ready for 3.30 am. At 3.45 am, our artillery opened out a terrific barrage on the enemy front line. At 3.50 am exactly we got over our front line and made our way towards the enemy. It being dark and a terrific din on all the time, I managed to get entangled in some barbed wire, and on freeing myself I could not find the Lewis Gun team of which I was No 2 and carried the spare parts bag. On two separate occasions I was blown off my feet by our own bursting shells but got up untouched, and I found I had lost all direction and was in the middle of the North Lancs who was on our left so I took half right turn and eventually stumbled on across the team in a Communication Trench of the enemy (We called it Cambria Drive). Ralf Tyson had just been hit in the hand (right). We did what we could for him and passed on, and established ourselves in what we thought was our correct position, but were informed later that we should be a little further forward. I accordingly left the gun and went scouting out in front for the party digging our strong point in front of Plum Farm. Finding the party I went back and brought up the gun and team. We got into a shell hole, cleaned the gun etc and dug deeper and connected up with the strong point. It was about 6 a.m. now and the 9th had passed through us. We noticed Plum Farm (which was a strong point of the enemy and well concreted) shake. The enemy had it mined and had tried to blow it up, but this failed. He shelled it heavily during the day, but I think it was too strong for him. The Tanks were an absolute failure, the ground being too soft, and their progress being exceedingly slow. Fritz put several out of action. We changed our position several times during the day, and one of the team (George) having gone down the line with a sprained ankle we were only four strong. Towards the evening the enemy

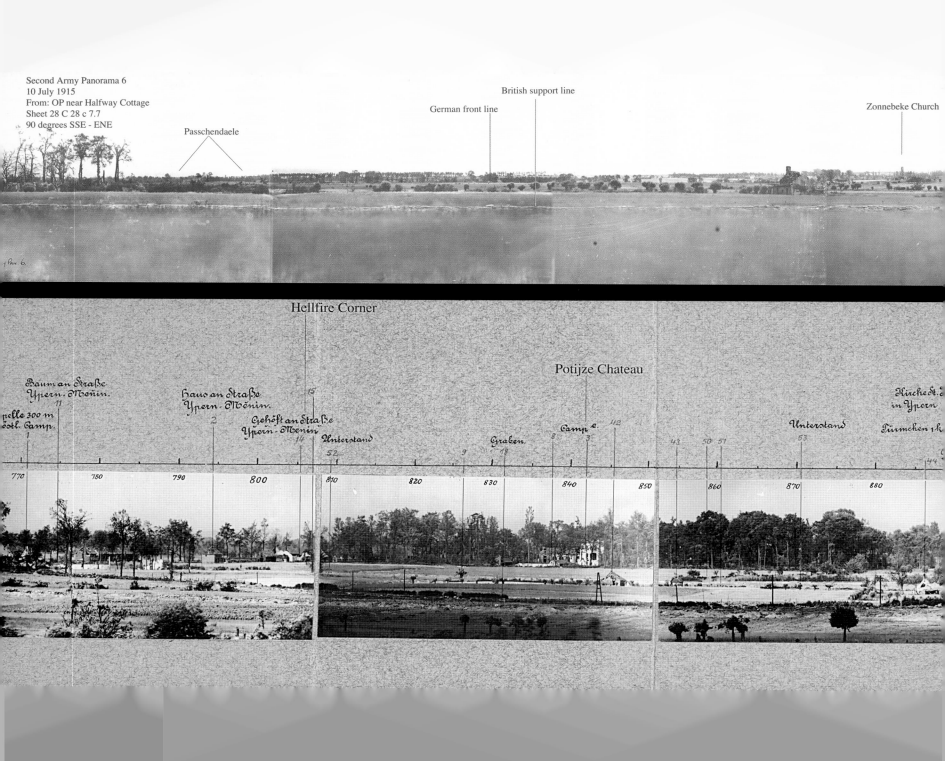

Second Army Panorama 6
10 July 1915
From: OP near Halfway Cottage
Sheet 28 C 28 c 7.7
90 degrees SSE - ENE

Passchendaele

German front line

British support line

Zonnebeke Church

Hellfire Corner

Potijze Chateau

Baum an Straße
Ypern-Menin.
11

Haus an Straße
Ypern-Menin.
2

15

Kirche St.
in Ypern

pelle 300 m
östl. Camp.
1

Gehöft an Straße
Ypern-Menin
14

Unterstand
52

Graben.
9   18

Camp
8   3

42

Unterstand

Türmchen st.

43   50 51   63   44

770   780   790   800   810   820   830   840   850   860   870   880

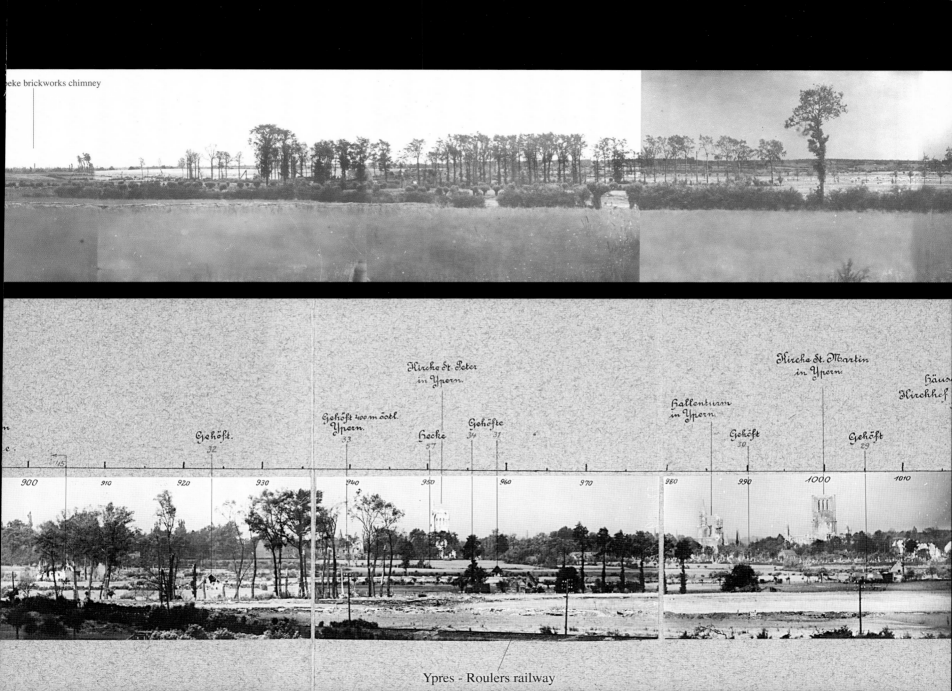

beke brickworks chimney

Kirche St. Peter in Ypern.

Kirche St. Martin in Ypern.

Häus...
Kirchhof

Hallenturm in Ypern.

Gehöft 400 m östl. Ypern.
33

Hecke
57

Gehöfte
34 31

Gehöft.

Gehöft
30

Gehöft
29

45

900   910   920   930   940   950   960   970   980   990   1000   1010

Ypres - Roulers railway

put heavy fire all over the captured ground and landed a shell on our trench killing two men next to me and wounding Pickering in the left arm, and myself being stunned only. The next I remember was being told by Sergt. Lewis to go for Stretcher Bearers, so I got out and rushed back to our supports and gave the necessary message. I remember nothing further till early next morning when I woke up sitting next to my pal Jack Sharp up to the knees in water and raining hard. I believe I fell exhausted and rather shaken after delivering the message. I was the only man left of the team. My rifle, ground sheet and valise having been blown up with the Lewis Gun. So I consider I had a marvellous escape.
PRIVATE WALTER HOSKYN, 5TH KING'S (LIVERPOOL REGIMENT)

The irregularity in line and speed of advance was universal: no one knew who was where. Aircraft had been in action, sketching the positions of visible troops on maps to drop them near infantry HQs. It was information that could not be acted upon. On the ground forward telephonic communication was constantly severed making runners the only reliable form of direct contact. Working in pairs (conveying duplicated information) they carried message maps from the foremost positions back to battalion or brigade HQ, where the information was passed back electronically – if the machinery was working. Again, turnaround time was too slow for commanders to effect any useful changes, but this had been expected – it was down to lower-ranking officers and NCOs in the field to make decisions on the spot. On Maxse's right Lieutenant General Sir Herbert Watts's XIX Corps, incorporating the 15th (Scottish) and 55th (West Lancashire) Divisions, found dozens of undamaged pillboxes facing them. Nevertheless, some managed to negotiate a route, vaulting Frezenberg Ridge,

crossing the Steenbeek, and also pushing on to positions near Gravenstafel. Once more troops arrived, few in number and on a fractured line. Not unnaturally, in the stirring mêlée of action and noise many men were inspired to push on in the belief that they were lagging behind. In truth they often formed the spearhead.

We left St. Julien close on our left. Suddenly we were rained with bullets from rifles and machine-guns. We extended. Men were being hit everywhere. My servant, Critchley, was the first in my platoon to be hit. We lay down flat for a while, as it was impossible for anyone to survive standing up. Then I determined to go forward. It was no use sticking here for ever, and we would be wanted further on; so we might as well try and dash through it. 'Come along – advance!' I shouted, and leapt forward. I was just stepping over some barbed wire defences – I think it must have been in front of Schuler Farm (though we had studied the map so thoroughly beforehand, it was impossible to recognize anything in this chaos) – when the inevitable happened. I felt a sharp sting through my leg. I was hit by a bullet. So I dashed to the nearest shell-hole which, fortunately, was a very large one, and got my first field dressing on. Some one helped me with it. Then they went on, as they were, to their great regret, not hit! My platoon seemed to have vanished just before I was hit. Whether they were in shell-holes or whether they were all hit, or whether they had found some passage through the wire, I cannot say. I only know that, with the exception of Corporal Hopkinson and one or two Lewis Gunners who went forward soon after, they had all vanished. It was one of the many mysteries of a modern battlefield! Allen was going on all right: I saw him going on in front: I believe he got to Aviatik Farm [see also Epilogue].
SECOND LIEUTENANT THOMAS HOPE FLOYD,
2/5TH LANCASHIRE FUSILIERS

Passchendaele Church, still entirely recognizable as such even without its tower, stood just over 2

Above
A key landmark with key observation of almost the entire battlefield: Passchendaele Church.

kilometres distant and would have been easily visible to troops mustering around Gravenstafel at this time. They suffered an unavoidable fate. The problem lay in overcoming dispersed pillbox and strong-point resistance; it was simply not something that could be choreographed in unison. The guns, normally the great partner in wave attacks with the creeping barrage, could be of no assistance when linear cohesion and planned speed of advance degenerated. The highest point reached and consolidated by the 15th (Scottish) Division was Pommern Castle. Ahead lay the village of Zonnebeke and beyond, the Passchendaele and Broodseinde ridges. These positions, some 400 metres from the jumping-off line, were the limit of their pursuit. Despite many dismissive remarks about the tanks, some machines had done sterling work before ditching.

With the day gradually becoming lighter and the possibility of assessing the difficulties of the ground ahead, we were able to make fair progress over what was almost an impossible quagmire, by careful driving and picking our way. Being in No. 9 Company 3rd Battalion, our second objective was the enemy's second line and the strong point Frezenberg. We were then to patrol this line until the second wave of tanks arrived and passed through us. By careful observation of the ground ahead and steering accordingly we made what could be called good progress in spite of the fact that the battlefield was a total mass of shell holes, great and small, smashed trenches and almost a quagmire owing to it being so low and almost no drainage. We were soon in front of the infantry and heading for the enemy second line and Frezenberg. Our guns had already been in action but as we neared these points we were being hit by heavy machine gun fire. The 6-pounder guns however began to have great effect on the Frezenberg stronghold, silencing the enemy machine guns and helping to overcome the strongpoint. At the second line we found the trenches had a number of concrete pillbox

machine gun emplacements standing quite high above the ground and causing a lot of trouble. It was therefore a source of great satisfaction to us inside the tank to see our 6-pounder gunners having such positive and splendid targets, and as we drove up closely (point blank range: 50–100 yards or so) to note the 6-pounder shells smashing these pillboxes. Needless to say this completely stopped any more fire from these machine guns and enabled the infantry to take the position. We were greatly helped hereabouts by a pre-arranged system of signals with the infantry – tin hats etc. on top of bayonets, indicating the position of what was holding them up, as with the very limited vision from within the tank it was most difficult to see this at times. Our 6-pounder gunners had done splendid work and continued to do so whilst we patrolled hereabouts for the next wave of tanks to pass through us.

PRIVATE WILLIAM DAWSON, C BATTALION, TANK CORPS

The ever-worsening ground conditions baulked all hope of further advance at Frezenberg. Once this had been accepted, it was a case of escaping to fight another day.

As our ammunition was running very low we returned to our lines. This was no joy ride in view of the terrible state of the ground and the fact that the Boche were now putting down heavy counter-artillery fire. However late in the afternoon we reached the place where we understood our HQ would be. I had been in the driving seat for 13 hours without moving out and of course nothing to eat or drink. During the return journey, owing to the many hundreds (possibly even thousands) of times I had to operate the clutch to enable the track gears to be changed for the purpose of steering clear of obstacles or bad patches of ground, my thigh muscles in my clutch leg suffered from cramp and exhaustion and I often had to use both legs – a rather awkward and difficult thing to do. The result was that when at last I got out of the tank, my legs gave way and I had to lie down for a while.

Needless to say both officer and crew were worn out by such a long time in action inside a machine with exhaust pipes

Right

Actions of the tanks on 31 July. Apart
from enemy action, it was the ground
conditions that caused the greatest
number of tanks to become disabled.

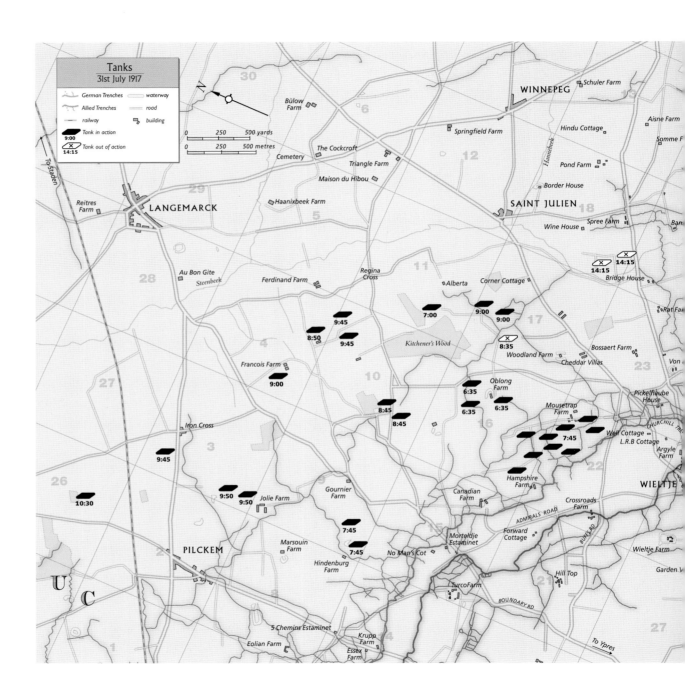

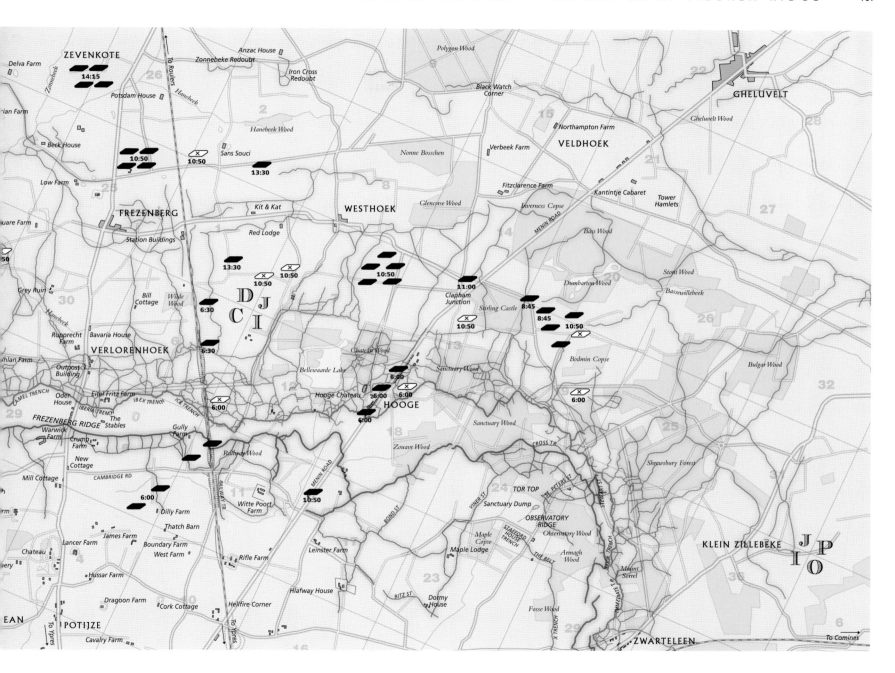

Delva Farm

ZEVENKOTE

Anzac House

Zonnebeke Redoubt

Iron Cross
Redoubt

Polygon Wood

GHELUVELT

14:15

26

Potsdam House

To Roulers

2

Black Watch
Corner

Northampton Farm

Gheluvelt Wood

28

Beck House

Hanebeek Wood

Sans Souci

Nonne Bosschen

Verbeek Farm

VELDHOEK

21

Low Farm

10:50   10:50

13:30

8

Fitzclarence Farm

Kantintje Cabaret

Tower
Hamlets

27

FREZENBERG

Kit & Kat

WESTHOEK

Glencorse Wood

Inverness Copse

MENIN ROAD

Station Buildings

Red Lodge

1

14

Bass Wood

Grey Ruin

13:30

10:50   10:50

D   J
C   I

10:50

11:00
Clapham
Junction

Stirling Castle

Dumbarton Wood

Stout Wood

Bassewillebeek

30

Bill
Cottage

Wilde
Wood

6:30

8:45

8:45

10:50

26

Rupprecht
Farm

Bavaria House

6:30

Bellewaarde Lake

Château Wood

Sanctuary Wood

10:50   10:50

Bodmin Copse

Bulgar Wood

VERLORENHOEK

13

6:00

32

Outpost
Building

Hooge Château

6:00

6:00

6:00

Oder
House

IBEX TRENCH   ICE TRENCH

6:00

26:00   6:00

HOOGE

CAMEL TRENCH

FREZENBERG RIDGE   The
Stables

IBERIA TRENCH

Eitel Fritz Farm

6:00

Sanctuary Wood

25

29

Warwick
Farm

Crump
Farm

Gully
Farm

Railway Wood

Zouave Wood

CROSS TR.

Shrewsbury Forest

New
Cottage

CAMBRIDGE RD.

RAILWAY TR.

MENIN ROAD

BOND ST.

VINER ST.

TOR TOP

PETERS ST.

STEVART ST.

Mill Cottage

6:00

Dilly Farm

Witte Poort
Farm

11

10:50

18

Sanctuary Dump

OBSERVATORY
RIDGE

Observatory Wood

KLEIN ZILLEBEKE

J   P
I   O

Thatch Barn

Lancer Farm

James Farm

Boundary Farm

West Farm

Rifle Farm

Leinster Farm

Maple
Copse

Maple Lodge

STAFFORD
HOUSE
TRENCH

THE BELT

Armagh
Wood

IMMEDIATE T.R.

Mount
Sorrel

36

Chateau

4

Hussar Farm

23

Dragoon Farm

Cork Cottage

Hellfire Corner

Hlafway House

RITZ ST.

Dotmy
House

Fosse Wood

X TRENCH

29

6

EAN

POTIJZE

To Ypres

Cavalry Farm

To Ypres

16

To Comines

ZWARTELEEN

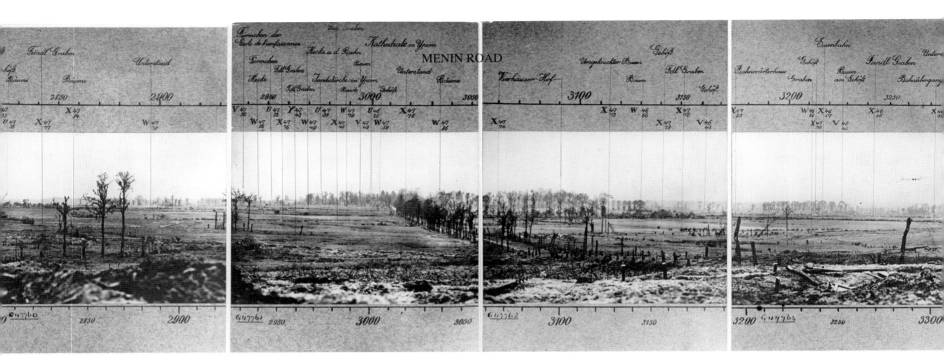

This German view from a position in Hooge looks down the Menin Road towards Hellfire Corner. On 31 July troops of 24 Brigade (8th Division) took the ground upon which Hooge Crater Cemetery (bottom) now stands. See map on next page. The modern view is taken from the nearest possible clear vantage point.

glowing red hot, a 40 gallon radiator boiling or nearly so, plus the noise of the engine, tracks and 6-pounder guns with the heat and fumes from the shell cases and the noise of machine gun bullets hitting the tank, with the red hot bullet splash coming in. We all quickly recovered, and being provided with a meal and tea felt the great satisfaction of knowing we had successfully carried out our task. We were one of only two tanks to return and the only one which had not had to use its unditching gear. I was very glad about this because to have to fix this to the track and later take it off meant exposing two members of the crew to very grave risk, especially if close up to the enemy, and this always caused me much concern.

About the time we got back to HQ, or a little before, it started to rain heavily, which continued almost continuously for three or four days. This was quite disastrous.

PRIVATE WILLIAM DAWSON, C BATTALION, TANK CORPS

Heavy rain began to fall in mid-afternoon. Digging in that evening Watts's troops would already have gleaned the state of affairs on their right, for they had been forced to halt and consolidate partly because of heavy enfilade (lateral) fire from their right flank, the higher ground of the Gheluvelt Plateau. If the enemy guns were able to shell them at will from here, the Germans were clearly not fully occupied in defending their own front. Ergo the neighbouring British attack must also have failed.

The boundary between XIX Corps and Sir Claud Jacob's II Corps (8th, 24th, 25th and 30th Divisions, plus 53rd Brigade from 18th (Eastern) Division) was the Ypres–Roulers railway line. Jacob's sector, bisected by the Menin Road, formed the heavily wooded approach to Gough and Haig's most tormenting objective – the plateau. Three full divisions had been earmarked to crack it. The going was expected to be better on these more sandy slopes, but woods and not crops had been planted here for a reason: the clayey ground was often too wet to warrant cultivation.

The 30th Division's task was to advance through Stirling Castle, diagonally cross the Menin Road and attack Glencorse and Polygon woods. It was as if the enemy had been pre-warned. Struggling out of the mess of fallen trees and stumbling up the tortured slopes, they had no hope of keeping in touch with the creeping barrage. The men had identified routes by noting the shape of woodland on the skyline. Visibility on the day was generally poor anyway, but in the welter of noise, smoke and fumes they all looked horribly similar. Some units lost direction, veered towards the wrong targets and left wide gaps unassaulted. The Germans, meanwhile, laid low until the curtain of British shells passed by, then surfaced to create havoc from support positions. Shrapnel fell in sheets. The slowed pace of advance was neither visible nor properly communicated to British gunners, whose neat creeping barrage gradually pulled away, leaving the troops exposed to fire from the innumerable concrete emplacements speckling the hills, now sitting inside the barrage zone. As elsewhere, many were unknown and undamaged – and out came the garrisons to cut the British down. Although the lightly held enemy front (blue) line fell, the confusion immediately transferred to supporting British troops, 53 Brigade of the 18th (Eastern) Division, which was due to pass through the 30th and continue the advance.

The second barrage (for the attack by our Division) started at the scheduled time and place – 12.30 p.m. near Glencorse Wood. Thanks to the failure of the 30th Division we were not anywhere near our proper position and the barrage was therefore of no use to us. Nevertheless, the Battalion carried on from where they were, and did what they could. The advancing was trebly diffi-cult without the barrage, and the result was that the front troops finished up somewhere near Glencorse Wood, instead of the scheduled position – halfway across the race-course in Polygon Wood. We got one telephone wire to Brigade. But visual sig-nalling was useless, owing to the bad visibility – misty, with low-lying clouds. A very big enemy howitzer – probably one of the famous 16 inch – was dropping occasional shells about half a mile or more to our left, and even at that distance I could not help wanting to 'duck' when one of these shells came roaring over. Late in the afternoon we moved with Batt. Hdqrs. to the left, where the road was not on such a high bank. Here, we found a tunnel [Hooge Tunnel] running under the centre of the road – evidently an enemy communication trench. The tunnel had been broken or blown in at intervals by our heavy shells. The parts left intact had already been examined by the R.E. and marked 'Safe'. In the tunnel were many enemy telephone lines – all kinds of wire. It had been supplied with electric light too, many of the bulbs remaining – (Wotan 'Centra'). We remained in a portion of the tunnel until 9 p.m., when we were ordered to move. The enemy was shelling the road as we got out of our hole, so we 'got a move on'. We went down the road towards Ypres for about 250 yards, stumbling over dead bodies, barbed wire, 'pavé' setts, etc., falling into shellholes every few steps. One of the scouts (Philips) was wounded by one of the shells, a splinter passing through both legs at or near the knees. Our Padre was with us, and he said to one man (referring to the shelling), 'Warm isn't it?' The man replied (not noticing who he was speaking to, in the darkness and confusion), 'Huh, it's ------- hot, I think.' We turned off the road to the left and found our way to Ridge Trench near Zillebeke. Here we spent the night.

PRIVATE S.T. FULLER, 8TH SUFFOLK REGIMENT

The 18th (Eastern) Division's assault petered out in bloody chaos. On their right the 24th

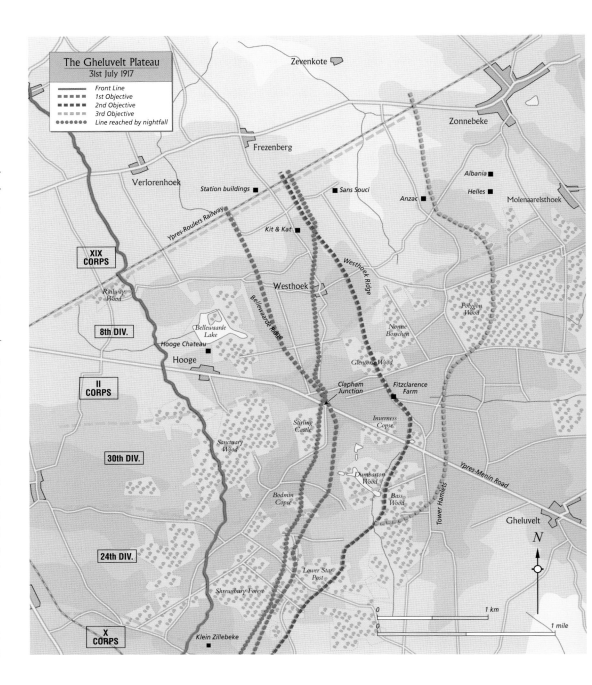

Left
Left
The attacks upon the Gheluvelt Plateau, 31 July 1917.

Following pages
The precise area of attack of 24 Brigade (8th Division), then and now. The troops emerged from all the trenches pictured. The panorama is from 6 July 1915: Second Army pan 5.

Division encountered identical problems. The task of forming a defensive flank was hopeless – there was no one to defend.

Forty-eight tanks had also been allotted to II Corps to assist their assault. Nineteen arrived at the front line – all late. As soon as they ventured off the Menin Road to assist the infantry, like Venus flytraps the mud-filled shell holes claimed them as victims. Water rushed in through the sponsons, swamped the engine and the machines became irretrievably stranded – and, like so many others, a fine target. Those few that avoided ditching, although usefully drawing fire, were unable to deal with pillboxes sunk into the earth to roof level – apart from anything else they were almost impossible to spot. The tank crews did all that was humanly possible to keep the machines moving and fighting, but it was no good – first the ground conditions and then the enemy defences prevailed. The Germans appeared happy to wait until the machines reached certain positions before calmly picking them off one by one. All but one that went into action along the Menin Road that day were knocked out, forming the nucleus of what later came to be called the tank graveyard. But the most serious problem for the infantry was German shelling. In this sector it fell with such intensity and accuracy that officers questioned each other as to what on earth had happened to their own counter-battery fire. Storms of British shells had been sailing over their heads day and night for weeks, so how could the enemy guns possibly not have been silenced? Only the RFC could answer the question. Despite the poor weather, it was essential that some flew.

31 JULY

As I dare say you know the Push has started today so I'll tell exactly what has happened as far as I am concerned. To begin with Zero Hour was fixed for 3.50 a.m., so at 3.15 a.m. we were all called to stand by our machines. I managed to get a couple of boiled eggs and some tea. The weather was most hopelessly dud. The clouds were at 800 so we had to fly at 700. This was almost suicidal as a machine is a very big and easy target. However, as we were the contract Patrol Flight we had to go up and try to do something. The other flights have been on the ground all day. I left the aerodrome at 5.30 a.m. and scraped over houses and trees etc until I got to our guns. Here the fun started as there was, so experts tell me, the worst barrage that has ever been known, and I had to fly through it.

I could hear and occasionally see the shells and every minute I was expecting to see one of my wings vanish. However, nothing hit us until we got over the lines (which had been pushed forward considerably) and here in 8 minutes we got 30 holes through the machine from machine guns. Ten of them passed within a few inches of Woodcock. The wireless transmitter, valued at £200 disappeared. Three spars on the wing were broken and lastly a bullet went through the petrol tank. I smelt a smell of petrol and in a few minutes it all came rushing over my feet and legs. How we got back, I don't know, it seemed the longest journey I have ever made but eventually we landed safely. I had to write out a report on the flight and then had a shave and was just going in to have some breakfast when I go orders to take up another machine to try to find the 30th Division who had got lost. So, off I went again and tootled over our lines for an hour. The first thing that happened was that the wireless transmitter again disappeared, leaving only a big hole in the fuselage. After this we weren't hit quite so much as before. Meanwhile we were called to the infantry to light flares for us; but as they wouldn't do this we had to draw the fire of the Huns onto ourselves so as to discover where the enemy line was and deduct ours from it. We managed to do this fairly successfully and came back unhurt,

Immediately we were put into a car and taken to Corps

Bellewaerde lake behind trees

Trees lining Menin Road

The Culvert

WING HOUSE

Support line (Br.)

Bull Farm

Hooge Chateau

The Wall

Front line (Br.)

Headquarters where we interviewed several old generals and Brass Hats, so altogether we had a pretty busy morning.

This afternoon it's been raining so we've had nothing to do. It's an awful shame the weather is so bad, as given fine weather we could have done some much better work and chased the Huns for miles. Our only casualties are two missing. I shall not tell you anything about how we are getting on with the Push as I am not certain myself; but I think they are getting on better further north. We have not done at all badly, but we've had a lot of opposition.

LIEUTENANT JACK WALTHEW, NO. 4 SQUADRON,
ROYAL FLYING CORPS

Gains were more meagre against the Gheluvelt Plateau than in any other sector, and it was indeed this serious lack of progress that had permitted German artillery to fire in enfilade against XIX Corps.

Plumer's diversionary Second Army push on the northern and eastern slopes of the Messines Ridge turned out to be of negligible benefit to their comrades in the Salient. Only small parcels of territory were wrested, the most useful being that around Klein Zillebeke and Hollebeke.

31.7.17

At 4 a.m. in spite of most atrocious weather the attack was made on a 14 mile front, French and Belgian troops co-operating with the British on the left. We were the extreme right, the battalions being engaged being the 11th R.W. Kents and 18th KRRC. The 123rd Brigade were on the left of the Canal advancing to Hollebeke Chateau. Our objective was Hollebeke Village. Fritz spotted the preparations for the attack soon after 3 a.m. and shelled our front line unmercifully, so that we had suffered a large number of casualties before the attack commenced. Fortunately for me my duties did not compel me to leave the sap, although we were all 'standing by' for emergencies. The KRR's met a very strong

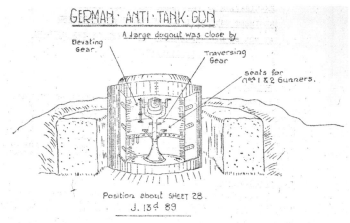

resistance and suffered accordingly. They should have actually taken the village but those who managed to get through at all lost direction with the result that the Kents, whose progress had been better, found themselves with an exposed flank which was subjected to a fierce machine gun fire. Colonel Corfe organised an attack on the village and by 10 a.m. the final objectives were being consolidated. The prisoners taken numbered about 100. From what I can gather by reading between the lines of the various reports that have come through the resistance has been so fierce that only in a few places has the final objective been reached. If all the attacking Divisions have been in the line as long as we have it is no wonder that they have failed. For 8 days our men have been in the trenches under the worst possible conditions regarding weather and shell-fire and to expect them to make a successful advance now is asking too much. The state of the country is indescribable owing to the recent rains and the naturally marshy nature of the ground churned up into a filthy sloppy mass by all manner of shells. Rifles and machine guns are choked with mud and are unusable. All our rifles were collected this afternoon for handing*

Left
British sketch of a German anti-tank gun situated at Stirling Castle near Clapham Junction, an area soon to be known as the Tank Cemetery.

Right
The effects of British gunfire on the bend in the Menin Road near Clapham Junction.

Below
Proof of the efficacy of a single gun. Disabled tanks at Clapham Junction, and the 5cm gun that, although manufactured in 1891, did serious damage to them.

over to the Kents but some others came up from the Transport Lines just in time. In the scramble I lost my own rifle but got another which was in nearly as good condition.

SAPPER ALBERT MARTIN, 41ST SIGNAL COMPANY, ROYAL ENGINEERS

Across the battlefront as a whole the first day might be characterized as an enterprise typical of the British mould: early optimism and promise, great dash, slow disintegration, fading communication, variable success. Progress was excellent on the far left, fair in the centre where some objectives were attained and negligible on the right. At Railway Wood and in the Observatory Ridge sectors the British had been able to sweep across the German front and support lines. Here, the Messines psychology had again helped, for these had long been mining areas, and a fearful enemy responded by either reducing garrisons in the line to a bare minimum, or evacuating altogether. Having raced over the *vorfeld*, however, the British, both man and machine, ran into a wall of steel and lead in the battle zone.

CLOSE OF DAY

Although von Armin and von Lossberg's strategies prevailed on 31 July, it was at an equally heavy cost as those they had largely thwarted. This too was integral to Sir Douglas Haig's wider thinking for the battle: a continuation of the attritional approach launched on the Somme. Again like the Somme, however, the German defensive performance had been superlative, especially the work of most *Eingreif* units. But surely after such a day Charteris' suggestion of imminent enemy collapse was now even closer to reality? With a

limited supply of reserves and a battlefield full of exhausted troops, each in the full knowledge that the Tommies would soon come knocking again, future German prospects were not just unappealing, they were ultimately hopeless – or so Charteris would have GHQ believe. As for the British, they could take heart from the fact that the new tactics and weapons devised to neutralize pillboxes had, on the whole, worked more than adequately; if only enemy counter-attacks, hidden emplacements and batteries could have been better dealt with, the territorial gain of around 20 square kilometres might well have been greater. But then there was the rain. It created havoc along the entire Salient. And there appeared to be no let-up.

01.08.17

Appalling wet day which is spoiling offensive. Dugout beginning to collapse.

02.08.17

Still living at long range; too muddy to move. Rotten bad luck being unable to follow up initial success of offensive.

03.08.17

Horrible wet day. Attempted to build new Gun Position across canal. Rather heartbreaking in the rain.

CAPTAIN EDMUND GIFFARD, 75 BRIGADE, ROYAL FIELD ARTILLERY

Once more, this time courtesy of Mother Nature, the Germans were presented with time to adjust and reinforce. Now, as they were preparing a second strike, was the time to harass the British to the maximum. Apart from the already churned-up nature of the ground and the continued heavy shelling, the expanded battlefield swarmed with men and animals – a deadly blend.

The Bluff

Lodge at O 4 c 5.4

The German artillery are lively and causing us a lot of casual-
ties. One orderly, an Irishman says, 'I know what I would like
to know, what day it is,' says one, 'No to have a leave, no to have
a nice soft Blighty one, no, well Mike, what do you like?' A shell
drops near them, one says, 'I would like to be behind that
German firing that gun with a nice big stick in my hand then I
would be happy.' This is about the worst of the war, mud every-
where and dead lying in hundreds, an artillery man with a pack
mule pass me going up, then suddenly they disappear. I lose my
footing and fall in a shell-hole full of mud and water, up to my
neck, I try to scramble out I catch a loose duck board; an orderly
passing says, 'Hello Taff, shipwrecked?' Smiling, but he pulls me
out. I am sure there are bodies in that hole, and I have been tread-
ing on them. I tell the orderly of the man and pack mule he says
he saw them fall in the shell hole but they didn't get out.

The Germans are giving us hell. Next day going up a
shell bursts a distance away. Up jumps an officer; he has his
arm blown off. Raving mad, shouting, yelling, running about in
the open. Nothing seems to touch him. At last he falls in a hole
full of mud. He is got out exhausted but mad, staring in front
of him and whimpering all the time. It is a trial here up and
down, and hard to find anyone.

Private Charles Heare, 1/2nd Monmouthshire Regiment

The experiences of 39th Division engineers and medical teams illustrate the general picture and can be extrapolated elsewhere, except on the right against the plateau. By 6.00 a.m. on 31 July, Field and Pioneer companies had already been in action repairing and extending tracks for guns and pack transport and patching the network of roads. Little protected from German shells it was a hazardous task, yet by noon a route had been cleared across the old enemy front line near Mousetrap Farm. By

Eikhof Farm

Damm Strasse

Pheasant Wood

Above
The Bluff sector near Hollebeke as pictured on 21 May 1917. It was from the woods in the distance that 41st Division troops attacked Hollebeke on 31 July. Second Army pan 114.

3.00 p.m. it had already reached Alberta, a position near the German third line beyond Kitchener's Wood. This strong point had been taken earlier with the help of two G Battalion tanks. They had been partly guided there by infantry pointing out difficult ground on behalf of tank commanders whose vision through small observation flaps was impeded by smoke and dust from the barrage. The tanks' remit was to seek out pockets of resistance – machine-guns in shell holes, pillboxes, etc. – and deal with them. The following description shows just what tanks and their crews were capable of once they had identified a target – and with a bit of luck. On 31 July tank G47 made one of the deepest penetrations into German territory.

I straightened up a bit and made for Alberta, in front of which I saw the 17th Sherwoods who were waiting for the barrage to lift and for the machine-guns at Alberta to be silenced. I travelled along three sides of Alberta and poured in a good fire, and as our own barrage had not lifted yet we reversed and went round the three sides again. Three machine-guns were certainly engaged about here, two in the strongpoint itself, and one on the right. We all had a chance of shooting. About this time five of our six guns were out of action and I was able to fire through the front flap with my revolver, and it must have had good effect for when the barrage lifted the infantry were able to go to the strongpoint without any resistance and we soon saw a party with machine-guns come out and return towards our lines as prisoners. The 17th Sherwoods at once consolidated and I sent my first pigeon off.
SECOND LIEUTENANT JOHN ALLDEN, G BATTALION, TANK CORPS, COMMANDING TANK G47

G47's action, coming at emplacements from the rear and threatening not only the garrison inside but their line of retreat, was found to be the most effective – if it could be achieved. Second Lieutenant Allden then moved on, became ditched in a shell hole, 'abandoned ship', went back to HQ at Hilltop Farm dugout for fresh orders, returned to the tank, dug it out at the second attempt and eventually managed to limp home. The entire escapade took forty-five hours. The crew had been very lucky to escape the clutches of the sucking Flanders geology, 'bellying' proving as much a hazard as uncontrolled German guns. Only one form of dedicated anti-tank weapon was encountered on XVIII Corps front, a small, rail-mounted affair sited just north of St Julien. Aptly, it was chased away by G47 and G48.

By 1.00 a.m. on 1 August the sappers completed the track connecting Admiral's Road to Alberta. Ostensibly it was 'ready for wheeled transport', but because of the pouring rain and mud the route was almost instantly impassable. At the same time the engineers brought forward artillery bridges for streams and ditches to allow field guns to move forward. Having arrived at new locations the gunners now needed to dig a pit for protection against shell splinters, build a timber gun platform and erect some form of camouflage to veil their efforts from both air and ground observation.

Meanwhile, parties from 225 Field Company were detailed to find that vital element, drinking water; on their entire divisional front (39th) just one clean well was located, at Racecourse Farm. They calculated that it could provide each man with no more than two ladle scoops per day. All further supplies until new sources could be found had to be carried forward over open ground in petrol tins and small horse- or mule-drawn bowsers. A party taking twenty-six mules went forward in the afternoon loaded with material with which to build strong points, whilst in the evening dumps of basic RE stores of wire (60 rolls), screw pickets (340), shovels (320) and sandbags (500) were established. The conditions obviated the use of any of it.

2/8/17

Filthy wet day: but they had attacked again at 8.00 a.m. and been equally hammered. The East Lancs this time. I went up, and damned nearly got stuck in Manchester [trench]. I had to delay a quarter of an hour to dig one chap out of the filth. Monk and I both went in to our hips. When we got up, I saw the whole show had been a wash out: the men were back in the old posts, hardly having moved forward a bit: the Bosche sniping like fury from trees etc., and they had excellent targets, as the attackers were being relieved by the R.B.'s [Rifle Brigade]. I made a report of the thing: my digging and wiring stunt was off. It took Monk and myself two hours to get up, and any men loaded with wire etc. would have been irretrievably stuck. When I got back, having been properly shrapnelled most of the way, I heard that Jenks had been killed, and Pennyewick wounded by those same snipers. Damn them: Jenks was one of the best. Robertson took over command of the Company pro tem. Jenks' funeral is coming off tomorrow.

SECOND LIEUTENANT J.T. GODFREY, 104TH FIELD COMPANY, ROYAL ENGINEERS

Whether walking or digging, the mud sapped every ounce of energy. It was easy enough to get the stuff onto one's spade, but almost impossible to throw it off; men scraped it from the blade with their fingers. As they slopped out a new line, so

Above
Alberta blockhouse, neutralized by tank G47.

others built and repaired bridges, cleaned captured pillboxes, buried the dead, evacuated the wounded, wired, reversed fire-steps in the remains of captured trenches, cut down trees in woods behind the line to open up fields of fire for the heavy guns, erected screens and camouflage, and carried, carried, carried, lugging forward the essentials of warfare through the mire. Although never at the firing line, on 31 July the four 39th Division sapper units lost seventy-six killed or wounded. The plight of the medical services striving to reach, treat and evacuate the many wounded dispersed across the battlefield was yet more distressing, as Major James Rogers, Medical Officer for 4/5th Black Watch, noted in his post-battle report on 2 August.

The battalion moved up over the Steenbeek at 10 a.m. and I followed about 250 yards in the rear. C Company got about as far as the site I had selected for an Aid Post. I saw almost immediately that they were held up by machine-gun fire and that they were having casualties. I decided to form an Aid Post where I was. It was evident that the stretcher bearers would find it difficult or impossible to evacuate wounded, so I decided to push on and take my chance. My orderlies and myself got on safely by short rushes and taking shelter in shell holes which were very plentiful. I was kept busy dressing wounded the whole time. I was unable to evacuate stretcher cases as there were practically no bearers left and only one stretcher. Besides, it was impossible to get a stretcher back due to the machine-gun fire. I put the stretcher cases under the best cover available and got any walking cases to try and get away when they felt able. I got in touch with the Signalling Officer and asked if he could get a message through saying where I was and asking for assistance. He did not get back to HQ, I understand, until 3 p.m. The Boche began to get round our right flank and casualties became more numerous about 4.30 p.m. The Boche counter-attacked on our right flank and we were being enfiladed and the order to retire was given. I told the remaining walking cases to try to get back as best they could. The stretcher cases I was loathe to leave, but there was no way of getting them back. Those I came across I dressed in shell holes. I eventually got behind a line held by the

Right
XVIII Corps map showing the route of the track taken forward to Alberta which became instantly unuseable. It was later christened Track X and now has a small cemetery of the same name along its route near Admiral's Road.

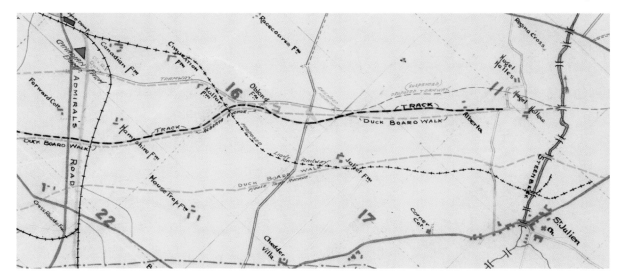

Notts and Derbys and the remnants of our battalion. I found a suitable site for an Aid Post at Alberta about 600 yards from the firing line. My orderlies were all wounded and I had lost all my dressings. My corporal of stretcher-bearers was wounded as also were most of the bearers. I had tried to get in touch with OC Divisional Collecting Station but the runner was wounded. I did what I could for the wounded who came from several battalions but could not do much as I had so few dressings, no stove, no food. I could not label the wounded as I had no tallies [similar to old-fashioned card luggage tags]. About 8 a.m. August 1st, six stretchers and 24 bearers turned up. The bearers and stretchers were only sufficient to evacuate the wounded in the Aid Post but not the wounded up front. There were no dressings sent. I proceeded with the Padre and 12 bearers to the front lines. We were fired on most of the way by a sniper, but with indifferent success on the part of the sniper. The going was very

heavy and it was evident that even six bearers were too few as not only was the mud knee deep in places or deeper and the ground so broken up by shell holes, but also the distance to the Divisional Collecting Station was too great. As soon as I was relieved I proceeded to the DCS to explain the situation to the OC. The RAMC bearers did their best but the work was too heavy for them as the state of the ground was terrible. The casualties of the men are between 300–350 as far as I know [the actual figure was 269]. I myself received a bruise from a M.G. bullet at side of knee and another on thigh from piece of shell, but I am quite able to carry on. Three machine-gun bullets elected to pass through my clothing instead of myself for which I am duly grateful. We move up to 1st German Line at 2.30 p.m. this afternoon.

Major James Rogers, Medical Officer,
4/5th Black Watch (Royal Highlanders)

Right
Mules fitted with specially designed saddlery to transport GS (General Service) shovels.

Below
164 infantry Brigade (55th Division) map showing the positions and nature of critical supporting works carried out prior to the attack.

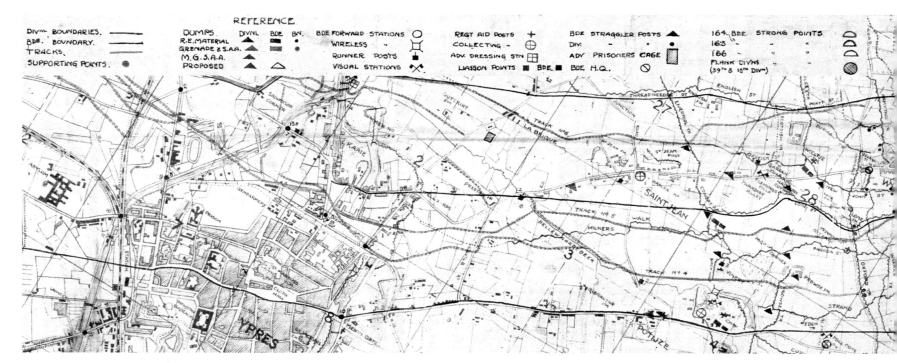

The action in the north had been a highly successful one for the French and British. The 38th (Welsh) Division post-battle report was one of the first to arrive at GHQ. It is an excellent indication of the variability and strength of German defences in front of Ypres. Survey teams noted no less than 280 concrete emplacements in the 38th Division sector alone – aside from the French attacking front, it was the weakest-defended sector of the entire battlefront.

2 AUGUST

Raining hard again. The men went out to clean up some of the concrete MG emplacements of the Bosch. We started on one in Hey Wood, a beauty, intact, concrete 6 feet thick, but in such a dirty state. We cleaned it up and built a sandbag

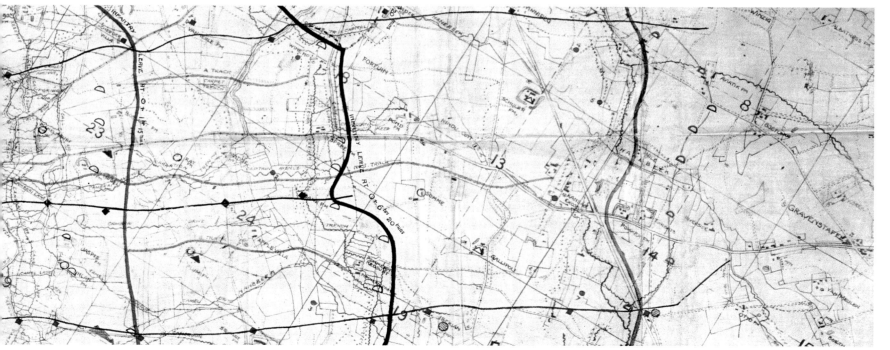

parapet in front of the door as it faced the wrong way. Mason and I went reconnoitring for others. In the 'Blue Line' there were dozens, full of water and wreckage. Some were sound, one had been shifted bodily by one of our big shells. This trench was in an awful state; we saw several dead Germans and in one dugout 2 wounded Germans, of whom we told the RAMC, so that they might clear. We looked too at several of the farms; the concrete in these was completely wiped out. The heavy shelling on this part and the heavy rain made the ground awful, up to your waist in mud. Finished the dugout at Hey Wood and made a reconnaissance of other concrete dugouts; nearly all were smashed. One we found full of German dead, dead for many days too. In another dugout, evidently an officers' mess, a shell had penetrated right through and killed the lot. There was a third instance of a dugout which evidently refused to surrender and, as the occupants came out, they were clubbed. There were 30 dead Huns outside this, all with their heads smashed in. As far as British dead, there were very few. I saw several Irish Guards and Grenadier Guards, one with his Bible in his hands.

LIEUTENANT HAROLD RIDSDALE, 76TH FIELD COMPANY, ROYAL ENGINEERS (GUARDS DIVISION)

Enemy dead were removed from useable pill-boxes to lie with those who had fallen in the open. Their interment would follow when labour became available, but always after burial of British casualties. This task was overseen by a Divisional Burial Officer (DBO). Under his command each brigade supplied an NCO and three men to guide infantry burial parties to their tasks, supervise the work, help properly mark graves, record personal details and gather the effects of each casualty. The interment itself was always attended by a chaplain. It was also usual for chaplains, dressed as ordinary soldiers without mark of rank or calling so as not to be a 'target', to go forward with their unit in attack. Their task was not to fight but help the wounded and medical teams.

I would be with the forward Aid Post in a dug-out on the site of a trench just a few hundred yards behind the actual fighting line. Like all other Officers I had to leave my Officer's tunic and Sam Browne belt behind and wear a Tommy's tunic when we went into action, as an Officer in the usual uniform was too much of a target for enemy snipers. This little Aid Post was run by an Aid Post Sergeant, a Corporal, and the M.O. (Medical Officer). It was to this forward Aid Post that men would come for an inspection and preliminary dressing of their wounds. When hard pressed I helped to cut away the clothing and expose the wound. The M.O. or Sergeant would apply a picric acid dressing and I would then write the label detailing the nature of the wound with the man's name and number and he would then be sent (or carried) down as opportunity offered to the Adjacent Dressing Station a little further down the Line. This was organised by the Field Ambulance attached to the Brigade – the 151st in our case. From there the men would be sent down to a C.C.S. (Casualty Clearing Station) and so right away down the line to a Base Hospital. I had to keep a Tally Book of all the cases treated in our Aid Post. In it I entered every man's name, rank and number, the nature of his wounds and the treatment given and the time of morphia, if administered. Sometimes a man was obviously dying and past all human aid. In this case I would do what I could to help him in his last moments, pray quietly with him, and if he expressed the wish, I would take down his last message and send it to his home. This was a very sad and sacred part of one's task and one about which it is obviously difficult to say much.

During the bitter Passchendaele fighting when the forward Aid Post occupied one half of a concrete Pill Box originally built by the Germans, no less than 376 men were treated during the three days and nights which we spent there.

REVEREND E.V. TANNER MC AND BAR, ATTACHED 2ND WORCESTERSHIRE REGIMENT

Above
Interior of a stretcher bearers' base near Boesinghe, with a casualty ready for burial. Note the stack of crosses on the right, and the bloodstained stretchers against the wall.

Below
31 July. A collecting post near an observation balloon position at a farm close to Elverdinghe Chateau. The first wounded troops of the battle are arriving for treatment.

One hundred and seventy-nine chaplains lost their lives during the war. Whereas ideally a body would be brought to a recognized burial ground, it was often necessary for hygiene reasons or because of local activity to bury men where they had fallen, and as soon as possible. Experience of previous summer fighting showed that simply by the action of flies a man could entirely disappear in eight days, leaving only a skeleton. When battlefield burials were necessary, names, numbers and locations (trench map references) of each casualty were taken and immediately passed on to the DBO. All personal items were removed and sent by post to relatives. It will be seen that a huge amount of correspondence developed upon the Chaplaincy.

There were not many occasions when the post did not bring with it a letter from some anxious or bereaved relative asking for information about their husband, brother or son.

And quite frequently something of this kind:-

'Dear Sir, I have just heard the terrible news that my boy has been killed in action. He was such a good lad, always cheerful and I do miss his cheery letters. Can you tell me what were his last words before he died (or) Can you send me the watch (or) ring) that he was wearing (or) I should be grateful if you could send me a photograph of his grave.

Poor souls, how little did they realise the awful conditions of modern warfare.

REVEREND E.V. TANNER MC AND BAR, ATTACHED 2ND WORCESTERSHIRE REGIMENT

It was battlefield graves, so often lost as a result of subsequent action, that generated the huge number of British headstones in the Salient simply inscribed with the words 'Known Unto God'. Their names will be among the 102,000 engraved on the three main memorials to the missing in the Ypres Salient – on the Menin Gate, in Tyne Cot Cemetery and at Ploegsteert. It is also the reason why such a small percentage of the remains that are still so regularly found today are identifiable. The 'lost' graves are poignant signs of every man's greatest fear, that of 'lying out': being wounded, unable to move, unable to attract attention, and exposed and alone in no man's land.

I noticed that the more experienced men made agreements with their pals, that whatever happened and no matter how bad things got, they wouldn't let each other lie out; if they could do anything at all, they would. They took terrible risks. I didn't know what it meant until we got to Yeepree because I'd not seen a big attack before, but they were there in hundreds, maybe thousands; bodies all over the battlefield. You knew all of them must have probably died in pain, but you know, you could cope with that sometimes, the pain, because the body does something that stops the pain reaching your brain. I can vouch for that myself when I was hit. So, no, it wasn't that, it wasn't a physical thing, it was being alone, especially at night, with the feeling that no one knew where you were and would never come and get you in. Men in agony make terrible sounds; you didn't seem to hear them during the day because there was always noise, but you knew they were there waiting for you. At night it was awful, just awful. It sounds callous but you prayed for a busy night so as to cover up those awful noises. The medical blokes did everything they could, they were out all night every night even though the risks were serious. Some of those lads at Ypres lay out for days before they were picked up. God knows how many never made it and died alone? Thousands? There was a horror in that for all of us. I can tell you, a lot of them lay there for months. We could see them still lying there in December, January, February.

PRIVATE BERT FEARNS, 2/6TH LANCASHIRE FUSILIERS

The 31st of July was just the first day of months of such agonies for both sides.

POST-MORTEM

5 AUGUST 1917

Dear Mamma,

I have been at the War. I have seen a battle. I will not say I liked it, and yet it was wonderful beyond all expression. Where to begin and what to tell you is the question. I was lucky to get a copy of yesterday's paper and saw in it an article by Philip Gibbs on our part in the operations of last week. He appears mainly to have been struck by words that 'loomed through the mist'. As for me, the thing that struck me most, and stuck to me most, was the mud. Imagine a belt of land to a depth of about a mile, all churned up into heaps and hollows so that scarcely any grass is visible. I would say that it looked as if it had been ploughed into furrows six feet deep and then harrowed, but it is not regular like that. Imagine next that into all the hollows has been poured a sort of thick soup, one to two feet deep, bridged in places by planks which almost always sink when you step on them. That is the ground we took from the Germans last Tuesday, and there our men had to stand in drizzling rain for six days and nights after the first advance. The shelter they had was only a pretence consisting of smashed dugouts.

I myself had a delightful little hole back in our own old trenches. But I used to visit the men and their Officers daily, and I know what they suffered. Some of them had to give in and limp with swollen feet to a more or less comfortable place further back. It is a wonder that any of them were able to stand it. Wet through for six days, legs caked in mud, boots reduced to paper, nerves on edge, sick with apprehension and shock, there they remained on the alert because their Officers were prepared to stick it with them, and their Officers cheered them up because they knew that it all depended on them. The whole place was floating in mud and heroism. As for the first assault on Tuesday morning, we were in that and we did so well as to earn the special congratulations of the General. We had casualties, and no congratulations except the approval of God are anything but a mockery to set against death and maiming, even of one man. I myself ran comparatively little danger, I am thinking of the Company. That was the pitiful side of the affair. The heartening side of it is in the fact of our success, and I think there is not a man of all the thousands here who is not pleased and proud that we did what we set out to do and prepared the way for more.

Then there is the wonderful side of it, the spectacle of the immense engine of War moving in perfect harmony – guns, infantry and 'tanks'. Of that I am not allowed to speak much, but I am certain that no man living has seen anything more wonderful than the sight I looked on last Tuesday. Some day I will spin you a long yarn about it all. Meantime I am indignant that you should have known at home better than we did out here when the attack was due to take place, and that London newspapers should publish in headlines what none but Commanding Officers are allowed to know in the army in the field. What an undisciplined public! What a weak Government! What a wonder if we win the War!

Best love to all.

From your affectionate son,

Willie

CAPTAIN WILLIAM FERRIE, 196TH MACHINE GUN COMPANY, 55TH (WEST LANCASHIRE) DIVISION

In the entry for Wednesday, 1 August, Sir Douglas Haig's diary records 31 July 1917 as a 'fine day's work'. The losses, about 27,000, are described as 'small', which by comparison to the numbers he had grown used to since the Somme, was a truth of sorts. Brigadier General Charteris appeared that same day with a report stating that German divisions were being swallowed up by continuing actions all across the Western Front, and that the first day's prisoners at Ypres proved to be of a 'poor stamp', with morale lower than any previously encountered. Their disintegration was assured if, as the Germans had failed to do at First Ypres, the

Above

A roadside dressing station near Boesinghe, 31 July. In the foreground an injured RAMC man is being treated by his colleagues.

British kept kicking at their door. Gough had already been given permission to carry on with operations as planned but with the rigid proviso that the British guns *must* this time dominate in all areas. For this to be at all feasible, said Lieutenant General Sir Herbert Uniacke, Fifth Army Artillery Commander, two full clear days were required for aerial observation and sound ranging. The RFC had struggled with the poor flying conditions, being forced to use klaxon horns to encourage troops on the ground, who were more and more inconspicuous in the mud as the day wore on, to light flares to reveal their positions – an unnatural thing to do when one is aware that the enemy too sought the self-same information. It seems apt that on this day of continuous and worsening rain Haig should also have attended another meeting about landings on the Belgian coast. His troops in the Salient would have benefited from being amphibian.

AUGUST 2ND

It rained all last night and the whole of today, with the natural result that everything was beastly wet, and the mud was muddier than ever. Our move is postponed on account of the ground being too soft to move the guns. We fired most of the day on the Hun back trenches.

AUGUST 3RD

Still raining. Great difficulty experienced with the guns owing to the trails and wheels sinking so deeply into the soft, wet ground. The whole battery had to heave on one gun every time it had to be pulled out to switch. Every conceivable means was adopted to try and prevent the trails sinking so deep, but none were very successful. Bundles of faggots and brushwood placed behind the trails, perhaps gave the best results. The men are having a very heavy time of it.
LIEUTENANT E.C. ALLFREE, 111TH SIEGE BATTERY, ROYAL GARRISON ARTILLERY

The extraordinary two-hour relocation of 39th Division's field guns on the morning of 31 July was a thing of memory already, a remarkable feat. But move again all guns must, for operation orders for two more thrusts were now issued by General Sir Hubert Gough. As for the tanks, they had many a skirmish to come, for despite the rash of broken machines strewn across the battlefield, and although seldom a battle-winner, their fire-drawing and pillbox-busting capabilities had certainly been valuable and saved many a life. Seventy-seven of the 117 machines employed on 31 July had ditched, most 'bellying' in the soft mud. The panoramas show how German gunners were now presented with splendidly visible and vulnerable targets, and plenty of time to destroy them. Major General Elles requested his machines should not be used again until conditions *improved* – the word was subject to individual interpretation, an interpretation that was not shared by General Gough and the Tank Corps.

The battlefront remained relatively quiet on 2 August except for two German counter-attacks on Pommern Redoubt. Both were driven off. It had not yet stopped raining for more than an hour or two and forecasts were suggesting continuing grim weather. Gough was therefore forced to keep his powder – and plans – dry, and wait. As he kicked his heels, Sir Douglas Haig accentuated the need for patience and ordered something the Germans were quite unable to contemplate – the relief of every division in the line. Not for the last time, sappers and medics were excluded.

THURSDAY AUGUST 2ND

A quiet day – very little shelling – still torrential rain. Cases are coming down more slowly now. Total stretcher cases up to 5 p.m.

today is 298. The real reason is that there are still scores of badly wounded up in the front line, but it is impossible to get them down owing to the sniping and machine gunning. Our bearers are getting very done up and I have had to draw on the whole of the reserve bearers from the 58th F.A. We had a lively time at Onraet tonight as Fritz gave us a gas shell bombardment. It was probably meant for the batteries but the wind brought it all over us as well. He was using the new mustard oil shell and our curtain did not keep much out. However there was plenty of wind and it didn't hang about long enough to do us any harm.

FRIDAY AUGUST 3RD

Still the same continual downpour. Things are getting desperate with the poor old Division and it seems as if we are not going to be relieved. The men are in a terrible condition and are living up to their waists in water and mud in the front line and shell holes and all the time are being heavily shelled and sniped. This morning the O.C. and 2 officer of the 43rd Fd. Amb. came up to see round the area and system of evacuation. They were in orders booked to arrive at 11 a.m. but I am blowed if they didn't come up at 10 a.m. whilst I was having breakfast after being up all night and I had to take them up to the R.A.P.'s at once. I wasn't at all pleased. It was very quiet, but raining torrents and I finally got back wet through and with nothing dry to get into. They didn't know when they were going to take over and obviously were not a bit keen at the idea at all and I don't blame them! The C.O. sent up a rum ration today which was a blessing and helped to warm the men up a bit. The Cheshire M.O. dropped in tonight and said they were relieving the Wilts later on tonight and that they had heard they were in for 4 days – also that the Division is in till the 12th – so we are resigning ourselves to the inevitable and consider that there won't be any need to relieve the division soon as there won't be any left to come out.

TUESDAY 7TH AUGUST.

We really are coming out tomorrow.
Major A.G.P. Hardwick MC, 59th Field Ambulance, 19th (Western) Division

The reason behind Major Hardwick's relief and delight was that on Saturday, 4 August all extant operation orders were cancelled. Concentration now centred not upon fighting but communicating.

4 AUGUST

The section was repairing the footbridges across the Canal, all of which had been smashed. We made two good ones and just at the end lost two men, Turner and Rossiter, Turner being seriously hit. The sun came out and it stopped raining, the first time for a week.
Lieutenant Harold Ridsdale, 76th Field Company, Royal Engineers (Guards Division)

The sun may have chosen to reappear on the 4th, but it was the 10th before Gough was able to crack his offensive whip again. In the meantime GHQ had learned of German reserves arriving from the Champagne front, the fresh divisions entering the central battleground in front of Zonnebeke, the sector considered to be most in need of bolstering to protect the Gheluvelt Plateau. What most concerned Sir Douglas Haig and his advisers now was that the next attack should be properly prepared and supported by artillery, the infantry not being allowed to stray beyond the guns as they had done in the initial foray, thereby presenting *Eingreif* troops with golden counter-attack options on a plate. Distances were halved. An advance of two thousand yards, less than two kilometres, was his maximum recommendation. And that advance *must*, he said, be against the Gheluvelt Plateau, for unless this was wrestled into British hands no move against the Passchendaele–Staden Ridge was ever going to be viable. On the battlefield men caught their breath, but hostile attention was persistent and sleep came without rest.

Below
German dead in their positions on the Pilckem Ridge severely damaged by the British bombardment. Photograph taken before the heavens opened during the afternoon of 31 July.

2ND AUGUST 1917

My dearest Dad and Mother,

I intended writing you quite a long letter but I feel too utterly fagged, after the adventures of the last two days. I have been sent down to the Transport Lines for a rest, but shall probably have to go up to relieve another officer tomorrow. I can't write anything of the details of the Battle but I can say that it is the most awful and ghastly affair imaginable and I pray to God that it ends this awful war. For a good description I commend you to Phillip Gibbs' article in the Daily Telegraph which is extremely good although no one can convey the horrors and awfulness of the real thing. I should be pleased if you will get me a Telegraph of August 1st and save it for me (or another paper of same date). Well, dears, I don't doubt that it will be a relief for you to know that so far God has seen fit to answer our prayers and brought me safely through. I also prayed that He would bring my Platoon through which He has also done. It was most remarkable but I had not a single casualty in my Platoon during the attack and only two Blighties afterwards. I prayed for strength to carry thro' with and that He would give me courage and I can honestly say that although I shuddered at some of the sights I never funked the stunt at all. The men were simply great and I was awfully proud to lead such men. Although I am very glad to be temporarily out of it I wouldn't have missed it, for everyone proclaims it to be the greatest battle of the War and as such the greatest Battle in the History of the World. May God grant that we may exploit our success and bring about the peace which we all so earnestly desire. Please wish Dil very many happy returns of the ninth for me and tell her I hope she likes her new career.

> *So long, dears, and don't worry. Love to all,*
> *Ever your own Boy,*
> *Glynne*

P.S. I am just going to remove some of the fur from my chin and the mud and blood of three awful days from my hands.

SECOND LIEUTENANT J.G. MORRIS, 16TH SHERWOOD FORESTERS

A new cadence of battle was forming. It was accompanied by the traditional lilt of cynicism.

The boys came out to join us and they looked the worst I had ever seen them. They were mostly caked with half-dried mud, very weary, unshaven and bedraggled. The conditions had been a worse enemy than the Germans, and they sank down where they were and fell asleep. The next day, after hours of cleaning their uniforms, they were in great form, knowing what they had left behind. When they heard the official communiqué of the battle, that 'all objectives were taken on a fifteen-mile front', they were astounded. They had thought it had been a wash-out. Two nights later the 11th Queen's relieved us and we went further back to the familiar camp at Scottish Wood where we were in reserve to the 123 Brigade. We were reorganised. And refitted out and so prepared to receive another visit from the red-capped staff of the Divisions, and of course, the parrot-like words of appreciation were delivered. Any one of us, by now, could have made the well-worn speech of appreciation, and probably have made them sound a little more humane. We all put a brave face on things but what a pity that the Staff did not pay us a visit some few days earlier.

RIFLEMAN GERALD V. DENNIS, 21ST KING'S ROYAL RIFLE CORPS (THE YEOMAN RIFLES)

A certain exhilaration and rush of optimism and faith always accompanied a big push, and there were not a few men who, believing an end might be in sight, had looked forward to 'proving themselves' in battle. Some found that they actually enjoyed the entire state of being at war.

JULY 27TH, 1917.

I was charmed to get a letter from you to-day and to hear that things are progressing so well. I was delighted to get the Illustrated Sporting and Dramatic News with the photographs of the Dulwich College O.T.C. How it does warm my heart to see even a photograph of the old College and its surroundings! I note that, barring Scottie and poor Kitter, there isn't much change in the officers of the Corps. What excellent fellows they are! Give my love to them all. Many thanks for the last parcel containing among many acceptable things a Gaboriau detective novel. I was very anxious to read this and compare it with good old Sherlock Holmes, whom I still worship as much as ever.

I have just completed two full continuous years of service in this country. Well, cheer-oh, old boy! Best luck and much love to you all!

P.S. – Have you ever reflected on the fact that, despite the horrors of the war, it is at least a big thing? I mean to say that in it one is brought face to face with realities. The follies, selfishness, luxury and general pettiness of the vile commercial sort of existence led by nine-tenths of the people of the world in peacetime are replaced in war by a savagery that is at least more honest and outspoken. Look at it this way: in peacetime one just lives one's own little life, engaged in trivialities, worrying about one's own comfort, about money matters, and all that sort of thing – just living for one's own self. What a sordid life it is! In war, on the other hand, even if you do get killed you only anticipate the inevitable by a few years in any case, and you have the satisfaction of knowing that you have 'pegged out' in the attempt to help

your country. You have, in fact, realised an ideal, which, as far as I can see, you very rarely do in ordinary life. The reason is that ordinary life runs on a commercial and selfish basis; if you want to 'get on', as the saying is, you can't keep your hands clean. Personally, I often rejoice that the War has come my way. It has made me realise what a petty thing life is. I think that the War has given to everyone a chance to 'get out of himself', as I might say. Of course, the other side of the picture is bound to occur to the imagination. But there! I have never been one to take the more melancholy point of view when there's a silver lining in the cloud. Certainly, speaking for myself, I can say that I have never in all my life experienced such a wild exhilaration as on the commencement of a big stunt, like the last April one for example. The excitement for the last half-hour or so before it is like nothing on earth. The only thing that compares with it are the few minutes before the start of a big school match. Well, cheer-oh!

LETTER TO HIS BROTHER FROM LIEUTENANT HENRY PAUL MAINWARING JONES, MACHINE GUN CORPS (ATTACHED TO TANK CORPS)

Jones' parents later wrote: 'This was our son's last letter. A few days later came a field postcard from

Above
When the rains came. Artillerymen faced colossal problems even when moving the lightest of field guns. At least thirty-two men are struggling here. A horse team stands by.

Below
These front-line trenches at Railway Wood formed 23 Brigade's (8th Division) jumping-off position on 31 July. Second Army pan 88, 11 September 1915.

him, bearing the date July 30, the day before the battle in which he was killed. After that, silence – a silence that will remain unbroken this side of the grave.'

Henry Jones is commemorated on the Menin Gate, Panel 56. The circumstances of his death were unusual, and first related to the family by his commanding officer, Major J.C. Haslam:

AUGUST 2ND, 1917

Your son went into action with his Tank, together with the remainder of the company, in the early morning of July 31st. He was killed by a bullet whilst advancing. From the evidence of his crew I gather he was unconscious for a short time, then died peacefully. I knew your son before he joined the Tanks. We were both in the 2nd Cavalry Brigade together. I was delighted when he joined my company. No officer of mine was more popular. He was efficient, very keen, and a most gallant gentleman. His crew loved him and would follow him anywhere. Such men as he are few and far between. I am certain he didn't know what fear was. Please accept the sympathy of the whole company and myself in your great loss. We shall ever honour his memory.

J.C. Haslam (Major), No. 7 Company, C Battalion, Tank Corps.

A member of Henry Jones's crew, Corporal D.C. Jenkins, also wrote in sympathy:

I have been asked by your son's crew to write to you, as I was his N.C.O. in the Tank. Your son, Lieut. H.P.M. Jones, was shot by a sniper. The bullet passed through the port-hole and entered your son's brain. Death was almost instantaneous. I and Lance-Corporal Millward, his driver, did all we could for your son, but he was beyond human help. His death is deeply felt not only by his own crew, but by the whole section. His crew miss him very much. It was a treat to have him on parade with us, as he was so jolly. We all loved him. Fate was against us to lose your son. He was the best officer in our company, and never will be replaced by one like him. I and the rest of the crew hope that you will accept our deepest sympathy in your sorrow.

These were just two of tens of thousands of letters of condolence to be written by commanders, colleagues and 'pals' during Third Ypres.

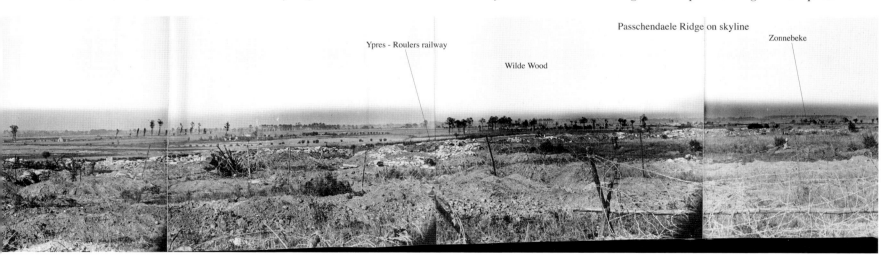

Ypres - Roulers railway

Wilde Wood

Passchendaele Ridge on skyline

Zonnebeke

CHAPTER NINE

Dog Days – August

3.8.17

Fritz is not taking it lying down, and although the country is in such a bad state that infantry operations are almost impossible, yet his artillery is particularly active especially on White Chateau and here (Spoil Bank). To go out of the sap is to court death, especially on the canal side. On that side I limit my journeys to one a day, viz. when I get water for a wash. This morning when I went out six pieces of shrapnel whizzed down within a few inches of me, and I was out less than a minute.
Sapper Albert Martin, 41st Signal Company,
Royal Engineers

Although much of the ground lost during Second Ypres was regained on 31 July, the statistic gratified few. Results were deeply disappointing and the cost as leaden as the weather. The Germans were certainly shaken, but their guns remained dangerously uncowed. And in the space of twelve hours the weather had helped create a mire that in impeding British activity and momentum would buy the enemy precious time to adjust tactics and dispositions. Although far from deep, the battle area that the British now occupied presented a logistical nightmare. Routes had ceased to exist, every hollow in the landscape was filled with water, and road metal – stone – simply disappeared in the apparently bottomless morass. Even the lightest of field guns soon became stranded.

The conditions greatly diminished the gunners' prospects, not only in the transport and stable laying of weapons, but their potential effect upon the backbone of German resistance – concrete. The pillbox defence was a modern variation of Vauban's classic geometrical fortress designs. Given a gritty garrison of defenders, they were capable of holding out until someone could get close enough to sling a charge or bomb through a door, embrasure or roof vent. With thousands of dispersed emplacements studding the projected British battle zone, each a miniature fort, their destruction by shelling now appeared as much a matter of luck as judgment. They were found interred along the lines of hedges, roads and ditches, within farm enclosures, and within houses, cottages and farm buildings, all lurking unseen and often undetected until their protective brick or earth 'shell' had been blown away. Curiously, the best indication of their presence was through latent signs of trench tramway lines used during construction. Even though the track itself had perhaps long been removed, a tell-tale trace on the ground was sometimes left, its profile being too regular for an infantry track.

It required no less than a direct hit by a large-calibre shell – at least 10-inch – and a hit *at the correct angle* (i.e. steepling howitzer fire) to have any true hope of neutralization. Glancing blows were ineffective. The very size of the emplacements – mere spots upon the landscape (the majority holding an average of a dozen men) – made it a huge challenge even with the great numbers of guns at the disposal of the British. It is interesting to note that most extant pillboxes in the Salient today show few battle scars. Many of the shattered examples one can find were not, in fact, damaged at all in 1914–1918. When the price of steel skyrocketed during the Korean conflict in the 1950s, hundreds were blown up to salvage the suddenly valuable steel joists used in roof construction. From 1920, when the populace began to return once more to farm the land, thousands were entirely erased, whilst many hundreds in more convenient positions were put to use as animal accommodation and storehouses. Ironically, during the early days of the Second World War, before the Dunkirk evacuations, they provided excellent protection from air attack – from both Allied and German planes.

In early August, Haig was typically sanguine about the problem of concrete. Regarding emplacements on the Gheluvelt Plateau that because of the weather could not at present be pinpointed by aerial photography (they had clearly also been unknown before battle), he noted that: 'Two German maps have luckily been captured, giving the exact positions. They can now easily be destroyed – but a 15-inch howitzer is necessary, as the emplacements are strongly built of cement. Jacob is quite confident of being able to capture and hold the ridge at his next attempt.' By the 18th of the month he had lost all such confidence. 'Easy' destruction of pillboxes in sodden conditions was optimism indeed – an Army Corps could expect to have no more than two 15-inch and half a dozen 12-inch guns on its books, and even these fearsome weapons relied largely upon luck. As fresh ground was occupied, Royal Engineers surveyed every aspect of the

Above right
Pillboxes exposed by shellfire.

Right
A diagram of a pillbox built inside a farm building. Such constructions were a common feature of German defences in the Salient, every farm being a potential candidate.

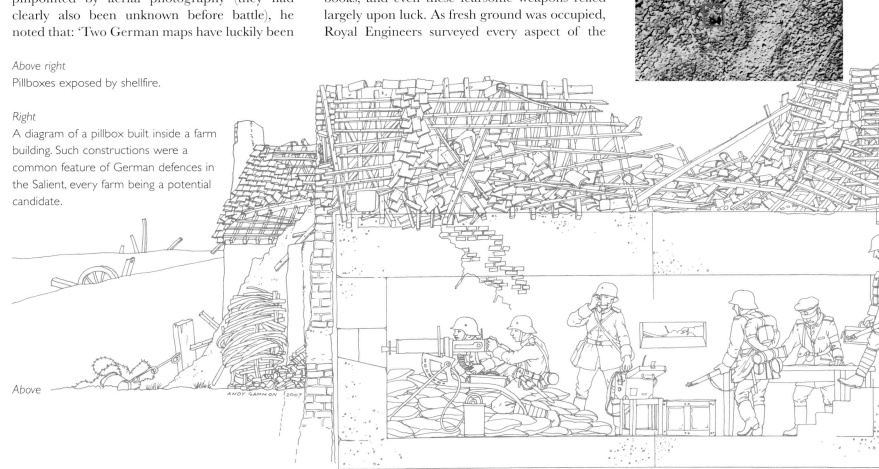

Above

ANDY GAMMON 2007

enemy defences, passing on reports to the Chief Engineer at GHQ. Their history later noted that:

Even a near miss by a 12-inch shell, exploding in the soft mud outside, would only tilt the block of concrete and leave it still in occupation. A direct hit on the roof would often kill all the occupants by concussion, but the enormous expenditure of ammunition required for the systematic destruction of so many of these strong-points resulted in further increasing the sea of mud. Time after time the assaulting infantry, after wading across the terrible ground, would find unsuspected machine-gun posts untouched by what had seemed a totally destructive bombardment.

Shelling, never as exact a science as required, often relied less upon accuracy than intensity, i.e. a 'destruction shoot' upon a strictly limited area. The more numerous the hardware – the guns – the more constrained and concentrated the barrage, and the more likely the chance of reducing resistance within that area. Indeed, this riot of shelling, though perhaps not demolishing concrete structures, could at least reveal secret locations by blowing away the camouflaging earth caps. The pillboxes could then be spotted from the air, registered and further molested by the guns, and, most importantly of all, incorporated in infantry attack plans. This became the prevailing approach.

It also had to be acknowledged that the Flanders geology and climate would, apart from localized achievements, ultimately defeat the tanks, and likewise make cavalry redundant. The great swathe of pillbox-studded ground could only be conquered – that is, occupied – by the military 'software' – troops.

For infantry ground attack the tacticians fell back upon the pre-war application of 'fire and movement'. The method was a simple though hazardous one requiring one party to maintain suppressing fire to keep enemy heads low whilst another moved stealthily forward to engage in close combat. Shell-hole strong points could be contained or neutralized by mortar and rifle-grenades, but pillboxes each demanded an individual approach: they were physically immune to small ordnance and, as an integral part of a resistance network, potentially defended by fire from a host of other emplacements, concrete and otherwise. Close co-operation between attacking parties was therefore crucial. Ypres offered as many opportunities for this gruesome contest as anywhere on the Western Front. The German defence was based upon the machine gun fired from within, upon or outside (in nearby shell holes) the emplacement. In these miniature, self-contained sieges – a battle within a battle – the Lewis gun was a key British weapon. Much lighter than a Vickers and far easier to man-handle, it could be fired from the hip if necessary. The plan was to approach close enough to engage a chosen position utilizing whatever cover was available, to a point where one could maintain accurate and persistent fire at embrasures and/or external garrisons, whilst riflemen and bombers crept around the flanks in a series of rushes from shell hole to shell hole. Except for the final stage – the close-contact coup de grâce – grenades had limited application. During a push, dozens, even hundreds, of these miniature offen-

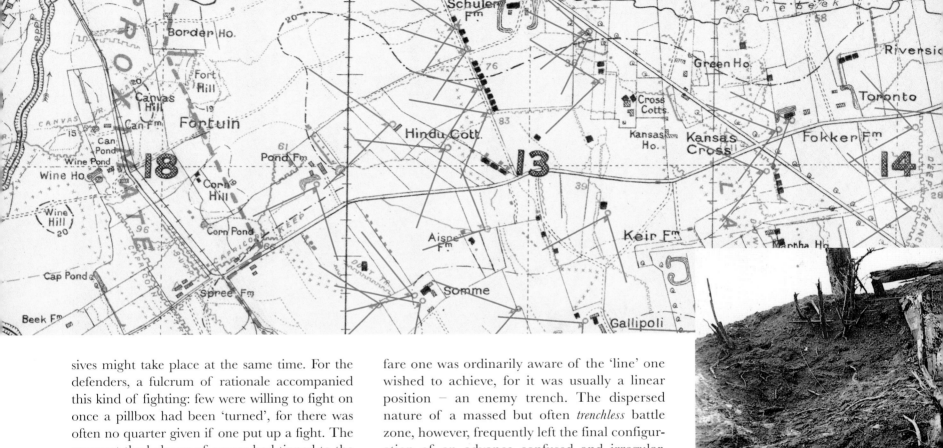

sives might take place at the same time. For the defenders, a fulcrum of rationale accompanied this kind of fighting: few were willing to fight on once a pillbox had been 'turned', for there was often no quarter given if one put up a fight. The moment the balance of power had tipped to the attacker, most garrisons found it was wise to concede. In one authenticated case British troops captured a pillbox to find the body of a German officer with his hands tied behind his back. The garrison had wished to surrender but their officer refused, whereupon the men tied him up, killed him and capitulated.

There was, however, a serious corollary to 'pillbox warfare'. In conventional trench war-

fare one was ordinarily aware of the 'line' one wished to achieve, for it was usually a linear position – an enemy trench. The dispersed nature of a massed but often *trenchless* battle zone, however, frequently left the final configuration of an advance confused and irregular. Whereas one pillbox might take minutes to dispose of, another could hold out for hours, even days in many instances. And once the chaos of combat had subsided, each individual attacking group was left with the problem of deciphering who owned which strongpoint. This was the serious predicament encountered in the central sectors on 31 July. Often the only way to differentiate the locations of friend and

Left
Trench map marked with the fields of fire of suspected German machine-gun. There were always more than expected. Note how many are in open ground. The dotted red line is the British front line.

Right
German batteries near Langemarck picked out by British counter-battery fire.

Below
The result of fire-and-movement tactics. British and German troops lie dead behind a pillbox.

foe was to deliberately expose oneself and wait for the result!

Once a 'line' had been annexed, the problem transferred to the other side. The deluge of high explosive sent over by the British to destroy emplacements and subdue and harass German defences was subsequently returned with interest, either in preparation for counter-attack or simply seeking to annihilate. The moment *any* force showed itself in the open, however, an SOS barrage, signalled to the guns either by telephone, Very light or rocket, could be expected (both sides tried to mimic each other's light signals to confuse the artillery). This was a rapid-response tactic, calling down high-intensity shelling usually employing a mix of shrapnel and high explosive. Given good conditions and communication such a barrage could practically wipe out a body of attacking troops, or at the very least seriously baulk their movement by its frightfulness. Hence the absolute necessity for effective counter-battery work *before* an attack took place. It was this tit-for-tat, split-second reactive gunnery that characterized the Third Ypres artillery campaign. As a result of the deluge of steel hurled back and forth during this battle especially, after the war the pastures of Flanders yielded – on first clearance alone – six unexploded shells per square metre.

Safety could be found underground, but there was no such accommodation in the August battle zone: in attacking on 31 July the British had passed beyond the critical interface separating security and severe peril. Those in support or reserve could still occupy the great dugout systems installed before battle, but thanks to the competence of German gunners, they too held idiosyncrasies and dangers.

12.8.17

The Huns have made some fierce counter-attacks on our left today but only treated us to the usual quality of shells. This evening we heard that we are to be relieved tomorrow. Thank God. Although we have spent most of our time in the comparative security of the saps [all-embracing RE term for tunnels/dugouts], this period in the line has been most trying and exhausting. By day and night the Hun has kept up a continual harassing fire, mainly of H.E.'s and gas shells. The entrances to the saps are covered at night with double gas curtains which are daily saturated with some mixture intended to neutralise the poison. They give a certain amount of protection but are not much good against persistent gas-shelling. Every night when the weather has been favourable Fritz has treated us to a heavy dose of gas-shells and each time the gas-guard has had to wake us and we have been compelled to wear our masks for a couple of hours at a stretch. We also use fans (pieces of thin wood on handles) to fan the gas out of the tunnels. Owing to the gas-curtains being kept down at night and the ventilation shafts being shut the air in the tunnels becomes most fetid. 70 or 80 men crowded in one of these galleries, many with wet clothes, and all in a filthy dirty condition, breathing the same air over and over again, their bodies stewing in the close damp atmosphere and exuding all manner of noxious odours – this alone is sufficient to make us ill. It is positively choking to enter the tunnels in the early morning, before the curtains have been raised and a draft created. You choke and splutter and gasp for breath, but if you have slept in

it you do not notice the aroma; you only realise that you have got a rotten headache and feel beastly sick. But foul air is better than poison gas, and dugouts are to be preferred to shell-holes.
SAPPER ALBERT MARTIN, 41ST SIGNAL COMPANY,
ROYAL ENGINEERS

This kind of indirect deterrent action was seen across the entire Salient, creating crises in feeding, resting, watering and relieving troops. Soon the Germans were to employ heavy delayed-action shells that penetrated to 10 metres or more before exploding, blowing in the dugouts or gassing (by the action of carbon monoxide) those sheltering inside. Outside, the risks were so great as to be incalculable, especially at night. No matter where one was working in the Salient, one could expect unwelcome attention from the German guns.

8.8.17

Had a tough business to get up the rations this evening. We met the transport at the brickstack and found that in addition to the rations was a very large quantity of stores which would mean us making three or four journeys. The Transport drivers are generally content with dumping the stuff off whether we are there or not and then getting back out of it at a gallop. I can't blame them for this is a most 'unhealthy' spot and Fritz has got the roadway taped to a nicety. However this evening Driver Ashford ASC [Army Service Corps] offered to try and get his G.S. Wagon over the shell holes up to the sap entrance. It was some game but in crossing a mixture of trench tramway lines and shellholes, one of the horses fell, the front of the wagon slithered into a shell hole, the rear got caught up in a broken tram rail and one of the wheels came off, while the rations and stores spread themselves about the country. This was cheerful as Fritz was bumping us pretty merrily. We set to and emptied the wagon and unharnessed the horses; then lifted the wagon up on to fairly level ground, replaced the wheel, turned the wagon around and put the horses in again. It was useless trying to

Above
Accurate German counter-battery fire falling upon camouflaged 8-inch howitzer positions near Boesinghe on 17 August.

Left
Equally accurate British work.

get the wagon up any further so it set off back again. I admire Ashford for attempting what none of the other drivers would think of doing. It was raining all the time and we were soon wet through. Before we came out I took the precaution of removing my shirt so that I should have something dry to put on when I returned. I fell into a shell hole with a heavy box of rations and the bacon got covered with mud.

SAPPER ALBERT MARTIN, 41ST SIGNAL COMPANY,
ROYAL ENGINEERS

In the tortured ground beyond the dump lines, the geology demanded especial respect and attention. The prime example of how adverse conditions so often crushed British aspirations can be found in the efforts of the sappers during the battle. Whereas in earlier actions the majority of Field, Tunnelling and Pioneer company troops would have been employed on constructing strong points, new trenches, dugouts, water supplies and other aspects of fieldwork requiring specific skills,

during Third Ypres almost the entire sapper establishment, plus tens of thousands of attached troops, were from the first day concerned solely with roads and tracks. Already it had become necessary to build double-width duckboard routes for the use of stretcher-bearer parties – four men per casualty was often the minimum. In a desperate effort to make them a little less visible, new timber boards were smeared with mud before laying. Because installing communication trenches in the forward zone was out of the question, infantry traffic could only be surface based. The extension of water pipelines, as seen in the extraordinary schemes installed on the Somme in 1916, was equally impracticable, for in the Salient there was no hiding from enemy eyes. Regardless of the climatic conditions, the desperate need for permanent work on roads and tracks throughout the battle led to the situation whereby even when divisions were relieved, Field and Pioneer companies were forced to remain behind simply to try to tackle the avalanche of labour required to rebuild what one's guns had had no choice but to destroy. Destroy and rebuild – the sequence was unavoidably interminable. As the weeks passed and the guns endlessly bellowed, the ribbon of devastation widened, making the task of transport drivers and sappers' practically Sisyphean.

BATTLES OF THE SPURS

And so it was within this new environment that Fifth Army continued their mission on 10 August. Rain had fallen every day but two since 31 July, and the ground conditions remained deplorable. Battered by German guns, again insufficiently suppressed, II Corps (18th and 25th

Divisions) attacked on a 3-kilometre front astride the Menin Road. Having worked in and around the line for almost a week the troops were drained before taking up their positions.

Hardly anyone slept that night. There was too much coming and going. Runners, stretcher-bearers, gunner officers, signallers, Stoke mortar teams, and others made perpetual traffic during the darkness. I sat up and wrote a last letter home by shaded torch-light. A dismal epistle, in the form of a last will and testament. Then and there I could do nothing better. Even the ridge we had left looked impossible to get back over, and I was about to go the other way, forward into the more concentrated blast of an attack in a few hours.

The sergeant roused everyone an hour before zero, and repeated orders to sections. Rum was issued. I went along to inspect the men. Bayonets were fixed, cartridge clips and grenade pins loosened. Some men had collected boxes, others had dug holes in the trench side, or placed small ladders to help them to clamber out. They stood facing the parapet, jaw muscles rigid, bayonet-points under cover – waiting. At two minutes to zero I took a good swig of neat whisky, saw the nearest men all tensed ready to climb out, and put my whistle to my lips. My heart thumped heavily.

Second Lieutenant John Lucy, 2nd Royal Irish Rifles

The objective was to make a firm lodgement on the Gheluvelt Plateau, General Gough requiring an advance of around 800 metres. Despite facing an even more exhausted and traumatized enemy that had been in the line since before 31 July, results were meagre, largely due to the German 'secret weapon' – the counter-attack. The British failed to progress anywhere more than 400 metres, failing completely on the right-hand half of the front. The only joy was in 74 Brigade's (25th Division) capture of Westhoek, a tiny hamlet

beyond the Bellewaerde Ridge that had temporarily been in British hands on 31 July. Once more, confusion dominated the undertaking.

Exactly to the second pandemonium broke loose. I blew my whistle and was up and over, looking back to see my trench rapidly emptying. Only two men were still struggling to get out – slipped off boxes or something. Good enough for me. I broke forward into a trot, gripped my whistle between my teeth, pulled a bomb from my haversack, and threw away the pin . . . My boots struck hard on road metal – part of Westhoek, and I did not know it. There was not a brick left upon a brick. Now I became exhilarated. My men appeared to be going well. On my right they were in advance

Above
Royal Engineers using barges as a bridge base to traverse the canal near Ypres. This is Bridge 4 at Essex Farm.

Above
Captain W.F.C. Holden's painting of Bridge 4 looking from the opposite bank. The cutting through the embankment still exists. Holden worked with the RE camouflage service.

Right
The original Bridge 4 pictured in high summer 1915. It was still in use (for foot traffic only) during the 1917 battles, crossing the canal adjacent to the heavy bridge above.

of me, and some of them had entered our own creeping barrage . . . Before us a heavy pall of smoke hid the German position. Dim figures with hands up tottered towards us out of the clouds. We waved them on to the British line. Then the British barrage checked according to plan. The sudden withdrawal of that tumultuous noise gave me a physical shock, and gave me the sensation of being deaf. I found myself with about twelve men standing where a German trench had been. Battle gear and odd rags of uniform lay scattered about the torn earth. Parts of bodies stuck into the air above a zig-zag grave – the trench. Only a few small groups of enemy, most of them bareheaded, came to us with hands upstretched. We waved them away back to our lines. They thanked us in gestures with their descending arms . . .

On my left my Lewis gun section clambered on to the roof of a German pill-box, and one of our own shells came and blew the whole team off it. Most of them rose and appeared to be unhurt. The pill-box was occupied by Germans, who began to stream out, hands in air. A young subaltern suddenly appeared from the left attracted by the procession, and went to meet the Germans, poking his gun at them. A tall German officer suddenly stepped forward from behind his men, fired his parabellum at our officer, and missed him. The subaltern fired back, but his hammer clicked on an empty case. He coldly broke his gun, loaded up, and killed the enemy officer. The German men scattered like hens in fear. The young officer collected and counted them, and gave a signed note to one of them showing he had captured them . . . The country in front was remarkably quiet. One silly British gun kept placing a shell on the ground behind our backs. The co-operation aeroplane suddenly appeared from the rear, flying very low, and I lit three flares. It wheeled away right.

SECOND LIEUTENANT JOHN LUCY, 2ND ROYAL IRISH RIFLES

If Westhoek was the sole advance of the day, it meant that units to either side of John Lucy's sortie had made no progress. The line was therefore fractured, putting his vanguard party in danger of being outflanked.

Collins, wounded through the arm, came up and said: 'Hallo, Luce. How goes it?' I told him. Then he asked quizzingly: 'Have you any idea where you are?' I said: 'Not the faintest.' 'Well,' he said, 'all the other platoons are behind you, and you had better get back into line, you have gone too far forward.' This surprised me, and at the time I could only feel foolish at being carried away by the excitement of the attack. About now the Germans realized that they had lost their trenches, and they opened with their guns on the captured ground. I moved back with six men, and told the sergeant to cover me from any ground attack, and to follow with the rest. We lost four or five men in that simple operation, and it was only when I got back in line with the other platoons that I saw I had

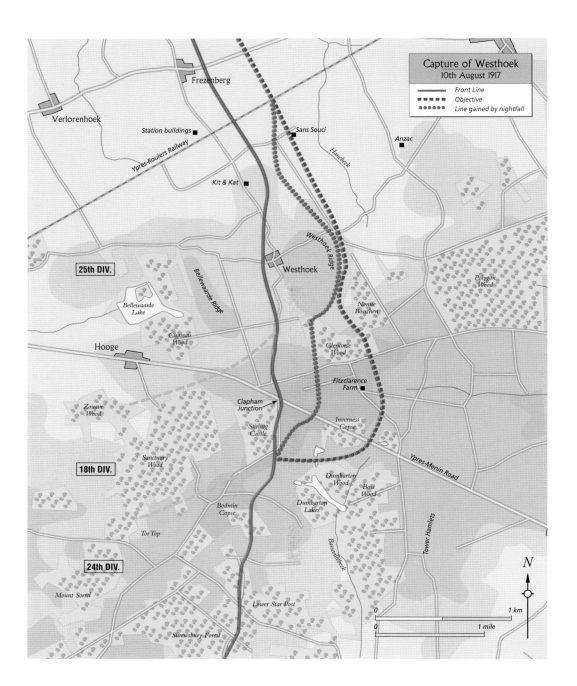

Left

The small but costly 25th Division advance that annexed the village of Westhoek on 10 August.

but eight men left out of thirty.

The ground about showed the reason. It was covered with a close network of concrete pill-boxes, whose garrisons must have raked us with machine-gun fire as we passed through. We took station in a small trench on the British side of one of the captured pill-boxes. Exhaustion and reaction came now. We dug a little to improve the post. Stretcher-bearers appeared from the rear, and moved openly across country collecting the wounded. My little command slumped down and most of them fell asleep. One man had to be dragged into the trench from the open, where he lay spread-eagled on his back, snoring loudly under a fresh enemy bombardment which increased in volume and intensity every moment.

We were relieved that night and marched back from Ypres to rest and reorganize in billets – a small unit of seven officers and one hundred and forty men.

SECOND LIEUTENANT JOHN LUCY, 2ND ROYAL IRISH RIFLES

On Lucy's right flank, a decent initial incursion into the plantations of Inverness Copse and Glencorse Wood once more struggled to hold out; the British were forced back to positions on exposed ground in front of the woods. By midday the shoulder of the plateau had not yet been gained and though many appeared tired and drawn the performance of the German guns indicated their line was far from crumbling. There were more than 2,200 British casualties on the day. It was chaotic and dispiriting.

Men of our Battalion kept straggling back all day. There were men from every one of our Coys., and they said they had been 'led wrongly' by their officers when the Battalion had moved up, had got lost, been 'spotted' by Fritz and heavily shelled, then getting scattered and more 'lost' than ever. Many had been on other Divisions' fronts, some had wandered into Ypres etc, etc. One of our officers was reported to have blown out his brains on discov-

ering that he had missed the right road. Altogether, about 70 of our men came back to the camp. From their various stories we gathered that the Battalion was badly disorganised and scattered all over the place. They should have 'gone over' that morning, but were not in their proper position when the barrage started.

PRIVATE S.T. FULLER, 8TH SUFFOLK REGIMENT

Strangely, Haig did not countermand Gough when he proposed plans for his next step, set for 14 August. Despite agreeing and acceding to his C-in-C's explicit requirement that all efforts must be concentrated upon annexing the plateau, he now decided to tackle almost the same battlefront as 31 July: a huge assault stretching from Bixschoote in the north (again involving Anthoine's French on the left flank) to beyond the Menin Road. Five British corps incorporating nine divisions were to be involved. The key point was that the plans had been founded upon the expectation of greater British success during the 10 August venture. Haig uttered not a murmur. Did this signify tacit agreement? Gough, although postponing the assault for forty-eight hours, carried on regardless. In correspondence with British Official Historian Sir James Edmonds during the Second World War, Gough maintained that the plans had not only been agreed by Haig, but encouraged.

LANGEMARCK: 16–18 AUGUST

AUGUST 16TH

I was called at 4 a.m. It was still quite dark. I got up, fetched the necessary particulars of the lines and elevations which we had worked out last night, from the map room; gave the battery 'Action', and saw each gun properly laid. At 4.45 a.m. our first shells were to burst on the appointed targets; so at 4.44.30 a.m. (allowing 30 seconds for the calculated time of flight) I gave the

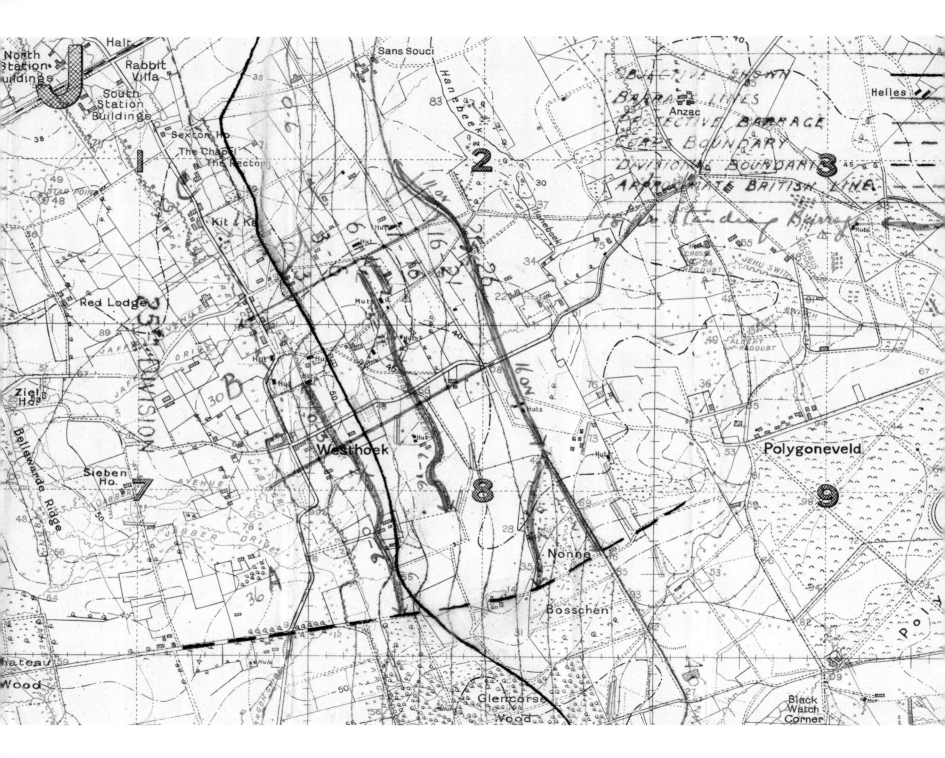

Left
25th Division's barrage for their Westhoek venture.

Below
Mr Harry Patch of 7th Duke of Cornwall's Light Infantry, 20th (Light) Division, is believed to be Britain's last surviving infantry veteran of Third Ypres. Mr Patch crossed the Steenbeek to attack Langemarck on 16 August. See also page 135.

order 'Fire' and the barrage had started, and the Infantry were 'going over the top'. I remained on duty till 8.30 a.m. lifting the barrage at the appointed times. We had the satisfaction of hearing, later in the day, that the Infantry had gained their objectives with comparatively light casualties. They had advanced over the River Steenbeek, and captured Langemarck.

Lieutenant E.C. Allfree, 111th Siege Battery, Royal Garrison Artillery

The Battle of Langemarck began at 4.45 a.m. on 16 August. Although it dawned a dry but overcast morning, the two previous days had seen heavy rain; ground conditions were still dreadful. Like the Westhoek garrisons, many German units, especially those facing the left and central sectors of the attacks, had served in these trenches without a break since 31 July; they were utterly worn out. As luck would have it, the British attack fell precisely as they were at long last being relieved. Anthoine's French, once more presented with limited objectives, again achieved complete success, advancing up to the St Jansbeek with only 350 casualties. It is said that the overwhelming concentration of heavy guns was the root of this success, but in fact their artillery was also busy assisting both the Belgians to the north and units on the British left flank. With this high-explosive support, Cavan's XIV Corps obliged by capturing the bastion of Langemarck and consolidating almost a kilometre beyond on the spur between the Steenbeek and Kortebeek.

Dear Mother,
Your prayers, I think, have been answered, and I have come through all right. We had a grand day and took all the objectives allotted to us. On our part of the front the whole thing was a great success. We had the Boche absolutely snookered. One part of our line was held up by a strong point and the Regiment in front could not get on, so B Company came to their rescue, and took it for them and forty prisoners. We then pushed on and took our own objective and two machine-guns. We had great sport. Afterwards they tried to form up to counter-attack us and we absolutely smashed them with our machine-gun and rifle fire. I shot dead five Prussian guardsmen, one of whom was not killed at once, but died in a few moments after we got there. He seemed a bit fed up about it.

Captain Walter Ewbank MC & bar, 1st Border Regiment

Cavan had been shrewd: although there was nothing he could to do ameliorate the going for his troops, each had been issued with a clean replacement rifle. One man attacking on this day was Harry Patch, part of a Lewis Gun team in the 7th Duke of Cornwall's Light Infantry, and at the time of writing believed to be the last surviving Great War veteran to have served in the infantry during Third Ypres.

On Cavan's right, straddling the St Julien village sector, Maxse's XVIII Corps once more had prepared another assault on the same ground as Z-day. During 31 July they had been forced to withdraw to the village itself, and since then the Germans had re-established solid defences. British gunfire was weaker here than on the left flank, and yet again enemy batteries were insufficiently checked despite improved observing weather. Plodding through the morass either side of the Steenbeek, the infantry were almost entirely neutralized by concentrated enemy SOS barrages. The action exemplified how von Lossberg's battle zone had been designed to function. It produced a heavy casualty list, and an uncharacteristic and deeply troubling setback for Maxse, recognized as one of the most meticulous

Left and opposite
Langemarck village with the largest
German military cemetery circled,
Langemarck Nord, which before the
battle contained 10,143 marked graves.
The aerial photograph on the left was
taken in June 1917 when the cemetery
was relatively undamaged. The picture on
the *right* is from August: the site has been
swept away. The powerful Wilhelm
Stellung positions run along the top of
the cemetery – see also pages 220-1.
Inset top: the pulverized remains of
Langemarck Church and (*below*) as it was
shortly before the battle.

Below
Another sketch to assist the British
infantry.

Langemarck   Church
Sheet 20U 22 d 72

planners in the British Army. Other aspects of the attack also pointed to the future complexion of battle: beyond St Julien just a handful of strong points had been able to stymie the advance. As soon as was feasible the tanks would be sent in to deal with the problem, but with September and autumn knocking at the door their utility was likely to be short-lived.

The most awkward sectors on 16 August belonged to Watts's XIX Corps, attacking the high ground of Hills 35 and 37 protecting Zonnebeke, plus the spurs reaching down eastwards from the Gheluvelt Plateau towards the Ypres–Roulers railway.

When we first went up in the gathering night, Ypres was a wonderful, terrible and heart-rending sight. A mass of ruins and that is all, but one saw visions of the Cloth Hall as it used to be. And now – a gaunt brick wall on one side; the rest – heaped up debris. Then the barrage on the morning of the attack [16th August].

At 4.30–5 am it was getting light and the horizon – the line – was a dazzling line of rushing light of all shades – blue, red and yellow predominantly. One thought of the Germans and it seemed wonderful that any could live through such a terrible inferno. These barrages make me personally feel exultant, horrified, tremendously strong and capable of doing anything, bitterly resentful against the war and the awfulness of it and almost fiendishly glad at the strength of our guns and of the terror of the Germans. Until one thinks of what is to follow!

The sights – awful. Dead horses, some blown to pieces, others with their entrails spattered all over the road. Blood, mud, filth, frightful smells, shattered men – one sees but passes them by almost without a shudder. One eats ones food beside dead men without a thought, where, before the war, the very thought would have turned one sick. One sees one's own comrades killed and lying in pools of water, face downwards – it is all terrible but fortunately perhaps one does not feel it extremely.

By six o'clock the casualties were coming down fast and we were kept very busy indeed loading and unloading cars and giving a hand wherever needed until after 10 am. I was then told to turn in until 8 pm and had just got my puttees off when I was hauled out again and ten of us (2/1st) were sent up further to be attached to the 3rd Londons. We went up the Menin Road as far as the Hooge Tunnel. Before getting into*

* The Hooge Tunnel was a German-built structure. Installed during 1915 it ran at a depth of 3 metres beneath the Menin Road from Hooge to beyond the crest of the plateau between Clapham Junction and Gheluvelt. The tunnel allowed unobserved access and egress to and from the front line.

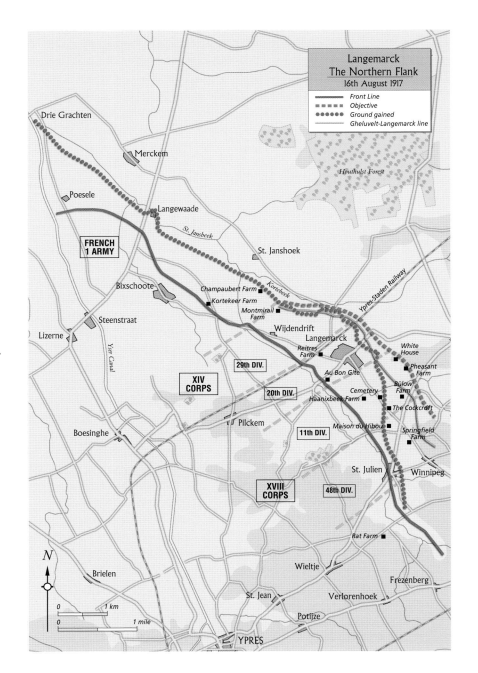

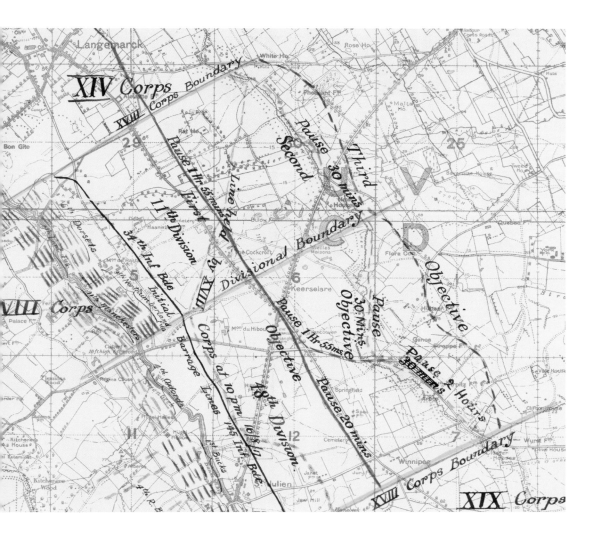

Above
11th and 48th Divisions' forming-up positions and objectives for 16 August attack.

Left
The results of British 16 August endeavours on the northern flank.

the tunnel we had a most unpleasant 20 minutes hugging the earth in a more or less filled in trench. The Bosche evidently saw us for he sent over salvoes of whiz bangs which almost brushed our hair and I expected any moment we would get one in our midst. Yet we dared not move for fear of getting them right at us. Finally we were able, in a momentary lull, to dash back to the tunnel – quite a wonderful place this – about 6 feet high and 3 to 4 feet wide, splendidly made and fitted with innumerable wires. Here one was in comparative safety for direct hits seemed only to shake the place. But the atmosphere was terrible. We found we had had all our trouble for nothing for we had come the wrong way and had to retrace our steps to Hooge Crater where we found a German concrete place with the officer we were seeking inside. After some tea we went from there, up through Chateau Wood to the Aid Post and there had another unpleasant half hour's sitting in a scooped out hole waiting for cases. This time they sent over 5.9's that literally shook the earth all around. However no harm came to us and finally we got down with a case and stayed the night in the concrete 'dugout'. It was a most uncomfortable night as we were packed like sardines but we couldn't grumble as we were safe, 5 direct hits on top failing to do more than shake the place.

On the way up to the Aid Post in the evening we met people rushing back saying 'you can't possibly go up there. It's murder, the Germans are advancing and everyone is being killed.'
Private H.L. Chase MM, 2/1st London Field Ambulance, RAMC

Almost every British assault was crushed. Small gains were made on the boundary where Watts's Corps adjoined Maxse's east of St Julien, but that was it. As the troops battled through the mud and uncut wire, for the guns had performed especially poorly here, the creeping barrage crept away too swiftly, leaving large bodies of men exposed. In addition Watts's troops had spent too long in the line, were seriously under establishment, and had squandered precious energy toiling on engineering and supply work before going into action. And they had been presented with an uphill climb towards the most heavily fortified sector of the 16 August battlefront. Every one of the numerous farms dotting the contours was a bastion and only a handful had been neutralized by British shellfire.

It was time to be off. The enemy was putting down a heavy bombardment in front of us, but most of the shells were falling in the same places, and before leaving the safety of the trench we worked out a zig-zag course for ourselves, so as to avoid them. We tacked across the sea of death. In a straight line we had only a thousand yards to go, but it took us nearly an hour. The sun came up above the horizon in front of us as we were going. The long summer day had begun.

Up to this time everything had gone well for us. We had arrived at Bank Farm, we were in good time, our party had suffered no casualties, we had not even been particularly frightened, none of the shells had fallen close to us. Now we were to go up the slope on the other side and find out where our infantry had got to.

But we never went beyond Bank Farm. I saw one of our machine guns firing from a trench at a short distance on our right. If the attack had been successful there ought to have been no German within range of a machine gun from here by this time. And machine guns were generally fired over open sights. If those gunners could see the enemy then he could see us. Vernon also had seen the machine gun firing and had drawn his own conclusions. 'We'd better find out what's happened before we go any further,' he said.

We separated. There were plenty of people to ask, but no one could tell me much. No one that I saw was doing anything, everyone looked as though he was wondering what to do, except those who had already decided to do nothing. Then I saw Tommy Rust, one of A Battery's officers, and a friend of mine. I knew he had come up the night before, he was acting as liaison officer to the infantry, he would be able to tell me. He was a very smiley person as a rule, but he did not smile now. It had been all right at first, he said; then the infantry had met a counter-attack;

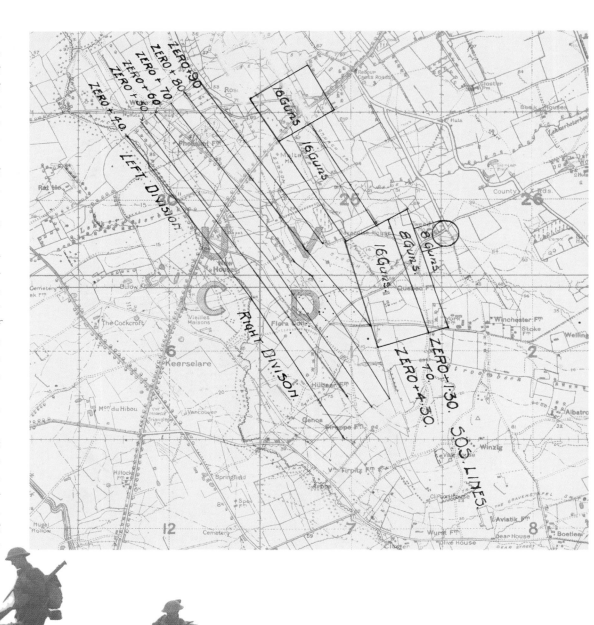

Above
German sniper and observer in action from breastworks near Langemarck.

Left
XVIII Corps machine-gun barrage plan to cover the advance of their two divisions on 16 August. Note specific targets for selected numbers of guns at different times after zero and that most of the fire is to be directed beyond the final objective.

Left
20th (Light) Division troops advancing at Langemarck on 16 August.

and the pill-boxes had shot at them from behind.

'We must tell Brigade what's happened,' I said.

'We can't,' Vernon said, 'there's no line.'

'Is it down?' I asked. I thought he meant it had been cut by shellfire.

'I don't think it's ever been up.'

'What do you mean?'

'I don't think there's ever been a line back from here.'

So there was nothing we could do. The attack had failed, our men were back where they had started. All our guns would be doing no good at all. Adding on a hundred yards to their range every few minutes as though the infantry were close up to the curtain of fire. But the infantry was back here, what was left of them.

SECOND LIEUTENANT P.J. CAMPBELL, 150 BRIGADE, ROYAL FIELD ARTILLERY

Gains were minuscule and practically worthless, losses shocking, but worst of all was the severity of German gunfire. The British counter-battery work, although benefiting from a few days clear weather, appeared to have failed, and communication had almost completely broken down. Alongside units to left and right, P.J. Campbell and his colleagues only managed to reach the original British jumping-off positions before coming under most severe shellfire.

There were two pillboxes at Bank Farm, both very strong, but one was the headquarters of the infantry battalion, the other a dressing station. There was no room for us in either. There was a trench at the side of the pill-boxes, but it was so wide and shallow that it was almost useless for protection. But in one place there was a low wall beside the trench. It was on the wrong side of the trench, the non-German side, so that one was completely exposed on the side from which the shells were coming, but it was better than nothing, and we made our way to it quickly. Half a

dozen other artillery officers were already there, sheltering behind it. We joined them, crouching down at the bottom of the shallow trench, with the wall behind us. I was at one end, Vernon was next to me. I did not know where our signallers were, I hoped they had found some sort of shelter, but the shelling was too heavy to go and look for them. I hoped it would only last for five or ten minutes, concentrated shelling was usually over in a short time. But it went on. Some of the shells fell very close, and they were big ones. I flattened myself against the earth and the wall. The dressing station was about twenty yards from me, on my right, I was the nearest one to it. There was not room inside for all the wounded men who had been brought there. Some had to be left outside, or were taken outside if they were hopeless cases. They were a long time dying. Unconscious they may have been, but they heard the shells coming. Their crying rose to a scream as they heard the sound of one coming, then fell away to a moan after the shell had burst. I learnt to distinguish the different crying voices. Sometimes one stopped, and did not start again. It was a relief when this happened, the pain of the crying was unendurable. But there were new voices. The crying never stopped, the shelling never stopped. Then I stopped noticing the crying voices. I was conscious only of my own misery. I lost all count of the shells and all count of time. There was no past to remember or future to think about. Only the present. The present agony of waiting, waiting for the shell that was coming to destroy us, waiting to die. I did not speak to Vernon, Vernon did not speak to me. None of us spoke. I had shut my eyes, I saw nothing. But I could not shut my ears, I heard everything, the screaming of the shells, the screams of pain, the terrifying explosions, the vicious fragments of iron rushing downwards, biting deeply into the earth all round us. I could not move, I had lost all power over my limbs. My heart throbbed, my face was burning, my throat was parched. I wanted a drink, there was lime juice in my water-bottle on my back, but I could not move my arm to pull it towards me. I could think of nothing but my own suffering.

SECOND LIEUTENANT P.J. CAMPBELL, 150 BRIGADE, ROYAL FIELD ARTILLERY

From near Pommern Castle
23/24 August 1917
Sheet 28 D 19 a central

Wieltje - Passchendaele Road

Martha House

Kansas Cross

Passchendaele   Ri

Passchenda

Passchenda

By mid-afternoon the battle was all but over.

We went outside. It might be more dangerous out there, but I could not endure the moaning of the dying man. I'd had as much as I could stand for one day. Anyway, we had been told to look out for enemy movement. We found a place about a hundred yards in front of the pill-box, and our signallers laid out a line to it from the telephone pit. There was a small patch of flat ground on which we could lie down and a shell-hole close to it in which we could shelter if we had to. But we did not have to use it, no other shells fell close, the peace and stillness of a summer afternoon seemed to have descended on the battlefield. There was peace behind the German lines also; I could see no movement anywhere. Down the hill to Bank Farm, up again on the other side. Somme, Gallipoli, Iberian – there they were, low grey slabs of stone in a desert place, like the huts of primitive man. And beyond that ridge there were other ridges. I counted three or four, there was grass on the furthest one. I could see grass and trees and red brick houses, the village of Passchendaele again. Some way to the right, but almost due east of where we were lying, a grey obelisk stood out on a hillside. That was Zonnebeke church, all that was left of it, the village had gone, only this one wall of the

church remained. The sun beat down on us, there was no shade anywhere on the battlefield, there was no variety of colour, just the hard brown of sun-baked mud.

SECOND LIEUTENANT P.J. CAMPBELL, 150 BRIGADE, ROYAL FIELD ARTILLERY

The right flank again belonged to Sir Claud Jacob's II Corps. His attacks went in with scant acquaintance with the exact positions or quantity of enemy strong points and without being aware that the Germans had created a new forward outpost zone. Initial progress, dictated of course by a creeping barrage, was acceptable. Then the troops hit bad ground and once again the shield of bursting shells absconded into the distance. Now, *Eingreif* troops fell upon the British. In the entire attacking sector a few yards were snatched in just two spots, astride the railway and in front of Westhoek village. Still the plateau glowered down upon a Fifth Army that by the end of the day was 15,000 men lighter. The final British positions were more indistinct than ever.

Above
Fifth Army pan 117. The view from the high ground of Hill 35 looking towards the Passchendaele and Broodseinde ridge. This territory was attacked by 55th and 15th Divisions on 31 July, but not captured (by 55th Div) until 20 September.

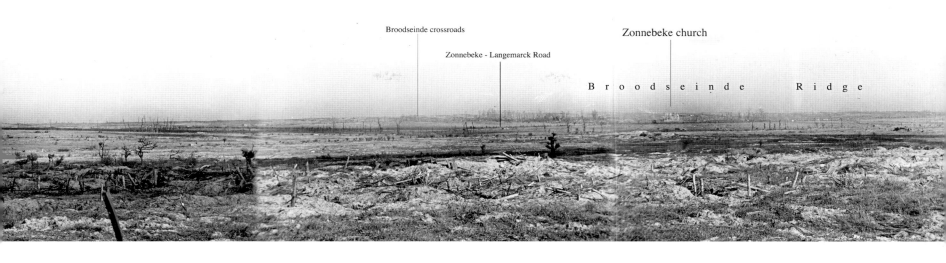

Broodseinde crossroads

Zonnebeke - Langemarck Road

Zonnebeke church

B r o o d s e i n d e   R i d g e

Below
Eingreif troops await the call.

16 AUGUST 1917

Before tea I learnt through the Battalion orderly room that all had not gone well as we had been held up by strong points and pill boxes such as Mon du Hibou, Springfield, Winnipeg etc., chiefly I think owing to no tanks having been used and that our consolidating parties (5 platoons from A, C and D Companies) had suffered very badly in casualties having to lie out in the open till they were required; Cecil Langham, the C.O's son who was i/c of the whole party has been killed which is awfully sad and will be a great blow to the colonel [Captain C.R. Langham, 5th Royal Sussex Regiment, died 16/08/17, buried Vlamertinghe New Military Cemetery] and Green (a sub in D Coy) is missing, believed killed. As the parties have not all arrived back yet it is still impossible to give any figures. During the afternoon I started getting diarrhoea which is a beastly nuisance. After tea at 6 p.m. I relieved Cole on the O.P. for the night, getting up there without trouble and passing some of the remnants of our D Coy consolidating troops returning. I found the view from the O.P. was much changed; the country in front of the Langemarck ridge was utterly strafed and Poelcapelle church as a habitable structure no longer existed, however the Bosche were still in the Langemarck line for I could see *them moving about in small bodies on the ridge before the light faded. We apparently now hold a line back on the Steenbeek on the left, opposite Mon du Hibou, Triangle Farm, and then along about 400 feet in front of the river though everything is uncertain and neither the enemy or ourselves know exactly where we are.*

LIEUTENANT GERALD BRUNSKILL, 5TH ROYAL SUSSEX REGIMENT (CINQUE PORTS BATTALION), ATTACHED TO XVIII CORPS RAILWAY CONSTRUCTION

Langemarck, captured by 20th (Light) Division, was the sole bright spot in a dismal day. It has been said that Gough attempted to blame the failure on the Irish troops of 16th and 36th Divisions, who apparently 'did not like the enemy's shelling'. They sustained almost 8,000 casualties. Yet Gough's alleged sequence of denigrating remarks about these units (Watts too had indicated his displeasure to the C-in-C) did not gel with the reports Haig was receiving about the two units being subjected to exhausting pre-battle activities, a full day's fighting without relief, and the ineffectiveness of British artillery. So the C-in-C's dismissal of the disappointing results was typically blithe. Although just a handful of British units had been able to achieve their designated objective, he dubbed it an 'undoubted success'. The conclusion was based not upon territorial gain, but the perceived scale of destruction of German manpower and the disruption of several counter-attacks. His indissoluble optimism was brilliantly illustrated on 19 August when at a meeting with senior staff officers he yet again suggested that final victory was 'near' and could be achieved by Christmas – if the present attrition rate could be sustained and British troop numbers constantly augmented. Did it mean he had shelved the possibility of breakthrough? The following day Charteris told Haig that a full twenty-nine German divisions had already been 'exhausted' in Flanders, reiterating the 'inferiority' of replacement units. Why, after three weeks of bitter fighting, this had not been reflected by greater success, was not mentioned. Haig's diary during this strange period of indetermination is full of 'ifs': *if* the weather had been finer, *if* the guns had performed better, *if* he had had more luck during earlier encounters, *if* an original scheme had been employed, *if* the RFC had been able to retain their erstwhile total control of the air. On 17 August Gough himself precipitated dramatic action from the C-in-C by outlining the next stage of the offensive. Tolerance of his impetuous approach was wearing thin at GHQ, and the five proposed 'line-straightening' attacks over a period of a week appeared disturbingly similar to the costly ventures pursued by the British during the latter part of the Somme campaign. Fortunately a shortage of fresh troops forced amendments. Although diverse minor local actions to secure awkward outposts and

strong points were occurring daily across the Salient, just two main attacks took place.

19.08.17

At 4.45 a.m. assisted in attack by XVIIIth Corps. Went down with Seigne to reconnoitre the country the other side of WIJ-DENDRIFT. Appears practically impassable for artillery, one mass of crump holes and nearly under water. 5 p.m. Brigade positions were rather heavily shelled by 8" and 5.9" till 7.30 p.m.: two dugouts blown in and some ammo and camouflage destroyed, fortunately no casualties to Battery. Men behaved well – a few showing the strain a bit.

CAPTAIN EDMUND GIFFARD, 75 BRIGADE,
ROYAL FIELD ARTILLERY

Right
The costly and largely unprofitable operations during the middle weeks of August.

Below
One of many German machine gun crews sited in trenches rather than pillboxes.

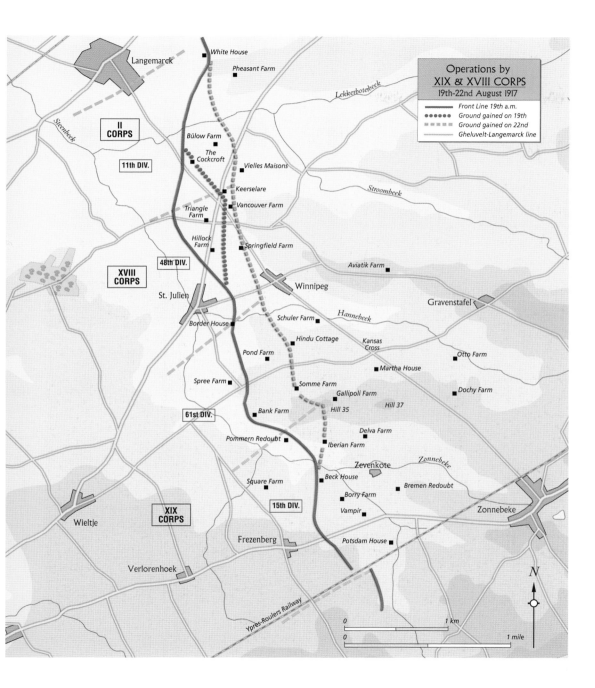

In the first venture on 19 August, Maxse's 48th (South Midland) Division (XVIII Corps) attacked a carbuncle of five apparently impervious fortified farms and pillboxes around Maison de Hibou north of St Julien. This string of positions, immediately in front of the British line, were heavily defended by machine guns and had already blocked earlier approaches. They could be expected to do so again. Despite generally bad ground, a few days without rain persuaded Maxse that tanks might be employed here, for the emplacements were just about within reach of roads and tracks. Under cover of aircraft, artillery and machine-gun barrages (that also masked engine noise), and veiled by dense smoke, fifteen minutes before 5.00 a.m. eleven machines rolled onto the St Julien–Poelcappelle road. Seven made it to Hillock Farm which was deserted. Moving on they passed Maison de Hibou – which was clearly occupied. As was now their habit, the tanks cruised past, neutralizing it from the rear, then continued on, leaving the infantry to mop up, occupy and consolidate. The strong points of Triangle Farm and The Cockcroft, both of which had been in British possession on 31 July, were next to fall. After two hours of fighting the line had been nicely straightened and secured. Five tanks managed to return and total casualties (tank personnel and infantry) numbered just twenty-eight, only two of which, both tank men, were fatal. By achieving surprise the machines had driven the Germans to seek cover, from which they were winkled out to surrender or to run away. It was a model victory that set many a tactical mind thinking about the greater application of tanks in battle.

One man who was about to begin his task of

recording Third Ypres was Australian official photographer Frank Hurley. An inveterate (and famous) adventurer, he had taken part in Sir Ernest Shackleton's ill-fated attempt to reach the South Pole, Mawson's later Australian Antarctic expedition and several other hazardous excursions to inhospitable places.* His photographs are some of the most iconic and telling images of the war; the accompanying diary, written from the standpoint of an observer often working at the very sharpest end, reveals a fascinating personal view of the evolution of Third Ypres. Hurley arrived in the France on 21 August.

At Boulogne Captain Bean (later to write the official history of the Australian forces during the war) was awaiting us with the two cars and we conveyed all our goods to safe storage. After an excellent meal – by the way the French bread is far superior to our British War loaf – we left for Headquarters, which are situated in Hazebrouck. One is scarcely conscious of war, except for the great numbers of transports and khaki men. To me the ride was filled with interest – everywhere tiny villages were surrounded by closely cultivated lands, and the golden grain, partly mowed, lay in long rows of sheaves, with here and there great conical ricks. The roads were in excellent order and planted on each side with long rows of poplar and other trees. Darkness soon came on and before reaching St Omer we took a wrong turning and rushed into a flock of sheep. These scattered at our unexpected visit and fortunately we only damaged two. Bean endeavoured to arrange the damage with the herdswoman without success. Naturally she assessed the damage exorbitantly. After much haggling we proceeded on our way, and as we wended our way towards Hazebrouck the sky gradually grew brighter with

the flickering quiver of hundred of guns in action. It was the most awesome sight I have ever seen. As we neared Hazebrouck the guns could be heard almost synchronising with the flashing.
<small>CAPTAIN FRANK HURLEY, OFFICIAL PHOTOGRAPHER, AUSTRALIAN IMPERIAL FORCE</small>

Hurley was witnessing the build-up to the second attack of this period. Only later was he to realize at first hand the reality of the 'awesome sight'. The territory south of Frezenberg, which the Australian would grow to know well, formed the core of the 22 August thrust for Watts's 15th (Scottish) and 61st (South Midland) Divisions (XIX Corps). The troops left their trenches, again at 4.45 a.m., advancing up the gentle slope of the St Julien Spur. Results were far less satisfactory than the previous stunt.

AUGUST 18TH – *Took over ADS (Potizje Chateau) formally at 5 a.m. Line as when we left and the Irish made no advance. Fair number of wounded during day. Leslie up at 6 a.m. and Baughman (American) of the 47th. Enormous numbers of aeroplanes up in afternoon. One of our men hit in the doorway and a piece of hot shell lodged in the seat of his breeches. Persistent shelling in night and the dugout entrance blown in. Stung in hand by wasp. Very painful and much swelling of hand. Not many wounded in night.*
AUGUST 19TH – *2 bearers wounded at Frezenberg, and got away with difficulty. Heavy crumps all round us, some very near. Another man hit in the doorway. This went on from 11.30 a.m. to midnight. Intense barrage of 5.9's on road. One ambulance car knocked out at noon. Three stretcher dumps round us blown up. Some 70 of them in matchwood. Three direct hits on building. Amputated leg of Lt. Templeton. Captains Knox and Black of Australian Artillery in. Former died next morning. Leslie while trying to get back to Potizje hit in hand and concussed. Sent back to Poperinghe (for rest of show). At midnight a dump set*

Above
An abortive British attempt to capture a pillbox. As was so often the case, the valuable soldiers' boots have been removed for German use.

Right
Official Australian Photographer Captain Frank Hurley poses on the footbridge over the moat at Ypres. A new bridge exists today on this exact spot. The ramparts behind were honeycombed with relatively secure dugouts, one of which housed the famous trench newspaper, the Wipers Times.

*Sir Douglas Mawson, celebrated Antarctic explorer who accompanied Shackleton on the expedition of 1907–9, organized and led his own Australian Antarctic Expedition in 1911.

alight 500 yards down road, mostly smoke bombs and Very lights. Stopped all cars till 1 a.m.

AUGUST 20TH – *Inspected damage to the estate.*

AUGUST 22ND – *General attack by us at 4.55 a.m. 100 stretcher cases through by 11 a.m. We have been beaten back to our old lines again. Huns have been coming on in mass formation, firing from the hip. Shelling is worse at 8 p.m. Some planes brought down (Huns) at 8 p.m. 44th Bde. reach their objectives. Have felt the effects of gas all day. Nausea. Cough. Sore throat. Brigade Major of 44th severely wounded. Two of our men hit. Took Lt Robertson GSW [gun shot wounds] chest. Many wounded in night. It is beginning to rain.*

AUGUST 28TH – *Very strong gale of wind and rain. Cold and uncomfortable in elephant [shelter]. Lice also very troublesome. An Irishman in who had lain in a shell hole with 2 wounded in No Mans Land for 11 days. When they died he crept back. Sun in afternoon. Story of the Colonel and the Royal Highlander kicking out the brains of an outpost of one officer and three men. Huns. At 10.30 p.m. the expected happened. Shell fell near elephant at B. House and wounded Matthew and Gray, killed 7 and wounded 12 stretcher bearers (Regimental). Replaced one man's colon through the axilla. Elephant at Annexe shelled and*

MO killed, his orderly and one of my men, Private Priest. Peaceful night.

AUGUST 31ST – *Wash and clean up. Delousing process long and pleasant. New man, a New Zealander called Berry. Warren has gone to a Regiment. At 10 p.m. a Hun flew twice down the main street machine-gunning. There seems nothing to stop him. Tomorrow we go to Arras region by bus and train. Laus Deo.*
Major Martin Littlewood, 45th Field Ambulance, 15th (Scottish) Division

Despite a terrific bombardment not a single strong point had been neutralized by the guns, the ground was as mucky as ever and enemy resistance underestimated. Again, incursions were isolated, and summarily brushed away by counter-attack. Yes, the line had been advanced a little, but the casualty count approached a crippling 3,000 men. Finally, on the southern flank elements of II Corps continued to bludgeon a way towards Gheluvelt, again blunting their swords against Inverness Copse. Returning heavy rain curtailed fighting to two days, but the pattern

had again been preserved: no progress against the plateau. Typically, British and German High Commands offered differing opinions on the result of the day's fighting as the following extracts from *The Times* of 23 August illustrate:

BITTER FIGHTING AT YPRES
FARMS AND REDOUBTS CAPTURED

THE FOLLOWING TELEGRAPHIC DESPATCHES WERE RECEIVED FROM GENERAL HEADQUARTERS IN FRANCE YESTERDAY:

9.12 P.M. *Successful operations were undertaken by our troops this morning east and north-east of Ypres for the capture of a series of strong points and fortified farms lying a few hundred yards in front of our positions astride the Ypres–Menin road and between the Ypres–Roulers railway and Langemarck. Bitter fighting has taken place at all points. The enemy has again launched repeated counter-attacks, which have suffered heavy losses from our artillery and machine-gun fire. The struggle was particularly fierce in the neighbourhood of the Ypres–Menin road, where the enemy fought desperately to retain command of the high ground. Here our line has been advanced to a depth of about 500 yards on a front of about a mile. A position giving important observation eastwards has been captured by us, and our troops have established themselves in the western portion of Inverness Copse. Farther north our line has been carried forward on a front of two and a half miles to a greatest depth of over half a mile.*

The garrison of the captured farms and strong points resisted with great stubbornness. In many cases isolated positions were only reduced after fighting lasting throughout the greater part of the day. In these operations we have captured over 250 prisoners, but by reason of the obstinate nature of the fighting the prisoners taken by us bear a more than usually small proportion to the losses inflicted on the enemy.

GERMAN OFFICIAL REPORTS, AUGUST 22ND:

Front of Crown Prince Rupprecht. In Flanders the artillery duel on the coast, and from Bixschoote to Warneton, was again intense during the evening. Early yesterday morning, after a vigorous wave of fire to the north-east of Ypres, a strong English attack took place near St. Julien. It was repulsed.

EVENING. – *In Flanders British attacks east of Ypres, which began this morning, extending over a 15-kilometre [9 mile] front, failed, the enemy suffering heavy losses.*

Right
One of the infamous duckboard routes that fingered their way forward towards Passchendaele. This is a double track fitted with anti-slip wire.

Inset
In the midsummer conditions, it was essential that bodies were quickly buried, be they friend or foe, to avoid scenes such as this.

Below
A German aerial view of the winding British duckboard track that crossed the Steenbeek (by now a vast quagmire) south of Langemarck, heading in the direction of Poelcappelle.

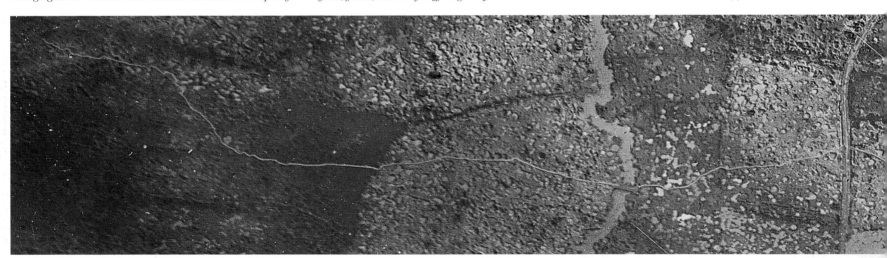

The battlefield was now becoming an ever-more difficult place both to find one's way around and to work in. As sequence upon sequence of bombardments crept slowly forward, the landscape was literally torn to shreds, leaving hardly a trace of human habitation save brick heaps and the ubiquitous and apparently indestructible pillboxes.

AUGUST 20TH

We then proceeded on foot over the Canal, over the Ridge the other side, past our old O.P. at Captain's Farm, down the slope towards the River Steenbeek, over an improvised bridge, past the Wijdendrift (which was a strongly concreted building, the Boche had occupied, and which we had fired at on former occasions), then over a wide, flat, open expanse, pitted with shell holes, wet and marshy in places, with dead bodies lying about (both British and Boche) in various attitudes as they had fallen, some half in shell holes and half out. We then reached what had been a Boche communication trench, but which was now no more than a battered bank of earth. We followed this forward, taking advantage of such cover from observation as it afforded, till the telephone line, which was guiding us, led us to a Boche concrete pillbox erected in what had been the trench. This was the O.P. – officially known as 'F.A.'. (I do not know what 'F.A.' stood for, but every O.P. had some official reference number or letter). 'F.A.' was a loathsome spot. I am afraid my powers of description are not equal to the task of conveying to others anything like a true mental picture of it. But F.A. was to be our O.P. for the next two months, and during that period it was the chief bugbear of my life. I measured time from one O.P. day to another. Perhaps the worst feature was that it was so isolated and far from home. It seemed far out into the Interior of Hell. So far forward over those miles of desolate battlefield, now so swept by shell fire, that neither tree nor house nor blade of grass was left – nothing but brown shell-pocked earth, with here and there some bare splintered tree trunks, which had once formed a wood, or a few bricks,

which had been a farm. You might stand in the ruins of Boesinghe, and look across over this barren land to the top of the Ridge, where shells might be bursting, (they so often were) sending up fountains of earth and smoke, but the O.P. was far beyond that. You might get over the Ridge to Captain's Farm and look across more barren land to the valley of the River Steenbeek, where shells might be bursting (they so often were), but the O.P. was far beyond that. You might get over the River, and look across another equally desolate, but muddier, expanse towards a ridge of earth, along which shells might be bursting (they so often were), and the O.P. was there, far along this earth bank that had been a trench. So far from life, and, as it seemed, so near to death. So far from your friends and from assistance should you need it. It was a long and tedious walk over those interminable duck boards, winding between shell craters; and as you plodded along with various impedimenta suspended around you, it was hard to exclude from your mind that at any minute and at any stage, that fateful shell might burst in your path. Some part of this area, over which our route lay, was always being shelled. It was just luck if you were to happen to be on that particular spot at the time or not. At times, of course, you could see in advance where the shells were falling and make a detour to avoid that particular spot. On arriving at F.A., we find it consists of a concrete pill box – pretty strong and massive, giving one a distinct sense of safety. It would probably stop a direct hit from a 4.2 shell. There is an inner chamber about 3 ft. 6 ins. or 4 ft. high inside. The outer chamber is a bit more lofty and has an aperture in the roof. Probably the Boche used this in some way for observing, but the aperture is useless to us for that purpose. The entrance is in the left hand side as you face the Boche, and around this has been erected a low barricade of sand bags, forming a low wall, over which, by standing outside the pill box, one can observe without exposing oneself to the view of the Boche.

After the walk there, it seemed a little haven of refuge, but it was not a savoury spot. Just the other side of the sand bags, about two yards from the entrance to the pill box, was a dead Boche, lying with his face in a shell hole; a few yards down the

Right
Low-level German aerial of a section of the Wilhelm Stellung east of Langemarck Cemetery. The waterlogged borrow pit to the front and the shadow cast behind tell us that this was a breastwork construction rather than a trench. It is packed with troops (note helmets), both in fire bays and simple secondary excavations dug into the parados at rear. See also British breastwork position on page 36.

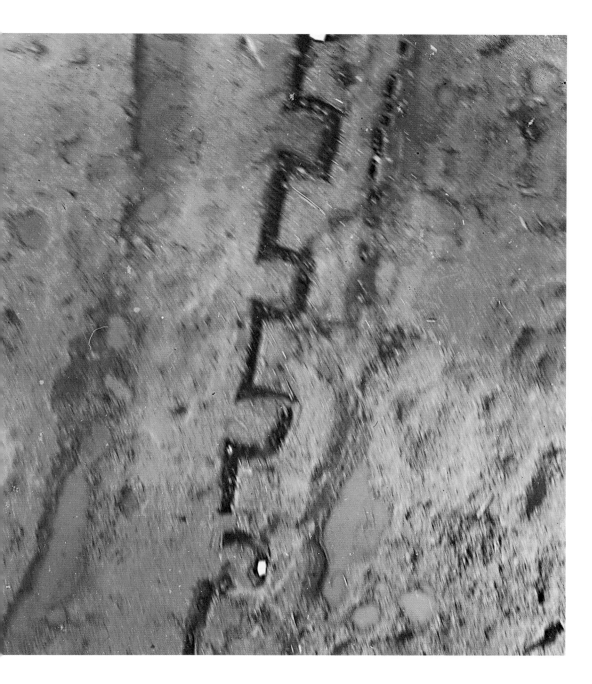

trench behind us was another, and just in front of us was a dead British Tommy. They never got buried – it was not worth exposing oneself to the Enemy to perform the task. Each time I went to the O.P. I saw them rotting away – getting thinner and thinner – till at last they were actually skeletons in discoloured uniforms. In the meantime great green-bodied bluebottles swarmed over them, and it was only with difficulty that one kept them off one's bully beef or sandwiches, when partaking of lunch. I suppose they rather fancied a change of diet. At night, I think they went to roost in our pill box. The interior was not exactly enticing. It swarmed with these flies, and probably with other things as well.

The Major gave orders to have this cleared out, and the next time I visited the O.P. I found it in a vastly improved condition, thanks to the efforts of the telephonists. But on this first day, in spite of its unsavoury condition, we were glad to take refuge in the innermost chamber on several occasions, as periodically the Hun did a shoot on us and dropped his beastly shells all along the trench. He probably suspected that his old concrete dugouts were being used by us as Artillery O.P.'s. The view from F.A. was fairly extensive. On our left front was Houthulst Forest, on our right front was Poelcappelle, and to our right flank, and fairly close was the remains of Langemarck.

LIEUTENANT E.C. ALLFREE, 111TH SIEGE BATTERY,
ROYAL GARRISON ARTILLERY

Gough's response to the setbacks was to augment subsequent attacks with extra troops. The move did not approach the heart of the problem – the imperfect performance of the artillery, both in subduing German strong points and batteries. Discounting the accuracy and persistence of hostile counter-battery fire, their lot was a difficult one.

We had very great trouble with the guns, owing to the difficulty in pulling out when switching on to a fresh line, or when the top traverse on the guns became exhausted. This was caused through the ground being wet, and the soil very clayey. The trails, after firing a number of rounds, would become very deeply buried, necessitating much digging with pick and shovel and strenuous heaving to get them out – thus some time was unavoidably lost, and the full allotment of rounds on each target could not always be got off in the time. The fact that the guns had been placed in dug out pits was, to a large extent accountable for this.

LIEUTENANT E.C. ALLFREE, 111TH SIEGE BATTERY,
ROYAL GARRISON ARTILLERY

Subsequently, more piecemeal attacks failed, including a fourth on 27 August launched with two tanks against Inverness Copse. The three Fifth Army corps engaged in so many attacks since 16 August were now acknowledged to be dog-tired. Yet the same day Gough drew up plans for another crack on the last day of the month. The Tommies gradually grew to learn of French success on their left.

22ND AUGUST.

The Battalion is still out of the line but go up tomorrow night taking in two days rations. The Bosch has raided us almost nightly since the stunt, but not so much shelling of back areas. A French Interpreter (the Count, we call him, whether he is, I don't know, but a good fellow all the same) called this morning. He told us a bit more about the show as he was Liaison Officer and went over with D Coy. The French only had 15 casualties in the Battalion next to us. He says our guns killed nearly all our men. It certainly is remarkable that we should have 170 casualties and they next door only 15!! Their 75's, he says, were a bit short at first, but immediately corrected. Ours did it but said afterwards it was the Bosch. Bosh they meant probably . . .

He also told us that five men took a strongpoint which contained several machine guns in gun placements with concrete two or three metres thick which were impervious to their shell fire. The place was thought to be a farm – so it has been once. It held

up the whole of the advance on that sector. The five men crept forward from shell hole to shell hole and once up against the wall were able to launch in bombs and forced them to surrender. About forty got away but those five fellows sent back 122 prisoners the Count informs us. We, of course, would have launched Coy after Coy probably through a beautifully fire-swept zone.

*In the last two nights air raid the Bosch dropped bombs on three of our CC [casualty clearing] Stations near St SIXTE – Nos 4, 47 and 61, and the Count informs us that he inflicted 113 casualties on our wounded – not **all** ours. He killed 21 of his own, the swine. Apparently he had a CCS (or dressing station probably) in the area we won from him and which must have come under our barrage. Hence the retaliation, no doubt. I only hope he has taken it behind from our aeroplanes where the chicken got the axe.*

CAPTAIN (QM) ERNEST KIRKLAND LAMAN MBE MC,
2ND SOUTH WALES BORDERERS

As Ernest Laman intimates, troops in reserve and at rest were by no means immune to hostile molestation. At every meteorological opportunity German aircraft bombed camps, towns and villages by night, whilst during the day planes were 'more numerous than birds'.

AUGUST 25TH 1917

My dear Aunt Nellie,

Thank you very much for your letter of the 20th and also the magazines, both of which I received safely.

I'm afraid we have been having rather a hot time out here lately as we have made several attacks and, of course, we get just as much to do as any other arm of the service. During an attack my special job is to go out and discover how far the infantry have advanced and then to bring the news back to Headquarters. In order to do this successfully it is necessary to fly very low, and not only do we run the dangers of Machine Guns from the ground, and 'Archie', as the Hun Anti-Aircraft guns are called, but we also frequently get hit by our own shells during their flight through the air. So it is a particularly unhealthy job.

As yet I have failed to come back without having some part of my machine hit. Of course I get it worse at times than I do at others. Four times I have been shot through either my oil or petrol tanks, which has necessitated a hurried retirement; and once I got hit in the engine which brought me down just inside our own lines. Luckily, although the machine was crashed to matchwood, my observer and I both escaped unhurt. But the former had his nerves spent by the experience and has gone back to Blighty for a rest – I wish I was the same.

When there is no push on I am employed in registering the Artillery on certain targets. This is a much safer job as we can fly higher up. And at times I also take photographs of Hunland. Of course we are often attacked by enemy machines but they usually clear off after a short encounter provided your observer does some good shooting. However, they never attack with less than two which makes things more lively – once I had to fight five but managed to hold them off until three more of ours came and chased them away.

The great thing though about the R.F.C. is that we can always be certain of getting back to comfortable quarters which, I think, more than compensates for the excitements of the day.

Your very affectionate nephew,

Jack S. Walthew

LIEUTENANT JACK WALTHEW, NO. 4 SQUADRON, ROYAL FLYING CORPS

On 28 August, as an unofficial truce was observed to clear the battlefield of wounded and bury the dead, Haig implemented an important rearrangement of responsibilities. It was definitive – Plumer, not Gough, was to oversee future actions against the Gheluvelt Plateau. Plumer's first request was a three-week planning and preparation period to try to devise a method of dealing with the German defence. It was granted.

His key aims were to: a) neutralize enemy guns; b) create a more flexible system of attack against dispersed strong points; c) select targets according to the troops' capabilities, not the commander's 'fantasies'; and d) make certain that tactics allowed for sufficient fresh troops to fight off inevitable counter-attacks.

There was now a little time for relief, rest, leave for a lucky few and for the troops to try to convey recent experiences to those at home. It was known that the censor would spoil any over-descriptive letters, so to offer a flavour of life men resorted to speaking of what would at first sight appear mundane. A topic high on the list of hundreds of thousands of letters was the filigree of duckboard tracks covering the Salient, for there were few who escaped being on carrying parties. The duckboard was a staple part of everyday life, almost looked upon in the same curiously fond way as bully beef, and plum and apple jam. It was an inanimate but ubiquitous object that one could grouse about. Or was it inanimate?

25/8/17

As usual

B.E.F.

My Dear Mother

Here we are on the right side of offensives and things and free to breathe again for a bit. Well, we have had long enough of it; as you have heard our affair on 18th was quite successful; it was quite fun in its way, and no one worried at all. The noise and confusion everywhere, and the various sights have one almost numb at first, and then everything becomes quite natural, people stroll about with cigarettes going strong and so on just as if it was a parade, and everything works out like a pageant of old. The barrage is a marvellous sight, you can see a perfect line of shells bursting forwards a few yards ahead, and see, in the dull light of dawn, the sudden curves of light from the fuses of the smaller shells as they shower down just over the heads of the men in the front wave; it is marvellous how even a fly is left alive after; in fact even the flies did get shell shock, and for a while we saw them crawling about on the ground in quite a helpless state. The whole landscape is brown – not a blade of green anywhere – nothing but shell holes, and each one at that having been made several times over. A railway embankment even requires a trained detective to spot it, and as for farms, there is nothing to be seen up to half a brick; the only indication is by the shell holes being specially watery from the surrounding moats which formerly existed. Walking along the advanced duckboards is not at all what it would appear, in the dark after rain every fifty yards safely traversed is a thing to be thankful for, and a mile is worth writing home about. I will deal with a few types of board I noted last Sunday night, only a few because to be exhaustive would be to become an author of much accomplishment and experience.

There is (a) The Good Duckboard and the well-made and well-set duckboards, only this generally is off the track to one side or other and is quite outside the scheme of things; it needs a special detour to walk over it. Otherwise all duckboards are bad. These bad ones are divisible into two classes:

Those obviously bad and obviously to be avoided. A rare class.

Those looking safe, but being black at heart, with 'biles of jet' to quote our friend Chaucer. Each of these, and their name is legion, is willing to sacrifice a rung if it can thereby sprain an ankle, and to sacrifice itself if it can break a neck.

Take one of these, imagine yourself moving along half asleep loaded up with all the lares and penates of a pillbox war. The man in front steps on a firm duckboard and moves on; now, all unbeknownst to yourself that duckboard has pivoted midway and his end has gone down and yours up. The next step ruins you, your foot catches neatly under the end and over you go, all the electricity in your body crashing out in simultaneous sparks, and every belonging you have hanging in clusters round your neck never to be readjusted till the end of the march. That is the com-

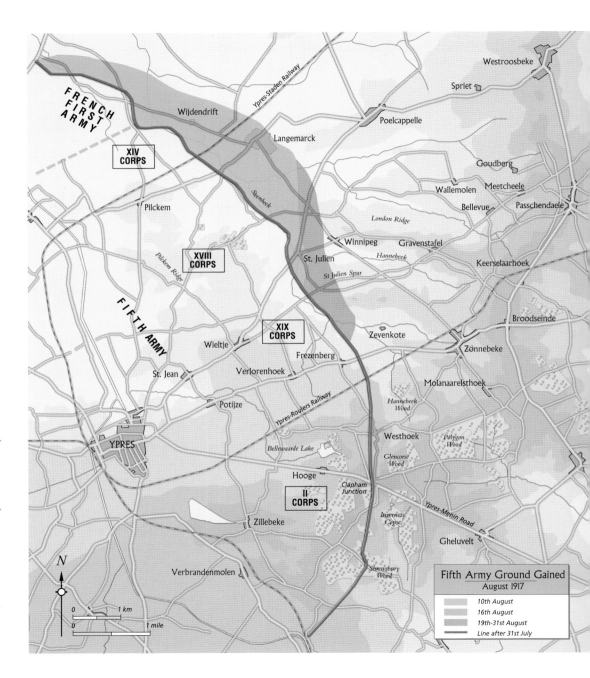

Above
Second Lieutenant J.G. Morris, 16th Sherwood Foresters.

Left
The meagre sliver of ground gained by Fifth Army during August.

monest and most innocent of them.

The next worst is the one slightly tilted sideways. When dry this is harmless, but after a spot of rain it becomes a form of extreme danger. You step firmly on it and your leg shoots off with quite a high muzzle velocity. The counter for this is to shoot out all limbs violently in a sort of spiral, this makes all hangings (glasses, waterbottle etc.) fly round in unison; sometimes the fall is checked, but generally one crashes violently on one's hip in spite of all these speedy precautions.

There is another kind that suddenly lunges up sideways and deposits one in a shellhole full of water by the side – not so common.

The worst one I passed on Sunday was of the following type. It led steeply down the edge of a big shell crater (a ridiculous thing to do anyhow). It led on to a level one below, and then up another on the far side. It was wet so the only way to get down the board was to take a deep breath and then with short sharp paces run down it, and hope to reach the level one before anything happened, but no. I drew the deep breath, gritted my hands and clenched my teeth and started the run. The duckboard waited till my speed was great enough, then calmly tilted over sideways and left me knee deep in soft slushy mud; the board then flopped back and awaited the next victim.

The worst board of all though I ever heard of was one of perfectly devilish cunning. Enter victim cheerfully. On stepping onto the duckboard it at first held till all his weight was on and then down went his end and the other end sprung up so violently that it hit him in the face and stunned him. Meanwhile his legs had dropped into the gap formed at his feet, and the duckboard then dropping back into its previous position, severely lacerated and almost broke both his legs, the whole operation done with the speed and neatness of a skilled operation by a doctor.
SECOND LIEUTENANT RONALD WILSON,
4TH WORCESTERSHIRE REGIMENT

SEPTEMBER

Rainfall is less on the average than in August and considerably less than in October, but it is greater than in the spring months, April and May. As, however, the ground is generally dry, only heavy rains affect the conditions seriously. The smaller amounts, which are sufficient in spring to make the ground very difficult, leave it firm and hard in September. Nearly every year there is one spell of at least a week's duration of dry weather. Very dry Septembers occur about 1 year in 4, 20 or more days being free from rain. Evaporation is nearly as high as in the preceding summer months, so that much of the rain which falls is removed directly. Mist or fog is common in early mornings. Gales and high winds are about as frequent as in August and less than half as frequent as in October.
METEOROLOGICAL SECTION, ROYAL ENGINEERS,
30.8.17

For the first week of September Sir Hubert Gough continued to press more XIX Corps attacks in the central sectors. Every one was abortive. After the fifth such venture failed, cut to pieces by untouched machine guns situated on a rear slope, Haig grew so concerned that he visited individual Fifth Army divisional commanders to gauge their assessment of recent actions and stance upon future missions. There was no accord. Meeting Gough personally, Haig made it plain that since the date for Plumer's attack on the plateau had now been fixed for 20 September (this had been suggested on 29 August in the first draft of attack plans), his own endeavours should be wound down. It was not a direct order, but the General yielded. Gough's supremacy in the Salient was over.

So ended the first phase of Third Ypres. Apart from 31 July and the minor tank-led triumph of 19 August, results had been disappointing. Casualty figures for August almost touched 68,000. In the lead-up to Plumer's first venture lives also continued to be lost; the Germans knew the battle was far from over, and shelling and skirmishing was ceaseless.

3RD SEPTEMBER 1917

Dearest Dad and Mother,

I received your excellent parcel today – thanks awfully. I am not going on that course after all [he had volunteered to train to command a Pioneer Company], owing to something more important coming off. I can't say too much, but we are going in training tomorrow, but don't worry as it is highly probable that I shan't have anything to do with it as it is my turn to stand down. I have volunteered to go if necessary. Haven't time to write a lot. Fritz bombed us here last night with some pretty heavy stuff but as we were in bed we stayed there excepting to keep going to the door to see if any machines were being brought down. At last we dropped off to sleep and as we were all here this morning it is safe to assume that he didn't hit us.

Love to all. In great haste.
Ever your Son,
Glynne

SECOND LIEUTENANT J.G. MORRIS, 16TH SHERWOOD FORESTERS

On 13 September, whilst holding the line in Shrewsbury Forest, Glynne Morris was badly wounded and taken to X Corps Advanced Operating Centre, 140 Field Ambulance. The medical care provided and the emotional support extended to his family were far from unusual.

13TH SEPTEMBER 1917

Dear Mrs Morris,

I do hope you will have this note before learning from the War Office. Your son Lieutenant J.G. Morris was admitted to our Ambulance about 9 o/c this morning suffering from abdominal wounds, and is very dangerously ill. He was operated on shortly after admission, is just as well as we can expect. He is young and strong and we hope with God's help to pull him round for you. I will write again tomorrow and tell you how he is. Need I say how deeply we sympathise with you in your anxiety for your brave lad.

Yours Sincerely
[Sister] Annie Wright

14TH SEPTEMBER 1917

Dear Mrs Morris,

I am so pleased your son is considerably improved this morning. He had a very fair night, and tho' not out of danger is holding his own well. He is very bright and very hopeful and makes a very good fight for recovery. If he continues to improve I will write in three or four days time, if not I will write daily. He asked me to say he would write himself shortly.

Yours Sincerely
Annie Wright

16TH SEPTEMBER 1917

Dear Mrs Morris,

Your Son Lieutenant Morris is still in the Ambulance (140th). He had a very restless night and isn't quite so well this morning. All the surgeons and nursing can do is being done for him, he suffers very little pain, but just seems tired out. Tomorrow, I hope to have a better report for you, and believe me that we will do all in our power to send him back well again to you.

Yours Sincerely
Annie Wright

19TH SEPTEMBER 1917

Dear Mrs Morris,

I promised to write again telling you of your son's condition. He is still alive but his condition is not as satisfactory as we could wish. He slept well last night and if anything this morning he is a little stronger. He has every attention and comfort possible and we pray we may yet be able to send him down to you. His batman is here and asked me to acknowledge a parcel you sent to Mr Morris. I will write again in a day or two. You have our deepest sympathy in your anxiety and rest assured no one will spare themselves if it is to save his life.

> *Yours Sincerely*
> *Annie Wright*

21ST SEPTEMBER 1917

Dear Mrs Morris,

Your son, I am so sorry to say is not nearly so well this morning. He had a very restless night and his condition causes much anxiety. He does not appear conscious of pain and takes no interest in life. Will write again tomorrow. I am so sorry for you so far away from your boy, but we give him all possible care.

Believe me.

> *Yours Sincerely*
> *Annie Wright*

22ND SEPTEMBER 1917

Dear Mrs Morris,

Lieut. Morris had a much better night but I regret to tell you that the surgeon holds out very little hope of his recovery. He has no pain, lies today as if asleep taking no interest in anything.

With much sympathy

> *Yours Sincerely*
> *Annie Wright*

23RD SEPTEMBER 1917

Dear Mrs Morris,

Your wire came this morning just an hour too late, your dear boy having passed peacefully away at 9 o/c. Sister Rickard was with him and took this little piece of hair for you. She also put some white flowers in his hands in your name, she was very, very good to him and he seemed to prefer her looking after him. It may be of some comfort to you to know he didn't suffer, only from the very first seemed tired out. His wound which was an abdominal one did very well indeed. I cannot tell you how sorry we are not to have been able to save him for you, but really if you had only seen how wearied he looked you would not grudge him to rest. With deepest sympathy with all his friends,

> *Yours Sincerely*
> *Annie Wright*

If you write giving his name, rank, Regiment and time of death to the following they will later on send you a photograph of his grave: Director of Graves, Registration and Enquiries, War Office, Winchester House, St James Square, London.

John Glynne Morris is buried in Reninghelst New Military Cemetery in grave IV.D.5. He is one of 99,100 Second and Fifth Army casualties recorded between 31 July and 14 September 1917.

It might be thought that some political intervention, or at least an indication of concern, might have been received at this time from the War Policy Committee. Not so. Despite being kept fully informed by Sir William Robertson, they appeared to take no interest. Since the last fractious meeting in June there had been no more, and would not be until the end of September. Sir Douglas Haig, Robertson, Charteris and Co. were left to pursue their goals as they saw militarily fit. Regarding the Western Front there seemed to be a mild case of loss of nerve in Lloyd George; he asked no questions about what had been a dreadful month in Flanders, and still promoted Italian ventures at every opportunity. Playing his own political game, Haig happily sanctioned the shifting to Italy of 100 French guns from the successful northern flank of the battlefield – but with the proviso that he wanted them back in time for the coastal attacks, which were still very much on the agenda. As far as the C-in-C and GHQ were concerned, there was only one real enemy: it was not the Turks in Palestine, Salonika or Mesopotamia, nor the Austrians in Italy, but the Germans on the Western Front.

From this point onwards the battlefield and the nature of battle was to make its first radical change. Gough's apparent blundering and Haig's bizarre non-interference were over. And these were not the only changes. As Plumer appeared, so the rains disappeared, replaced by long, warm, dry days of sunshine. As the ground baked, so a fresh tactical cauldron was devised in which to immerse the Germans.

25 AUGUST

In the morning I did the rounds of the 'red tabs' [staff officers] endeavouring to make arrangement for the transference of the men's rations and for sundry affairs to Steenvoorde. What absurd and unnecessary formalities I had to go through, and now I am further off than ever. My contempt and disgust for army administration increase with every trifling matter I have to see headquarters about. Things that could be settled in five minutes take usually ten days! And why? Because it has to pass through a score of unnecessary channels that seem to have been created to find soft jobs for the 'string-pullers'. The surrounding country is in glorious condition, the harvesting is nearly at an end and the golden sheaves are being built up into great cone-shaped ricks. The winding roads are dark with the deep shadows of poplars and other trees, and are just alive with the endless processions of transports coming and going from the battlefield. Collectively, it's the most beautiful rural country I've ever been in.

26 AUGUST

Bean, Dyson, Lindsay, Wilkins and self (and batman) motored out in the two cars to Voormezele and made our way up to Hill 60 on foot. From Voormezele there is absolutely no cover, all vegetation being absolutely swept away by the fire which has continued over it for over two years. It is about two miles up to Hill 60, a miserable, desolate, shelled waste, over which shells scream and the heavy artillery, with the roar of a thousand thunders, belches them forth in an endless stream. The bursting of Boche shells in one's immediate vicinity added to the excitement of the tramp, but rather detracted from one's admiration of the surrounding desolation. During the afternoon Blake and I strolled out to an advanced position in front of Hill 60, over the recently-won ground. What a devilish sight it was. Everything to the horizon has been shot away. Photographed the interior of the Elephant Iron dugout of the O.C., Major Morris of the 105th Howitzer battery. Blake on left,* Ikin centre, and Major Morris right.
Captain Frank Hurley, Official Photographer, Australian Imperial Force

* Footnote in diary: Captain L.R. Blake went right through the war with the artillery and was killed on the morning the Armistice was signed, 11 November 1918. Like Hurley, he too had been a member of the Mawson expedition.

Right
The photograph of the artillery HQ near Hill 60 taken by Captain Frank Hurley that corresponds to his diary entry of 26 August (left).

CHAPTER TEN
The Menin Road Ridge, 20–21 September

20/9/17

Dear Mother,

If it were not for the men who have spared me on this fierce day and who are lying around me and looking timidly at me, I should shed hot and bitter tears over the terrors that have menaced me during these hours. On the morning of the 18th, the dug-out, containing seventeen men, was shot to pieces over our heads. I am the only one who withstood the maddening bombardment of three days and still survives. You cannot imagine the frightful mental torments I have undergone in those few hours. After crawling out through the bleeding remnants of my comrades and the smoke and debris, and wandering and fleeing in the midst of the raging artillery fire in search of a refuge, I am now awaiting death at any moment. You do not know what Flanders means. Flanders means endless endurance. Flanders means blood and scraps of human bodies. Flanders means heroic courage and faithfulness unto death.
Your Otto

LETTER FROM UNKNOWN GERMAN OFFICER (PRISONER).
SECOND ARMY INTELLIGENCE SUMMARY

German GHQ readily admitted that the fighting had cost them heavily, and not only in Flanders but elsewhere on the Western Front where the French too were pressing attacks, partly on behalf of Sir Douglas Haig and partly to claw back territory that had been lost the previous summer. That the British were going to continue to pursue their Ypres ambitions was without argument. The sense that tactics were about to change was also evident, for history told the Germans no British commander would order a lengthy respite during prime campaigning months without good reason. That reason was Fifth Army's blend of profound loss and meagre gain. It was clear to Rupprecht, von Armin and von Lossberg that the initial phase of the battle had concluded, but what was to follow?

The British were about to shift from Gough's steeplechase dash to Plumer's relay race – at walking pace. From now on every stride was to be short, sure-footed and utterly decisive.

TUESDAY, 19 SEPTEMBER

Bean, Wilkins and I set off at 1 p.m. to take up suitable positions for the great event tomorrow. Bean, who learns all information at Headquarters, informed me that we are undertaking a new system of attack. At 5 a.m. the artillery will all simultaneously open a barrage on the Boche front lines for a period of an hour or so. This is intended to engage his artillery and demoralise them. The machine-guns will play on his infantry. At a specified time the barrage will be lifted and our troops will dash over into the enemy's lines. This objective secured, a second barrage will take place, and the second wave of infantry will again move forward over the area controlled by this barrage. The third and final barrage will take place about 9.30 a.m. It will isolate

Below
Crown Prince Rupprecht, exuding confidence, inspects his troops.

Above
Railway-mounted 12-inch howitzer of 104 Siege Battery, Royal Garrison Artillery, being prepared for action near Salvation Corner north of Ypres.

Following pages
A segment of a vast 178° German panorama taken from Passchendaele Church tower in July 1916. The field of view extends from Gheluvelt on the left to Zonnebeke and encapsulates the infamous Gheluvelt plateau territory including Polygon Wood and the Broodseinde Ridge. Note the several German cemeteries pictured. None exist today. See also pages 288-9 for a closer view.

the third section of the enemy's lines and our infantry will advance at 10 a.m. The barrage will be maintained for some time so that our position may be consolidated. Altogether we expect to advance 1500 yards over a frontage of about 15 miles.
CAPTAIN FRANK HURLEY, OFFICIAL PHOTOGRAPHER, AUSTRALIAN IMPERIAL FORCE

The plan Sir Herbert Plumer and his Chief of Staff, Harington, delivered to Sir Douglas Haig at Cassel on 29 August described the sequence of limited assaults minimally outlined above by Hurley. Their twin foundation was patience and methodology. The goal was not only to gain the requisite ground but to be able to hold – firmly and permanently – all newly won positions against counter-barrage fire and counter-attack. Five separate stages were proposed to capture the 4-kilometre band of territory now separating the British from the heights of the Passchendaele Ridge. The primary target remained the Gheluvelt Plateau. For stage one it was incorporated into a Second Army battlefront of around 6 kilometres stretching southwards from the Ypres–Roulers railway to the Ypres–Comines canal. Although strictly un-Haig-like in its limitations, the C-in-C made no attempt to amend or alter the overall plan, for Gough's recent performances were lesson enough that modification was urgently required, and Haig was well aware of Lloyd George's political sword of Damocles dangling over his offensive.

For the attacks to have any hope of success Plumer demanded colossal artillery presence – greater again than anything yet employed. He borrowed ordnance from First, Third and Fourth Armies, bringing together almost 1,300 heavy naval guns and howitzers and over 700 field pieces. With a gun every 5 metres firing on a nar-

row front upon a shallow depth of battlefield, the density of shelling was almost fourfold that of 31 July. Opposite, the Germans, it was believed, deployed around 550 guns in defence.

Second Army comprised X Corps (General Sir Thomas Morland) and 1 Anzac Corps (General William Birdwood), with the 19th (Western) Division of IX Corps (Lieutenant General Sir Alexander Gordon) providing a defensive flank along the Ypres–Comines canal. Fifth Army too was taking part. Deployed upon a 7-kilometre battlefront on Plumer's left, north of the Ypres–Roulers railway, they were to apply identical tactics over a similarly defined width and depth of attack against the slightly elevated contours guarding Poelcappelle, Westroosebeke, Gravenstafel and Zonnebeke: jumping-off positions for later attacks upon the main Passchendaele Ridge. Gough was able to count upon twice the 31 July concentration of gunfire. Maxse's XVIII and Fanshawe's V Corps were to form the spearhead, advancing shoulder to shoulder with I Anzac Corps whose direction of attack was straight along the railway. The 20th (Light) Division (XIV Corps) were given the ostensibly less demanding job of advancing on the northern flank in front of Langemarck up to and including the Lauterbeek. Although Plumer was renowned for his tactical diligence, even at this critical stage in proceedings it appears that some planning conferences were not always electrically charged.

Yesterday I had an interesting experience. I attended a divisional conference. The Major-General was there, and the Brigadiers were there, and the Colonels of infantry battalions. We sat round a table, each with a sheaf of foolscap and a pencil in front of him, and all got very bored and tired. I can testify that neither

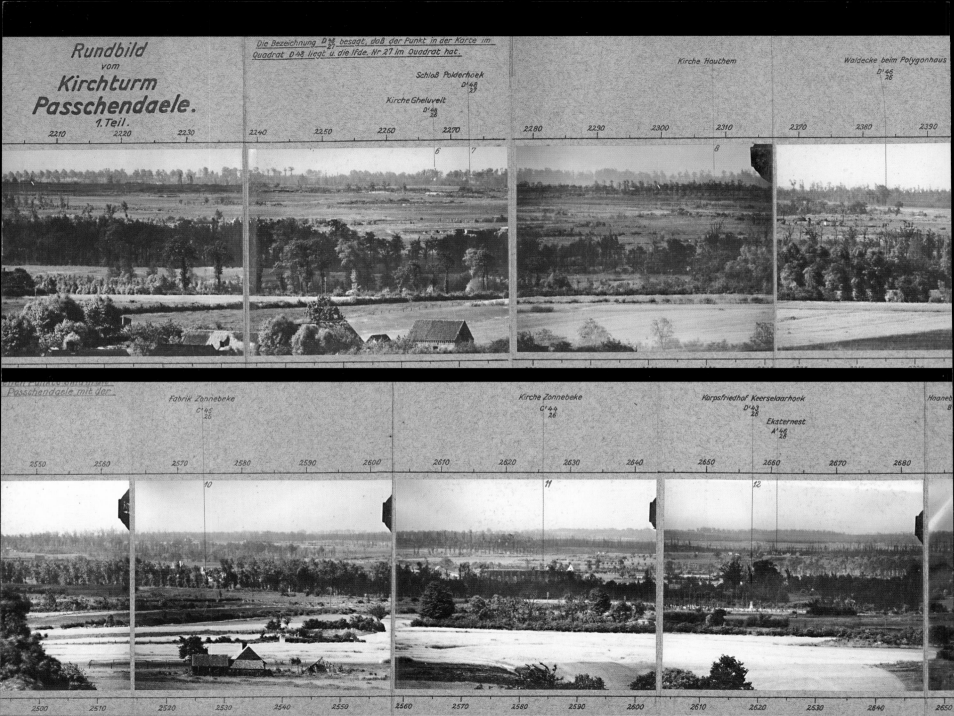

Rundbild
vom
Kirchturm
Passchendaele.
1. Teil.

Die Bezeichnung $\frac{D\,48}{27}$ besagt, daß der Punkt in der Karte im
Quadrat D 48 liegt u. die lfde. Nr 27 im Quadrat hat.

Kirche Houthem

Waldecke beim Polygonhaus
$\frac{D^{1}46}{26}$

Schloß Polderhoek
$\frac{D^{1}48}{27}$

Kirche Gheluvelt
$\frac{D^{1}48}{28}$

2210 2220 2230 2240 2250 2260 2270 2280 2290 2300 2310 2370 2380 2390

6   7   8

...teil Punkte sind u... te
Passchendaele mit der

Fabrik Zonnebeke
$\frac{D^{1}45}{26}$

Kirche Zonnebeke
$\frac{C^{1}44}{26}$

Korpsfriedhof Keerselaarhoek
$\frac{D^{1}43}{26}$

Eksternest
$\frac{A^{1}46}{26}$

Hooneb...
8

2550 2560 2570 2580 2590 2600 2610 2620 2630 2640 2650 2660 2670 2680

10   11   12

2500 2510 2520 2530 2540 2550 2560 2570 2580 2590 2600 2610 2620 2630 2640 2650

Die mit roten Zahlen versehe.
Karten auf dem Kirchturm i
gleichen Ziffer bezeichnet.

Regimentsfriedhof Res. Inf. Rgt. 248
C¹45
26

Korpsfriedhof Broodseinde
D¹44
26

Jägerfriedhof Broodseinde
D¹44
27

Eisernes Kreuz Wäldchen
C¹46
27

2410 2420 2430 2440 2450 2460 2470 2480 2490 2500 2510 2520 2530 2540

9

2340 2350 2360 2370 2380 2390 2400 2410 2420 2430 2440 2450 2460 2470 2480 2490

Bhf. Zonnebeke
C¹44
28

stift
44
27

Brigadehof
C¹43
28

Villa Haanebeek
B¹45
27

Schule
A¹45
28

Kapelle
A¹45
27

Zementhaus
A¹45
28

Aussichtsturm a.d. Kemmel

Katzenhof
A¹45
29

Pappelhof
A¹45
30

Engländer Wäldchen
Y¹45
30

2700 2710 2720 2730 2740 2750 2760 2770 2780 2790 2800 2810 2820 2830

13

14

2670 2680 2690 2700 2710 2720 2730 2740 2750 2760 2770 2780 2790 2800 2810

the Brigadier-General on my right nor the Lieutenant-Colonel on my left can draw. The first was fond of railway engines, as far as I could make out over his shoulder; the Colonel tried men's faces, but neither one nor the other was any good. After two hours of hearing other people talk we went back to our own quarters for tea – with oatcakes from Manuel and Webster.
CAPTAIN WILLIAM FERRIE, 196TH MACHINE GUN COMPANY,
55TH (WEST LANCASHIRE) DIVISION

Part of the reason for this lack of electricity was that with Plumer's new tactics far more responsibility was devolving from Division to the lower-ranking officers from brigades and battalions actually involved in the fighting. The character of command and control was changing.

Although the Germans had been forced to relinquish certain important forward positions – Pilckem, Frezenberg and parts of the Westhoek Ridge – and suffered heavy loss in the process, there still lay a great depth of heavily fortified territory for the British to win. Enemy interference was guaranteed, so a profound knowledge of the terrain was becoming more and more essential as the advance progressed.

11.9.17

A relief model of the ground over which our next advance is to take place has been made in an orchard on the other side of the road. I have been and had a look at it. We are going to the north of Ypres-Comines canal and our objective is a spot called Tower Hamlets. The ground sinks down to a little stream, then rises again, and our task looks pretty formidable. We expect to get our orders to move at any time. We had had a good rest and can't grumble although the weather has not been so good as it might have been. But the return to the line is always viewed with certain misgivings and forebodings, but no man shows his heart to another and we forcibly thrust

ourselves into an appearance of carelessness and nonchalance.
SAPPER ALBERT MARTIN, 41ST SIGNAL COMPANY,
ROYAL ENGINEERS

Both sides knew that good weather was the only thing that could unlock the German defence. August ended as poorly as it had begun, but although the RFC were so often grounded, things were about to change.

AUGUST 31ST 1917

My dear Uncle Tom,
Thanks very much for your letter of the 28th Aug. and the cigarettes, both of which I have just received. Luckily we are having gales and rain just now so no flying. Consequently I may have time to answer some of the numerous letters of birthday wishes which I have had today. This bad weather has just come out at a very opportune moment as we had been having a very hard time lately, and needed a rest very badly. Just at present I am fostering an aggressive spirit by chasing and killing the numerous ear-wigs which have their being in my tent. So even when we are prevented from flying my love of war prompts me to acts of slaughter.

I'm afraid I have no flying news to tell you as I have not left the ground for three whole days and nights. But I have spent most of my days killing ear-wigs and sleeping. In the evenings, when we are quite sure the weather cannot clear before it gets dark, I usually go to one of the towns or villages round here and have a look at them, get supper at some restaurant (nothing like the Holborn) and then come back. But I think this weather is too good to last and I expect I shall soon have to fly again.

Well, cheery-oh! – Excuse this short letter, but I have such an awful lot more to write.
With love,
Your very affectionate nephew,
Jack S. Walthew
LIEUTENANT JACK WALTHEW, NO. 4 SQUADRON,
ROYAL FLYING CORPS

Above
The troublesome dust noted repeatedly in his diary and photographed here by Frank Hurley. Although there were many such days in September and early October, such an image is counterintuitive to the popular perception of Third Ypres.

Below left
A ration party preparing to set out with their loads. Food was packed in a pair of sandbags that were tied together and hung over a shoulder or round the neck. Note the fine weather.

Below

Bottles found on the battlefield. None are army issue products. They include Camp Coffee, HP Sauce, Bovril, and an intriguing concoction marked as 'lung tonic'.

September was to bring less and less rain, and long days of uninterrupted sunshine, so much so that dust was to become a nuisance. Whilst Plumer's preparations continued, essential reliefs took place across the Salient. Fresh troops moved in, took stock of the unenviable and unattractive surroundings and made temporary homes of captured positions. With the enemy everywhere still in commanding positions and very much on the qui vive, a strict order of activity accompanied these activities.

This was the most difficult part of the journey for the Germans were always on the lookout for relieving troops and ration parties, and would put down a barrage along the Steenbeek and through the village if he saw much movement. He would accompany this with a hail of machine-gun bullets. It was a nervy job getting through Langemarck but we got through alright. The village was absolutely ruined, here and there you could see pillboxes now occupied by us, Very lights were sent up continually by the Germans and by their light you could see a good distance. Several times we passed dead bodies and all around was one awful scene of desolation. We got to the Langemarck-Poelcappelle road and soon came to 'Fly Dug-out' (given its name because of the quantity of flies always in the pillbox). Here we met platoon guides and I got the guide for my two platoons and was taken by him to the platoon positions which were a good number of isolated positions making the support line, Company HQ being at Fly Dug-out. As it was the middle of September, the days were quite warm and the nights were just comfortable, but the mornings were rather cold. After reporting to Peard (Company commander) and getting instructions from him, I went back to my platoons and got to work on my own portion of the trench. We got a door from nearby and made a roof and covered it over with grass and earth and managed to make a fairly decent shelter though it was small and rather cramped. Just before dawn I went round the line and issued rum to the men. There was always an issue of rum when in the front line and a tot did a great deal of good just before dawn, it warmed one up and helped one to get to sleep. After going round with the rum, I returned to my shelter and went to sleep. About mid-day I woke up and Halford cooked a stew of onions and Maconochie on a Tommy-cooker. Rations were brought up in sand-bags by the men when they came up the line and consisted of bully-beef, Maconochie, jam, army biscuits, margarine, onions, milk, sugar and tea, and some pickles. There was also an issue of Tommy-cookers. These were small tins filled with solidified paraffin. You lit them with a match and when you had finished cooking put the lid back on so they could be used again. After a good lunch I peeped over the top of the trench. It was a lovely September day and I could see a good distance. We were in a small plain between the Pilckem Ridge, where our guns were, and the Passchendaele Ridge, where the German guns were. Both front lines were in the plain.
SECOND LIEUTENANT GEORGE MCMURTRIE,
7TH SOMERSET LIGHT INFANTRY

Although relative bliss for the troops after the swamps of August, the timing of the climatic amelioration was also in a way unlucky for the British, for the three weeks of Plumer's preparations turned out to be generally fine: prime fighting weather that could never later be clawed back. Although sunshine and warm winds sucked the moisture from the earth, inside the only real cover on the battlefield, captured pillboxes that were universally sunk into the ground, conditions were sometimes grimmer than in the trenches.

On the night of 19/20 all my guns went into position, Henderson being in charge at Rat House, and Pulley, Webb and Holmes at Hannixbeek. I moved my Company H.Q. of myself and two runners to Ferdinand Farm. The lack of accommodation on zero night was appalling. It was death to be outside of concrete as the Germans were continually shelling. At the farm itself there were three concrete buildings – one was advanced Signal HQ for Brigade, one was full of machine-gunners of the 164 Company who were to go forward and consolidate the blockhouses and one was a company HQ, shared by Hughes of 154 company and myself. This pill-box we were in was perhaps twelve feet long by ten feet wide inside and had about two feet of water in the bottom – the height between the top of the water and the roof being about five feet. The entrance of course faced the German line, as it was a captured position by the division on the 31 July. It had a large shelf in it built by the Boche for men to lie on some 3 feet above the floor, and this was still one foot above the water level. In this, I, Hughes, his second in command Lawson, his section officer going forward to consolidate, a trench-mortar Captain, and some six servants and runners spent the night. One could not stand upright, or lie down, just crouch in a corner. The water underneath smelt abominably, it was floating with stinking old tins, refuse and excreta, and had an oily look. Whenever it was stirred up by someone entering or the underneath concussion of a shell bursting nearby, the smell was overpowering. At the door of the pill box was a huge 9.2 or 12-inch shell hole with some six feet of water in it. Over the shell hole was a plank, the only means of getting into the shelter. In the shell hole was a month-old inflated corpse of a Boche – we called him our barometer, as one day he floated and the next day he sank. The pill-box was of course lousy.

Lieutenant Douglas Wimberley,
232nd Machine Gun Company

The heaviest British guns attended to the toughest targets, employing a proportion of armour-piercing shells alongside HE to pierce, shake, crack or lift concrete emplacements – anything to neutralize the garrisons and drive them out into the open.

Extracts from captured German letters distributed in Intelligence summaries illustrate how demoralizing the British artillery could be.

EXTRACT FROM LETTER WRITTEN BY A LANCE CORPORAL IN THE 19TH RESERVE INFANTRY REGIMENT TO HIS WIFE.

Yesterday night we had to put up wire again, an utterly useless proceeding because everything is shot away again at once. It was very still and we did not like the idea of going, so I went to our blockhouse of my own accord. On the way, frightful artillery fire began; I had, however, by this time got into the blockhouse. I simply refused to go with the others even though they put me under arrest. Suddenly the English commenced to bombard the blockhouse with heavy shell. They kept it up for half an hour but luckily it stood firm. A few hours previously they had shot another to pieces; 17 of the occupants were killed and only two wounded. Our Sergeant has gone mad. A wireless message has just come that another dug-out has been shot to pieces . . . again many dead and wounded . . . We are now only about 35 men.

The devastating effects of gunfire upon the human nervous system was now something that doctors on both sides of no man's land were beginning to better understand. Slowly, shell-shocked men were being treated not as malingerers, and punished, but genuine cases to be carefully examined and questioned. More than 20 per cent of discharges during 1917 were as a result of some kind of neurosis. As the numbers and power of guns grew and bombardments became ever more violent, so more and more men were affected; the affliction might strike down anyone from the youngest recruit just arrived in the trenches, to the most experienced professional soldier. In the line it was accepted that everyone had a breaking point, but around the world doctors and psychoanalysts, divorced from the true conditions of the battlefield and, like us, entirely unable to comprehend either the environment or circumstances, concocted a vast

Above
The spring in the step of these soldiers is due to the fact that they are moving out of the Salient towards a period of rest.

Right
Careful reconnaissance of enemy positions and strengths made before the 41st Division's attack on the Tower Hamlets sector on 20 September.

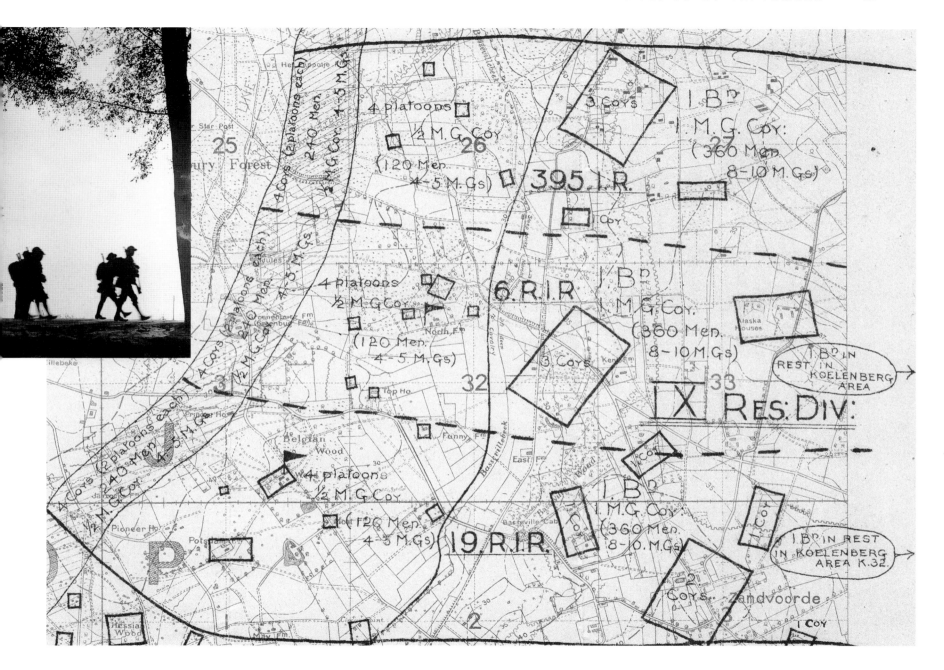

range of widely differing explanations for break-down. It remained a mystery, however, for the onset and symptoms of shell-shock could be attributed to so many events, from the daily sight of death and decay, to being buried alive. An attack of 'nerves' could happen at any time.

While bombs were being dropped in Poperinghe a few nights ago close to 'B' Co transport lines, one man, Private Saunter (who had previously had shell shock) got it badly again. An R.A.M.C. Sergeant, who thought he was merely windy, went over to him and said 'Pull yourself together, my man, it's all right', where-upon he received a terrific biff on the nose subsequently having to go to hospital! Poor Saunter then ran amuck, and being a pretty hefty chap, laid several people out before he was finally captured and sent to hospital also.
LIEUTENANT GERALD BRUNSKILL, 5TH ROYAL SUSSEX REGIMENT (CINQUE PORTS BATTALION), ATTACHED TO XVIII CORPS RAILWAY CONSTRUCTION

Year on year men had volunteered. They did so to do their duty, not to break down. As early as 6 December 1914 when artillery firepower was almost trivial compared to Third Ypres, Major Valentine Fleming of the Queen's Own Oxford Hussars wrote: 'The men have realised the fact that it's safer to sit in a trench than to get out of it and run away.' In the Salient there was indeed nowhere to run.

It was decided that reciprocity was the best medicine as regards counter-battery work; just as German gunners delivered their daily cascades of gas shells, so too would the British. The traditional creeping barrages would protect the infantry, making sure to slow down as the men annexed fresh territory and as each wave was relieved by fresh battalions. A few hundred metres ahead the guns were to deploy a 'searching barrage' to deter supports and cut off supplies, and beyond, 1,000 metres ahead of the leading wave, no less than four linear screens of heavy protective shellfire. There was more. The British already employed machine-gun barrages, but on 18 August Sir Douglas Haig had attended a demonstration near Etaples to watch thirty-two Vickers guns simultaneously deluge trench lines and boxes of ground at a range of 2 kilometres plus, similar to the tactics so profitably employed by the Germans during the Somme. He was impressed. Alongside the artillery, Plumer's machine guns would therefore fire torrents of lead over the heads of each successive wave *as they were attacking*, further suppressing German shell-hole-based defences and any massing support or counter-attack troops. There were sufficient weapons in the seventy-three machine gun companies present in theatre to potentially place a Vickers every 25 metres along the entire front. All this was to take place simultaneously *and* continue for the duration of the attack. The combination, it was hoped, would profoundly affect German morale. Three and a half million shells were placed at Plumer's disposal, for above all other considerations he was all too aware of what the C-in-C's insistence upon extended objectives had done to his own men during the latter stage of Messines; this time he was determined not to let them stray beyond the range of the guns.

12 SEPTEMBER

Early start for Voormezele to visit the 54th Battery Australian Siege Artillery. Great numbers of Australian troops are converging on the sector between Ypres and

Right
German map segment showing the location of every British battery in the Salient. The insets show the sites (and companion photograph) of one of the several railway-mounted howitzer positions.

Below
Unloading 15-inch howitzer shells on the Menin Road. The shells each weighed 1,400 lb (636 kg), created a crater 15 metres deep and 15 across, and flung steel splinters up to an effective, i.e. lethal, range of 800 metres.

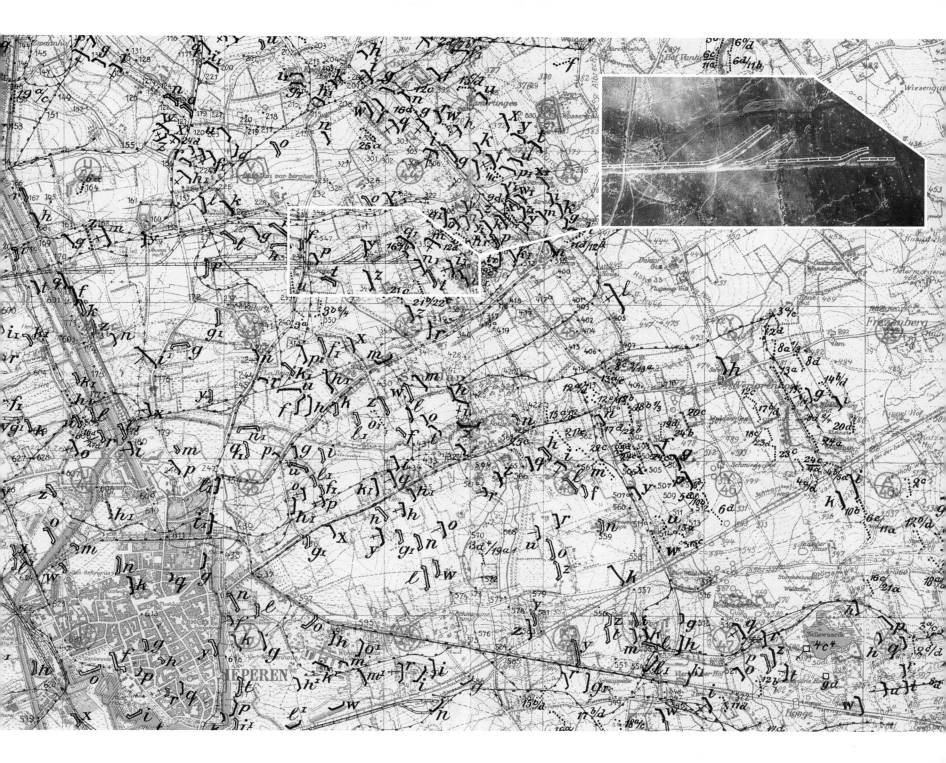

Voormezele and there are everywhere evidences of a great 'push' or blow being dealt against the Boche very shortly. Immense dumps of munitions are accumulating, and it is gratifying to see that there is a great abundance of them. The roadway is practically lined on one side with heavy naval guns. In Voormezele itself I saw one enormous Howitzer of 15-inch calibre. This ponderous beast, for there is something hideously lifelike about it, fired a projectile weighing 1120 pounds! Great numbers of projectiles lay by it looking like a litter of fat pigs. The circumjacent country is crowded with guns of all calibres, from 18-pounders in the advanced positions, up to the 12-inch in the retired. The artillery complain there is insufficient ground on which to place their machines. The country in every direction along this sector is a tremendous concentration of ordnance and ammunition dumps. If the weather will but hold favourable, we should be able to deliver a crushing blow for there is no limit to guns or ammunition. One realises the impossibility of rapid advance, even should we be able to break through the Boche lines, for the weight of these titanic weapons makes them so cumbrous as to be practically regarded as fixtures.

CAPTAIN FRANK HURLEY, OFFICIAL PHOTOGRAPHER,
AUSTRALIAN IMPERIAL FORCE

There was a problem here. The fixed nature and dense concentration of British batteries – almost all visible as soon as they fired – offered enemy gunners a huge choice of targets. Opposite British muzzles the German batteries were still as dispersed, mobile and subfusc as ever. A few did not exist at all – except as canvas and timber dummies, whilst others displayed all the sound and fury without being guns at all. From the air these 'batteries' appeared as covered gun pits, but in fact consisted of no more than a linear sequence of small boxes made of thick cardboard, bound with four layers of tarred twine. Each separate box contained 70 grams of nitro-

cellulose with a hole in the top where a wooden plug secured a piece of safety fuze. The fuzes varied in length, and the free ends led to a canvas folder containing an igniter of 5 grams of nitro-cellulose. When 'fired' the flashes and reports of each box exploding in sequence occurred at intervals of 35-40 seconds, exactly mimicking those of a field gun, attracting the attention of British flash-spotters and sound rangers, and drawing valueless gunfire. Meanwhile many 'real' German batteries simply remained silent, hibernating beneath camouflage until the chosen moment. None of this was evident to the casual observer, for whom the German guns had turned the Salient into a charnel house. Although there had only been a few raids during first two weeks of September, more than 10,000 casualties were sustained by the British, a large percentage of which were at the hands of the German guns.

FRIDAY, 14 SEPTEMBER

We left the city by the Menin Gate, or rather where it used to be, and I left Wilkins [camera assistant] and proceeded on foot along the Menin Road to our advanced batteries. This is a distance of about two miles – the liveliest two miles I have ever walked. It is along this way that all our supplies and ammunition must go to the Ypres front. It is notorious, and being enfiladed by the enemy's fire is decidedly the hottest ground on the whole front. The way is strewn with dead horses, the effect of last night's shelling, and battered men's helmets that tell the fate of the drivers. The Boche was very active around Hellfire Corner and his 5.9's were bursting around there in rare style. His spotting balloons could be clearly observed and doubtless his precision was due to their observation. The trees along the Menin Road are avenues of shot-away stumps and the surrounding lands ploughed up with shells like a sieve. The stench is frightful, and even the old-stagers dodge this charnel-like thoroughfare. I saw the Boche put out of

Above
30 September. German shells searching for targets along the Menin Road, a highway that was packed day and night with traffic.

Left
A German battery position spotted as being bogus.

action one of our batteries and explode the ammunition dump by a direct hit. I had to seek shelter in an adjacent dugout owing to his barraging the road, shells dropping along in a trail-like succession. One lives every moment in anticipation of being blown skywards and to drive down on a limber, racing from shellfire and bumping over a shell-torn road is keener excitement than even I relish. Accretions of broken limbers, materials and munitions lay in piles on either side, giving the road the appearance of running through a cutting. Any time of the day it may be shelled and it is absolutely impossible owing to the congested traffic for the Boche to avoid getting a coup with each shell. It is like passing through the Valley of Death, for one never knows when a shell will lob in front of him. It is the most gruesome shambles I have ever seen, with the exception of the South Georgia Whaling Stations, but here it is terrible for the dead things are men and horses.
CAPTAIN FRANK HURLEY, OFFICIAL PHOTOGRAPHER, AUSTRALIAN IMPERIAL FORCE

With the Germans still retaining the higher ground, many British batteries could also be engaged by direct observation as well as from the air, for despite the guns being camouflaged, their muzzle flashes instantly gave away their positions. Being largely on lower ground, without aerial assistance the Royal Artillery could not see the objects of their attentions for they lay either behind the ridge or in the valleys between spurs. Whereas once the cavalry had been the eyes of the guns, now it was the camera and observer.

The short wave tuner enabled you to receive with headphones messages which were being sent in Morse from the air by pilots and observers. You could record that on your message pad and transmit it to your battery commander. You opened up your station when the machine came up from the squadron and called you at the battery. You had your own specific call signs which you recognised immediately. From then on observers asked you to

stand by. He had already been told the target on which he'd got to range [the guns]. The shoot would commence by your signalling to the observer by means of an American white strip about two feet wide, weighted at each end and put out in the forms of letters such as 'K' or 'L' or 'N' or 'D', as the case may be in accordance with the code. As he was approaching the target he would give you what was called a 'G' signal, which meant 'fire'. You would pass that signal to your battery commander who would then give the order for one of his guns to fire.
WIRELESS OPERATOR LESLIE BRIGGS, ROYAL FLYING CORPS

As the gun fired so the plane would be heading towards the target, ready to register the fall of shot, and hoping to be nearby as the shell struck. Having achieved this the pilot turned the aircraft whilst the observer calculated the required adjustment ready to signal it back as the plane flew in the homeward direction where the signal was strongest.

He was able to correct where the shell had fallen by means of a device called the 'clock code'. It comprised of a circular disc of transparent material which had twelve radial lines coming out from the centre of a pin, and eight concentric circles. The observer would fix that device on to his map on his dashboard in the cockpit. He would register where that round had fallen by giving the correction on direction based on one or other of those twelve lines corresponding from one to twelve around a clock. Then the rings would be varying distances from the target, and they were lettered 'Y' 'Z' 'A' 'B' 'C' 'D' 'E' 'F', with the inner ring being ten yards from the target . . . If you got a correction coming back 'A9', it would mean that the round had fallen within 50 yards of the target at nine on the clock.
WIRELESS OPERATOR LESLIE BRIGGS, ROYAL FLYING CORPS

After signalling, the plane would once more turn back to the target area to observe the next fall of shot. By repetition of this sequence gunners were able to adjust their direction and distance until the signal 'OK', signifying a direct hit, came through; then the entire battery set their sights to pulverize the spot. Given fair weather and manageable retaliatory action from German planes and anti-aircraft guns, the system worked well, and an aircraft could continue observing and sending back messages signalling (and sometimes photographing) the accuracy of the concentrated fire, i.e. monitoring the destruction of the target, before finally signalling 'CI' – 'coming in'.

The concentration of British artillery was by far the greatest of the war to date. Surely the massive onslaught of steel was enough to release the German grip on the plateau?

SATURDAY 15 SEPTEMBER

All the guns in the vicinity, hundreds in number, opened fire precisely on the stroke of 4 p.m. The effect was terrific, with simultaneous burst hundreds of shells went screaming and hissing away to the enemy's line. Then independent firing continued for half an hour. The din and roar kept up of the concentrated fire from the massed cannon and screaming projectile is beyond me to describe. Our aeroplanes hovered by circling over the battery groups, and sent down wireless reports of the results and also directed the fire and ranges. The Boche returned the fire on one of the heavy batteries with wonderful precision. Our artillery men speak in high terms of the enemy's gunnery. While though we send over much greater quantities of projectiles, his precision is admittedly superior.

CAPTAIN FRANK HURLEY, OFFICIAL

PHOTOGRAPHER, AUSTRALIAN IMPERIAL FORCE

Hurley's latter comment – the superiority of German gunnery – is telling. Although there was never more than the lightest of showers during this initial bombardment period, low cloud hampered British aerial observation. As the build-up progressed batteries recorded an instant hostile response as soon as they opened up. It was to decrease only slowly as the days passed towards zero. In addition, on most afternoons flights of German Gothas appeared to bomb all kinds of British activity. Bombing was now almost round-the-clock, with attacks on camps, railheads and other key positions, some far behind the lines. Although casualties were seldom heavy, it served to sap the strength of resting troops. The question now facing the British was whether the strong points had been better neutralized than the enemy's guns.

The most eye-catching aspect of Plumer's battle plans from the infantry's point of view was that they were presented with objectives that appeared extraordinarily meagre by comparison to Gough's requirements during August. The primary Second Army targets were again the woods and copses that had baulked II Corps, but the new arrangements that were practised day after day turned the loose but successful fire-and-movement tactics against pillboxes into a recognized discipline. Now, the breakdown of communication experienced at the parapet interface was largely eliminated, for the old battalion or brigade

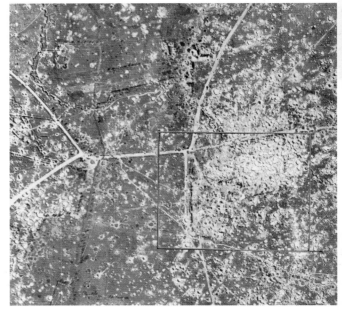

Above
Desolation and corruption on the exposed track that traversed the Westhoek Ridge.

Left above and below
Concentration barrage with heavy calibre shells to neutralize pillbox groups. Tower Hamlets sector.

prised three 'bounds'. Because the German outpost zone was known to be less strongly held, it was decided that the first assault wave also need not be as strong. As the battle zone was entered and resistance grew, successive leapfrogging units became progressively more numerous and robust. In this way the battle zone should receive a more than adequate attacking punch. The final bound, which would most likely bring troops into contact with the *Eingreif* units, was to be the most forceful. Unlike previous endeavours, having only leapfrogged but not yet engaged the enemy, this third wave would also be fresh, energetic and resilient. It was here that the most telling losses could be inflicted upon the enemy. Neutralization of the highly trained counter-attack units was the Germans' greatest fear — for everything depended upon their competence in halting any potential breakthrough.

The British attack sequence was to be interrupted by two halts to allow moppers-up to comprehensively clear captured ground. The first was forty-five minutes, the second about two hours, each being calculated to make sure that the subsequent heavier waves of men had time to get into suitable jumping-off positions for their respective 'stunts'. Attacking distances, although variable according to locality, were proportionate to the nature of each of the enemy's defensive belts: approximately 800 metres for the outpost zone, 500 metres for the battle zone, and 300 in the 'counter-attack' zone. Once the latter had been reached immediate deep consolidation would take place, ready to tackle the inevitable hostile response. As for reserves, 25 per cent of the attacking force would hang back close behind the action, ready to be called upon in case of

fighting unit was broken down into several smaller self-sufficient bodies, each with their own complement of machine guns, riflebombers and moppers-up. It was hoped that once versed in the new techniques junior commanders on the spot would be able to work more flexibly and independently to attain their purpose. If each successive wave, similarly armed, performed in the same fashion, decision making should be quicker, progress steadier and consolidation firmer.

Each of the five steps to the ridges com-

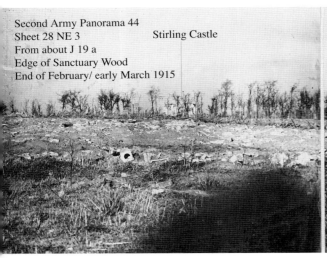

Second Army Panorama 44
Sheet 28 NE 3   Stirling Castle
From about J 19 a
Edge of Sanctuary Wood
End of February/ early March 1915

problems and to help against counter-attack if necessary – by commanders on the spot. After a month of Gough's mechanical ventures, it was refreshing to see new methodical thinking being put into practice. The sappers too were employing fresh ideas.

On September 17th we were moved forward into the Salient past Hellfire Corner (which was well named) to the Frezenberg Ridge from which, on 20th our infantry attacked. In front of us was a valley in which ran a stream, the Zonnebeke, and the left of our part of the front was on a railway embankment which crossed the valley from our ridge to that occupied by the Germans, the stream flowing through it in a culvert. To stop our advance the Germans had blocked this culvert and created a lake between our lines and their own. On their side of the lake they had built, inside the scattered farmhouses and out of sight, a series of very strong reinforced concrete pill-boxes, from which they had effectively stopped former attacks, the gunfire for which had however blown away all the sheltering walls of the houses, so that they were now visible. Such was the picture from 'Kit and Kat' our

forward H.Q. before the battle. The Sappers played the following part in the success which followed: with an infantry patrol, at dead of night, two nights before the battle, we approached to within 100 yards of each pill-box and planted there a peg, the side of which, facing our way, was painted with phosphorus paint, and glowed in the dark. The next night, with these pegs as guides, we laid out tapes around the shellholes and leading to the pegs. During the night the attacking troops were led down these tapes, and placed by their officers as near the pill-boxes as possible. Meanwhile, and this was my job, a section of Sappers crawled along the railway embankment to the choked culvert, and after getting very wet succeeded in removing the sheets of corrugated iron which stopped the flow. That quickly drained the lake, and incidentally flooded out a lot of German trenches on the other side of the bank. We then carried down a lay of portable footbridges and put them across the Zonnebeke. When the barrage opened just before dawn the infantry, already close to the pill-boxes, with some of our sappers carrying big explosive charges made in the prison [Ypres prison was used by the RE as a small factory for specialist items], crawled up and dropped into the machine-gun openings these charges, also some phosphorus

Above
Panorama taken in 1915 from the British front line in the Tor Top sector near Sanctuary Wood.

Right
Australian tunnellers at work extending dugouts in the Hooge crater on 18 September. These important and extensive workings were used as forward tactical headquarters.

bombs. These latter were most effective. They set fire to anything they touched, and made violently sick anyone not burnt or killed by explosion.
CAPTAIN J.E. MARCH MC, 90TH FIELD COMPANY,
ROYAL ENGINEERS

Across no man's land German intelligence came to the conclusion that an attack on 20th was 'not improbable' and ordered that from the early morning British trenches and gun positions be subjected to annihilating fire. All was set and Plumer was about to face his first test.

FIRST STAGE –
THE BATTLE OF THE MENIN ROAD

19.9.17

This morning I came up out of the tunnels and had a wash in a shell-hole. Then I went to the top of the bank and had a look around. It was not safe so I didn't stay long. Looking towards the enemy (the front line is about 400 yards away) the land dips down

W.F.C. HOLDEN
CAPTURE.

.Menin Road.

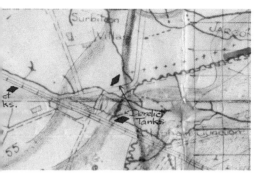

Above
Segment of hand-annotated trench map marking knocked-out British tanks near Clapham Junction on the Menin Road.

Left
Another W.F.C. Holden painting: the Clapham Junction area. The colour of the ground is accurate; beneath less than half a metre of dark topsoil, the Flanders geology is various shades of yellow and russet clay mixes.

into a slight valley and on the hill beyond stands Gheluvelt, which at this distance appears hardly to be touched. Tower Hamlets, our objective, is this side of Gheluvelt but on the other side of the valley. I counted a dozen derelict tanks and we call this neighbourhood 'Tank Cemetery'. Looking backwards over Zillebeke Lake, Ypres stands out grisly and white like a ghost of a city, and really that's all it is. This spot is certainly a vantage point. No wonder Fritz pays it so much attention. With the exception of short bits of trench at the entrances to the saps [tunnels] the only shelter is to be found in shell-holes, and half of these are filled with water. The horses with the rations cannot get right up here, so each night all men not on duty have to form a ration party and go and bring them up. Returning, I got into the trench and was almost up to the door of the sap when a shell burst on the parapet and I was covered with mud and dirt, one piece giving me a nasty whack on the top of the shoulder. I thought no more about it until later in the evening when something caused me to put my hand to the spot and I found a long scratch, no worse than a kitten would give. I am rather surprised because all I felt at the time was a thud as if a heavy clod of earth had struck me. Thank God it was no worse, though at times the strain of this existence makes one long for death.
SAPPER ALBERT MARTIN, 41ST SIGNAL COMPANY, ROYAL ENGINEERS

In his dugout at Mount Sorrel Sapper Martin occupied one of the highest contours on the right flank. The corresponding elevated ground in the central sector, the Zonnebeke Ridge, belonged to the 55th (West Lancashire) Division. Both had the benefit of the driest ground on the battlefield, but neither was in a position to appreciate it.

19/9/17, WEDNESDAY.
Woke up at dawn. Nothing doing all day except very heavy bombardments by our artillery. We saw the effect from the top of our dug-outs. The day was fine, sun shining nearly all the time. We saw our objective (The ridge Hills 35 and 37) being blown up.

There was perfect hell going on. Pommern Castle slightly to the left was also getting its full share of shells. After tea it started to rain, which made things very unpleasant as we moved up to our position at dusk. We followed a light railway for a little while, then a duck board track. It was pitch dark and we had a very rough passage. Flare lights kept lighting up the desolate scene. We seemed to be walking round in circles, but arrived in our positions about 2.30 am in the morning. Going up the smell was terrible. Dead from July offensive were still lying about. Mules and men lying on either side of the track. Falling over such objects was anything but a pleasant thing.
PRIVATE WALTER HOSKYN, 5TH KING'S (LIVERPOOL REGIMENT)

On the night of 19 September, beneath the cloak of darkness, eighteen assaulting brigades numbering 65,000 men silently streamed along cross-country tracks to take up their allotted positions. It mizzled all that evening, heavily enough to turn the surface into a slippery, soft porage and fill the myriad craters. Just as the troops were thoroughly soaked and thoroughly miserable, the rain ceased.

Curiously, the conditions troubled Gough. At 11 p.m. he telephoned Plumer to suggest that perhaps a postponement might be wise. Having consulted 'Meteor' (the military meteorologists), who said that apart from a risk of the odd thunderstorm the barometer was looking pretty fair, Plumer said no, the attacks would go ahead. Over 1.5 million shells had already deluged the German positions; now the fire would redouble.

THURSDAY 20 SEPTEMBER
We were just walking along the Menin Road in the twilight near Hellfire Corner when our barrage began. Simultaneously from a thousand guns, and promptly on the tick of five [the attack actu-

ally began at 5.40 a.m.], there belched a blinding sheet of flame: and the roar — nothing I have heard in this world or can in the next could possibly approach its equal. The firing was so continuous that it resembled the beating of an army of great drums. No sight could be more impressive than walking along this infamous shell-swept road to the chorus of the deep bass booming of the drum fire, and the screaming shriek of thousands of shells. It was great, stupendous and awesome. We were glad, notwithstanding, to reach the more or less sheltered site of the mine crater at Hooge, wherein are excavated the dugouts of the Brigade Headquarters, some 25 feet below the level of the ground. Last night's rain had made things frightfully sloppy and muddy: the dugouts being no exception, as the soakings percolated through the roof and oozed through the walls. [in an earlier diary entry, Hurley had noted that the Australian tunnellers constructing Hooge dugouts referred to this ooze as 'hero juice' on account of the piles of bodies buried above them over the years]. This filthy liquid had to be incessantly pumped out, but even then it left the passage ways deep in slime. Anyhow, it was shellproof, and I was grateful to be inside for a brief lull from the frightful din without. A large number of prisoners were captured and sent in. This body of men, which came into the crater a little later, were in an extremely poor condition, haggard, emaciated and dejected. Many were mere boys and shadows of men. One could not help feeling regret for these wretched prisoners, forced into the front line no doubt on account of their inferiority and intended merely as buffers, whilst the finer troops were held in reserve. It was one of the most pitiful sights to see the wounded coming in, many of our men being carried on stretchers by Hun prisoners, others with their arms around each other's necks being assisted by friend or foe, and all eager to get away from the horrors of the combat. Bitterness and hatred were forgotten; for after all we are all but men, and this frightful scene of carnage seemed to bring each back to the realities of humanity and to hold them spellbound by the horror and terribleness of their own doing.

CAPTAIN FRANK HURLEY, OFFICIAL PHOTOGRAPHER,
AUSTRALIAN IMPERIAL FORCE

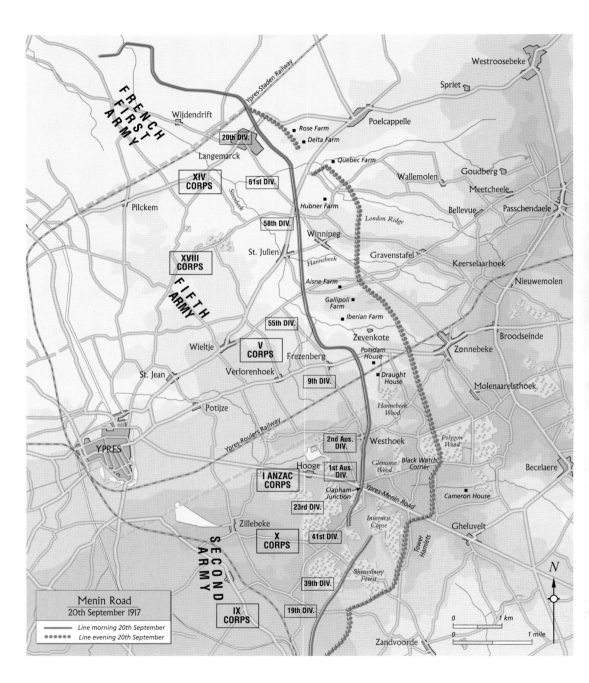

Menin Road
20th September 1917

—— Line morning 20th September
••••• Line evening 20th September

Inset
Three traumatized German prisoners captured in the attack on Vampir(e) Farm on 20 September.

Below
Friend and foe assist each other through the quagmire.

In the mist of the early autumn morning of 20 September the renewed assault on the Gheluvelt Plateau began. Despite the rain the ground was firm and the going relatively good. Tanks were again in action. The initial waves of infantry moved off about 150 metres behind the creeping barrage at a rate of 25 metres per minute. Far ahead the protective barrages, without precedent in intensity and organization, formed dense curtains of covering and suppressing fire. The plateau was held by three divisions of tired German troops who had been in the line for three weeks without relief.

20.9.17

I was awake when the attack started at 5.40 a.m. so I went up on top to watch it, but the barrage on both sides was so heavy that it was impossible to see any movement because of the smoke, but along the line of attack shells were bursting in dozens at a time. I shaved and washed in a shell-hole and about 8 o'clock climbed to the top again. It was evident that things were not going so well as anticipated – the line had moved forward but it was still far from the final objective, and there was no doubt that Fritz was putting up a very fierce and stubborn resistance.

SAPPER ALBERT MARTIN, 41ST SIGNAL COMPANY, ROYAL ENGINEERS

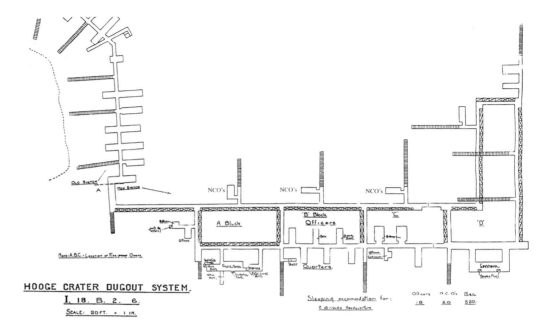

HOOGE CRATER DUGOUT SYSTEM.
I. 18. B. 2. 6.
SCALE: 20 FT. = 1 IN.

The hurricane of shells and speed of attack was actually peeling open the outpost zone along much of the attacking front. On the Menin Road tanks wallowed in the infantry's wake. Locally, however, resistance was fierce, and showed the potential capabilities of the German system should the British be unable to sustain such a dazzling bombardment. In

Above
Plan of part of the Hooge crater dugouts. Fifteen stairways, known as inclines, are marked here, plus bunked galleries (hatched) for other ranks and separate chambers for officers' accommodation, administration and messing.

Above
20 September. Two tanks knocked out near Stirling Castle, and the bodies of two British soldiers believed to have been killed whilst using them for shelter.

Left
Panorama section showing the exposed slopes of the Menin Road Ridge, with a further brace of disabled Mark IVs.

several unsuspected places single machine guns escaped the shells and baulked the advance.

20/9/17, THURSDAY.

The fatal day for thousands found us wandering about for our positions. On arriving there I got my Gun team into two shell holes and set them to work to dig for their lives to get head cover. Fritz was shelling and machine gun bullets were flying round. The men and self were absolutely done up and tired when we had finished and as it was raining just a little I handed my rum flask round and we all felt the benefit of it. It was a godsend to all. Unfortunately for us a trench mortar battery of ours opened out about 25 yards to our right and Fritz was trying to find it with shells and we had an exceedingly anxious time of it. We were repeatedly covered with debris caused by his shells. Then the word came about 'Half hour to go. Fix bayonets. Load Lewis Gun' and I saw that all my section were ready. At 6.40am we got the word 'Over with you' and we all moved off, my section following me up. On arriving at our Front Line positions Fritz opened his barrage on us and we were in the thick of it. He was not three minutes after us in opening out. Shells were bursting and men falling right and left. Fritz had a 'Pill Box' or concrete dug-out directly in front and alongside was a smashed up 'Tank' which was put out of action there on 31st July. Both places he was using as machine-gun emplacements and causing great havoc. We could just see it in front and we opened out on it. A Gun team was knocked out just in front of me and my No. 1 on the Gun had reported the loss of my gun to me. So I ordered rapid rifle fire. We could see Fritz moving about behind the now partly demolished Pill Box but he held us up for about an hour. During this time I had expended all my ammunition but filled all up again from a wounded man's equipment. Then Fritz did a thing I will never forgive him for, I was only 150 yards from him now and saw it myself. He raised and waved a white flag with a red cross on it as if to surrender. About 20 men went over to take them prisoners. As soon as they got within range Fritz threw a hail of bombs which we call 'Potato mashers' and put the whole

lot out of action. This happened on the left of the Pill Box. The men on the right were able to take a little advantage and get closer. At last he came out (about 12 of them) waving the same flag and marched in file towards us, expecting mercy from us, after doing such a foul thing. I am very glad to say every man of them paid the penalty and although they are all dead on that account I swore I would not take a prisoner.

Private Walter Hoskyn, 5th King's (Liverpool) Regiment)

Pillboxes were dealt with in the manner that had been rehearsed, highly personalized miniature encounters in the great maelstrom of the wider battle. Revolvers, trench clubs, the bayonet, and Mills grenades were of little use until fighting was at close quarters. Instead, smoke was extensively used, blocking enemy vision whilst parties encircled their emplacements.

As soon as the barrage opened onto the enemy, I jumped out of the assembly trench to get as far away from our assembly trench as possible before the German barrage opened out. I were well clear when the enemy replied to our barrage in which several of our men got caught, being late in climbing out of the trench. As soon as the barrage lifted off our first objective I were there, and I thought I saw a movement as I passed a dugout so I threw a bomb in as I passed by, but the lights were not too good yet. I saw the Welsh retiring as I got onto our right flank. I shouted at them to stand fast but they took no notice, then I shouted 'Are there any Officers here?' and one man near me turned round and said 'Yes I am.' He had a pip on the shoulder. I told him to stop them as they would get it worse going back than forward. I never forgot his reply. 'What can I do?' I replied 'You have a revolver, haven't you?' but I didn't wait for his reply as I saw the barrage lift off the Pill-Box in front. I ran for it and, just looking around the corner, I saw two sentries. They jumped, I had the pin out of the bomb, just holding the level with my fingers. I took my head back and slipped the bomb round. As soon as it exploded I went round. The Germans must have got into the Pill-Box before it exploded. I had no more bombs and looking around for help I saw Lieutenant Colvin* with 2 men at another Pill-Box which were in ruins about 30 yards on my left. I waved them over, Colvin were the first to reach me. He asked 'How many have you got there, Gerrard?' I told him I had only seen two who were on sentry and I wanted two bombs to get them out. He got two bombs off one of his men, gave me one and we threw one into each entrance together. One exploded slightly before the other. As the second bomb exploded they started to come out with their hands up, the first man who came out of my entrance were a smart chap over six feet. They must have thought they were surrounded, he was without tunic. I think he was the Officer, he just looked around with an expression of surprise on his face, then he looked at me and, smiling,

nodded and went the way I pointed. I have never seen a man take it like this when he has just been captured. He was not scared, or vindictive, he just went with an amused smile on his face. He must have been a grand chap to take it like this. You usually see them scared and trembling or they glare at you, and he was the only German I was sorry to see killed when some of our chaps saw them coming around the Pill-Box with their hands up they rushed for them, and a German machine gun played onto them and the Officer got killed along with some of our men who were after souvenirs off the prisoners.

PRIVATE JAMES GERRARD DCM MM,
9TH CHESHIRE REGIMENT

* Footnote: Second Lieutenant Hugh Colvin was awarded the VC for his part in the capture of the pillbox at Potsdam Farm whilst Gerrard received the MM for taking two messages to Headquarters over open ground under fire.

Passchendaele Village

Railway cutting near Tyne Cot

Left
German trench and pillboxes captured
by 9th Division troops on 20 September.
Simple shelters have already been
erected.

Below
Panorama 127. The pulverized battlefield
in front of Zonnebeke and the present
view from a nearby position. Within two
weeks the battlefield had been fitted with
a vast infrastructure of roads, tramways,
tracks, pipelines, cableways and gunpits.
See page 300.

Pillbox fighting showed the true worth of the lighter Lewis guns, now numbering thirty per battalion. Normally difficult and cumbersome to handle, and with only six seconds of fire before the ammunition drum was empty, the Lewis was not an ideal weapon for general static trench warfare. When it came to the kind of fighting now required in the Salient, however, it was grand for 'pillbox-busting', a clash where absolute accuracy was perhaps less important than the sensation created by intense automatic fire upon a potentially ensnared defence.

For nearby shell-hole-based resistance – an equally serious barrier – a battalion could now count upon the talents of sixteen trained rifle-grenadiers and eight rapid-firing Stokes mortar crews. The heavier Vickers machine guns followed the advancing infantry, and when events dictated laid down long-distance barrages to supplement artillery. The key lay in keeping weapons working in a muddy or dusty landscape full of concealed enemies.

After taking the Pill Box I got my team together (minus the gun) and pushed on, ordering them to keep the Gun ammunition, as it would be welcome on another gun at the objective. We were now on top of Hill 37 and I observed some 5 Germans in a shell hole, and just in front of me were one or two of our wounded, so I could not fire. However I covered them and they came out like sheep with their hands up, and I sent them to the rear. I had no sooner done this than Fritz began to sweep us with machine gun bullets from other Pill Boxes and we had to get down. I told my

Broodseinde Crossroads   Zonnebeke station   Zonnebeke Church   BROODSEINDE RIDGE   Ypres - Roulers railway

men to follow me, but when I arrived at Gallipoli Farm I was alone and in the midst of a series of Pill Boxes. We had taken 6 more without any trouble, capturing about 50 prisoners in them but the ones in front were occupied. I could do nothing by myself, so had a look round. I was well in advance of our boys and in a tight corner, a sniper was on my right, but I could not locate him and a machine gun on my left, and I was under their cross-fire. However another L/Cpl out of 4 Platoon came up to me then and we were discussing what should be done, when a bomb hit me on the leg and rolled between us. I can tell you we did not think about machine guns then but risked everything and landed safely in the next shell hole. There I discovered two of my platoon and 2nd Lieutenant Hassop, and we had a consultation. Here we were for about an hour, held by the sniper who had seen us move and was firing at us, we could see the strike of his bullets on the side of the shell hole so had to keep low. Being by ourselves and unable to do anything, we at last decided to try and get back for a little help. I had stuck to my spade, so we took it in turns to dig ourselves out. We got to the next shell hole at last and from there made short dashes back to the main body.

PRIVATE WALTER HOSKYN, 5TH KING'S (LIVERPOOL REGIMENT)

Thankfully for the British and Australians, the improved performance of the gunners extended to counter-battery work, and although isolated German SOS barrages caused breakdowns in some places, harassment from hostile artillery was thankfully more disjointed than usual. The Australians also managed to quickly capture Anzac House on the Westhoek Ridge, the observation and command post that had directed such devastating enfilade gunfire across the northern battlefield during the August attacks.

During the afternoon, the Hun shelling along Bellewaarde and Westhoek Ridges got pretty hot and several came pretty close. One

large one landed about 10 yards from the pill box whilst I was trying to tie a radial artery, and covered us with mud and dirt. My fingers all became thumbs and I wasn't much use for a minute or so from fright. We could see Anzac House about a mile away with shells falling all around it. This was our final objective. One stretcher bearer was killed, and two wounded on the Bellewaarde Ridge this afternoon. This day seemed very long to me. About 5 o'clock saw our batteries beginning to move up, and large parties of pioneers building a road across shell holes, in order to get the guns up over Bellewaarde Ridge. Several shells landed amongst these parties during the afternoon, and they had very large casualties. As fast as they build the corduroy road, the Hun kept blowing it up with shell. About 5.30 pm our bombardment ceased but the Hun kept pasting Bellewaarde Ridge and the lake.

CAPTAIN DONALD COUTTS, AUSTRALIAN ARMY MEDICAL CORPS, REGIMENTAL MEDICAL OFFICER TO 24TH INFANTRY BATTALION, AUSTRALIAN IMPERIAL FORCE

The morning mist quickly cleared to reveal a bright sunny day. With the outpost zone overrun, each position in the battle zone was attacked by its own dedicated assault party. These rearward defences were subdued rather than destroyed largely by shellfire, for the new irregular fire-pattern ensured that the Germans soon became aware that the moment one barrage had passed over, a fresh one was certainly on its way sooner or later. Those troops unprotected by concrete were therefore forced to keep low. Gradually the British were closing in on Zonnebeke, Polygon Wood and Gheluvelt. The aforementioned Menin Road (Hooge) tunnel with its several entrances and extensive shelter became one of the most important features of the northern battlefront, sheltering hundreds of men and incorporating several dressing stations.

Unhappily for me my movement coincided with that of a large and slow-moving tank which immediately drew the special attention of a German howitzer. I do not remember how many shells were fired but one of them landed at my feet smashing my elbow and piercing my right knee. Although I was hit also in the head I felt almost nothing except extreme thirst. I was still able to hobble along with bent knee and proceeded to dismiss myself to the rear. There was an advanced dressing station within a hundred yards or so where I was offered brandy and a sling for my arm. Whilst I was in the dressing station another tank came wobbling up, passing with one of its caterpillars over the end of the dressing station. All the inmates bolted for the door for safety and I

continued on my way along duck-boards to the rear till I met two stretcher bearers vastly relieved by the prospect of picking up a proper passenger at that point. In the advanced operating hospital which must have been near Poperinghe, I regained consciousness in comfort of both body and mind. It was not apparent to me that I had lost a limb. The nervous system remains unaltered by an amputation: nearly fifty years later I can still 'feel' my right hand and each individual finger, though it gives the impression of being attached at the end of an elbowless stump. For some reasons I remained in ignorance until visited by those who were anxious to break the news gently; and I remember the few but kindly and helpful words of the doctor who had operated.

CAPTAIN J.R. BELLERBY, 8TH WEST YORKSHIRE REGIMENT, ATTACHED 248TH MACHINE GUN COMPANY

On the central battlefront Plumer's Second Army achieved almost all its objectives. On the right his 19th (Western) Division captured two important woods, Bulgar and Belgian, to form a firm flank. The strategic village of Zandvoorde now lay before them, screened for much of the day by a smoke barrage laid down by British guns to obscure enemy observation. On their left the 39th Division began well, but came to suffer

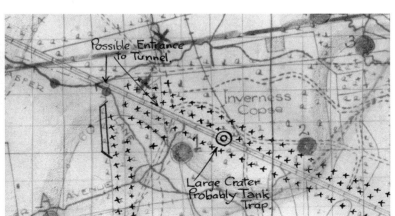

badly through hidden machine guns firing diagonally from the left flank, the 41st Division front. Nevertheless final objectives were attained. The 41st had probably the most hazardous approach, needing to negotiate the wide marshy valley of the Bassevillebeek in order to reach their prominent objective on the high ground beyond, Tower Hamlets, from which heavy fire had originated that held back the 39th Division. Despite fine, organized shooting, the British guns failed to neutralize the immense strong points on this important ridge spur, leaving a swathe of untouched pillboxes in treacherous positions near the crest of the plateau, and an adjacent group of fortified farms to the south-east known as The Quadrilateral. Both 41st and 23rd Divisions were not just baulked, but cut to pieces by the ferocity of the fire, so chronicles of this action are rare.

20.9.17

I have been on duty in the signal office a good deal during the day and little bits of information have been trickling through regarding the progress of the attack. Putting them all together the situation seems like this. Fritz had occupied some of the derelict tanks lying in no man's land and had made strongpoints of them. He fought desperately and disputed every inch of ground, and his snipers remained at their posts, hidden in tree trunks etc., and even after our troops had passed them and continued to shoot our men from behind. One of them was captured badly wounded, and Colonel Carey-Barnard* coming up, raised his revolver to kill him but, seeing his terrible wounds, refrained, and the wretch then pointed out where one of his sniping comrades was hidden. A machine-gun post in a pill-box held our men up for a long time. Our artillery played on it but could not get a direct hit. The Hants could get no further. They had lost all their officers and a great many men. Colonel Corfe of the Kents tried to rally the men but was soon hit by a bullet in the shoulder, but he held on until the post had been outflanked. Then he collapsed.

SAPPER ALBERT MARTIN, 41ST SIGNAL COMPANY, ROYAL ENGINEERS

* Colonel Carey-Barnard appears to have been quite a character. According to Sapper Martin, the Colonel's dog once 'absented itself without leave for a couple of days and on its return he awarded it Field Punishment No. 1. It was tied to a tree and fed only on biscuits and water for a prescribed period.' He also returned his cook to his company for failing to produce an egg and bacon breakfast in the welter of the Messines Ridge Battle.

Above
Panorama segment looking across the Gheluvelt plateau.

Right
13th Durham Light Infantry (69 Brigade, 23rd Division) awaiting the whistle for their Veldhoek attack on 20 September.

Inset
Final preparation of the Durhams: one GS shovel per four men. The photograph portrays the tension of the moment.

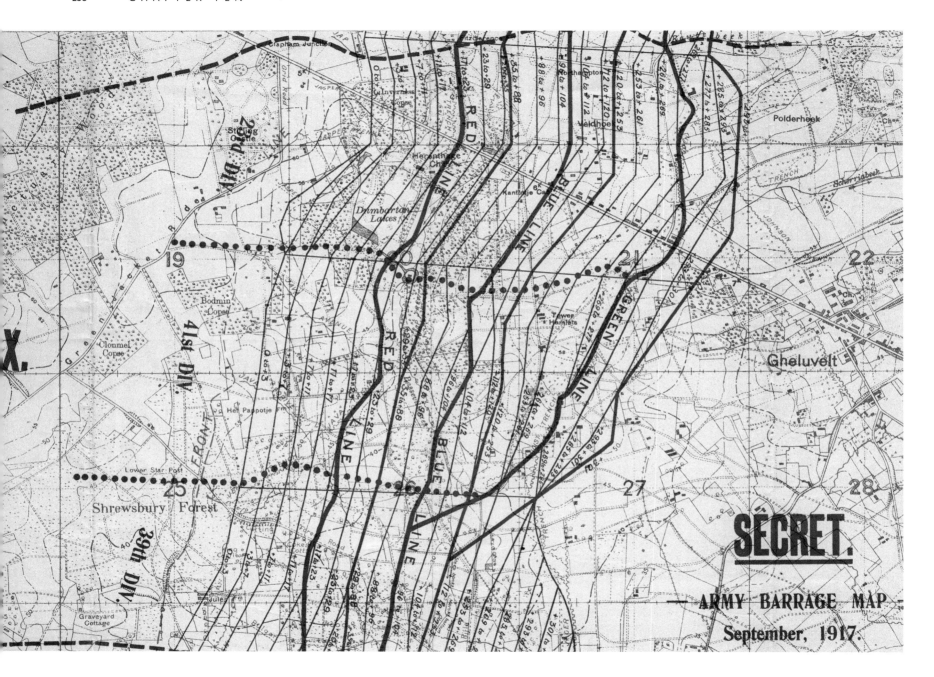

SECRET.

ARMY BARRAGE MAP

September, 1917.

Above
Tower Hamlets appears totally obliterated, but the pillboxes survived.

Left
Barrage map for 20 September showing red, blue and green objectives, and covering the attacking front south of the Menin Road.

The attacks on Tower Hamlets came to rest short of the final objective. With I Anzac Corps (1st and 2nd Australian Divisions) capturing all their objectives across the Menin Road and beyond to the junction with Fifth Army near the Ypres–Roulers railway, the breakdown left an unattractive belly in the new British line. In the chaos and disappointment, not unsurprisingly local belief was that the entire advance had followed the same dismal pattern.

20.9.17

It is now apparent that the attack has fallen far short of what was expected. I expect tomorrow the English papers will be shouting the news of a great victory, but it has been a ghastly and murderous failure. A reinforcement arrived for us this evening – a young fellow just out from England. It's ridiculous to send a new recruit up to a place like this. I was surprised to see some Military Police in the tunnels [Canada Street tunnels, Observatory Ridge]. They are the warriors who infest the rest areas and spend their time 'running' poor Tommies who leave cycles unattended for a few seconds. Their business up here is to prowl round the tunnels looking for men who have taken shelter when they ought to be outside. A miserably ignoble trade.

SAPPER ALBERT MARTIN, 41ST SIGNAL COMPANY, ROYAL ENGINEERS

In fact, on the plateau every targeted wood and copse had been engaged, taken – and left behind. Only Tower Hamlets had resisted. As soon as objectives had been reached the British consolidated by fortifying strings of shellholes. In some places short sections of fire trench were constructed. A new lesson was learned here: such anomalous linear features amongst a sea of craters were easily spotted from the air and received severe hostile artillery attention. Throughout the battle German observers on the ridges had been able to guide the guns onto the less challenging targets of support and auxiliary troops moving and working behind the lines.

It was now about 2 p.m. and we were not half way to our objective, but reinforcements were coming up. A shell got rather close and I got a piece in the back of my left hand, but thought nothing of it. At 2.30 p.m. the reinforcements were up to us. One of them noticed my hand, which was covered in blood and feeling stiff and sore, he bandaged me up and told me to clear off, as it was sufficient to go down with, I did not think so, but I had had enough so went down. After staying about an hour and having a good rest at the Field Dressing Station I got my ticket to proceed off the battlefield. I gave up all my food rations and water bottle and followed the track down which the stretcher bearers were going. I only got a little way down when shells began to fly quite close so had to take cover behind another pill box. What surprised me here were the shells sticking to the concrete walls unexploded, just the base of them showing. After a little while I proceeded and got on the 'Fatal Wooden track' leading to St Julien. Disabled Tanks and men were lying right and left, and huge shell craters were in the track and all round it. Nevertheless Labour Battalion men were persevering and putting fresh bundles of sticks and logs of wood down. Now I came in amongst our Field artillery and they were hard at it. Limbers, GS Wagons and other vehicles were bringing up 18-pounder shells etc. In fact the place was thickly strewn with shells. I had just got past a number of such wagons after a little difficulty when all of a sudden our guns stopped firing and overhead appeared a German aeroplane, closely followed by our anti aircraft guns which were giving him a very warm reception. I had now arrived at our original Front line trench so I got down a mine shaft out of the way of shrapnel etc. I think I

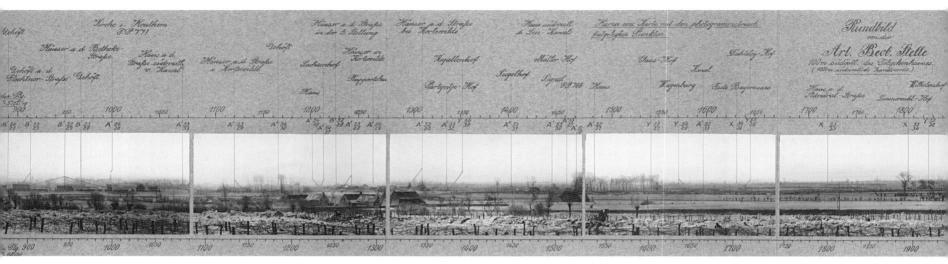

was here for about quarter of an hour till the fun was over and Fritz went back. I saw a number of German prisoners passing down, helping wounded men and carrying stretchers etc. They seemed jolly glad to be on their way out of it.

PRIVATE WALTER HOSKYN, 5TH KING'S (LIVERPOOL REGIMENT)

A number of Victoria Crosses were won on the day, several for individual gallantry in taking pill-boxes, even groups of strong points, single-handedly. Such actions illustrated how defenders were more than willing to throw in the towel once a position was outflanked, for the penalties meted out for perceived excessive resistance were ruthless. The British protective barrages were sustained, falling up to 2 kilometres beyond the foremost positions to catch *Eingreif* troops. Expecting deeper penetration, they were thus forced into a 'killing zone' themselves, but one of British making. In places it had even been possible to so arrange the barrage as to

advance and meet the enemy. Though numerous and heavy, every counter-attack on the plateau was felled, with grave German losses.

Plumer and Harington's tactics appeared to have prevailed. British and Australian troops were well up onto the plateau now. For some of the old lags, the village of Gheluvelt, last seen during the November 1914 retirement, now lay almost within touching distance once more. Beyond could be seen unsullied green fields, all the way to Brussels. Another ribbon of Flanders had been pulverized to achieve the view. The guns ruled the battlefield. It was a scene of devastation few had witnessed before.

I pushed on up the duckboard track to Stirling Castle – a mound of powdered brick from where there is to be had a magnificent panorama of the battlefield. The way was gruesome and awful beyond words. The ground had been recently heavily shelled by the Boche and the dead and wounded lay about everywhere. About here the ground had the appearance of hav-

Above

1916 German panorama taken from the defensive lines running through Zandvoorde, which with Gheluvelt was hoped to be the next British objective when the Tower Hamlets ridge had fallen. Neither village was taken during the battle.

ing been ploughed by a great canal excavator, and then re-ploughed and turned over again and again. Last night's shower too made it a quagmire, and through this the wounded had to drag themselves and those mortally wounded pass out their young lives. I saw a horrible sight take place within about 20 yards of me. Five Boche prisoners were carrying one of our wounded in to the dressing station when one of the enemy's own shells struck the group. All were almost instantly killed, three being blown to atoms. Another shell killed four and I saw them die, frightfully mutilated in the deep slime of a shell crater. How ever anyone escapes being hit by the show-ers of flying metal is incomprehensible. The battlefield on which we won an advance of 1500 yards was littered with bits of men, our own and Boche, and literally drenched with blood. It almost makes one doubt the existence of a deity — that such things can go on beneath the omnipotent eye. The Menin Road was a wondrous sight with stretchers packed on either side awaiting transport, and the centre crowded with walking wounded and prisoners. On returning via Ypres I saw a large number of these latter enjoying a great meal of white bread and cheese. The poor devils were ravenous, and I am pleased to say that our fellows treated them kindly, not as en-emies, but as fallen heroes, for indeed these men were, for our mighty artillery bombardment fairly tore the earth into fur-rows. God knows how anyone could escape it unless in the safety of the impregnable pillboxes.

CAPTAIN FRANK HURLEY, OFFICIAL PHOTOGRAPHER,
AUSTRALIAN IMPERIAL FORCE

The hideous state of the battlefield was not only evident to those on the ground.

20 SEPTEMBER

Day of great push. Counter attack and contact went up. Rained and clouds low so didn't go up all day.

21 SEPTEMBER

Went up with Dorey on DX87 at 3 p.m. Huns rather plentiful but didn't bother us. Some of the shell holes appear quite red from air owing to blood. Horrible sight. This was confirmed by other pilots so was not imagination.

LIEUTENANT H.A. BLUNDELL, NO. 21 SQUADRON,
ROYAL FLYING CORPS

Fifth Army employed Plumer's tactics and achieved similar successes, annexing almost all of the Langemarck Line despite being able to employ fewer belts of barrage fire. Many of Gough's men had also been subjected to a hostile barrage almost on the stroke of zero (again 5.40 a.m.), and their low-contour approach was more sticky and difficult than that of the plateau or Zonnebeke approaches. Mud, marsh and the *bekes* should have made the going heavy and slow, and more difficult for the troops to follow the creeping barrage, but their training had also included study of the most awkward spots. These were carefully avoided. Conditions were worst on the far left flank where two brigades of the 20th (Light) Division failed to fully overcome Eagle Trench (actually a breastwork) and were unable to make intended progress; on their right, however, 51st (Highland) and 58th (London) Divisions were entirely successful. The imbalance left a dog-leg in the line, but German counter-attacks were nevertheless swept away. As usual, as combat subsided clearing the wounded became the most critical task.

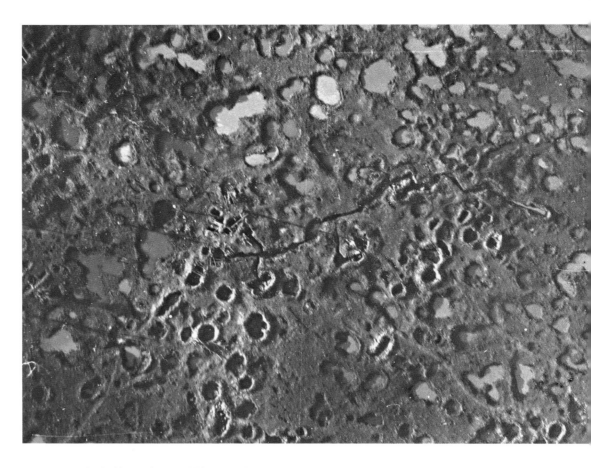

This time St Julian and beyond. Janet Farm and Cluster Houses, this again was an awful journey and having to take orders from a certain officer made it doubly hard. He was white livered and yellow, anyhow he was on this occasion when it required nothing but courage and nerve and a little spot of kindness. Being shelled heavily we took refuge in Janet Farm, another German concrete strongpoint. This so called officer forced us out and seeing we were reluctant to go said he would shoot us, so we were between the devil and the deep blue sea. I have never seen a man in such a state before. I think he must have been mad at the time. Anyway out we went and eventually reached Cluster Houses, at least some of us, I was a man short in my squad. So asked for a volunteer. One man promptly did so, a fine, well built

young man, who for his devotion was killed instantly on the back of my stretcher. I was at the front; I heard the shell and shouted 'down', but he wasn't soon enough. This was heartbreaking. Here we were caught in a barrage and all we could do was to drag stretcher and patient into a shell hole and hope for the best. And this we did for over an hour. I wrote to this young man's mother. How these mothers have suffered.
SERGEANT NORMAN FERMOR, ROYAL ARMY MEDICAL CORPS

With the help of armour, rectification was attempted the following day. The tanks attached to elements of 20th (Light) Division were disabled in Langemarck long before reaching

Above and right
The only form of cover on newly-won territory other than captured pillboxes and a few shattered trenches was the shell hole. Here, British troops (whose helmets can clearly be seen) have deepened and connected several to form a strongpoint. See also page 343. Connecting trenches, as seen in the example on the right, were susceptible to flooding. This picture is actually from 31 July, but is representative of practices throughout the battle.

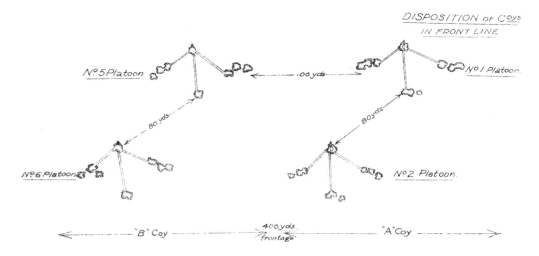

DISPOSITION OF COYS
IN FRONT LINE

N°5 Platoon   .100 yds   N°1 Platoon

80 yds   80 yds

N°6 Platoon   N°2 Platoon

"B" Coy   400 yds frontage   "A" Coy

Above
Corps instructions on how to form
defensible shell-hole strongpoints.

positions from which help could be rendered. Although Eagle Trench finally fell on the 23rd, the line could not be brought far enough forward to conform with Maxse's XVIII Corps positions. On the morning of the 21st, 123 Brigade of 41st Division also tried to erase the unsightly belly on the southern side of the battlefront in front of

Tower Hamlets. It was a chaotic endeavour and, for some, a bitterly hard introduction to the Western Front.

21.9.17

At 8.30 this morning the Sergeant sent for me. He directed me to take Cochran (the new man) and go to Sgt. Jordan and bring back two drums of cable. It was wanted urgently as all our lines had been blown to smithereens and our supply of cable was exhausted. Immediately I got out of the sap [Hedge Street tunnel] I knew we were in for a rough journey as Fritz was giving us a most terrific shelling. Every conceivable type of shell was bursting all around, whiz-bangs, H.E.'s, H.V.'s, liquid fire, gas shells and all manner of shrapnel, the latter bursting a dozen at a time. When we got to the end of the little bit of trench I scrambled out, but Cochran lost his head and shouted out, 'Don't, go, don't go, we shall get killed.' It was no time to be nice so I told him not to be a fool but to come along, and I caught hold of him and pulled him up on to the parapet. A shell burst a little way away on our left and out of the smoke emerged two men one supporting the other who had been badly hit. Another burst on our right and Cochran threw himself behind a pile of duckboards. I fetched him out and he hung on to my coat and tried to pull me into a shell-hole. I coaxed him and cursed him but he hadn't a ha'porth of nerve and I literally had to drag him along. It was a thousand times worse than going by myself. When we got to Canada Tunnels he recovered himself somewhat. I found Sgt. Jordan, an old soldier, and he refused to let me have the cable because I had not brought a demand note signed by an officer. He actually wanted me to go back and get it. I thought many strong things but didn't say them. I talked nicely to him, pointed out the urgency, and told him what a nice fellow he was. Eventually he agreed to let me have the two drums if I promised faithfully to bring back the demand note at once. I was in the mood to promise anything though I had not the slightest intention of keeping any promise I might make. The drums weighed half a hundredweight [25 kg] each, which is quite as much as any man would like to carry over this churned

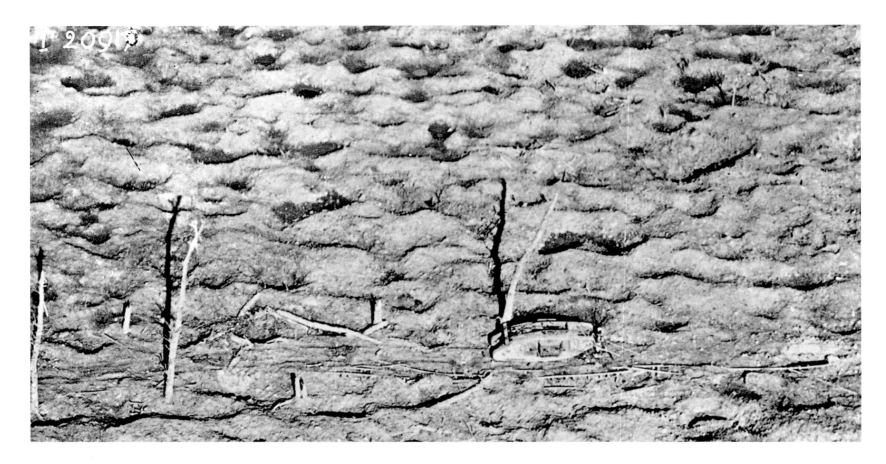

and muddy country. Before we left the tunnels I gave Cochran a good talking to and told him that we had got to get back to Hedge Street in the quickest possible time; therefore he had better not act the giddy ox but keep close behind me and only duck into shell-holes if he saw me do it. I glanced back two or three times and saw that he was following, although the distance between us was increasing. After jumping over a fragment of trench I proceeded for about 50 yards before looking round, and then Cochran was nowhere to be seen. I dumped the cable and was just going back to find him when he scrambled out of a trench, trembling and blubbering worse than ever. In his fright he had failed to jump over

the trench, and dropped down right on to a dead body. It was some job to fetch him along after that, but at last we got into the tunnel. The distance was only about 300 yards each way, but it had taken us 2 solid hours.

Sapper Albert Martin, 41st Signal Company, Royal Engineers

The following day Albert Martin's diary revealed another facet of the fighting and the 41st Division's failure; this time he observed the opposite end of the military ladder.

Above

A remarkable low-level aerial photograph believed to show the tank D41, Dracula, forging a lone passage along the St Julien–Poelcappelle road on 20 September. Its unditching beam can be seen attached to the top rear; it would probably only be required after the tank left the road and entered the perilous crater fields to each side.

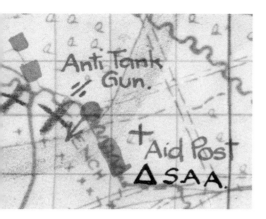

Above
Map segment showing the positions of a German anti-tank gun, machine-gun post (with arrow), an aid post and a small-arms ammunition cache.

Below
How anti-tank guns were protected and used in the Salient. The shelter is a similar steel-reinforced concrete construction to a pillbox.

22.9.17

Last evening Fritz treated our front line to a hurricane bombardment and developed a counter-attack. Our men were quite exhausted and it is no wonder that some of them started to retire without receiving orders to do so. Colonel Carey Barnard and Major Pennell (KRRC) drove them back at the point of the revolver. For some time the position was extremely critical, but our artillery managed to stop the counter-attack. The troops are all mixed up, men of different units and even different Divisions, are huddled together in shellholes. The Brigade Major has been up the line and has sent a secret report into Division. There is no doubt of the seriousness of the situation for on the phone I overheard a most amazing conversation between our Brigadier [122 Brigade] and the Divisional Commander [41st Division]. The Brigadier was very firm in his insistence that our infantry is thoroughly exhausted and totally unable to make any resistance if the Huns attacked. They would break right through our lines if once they got beyond our artillery barrage. The Div. Commander tried his hardest to get the Brigadier to say that we can hold on for another 24 hours, but General Towsey wouldn't take the responsibility of making any such statement. Lawford, of course, is looking to the laurels of the Division and the honour that will fall to him. When General Towsey told him that the men could get neither rations nor water he merely replied, 'Let them take the iron rations from the

killed and wounded.' This conversation lasted about half an hour and I expect it will result in a speedy relief.
Sapper Albert Martin, 41st Signal Company,
Royal Engineers

Relief arrived within hours. Apart from the Eagle Trench and Tower Hamlets sectors, overall it had been an excellent battle for the British and Australians. Communication, mainly by lamp, runners and pigeons, had been relatively uninterrupted throughout the fighting, and on the whole the guns had performed excellently, both in attack and in defence, breaking up counter-attacks. Now, Field and Pioneer companies were extending cable trenches as close to the firing line as possible. In the air clear skies had also helped observers to send almost 400 wireless messages, a substantial number of which instantly directed British artillery towards fresh targets to be neutralized before the next step. Above all, it was the shattering of every German counter-attack that most delighted Plumer, Gough and Haig. By nightfall on 23 September the *Eingreif's* fearsome power had been seriously blunted. Over 3,000 prisoners languished in the cages, and a good proportion of the plateau was now in British and Australian hands. It was a significant achievement, and one that forced von Armin to look again at his defensive tactics.

Sir Douglas Haig in his diary describes as 'slight' the combined Second and Fifth Army casualties of 20,255. The casualty/gain balance was actually far more favourable than usual, but to continue in such a way was going to require a constant stream of reserves, derived from other sectors of the Western Front or untested new drafts from the UK. In theatre the losses, as

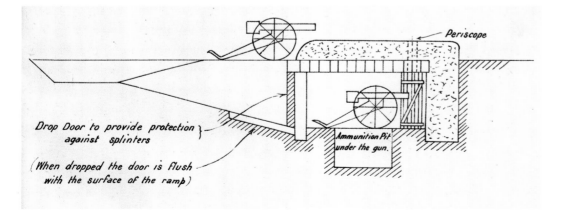

Periscope

Drop Door to provide protection
against splinters

(When dropped the door is flush
with the surface of the ramp)

*Ammunition Pit
under the gun.*

always, were accepted by the troops. Plumer's careful administration had been appreciated: men had gone into battle fresh and rested, been relieved within 48 hours and could expect a decent period out of the line before returning. During the next few days numerous German attempts were made to claw back some of the lost ground, especially the higher contours. Every incursion was expunged. Elsewhere, the ancillary industries of war were in full flow with men making and repairing roads, installing cables, draining, digging fresh positions for the guns, evacuating wounded and burying the dead. Pack transport streamed back and forth, and fresh tracks and tramways appeared. At the same time the entire Salient, still under hostile observation of course, was in the process of being screened with row upon row of hessian and canvas 'walls' stretching miles across the battlefield, baulking enemy view of British activities. This was all very necessary for Plumer's next step was to take place soon, on 26 September. The Germans knew it was coming and made life as tough as possible for all concerned in making the arrangements. As usual roads and batteries naturally received the harshest treatment; no sooner was a track or tramway started than it was shelled; day and night the German guns harried reliefs, supply columns and transport with HE and gas. But this was no more than the British expected after such a triumph. What counted was that someone was at last investing profound thought into solving a problem that had appeared intractable. Despite the triumphs of 20 September, the men, long inured to the kind of optimism enjoyed by Sir Douglas Haig, were phlegmatic; the future was still opaque.

BEF 25.9.17

My Dear Father,

This letter will be neither a long, nor, I am afraid, a cheerful one, for I am feeling quite the reverse of cheerful. A few hours under bombardment, with the knowledge that one may at any moment be blown to pieces, gives one a wonderful insight into the characters of one's comrades: and living under these conditions you take either a violent – and often inexplicable – antipathy, or feel a real love for your fellow sufferers. We have lost from our section one of the most sweet-dispositioned men I have ever met, who was killed on the same day on which he was Gazetted for the Military Medal. Those who have never seen death, other than as a peace-

Near Garter Point. A typical scene acted out every day of the offensive: a party of stretcher bearers carry a casualty back along duckboard tracks. The carry was often one of several kilometres; the risks, especially at night, are self-evident.

Telephone cables being laid by Australian signallers and linesmen on 21 September. The protective 'bury' here is around a metre and a half in the foreground but is being deepened by a second party behind. The cable systems are occasionally uncovered today.

ful passing over, cannot realize the horror of a sudden and violent end. You may be walking along happily enough, when suddenly there is a cry from your companion, and he lies dying at your feet; or worse, you leave him for a few minutes and return to find hardly a trace of him remaining. Dead and mutilated bodies everywhere; streams – apparently endless – of wounded; numbers of the relieving troops wiped out before they even get up to the line: the whizz and whine and shriek of shells: deafening crashes. The trail of blood along the duckboards which lead back over the mud. The stench of corpses, gas, HE: one's friends falling all round: the earth mutilated in a wilderness of shapeless craters. This doesn't make such a beautiful picture, though doubtless it all serves a useful purpose. At least those who would carry on the slaughter for ever have the satisfaction of knowing that it doesn't so much matter if all the reserves are killed; the best of the country's manhood is already dead. You may think me unduly morbid, or even worse – for indeed it is by no means uncommon to see men's minds quite unhinged: but I am quite my normal self, only feeling very grieved and even more than usually bitter against the war – for-ever-and-everites. Against the Germans, too, I feel very strongly, after seeing them deliberately bomb a hospital by daylight from a very low altitude.

Well, I suppose I must try and be a bit more cheerful, which should not be very difficult as I think we shall very shortly be going back for a long rest to recuperate. I've just had a long overdue letter from AF dated 14th., in which she tells me my letters have recently been more interesting, so now I feel bound to try and keep up the high standard. If one puts in the background for a moment the object of it all, the colossal preparations for a stunt are interesting. Strings of lorries laden with shells, trench boards, men, wagons full of food, bombs, ammunition, petrol, tins full of water. All along the roads are 'dumps' where tons of stores are piled; often at night, one sees a great glow in the sky and knows that somewhere an ammunition dump has gone up. Trains and light railways, too, are used, and one wonders where it can all come from. It was a wonderful sight the other morning when the weather cleared to see hundreds (literally) of aeroplanes with which the sky seemed crowded; indeed there wasn't room for them all up there, for I saw two collide and come crashing down.

We are having absolutely perfect weather: misty mornings followed by cloudless days, only it is becoming rather cold at night.
PRIVATE CHARLES BIRNSTINGL, 9TH LONDON REGIMENT (QUEEN VICTORIA'S RIFLES)

Misty mornings and cool evenings signified that autumn was drawing close. Soon, the climate could again be expected to pose problems for the British.

Left

A Frank Hurley picture from 20 September, showing the view looking back from Stirling Castle towards Hooge crater, with 1st Australian Division men moving up to the attack on Glencorse Wood. The shell burst looks relatively benign, but at the moment the picture was taken three men were killed and several seriously wounded. The body language of some of the men at the front of the column indicates their understanding of the repercussions.

Another Blow Struck – Advance east of Ypres – Important Positions Won – Fight for Final Objectives – 2,000 Prisoners Taken

THE FOLLOWING TELEGRAPHIC DESPATCHES WERE YESTERDAY RECEIVED FROM GENERAL HEADQUARTERS IN FRANCE:

10.6 A.M. – We attacked at 5.40 a.m. this morning on a wide front east of Ypres. Satisfactory progress is reported, and our troops have already captured some valuable positions.

10.6 P.M. – Our attack this morning east of Ypres was made on a front of about eight miles between the Ypres-Comines Canal and the Ypres-Staden railway. Great success attended our troops; positions of considerable military importance have been won and heavy casualties inflicted on the enemy.

The assembling of the regiments detailed for the attack was carried out without incident, although rain fell steadily during the night. Our first objectives were captured at an early hour, including a number of concreted strong points and fortified farms, for the possession of which heavy fighting had taken place during previous attacks.

North Country regiments carried Inverness Copse. Australian troops stormed Glencorse Wood and Nonne Boschen. Scottish and South African brigades took Potsdam, Vampire, and Borry Farms. West Lancashire Territorials carried Iberian Farm and the strong point known as Gallipoli.

Our troops then advanced to the assault of their final objectives. On our right English county troops reached the line of their final objectives after sharp fighting in the woods north of the Ypres-Comines Canal and in the neighbourhood of Tower Hamlets.

In the centre North Country and Australian Battalions penetrated the German positions to a depth of over a mile and captured the whole of their objectives, including the hamlet of Veldhoek and the western portion of Polygon Wood. Further north Zevenkote was captured, and London and Highland Territorials carried a second line of farms, including Rose Farm, Quebec Farm, and Wurst Farm, on the line of their final objectives.

During the morning the weather cleared, and our aeroplanes were able to make a more active part in the battle, indicating the position of our troops and reporting hostile concentration to our artillery. In this way a number of German counter-attacks were broken up, while others were repulsed by rifle and machine-gun fire of our infantry.

No accurate estimate of the number of prisoners captured can yet be given, but they are known to exceed 2,000. We also captured a few guns.

GERMAN OFFICIAL REPORT, SEPTEMBER 20:

FRONT OF CROWN PRINCE RUPPRECHT. – *In Flanders the strong artillery duel lasted throughout the day between the Houthulst Wood and the Lys with undiminished intensity. Bursts of fire of the greatest violence were directed in turn on some sectors of our defence zone. The night did not interrupt the increased fighting activity of the massed artillery.*

Formidable drumfire in the early morning was followed at day-break, according to reports at present to hand, by strong English attacks on a broad front.

EVENING. – *The battle in Flanders is still in full swing on the English front from Langemarck to Hollebeke. In the foremost part of our defensive zone bitter and fluctuating fighting has taken place since the morning.*

CHAPTER ELEVEN
Plumer's Second Step – Polygon

We start today for business. The battalion is very fit and marches well and it is second to none in its own opinion and so its morale is splendid. It is now well trained and has a fine sprinkling of boys of 19 years and a good seasoning of older men. The men are all right, the NCO's heaps improved and the officers much better. And so with eager hearts and great determination and knowing we shall beat the Bosche we start off for the Third Battle of Ypres.

CAPTAIN N.P. PRITCHARD MC, 20TH MANCHESTER REGIMENT

After the accomplishments of the Menin Road it became clearer than ever that Sir Douglas Haig believed the German Army to be on the point of disintegration. His especially buoyant disposition precipitated behaviour similar to that which had followed late successes the previous year on the Somme, when he ordered Rawlinson and Gough to draw up plans to break out and aim for

Left

A house in Zonnebeke being used as a German headquarters. The regiment's number is painted on the shutters, whilst the sign over the door assists newcomers to orientate themselves.

Below

An ostensibly deserted Zonnebeke village in early spring 1916. The church roof and once distinctive modern square tower have long gone. Many hundreds of German troops are secreted in the ruins.

Cambrai 30 kilometres distant. Haig once more contacted Admiral Sir Reginald Bacon to discuss renewed possibilities for attacks on the Belgian coast. The aspiration was to advance in the coming fortnight as far again as the troops had managed during the first seven weeks of battle, about 6 kilometres. That, however, was only the first phase: Roulers and Thourout, the key German supply nuclei originally marked down as potential targets for Day Two of the offensive, would immediately follow. And so on, driving the Germans to the Dutch border as in the original offensive scheme. Bacon said amphibious land-

ings were possible at any time up to early November, when changes in tides would make things considerably more awkward. Be prepared, said Haig. Despite Charteris' cheering intelligence summaries, however, on the battlefield there were no valid physical signs of German collapse. On 25 September GHQ received a genuine wake-up call. Preceded by a deluge of shells almost as intense as that which the British were now accustomed to applying, two fresh German divisions launched a heavy counter-attack against a section of the Wilhelm Line south of Polygon Wood.

1 a.m. of 26th. when I make this entry – just developed [photographs] – tired as the devil. Been at it since 8 this morning. Went to Anzac Heights – had a hell of a time in the midst of heavy shelling – battlefield terribly torn, like a heavy sea. Boche sends 'barrage terrific' on to Inverness Kops [sic] and Glencorse Wood – great many casualties. He evidently anticipates our next stunt and is amassing great reserves and concentrating artillery – on the eve of a great battle. Boche shells our communication ways all day – smashes up the Menin Road – wagons, dumps, and everything ablaze, dugouts smashed in. Wilkins and I nearly blown up by a dump which exploded only 100 yards away; hit with flying wood and mud. Thank God we are unscathed. Gothas come over and bomb; altogether the hottest affair I have been in – shells bursting everywhere. Battle comes off tomorrow – great uneasiness and anxiety. Things seem unsettled and a trifle demoralised by the superb Boche shelling. We are off to cine affairs at 7.30 and wish the day was well over. I must have a few hours sleep.

CAPTAIN FRANK HURLEY, OFFICIAL PHOTOGRAPHER,
AUSTRALIAN IMPERIAL FORCE

The enemy penetration was considerable – almost half the ground that had been won in front of Polygon Wood on the 20th was reclaimed. And it came at a bad time, for British and Australian troops were in full preparation for the second stage. This preparation was partly the reason for the enemy success, for at the very moment of their assault the 33rd Division was in the process of relieving the 23rd. Confusion reigned. Without an established trench infrastructure to control traffic, reliefs were doubly complicated, taking far longer than normal. The attacks were halted through a fortunate loss of German direction in dense early morning mist, a perfectly pinpointed SOS barrage from British guns, and by enfilade machine-gun and mortar fire from the exposed northern flank. Plumer's losses were not serious and ultimately little ground was ceded – an average depth of around 200 metres, but the shock of a full day of bludgeoning by an ostensibly beaten enemy was a little disquieting. The most significant repercussion was the loss of part of the planned jumping-off line required for the 26th. Apart from describing conditions during the day, Frank Hurley's diary entry also reveals something else the British had not been expecting: German artillery appeared to be growing not weaker but more potent, and it had lost none of its supreme accuracy. Instances of 'bracketing' – intense, precisely-concentrated fire – were now a constant feature. The troops were being harassed in this way, regularly, heavily and in great depth, across the entire Salient.

SEPTEMBER 14TH, 1917
Battery again, same job. Fritz shelling all around us, no-one hit.
SEPTEMBER 15TH, 1917
Up at the Battery again. Fritz nasty from the start, putting over some very heavy stuff. Worked again on the first cook-house making it stronger. Had to knock off and get inside it all the afternoon. Shells lobbing as close as possible without a direct hit. At 4 p.m. all our guns opened up at once, that shut him up. Were able to complete our job. Our batteries stopped after about half an hour and Fritz started off again worse than ever. Dashed for the brick kiln for better shelter. Found he had got one direct hit and smashed the wireless place. Got inside the new cook-house. We got another hit, the shell coming right through the tunnel further along from us. Killed two men, buried several and wounded one officer and two or three men. Major gave orders for every man to clear out from the battery. Everyone had the wind up pretty badly. Dashed for our lives falling over wires and holes. Got a lorry and reached rest camp safely about 9 p.m. Men coming in all through the night. Some shell-shocked. Worst shelling I have experienced.

Background
A heavy German Minenwerfer shellburst, a scourge of trench warfare for the Allies.

Below
The only form of transportable shelter on the battlefield: elephant shelter sections.

Bottom
Forward observation officers tentatively peek over the ruins of a farm to monitor fall of shot and enemy movements.

SEPTEMBER 16TH, 1917 (SUNDAY).

No one going up to the battery to-day. Going to walk up to our head-quarters for pay and mail (much pleasanter).

Sapper G.T. Marwood, 5th Pioneer Battalion, Australian Imperial Force

Certainly, British counter-work appeared much improved, but from the growing weight of hostile steel bursting on batteries and transport routes each successive day, it was clear that fewer enemy guns had been destroyed than Haig and Plumer had hoped. Were absolute proof required, it could be found in British gunners' casualty lists during this period: it had almost doubled in the space of a fortnight. It may have been partly due to the forced hiatus whilst weapons were shifted and re-registered following the advance of 20 September that allowed the Germans to take advantage. But their artillery were largely still out of sight of British ground observers, and still shifting between battery positions (as a rule, each had three pre-prepared alternative sites); it was easier and faster for them to pull guns back to new pits than drag them forward, as the British were forced to do. Their ground had not been bludgeoned, the guns need not be turned to be moved (again, as the British had to do), *and* ammunition routes and supplies were already fully established in rearward positions. Statements from prisoners also revealed that British observers were further confused by the unexpected moving *forward* of German batteries at night; in these instances a single gun was left behind to draw fire whilst the rest operated from the fresh locations. The faster the British could adjust, the sooner they could respond – a situation entirely appreciated by the enemy. A later

Hurley diary entry exemplified the problem:

I had a rare tour in our advanced positions, especially as the enemy sent down a heavy barrage. I had all the excitement I wanted snapping shellbursts from a shell crater. Walking through a barrage makes one feel their very enormously great insignificance; for the impression is that the entire cannonade of the Boche is being turned especially in one's direction. His artillery is so organised, however, that it is possible to circumvent his aims by skirting the fringe of the barrage. I went into several of the captured pillboxes and was surprised at their solidity. These are really nothing more than fortifications in commanding situations. The roof is proof against almost any shell, being generally five to six feet thick of reinforced concrete, the walls about three to four feet. A shell hitting them just flakes off a small slab. The barrage is so terrific that it sweeps the ground as if with a rake of steel and combs out the greater number of the foe, whilst the remainder are so terrified with its terribleness that little fight is left in them. Still, many gallantly hold out in the concrete pillboxes and other strong points until our bayonets stuck through the loop holes or a Mills bomb dropped down the ventilator announce that we have arrived.

Captain Frank Hurley, Official Photographer, Australian Imperial Force

So precise was German shooting that a barrage could often be comfortably skirted. If under attack, British gunners were allowed to vacate the battery, but only if it was not required for action. The guns themselves, of course, were immobile. Already crowded, with each step towards the Passchendaele Ridge they were being forced into a tighter pocket. From dry, undamaged, stable ground behind the ridge, bit by bit the Germans proceeded to damage the prime lever for British progression. The main problem was that there was no hiding place.

It was the first time I was in sole charge. During the morning we carried out a programme of firing on various points inside the German line, and at lunchtime my batman brought me his usual savoury mixture of broken army biscuits, meat and onions. I had scarcely finished it when there was the noise of an approaching five-nine, and it burst uncomfortably close, just in front of the battery position. A few seconds later it happened again, and the shell burst just over the position. Two more, one over and one short, made it clear enough to us that we were, in the words used, 'bracketed'. That is, some German battery knew where we were and were ranging on us. This was a situation well-known to every gunner-officer. The rule was that if the infantry were out of their trenches, either on an attack or, if they were being counter-attacked by the Germans and had put up SOS rockets, the gunners HAD to stay by the guns and continue firing until they were, if necessary, completely destroyed. If, however, the battery was only engaged on such harassing fire or an area strafe, or on engaging some German battery in the course of counter-battery work, then, if you were bracketed, you could take your men out of the position, e.g. on a flank, and wait until the hostile fire stopped. I was always terrified that I should have to stay by the guns or go back to them and be massacred, as happened to a neighbouring heavy artillery battery. The difficulty was that you had to be sure, or reasonably sure, that you had been bracketed, and that the shells were not just 'stray rounds'. If you took the men out of the position unnecessarily and too often, you might well acquire the reputation of being a 'windy bastard'. If, on the other hand, you left the men too long and lost members of the battery, your powers of judgment were frowned upon. So there was always this dilemma. On this occasion, we were both perfectly clear that we had been bracketed, and so we took the men away to a flank, into some trenches of the old German front line where they would be safe. At intervals we went up and down the line to see if the people were all right, and thank God they were. In a few minutes the fire got very much worse and we estimated that probably about three German batteries were concentrating upon us, intending what was known as a 'shoot to destruction'. After,

I suppose, a couple of hours, fire slackened and we went back to see what had happened. We found that all our guns were out of action. One had been blown bodily over backwards, and the other three were hit. One was repairable on the spot, but the others would have to go back to be replaced by the ordnance people. The Germans had a nasty habit of waiting a few minutes after the end of a destructive shoot and then starting it again for a few minutes, so catching people who had come back prematurely to the position. They did it on this occasion, and we fled, thanking heaven that we had not got the men back yet.

Lieutenant Cyril Dennys, 212th Siege Battery,
Royal Garrison Artillery

In the German infantry too, changes were also being made to counteract Plumer's tactics. The following order, received by the 18th Reserve Division on 26 September 1917, laid down a fresh scheme of work:

WORK AT THE PRESENT TIME IS RENDERED VERY DIFFICULT, AND IN PLACES IMPOSSIBLE OWING TO:

The great superiority of the enemy's artillery which destroy everything visible.
The enemy's airmen, who dominate our zone of defence, and report everything to their artillery.
The broken up state of the roads, which prevents material from being brought sufficiently far forward.
The depth of the surface water.
The enemy's facilities for ground observation, up to and beyond the artillery protective line.

THE WORK PLANNED INCLUDES:

Wiring the banks and streams and outpost positions.
The construction of strong points for small bodies of infantry with light machine guns, to act as points of support and also to obtain flanking fire.
The provision of splinter-proof shelters in shell holes.
The construction of dug-outs.

Above
German machine-gun crew in front of Poelcappelle.

Right
German aerial of vulnerable British camps near Elverdinghe.

Below
A fresh German idea to form pockets of resistance. Shallow camouflaged underground shelters with some overhead protection (concrete) and individual Siegfried frames (one-man shelters – see page 425). Only useful in ground where the water table was low enough.

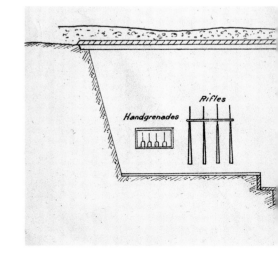

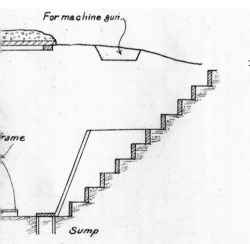

The construction of infantry and machine gun nests. The construction of the artillery protective line by the emergency garrison, under the direction of the pioneers. Stress is laid upon the work of providing splinter-proof accommodation for all supports.

The order reveals the efficacy of the British bite-and-hold approach, but it also indicates future complications, for this new format again altered the dispositions of German troops across the battle zone, breaking them down into smaller more independent groups – just as Plumer had done in attack – and drifting away from the pillbox as the manifold heart of defence. Shell holes fitted with

some form of shelter from weather, splinters and shrapnel now assumed the core role. Yes, they were more vulnerable, but being abundant and widely dispersed, and camouflaged, they were likely to be more difficult to spot and target by FOOs and therefore less likely to be hit. To counteract the change an even heavier volume of British shells would be required – a destruction shoot on a 'broadcast' scale. In the air too German nocturnal bombing visits were becoming yet more frequent, with the rear areas around Poperinghe, Steenvoorde and Hazebrouck now being regularly molested. Given good flying conditions, bombs fell all night.

Almost get to 'Blighty' again tonight. Three or four of us are sitting in tent about 7.30, and four or five bombs drop right in the camp. Our tent was riddled with holes, yet not a man was scratched, not so the units, Buffs especially. It was a ghastly sight. Bodies lie everywhere as several tents and huts are completely done in. It is a mercy that 75% of the men are out in Cafés or somewhere like that. Then starts a night of nights, there must be dozens of them, for they work in relays, no sooner has one looped the loop and dropped his load, another is anxious to get his business done and back to a warm bed. This continues right through to the morning, with just sufficient intervals to enable us to get comfortable. Every time he comes we get the 'Wind Up' pretty badly, for it is immediately overhead and we expect another handful. Still 'Pop' [Poperinghe] is a veritable 'Butcher's Shop'. He lays the poor chaps out in hundreds.
PRIVATE ROBERT CUDE MM, 7TH EAST KENT REGIMENT
(THE BUFFS)

By moonlight, the numerous, vast, tented and hutted camps were easy to spot; should the bombs, which burst at knee height, miss their intended human targets they were likely to cause at least some death, destruction or mayhem in the adjacent horse, mule and wagon lines. Tents were quickly camouflaged (with paint) and protected by sandbag walls to intercept flying fragments that would otherwise scythe through the canvas and the occupants, whilst at the same time anti-aircraft and searchlight batteries sprung up around every camp.

Yesterday we rested at our billets, and today we had but a three hour march to Clyde Camp (tents) near Poperinghe. We are now in the back area of the 'Bloody Salient' and the whole countryside is dotted with camps. Thousands upon thousands of men seem to be located in this neighbourhood where the Third Battle of Ypres has already been in progress for some weeks or months. A fleet of Jerrys' planes came over and bombed the camps and town. I was standing outside my tent, when suddenly, in the trees about 400 yards from where I stood, bursts of flame appeared simultaneously with four loud explosions. That was the first load dropped, and landed right in a 'Tommy' camp lines, killing 22 and wounding many more. After that, bombs seemed to be dropping everywhere, while machine guns and 'Archies' were madly firing at the planes, which at times could be plainly seen as they were caught in the rays of the searchlights focussing on them from all angles. The air began to buzz and drone with the falling fragments and nose-caps of the 'Archie' shells, and when a nose-cap came whizzing to earth, landing with a thump almost at my feet, I beat a hasty retreat to my tent, little thinking in my haste that I would be no safer beneath its canvas walls than out in the open.
PRIVATE N.M. INGRAM, 3RD WELLINGTON REGIMENT,
NEW ZEALAND EXPEDITIONARY FORCE

By day too aerial harassment was persistent, but in general the British still held control of the skies. In September alone the RFC guided the guns onto more than 9,500 targets, mainly German batteries, and took almost 15,000 aerial photographs. Scouts were ubiquitous, pouncing upon enemy fighters and downing several German aces. If conditions were favourable the air buzzed with swarms of British machines, half a dozen different makes of fighters scudded back and forth at around 10,000 feet, protecting the plodding artillery spotters far below.

Frank Hurley found himself desperate but entirely unable to capture the essence of daily events in the Salient in a single photographic frame – infantry attacks, shelling, aerial combat and tanks. He felt compelled to apply for permission to produce 'modified' images by which the public could gain a more authentic visual grasp of the true texture of warfare in Flanders, unconstrained by the limitations of his viewfinder.

Had a lengthy discussion with Bean re. pictures for exhibition and publicity purposes. Our authorities will not permit me to pose any pictures or indulge in any original means to secure them. They will not allow composite printing of any description, even though such be accurately titled, nor will they permit clouds to be inserted in a picture. As this absolutely takes all possibility of producing pictures from me, I have decided to tender my resignation at once. I conscientiously consider it but right to illustrate to the public the things our fellows do and how war is conducted. They can only be got by printing results from a number of negatives or re-enactment. This is unfair to our boys and I conscientiously could not undertake to continue the work.
CAPTAIN FRANK HURLEY, OFFICIAL PHOTOGRAPHER,
AUSTRALIAN IMPERIAL FORCE

Hurley tendered his resignation immediately following the denial. His reputation and dedication, not to mention the quality of his work, led to Headquarters coming through with limited authorization on 6 October and, fortunately for

Above
Driver J.C. Humphries of the Royal Army Service Corps with his dog in a camp near Poperinghe. The tent has been protected by the addition of corrugated-iron walls. It is likely that a layer of sandbags was also present.

Right above
Three German soldiers taking refreshments in their Polygon Wood pillbox. The wood still hides several examples.

Right below
The hunted and the hunter. German Zeppelin Staaken bomber and Nieuport fighter.

future generations, the resignation threat was withdrawn. Hurley was to leave Flanders just as the Passchendaele chapter closed and exactly one year to the day before the war itself came to an end.

POLYGON

Such was the atmosphere on and above the battlefield on the eve of Step Two of Plumer's design. In five days time it would be October. Haig's strategic barometer still appeared to be rising. The weather, for the present, was fine, indeed the ground was parched. Shell bursts threw up vast clouds of what Hurley called 'frightful dust', as did vehicular and horse-drawn transport and troop movement on the roads. The Germans were indeed rapidly approaching the limit of military, human and materiel endurance. Many units had been engaged

several times over and wastage was making itself felt. Daily, Crown Prince Rupprecht, commanding the *Flandern* forces, scanned the Flanders skies for the low, grey clouds scudding in from the west that would carry the only thing that could save him: rain, and as much as possible. So too did every eye at British GHQ. Autumn habitually brought guaranteed downpours, plus plunging thermometers, shorter days and milky sunshine; a combination that guaranteed ever-longer drying periods. Resist until winter set in, therefore, and the great threat of British breakthrough could entirely vanish. Rupprecht fervently prayed that the next attack would not follow swiftly, for he had few reserves available; the Russian front too, was still active; he could count on little support from there. It was simply a question of time. Plumer did not oblige him with more than a moment.

Having scrutinized the modified line following the German counter-attack of the 25th, Plumer did not see any necessity to seriously amend the plans. The battle, another dual Second/Fifth Army endeavour, would go ahead without change. Gough's XVIII and V Corps took the northern sectors, and Plumer's I Anzac and X Corps the southern. At just under 8 kilometres it was a narrower battlefront than the Menin Road enterprise, a change brought about by difficulties encountered in moving battle materiel forward, especially guns, many of which were still not in position by zero hour (5.50 a.m.), and also because of the telescoping of preparation time: now just days separated major military actions. Contracting the battlefront, therefore, did not further condense British artillery firepower as had been envisaged.

SEPTEMBER 25TH, 1917

We had orders to report back to the company this morning. When we got back we were told to move off at 3pm, that is the machine gunners, to take on anti-aircraft work up the line. We arrived about 6pm. We found our position had the nice peaceful name of 'Hell fire corner'.

SEPTEMBER 26TH, 1917

The place well deserves its name. Fritz must have put over about 300 shells during the night, some gas, we got very little sleep though we have got a decent dug-out. We have mounted our gun and are on duty. There are six of us, Fred and Tom are here of course. One man does a two-hour spell during the day time and two men do two hours together at night. The big strafe started this morning. Fred and I were on duty in the early hours 2 to 6. Our barrage started just on our left at 4.30. The batteries all round us opened fire at 5.30. It was like Hell let loose but very effective. Things were fairly quiet, just a few shells flying about, dawn just breaking when at a signal every gun for miles opened fire. We could see the flashes for a great distance along our line which at this point is horseshoe shaped, the top being towards Fritz. Our post is near the Ypres-Menin road. The Australians went over the top and took their objectives alright and the barrage was kept up all the day while our men dug in. They have taken the last ridge, now comes the Menin plain, 15 miles of flat country known as the racecourse. I think Fritz will have to go back that distance as he will be under observation from our side for miles. I had a narrow escape today. I was off duty and sitting in the dug-out reading the 'Sunday Times' Katie had sent me when a shell burst right on the roof of our dug-out and came through just where the doorway was. My bunk was next to the door but luckily I was sitting on another chap's bed farthest from the door. The man whose bunk was under mine was wounded in both feet, left thigh and both arms. The fellow beside him had his face blown in. We dressed their wounds and carried them to the dressing station. There was quite a procession of wounded coming along from the front line and as we went down a Fritz aeroplane dropped a bomb just behind us but fortunately hit no

one. The paper I was reading was torn to rags and I felt like a hot blast down my right leg but that didn't even mark me although it was sore for a while.

SAPPER G.T. MARWOOD, 5TH PIONEER BATTALION,
AUSTRALIAN IMPERIAL FORCE

The morning of Wednesday, 26 September was quintessentially autumnal, still and misty, with a warm sun waiting to break through. The mist created bloody initial problems for both sides. As

Above
Australian troops head across the Grand Place (today, Grote Markt) towards the Menin Gate and, beyond, the trenches.

Below
British 10-inch railway-mounted naval 'pillbox-busting' gun, shrouded against German view near Hellfire Corner. The ammunition has also been camouflaged.

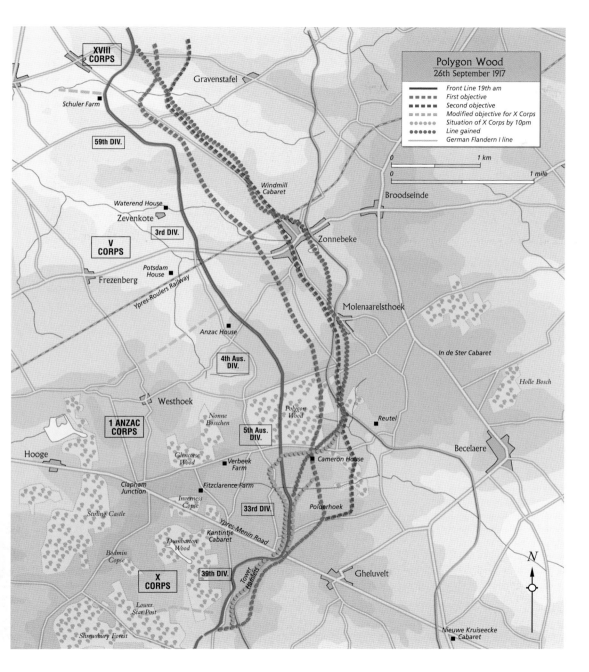

Polygon Wood
26th September 1917

Front Line 19th am
First objective
Second objective
Modified objective for X Corps
Situation of X Corps by 10pm
Line gained
German Flandern I line

0   1 km
0   1 mile

the map shows, the distances to final objectives for the British and Australians varied considerably according to sector. In the perceived toughest area, Tower Hamlets south of the Menin Road, the 39th Division were required to do little more than straighten the line by making a 400-metre advance that would bring them onto the highest contour level with Gheluvelt, the village itself being saved for the next step. In the neighbouring 33rd Division's sector north of the road a slightly greater advance was required, enough to excise the potentially problematic muddle of tortured timber that now comprised Polygon Wood. Likewise in Maxse's northernmost sector: two leaps each of 400 metres would nicely straighten the line, ready for assaults upon Passchendaele and Poelcappelle, and enough to bring the field guns tight up to the line but under cover of the ridges around Gravenstafel. Curiously, the 58th (London) Division's jumping-off line in front of Aviatik Farm almost exactly complied with the furthest advance of British troops on the first day of the offensive. The mortal remains of 39th and 55th (West Lancashire) Division men still lying where they fell almost two months earlier were testimony enough of those early wasted efforts.

It was in the central sector where Plumer asked most of the troops. The 3rd Division (V Corps, Fifth Army) and 4th Australians (I Anzac Corps, Second Army) were to gain a firm foothold in Zonnebeke, a long-fortified village bisected by the Army boundary, and one in which the Germans had made themselves most comfortable over a period of more than two years. The first of the three major rear defence lines, *Flandern I,* traced a treacherous barrier across the lower slope of the Passchendaele Ridge, passing through Zonnebeke's eastern outskirts.

The battle was to follow a similar pattern to the Menin Road. Somewhat indifferent results on either flank, but excellent progress in the centre. Tower Hamlets at last succumbed and much of the ground lost in the enemy counter-attack of the previous day was regained. The artillery were superlative, stably embedded in their pits the guns created sandstorm-like conditions, lifting great clouds of smoke and dust across the battlefield, combining with the mist to disorientate enemy eyes. Having completed their persecution of Glencorse and Polygon Woods, the shredded stands of timber fell to the bayonet. One eyewitness illustrated the ferocity of the Australian attack:

I was over Polygon Wood just subsequent to the attack, and can honestly say that I have never seen so many Bosches bayoneted in my life. Every 'Pill Box' and concrete redoubt was the centre of a mass of 20 or 30 Bosches, and the pleasing part of it was that a very large proportion of them were bayoneted in the throat.
OFFICER'S REPORT, I ANZAC CORPS INTELLIGENCE SUMMARY, SEPTEMBER 1917

Australian losses too, however, were severe; enemy snipers skulked in the splintered choirs and from hidden pillboxes machine guns spat. For their grim resilience here, the Germans would be made to suffer at their next encounter with the Diggers. Zonnebeke held out a little longer than Polygon, but eventually the last snipers were cleared from the ruins, and as the entire village fell into jubilant Anzac and British hands field-grey clad figures could be seen streaming up the slope to the sanctuary of the

trenches, pillboxes and blockhouses of the Broodseinde Ridge.

By the end of the day, most of the main central sector objectives had been secured. As fighting subsided reliefs were quickly instigated, and for the next week more counter-attacks were

Left
British aerial of Polygon Wood in June 1917, with the pre-war Belgian cavalry training ground clearly visible.

Below left
The wood during the battle, with shells bursting. By mid-October it had been swept from the map.

Below
Fallen Scottish troops of 3rd Division (possibly Gordon Highlanders) on the approach to Zonnebeke village.

Top
The Butte in Polygon Wood was originally a shooting ground for Belgian cavalry. The Germans filled it with tunnelled dugouts which British and Australian tunnellers later extended.

Above
German troops captured in the Polygon attacks.

Right
Portable flamethrowers, Flammenwerfer, were employed more as a terror weapon than a killer. The Germans hoped their use would cause enemy troops to panic and break.

recorded across the entire line. Some employed gas, others flamethrowers, several were supported by ground-attack aircraft, but all were driven off. Casualties stood at 15,500 for the day, but this was deemed satisfactory for the key central battle-front was still moving forward at the required tempo. In addition, rapid consolidation and wrecking of counter-attacks had again been exceptional. As both sides licked their wounds, it was plain to see that enemy troops were vanishing from the attritional equation at an agreeably greater rate than British.

SEPTEMBER 28TH, 1917

Things still quiet. Fred and I had the 10 to 2 watch last night. It was rather ghastly to see in the moonlight wounded men limping by and stretcher bearers carrying out the badly hit. When I say things are quiet it is only by comparison for I have [tried] several times to count up to three quickly without a gun being fired and have never succeeded. We are not getting much shooting now our planes are up in scores and Fritz is keeping well back. I think we will be relieved to-day and go back to the rest camp there to do duty on a gun for a few days. We can do with it too as the noise gets one's nerves going. I had to stop my ears with

cotton wool during the bombardment to lessen the concussion. Weather still holds good.

SAPPER G.T. MARWOOD, 5TH PIONEER BATTALION, AUSTRALIAN IMPERIAL FORCE

Haig, Gough and Plumer met again on 28 September. There was a sense of exhilaration in the Commander-in-Chief's manner. All was well on the ground, and by their relentless action German ground-based observation was being seriously disrupted by the guns; shellfire had erased so many posts that increasing reliance was being invested in the much more vulnerable balloon. If Step Three was successful in capturing the rest of the plateau and the Broodseinde Ridge south of Passchendaele, it would not be unwise, he was now prepared to suggest, to make the next undertaking a somewhat greater stride, not only securing the rest of the Passchendaele Ridge but going on to exploit any and all perceived German weaknesses (i.e. get the cavalry and tanks up and drive through to Moorslede or Roulers). Indeed, he had already called the cavalry forward as far as Clapham Junction. Knowing Haig, the suggestion was not unexpected, but both Plumer and Gough, comfortable in the achievements of their men thus far, both expressed reservations. Too premature, they said, the Germans still had several lines of organized defence beyond the ridges, plus a considerable body of uncowed artillery; the golden British rule (nicely illustrated on too many occasions until recently) of advancing beyond the range of one's own guns would be broken. Let's complete the occupation of the ridge before we strike out towards open warfare, they pleaded. Haig responded by saying that all

he wished to do was be prepared for break-through if the opportunity arose. When? Possibly following Step Four, timetabled for 10 October. Remember, the Germans were crack-ing fast – 'teetering' was his chosen word – and the way things were going at present they could crumble at any moment . . . so he had been dependably informed by Charteris. So they must be prepared. Transportation staff had guaran-teed that given a little notice they could have the required reserves in place on the battlefield touchline within four hours. With the old railway lines from Ypres repaired, these men could be brought up at least as far as Zonnebeke, Zillebeke and possibly Langemarck, ready to strike a 'good, vigorous blow'. Besides, said Haig, the ground beyond the Passchendaele Ridge would not be so torn up as it was in front, so cav-alry and tanks could be very effective. Two divisions of mounted troops and five battalions of tanks were called forward. Curiously, as October loomed even Charteris now expressed misgivings about attempting too much so late in the campaigning season, privately noting that, 'Unless we get fine weather for all this month, there is no chance of clearing the coast.' Despite the honesty of the statement, it was a little cheeky considering he had nurtured the C-in-C's beliefs and enthusiasms by an almost endless chain of carefully selected and massaged reports.

Far right
Water-carrying party using Yukon packs. Near Polygon Wood, 27 September.

The desolation of the Glencorse Wood and Inverness Copse sectors as photographed by Frank Hurley on 26 September. A German counter-attack is being fought off in the middle distance.

Left
Upon Sir Douglas Haig's orders British cavalry move forward along the Cassel–Poperinghe road near Steenvoorde on 14 September. They reached positions as far forward as Clapham Junction but once more could not be further employed.

The politicians still appeared calm – GHQ had heard not a peep from London in weeks. In the meantime, whilst preparations were made for the next operation, the excellent dry weather continued. As Monday, 1 October dawned, all looked set fair for another progressive leap. On the mainline standard (full) gauge railways serving Flanders, the month was to see the greatest activity of the war, with an average of 261 trains a day delivering men and materiel into the Salient, returning with wounded bound for coastal hospitals and Blighty. A confident Australian Official Photographer, out on the battlefield with movie camera, was excitedly preparing for more action.

2ND OCTOBER

It was very quiet and there was no great artillery activity. I noticed all the artillery is ready for another 'stunt'; they are all registered and have great supplies of ammunition on hand. I am getting to know where the Boche are most likely to shell, and avoid them. It was Joyce's [Hurley's assistant] first day on the battlefield and his comments and dodging when shells came over rather tickled me. I have become a fatalist. I took over 400 feet of Cine film of glimpses of the Menin Road, the effects being extremely fine on account of the frightful dust. We appear on the eve of another battle, and the roads on the way home [to Steenvoorde] were just a stream of men and transport.

3RD OCTOBER

The battle is to come off tomorrow and we intend taking the ridge in front of Zonnebeke. The weather is becoming very wintry and considerable rain fell during the night. Given two fine days we will gain our objective beyond doubt. The mass of artillery is appalling and nothing can withstand against it. Our supply of shells and munitions is endless and one cannot but feel sorry for the wretched devils on the Boche side. Germany cannot win and might just as well give up, without further slaughter. Nothing can withstand our artillery, for when we intend taking a position we simply blow it to pieces with the guns and then scour it with infantry.
CAPTAIN FRANK HURLEY, OFFICIAL PHOTOGRAPHER, AUSTRALIAN IMPERIAL FORCE

Hurley would never have to contend with dust in Flanders again.

CHAPTER TWELVE
Broodseinde

> The month is frequently one of heavy rainfall. On average it is the wettest month of the year so far as total amount is concerned. It rains on the average every other day and in some years 3 days out of 4. Evaporation is about two thirds as great as in September; rainfall being greater, this leaves about twice as much water to be got rid of by drainage or percolation. Mist or fog is common in early morning and sometimes lasts all day. Gales or high winds are nearly as frequent as in winter: about 1 day in 5 on average.
>
> REPORT FOR BRIGADIER GENERAL CHARTERIS BY METEOROLOGICAL SECTION, ROYAL ENGINEERS

From the meteorological point of view the month began adequately, with just the odd shower. As for other forms of precipitation, the forecast was far from pleasing:

TUESDAY OCTOBER 2ND

The last two nights have been rotten. A blazing full moon and from 9 p.m. onwards each night we have had Boche planes over. On Monday two bombs were dropped just 100 yards off our edge of the camp. It is not at all nice, as canvas tents don't protect much. Last night Fritz pasted Westoutre, Locre (16 killed), Hazebrouck and the top of the hill close to our camp. It is not doing our shellshock patients any good. Still gorgeous weather – no signs of that 'leave'.

MAJOR A.G.P. HARDWICK MC, 59TH FIELD AMBULANCE, 19TH (WESTERN) DIVISION

On 30 September Fourth Army Commander General Sixt von Armin and Crown Prince Rupprecht issued orders that once more reorganized German defensive strategy in the Salient. Regarding the guns, they now required relentless pre-battle work, concentrating on British forming-up and machine-gun positions, roads, tramways and duckboard tracks, plus greatly enhanced night-time harassment both on the ground and from the air to inconvenience and

Above
27 September. 45th Australian Infantry Battalion troops prepared for hostile gas shell attacks. The pillbox is Garter Point.

Right
Passchendaele village during the summer before the battle with (*inset*) free movement in the streets, cafes and shops.

interrupt reliefs and supply, and aggravate resting troops. And yet more gas would be employed against batteries and transport routes. The frequency of raids was also to be increased, the purpose being to force the British into holding their line more strongly between attacks, thereby offering German guns more profitable targets, whilst at the same time baulking plans to buy time until the rains came. Although bravely pressed, most of their counter-attacks had been rendered largely ineffective by excellent British gunnery; this too had to be stopped. The new scheme partly reverted to the old style of defence: a strongly held *vorfeld*. But there was a key difference: the line was

Top and above
The view northwards towards Broodseinde from the top of the Polygon Butte. Panorama 101, left half.

Right
Poelcappelle village as pictured on 13 September. Adjusted German tactics meant that whereas the strong point at centre had become British property, the long low pillbox beyond remained firmly in enemy hands, severely narrowing no man's land.

to be placed as close to the British as possible to make their gunners think twice about employing annihilation barrages. As for machine guns, they were now required to drench the battlefield with fire. Weapon numbers were to be hugely augmented by dispersing every machine-gun company in the reserve battalions in the forward zone to produce an awesome density of flying lead. The idea was to baulk the *first* attacking wave rather than allowing incursion into the battle zone. The final change was in counter-attack tactics: whilst the *Eingreif* troops would still wait further to the rear in case of deeper penetration, supports would be thrown in immediately a hostile attack was under way. Times were desperate for the Germans; if these policies failed, there was nowhere else to go. As the tactical ball was firmly struck back into the British court, their preparations were in full swing. In this new battlefield milieu it was now no longer uncommon for more senior officers to go out and examine their line before an action. Lieutenant Colonel R.T. Fellowes of the 1st Rifle Brigade (4th Division) was keen to appre-

ciate the dispositions of his troops and examine the ground that lay before them. The battlefield had to be seen to be believed.

OCTOBER 1ST, 1917.

We've been pretty busy the last three days, what with arrangements for the battle and for the relief to-night. Have had to write operation orders early, as once in the line there won't be much time or opportunity to sit down and write. We've issued all the S.A.A., bombs, grenades, flares, sand-bags, tools, rockets, etc., that we've got to carry, and are now pretty ready. We've been bombed every night we've been here, and have had very disturbed nights. Harston and I went off one morning at 4.0 a.m. and got back at 11.30. We reconnoitred all the forward area and by crawling from shell-hole to shell-hole, in and out of smashed trenches, and wriggling along on our tummies, we managed to get up to just behind the front line – a so-called line – really only a series of isolated posts, some in single shell-holes, some in shell-holes that have been connected up. It was rather exciting work as most of the time one was in full view.

The fact that 'excitement' was less evident in the front line than in the rear areas was evidence of the change in enemy tactics.

Quite a fair relief in the brilliant moonlight. I went round the line after we had settled in. The line was held simply by a chain of isolated posts – some in connected shell-holes, and some in short lengths of trench. We had quite a quiet time up there actually in the front line, but got very heavily shelled in rear from 9.0 p.m. to 6.0 a.m. next morning. H.Q. were right in the middle of the Boche barrage line, and from 4.0 a.m. to 6.0 a.m. the shelling was intense. About twenty of us were cooped up in the pill-box, and what with the flies and heat and atmosphere, life was far from pleasant. One couldn't move out by day as one was in full view. The whole of the night of the 2nd I was out round the line and later on helped to lay out a new trench-board track across the waste of shell-holes, and then had to take a party of guides down the track and show it to them for the relief the next night when we were relieved by the Somersets and Hants. Each Battalion relieved one of our front line Companies, and no less than three Battalions came in and formed up for the attack next day in the area occupied by our two Companies. It was rather a complicated relief in consequence, and was eventually over at 1.30 a.m. on the 4th, when we moved back to an area near Pilckem with H.Q. in Jolie Farm – merely a tunnel under some ruins!

LIEUTENANT COLONEL R.T. FELLOWES, 1ST RIFLE BRIGADE

Whilst reliefs took place and guns and ammunition were dragged forward, so selected parties from every unit went out to reconnoitre their new 'patch', get to know in and out routes, locations of aid posts, and the sites of various HQs.

This morning a party of us were detailed to go forward to the reserve lines and there to spend the day, returning this evening to guide the Companies up. We are snugly 'set' in an old German trench, but those of us who are new to war have been prowling about looking for souvenirs. Stan Allan, my hardcase pal, who is forever prowling, no matter where we are, came across a dead Jerry's leg sticking out from the side of a large shell hole. The German style of boot being new to us, he wished to inspect them

more closely and getting a firm grip of the toe and heel, he leaned back and heaved, but to his disgust and consternation the boot remained 'put' and the leg came away at the hip, Stan and his 'souvenir' falling together to the bottom of the shell hole. As the scent was not exactly of violets, he lost no time in scrambling up the side and leaving the boot to its owner. Whilst in the act of passing a pill-box which had been partly uprooted by a heavy shell at some time or other and was lying all askew in a bed of mud, curiosity prompted me to stop and have a peep inside. One look was sufficient. In its dungeon-like gloom I could see it was half full of black, evil looking water in which was floating, amongst several wooden planks, the greatly enlarged body of a Hun, probably three months 'gone'. The smell was vile, unclean and evil. What other things lay beneath those rancid waters, God knows, I did not stay to investigate further.

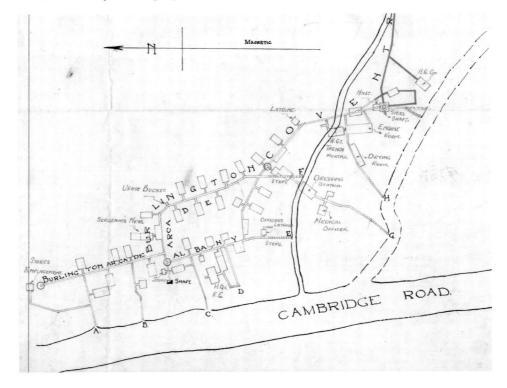

Above
Railway Wood dugouts during the battle. The wood itself, which once sheltered the entrances protected by the corrugated iron, is long gone.

Left
Plan of part of the Railway Wood or Cambridge Road dugout system. Every branch of the army was catered for underground. The dugouts extended northwards more than 150 metres, then branched east and west into the mining system.

This is certainly an 'interesting' area. All roads and tracks except the Menin Road have been totally obliterated by shell fire, but Engineer and Pioneer Battalions are rapidly replacing them by corduroy plank roads for wheeled transport and guns, and duckboard tracks for men. There are no trees, no houses, no countryside, no shelter and no sun. Wet, grey skies hang over the blasted earth and the bleak, gloomy atmosphere of the place seems to depress one's mind and fill it with dread foreboding. Long strings of weary mud-bedraggled mules can be seen plodding along the greasy shell-swept tracks, laden with ammunition for the eighteen-pounder guns. Now and again one of these animals would step off the track to flounder, hopelessly bogged, in the mud and ooze. The old mule may be a stubborn brute at times but he has a heart of oak. No horse could give the service which he provides and he is indispensable in country such as this, where the gun and transport limbers cannot leave the corduroy roads without instantly becoming bogged to the axle. We are due to go over the top on the morning of the 4th, our advance is to be strictly limited to about 1700 yards and our objectives are Abraham Heights, Gravenstafel Village and Waterloo Farm.
PRIVATE N.M. INGRAM, 3RD WELLINGTON REGIMENT, NEW ZEALAND EXPEDITIONARY FORCE

Not a few such parties were bewildered by the uniformity of the terrain. Major features such as the remains of Passchendaele, Zonnebeke, Westroosebeke, Houthulst Forest and the ridges capped with blockhouses were easy enough to identify, but in the shell-tortured region between Ypres and the present front lines nothing, not even the pillboxes, were fully identifiable until one was able to read the painted name or map reference. For newcomers, the first 'trip up' could be a most confusing affair.

In the afternoon, Major Fraser wanted someone to go up the line with him, to find Railway Dug-out. Captain Stevens said he would carry on in the dressing room, so I went with him. Walked along the railway to a place called Little Wood, and asked several people if they knew of Railway Wood. Called in at our Artillery Hdqrs. to ask the way, and found we had gone much too far. Some shelling of the battery whilst we were here. Decided to go on to Rabbit Villa. Not far from Anzac House. Found the place in a cement dug-out near the railway embankment. It was a clear afternoon, and we had a very fine view of Zonnebeke in the valley in front of us. Just behind it we could see Passchendaele, and the German front line beyond. Could see our shells landing all along the German trenches, and sending up clouds of smoke and dust. Returned along the railway to Cambridge Road, and found Railway Wood. Passed two crashed aeroplanes on the way. We walked past a battery of heavy howitzers that were firing at the time. African negroes were loading the guns and carrying up the ammunition. The noise deafened my left ear for some time afterwards. After some searching found the dug-out. It was a very large and deep dug-out which would hold two or three battalions. We walked along underground for about 300 yards, when we came to 6th Brigade Headquarters. They knew nothing about quarters for A.M.C. This was the largest dug-out I have ever seen. We walked for about half a mile under ground. It was lit throughout by electric lights and pumps were working all the time keeping it dry. Through one part was an underground tram line for carrying rations etc. Came up to surface again and had a look round for A.M.C. with no success. About dark the Hun commenced to shell the Howitzer Battery here, so we returned to A.D.S.
CAPTAIN DONALD COUTTS, AUSTRALIAN ARMY MEDICAL CORPS, REGIMENTAL MEDICAL OFFICER TO 24TH INFANTRY BATTALION, AUSTRALIAN IMPERIAL FORCE

Railway Wood (also known as Cambridge Road) dugout was one of the largest and most complex underground accommodation schemes in the Salient, incorporating headquarters for every branch of the Army and bunked accommodation for many hundreds of men; it was literally an underground village, and still being extended. Originally connected to the vast but now defunct mine system that stretched from north of the railway, under the Bellewaarde Ridge and almost to Hooge, the dugout was built by Royal Engineer tunnellers during 1916 beneath a stand of dense woodland – clearly marked on trench maps as a wood; by mid-1917 every tree had entirely disappeared, leaving just a wilderness of holes and battlefield detritus. The entrances to the system, of which there were at least fifteen, were also now so inconspicuous amongst the debris that the men failed to spot both wood and dugout.

4 OCTOBER 1917

At 2 a.m. I was called and went up to the new O.P. with Private Thomas F.W. and a telephonist, on the way we met Corporal Oyler and the working party returning. They had completed digging the O.P. and had laid wires to it and to an adjacent pillbox beside 'Arbre' from the advanced cable head, a pill box a few hundred yards behind. After a fairly quiet walk in the dark we reached the O.P. at 5 a.m. and set about testing our lines and getting everything before zero hour 6 a.m. Shortly before this however, the Bosche, possibly knowing our intentions put down a sudden and fierce barrage on the top of our ridge – I happened to be right on top checking the cable to the pillbox and just at the moment the barrage started, got my pack on my back completely tangled in several wires which I had thrown over my head – this was very awkward and after vainly endeavouring to get free, slipped my pack off and left it and made an undignified sprint for the pillbox which was luckily only a short distance away. After the barrage had slackened, I found that the O.P. had been badly damaged and the wires to it cut – we had no time available for repairs so moved with all the gear we salved into the alternative position in the pillbox which did not give such a good view but was a good deal safer. This pillbox was also used by

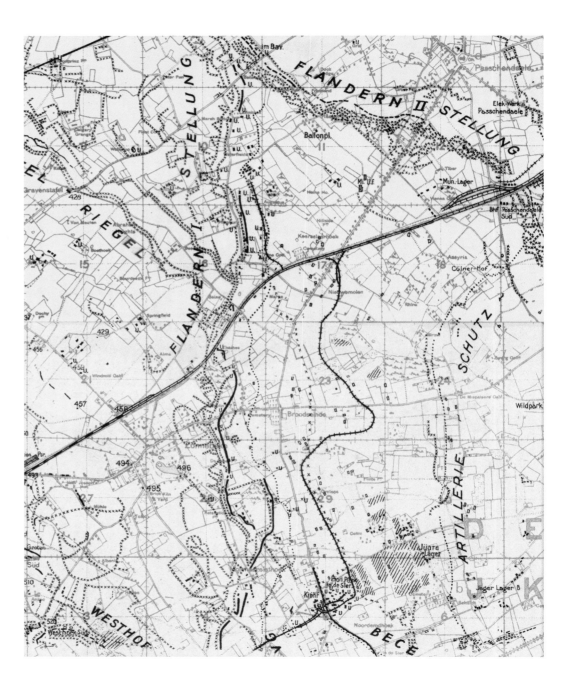

Left

The first target for the October campaign: the Flandern I Stellung. The line runs through Tyne Cot cemetery just above the bend in the railway (see cluster of U's – unterstand – pillboxes and blockhouses) and on along the Broodseinde Ridge towards Becelaere. Flandern II protects Passchendaele village.

some heavy gunners who had cleared out the dead Bosches who were in it when I had last visited it and built up the side facing the enemy as a shell of ours had pierced it and blown this side right out. The gunners, whose F.O.O., Lt Cardew, was observing, had named the place 'Barker O.P.'. Close by I found a cement barrel with the label of an English Portland firm dated since the war started!* How is it done? Hardly had we settled down in Barker O.P. when the barrage started, the most wonderful and awe inspiring spectacle I have ever witnessed and heard. 6 a.m. on a cold, damp, misty October morning – everything quiet save an occasional rattle of machine gun fire or a lonely gun sounding in the distance, nothing to be seen save the flicker of the 'Very' lights, for it was still dark – suddenly as the watch hands point to the tick of 'zero' 3 or 4 red gun flashes from our rear, as many cracks and then the whole line bursts out into a maze of flashes; into a thunder of booms and cracks; into a regular swish and swirls of shells of all calibres flying overhead. The noise is absolutely deafening and even in the pill box you have to shout hard to make the man beside you hear. Looking out forward though the slot, the flashes of the shell bursts, the air full of Very and coloured lights and smoke and the crack of rifle and M.G. fire makes you feel bucked you are not down there a few hundred yards in advance, but you are not so bucked when a few minutes later the enemy counter barrage crashes down on the ridge which (you had perhaps forgotten in your excitement) was their barrage S.O.S. line!

LIEUTENANT GERALD BRUNSKILL, 5TH ROYAL SUSSEX REGIMENT (CINQUE PORTS BATTALION), COMMANDING LANGHAM SCOUTS

In the main central assaults Fifth Army again used Maxse's XVIII Corps. With the help of tanks his 11th (Northern) Division temporarily cleared Poelcappelle before towards evening

* British Portland cement, exported commercially to neutral Holland, was being sold on to Germany. Similar observations had been made on the Somme in 1916.

counter-attacks succeeded in wresting back a part of the bludgeoned village. Using mainly the roads the tanks performed brilliantly. At dawn the monsters crawled forward from St Julien. An extraordinary eleven of twelve machines arrived to skirmish through the network of Poelcappelle's streets, each of which concealed concrete emplacements in houses and gardens.

The 12 Fighting Tanks of this Company reached St. Julien without incident and in very good time on X/Y night and lay safely concealed there under special brick rubble camouflage netting until midnight Y/Z night. Then they moved up the Poelcappelle Road where they awaited Zero close behind our front line and well in advance of the attacking infantry. One Tank was here forced to withdraw through serious mechanical trouble. The Section destined for Terrier Farm etc., lay in advance of the other two sections who were to proceed straight up the road into Poelcappelle. At Zero the Tanks moved forward past Delta House, where a Machine gun was silenced by 6-pounder fire, but had to wait at Retour Cross Roads some 20 minutes for the barrage to lift and for our infantry to come up. Those leaving the main road at this point were unable to distinguish the branch road that they were supposed to take but managed to follow their allotted routes with sufficient accuracy by the use of previously noted three land-marks and the help of their compasses. Though they only occasionally found themselves on the obliterated roadway (recognised by odd patches and heaps of metalling) the going was better than had been feared and in places quite tolerable. Gloster Farm had the appearance of a large timber dump but was recognised for what it was and vigorously bombarded with 6-pounders. This bolted a number of the enemy who gave easy targets to the Lewis gunners. A Tank then moved close up to the Blockhouse, causing the remaining garrison to surrender to our waiting infantry. Two Tanks crossed the Lekkerboterbeek in the neighbourhood of Terrier Farm without realising it until they were well over – there being very little water in evidence. This strong point had apparently given in to the infantry on the fall of Gloster Farm and, no further assistance from the Tanks was needed. The Tanks detailed for Poelcappelle and beyond moved into the village with the infantry and safely negotiated the very badly crumped area at the 'V' junction. Those allotted to the Tragique and Red House Roads saw that the infantry were already well in possession of their objectives so did not attempt the very unfavourable approaches thereto – but joined the village section in their hunt down the main street and out to the far end. There were a number of concrete Mebuses still occupied – but the 6- pounders and special bombs bolted the garrisons in every case who were then either killed by Lewis Guns or case shot [thin-cased 6-pounder shells filled with lead balls – literally an oversized shotgun cartridge] or taken by the infantry. The mound at Meunier House was conspicuous and un-missable and this strong point was also successfully engaged by 6-pounders – a considerable number of the retiring enemy being shot down by Lewis Guns on the slope of the hill behind it. Case shot had many opportunities of proving its value. One Tank Commander in searching the pockets of a German Officer he had himself killed, on the chance of finding orders or other documents, came upon a map showing the disposition of MG's N.E. of Poelcapelle – now on our immediate front. This was despatched to the Corps concerned. Five boxes of S.A.A. Ammunition were carried up on each Tank and were handed over to the Infantry who had been warned to expect it. There was considerable competition for the Ammunition between the infantry and Machine Gunners, the demand in most cases exceeding the supply. In some cases Lewis Guns and drums were given to detachments in need of them, objectives etc., were pointed out to infantry and shown them on the Tank charts – and close cooperation seems to have existed generally between Tanks and infantry throughout the Battle. Having ascertained that the infantry had no further need of them – the Tanks withdrew at Zero plus 6 hours in accordance with orders and proceeded back down the Poelcappelle–St. Julien Road.

(OFFICIAL ACCOUNT DRAWN UP FROM REPORTS OF TANK COMMANDERS)

It was a display of organization and co-operation at its best. Above the battlefield, supporting aircraft were presented with one of the most extraordinary and terrifying tasks of the war: the pilots were required to enter the battle zone beneath a parabola of super-concentrated shellfire, and attack any sign of hostile troops.

Our task was to fly into that tunnel below the flight of the field gun shells, look for any target we could see – any Germans in trenches, enemy machine-gun posts, anything at all – shoot it up, fly through the tunnel and come out the other end. We were warned that we must not try to fly out sideways, if we did we would almost certainly meet our own shells in flight and be brought down by them. Once we entered the 'tunnel' there was nothing for it but to carry on and go through to the very end. We flew in pairs. I led, being flight commander. I and my companion flew to the south of the tunnel, turned left and entered it. Instantly we were in an inferno. The air was boiling with the turmoil of the shells flying through it. We were thrown about in the aircraft, rocking from side to side, being thrown up and down. Below was mud, filth, smashed trenches, broken wire, limbers, rubbish, wreckage of aeroplanes, bits of men – and then in the midst of it all when we were flying at 400 feet I spotted a German machine gun post and went down. My companion came behind me and as we dived, we fired four machine guns straight into the post. We saw the Germans throw themselves on the ground. We dived at them and sprayed them – whether we hit them, we didn't know. There was no time to see – only time to dive and fire, climb and zoom on to the next target. We saw a number of the grey-green German troops lying in holes, battered trenches that had been trenches and were now shell holes. We dived on them, fired and again we were firing at a target which we could not assess. We were being thrown about. A third time we dived on another target and then our ammunition was finished. We flew on rocking out of that inferno, out of the 'tunnel' and escaped. I felt that never at any time had I passed through

Above
The St Julien Poelcappelle road as it was in 1915. This was the sole firm route in the northern sector.

Right
Segment of July 1916 panorama taken from Passchendaele Church showing Poelcappelle Church in verdant pastoral countryside.

Kirche Poelcappelle

A' 39
26

3820   3830   3840   3850

44

such an extraordinary experience when we ourselves were shut in by a cloud of shells above real damnation on the ground.
CAPTAIN NORMAN MACMILLAN, NO. 46 SQUADRON, ROYAL FLYING CORPS

The problem Maxse's infantry now faced, however, was precisely what von Armin and Rupprecht had intended, and one that Macmillan and his RFC colleagues were required to resolve: the two sides were so close together – literally a matter of metres in places – that British guns could no longer be sure of hitting only the enemy positions, and were therefore loathe to open fire. In order to complete the conquest of the village the British would have to withdraw their infantry temporarily, hope that the Germans had not done likewise, shell the entire position, and attack again – with tanks if possible.

On the battlefront boundaries, Houthulst in the north (XIV Corps – Fifth Army) and Polygon in the south (X Corps – Second Army), the attacks needed to be sufficiently strong to support and protect the central effort with a limited advance of their own, creating the best line for the next stage. At Houthulst the German defences along the edge of the wood defeated all progress. Despite the period of relatively dry weather, troops were seriously slowed by heavy ground on the low, wet, flat approaches and again lost touch with their creeping barrage, despite it falling at a more leisurely rate than elsewhere. The struggling troops presented simple targets. There were few territorial gains but many losses, almost 1,800 men, many of which were sustained during a German barrage before the attack had even begun – exactly as von Armin had requested.

A visit round the front of the Brigade after dark by Harston, the Brigade Major, showed that our left had no protection whatever and that we were about 300 yards short of our objectives and that 19 Metre Hill was not held by us. He and I wandered about all night and moved 'B' Company to gain touch with the Hampshires and made them face north along the Laudetbeke and thus form a defensive flank. It had rained most of the day and the country was in a terrible state of mud and slime; the sides of all the shell-holes crumbled as one walked round them, and the desolation of it all was awful. There was a good deal of chaos and confusion on the battlefield, and the whole country was littered with men of nearly a dozen different battalions trying to find their way about. The question of reorganising a front after a battle in this crater and shell-hole fighting, where there are no trenches to recognise and no landmarks, is an extremely difficult one and it's almost an impossibility to reorganise in time to be ready to make a fresh attack under forty-eight hours. We did well on the 4th and made an advance of about 1,000 yards on the Brigade front, while the 33rd Brigade on our right got into Poelcapelle. It was fairly quiet during the night, though the Boche shelled the tracks across country a good deal.

LIEUTENANT COLONEL R.T. FELLOWES, 1ST RIFLE BRIGADE

The story in the south was initially similar. The Second Army's main objective was to clear the final quarter of Polygon Wood and push on beyond to Polderhoek and Reutel. The landscape beyond Polygon was more incised than elsewhere, the valleys sodden, the *bekes* swollen and still swelling with the rain; on the higher ground beyond lay the heavily defended ridge dotted with patches of woodland, each dense with wire and concealed pillboxes. Knowing it to be the final piece of the Gheluvelt Plateau jigsaw, the German artillery pounded the ground, not only here but across the entire Salient.

Only after a succession of assaults did most positions fall. The cost was ten casualties per metre of gained ground, but at least a little less of the dismal Gheluvelt Plateau now remained in German hands. In the central sectors Second Army persevered with the recently successful Anzac I and II Corps, the latter comprising both Australian and New Zealand troops.

By a dreadful coincidence, into the fine early morning mist and drizzle on the Broodseinde Ridge, a heavy German force of Guards was forming up ready to move forward. First, the crushing British barrage fell upon them – the 'heaviest yet experienced' German sources later said – and there were also serious losses in guns. By pure bad luck the Guards were about to launch Operation Hohensturm, a powerful counter-attack with the object of regaining the high ground west of Zonnebeke. As they advanced into the murk at the marshy foot of the west slope of the ridge, the 1st Australian Division appeared. Since suffering so heavily in the Polygon Wood attacks they were in no mood for taking prisoners. The result was a bloodbath – in a mudbath.

4 OCTOBER

The battle was fought in a misty rain – heavier falls have taken place overnight, so that the entire battlefield was a great quagmire of mud. It is marvellous what conditions our fellows can and will fight under. The entire country is ploughed into waves of pulverised muddy earth, the craters being filled with water, so that it is extremely difficult to move about. During a battle the whole back area is abustle with fatigue parties and stretcher bear-

Above
German prisoners captured by 11th Division at Poelcappelle during the battle for Broodseinde. The 'cage' was at St Jean.

Below
On the slopes of the Broodseinde Ridge, two young German casualties lie dead, caught in the massacre in the mist fought between German Guards and the 1st Australian Division on 4 October. Pictured on 14 October. See map right.

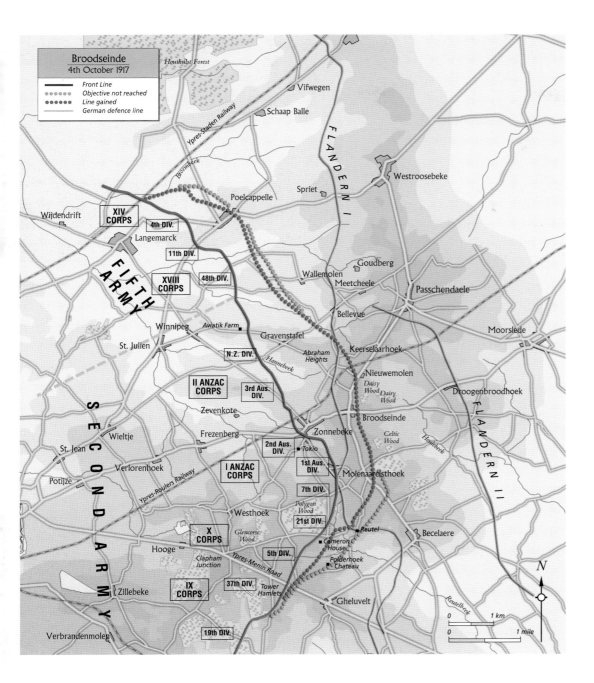

Broodseinde
4th October 1917

— — — Front Line
∙∙∙∙∙ Objective not reached
●●●●● Line gained
——— German defence line

ers, streams of prisoners under escort, supply columns, etc. Shells burst in paces where the Hun knows there are likely to be numbers of men, but the work goes on and the whole process continues, as though some great game was being enacted. I don't know whether one becomes callous or turns a fatalist, for the wounded and dead scarce make any impression, and one is absolutely heedless of the fact that his turn might be next instant. It's a damnable business. I wake up in the morning as though I had passed through some weird wild dream. It's impossible to realise that men are just murdering each other around you, and that you are in the heart of a great battle. The frightful roar of the artillery and scream of shell though brings one back to reality, but even it passes off as soon as you leave the scene of battle, and when I am back again in my cosy room at Steenvoorde I quickly forget the horrible doings of the day, and after a good dinner develop my plates and then turn in with no more thoughts for the day than if I had been at business the whole while and just returned from a late evening working overtime.

CAPTAIN FRANK HURLEY, OFFICIAL PHOTOGRAPHER,
AUSTRALIAN IMPERIAL FORCE

Part of the reason for Australian success at Broodseinde was the unexpected cessation of German artillery at a critical time – just as the Anzac attacks went in. The opportunity was eagerly grasped and losses consequently small. The cause of the break in shelling lay with the poor visibility so that the German gunners no longer knew where the Guards were. Curiously, on 1 October, the British had carried out a study to determine how visible men were under Flemish autumnal conditions at different times around dawn and with different backgrounds. Half an hour before dawn figures (two men carrying rifles at the high port) could be spotted at 150 yards (against a ploughed field); at dawn the distance was 217 yards. As the light increased, however, so too did morning ground mist. Half an hour after dawn they were visible at 147 yards. In full daylight, an hour after dawn, the mist made not just the men but *any* object completely invisible up to 200 yards away. It appears that future attacks utilized this data when timing their advance, for almost all were launched thirty to forty-five minutes before dawn when the light was low but visibility reasonable: morning mist was more likely to interfere with German reaction than British action. The view from the air offered further meteorological curiosities.

The reference to mist has brought to my mind the first occasion on which I was permitted to fly during the early morning. I was impressed by the fact that although, at take-off, the morning was bright and clear, a few minutes later, from two thousand feet above, the earth was shrouded in mist through which hillocks and tree-tops protruded. So impressed was I by this phenomenon that, to my mind, it vindicated completely our senior observer, Ferguson – a Canadian. Some time previously I had been orderly officer on duty in the squadron office when Ferguson had reported at about

8 o'clock in the morning. He and his pilot had then just landed. Blandly, it seemed to me, he had told Major James that he had been unable to see the target for mist. It was a glorious autumn morning. I had, there and then, deplored our commanding officer's gullibility and had wondered why Ferguson was held in such high esteem in all three flights of the squadron.

On the same flight I noted a second phenomenon which, to me, was of almost enthralling interest. This was that a shell bursting within a pall of ground mist had caused to agitate the mist surface to expanding, rippling circles, identical in appearance to those circles which form on placid water which is struck by a stone. I watched, and saw other bursts effect the same result.
SECOND LIEUTENANT T.E. ROGERS, NO. 6 SQUADRON, ROYAL FLYING CORPS

The mist was down at Broodseinde on the morning of 4 October. It was most unusual for two forces to meet head on in mutual attack, and until the German gunners could be sure of where their troops were on the battlefield, firing had to stop. Once the grim situation was revealed they then needed to alter the fire pattern from *Vernichtungefeuer*

Above
Laying a tape line for a duckboard track on a misty morning. Such weather was a boon to the troops, shrouded as they were from German view until the mist cleared. A huge amount of exposed work was done at such times.

Right
Right
4 October. Near Flinte Farm: the new Australian front-line positions on a freshly pulverized Broodseinde Ridge.

Below
Panorama 101, right half. The desolation of the Polygon–Broodseinde battlefield as seen from the Butte. This lonely landscape hides thousands of men.

(annihilating fire) to *Sperrfeuer* (defensive barrage). But the same problem still pertained: exactly where were they to drop it? Indecision turned to chaos, the guns remained silent, and the ridge fell.

I saw one of the 'best' sights I have seen in the war. Where the Huns had been massed and formed up for the attack they lay there dead in thousands – it was grand to see them – good dead Huns absolutely in piles. I have never seen so many 'stiffuns' before, and it is only when you see sights like this that one realises what a hiding 'Fritz' is getting. Every other shell hole in this area has a dead Hun or part of one in it and some had as many as five in them. How the Kaiser would have liked to have them for 'fat'. Well, for these four days the shelling was terrific and one wonders how a soul can come out of it all unhurt – but yet we do, and plenty of us at that. I don't think many live Huns get out as for every shell he gives us he gets about 20 in return, or so it seems to us anyway. I don't know exactly what the proportion is, but there's a tremendous difference. The conditions were very bad – rain most of the time and no shelter – mud and slush from top to bottom, and it was 'some' cold. Wet feet and wet to the skin with a cold wind blowing and plenty of mud and rain all night and all day in a bit of a shell-hole half full of water. It is really a wonderful thing that men can stand over here. From this they all come out and after half a day's sunshine they are all dry and as happy as sand-boys. Treatment only half as bad as ordinary home life would probably give us rheumatism and all sorts of dog diseases, but really I have not seen even one man with as much as a cold. The only ill-effects they suffer is that some men get swollen feet from the wet and cold, but that only lasts for a day or so when they get out and are able to keep dry.
CAPTAIN EDWIN TRUNDLE, 26TH INFANTRY BATTALION, AUSTRALIAN IMPERIAL FORCE

It was a serious defeat and the Australians were now installed on some of the highest ground in the Ypres Salient, ground that had been German property for years, and another bite had been

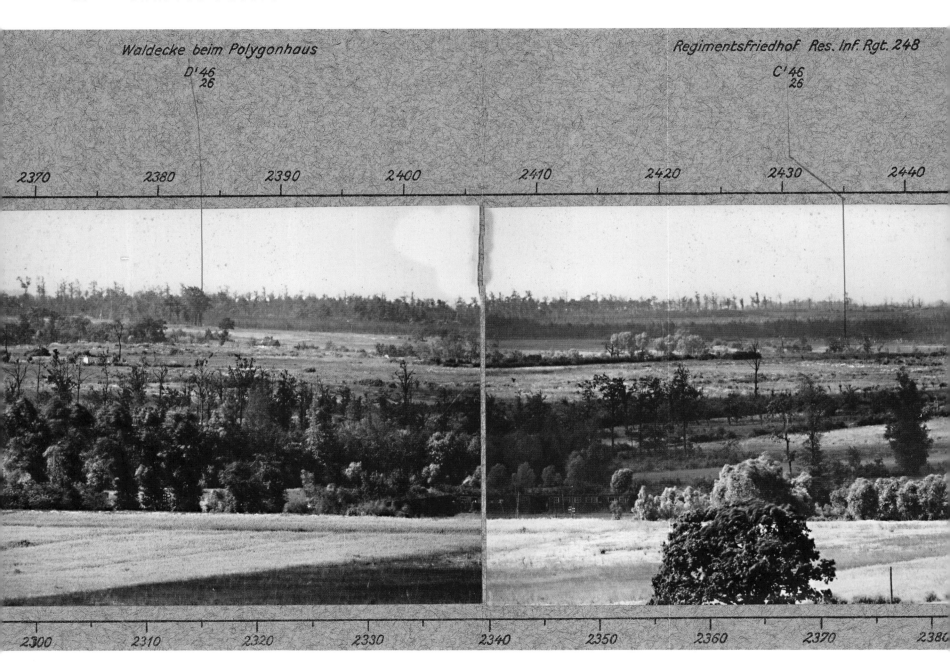

Waldecke beim Polygonhaus

Regimentsfriedhof Res. Inf. Rgt. 248

D¹ 46
26

C¹ 46
26

2370   2380   2390   2400   2410   2420   2430   2440

2300   2310   2320   2330   2340   2350   2360   2370   2380

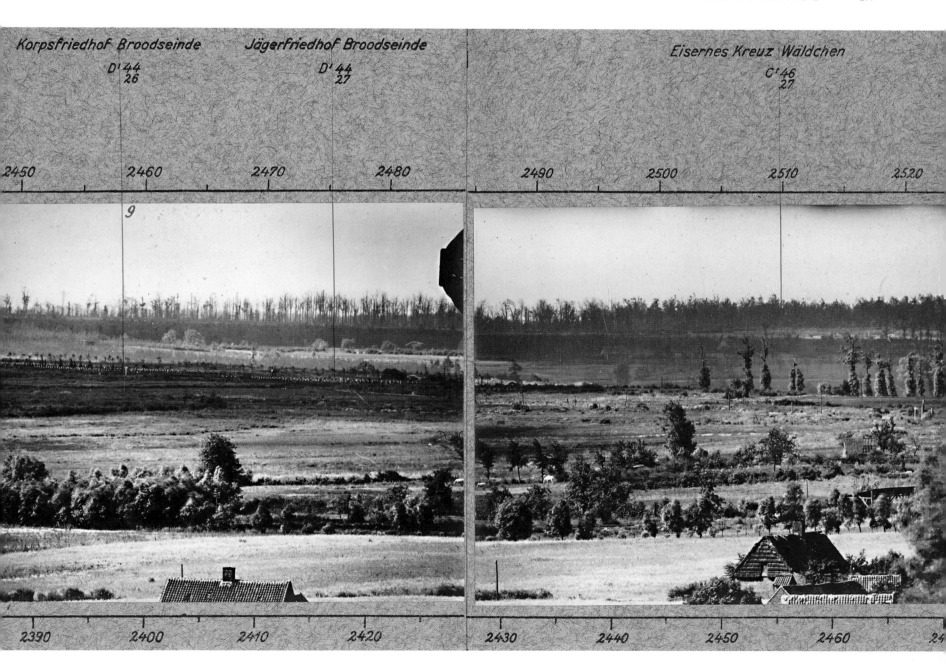

Korpsfriedhof Broodseinde   Jägerfriedhof Broodseinde   Eisernes Kreuz Wäldchen

D'44   D'44   C'46
26   27   27

2450   2460   2470   2480   2490   2500   2510   2520

9

2390   2400   2410   2420   2430   2440   2450   2460   24

taken out of the Gheluvelt Plateau. It carried priceless rewards. A glance westwards back towards Ypres revealed all the odious positions that the British had held for so long: trenches, tracks and roads stood out upon the tortured ground all the way to the shattered town and beyond, and the muzzle-flash of every British battery was clearly visible. To the east, however, lay an unsullied pastoral Flemish landscape of green fields and villages, with church spires pricking the sky as far as the eye could see into the haze. The last time Allied troops had gazed upon

this view had been in October 1914. Now they too could see German muzzle-flashes; from now on, day and night each was noted, plotted by compass, cross-referenced with other observations and passed to the artillery for action.

To the left of Broodseinde II Anzacs also performed well, although the fighting was considerably more demanding than earlier actions.

The attack has commenced – now for it!
A cataract of steel flows roaring, at tremendous pace, over our heads. Machine-gun bullets make a strange whistling

Previous pages
The Broodseinde Ridge sector seen from Passchendaele Church in July 1916. The high ground is dotted with three German cemeteries, containing 1,057, 5,963 and 567 graves. None exist today. The picture illustrates the area captured on 4 October by 1st and 2nd Australian Divisions.

Above
Panorama 125. The Zonnebeke and Broodseinde battlefield soon after capture. A fresh transport and shelter infrastructure is already fully in place, with plank roads, duckboard tracks – and the critical ingredient, signage.

sound as they pass overhead on their lethal mission. The Huns send up their bright coloured 'S.O.S.' signals and their gunners are not slow to answer the call. Their machine-guns rattle out their message of death and their whole available artillery vomits forth its message of hate as it lays down the counter-barrage – a curtain of flame, mutilation and death, lashing the earth with its fury, through which we must pass before we can come to grips with the Hun. Heavily laden, carrying rations, rifle, entrenching tools, shovels, bombs, extra panniers of ammunition and box respirator, we advance, skirting the edges of water-logged shell-holes under a rain of bursting shells and spitting bullets.

The noise is terrific. One understands nothing from one's shouting neighbour and seems half stunned by the unearthliness of it all. Thought and feeling are destroyed in the endless blast of sound. Never before, surely, has there been such a bombardment. Shells drop almost at my feet but, thank God! the mud is so soft that they bury themselves deep before exploding and thus decrease their lateral spread. My nostrils are full of the smell of explosive mixed with that of the stinking mud. A shell lands fairly at the feet of the leading men of my section. Up in the air, about 15 feet, two men go, spreadeagled in their flight. Two others are thrown to the ground, mutilated and bloody. Near the end of the section I am thrown momentarily off my balance, but stagger on while huge lumps of mud and pieces of shattered steel flop down from the sky, covering me with mud and filth. Immense swathes of smoke drift through the air and stinking gases hover over the tortured earth that the H.E. shells tear up again and again.

A large pill-box appears immediately before us and a rain of bullets lashes the air all around. Down we flop into a shell-hole, the Lewis Gun is set on the brink and we get into action in earnest. We have made contact with the enemy infantry at last. As fast as the drums of ammunition are used up we refill and hand to the No.2 of the gun who clamps them on and hands back the empty, while No. 1 peppers away at the loophole of the pill-box. Bullets hit with a WHACK! the earth about us and soon No. 2 rolls to the bottom of the shell-hole, hit in the temple with a ricochet, blood and brain-matter exuding from the hole. No. 3 immediately takes his place and we continue to lay siege, keeping up a concentrated fire at the loop-hole in the concrete pill-box from which the stream of lead is directed at us. Meanwhile other parties work around the flanks and suddenly the fire from the pill-box ceases as these parties get to the garrison with bombs through the rear doorway.

Private N.M. Ingram, 3rd Wellington Regiment, New Zealand Expeditionary Force

The Anzacs fought through a mass of concrete and advanced to take Abraham Heights and part of London Ridge, two spurs lying between three *bekes* that offered a satisfactory jumping-off point for an assault on Passchendaele itself – Plumer's Step Four. With British flanking support firm, the limited victory Haig now sought was very much in plain view, if only the troops could consolidate during the night. Now, as the light failed and enemy guns barked their bitter retaliation, the field of battle had again to be cleared, exhausted troops fed and reliefs carried out. One day of fighting such as this was enough, yet on this part of the front there was an isolated respite.

During the afternoon there is a mutual truce and the enemy Red Cross men can plainly be seen gathering in the dead and wounded on our front. All about us are our own dead and dying, lying in the mud in the drizzling rain. God knows when they will be removed as a vast sea of mud lies between us and the habitable rear from whence the stretcher bearers must come. Most of our own stretcher bearers have 'gone West' and we are physically incapable of removing them ourselves. A tally is made of our Company and we muster 30 men all told. All that is left of 120. We scout about looking for anything which might serve as a seat for our trench or provide shelter from the rain, but in our vicinity there is not a vestige of anything but mud, mud, mud. A few yards behind our trench lies one of our wounded in delirium. He is on his back, his head resting in his helmet which is a basin of blood;

Above

An advanced aid post near Zonnebeke station, with wounded waiting to be attended to or evacuated, 12 October. Pillboxes were an obvious choice to site such facilities.

Right

A RE dump next to the Menin Road near Birr crossroads. Note the timber or corduroy tracks. This material would be carried forward to more hazardous regions at night or under cover of mist.

he is making awful grimaces and appears to be choking. Someone goes over to him and discovers that his denture is stuck in his throat and he is certainly choking. The denture is retrieved but not before the fingers of the Good Samaritan are severely bitten by the delirious man. We go about tending our wounded, endeavouring to make them more comfortable, though God knows our efforts are but poor relief. All we can do is to lay them on a ground-sheet, cover them with another sheet and leave them in the drizzling rain and gathering darkness, alone with their thoughts and pain.

PRIVATE N.M. INGRAM, 3RD WELLINGTON REGIMENT, NEW ZEALAND EXPEDITIONARY FORCE

Although it was a blessing to be lifted from the battlefield, the numbers of wounded were too great for the meagre cover available: pillboxes. Being built for practicality rather than comfort, the average emplacement could hold few stretchers. Men were forced to lie in the open on the 'lee side' awaiting their turn for treatment within, or better still evacuation to the next stop down the medical line, a dressing station perhaps a mile from the front. Although still exposed, they were at least now with friends, with a degree of hope and no longer 'lying out'.

Being able to see the German guns from the newly captured high ground was one thing; stopping them speaking was another. Throughout the day hostile artillery punished the advance at every step.

Such things as ration and ammunition carrying, and burying the dead, fell to our lot. All these were carried out generally in the midst of heavy barrages. During the great attack of October 4, some of us had a wicked experience. For practically the whole of the day the Hun put down a heavy barrage, and we were engaged all the time carrying boxes of rifle ammunition, bombs and rifle grenades a distance of about 1,000 yards, forming a series of small dumps. This was done, of course, under the very nose of the enemy, who seeing what was being accomplished, promptly blew up the new dumps as they were started.

ACCOUNT OF ANONYMOUS SOLDIER 'N.R.P.', 12TH GLOUCESTERSHIRE REGIMENT (BRISTOL'S OWN)

With the darkness they continued to shriek, searching the ground for victims. In freshly captured pillboxes, the only cover, there had been no time to erect adequate barriers against incoming fire.

There came one shattering clang. In the infinitesimal fraction of a second, I saw the pigeoneer, his hands fluttering, his face twisted like a martyr's in the fire, leap upwards to the ceiling, and young Morgan, the runner, pitching forward on top of me. The candles shot up and died. I remember running trembling hands over my belly and legs, automatically searching for a wound. A complete silence fell. Then from the passage came one sigh, the simultaneous passing of life from the dozen men lying there. Another silence in which the pigeons began to coo and flutter; and at that there broke out from the aid-post a high shrilling. One of the orderlies had been half scythed in two by a piece of shell which had cleft him through the buttocks. The candles were relit by our shaking hands. The shell had fallen directly on the bomb boxes by the door, exploding the contents, smashing the stone and burying a number of those standing by. For a space of time we were all partially stunned and frozen by the shock. As we slowly recovered, one of the Rifle Brigade officers shot into the chamber and squatted down in front of Smith, shouting incoherently. His hair was grey-white, powdered with concrete, and stood on end. His face muscles leaped up and down as he gabbled. He was followed by a sergeant, who sank down beside him, and began shouting in his ear: 'E's gone, poor old Mac's gone, 'e's buried under the blasted concrete. D'ye 'ear?" repeating it again and again while tears trickled out of his eyes; but the officer had been deafened by the explosion and took no notice. With

Above

5 October. A YMCA stall distributing hot drinks to walking wounded of the New Zealand Division after they had captured Gravenstafel. In the ruins of St Jean.

eyes staring, he kept on chattering and waving his hands. We got them out at last and sent them back. Mackwood had given the poor aid-post boy a heavy dose of morphia, and the cries sank to groans and whimpers. He died half an hour later. The Rifle Brigade, without their bombs, went forward. Somehow the pillbox was cleared and the night ended. A bright uncompassionate day came in.

LIEUTENANT GUY CHAPMAN, 13TH ROYAL FUSILIERS

In London on this uncompassionate day, and despite the fact that the politicians had done and said nothing of import regarding the Flanders offensives for weeks, Lloyd George was letting it be known that he thought Haig had lost the plot. He was not alone. But after two months of inactivity, lack of broadcast discussion and apparent lack of interest, GHQ might have had fair reason to believe that the War Policy Committee had little right to intercede, even though nothing had gone according to the original plans upon which consent for the offensive had been established. When the Committee came together again on 24 September it was not to discuss Flanders, but Russia's deep troubles, events in Italy, the bombing of the British mainland by Zeppelins and airplanes, and an alternative to Flanders – the potential launching of a new campaign against the Turks in Palestine. French promises to launch diversionary attacks elsewhere to assist the Ypres endeavours had twice not been honoured. Like the Somme and Arras, nothing Sir Douglas Haig had pledged had yet been delivered. Lloyd George was more than just sceptical about GHQ's repeated promises, he – the entire Committee – had been misled, he suggested. There was some truth in this. On his sole visit to the Ypres sector in 1917 he had been taken to inspect the poor state of German

soldierhood. Lloyd George agreed, the prisoners were 'a weedy lot'. It was hardly surprising: by order of Fifth Army they had been 'weeded' of the fit and brawny.

The strategic waltz went on. The days following Broodseinde might have been a good opportunity for the Committee to call a halt. If the British now withdrew to consolidate the old German line running in front of Langemarck, through Zonnebeke and up onto the Broodseinde Ridge, destroying pillboxes in the vacated ground, a degree of observational and territorial parity might have been possible. No better opportunity for action was likely to present itself, as despite the recent advances no one could believe things in Flanders could get any worse. If Haig was not curbed now he was likely to take it as a sign of political acquiescence. Having berated all and sundry in the military, Lloyd George came close to making a wager with his committee colleagues, stating that when their political superiors, the War Cabinet, next met in three weeks' time, there would be no improvements to report from Flanders. It was an astonishing statement, suggesting that those concerned had almost lost interest in events. Having so sternly reserved the option of halting the offensive should plans go awry, they now appeared to relinquish or certainly avoid entitlements once so vehemently laid down before Haig and Robertson. There was no attempt to rein the offensive in, no desire for urgent discussion and it was ultimately this lack of urgency that legitimated continued fighting through October and into November. On the day before Broodseinde Ridge fell, 3 October, the War Policy Committee reconvened. Lloyd George ranted again, but still had no satisfactory concrete alternative proposals to offer. The meeting again ended without conclusion. They were to meet just once more.

The next day a great change was to come over the battlefield, and indeed the nature of the battle. Following the August deluges the ground had recovered well and although labour-intensive and remorseless, movement had become relatively straightforward. On the evening of 4 October the showers turned to real Flemish rain; by dawn the following day it was a downpour. The Ypres geology reacted customarily: low-lying areas turned into swamps.

After returning to the O.P., at 3 p.m. we spotted the enemy reinforcements approaching from the rear down the tracks on the slopes of the Passchendaele Ridge and entering the Staden line. We got the gunners on to this target where they did splendid work, one 60-pounder shell burst right in the middle of a platoon of Huns – a few men crawling away was all we saw when the smoke cleared. This shelling was undoubtedly the cause of breaking up an impending counter-attack. Later in this section we noticed a party with stretchers moving from right to left headed by a man carrying a large Red Cross flag. Little notice was taken of this at first, but as the party grew less and less, we realized that the wily Hun was in all probability extending a line of men in shell holes with machine-guns concealed in the stretchers. At 5 p.m., the 145th Infantry Brigade made a further attack – to clear up the situation which was in places obscure and we had a good view of the men going over.

During the enemy counter-bombardment Cardew, the gunner F.O.O. and one his signal orderlies were badly wounded, the orderly was outside and Cardew half way out of the pill box when a 4.2 shell landed nearly on top of them. I attempted bandaging but with little success as the wounds were too big. The officer had got it very badly in the stomach and was undoubtedly suffering from internal haemorrhage. By the grey-green look on his face I knew he was done for, poor chap. I was able to get on to his battery commander on the phone and carried out his work as best I could. We sent off for bearers, as far at the St Julien Dressing Station but none were forthcoming and the poor chaps had to lie out in the mud with waterproof sheets over them as we could not lift them into the O.P. through the small jagged entrance. Later, after I was relieved, they were got to the Dressing Station, six men to a stretcher owing to the appalling conditions, but Cardew died of wounds as I saw his name afterwards on the Casualty List. Chadwick took my place at 6.45 p.m. and I was not sorry to get away with Thomas, and we made as quick progress as we could down the trench board track, smashed and shattered every few yards on the Langemarck Ridge.

Lieutenant Gerald Brunskill, 5th Royal Sussex Regiment (Cinque Ports Battalion), commanding Langham Scouts
[Lieutenant John Haydon Cardew MC, 73rd Battery, Royal Field Artillery, was buried in Dozinghem Military Cemetery]

Those units that suffered the most severe casualties during the Broodseinde battle had done so because they were unable to keep up with the creeping barrage, and for this the state of the ground alone had been to blame. Things now could only get worse. It was precisely what the Germans had prayed for, but what would or could the British do? The leaden skies persisted.

7 OCTOBER
Left Steenvoorde at noon to pay the usual weekly visit, in the Ford, to the censor at Ralencourt. The weather, which has been very unsettled, broke and came down in a deluge the whole way. The wind was biting cold and the squalls which swept over the open country made things extremely unpleasant. Winter is coming fast and already the fine leafy avenues are shedding their leaves and gloomy skies bedismal the landscape.

Below
Shelled and repaired light railway track at Jabber House. Such lines were all too obvious in the landscape and received instant attention from enemy guns. Maintenance, night and day, was incessant.

8 OCTOBER

Savy aerodrome. The weather was too bad even to take the machines from their hangars.

CAPTAIN FRANK HURLEY, OFFICIAL PHOTOGRAPHER,
AUSTRALIAN IMPERIAL FORCE

Haig was undeterred, determined to press on, for Broodseinde had been another excellent venture with the majority of objectives gained and over 4,000 prisoners in the cages. With the return of the rain and lateness of season, both Plumer and Gough, and even Charteris, were for cessation and consolidation. Yet at the same time, on the eve of Step Four, Charteris still managed to sugar the pill of divergence, telling Haig that 'all [German] divisions had been seriously engaged and that there were few reserves left', and 'With a great success tomorrow, and good weather for a few more weeks, we may still clear the coast and win the war before Christmas' – statements guaranteed to fuel any field marshal's optimism. There was actually more than a grain of truth amongst the bluster. Ludendorff was profoundly uneasy about the scale of losses at Ypres. British breakthrough was still possible; it could not be allowed. He diverted to Flanders two Eastern Front divisions bound for Italy, and revisited Rupprecht's defensive tactics, sanctioning further augmentation and concentration of artillery, and the distribution of millions of metres of new barbed wire to slow down and destroy future British advances. His most fervent prayer was that the weather would continue to intervene. It was already crippling British efforts.

Although the attacks had managed to annexe many a useful contour, the Passchendaele sector and all the high ground to the west to Staden was still in German hands. The line now described was almost identical to that which the British had been forced to give up before the Second Battle of Ypres in April 1915 – a dangerously elongated pocket, precisely the situation that Plumer had made clear he wished to avoid after Messines. All were aware that without favourable weather the chances of further bite-and-hold success were drastically reduced. But was the offensive to be called off just as the troops were reaching touching distance of their strategic goal? On much of the present highly organic battlefield there were no structured lines to hold, none to fall back upon, just the minimum temporary cover required for a mobile battle. RE field company surveyors were now required to visit the most forward positions simply in order to locate and plot the troops' dispositions. Their findings would be delivered to Divisional HQ where a permanent staff of draughtsmen transferred the information to maps. It was only by this tortuous and dangerous way that commanders could come to any decision about planning their next moves.

It would take much time, much effort and a mountain of materiel to install fresh defensive infrastructure and unless the ridge was acquired much of this new work would still be overlooked by the enemy. So no, said Haig, having shed so much blood in reaching this tantalizing spot, the high ground *must* be taken. He persuaded himself that his troops could achieve the goal and get out of the blighted bowl of the Salient. If it had been put to a vote, it is possible that those who had served here in previous years might well have ticked the 'fight on' box: it was reviled beyond all other theatres.

I was in the Salient from late September '17 to mid-February '18. There was no one you met who did not curse Ypres, no one. The lads who had been there before, and especially the Second Army lot who had been there forever, they didn't seem to care what the sacrifice had been, just as long as they were on top looking down on the Germans, like we were that winter. Because they had had the life sucked out of them for years, they were determined to keep it that way – stay on top. It was only then that I understood how much the Salient was hated and for how long, because I had never been in a sector where the enemy could see everything you did. Yes, I thought, what a sacrifice the battle had been, but you see, you had to believe these lads when they said it because it was them who had suffered for years. When people say things with such passion you get pulled in, you have to believe. And I came to think that it was this hatred for the place that made our lads fight like they did – that terrible butchery – to get out of it once and for all, get out of that bloody Salient. When I had to kill, my actions were to do with fear, I had to shoot to survive, that's what I said to myself. There were some fellows, men who'd been out a while and probably seen a lot more than me, who were just out for blood. War changes you, you see, and you never got to know what they'd seen or done in the past. There was something in their eyes, they just wanted to kill – in any way they could, bullet, bayonet, anything; they didn't care. Nobody bothered, and it wasn't a permanent state. Although we had the upper hand when the LF's [Lancashire Fusiliers] left [the Salient] in February, because we held the high ground, I was damned glad to leave, because I had taken on that feeling of loathing for the place. Yet I had been far more frightened in Nieuport. Fear is a personal thing – there was many a time when I was trembling and others alright. At Yeepree you were often worried even when there was no need, just because of the reputation of the place. It's still with me today. God knows what those poor beggars felt when they had to give it all up again in April '18.

PRIVATE BERT FEARNS, 2/6TH LANCASHIRE FUSILIERS

The truth was that the Broodseinde attacks that took the British and Anzacs to within reach of greater gains had gone well largely through good fortune; the enemy had been in the wrong place at the wrong time, become confused, and deactivated their artillery in a key sector at a key moment. It was not something that could be repeated to order. Haig realized this fully, for it is recorded in his diary. Subject to compliance by Anthoine's First French Army, also about to re-enter the battle, he resolved to bring forward the date of the next attack by two days. Anthoine vacillated mildly, so in the end the Battle of Poelcappelle shifted just twenty-four hours from the 10th to the 9th of October. Before that, however, pressure was continually maintained on the most important sector, still the Gheluvelt Plateau.

Below
Australian Pioneers transporting duckboards to extend and repair tracks. Tens of thousands of infantrymen were also employed temporarily on fatigue work, or more permanently as 'attached' labour. Zonnebeke sector, 5 October.

On 8 October Sir Douglas Haig's diary records: 'I called on General Plumer and had tea. It was raining and looked like a wet night. He stated that II Anzac Corps (which is chiefly concerned with tomorrow's attack) had specifically asked that there be no postponement. Plumer was anxious lest the French should want to postpone. I told him that Cavendish (attaché to General Anthoine) had reported at noon by telephone that 'situation in First (French) Army for attack on 9th is on the whole satisfactory.' Gough telephoned to Kiggell as to postponement. He said Cavan was against it, but Maxse wanted to postpone. I ordered them to carry on.'

At the moment Haig sat down to write these very words his men were already experiencing a taste of what the future held for the British, Anzacs and soon the Canadians.

LANDSCAPE OF ARMAGEDDON

When night again fell we were still there, a mud-caked, filthy, bedraggled lot. It is impossible for me to truly describe the wetness, the sliminess and the stickiness of the all pervading mud. It clogged the fingers, filled the nails, smeared the face, ringed the mouth and clung to the stubbly beard and hair. The clothes were saturated with it, the mess-tins caked with it. To clean the mess-tin before using, one wiped a forefinger on one's shirt then rubbed

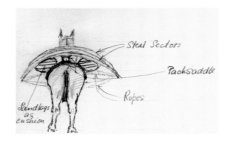

the inside of the tin to remove the mud and grease. Even so the mud got into the food and was gritty between the teeth. The skin of the face and hands was tightly drawn with it. Oh! the smell of it, the taste of it, the dampness of it and the filthiness of it. Those wounded who were still alive, and they were few indeed, were reached by the stretcher bearers about 11 a.m. and taken out. For twenty four hours, day and night, they had lain there exposed to the weather and shellfire, awaiting their turn to be taken out, a Herculean task even with six men to a stretcher. Water, brought up in petrol tins, and rations in sand-bags reached us about mid-day, the carriers well nigh exhausted with the effort to reach us with their loads. I noticed that the biscuits brought up and issued to us were thickly spotted with what looked like blood, and sure enough blood it was. Our Battalion transport, in charge of the Transport Officer, Lieut. Stables, coming up a road way back in the rear was held up by a traffic block in front. As there was no hope of making a detour they waited for the block to disentangle itself and while waiting a shell landed fairly amongst them killing the Transport Officer and several horses and wounding several men. Hence the blood on our biscuits. A Vickers machine-gun team arrived with their gun and after digging a T trench for it, began to clean off the mud preparatory to assembling. They were just a few yards in front of where I stood and I was watching them at the time, when suddenly a shell, one of our own, landed fairly in their midst. Up into the air went the gun and its team – not a man was left.
PRIVATE N.M. INGRAM, 3RD WELLINGTON REGIMENT, NEW ZEALAND EXPEDITIONARY FORCE

So it was raining again: what of the general battlefield conditions? In this respect, Private Ingram's testimony sums up almost every dilemma the British now had to contend with. For weeks, well-signposted dry weather 'cross-country' tracks were all that had been necessary to shift men, materiel, horses, mules and guns. Already scores of miles of duckboard tracks were in position for infantry use. Until the last few days, maintenance, although extremely hazardous beneath the eye of the enemy, had been relatively straightforward and quick. As soon as the rains returned, however, the system had to be radically reorganized, for the cross-country tracks became instantly useless, even lethal. At the same time an even greater number of men, all of whom required an unbroken supply of food, water, ammunition etc., now resided in a devastated area unserved by communication trenches. An apposite example of the simple differences a change in the weather can make is illustrated by the fact that a duckboard, made of porous softwood, weighed half as much again when wet. Until now they had been easily manhandled by troops. As was their mental suffering, the physical burden of man, horse and humble mule was about to multiply. The RE noted that:

Tracks for pack animals presented one of the most difficult questions in the whole problem of communications: mules especially were difficult to cater for; their feet are small and in wet weather sink into soft ground. Their intelligence also seemed to be as small as their feet, and they have an unequalled knack of slipping into inextricable places. Mule traffic over trench board track intended for troops was fatal and broke it up at once. Various patterns of portable track for mules were designed from time to time, but always had the great disadvantage of weight, and were difficult to handle in forward areas.

By nightfall on 4 October it had already become impossible to 'feed' troops and guns without creature assistance, but tracks for animals needed to be different to those required for men, and although the two species all too regularly met nose to muzzle, for the reasons given above it was actually prohibited for mules and horses to use infantry routes. Whereas a normal duckboard 'walk' for infantry was less than half a metre wide (they were often doubled), animals required at least thrice that width; should they not simply be carrying packs but pulling a wheeled vehicle, a water bowser perhaps, it jumped to an average 5.5 metres, requiring a vast amount of labour and material to build and maintain such systems. And of course animals could not deliver materiel beyond the end of a track; from here everything had to be manhandled. Thus the web of track and pathways that came to cover the Salient needed to be zealously organized, with each route marked as up, down, or two-way, fully signposted, fitted with passing places, and clearly marked at each end as to the permitted nature of traffic. As they were required for use by day and by night, to assist-direction finding some were lined with low pegs dabbed with white luminous paint. Invisible to the distant enemy, they saved thousands of lives.

Neither man nor animal was capable of delivering shells larger than six-inch, which weighed around 100 lb. No guns of heavier calibre could be got up into the forward artillery zone – they were simply unmanageable. For this work muscle power was unavoidable, for although ammunition could be delivered to a nearby railhead, further labour was needed to transport it to the final destination – the battery. Trench tramways became indispensable. Nine tramway companies were formed in early 1917. So successful was the scheme installed for the Battle of Messines, the units soon came to be assisted by large numbers of permanently attached skilled men, including temporarily

Above

A Decauville railway being constructed. The extraordinary speed of progress in track-laying can be gauged by the numbers of troops involved.

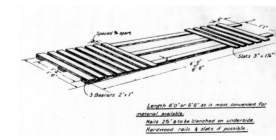

Left
RE pattern for a mule track. Wider and stronger than the standard duckboard, the slats were also closer-spaced to avoid the mules' small hooves snagging in the gaps.

Right
German light railway transporting wounded from the Hill 60 (Hohe 60) sector in May 1917.

unemployed tunnellers, and pioneers. All received special training in 'rapid track laying'.

The favoured gauge was the 60-centimetre Decauville. Essentially a light railway, given a trained gang it was remarkably fast to install and easy to repair. The route was first 'laid out' with telephone wire and pegs marking a centre line; then 'forming' took place, levelling the ground over a width of 3.5 metres and digging drainage ditches to each side. Rail-laying followed, with men bringing up, laying and spacing sleepers (wood or steel), carrying 5-metre rails forward, aligning and fixing them. As soon as the first length was laid trucks were put on the rails to carry materiel forward, releasing manpower for other work. As each truck was emptied at the 'end' of the line it was lifted off the rails to allow a second load to arrive, then relocated and taken back to the depot. As weight was gradually placed on the track, the ground beneath settled, so a gang of 'straighteners and lifters' was needed to pack the sleepers and maintain a level base. This task was unremitting whilst the line was in use. Decauville routes serving heavier guns ran from road-side or broad-gauge rail-side dumps to protected magazines adjacent to battery positions. Every route was plainly visible to the enemy, especially from the air, and a fine target for hostile artillery; as a result huge numbers of men were constantly employed on repair. On 12 October for example, 2nd Australian Railway Company alone were to record over ninety breaks in their lines.

With care and a great deal of sweat a tramway system could be devised whereby almost continuous and uninterrupted construction was possible – indeed, with an 800-man detachment,

the completion of 1.6 kilometres per six-hour shift, even over heavily shelled and wet ground, was not unusual. Trenches and ditches were negotiated with specially designed bridges. Haulage was either by hand ('push routes'), animal (horse or mule-drawn) or powered using a 4-ton, 20 horsepower, petrol-driven engine capable of pulling twelve trucks weighing (laden) 12 tons over level ground at just over 11 k.p.h. The schedule of tramway use was the most serious concern. A timetable as used on civilian railways was produced as a guide to confirm how much materiel might be expected on a certain route during a certain period, but usage times had to vary in case the enemy 'caught on' to the schedule. Large numbers of Decauville rails and sleepers can still be seen in the Salient today, used by farmers as fence and gateposts.

By the beginning of October 1917, however, no tramways had yet been made available in the forward area – they were all still to be installed in the coming weeks. All materiel for battle was manhandled to the front line.

Thus far the Salient had been destroyed ribbon by ribbon, the guns concentrating on that

narrow band of ground the infantry were required to capture. Immediately each band had been consolidated, sappers, pioneers, army troops, and tram and rail personnel moved in to repair the battlefield, make it 'habitable' by fashioning all kinds of shelters, install a network of roads and tracks, and create a system of signals. This latter, under the vigilant eye of the enemy, was as difficult a task as any work 'behind the firing line'. All exposed signal work – almost as far back as Ypres – was done at night. The ultimate purpose was to create an uninterrupted, integrated web that if necessary could connect headquarters to any given company in the front line, plus every other branch of the army, including artillery, balloons, survey, gas etc. It was regimental signallers who organized lines in the most forward command position: company headquarters, usually situated just behind the firing line. Connections between battalion and brigade were the remit of a Brigade Signals Officer. Behind them Divisional Signals oversaw connections to flanking units and, depending on the position of Divisional HQ, rearward to Corps. All these men were Divisional troops: 39 were employed at Divisional HQ, a section of 49 men at Brigade HQ, and 3 further sections of 25 looked after communications in the forward area through battalion to company level. From Corps HQ, 'L' Signals battalions installed and maintained the lines of communication, usually in the form of traditional airline telegraph, to Army and thence to GHQ in St Omer.

Naturally, the key area was the sharp end, the battle zone. Here, of course, the Germans had been able to build in a complex web of deep-buried telephone lines at the same time as

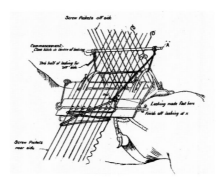

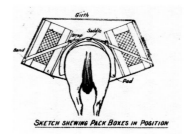

Left and below
Various articles of specialist kit designed by the Royal Engineers for horse and mule transort. Wire pickets, small-arms ammunition and (left) that most essential item, water.

installing the several defensive lines. As they fell back, the system remained largely viable. For the British, visual signals and runners were all very well during the commotion of combat, but as an advance progressed a more structured, reliable, extensive and permanent telephonic system was necessary. There was only one option: that which the Germans used – deep-buried cables. The geology of the Salient *during battle* could hardly have been less suitable for the work of the Signal

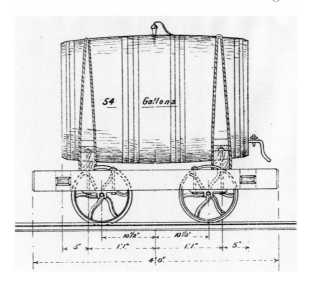

Service, for even when complete cable routes showed up clearly from the air; indeed, they had been a target for enemy guns since offensive plans had first been laid in early summer 1917. Subsequently, German shelling was systematic, with 'buries' being repeatedly targeted before each phase of the British attacks. At Arras and Vimy, both fought in chalk country, deep buries were possible right into the front lines. In many places caves and tunnels, even sewers, were employed. Behind the original 31 July front line, cables had been laid at a depth of 2.5 metres, safe enough to ensure unbroken communication; for forward buries the signallers' ideal was 2 metres, but in much of Flanders such depths were impossible to attain. Now, extending the lines across the sopping wilderness towards the foot of the Passchendaele Ridge,

Below
10 October. Wounded 66th Division troops being evacuated by light railway between Langemarck and Pilckem.

men faced a relentless trial. Main routes, of which there were several, at least one for each corps, consisted of not just a few spindly lines, but up to fifty pairs, a bundle as thick as ones arm of critical import. Very often, beyond Divisional HQ, a pair of dual lines were separately laid. Typically, a corps might require 1,600 kilometres of wire. Just over 402,000 kilometres of this 'trench cable' were supplied, and more than 703,000 kilometres of field (surface) cable. Where cables *were* able to be buried the routes followed not an obvious straight line but an indirect zig-zag, down one disused trench, up another, with fresh cross-country buries here and there, connecting the most forward single lines with battalion and brigade HQs on the battlefield itself, then running back to Division and Corps. Every headquarters dugout was interconnected, the cables running from the trench down inclined stairways into specially waterproofed chambers in which the signallers and their equipment were installed. The meandering route naturally consumed far greater lengths of cable, but offered the best chance of unbroken communication. Likewise, in captured ground pillboxes were most useful to the signallers.

Out on the battlefield, the moment a working party was spotted, it was shelled. Daylight reconnaissance parties to select and memorize (they could not be marked) routes for new lines consisted of one man only, usually an NCO. So sharp was enemy observation that the unfolding of maps and 'flashing' of notebooks was outlawed, for such signs signified something of greater importance than simple exploration of the battlefield. Just as this man was required to camouflage his purpose, so, in the absence of a cable trench, alternatives had to be found to obscure those sections of a route where lines could not be buried. The ultimate aim was to have every arm of the service interconnected.

Forward of Brigade HQ communication was required instantly; cable buries, although pushed through at extraordinarily rapid speeds, often a matter of hours after consolidation, were of no use when a battle was in progress. The least technical means of 'immediate' communication were runners, pigeons (12,000 birds were used during Third Ypres – they were especially useful in tanks, which carried two) and messenger dogs. Runners, who always worked in pairs to double the chances of a message reaching its destination, had a hard life. To assist, flags were planted at intervals along their various routes. At first they were spaced at 100 metres, but this soon proved too far, and was halved. Runners, admired by all, were the prime communicators.

A Runner's life is impossible to describe, unless one is intimately connected with war. It sounds nice to go a mile in daylight, but that mile at night, up and down shell holes impossible to walk round owing to the number of them, requires more than the average amount of quick thinking. In daylight it is a quick journey, sometimes a pleasant one, according to Jerry and his mood, but at night, with Jerry quiet, it is terrible; the strain that one is exposed to in finding their way and when Jerry starts to shell, the groping for cover. One has to cultivate one's sense of direction, it is a most useful sense. It is not unusual for us to wander around in a quarter mile circle, and hear not a sound of a human voice, yet, with the knowledge that if only you knew in what direction to take the 12 yards, you could deliver up your messages, and say, 'At last I am safe from Jerry – for a while at least?' The General Staff have realised to the full the difficulty under which the runners work, and an Army Order just issued states most emphatically that no runner is to be out alone at night, they must go in pairs.

It is a very wise precaution, for if one has someone to talk to, it eases the load considerably. Report Centres are established and the first one from Brigade is MONT BULGAR. To show a little of the difficulties that attend us on this journey, I will give a few details. From Brigade we have to strike due south – parallel to line – for distance of 500 yards. Here – if lucky – strike an old tree that has been felled. From here it is due east, or toward the line. Quite easy, but between this tree and our destination is the remains of an old canal, that has had its banks ploughed up, water abounds, but there is a thin smoke-like path across which on most nights cannot be seen except on knees, no lights dare be shown, however, granted you find the path alright, it is look out for squalls then, for these paths, even as duckboards are all marked on Jerry's maps, and periodically he drops a few right on the path. Now we are across the canal, we have to find what is left of a once decent trench, which, due in first place to neglect, and also the continued wet weather, is now not more than 3' 6" in depth, and then quite half that depth is nothing more than soft slimy mud. Once found, we trace the phone wires into a decent sized dugout. Then the messages are handed over to another Runner who carries then on to their ultimate destination, which is the forward Battalion. This runner has a matter of 500 yards to go in a straight line, but this part of the journey can only be done at night, as Jerry is not so

Top
A cable bury in progress at Hollebeke.

Above
First World War cable route uncovered during works along the Ypres–Roeselaere railway route in the early 1990s.

Above
This 1918 British communications pillbox near Gravenstafel formed a cable-head. Sited approximately a kilometre behind the front line, it would have been occupied by Signal Corps telephonists.

Below
A pigeon is fitted with a message tube. Like canaries for mining, pigeons were specially bred by the RE. Many thousands of birds were employed during the battle.

very far away that he could miss with a bullet. Battalion HQs are in a shell hole, and on this journey if the runner deviates at all, he is soon in Jerry's hands. No trenches here, only shellholes and one or two 'Pill-Boxes' and as Jerry is perfectly well aware that this is the only accommodation, it is usually very unhealthy to approach them.
PRIVATE ROBERT CUDE MM, 7TH EAST KENT REGIMENT (THE BUFFS)

Dogs could be a handy adjunct for they were quick and could be sent out day and night, but until 1918 were much more widely employed by the Germans than the British. Next came direct visual methods (flags and lamps), signalling via aircraft, Very lights and the variously coloured SOS rockets, the latter being the swiftest and most visible appeal for urgent artillery assistance. The gunners were not required to wait for orders if such signals were spotted.

My spine tingled as I detected a low, angry mutter from the front line – a growling, worrying rage of spitting machine-guns which grew until it transcended the swish of the rain and became a sustained uproar. I plugged in hurriedly to the Brigade line and hung on for the inevitable. No sleep tonight, that was certain; the heavies were getting under way behind us with a deep irregular booming. There were strange clickings and buzzings in the receiver, preparatory to the loud and insistent dot-dash-dot which meant they were calling me. I answered in an instant.

'Hullo! What? SOS!'

SOS! I dashed out to the guns, casting a glance across at the line as I ran; there was the signal, high in the sky over the trenches, three dropping stars of red fire that called for the artillery. The road became alive with running feet as the gunners heard my shouts; there was a clang and rattle of breechblocks, and two blinding flashes lit up the position.

They were off in good time. Right and left of us crash-

ing thunders and flames rolled across the sector as the bombardment developed; white and coloured lights played like fountains over the front line, flaring up through the rain to hover momentarily and drop like burnt-out meteors in the darkness. No ordinary trench-raid this; every gun in the sector was pounding away for all it was worth. The elements themselves seemed to take a hand in the tumult; the rain lashed incessantly; the louder the roar of the bombardment the higher shrieked the storm, tearing through the valley.

Nearly an hour later the drenched and shivering gunners crept back to their holes in the bank of the sunken road, the front having quietened down again. Calm succeeded the tempest, a hushed calm that seemed deepened by the crooning of the rain.
GUNNER AUBREY WADE, ROYAL FIELD ARTILLERY

During the campaign there was never any consistently dependable telephone communication with the forward area, so lamps, which could flash a message a good 2 kilometres in favourable conditions were employed alongside runners. Unfortunately, they laboured under the restriction of being able to send but not receive – except at the risk of the return flashes being seen, in which case one could expect an abrupt and severe rebuke. Where cover could be found, behind a pillbox for instance, the small Lucas lamp (designed by a serving artillery officer at the front) was by far the most effective means of conveying instant visual information. Pillbox-to-pillbox signalling, from doorway to embrasure, was extensively employed in the Salient, as were the many ditched tanks. Lucas lamps were small and could be used remotely with the signaller remaining under cover; they flashed messages very swiftly, lamp to lamp to lamp. Flags were proportionately far more hazardous. Each, however, was dependent upon prevailing conditions such as hostile fire, smoke and weather.

Aircraft were a most useful service. Although signalling via a 'ground panel' – literally a large louvred blind fixed to the ground that 'flashed' signals skywards by operators pulling on ropes – had been effective from time to time in the past, it was used with limited success on the Flanders battlefields. But aircraft were forever in the skies during an action, fighting, strafing bombing, photographing and gathering essential information about troop dispositions.

We were told on our own specialist parades that greater attention had to be paid to possible liaison with aircraft in the next stunt [Third Ypres]. If the plane released a white Very Light, this meant, 'Where are you?' The observer would look out for our battalion sign and our call sign sent with the panel. There was a slight variation in the two letter codes [called DD codes as everything was sent twice as a precaution] which had to be learned. They were: NN = short of ammo; YY = short of barrage; HH = lengthen range; XX = held up by MG's; ZZ = held up by wire; FF = enemy resistance; BB = enemy retiring; JJ = raise the barrage; PP = reinforcements; and WW = short of water. I was surprised to see the last one so put, as normally WW signified wash-out.

RIFLEMAN GERALD V. DENNIS, 21ST KING'S ROYAL RIFLE CORPS (THE YEOMAN RIFLES)

Message drops could also be effective, but they entailed an observer being able to appreciate events and troop dispositions above a confusing battle situation, note his perceptions in précis, then fly off to release a written message or annotated map in a tube over some prearranged dropping ground – often Shrapnel Corner near Ypres' Lille Gate, and therefore close to HQs tunnelled inside the town ramparts. By the time it was

received and acted upon, circumstances on the battlefield might well have changed dramatically.

The simple telephone line laid on the surface was the foremost and most common method of direct communication. But its installation and maintenance was dangerous and exhausting work, with linesmen out for hour after hour often under shell-fire, groping in and out of shell holes and trenches (often in the dark), following a defective line until a break was detected, mending it, testing and moving on to the next problem. The most technical procedures at this time were wireless and earth induction sets. By mid-1917 wireless telegraphy had not been sufficiently developed to play a signicant role in forward areas of the Ypres battlefields – the conspicuous aerials and their attendant crew would have been swiftly blown from the face of the Salient – but many systems were used by units in support. There were other less complex direct-transmission systems. The Fullerphone was one of two principal favoured kits. It worked by transmitting signals through the earth – induction. Through the use of a direct current and the signal being 'interrupted' many hundreds of times per second, only an identically set-up machine at the receiving end could decipher the Morse code. The introduction of this machine effectively eliminated a problem that had caused anxieties since the beginning of the war: the risk of enemy eavesdropping. Messages were sent and received by Fullerphone as far forward as Brigade HQ. Then there was the Power Buzzer. Also based upon induction, this system was simply a small sealed metal case which contained the machine plus batteries and coils. From it two cables were run out and attached to metal pins that were driven into the earth. On the top of the case were two terminals and a tapping key. It could send messages one way only.

Above

A headquarters chamber in a deep dugout near Hooge. Scores of such shelters were installed before the battle, and scores more afterwards during the winter of 1917/1918.

Lucas lamps being employed (above) from a trench and (left) in the open on Broodseinde Ridge.

Although originally mistrusted because of the apparent ease of interception through listening posts utilizing the self-same technology (evidenced on the Somme before 1 July 1916), it proved itself at Bullecourt in May 1917 and was widely used at Ypres where thanks to the artillery it was found that the Germans were far too occupied with trying to stay alive to do much eavesdropping. Eventually, the guns' total obliteration of the landscape effectively erased almost every enemy listening post. Power Buzzers were often used in the front line itself, passing messages directly back to Brigade. It served the purpose well. When an amplifier was eventually added two-way conversations could take place employing normal telephone equipment.

STEP FOUR

Both British and Anzac commanders were still generally content with progress to date, and indeed the style of progress. With the arrival of fresh troops and ordnance confidence flourished, and optimism rose at headquarters. Emotions were somewhat different on the field of battle itself. Since the end of July, some units had been sent into action several times. There was precious little to show for the effort and loss; morale was tumbling lower and lower; intoxication for the great offensive was long gone; stress, frustration and exhaustion accumulated, and physical and mental resilience dwindled. Many men were drained, devoid of hope, and with a growing sensation of insignificance.

Most men at this time could easily have run away; perhaps could even have died of fright. I admit I was so jumpy that there were moments when I hardly had myself under control. I knew, if we weren't moved out of the Salient soon for some long spell to recuperate, that I would be breaking down altogether. The endless shelling, the endless killing, were getting on my nerves. This was not fighting, this sitting in a shell-hole waiting to be blown up. I felt sure that one of these days I was going to cop it. Then I would say to myself that a shell has all of France to fall on and it's a million to one that it won't fall on me, and for a while I might feel better. At other times I could almost hear the hiss of the shell that was coming right at me, and would shut my eyes and think that all is over now. When I found myself still alive I would buck up, until the moping and the depression set in again.
PRIVATE WILLIAM GRAHAM, 6TH BORDER REGIMENT

Slowly the number of desertions, self-inflicted wounds and even suicides crept higher.

----------- was maybe 25 years old, dark haired and a decent-looking lad. Unlike most of us, he had good teeth; we all wondered why his were so strong and white and ours stained or . . . well, a lot of the lads didn't have any of their own left. He couldn't take shelling, this lad; from the start he just crawled into a corner of a dugout or a funk hole or anywhere, and shook like a leaf. A terrible state. Terrible. Nothing we could do or say had any effect, he was just made like that. It wasn't unusual, there were a lot of lads who suffered, all in different ways. Many a time I'd look at him and wonder why I wasn't doing the same. I thought sometimes there was something wrong with me, because I didn't crack up. Oh, I was regularly scared to death, you know, but it didn't come out like this lad. I just sort of froze all the while, closed my eyes and waited for the . . . well . . . whatever was going to happen. They should have took him out of it really because he was no good. No good either to himself or to us; someone had always to be looking out for him. I don't mean kick him out or anything like disgracing him, you know. No, they could have given him a job behind the lines on the roads or railways or canals, in an office, or on the docks, anything – at least he would know he was doing something useful, you know, productive for

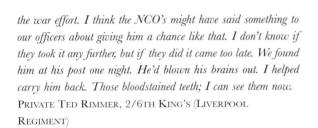

*the war effort. I think the NCO's might have said something to
our officers about giving him a chance like that. I don't know if
they took it any further, but if they did it came too late. We found
him at his post one night. He'd blown his brains out. I helped
carry him back. Those bloodstained teeth; I can see them now.*
PRIVATE TED RIMMER, 2/6TH KING'S (LIVERPOOL
REGIMENT)

As the Salient elongated, so far greater numbers of
'non-combatant' troops were subject to round-the-
clock attack. Roads as far back as Poperinghe
received their daily dose of shells and bombs,
extending the British 'battle-zone' to a depth of
over 22 kilometres behind the front line. Within
this band of misery almost a million men toiled to
hold the line, feed the offensive and manage the
consequences. On 8 October, Plumer's Chief-of-
Staff, Major General Sir Charles Harington,
gallantly stated that the British troops would find
the crest of the Passchendaele Ridge 'dry as a
bone'. Although the state of the ground now ruled
out any fresh tactics other than bludgeon and
bloodshed, GHQ was still awash with expectation.

*Arrived back to my regiment on the same day as they were leav-
ing the fight for a rest. One of my great chums was killed in
action on the 4th October. I was greatly upset. The Lincolns
went into action 660 strong
and came out with only 280,
most of those men I am sorry to
say were killed or missing and a lot
were caught in the bog, poor kids.
They did look done up when I saw
them coming along from the firing line. The day that they made
the attack the rain started and they were wet to the skin and
coated with mud. When we left the station to join our regiment
we had to walk 12 miles to find them and we were wet through
when we did find them. There are such a lot of men missing
that I have only one officer to cook for up to now. We are now
a long way from the guns for a little while, waiting for reinforcements. I have lost all my friends except one man.*
PRIVATE D.J. SWEENEY, 1ST LINCOLNSHIRE REGIMENT

Above

A method of gaining extra
secure cover quickly: the
construction of small dugouts
beneath suitable pillboxes.

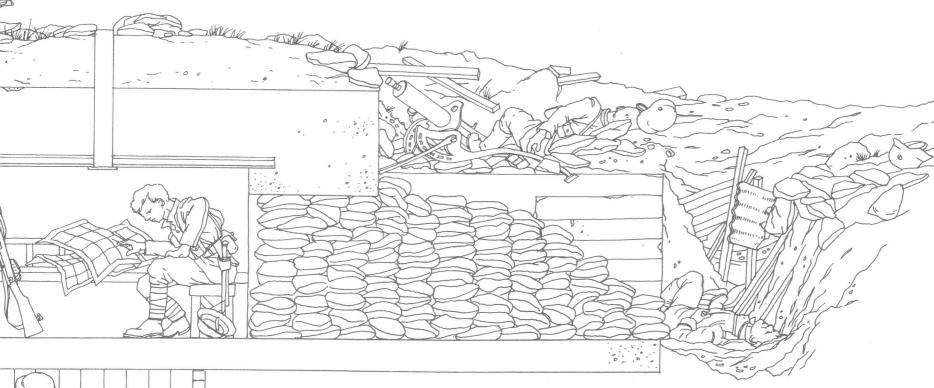

ANDY GAMMON 2007

It was also during this early autumn period of the battle that the true future expectations of the Staff began to reveal themselves. On 1 October, X Corps instructions from Second Army had included G.V.10., a brief document containing four points:

1. As the enemy have, as far as is known, no tunnelled accommodation in the ground over which the forthcoming attack is to take place, sections of tunnellers will not be attached to divisions as on former occasions.

2. The C.E. will arrange to attach one Tunnelling Officer to each Division for the purpose of reconnaissance as to the possi-

bility of tunnelling for Brigade and Battalion Headquarters.

3. In the event of such reconnaissance proving that tunnelling is possible at any point which the divisions considers suitable for a Headquarters, C.E. will detail the required tunnelling detachments. It must be understood, however, that the task of getting material forward will be difficult.

4. Divisions will take their own measures for clearing concrete dugouts and report number and position of those available for accommodation by our troops, through their C.R.E.'s

The document is an excellent indication of the prevailing mentality at Army HQ. Tunnelled dugouts required enormous amounts of labour, material and infantry assistance in their creation. Above all these considerations, however, was that of time, for many weeks were necessary to bring even a small dugout project to fruition. This was not an order dispensed by an army expecting breakthrough. And yet only a few days later Plumer was openly expressing confidence in the continuing offensive, whilst Harington informed a gathering of journalists that after the next two thrusts the cavalry would be ready to make their move.

For the recent actions, a glowing Commander-in-Chief was about to be further bucked by congratulatory letters from his American Expeditionary Force counterpart, General John Pershing, and British Secretary of State for War, Lord Derby. As usual the opinions of Lloyd George and Co. were discounted; with the backing of powerful colleagues at GHQ, Haig may well have persuaded himself he had an almost 'full house' of military and civilian support. The newspapers were still injecting concentrated doses of conviction, the London *Times* calling Broodseinde the 'most important victory of the year', at the same time farcically stating that 'the particular task which Sir Douglas Haig set his armies has been very nearly accomplished.' With such reportage – entirely obligatory as a result of government policy on censorship and 'tone' – what were the civilian population to believe? It was trumpeted too that almost 100,000 American troops were

already on European soil, with the promise of millions more, so perhaps Germany would soon make a bid for peace. But this qualified form of victory was not the kind Haig and a great many others still desired. There was no doubt, however, that in Flanders at least, more and more British troops of all ranks wished to hear their Commander-in-Chief call time.

Above
Disabled tank – although offering fair cover, it might have been a tempting target for hostile artillery.

BROODSEINDE
A DAY OF GREAT SUCCESS – OVER 3,000 PRISONERS

THE FOLLOWING TELEGRAPHIC DESPATCHES WERE YESTERDAY RECEIVED FROM GENERAL HEADQUARTERS IN FRANCE:

10.35 A.M. – At 6 a.m. this morning we again attacked on a wide front east of Ypres. Our troops are reported to be making satisfactory progress, and a number of prisoners have already been taken.

10.11 P.M. – Our attack this morning was launched on a front of over eight miles from south of Tower Hamlets to the Ypres-Staden railway, north of Langemarck, and has been completely successful.

All objectives have been gained, positions of great importance have been won, and over 3,000 German prisoners have already reached the collecting stations.

We are now in possession of the main ridge up to a point 1,000 yards north of Broodseinde.

The weather, which, during our preparations for the attack, gave promise of continuing to be favourable yesterday became settled. The wind steadily increased, and last night and throughout the battle has blown strongly from the west, at times with the force of a gale, and has been accompanied by storms of rain. These adverse conditions added to the difficulties of the advance and to the work of our airmen. Notwithstanding this, our aircraft performed valuable work, and afforded useful information from time to time both regarding the positions of our own troops and the assembly of the enemy for counter-attack.

The assault was delivered by English, Australian, and New Zealand divisions. Included among the English troops were battalions from 28 English counties. There were also a few battalions from Scotland, Ireland and Wales.

At all points rapid progress was made from the start. South of the Menin road, where only a short advance was intended, our objectives were reached at an early hour.

North of the road English battalions carried the hamlet of Polderhoek and Polderhoek Chateau, where sharp fighting took place, and drove the enemy from the numerous farms and small woods south and east of Polygon Wood.

Australian troops captured Molenaarelsthoek and cleared the houses on the Zonnebeke-Broodseinde road. New Zealand troops took Gravenstafel, and on their left other English divisions continued the line of our advance and reached the outskirts of Poelcappelle.

Within a short time of the opening of the assault our first objectives had been gained on the whole front of the attack. Our advance against our final objectives was carried out in accordance with the plan, and was attended by equal success. English troops took the village of Reutel and Noordemdhoek and secured the high ground overlooking Becelaere.

Australian regiments captured Broodseinde and established themselves well over the crest of the ridge, five miles east of Ypres, which gives observation eastwards.

On the left of our attack English troops carried the greater part of Poelcappelle village and secured the line of their objectives east of Poelcappelle church. The whole of our objectives had been captured before midday.

Information obtained from prisoners, and confirmed by identifications of German units and the number of German dead, establishes the fact that our attack anticipated by a few minutes an attack in force by five German divisions against our front from Polygon Wood to Zonnebeke. Our artillery barrage descended upon the enemy's troops as they were assembling, and the hostile attack never took place. Those of the enemy's infantry who escaped the fire of our artillery were overwhelmed by the advance of our infantry.

In consequence of the enemy's losses in the area of his intended attack, few counter-attacks have yet developed. Two counter-attacks attempted early in the afternoon east of Gravenstafel were in each case broken up by our fire before reaching our positions. Another counter-attack north-east of Langemarck resulted in severe fighting, but was unable to drive our troops from the positions gained by them.

Later in the afternoon three other unsuccessful counter-attacks were made by the enemy south-east of Polygon Wood.

The enemy's losses throughout the whole of the fighting have been exceedingly heavy, being greatly increased by the unusual number of German troops on the battle front at the opening of our attack. Our casualties have been light.

In addition to the prisoners taken by us, we have also captured a few guns and much other material.

'ONLY ONE KILOMETRE ADVANCE' GERMAN VERSION OF THE ATTACK

FRONT OF CROWN PRINCE RUPPRECHT. – *The enemy's fighting activity yesterday was similar to that of the preceding days. A strong destructive fire was directed deep into the territory behind our positions and against the Belgian villages and isolated sectors of our fighting area in the centre of the battle-front, where the most vigorous outbursts of fire were concentrated. Throughout the night the powerful artillery duel continued unabated from Houthulst Wood as far as the Lys. This morning it increased to drumfire. With the launching of strong English attacks in the Ypres Bend the battle in Flanders has again developed. With the other armies the fighting activity throughout the day mostly remained within moderate limits, due to bad sighting conditions, and it only revived towards the evening.*

EVENING

On the battlefield in Flanders the English during to-day's great attack penetrated only about one kilometre deep into our defensive zone between Poelcappelle and Gheluvelt. Especially bitter fighting still goes on to the east of Zonnebeke and to the west of Becelaere.

From the other fronts there is nothing of importance to report.

CHAPTER THIRTEEN

Climate Change – Poelcappelle and First Passchendaele

We were up at Nieuport on the coast for about two or three months waiting for some attack that was going to come off up there. It was all very cloak-and-dagger; we never got to know what the idea was. We waited and waited and nothing happened, and then we moved away somewhere inland. Everyone knew about the battle at Yeepree and I think it was towards the end of September we left Nieuport; we had heard it wasn't going so well, and guessed we might be going to join in. I forget the name of the place where we did the training for the attack [Arques], but we had good billets – our lot were in terraced cottages in a cobbled street. We could hear the battle going on quite plainly. The weather while we were there was grand, lovely countryside, and we practised our attack on trenches and farms, barns and haystacks with the other brigades. Turned out it wasn't a bit like the real thing! After a few days we marched off again and stopped at another little village called Winnizeele. The weather had changed for the worse, it was wet and had gone much colder. We went to a camp that was just a huge patch of mud. We stayed there a few days and got attached to the Aussies, the 66th [Division] were put with the Anzacs. Until then we had been Fourth Army, now we were Second Army. I think we stayed a couple of days or so, then we were taken by truck and dropped at Vlamertinghe; from there we marched right into Yeepree with all manner of other units and guns and supplies. There were wounded coming back, so the roads were jammed with everything from guns to buses because the battle was going strong up ahead; it was a hell of a noise, nothing like anything we had ever heard before. Everyone seemed pretty happy, because we were told we were advancing again. The walking wounded were the happiest, though, they were out of it for a bit. The gunfire gave us confidence; we thought it must be all our own! Stupid. We went into Yeepree, right through into the middle and past the ruins of the Cloth Hall – we were told to keep away from it, walk on the other side of the market place to the hall because of bits falling off when shells let nearby. I expected Yeepree to make more of an impression on me, but it was actually no worse than Nieuport – blown to bits. But the Salient had a reputation, you see, and we

hadn't been there before. I'll never forget something that happened there. As we walked past the Cloth Hall there was music, a mouth organ, and singing coming from a cellar in the ruins of a building on a corner opposite the Cloth Hall [today's Regina Hotel]. You couldn't see anything at first, it was coming up through the ground, but as we passed you could make out figures through holes in the pavement. They were singing one of those Keep the Home Fires Burning type of songs, and I found it very moving. It is one of the strongest memories I have of the war, and I often think of it. I found out later that there were thousands of men living like that under the Yeepree. Anyhow, we walked past and on through the Menin Gate and out into just . . . well, there's no words. The destruction was not so bad to start with, the roads were pretty good and there were still trees and buildings, railways everywhere, but when we crossed the old [31 July] front line there was just nothing but ruin as far as the eye could see – except for guns, hundreds, probably thousands of them, and of all sizes. Some were firing, others were covered with nets. With the big ones you could see the shell in flight for a bit as it left the barrel. It was an amazing sight. There were German shells falling too, but it was not so bad. We walked past the heavies and onto what I would call the battlefield.

PRIVATE BERT FEARNS, 2/6TH LANCASHIRE FUSILIERS

The 2/6th Lancashire Fusiliers were attached to II Anzac Corps. Their commander, Lieutenant General Sir Alexander Godley, had looked at the ground and felt the enterprise should go ahead as planned. Within the other corps selected to attack on 9 October opinions differed; Lord Cavan (XIV) was in favour, Sir Ivor Maxse (XVIII) against, General Anthoine (French Army, again on the left flank) stubbornly guarded, and Sir William Birdwood (I Anzac) absolutely opposed. Sir Hubert Gough himself was far from convinced. The final decision was Plumer's. He too had been for cessation of the entire offensive, but

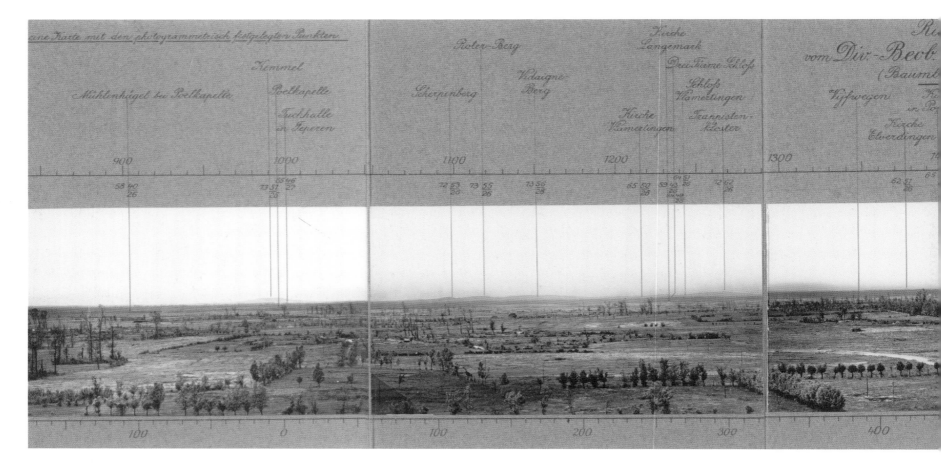

appreciated the repercussions on morale of pulling back, even to a well-defended line, having lost so many lives. The public and political outrage would be colossal, and it was not inconceivable that many a haloed GHQ head would roll. He decided that despite the conditions, a force of more than 30,000 British and 6,000 French would be sufficient to take Poelcappelle, push forward against Houthulst, extend the grip along the heights from

Broodseinde and firmly install the Allies on the threshold of the Passchendaele Ridge, placing them within touching distance of 'victory'.

Suitability of weather now appears to have been cast aside as a guiding principal. The sun was choosing to show itself only in short bursts, often exquisite dawns and sunsets, but somewhere in the Salient it rained to a greater or lesser degree almost every day. As forecast by 'Meteor', Mother Nature saved the worst for the two days preceding

Above
German panorama of April 1917 taken from almost the same spot on the Stadenberg Ridge as the 1915 example on page 138. The landscape is still relatively undamaged, and would remain so for the rest of the war. The comparison accentuates the extreme narrowness of the Ypres battlefields.

battle. Thanks to the low cloud base but especially strong and blustery winds, no flying and therefore no artillery spotting had been possible.

As a grey dusk gathered in the late afternoon of Monday, 8 October, the great caravans of troops earmarked for the following day's venture streamed through Ypres into the Salient. Those already installed roused cramped limbs to begin the trek to jumping-off positions. Many men like Bert Fearns had spent an uncomfortable two days crouched in muddy shell holes shrouded beneath groundsheets and gas capes. Whilst awaiting orders his Brigade (197) had been dispersed around a group of pillboxes known as Low Farm. The temperature was falling daily, winter was just over the horizon and driving rain now swept horizontally across the battlefields, blighting efforts to stay dry and warm. With legs wrapped in sandbags, the Battalion emerged from their holes, stretched and formed up for the

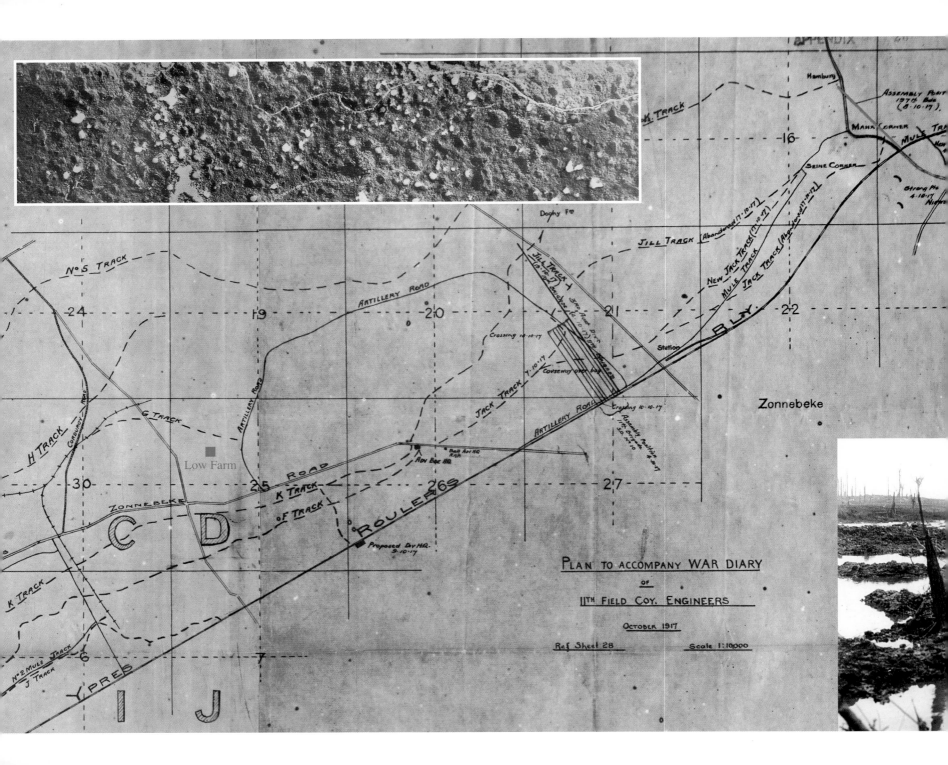

APPENDIX

KI TRACK

ASSEMBLY POINT
127TH Bde
(8·10·17)

MAHA CORNER

MULE TR

Hamburg

16

SEINE CORNER

Strong Pt
4·10·17

Nightio

JILL TRACK (Abandoned 17·10·17)

Doohy Fm

New Jack Track (17·10·17)

MULE TRACK

JACK TRACK (Abandoned 17·10·17)

JILL TRACK
(9·10·17)

Iron Fence Div'n
(6·10·17) 5th

No5 TRACK

ARTILLERY ROAD

24

19

20

21

Crossing 10·10·17

Station

Causeway over bog

22

RLY

Zonnebeke

JACK TRACK 7·10·17

ARTILLERY ROAD

Crossing 10·10·17

G TRACK

Assembly Position
11th Cy. 2nd
No 10

H TRACK

ARTILLERY ROAD

Low Farm

Batt Adv HQ Rah

Adv Bde HQ

CONDUROY ROAD

30

25

ROAD

27

ZONNEBEKE

C D

K TRACK

OF TRACK

ROULERS

26

K TRACK

Proposed Div HQ.
9·10·17

PLAN TO ACCOMPANY WAR DIARY

of

11TH FIELD COY. ENGINEERS

OCTOBER 1917

No2 MULE TRACK
J TRACK

6

7

Ref Sheet 28

Scale 1:10,000

YPRES

I J

Left
Plan drawn by 11 Australian Field Company showing roads and tracks available for the 9 October attacks, and (far right) the jumping-off point for the battle. Today it neatly bisects Tyne Cot cemetery. Low Farm, where the 2/6th Lancashire Fusiliers began their march into battle on 8 October, is marked.

Inset
German aerial view of part of this ground with a British Lattenweg.

Below
The Zonnebeke marshes. One of several treacherous mires which 49th and 66th Division troops had to negotiate during the night of 8 October to reach their jumping-off positions for the following day's attack.

march. They were expected to reach jumping-off positions at Dab Trench in the early hours of the following morning, allowing plenty of time to rest and feed before the attack, timed for 5.20 a.m. The War Diary entry for this period reads:

At 7.0 p.m. the battalion moved off in single file (route via 'Jill' track) to point of assembly. Owing to the state of the ground it took 10 hours to traverse a distance of under 2 miles.

A little more than two lines to describe one of the worst nights of the war. Through the combination of rain and 'obliterate and occupy' tactics during September, the sopping sea of craters before the Passchendaele Ridge had broadened. Only two main roads traversed the region, St Julien–Poelcappelle on the left, and Ypres–Zonnebeke on the right. Although primarily reserved for heavy transport, trucks, wagons and guns, troops always used them for dispersal before attacks. For those units stationed between the roads, there was only the ubiquitous duckboard track. The two II Anzac Corps divisions, 66th and 49th (West Riding), destined to attack side by side, had the use of three tracks, Jack, Jill and 'K'. Each comprised a narrow ribbon of wet, slippery timber that snaked and teetered around crater lips for 4 kilometres or more. To both sides of these narrow wooden causeways lay a lethal ocean of mud and water. Engineers had considered making them more direct, evading the crater field by perching the boards above ground on fixed trestles taking men straight to their destinations, but although this would certainly have produced the shortest route, the task required far more labour – and time – than was available. It was actually also unsound, for long experience

proved that duckboards bedded on the ground were more stable, less affected by shellfire and far swifter to mend than when 'suspended'. And most importantly for exposed troops, a track following a straight line was all too easy a target for enemy guns, day or night.

We were told to sit tight during the day, but were given jobs after dark – carrying parties mainly, rails, wood, ammunition and so on. There were plenty of pillboxes about for cover, but so many men had been brought up for the attack that it was officers only in there. We were put in shellholes around and about, and it was wet. We flicked the water out with our entrenching tool blades to keep the level down. You could look out from under your ground-sheet during the day and see working parties doing roads and tracks in a sort of wilderness of rubbish and muck, and field batteries digging in. The place was alive with men. It was a terrible sight because the shelling never stopped. They were helpless. We knew that was where we were going as soon as we got the order.
PRIVATE BERT FEARNS, 2/6TH LANCASHIRE FUSILIERS

Every unit faced dreadful ground conditions on their approach marches, but II Anzac were confronted by two serious obstacles, first the Zonnebeke valley, and then, beyond the Zonnebeke–Langemarck road, the shallow basin of the Hanebeek. Both were quagmires, and both were subjected to almost permanent searching hostile shellfire.

No one told us where we were going or what the ground was like, just that we were attacking the next morning and would have a rest and a feed beforehand. The name Passchendaele meant nothing to us then. It had been raining and blowing all day before we set off, and there were I don't know how many men on this single duckboard track – the whole of our battalion anyway. It was alright at first, but as it got dark you had to make sure to keep close to the fellow in front so as to follow the track, because it did-n't go in a straight line but meandered about round the shell holes. They [the Germans] must have known what was on because shells were falling all the time. They didn't do a lot of damage because of the mud, just covered you in muck. A lot didn't explode. If they'd been shrapnel they could have wiped us out. After a while bunches of men got separated a bit, and people started falling off the boards and shouting for help. Now, we had been told that if anyone fell out or got into trouble we were not allowed to stop, because if one man stopped we all stopped and we'd never get to where we were going. You could hear those poor blokes calling out from the darkness. It was pitiful. I found out myself a few days later that once you were in those shell holes there was no way out without help: the mud was like wet soap, you see, like it had been in a basin of water for a week; terrible stuff. You couldn't get any purchase to climb out, and the holes were brimming with water. You just got more and more tired with struggling; then you got chilled. We knew the poor devils were going to die if they weren't got out, and so did they. I tried to block my ears but it's not easy in the dark when you're carrying a rifle and pack and slipping all over the place trying to stay on eighteen inches of timber. Now, once the file broke up we were in a hell of a mess: sometimes you could see the bloke in front or which way the track went by Very lights or the flash of a shell, but most of the time we were like blind men: you had to slide one foot forward to see if the board was still there, then bring the other up, and so on – there were quite a few gaps caused by shells or maybe the board slipping away, so you had to stop to find where the track started again. You were on edge all the time, so you can see that progress was slow. You daren't look up, daren't take your eyes off the track, so the water ran down your neck.

We met a party of pack mules coming down the other way. Oh, the language! The track was meant to be one-way and only for infantry. I know we had to get off to let them pass, but one time when it happened later I think the poor things were shot by our officers just to get the path clear. We didn't know where we were going or how long we had to walk, we just kept going.

Hour after hour. Heads down. Then the duckboards ended and we came up on a road – the first bit of solid ground we'd stood on for hours. I was completely done up. We took shelter behind a big concrete pillbox [left-hand blockhouse in Tyne Cot Cemetery] and I fell asleep on my rifle, turned it upside down, put the muzzle on my boot and lay my head on the stock. It was light by then. I was so tired I didn't care if I lived or died; a bullet would have been welcome. I was woken up by an explosion or a gun firing close by or something.
PRIVATE BERT FEARNS, 2/6TH LANCASHIRE FUSILIERS

No one knows how many men were lost on the approach. The weather then mocked the exhausted troops. As they neared their destination the rain ceased, skies began to clear and the wind dropped away leaving a still, moisture-laden atmosphere. The 2/6th had been expected to arrive at between two and three in the morning for their 5.50 attack. It was now almost 7.30. Other units had attacked on time, but the whole assault was irretrievably fractured; as soon as news of the delays reached Second Army staff, they issued orders stating that no matter how late the various battalions turned up, the attacks should still go ahead. For the Lancastrians there was therefore no time to eat or rest. After twelve hours of trudging under shellfire, and with empty bellies, the troops went into 'action'. It was not only bellies that were empty. The men had nothing left to give.

Mr Kay came up and said, 'Come on lads, it's our turn', and we just walked round the corner of the pillbox and up the hill. It wasn't bad going but there was hardly a sign of any trenches. I didn't know then that we never got as far as any! The Germans didn't have much to fear from me that morning – there was no fire in my belly – no nothing. I staggered up the hill [this ground

Above
Man's vulnerability in the crater fields.

Right top
The Tyne Cot sector. Dab Trench (at top) runs through the present cemetery. The picture, taken in June 1917, shows a landscape with minimal damage, and the German cemetery at Keerselaarhoek on the edge of the railway cutting from which Bert Fearns and his 2/6th Lancashire Fusilier colleagues fought off a counter-attack on the evening of 9 October.

Right below
The same sector at the end of September. The German cemetery is still visible.

Far right
Creeping barrage plan for 9 October attacks. Use the bend in the railway above 2nd Australian Division as a reference point.

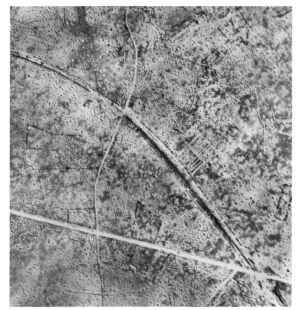

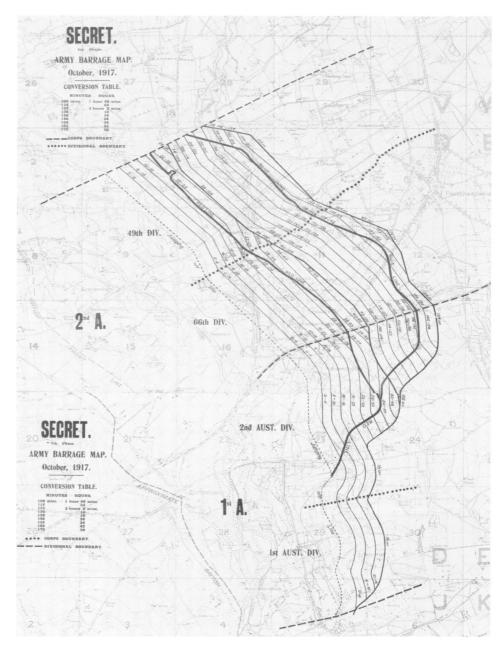

is now partly occupied by the Visitor Centre at Tyne Cot] and then dropped over a slope into a sort of gully. It was here that I froze and became very frightened because a big shell had just burst and blown a group of our lads to bits; there was bits of men all over the place, a terrible sight, men just blown to noth-ing. I just stood there. It was still and misty, and I could taste their blood in the air. I couldn't move. I stood there staring at the . . . just stood rooted. And then an officer, maybe Mr Kay again, came across and shouted that we were too far left, we must go half right and try to find other battalions on that flank. I'd prob-ably have been dead for 70-odd years if it hadn't been for him, because I just wasn't capable of moving without being jolted out of it. I don't remember any noise but it must have been hellish, and I never saw any of them [Germans], except dead ones, until that evening when they counter-attacked. The afternoon we spent waiting under shellfire and snipers, and looking for the Aussies on the right. I don't think we linked up at that time, and I could-n't tell you how far we advanced. You lose track of everything when you are exhausted. I know we went forward in the morn-ing, then came back a bit; and we ended up in a cemetery on the edge of the railway cutting. There were a lot of dead here – killed that day I mean – and they had not just been killed but horribly mutilated, heads bashed in and . . . Well, other things you can't forget. That's where the counter-attack came later in the day. It was going dusk I think and they appeared as a sort of clump in front of us. Up went our red rockets to call up the artillery. I can't think why the Germans didn't spread out a bit because it was like shooting at a crowd. They weren't rushing, just walking slowly towards us – I suppose they couldn't run on that ground. Anyway, I emptied my rifle into this dark mass, you did-n't even have to aim, just rapid fire, reload, rapid fire, and so on. It was over in no time, just broke up and disappeared; they didn't get near us. We must have put them off having another go because it went pretty quiet. I probably shouldn't have done but I crept into a pillbox and fell asleep – on the shoulder of a dead German offi-cer, it turned out. He hadn't a mark on him, but he had some nice binoculars that I 'borrowed'. Captain Chesnutt-Chesney

Background
Detailed barrage plan for 66th and 49th Divisions frontage.

Right
Private Bert Fearns.

Left and inset
The Tyne Cot area on 21 October. The Cross of Sacrifice stands upon the pillbox which can be seen in the middle of the picture. A fire-bayed Dab Trench runs

parallel to the road at left. The inset is a segment of an 11 October aerial. In it, attacking 66th Division troops can be seen taking cover in trenches and shell holes.

Above
Wounded from the attack being evacuated the following day.

Right
The remnants of the German cemetery on the railway cutting as pictured by Captain Frank Hurley on 6 November.

(commanding 'C' Company) later said it was looting and took them off me! I don't remember the next day much, but I do remember we were relieved by the Australians that night, 'You the LF's? Well piss off, we're here to relieve you.' We needed no second bidding. We moved to the right and slid down into the railway cutting then tried to follow the railway back to Zonnebeke. We came back in dribs and drabs and we could soon tell we had had quite a few losses because the cooks had prepared a hot meal for us at the asylum [the battalion had been ordered to remuster at the Ypres Asylum] and there was still loads of food left when we had all eaten. But we had been lucky because our front had been on the higher ground. The lads on our left were lower, and it was just a bog; they got hardly anywhere.
PRIVATE BERT FEARNS, 2/6TH LANCASHIRE FUSILIERS

Whereas 197 and 198 Brigades of the 66th Division had the higher ground astride the area now occupied by Tyne Cot Cemetery and up to the Ypres–Roulers railway cutting, the 'lads on the left', two brigades of the 49th (West Riding) Division, had been given the task of advancing up the valley of the Ravebeke, once a small stream, but now a wide morass that flowed down from

Passchendaele. Since 1915 this area had been christened Marsh Bottom by the British, and for good reason: annotation on tactical maps revealed the word 'impassable'. And so it was. No need for barbed wire here. On all but the very fringes of their attacking front the West Riding troops were engulfed in waist-deep mud. British guns had been of little assistance. Only a small percentage of those earmarked for the attacks had been able to get into position and once there the conditions beat the gunners. Every shell arrived plastered with filth and had to be cleaned; platforms slopped about, the guns were unstable eliminating any hope of accuracy. There was no creeping barrage – that had already drifted far up the ridge – and insufficient heavier guns targeting strong points and centres of resistance on the spurs to either side.

The men, fatigued and practically immobile, were cut down wholesale. By avoiding the lower parts of the Ravebeke, small parties of 49th Division men did manage to reach the upper contours, crossing the stream where the going was better. There they found new wire – much new wire – and resistance from not only woods and pillboxes but shell holes. Snipers were as plentiful as the Yorkshiremen were vulnerable. It was a pocket into which one ventured with little hope of return, and after six hours of fighting the few survivors had been forced back to their original starting point. The small advance made astride the Ypres–Roulers railway cutting almost reached the first objective, but also came to nothing; the territorial gain being perhaps 150 metres. On the right of the cutting, apart from a small (and abortive) diversionary assault against Celtic Wood, the Australians of I Anzac Corps were required simply to offer flank support and conform to 197 Brigade's final line. The latter turned out to be difficult, for although the Lancastrians hardly moved the line forward at all – just to Defy Crossing where the Passchendaele–Broodseinde road intersects the railway – the two Brigades, 6 and 7, of the 2nd Australian Division detailed to link up had spent three days as attached infantry, shifting and carrying, and road and track-building. After each night's toil, all that could be offered as sleeping accommodation was a water-filled shellhole. They were not only worn out when it was time to move forward, but suffering from the agonizing beginnings of trench foot and assorted other sicknesses, and down to almost half-strength. In the end 5 Brigade took on the task, eventually shifting the line the required few hundred metres, in doing so filching an added strip of ridge crest.

If the Lancastrians of the 66th Division achieved precious little for their efforts on 9 October they did, however, win one grim distinction: when Passchendaele eventually fell, the bodies of Lancashire Fusiliers were found in the village streets; they may well have been the first troops to reach Sir Douglas Haig's goal.

In XVIII Corps' sector a brigade each of the 48th and 11th Divisions pushed the British line a little further up the London Ridge, whilst among the ruins of Poelcappelle their initial advance was later driven back to the original jumping-off points. Although the troops engaged here had arrived in good time for their assault, the approach conditions were only marginally better than at Tyne Cot. And it was as if the enemy had been patiently waiting.

I spent a wretched night. I could hardly sleep. Every now and then I would wake, shivering with cold. I had a feeling that something was going to happen, that this might be my last day on earth. I was standing in for another fellow. Just my luck to be killed doing another man's job! Shortly after daybreak we moved off in artillery formation along the duck-boards. Two dead men, without equipment, without gasmasks and with no mark of shell-wounds, lay beside the track. Recalling the solitary grave behind the wood at the Somme, that made me wonder. The enemy barrage was falling between us and the start-line we had to reach. I studied carefully where the shells fell sparsely, in hope to make a safe dash through. It took us a quarter of an hour to reach the barrage. A party to the left had a shell right amongst them. Our leading sergeant went down. We scrambled on and were through. The trench awaiting us was shallow, so I and others moved into a shell-hole where I set up the Lewis-gun. We made a rough trench about five yards long. 'A' company had dug itself in fifty yards ahead of us and 'C' company behind. Prisoners were being herded back, a poor-looking lot and some of them

Below and right
The two sides of a message sent by Lieutenant J. Everard Smith at 6.45 on the morning of 9 October. The X on the map marks his position, with the tactical situation briefly outlined overleaf. This message would have been delivered to his battalion HQ by a runner – at great risk. Note line running through Tyne Cot, Dab Trench and the German cemetery.

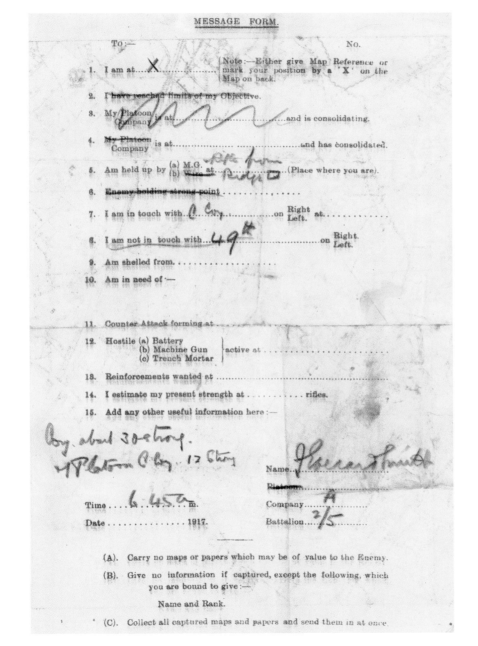

mere schoolboys. Some helped our wounded along or carried them on stretchers. Shells began to fall on the company behind us and at times I could see arms and legs being thrown into the air. Then the Germans shortened their range and shells began to fall among us.

PRIVATE WILLIAM GRAHAM, 6TH BORDER REGIMENT

The day also witnessed the final tank action of Third Ypres. Yet again, Poelcappelle and its web of negotiable lanes were the only possible sector where the great machines could be deployed. It was a different story to the previous attack of 4 October.

We crawled along in the relative silence apparently all alone until peering through the murk on either side of the road one saw little knots of infantry wearily ploughing their way through the quagmire representing the main axis of the victorious advance to Roulers. Round a bend we came upon disaster in the shape of a large tree, which had either been felled or blown across the road. The leading tank in trying to climb over it had slipped on the wet bark into the mud and had become ditched. Two other tanks had put on their unditching beams and had tried to crawl round the outside of the ditched tank and had themselves become ditched. There was a slight pause and then Skinner decided to lead the section over the tree, and by immaculate driving on the part of our drivers the three of us left crawled precariously up the trunk and slipped safely down the other side onto the road.

Our peace was then shattered by the opening barrage which came down a few hundred yards in front of us on what we imagined to be our objective, the brewery at Poelcapelle. It was impossible to hear or see anything except the black road between the horns of the tank and we crawled slowly on, conscious that the German defensive barrage had come down and that we were in the middle of it. Suddenly an ear-splitting crash filled the tank with the acrid smoke of an exploding shell through which appeared a tell-tale flame – we had received a direct hit.

The fire was on the starboard side of the tank and the driver with great coolness switched off and put it out with his Pyrenes [fire extinguishers]. The direct hit had been occasioned by a shell which came in through the starboard doors and hit the engine, and we were hopelessly immobile. There was nothing in sight, and all we could do was to evacuate the tank into the near-est shell hole. One gunner had practically lost his leg, he subsequently died, three others were more or less badly wounded. By this time we were in the middle of an absolute inferno. The last tank appeared in sight some twenty yards behind us com-manded by Rosy Stephens. We crawled back dragging our wounded with us and explained to him that the road was hope-lessly blocked in front and that to leave it was courting disaster in the shape of instantaneous bogging. The driver with quite extraor-dinary skill managed to turn his tank on that narrow road literally by swinging inches at a time until he was once more fac-ing in the direction of St. Julien and we withdrew down the road until we met the block we had passed previously and which now consisted of every tank which had started the advance except Hugh Skinner's, my own and Stephens'. We did our best to by-pass the chaos, but the morass was too much and we bogged half way round. A very brave advance stretcher party took off the man without a leg and the rest of us set off across a path we had found in the direction of home. We eventually found a dressing station to drop the rest of the wounded, who were by this time in a bad condition, but were halted outside by a military policeman who said is was reserved for the stretcher cases only. For the first time we were able to deal satisfactorily with an enemy met face to face.

Second Lieutenant Horace Birks, D Battalion, Tank Corps, commanding tank D30 (Dusky Dis)

Both tanks and infantry failed to make an impres-sion on the battered but infuriatingly resistant bastion. On the now all too well-known St Julien road tank crews soon to leave the Salient for Cambrai left behind their crippled machines; they were soon filled with wounded and dying

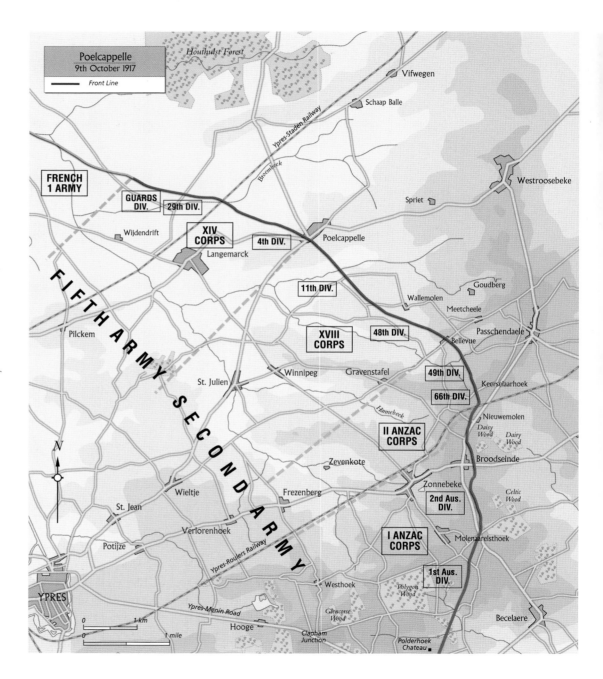

Above and inset
Aerial of October tank action. One machine has ditched in a trench; the other has crossed perpendicularly and attacked a shell-hole strongpoint (far right), clearly circling its target like G47 at Alberta.

men seeking shelter. Unable to be salvaged from such an exposed position, the tanks' presence created a serious problem by blocking one of the battlefield's arteries; the sappers came up with the only solution, blowing them into manageable fragments with portable charges.

Beyond Poelcappelle, the Guards and 29th Divisions (XIV Corps) both managed a small advance on better ground, but were held back by Maxse's failure to clear the village. The French, arriving in the right place and on time, claimed the honours of the day, advancing nearly 2 kilometres to the very edge of Houthulst Forest. That their line now rested in a swamp was the least of their problems: Anthoine's greatest fear was that he might be asked to enter the wood, for although blown to splinters it secreted hundreds of hidden and probably unsuppressable pillboxes.

There was a sense of tokenism surrounding the habitual German counter-attacks. They seemed to be launched more to show the British that they were still able and willing rather than to regain lost ground – for the meagre acres of muck they were ostensibly attempting to regain were as worthless to them as they were to the British and French. For those able to perceive it, the advance left the new Fifth Army line looking somewhat bent and disjointed.

On the other flank of the arena in front of Polygon, a small salient was pushed out by 7th and 21st Divisions. On their right, the battlefield's southern boundary, Polderhoek, was being attacked again, this time by two Brigades of the 5th Division; although the line here was relatively easy to reach, conditions on the Reutel battlefield were hideous, and the enemy as damnably resilient as ever.

8 OCTOBER

I got into my headquarters, which was a cellar belonging to a lodge, which in turn belonged to a chateau [Polderhoek Chateau]. This must have been a magnificent place in peacetime. Situated on a rise, surrounded by woodlands and with an extensive view across valleys and hills. The view was now all that remained. The chateau had disappeared and the adjacent country was utter desolation. We held the lodge, the Germans held the chateau. No actual buildings, except walls of the lodge or chateau, existed. They had been long since blown down by artillery. It was the cellars in both instances that were occupied. The cellar I found was occupied by D Company and brigade machine-gunners as their H.Q., but the most welcome sight of all was to see a candle

burning. I had not had a light for nights past, and its glow was very cheery. That the recent occupants were Germans was evident by the amount of German equipment strewn about. The sides of the walls were reinforced by blocks of concrete. We had reached another stage and wondered what was going to happen next. We were only fit to be literally carried out of the line at the first opportunity and given a night's sleep and some food (rations which had been sent up from the rear in double quantities seldom reached us. The carriers were either killed or unable to get through the barrage).

Small parties got through occasionally, and it was on these that we relied for sustenance. I had scarcely been in the cellar a few minutes when such a party arrived, bringing a supply of rations and rum. Under these conditions we fondly looked for relief, but instead I had a message at 10 p.m. by runner from Walters, asking me to go to his headquarters. Stuffing my pockets with grub and a bottle of whisky from D Company rations in case he was without food or rum, I returned with the runner, taking Sergeant Badger. Rain was pouring down; our condition was pitiable. Personally, my boots were full of mud and had been so for some days, and I was fairly wet through either by rain or perspiration. We were, without exception, all the same. We followed the runner over what seemed to be about a mile of ground. Although it was a very short distance, he had to stop every few yards to take his bearings. We found Walters at last. With him was Hutchingson, a subaltern. They were standing up to their knees in mud and water. They had no covering. Their shack (a ground-sheet stretched across the top of the trench) had fallen in. They were both shaking as if they had a bad attack of the ague and could scarcely speak from cold. I handed them down into the trench the whisky and food. Their expression of thanks was rather pathetic. With this tonic they recovered somewhat, and Walters told me he had operation orders for an attack on the chateau at dawn.

SECOND LIEUTENANT H.V. DRINKWATER, 16TH ROYAL WARWICKSHIRE REGIMENT (3RD BIRMINGHAM PALS)

Above
The pretty Polderhoek Chateau before the war.

Drinkwater and his men knew that in their weakened state the chances of even the most meagre success were remote. Cursing the staff for not making the effort to acquaint themselves with the situation, they nonetheless obeyed orders and began planning. Having agreed a scheme with his two fellow officers, each returned to their men whilst Drinkwater issued orders to his own NCOs. With no murmur of dissent the men traipsed wearily into the darkness to join their sections. There were no tapes upon which to form up, no one knew exactly who owned which bit of the battlefield, nor whether flanks were covered.

We were going over in two waves: A, B, and C Companies, supported by D Company, with the Norfolks on our left. Our particular objectives were the two pill boxes, A Company and the Norfolks dealing with the chateau; my platoon were in the first wave. Punctually at 5.30 a.m., just as day was breaking, the barrage opened on the chateau and pill boxes. We advanced, and in less than two minutes we were among the Germans, who were laying out in shell holes around them. Keeping well in line, we received and inflicted casualties, but our men were going strong, taking a prisoner here and there, and according to plan my platoon were keeping their eye on and making straight for the pill boxes, the Germans running before us as we advanced. I was the left-hand man of my platoon, so that I could keep them from straying with the party who were attacking the chateau. Glancing along the line as we closed up to the pill boxes, I saw my bombers crawling on their hands and knees close up, trying to find an opening to drop in bombs. My platoon machine-gunner, who was advancing with me, and slightly to the rear, carrying a Lewis gun, fell hit in the head. Hearing him fall down I looked round quickly and quickly back again, and saw a German stretched out in a shell hole. I let fly with my revolver. He was not more than ten

yards away, I missed, and he got up and bolted towards the pill boxes, while I dropped into the shell hole he had just left. Bullets were flying about in all directions, so I stayed a moment, glanced to the right, saw our men were still crawling up to the pill boxes, whilst on the left our other men, A Company and the Norfolks, appeared to be getting round the chateau. It all took only a moment and I was up again and going forward. We seemed to be making good headway, when for some unexplained reason my platoon and the remainder of the battalion on my right began to retire. Glancing to the right I found that there was not a soul between myself and the pill boxes, and looking quickly backward I saw the battalion retiring and were now some fifty yards to my rear. I dropped into a shell hole and glanced to the left. Our men were still attacking the chateau.

Drinkwater took cover behind a tree trunk and waited for his own men to return. None appeared.

I had a good view of the chateau being attacked, I was within a hundred yards of it. The Germans were putting up a good fight. One German from the top of the ruins was slinging bombs amongst our men. I could see him, but apparently they could not. But still our men kept crawling closer, taking cover in shell holes and behind fallen trees.

Still he was alone. There was no choice but to go back and find out what was happening and find men to support the continuing action. Judging the moment he bolted rearwards 'like a frightened rabbit', on the way stopping to assist a colleague wounded in the leg. Just as they reached the cover of a shell hole arm-in-arm, the two men came within view of the Germans in the chateau ruins. A machine gun opened up hitting the wounded man in the head, killing him

Below
The chateau in 1916.

instantly. Drinkwater dropped to the ground, crawled on and tumbled into a trench, landing amongst dead Germans and wounded British. The latter turned out to be remnants of his unit.

The attacks, both on the chateau and on the pill boxes, were failures. Gopsill [a platoon commander] was the only one to reach the chateau, and he was taken prisoner. In both cases we got to within a dozen yards, but could not push the attack home. I found the remnants of the battalion in charge of a Lieutenant, as Senior Officer, and two 2nd Lieutenants, and the men half-way up to their knees in mud. I waded along the trench and found Sergt. Badger. He had got the remains of the platoon together. From him I gathered that when the men had got to the pill boxes they heard the word given 'retire'. They should have known that it did not come from us, as the command is never given in the British Army. The Germans may have shouted it, or what is more probable our men were too exhausted to carry on.

Hostile counter-attacks were now their chief concern. Whilst a few men were detailed to crawl off in search of spare ammunition, rifles were hur-

riedly but carefully cleaned. All the newly gathered ammunition was equally caked in filth; it too needed cleaning. Next the trench itself had to be attended to, for it was knee-deep in mud. Fortunately no German attacks materialized, and as night fell rations arrived. Bucked by food, rum and the prospect of imminent relief, sure to come

Above

Panorama 102. The Polderhoek sector during the battle with severely damaged tank, and the same view today.

after such an action, the men hoisted haversacks onto weary shoulders and waited. Midnight came and went. As dawn was breaking a runner arrived with the news that the relief would take place that night. It rained for most of the day; the troops sat, watched and listened. As the light faded they prepared once more for relief, and waited.

Midnight came and no relief. At 3 a.m. we saw a number of men appear from the back and thought at last relief had arrived; but from the officer in charge we gathered that they had not come to relieve us but to reinforce us, and we were not being relieved that night. They were a company of the 14th Warwicks, with orders to reinforce us and attack again next morning. Quite memorable was the meeting and subsequent discussion between Sewell and the Captain of the 14th. Sewell pointed out with all eloquence the impossibility of our men again attacking, what was left of them could barely stand. Whilst agreeing, the 14th Captain nevertheless had orders to carry out the attack. They sat in the pill box both covered in mud, clothes, hands and face. By the light of a candle it was apparent how much each felt his responsibility. At daybreak the Captain went along the trench to see the position, and was sniped through the head. If this was intentional it was bravely done. Only a few moments before I had warned him of the dangers of the trench. By some means the second attack was cancelled. The men were almost ready to shoot themselves, or anyone else who came near them, as they took their packs off to stick it for another night. However, the reinforcement from the 14th Warwicks took on some of the strain, allowing our men to relax.

Before daybreak another ration party got through, bringing rum, cigarettes and food. They had had an awful time getting through. They said it was impossible to dodge the German barrage and they had had considerable casualties. My food for the two preceding days had been a piece of bread on the first and a piece of bread and cheese on the second, both taken from the dead. The rum, cigarettes and food were issued to the men. The cigarettes were particularly welcome. Some of them had not had a smoke for days. The ration party was followed by a runner from B.H.Q., saying that relief was coming that night certain. With that news we settled down for the day. The men had for the most part scooped holes in the side of the trench, and in these they sat, their legs hanging in the mud.

As the hours crawled by, three more men were sniped. They lay dead in the trench, and unburied. Rifles would no longer fire, and all machine guns were unserviceable save one which was missing its tripod and had to be fired resting on the parapet. As another evening approached, the men prepared again.

Sergeant Badger got ready what remained of my platoon, so that when the relief did arrive we could get quickly away. Towards 8 p.m. I was on duty, feeling too dead to wade up and down the trench. I sat in a cubby hole and dozed, like the men not on duty, hanging my feet in the mud. I was awakened by a sentry coming along and reporting that the Germans were using signal lights in the valley; so we all prepared for an attack. No attack developed, and we were still waiting when the relief arrived. They reported that the Menin Road was being very heavily shelled, and as far as they could gather so was the surrounding district. I was the only officer left of my company, and getting the men together as best I could, I told them of the conditions and warned them that if anyone fell out on the way no help could be given; that we had to go for all we were worth, to stop and help one man might mean half a dozen being hit. We set out, Percy de Vene leading the way

and taking with him a company, or the remnants of a company, which had not an officer left. We had not gone far when the shells came buzzing over. De Vene, not sure of the way, was leading us over shell holes and mud, the men slipping in all directions. Travelling over such would have been difficult to fit men; to us it was a form of torture as we wound round the craters. Representing half a battalion, we must have presented a pitiable spectacle, a few dozen men and a couple of officers. It was a blessing, perhaps, that the night was dark, the language was foul, and our appearance equal to the language.

Passing across the plateau, from Clapham Junction the men began the gentle descent down the Menin Road past Hooge and Birr Crossroads towards Ypres, heading towards some form of sanctuary. Negotiating the perennial hazard of Hellfire Corner they passed the heavy gun positions, hitching a ride with trucks which had just delivered one of many nightly cargoes of shells. Passing through Ypres the men eventually reached camp at Ridge Wood. Guided to their 'spot' by runners, the men threw off their kit and collapsed.

Major Quarry, second in command, was waiting for us, and from ten days of perfect hell I was transferred into a perfect paradise, a scene fitting for a banquet. During our absence the pioneers had been brought up and had built canvas shacks in the wood. The men were provided with a hot meal and a hot wash and somewhere to sleep under cover of sorts. Whilst for the officers – there were only three of us left out of seventeen who went up the line – a miniature fairyland presented itself. We were taken into a long canvas shack, brilliantly illuminated by candles and warmed by braziers. A table was laid complete with tablecloth; we had a hot meal. Arrayed along the table were more candles and bottles of wine. With a war on only a few miles away this was a magnificent performance.

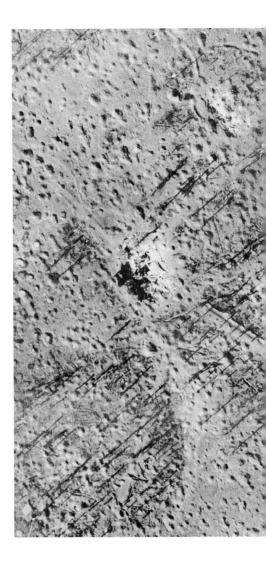

Above
Polderhoek Chateau and grounds from the air in October 1917.

Too tired to stand I was carried to bed, and sleep quickly brought to a close the horrors through which we had passed. We had accomplished nothing and had lost heavily.
SECOND LIEUTENANT H.V. DRINKWATER, 16TH ROYAL WARWICKSHIRE REGIMENT (3RD BIRMINGHAM PALS)

Beyond the appalling task of clearing the wounded, it was also a challenge for relieved troops and walking wounded to find their way back to Ypres. For those serving in the sectors between the two main roads, the railway line was the key. In the dark and without guides there was little chance of men being able to find forward track heads, so before battle commanders had given instructions that upon relief they were to move to right or left according to their attacking sector; in this way they were ultimately guaranteed to hit upon the track. Then it was only necessary to turn away from the Very lights and towards the origin of the heaviest gunfire – British, it was hoped – and follow the broken rails, embankments or cuttings to Zonnebeke where either the road or more defined duckboard routes led back to Ypres. Between Zonnebeke and Ypres the railway line itself was in a constant state of repair and improvement, for as soon as the Germans had been driven from the remaining section ridge it would become immeasurably safer and more functional, with connections to tramway 'branch lines' for artillery. The closer it was to completion, the quicker it could be made to serve troops and guns. Many hundreds of men were already toiling on the line.

OCTOBER 8TH–10TH, 1917
Our boys have taken further objectives. Weather very wet. Machine gun course finished. We go up on the railway today (10th). Expect to get rather wet and muddy.

OCTOBER 11TH, 1917
Went up to work on light railway today. Left camp at 6 a.m., back at 2 p.m. Fairly nice day, no rain, 'beaucoup mud'.
SAPPER G.T. MARWOOD, 5TH PIONEER BATTALION, AUSTRALIAN IMPERIAL FORCE

Whereas a few months earlier one would have been able to walk from Boesinghe to Ploegsteert without once showing one's head above the parapet, now across the Salient every trench had been almost entirely obliterated. Those that existed were no more than short lengths, dug on the spot. A strong point consisted of a parallel series of such slits. They were unrevetted, undrained (except manually by the troops), unstable and, being uncovered, susceptible to constant showers of mud from shell and small-arms fire. Here, mechanisms of rifles and machine guns became clogged the moment the protective covers were removed. There was no true 'line'. Many troops were not in a trench at all, but permanently crouched in the best-protected, i.e. deepest, shell holes they could find. Indeed, this was no longer trench warfare, but semi-open skirmishing. Gauging ones actual troop dispositions after an action became a game of join the dots, best played by airmen who were the only ones who could see the men, or rather the shape of their helmets, in the sea of mud. As rain continued to fall, water levels in the morass rose: the choice was to rise with it and become ever more susceptible to the constant and meticulous enemy sniper fire, or sit with one's lower half immersed in the water and the upper drenched and chilled. Whatever one did, it drew enemy attention and fire. To attend to his natural functions, a man was forced to leave this debatable sanctuary and find an unoccupied shellhole – a strictly night-time activity. Fever and trench foot, the latter a potentially fatal complaint which had almost disappeared from the Army's lexicon before Third Ypres thanks to fastidious construction and upkeep of trenches and daily inspection, made a fierce return. Given the ghastly conditions, the affliction could no longer, as once it was, be considered a crime perpetrated by the affected soldier. Unless relief was fast in coming, it was unavoidable. One Division at this time reported 1,200 men with symptoms of trench foot or trench fever.

TAKING STOCK

Whilst Sir Douglas Haig noted 9 October as 'very successful', his Chief of Intelligence, Brigadier General Charteris, considered it 'the saddest day of the year', concluding sullenly, 'We did fairly well but only fairly well. It was not the enemy but mud which prevented us doing better. There is now no chance of complete success here this year.' These sentiments were not communi-cated to his Commander-in-Chief. On 10 October Charteris wrote: 'He [Haig] was still trying to find some grounds for hope that we might still win through here this year, but there is none.' At the front, the hope was of a different kind. Relieving units were now lucky to find the positions they were to occupy, for many did not correspond with the map references given; the line was no line at all, but disjointed, zig-zagged, dog-legged and broken, with parties often isolated far from where staff at HQs thought their positions to be. And it was utterly squalid.

10 OCTOBER

The slope was littered with dead, both theirs and ours. I got to one pillbox to find it just a mass of dead, and so I passed on carefully to the one ahead. Here I found about fifty men alive, of the Manchesters. Never have I seen men so broken or demoralised. They were huddle up close behind the box in the last stages of exhaustion and fear. Fritz had been sniping them off all day, and had accounted for fifty-seven that day – the dead and dying lay in piles. The wounded were numerous – unattended and weak, they groaned and moaned all over the place . . . some had been there days already

Right
The return of the rains began to create the kind of battlefield conditions for which Passchendaele has become notorious. The positions seen on page 262 are now little more than ditches and ponds. The picture shows British positions in front of Westroosebeke.

Below
Mid-October. The view across the devastated Gheluvelt plateau as seen from a position near the Menin Road. Second Army pan 126.

Second Army Panorama 126
The Gheluvelt Plateau, October 1917
From near the Menin Road looking towards Polderhoek

Ruins of Becelaere village

Spire of Dadizeele church

. . . Finally the company came up – the men done in after a fearful struggle through the mud and shell holes, not to speak of the barrage the Hun put down and which caught numbers. The position was obscure – a dark night – no line – demoralised Tommies – and no sign of the enemy. So I pushed out my platoon, ready for anything, and ran into the foe some eighty yards ahead. He put in a few bursts of rapid fire and then fled. We could not pursue as we had to establish the line, which was accomplished about an hour later.
LIEUTENANT W.G. FISHER, 42ND INFANTRY BATTALION, AUSTRALIAN IMPERIAL FORCE

There had been no solid jumping-off line for the next assault, and everything had once more to be realigned if continuation was contemplated. For those who had enjoyed a break from the Salient, such as Frank Hurley, in France trying to photograph RFC activities, the vision upon return came as a shock.

10 OCTOBER

Day broke with the appearance of being fine, so went to aerodrome again. It turned out evilly, however, so I had to abandon my object and decided to return to Steenvoorde. As usual it cleared up on the return, and we had the displeasure to come home with a bright setting sun. Tomorrow, however, I intend being off at 6 a.m. and tackling the job again. The weather is turning extremely cold and it is evident that winter is with us. God help the poor devils in the trenches.

11 OCTOBER

But the best laid schemes of mice and men go astray, and so instead of going back to St Pol Flying Squadron I found myself 'lured' back to the battlefield (great emphasis on lured, for there is no place in eternity that is more hellish). My enthusiasm and keenness, however, to endeavour to record the hideous things that men have to endure, urges me on. No monetary consideration or very few others in fact, would induce any man to flounder in mud to his knees to try and take pictures. The past rains have made the place a great slough. One dares not venture off the duckboard or he will surely become bogged, or sink in the quicksand-like slime of rain-filled shell craters. Add to this the frightful walking, a harassing shellfire and soaking to the skin, and you curse the day you were induced to put foot on this polluted damned ground. A few bursts of sunlight allowed me to take a few pictures in the trenches on the Broodseinde Ridge; a heavy barrage of 5.9's were coming over at the time, so that I had a devilish tight time for an hour or so. Then the six and a half miles tramp back through the slush to Ypres, where the car has to be left, just about beat me.

CAPTAIN FRANK HURLEY, OFFICIAL PHOTOGRAPHER, AUSTRALIAN IMPERIAL FORCE

According to the British battle nomenclature committee, the 9 October endeavour was to be named Poelcappelle, for that village, although itself unconquered, was nearest to where the greatest gains occurred. Its annals list 4,000 British, Australian and French dead, and 13,000 wounded.

The first Battle of Passchendaele took place three days later. Before that, however, on 11 October as the dejected, exhausted, mud-caked survivors traipsed back to Ypres, and wounded still lay out awaiting succour, the War Policy Committee convened once more. Although Lloyd George was able to find ample support for his dour analysis of future prospects in Flanders, and equal enthusiasm for a crack at the Turks in Palestine, neither he nor anyone else were prepared to bite the bullet and suspend the offensive, for had they not promised to supply Sir Douglas Haig with the wherewithal to fight on until things looked like breaking down? And was not progress of a sort still being made? Sir William Robertson reported so. The Prime Minister required a clutch of powerful backers – military, not civilian – to have any chance of changing Haig's direction. If it proved that none but his own political clique would support him, what then was the alternative? Lloyd George appears to have lacked one and Haig appeared to know it. At the front, though, even the once ultra-judicious Plumer was now reconciled to almost eternal continuation, for the narrow foetid pocket which the troops presently held *had* to be broadened and straightened, otherwise the situation would resemble that of May 1915, where the British had been forced into muddled and ignominious retirement. Regardless of Haig and Charteris' convictions of imminent German collapse, he was all too aware of the importance of escaping the constrained and filthy quagmire in front of Passchendaele. This was the sole aim. Disregarding Gough's heartfelt pleas for pause, Plumer and his Corps commanders decided to forge on.

Above

12 October. Captain Frank Hurley's telling picture of Australian and British troops sheltering in funk holes, sharing the railway cutting near Tyne Cot with fallen comrades. Today this spot is relatively unchanged. See diary entry opposite.

12 OCTOBER

Last night I found a letter awaiting me from Captain Bean telling me of another battle which is to come off tomorrow. Our objective is Poelcappelle – about 800 yards advance. God knows how those red tabbed blighters at headquarters (60 miles from the front) expect our men to gain such a strong position when they have to drag themselves through mud. Curse them! I'll swear they were not within 20 miles of the firing line when this attack was arranged, the ground is impassable, and though it is essential that we should gain the 'key ridge' and put the Boche in the low hollow for the winter, I fail to see how it is possible to achieve this end without great loss, and then be evicted again owing to the artillery being in the unhappy position of getting bogged if they move up. Owing to Joyce (my Camera lumper) funking it, Wilkins and I set out in the car for Hellfire Corner (Menin Road 20 kilometres). Here we got on to the Zonnebeke railroad which has been shelled and blown to fragments during the past two years of straffing. It is now a raised bank of mud and bits of scrap iron rails. Already we are starting to rebuild it, and about 1000 labourers were at work rail-laying. It will be of incalculable value to support the front lines and artillery, as the roads will be impassable during the winter. It's a bloody work, however, for it is being constantly shelled and numbers are daily being killed. It is littered with bodies both of our own men and Boche. Things were reasonably quiet till we got near to Zonnebeke – But the mud! Trudge, trudge – sometimes to the knee in sucking, tenacious slime – a fair hell of a job under ordinary conditions, but with a heavy camera up and being shelled, I hardly thought 'the game worth the candle'. Nearing Zonnebeke we got into the Boche barrage, and as he was paying particular attention to the railway line (or rather what once was), it being the only possible means of communication with the front line about here: we had more than an exciting time. Shells lobbed all around and sent their splinters whizzing everywhere – God knows how anybody can escape them, and the spitting ping of machine gun bullets that played on certain points made one wish he was a microbe; under these conditions one feels himself so magnified that he feels every shell the

Boche fires is directed for his especial benefit. This shelled embankment of mud was a terrible sight. Every 20 paces or less lay a body. Some frightfully mutilated, without legs, arms and heads, and half covered in mud and slime. I could not help thinking as Wilkins and I trudged along this inferno and soaked to the skin, talking and living beings, might not the next moment one of these things – Jee – it puts the wind up one at times. We pushed on through the old Zonnebeke station (now absolutely swept away) up to Broodseinde and entered the railway cutting near the ridge crest. Shells began to fall just about a hundred paces ahead and their skyrocket-like whiz, without cessation passing too close overhead and bursting all around, induced us to retire. The light too, failed, and rain set in. We got no pictures but whips of fun. I felt great admiration for the stretcher bearers, who slowly plodded on with their burdens, trudging through mud and presenting a tempting target, for the enemy observation balloons had eyes on everything. It was impossible to bring in many wounded under these conditions, and many poor devils must perish from exposure. I noticed one awful sight: a party of ten or so telephone men all blown to bits. Under a questionably sheltered bank lay a group of dead men. Sitting by them in little scooped out recesses sat a few living; but so emaciated by fatigue and shell shock that it was hard to differentiate. Still the whole way was just another of the many byways to hell one sees out here, and which are so strewn with ghastliness that the only comment is, 'That poor beggar copped it thick', or else nothing at all. Our fellows, 3rd Division and the New Zealanders, obtained their objective, Poelcappelle, but were driven out again. We captured a number of prisoners though not many. We left the embankment near Zonnebeke Station and took to the Duckboards for home. These slippery slidy ways are the only possible routes over a vast slough of rain filled shell craters. It took me two hours solid walk to return and it was not until we actually got on the Menin Road and clambered on a passing lorry, that we felt we had once again cheated the Boche of his wishes and intentions.

CAPTAIN FRANK HURLEY, OFFICIAL PHOTOGRAPHER,
AUSTRALIAN IMPERIAL FORCE

Zonnebeke — La Gare.
De Statie.

Above and right
The infamous railway cutting under German rule in 1916 (above) and pictured, again by Hurley, in late October.

Left and insets
Zonnebeke station on 30 October 1917. The pictures illustrates the vast number of men (many of those seen here are from a British labour company) employed on battlefield infrastructure. Under daily persistent shellfire, they had no opportunity of shooting back. Inset: an evocative picture taken from almost the identical spot in 1913. No railway serves Zonnebeke today.

The German Ypres Corps situation reports covering this period stated that another big British attack would certainly be launched in the near future: preparations were being observed. British artillery had been regrouped – about forty batteries were thought to have been brought forward; railways and light trench lines were clearly being extended and roads remade. The British objective, it suggested, would be the possession of Passchendaele village and the adjoining northern and southern crests. An attack in the direction of Becelaere was also to be expected to effect a flanking movement and to drive a wedge in between the Ypres and Wytschaete Corps. They were absolutely correct.

PENULTIMATE PRIVATIONS – FIRST PASSCHENDAELE

OCTOBER 4TH.

We are doing nothing, just here. Today the line attack in front of us, and as far as we can gather it has been a fair success. Expect to be getting a move on soon, probably Sunday. No definite orders are available to move as yet. Rain commenced to fall again throughout the day, and is continued during the next, the 5th. It is perfectly sickening, it seems as though the elements themselves are in league with Jerry to hold us up as much as possible. 6th, another soaker, incessant pour all day long until evening, finishing with a bitter cold wind. Poor beggars in the trenches, to have to stand this wind after two days of soaking rain. It makes one wonder sometimes if there is a limit to human endurance. In the bitter cold, the Division band turns up, and gives us selections, for which we tender grateful thanks. Today, 7th is no exception to the run of weather we are getting lately, if anything it is a damned lot colder. Retire to bed early, fed up as usual. By the way, summertime ceases tonight, and clocks are put back 1 hour. Next day dawns beautiful, and sun shines as though it was sorry and wants to make amends for its non-appearance lately. A keen wind also helps to dry up the ground, and our spirits begin to soar aloft again. If this weather continues, we shall soon get our turn in the line done.

PRIVATE ROBERT CUDE MM, 7TH EAST KENT REGIMENT
(THE BUFFS)

The first battle for Passchendaele was pressed by XIV and XVIII Corps of Fifth Army on the left with Poelcappelle at the core, and again by II Anzac Corps immediately facing the village. The first thing troops noted were the many wounded British soldiers who had taken part in the attacks three days earlier still waiting to be evacuated from the battlefield.

We had a few days rest after the battle and then we were in again shifting and carrying like before. It was ridiculous. We shouldn't have been doing that at that time, we should have been getting the wounded in, all of us. You'd be carrying some damn lump of timber up and see these poor wretches staggering back, so weak they could hardly walk. We should have been up there with stretchers getting them back to dressing stations. I don't know why they didn't let us do it – all of us were willing. No one wanted to go back into that lot again, of course not, but you became fatalistic, you know, and I suppose I wanted to believe that if I got wounded then at least I'd be able to think that there would be help around if I was struggling. These lads could hardly put one foot in front of another. We were allowed to help them? Were we buggery. It was a disgrace, was that, and hard to forgive folk for.

PRIVATE BERT FEARNS, 2/6TH LANCASHIRE FUSILIERS

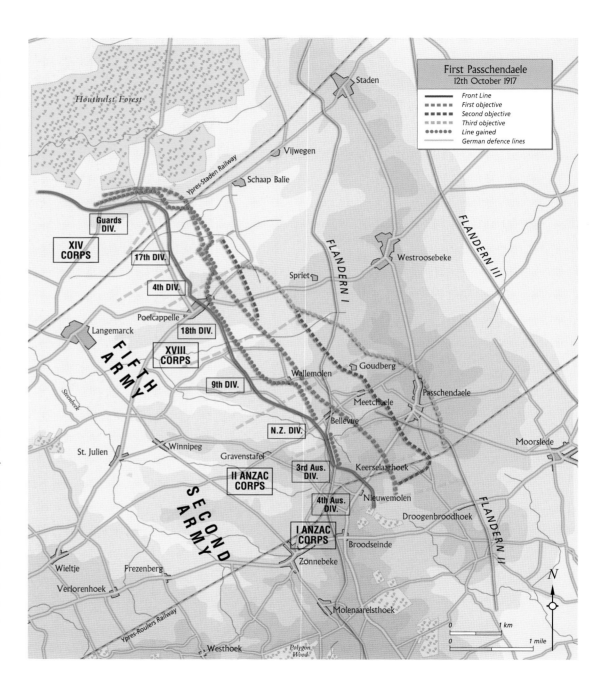

First Passchendaele
12th October 1917

- - - - Front Line
- - - - First objective
- - - - Second objective
- - - - Third objective
●●●●● Line gained
—— German defence lines

The infantry assaults which began at 5.20 a.m. were almost universally met with the thorniest facet of von Armin's new tactics: wire, dense thickets of it, freshly laid and uncut. The New Zealand Division, on the left flank, faced the worst. Although some men managed to find or cut a way through, the attack was again torn apart by converging machine-gun fire. It left the left flank of their neighbours, the 3rd Australian Division, wide open, whose failure in turn exposed their neighbour, the 4th Australian Division.

13 OCTOBER

The next day we were ordered to retake the line, and then our units sank to the lowest pitch of which I have ever been cognisant. It looked hopeless – the men were so utterly done. However, the attempt had to be made, and accordingly we moved up that night – a battalion 90 strong. I had A company with 23 men. We got up to our position somehow or other – and the fellows were dropping out unconscious along the road – they have guts, my word! That's the way to express it. We found the line instead of being advanced, some thirty yards behind where we had left it – and the shell-stricken and trodden ground thick with dead and wounded – some of the Manchesters were there yet, seven days wounded and not looked to. But the men walked over them – no heed was paid to anything but the job. Our men gave all their food and water away, but that was all they could do. That night my two runners were killed as they sat beside me, and casualties were numerous again. He blew me out of my shell-hole twice, so I shifted to an abandoned pillbox. There were twenty-four wounded men inside, two dead Huns on the floor and six outside, in various stages of decomposition. When day broke I looked over the position. Over forty dead lay within twenty yards of where I stood, and the whole valley was full of them.

LIEUTENANT W.G. FISHER, 42ND INFANTRY BATTALION, AUSTRALIAN IMPERIAL FORCE

The troops had lurched into the quagmire only to find the battlefield swathed with shrapnel, gas, lead and flying red-hot steel. Every unit lost heavily, each finishing a harsh day on or even behind the original jumping-off lines.

We moved forward, in artillery formation, to the edge of what had been the village of Poelcapelle, of which nothing now remained but heaps of rubbish, and the ex-enemy pill-boxes. On reaching the village, Battalion Headquarters stopped at a big pill-box, and the Company formed up for attacking. The shelling now was very heavy. Before long we heard that the 55th Brigade, which had attacked first, and through which we were to advance, had failed to reach their objective, and that our own men were losing heavily in trying to assist them by capturing the Brewery, an enemy 'strong-point' with the usual pill-box defences. Our C.O. and the Adjutant were up in the thick of it with the men. Saw a few prisoners come back – most of them young men, and all No. 477. One of them was wounded by one of their own shells near us, and lay on a stretcher beside us all day, there being too many of our wounded, who were attended to first. The R.A.M.C. chaps bound up his wound and left him until later. His wound was in the leg and must have been very painful for he often signed to us to cut his throat for him. At intervals he begged for 'coffee or vasser', and drank quite a lot of my water. J.C. ate sandwiches in front of him, evidently with the idea of tantalising him, but he was too far gone to worry about grub. We were heavily shelled all day, some of the shells coming from our left. One small man who was sitting a yard from me died of shock when a small shell burst about 15 yards away – he probably had a weak heart. The shell burst in an old shell-hole and none of the splinters came near us, but he said something like 'They'll hit me in a minute' – fell over on his side and died. At 3.25 p.m., J.C., who was standing in the doorway on the other side of the pill-box, was slightly wounded in the left shoulder, and lost the tips of two fingers of his right hand – splinters from a small shell which burst near. He started on the way out as soon as his wounds had been dressed. The enemy was shelling the ground behind us heavily and he had quite an exciting journey, but got through it alright. After dark the shelling eased off a bit and we managed to get inside the pill-box. There was quite a crowd – three Battalion Headquarters – the Royal West Kent's of our Division, and the 'King's Own', of the 4th Division, as well as our own Battalion. Two men inside had been blinded by mustard gas and seemed to be suffering great pain.

PRIVATE S.T. FULLER, 8TH SUFFOLK REGIMENT

No more than twelve hours had been required to bring the attacks to their knees. German guns, firing both from beyond the Passchendaele Ridge ahead and Houthulst Forest to the left, had the perfect range and direction to thrash the sector. *Englischer lattenweg* (duckboard tracks) were turned into lethal splintered and broken pathways, so subsequent assaulting battalions suffered in the same way as the 66th Division by extended, exhausting and often costly treks to start lines. The plight of British and Australian gunners, upon whom thousands of lives depended absolutely, was agonizing. Not only did trails bury themselves in the sludge, delivering their critical consignments short of the target, too often upon their own troops, but entire guns were now beginning to sink up to their axles and barrels. Gunners struggling the keep the guns firing paddled the pits to a thick, glutinous porage in which, if not careful, one would simply stick, immobile. It was hard enough to extricate men from the tenacious muck; shifting a gun was unfeasible without the help of caterpillar traction. Many field pieces became useless and had to be abandoned (they are still occasionally found today, complete). Conspicuous to hostile view the gunners suffered severe counter-battery fire without being able to make any worthwhile response.

Two days, and then another bombardment. Our guns were sticking it heroically, though the ground near the pits was continually ploughed by shells. Casualties had been numerous, and I missed quite a number of the old faces at the guns as I ran along with my messages; it was a wonder that anything was left of the position at all after the shelling it had been subjected to.

Still, there they were blazing away – flash, report, recoil; flash, report, recoil; banging off their ammunition as if they could never tire. What the object of attack was on this particular day nobody knew, and nobody seemed to care. It was enough that it was a 'show', and they had had such a surfeit of attacks that the gunners had nearly forgotten what it was like to have a night's sleep.

Bang . . . Bang! went the two guns, and all around the scattering repetitive flashes of the bombardment kept up the din. No rest – the attack was on – prisoners were straggling down past the guns, and wounded infantry in twos and threes with their hastily tied bandages soft red and white against the dirty khaki.

Here was a stretcher-party staggering along the wet duckboards with a horrid burden from which the blood leaked and spattered; they moved with uncertain footings, their shoulders sagging with the load, and as they reached our line of dug-outs there came the scream of a shell, a huge flash, a rending explosion, and the stretcher-party vanished.

A few yards away the guns were monotonously firing, their barrels red-hot, their breech blocks jamming and having to be opened with pickaxes for the next round; the gunners, faces blackened with oil splashes and smoke, mechanically slamming home the shells and staring sore-eyed through the sights. Midday found us still at it. The infantry had evidently failed again in their attack on Poelcappelle, although some slight advance had been made. Those terrible pill boxes were holding them up. Shelling had practically no effect on these six-foot-thick blocks of concrete, and the murderous machine-guns caused havoc in the ranks of the attackers. Urgent messages kept coming through asking us to concentrate on certain spots where wave after wave of the infantry had been buried back by

Above
One of many German guns in Houthulst Forest which were relaid to fire in enfilade against the Allied Passchendaele assaults.

the storm of bullets. The Fritzes must be fighting like the very demons of hell. Wounded were now coming down in a continuous stream, but the number of prisoners became significantly less as the day wore on, and it seemed indeed that we were engaged on a hopeless task.

A month of incessant attacks had failed to make any real progress on this sector. The loss of life had been appallingly heavy, and the severity of the fighting was having a bad effect on the morale of everybody concerned. Reinforcements of the new armies shambled up past the guns with dragging steps and the expressions of men who knew they were going to certain death. No words of greeting passed as they slouched along; in sullen silence they filed past one by one to the sacrifice. Now and again the flash and roar of a shell would leave a sudden gap in the procession, but they closed up with half-dazed, quickening steps. There was one less, that was all.

GUNNER AUBREY WADE, ROYAL FIELD ARTILLERY

It was hopeless and heartless to go on, and Plumer and Gough called off further action. During the day 13,000 spaces appeared in the ranks of the two armies. Recriminations for allowing the attacks to go ahead were not long in coming.

The general attack petered out – quite literally stuck in the mud. The infantry had suffered dreadfully – not only in actual casualties (which must have been very heavy) but in the physical and mental strain of the awful conditions of that 'front line', indeed of all the Salient stretching east of YPRES itself. I certainly shall never forget the men I saw filtering back - still disciplined and uncomplaining but indescribable horror in their pale unshaven faces and feeble beyond belief, like figures set in motion long ago but still retaining a faint modicum of impetus and energy, they moved uncertainly and slowly onto the broken pave of the Menin road. THIRD YPRES was a gamble with the weather – which let us down. But, this apart, can it be justified on any

count? I'm sure that the reply from all the troops engaged in it would be a most resounding 'NO'!

LIEUTENANT J.T. CAPRON, DIVISIONAL AMMUNITION COLUMN, 56TH (LONDON) DIVISION

And for the officers, there was the ubiquitous and never-ending corollary to all attacks.

Zero hour was 5.25am and as soon as the barrage started we followed about 30-50 yards behind. Unfortunately some of our shells fell behind and at one time we had to halt a short while to let it pass. As soon as we started we had a terrific machine gun enfilade fire from the right; quite a number of men fell near me and bullets were whistling through the air, although we hadn't much time to notice. We advanced about 500 yards and then dug in. Unfortunately a block house on the right held up the line and the 2nd Scots Guards. Snipers from the blockhouse caused a lot of casualties. Poor John Bibby, our Company Commander was killed by a sniper. Sergeant Collyer and Martin were also killed by snipers. I dug in but water trickled in after 3 feet so I had to hop over into Fox's trench. All our stretcher bearers were shot by snipers, whilst we like idiots, let their red cross men carry on. We had no rations and had to stand in water all day besides being drenched to the skin and having to sit on the wet mud. After midday Fox and I got out in front of our trench as it was full of water and dug another trench. I had Mycock (my runner), Walmesley and Fox in the trench with me. On my left was Sergeant Sudworth and Corporal Fleming. I had to eat my iron ration biscuits owing to having no food. We stood to half an hour before dusk. The Huns tried to relieve the blockhouse on the right but Simmons got a Lewis Gun on them and scattered them. We sent up Very lights periodically. The Boche shelled us at times but no damage done. I was nearly hit on the head by a nose cap whilst digging in during the morning. I kept watch with double sentries. We had no wire in front of us.

LIEUTENANT FRANK ENNOR, 1ST GRENADIER GUARDS

Like thousands of others before him, Frank Ennor was duty bound to write to the families of each of the men under his command who had died during the action. It was a grim and all-too-repeated task which although signalling the end of a life, often engendered such profound gratitude in response, it made the slow and fruitless crawl of the offensive yet harder to bear.

Dear Lieutenant Ennor,

It is with a broken heart I receive your letter. I am very grateful for your kind enquiries re. my darling's death. It was cruel of the Medical Board to send him to the trenches in his state of health. The grief is almost too much for me, and the nights of agony terrible. The longing for my Husband is greater than ever, but I can only call to the fold for help. I am glad you loved your men and may God bring you and them safely through the horrors and dangers set before you. Private Cliffs sent me a very kind and beautiful letter. I shall often read it in my hours of sadness with yours. I shall look forward for Private Cliffs' return to hear all about my darling who has been torn from me. The people of Torquay have been very kind to me in my greatest loss on earth, both men and women have come to mourn with me. My burden is very heavy for me to write or express myself as I should like but you who loved your men will understand. I shall pray for you and your men and trust you will return safely to your dear ones. Thanking you for kind letter and sympathy.

  Yours gratefully,

  Sophia Bolt

[Wife of Private William Henry Bolt, 1st Grenadier Guards, died 12 October 1917, commemorated on the Tyne Cot Memorial, Panel 9]

What had happened to cause such appalling failure? Apart from the planning being rushed, again it was mainly down to ground conditions. The guns had been almost impossible to move into position for the attack. Huge teams of men and horses were required to shift a single field piece through the sea of mud, making lucrative targets for German guns. Sentiments recorded during the aftermath indicate a growing sense of pointlessness.

Our poor devils are waist deep in water, and nothing in nature of warm food touches their lips, only tea, this latter is brought up in petrol cans and is usually cold when it reaches the line. If lucky, one may strike a can that is warm, but this is not much good when one wants for something hot. Battalions are being held up – as in preceding attacks – at Poelcapelle Brewery. This is not a building, but a mass of Trench fortifications with plenty of dugouts affording cover for a vast number of men. Our Artillery will not shell the place as the Staff think that it will make excellent winter quarters for the men. Whether they are wise or not, I will not venture to say, except that the casualties caused by the brewery being left as it is must run into several thousands. Lads dig in where they are or rather I should say, establish lines of shell holes where they are and the attack fizzles out. This is October 12th 1917, and we shall remember the date, for whatever one likes to call it, it will remain to us at least a heroic attempt to achieve an impossibility. Might mention that today Jerry starts a new stunt. About 20 Gothas, surrounded by 30 or more small fighting planes, came over to give us a taste of Culture. They make 3 journeys, and the number of bombs they dropped was – as they would term it – colossal. If a man was walking along, he would have a Gotha all to himself, and the casualties were in keeping with the number of bombs dropped. It put the 'Wind up' if nothing else.

Private Robert Cude MM, 7th East Kent Regiment (The Buffs)

The most ardent British and Australian prayers for a break in the dreadful weather were not answered.

Above

9 October. This battery of 3rd Australian Divisional Artillery has found a piece of stable ground from which to ply their trade. By the end of the month such positions were almost impossible to establish.

Right
Australian gunners trying to extricate an abandoned German field gun between barrages on 30 October in the Hanebeek area.

13TH OCTOBER SATURDAY

It rained like hell and blew a full gale all night and damned cold into the bargain. Thanks heavens we are not in the trenches it must be frightful.

CAPTAIN FRANK HURLEY, OFFICIAL PHOTOGRAPHER, AUSTRALIAN IMPERIAL FORCE

Frightful was certainly the mot juste, and not only on the battlefield. Whereas Hurley was able each evening to return to his 'cosy hut', such pleasures were seldom made available to those coming out of the line after action.

13TH OCTOBER

It is quite impossible to describe in words what the situation and the state of the country was like up there. It rained steadily the whole time, and the darkness at night was intense. This, added to the usual confusion and uncertainty that reigns on a battlefield the night of a battle, rendered reorganising and the locating of troops a superhuman job. Even in daylight it was almost impossible to find out where everyone was. Battalions were scattered over many square miles of country without a landmark anywhere. The country was one mass of shell-holes and it really came to having to search each shell-hole to see if there were troops in it or not! On relief we moved to Leipzig Camp, near Brielen, a long and weary walk back in the rain and darkness. Jock and I both went head over heels into a very deep shell-hole full of water and arrived soaked to the skin and one mass of mud from head to foot! Found very bad arrangements made for us and the men's comfort. Four Battalions were shoved into the middle of a mud waste with just a few shelters, while the officers of the whole Brigade had to live and eat and sleep in one small hut. The men had a hot meal, some rum and a dry pair of socks when they came in, and in spite of the perfectly ghastly time they had had they were as cheery as anything. They really are marvellous people, and every time I am more than ever filled with admiration at

their spirit. They way they 'stuck it out' living in the open, in mud and shell-holes, in torrents of rain, in bitter cold and under fire all the time was beyond all praise. I am proud beyond words to command such men. When we came out on the 13th, the Battalion had been in the trenches for eight days and nine nights in a tour of thirteen days, and had been through two attacks.

During the second phase we went into action with nine officers and 475 other ranks, and our casualties were Leetham and Greenup killed, Philip wounded and 156 total casualties to the other ranks. Total casualties since the 1st October when we went into the line – nine officers and 263 other ranks.

LIEUTENANT COLONEL R.T. FELLOWES, 1ST RIFLE BRIGADE

For the wounded, their lives totally dependent upon the action of others, the battlefield was a hell on earth.

On reaching the aid post we put a poor fellow who had been shot through the lungs – a gory mess of exuded and vomited blood – on to our stretcher and hoisting it to our shoulders started rearwards for the dressing station from whence we had been sent. Unencumbered as we were, the going out taxed our strength, but the return, with our burden, was the limit. Floundering knee deep in the ocean of mud we tortuously staggered along. Where the ground had been thick and soggy like porridge, it was now thin and sloppy like soup. In places where a few days earlier we had been able to walk on the dry rims of the shell holes and to avoid falling into them, we now had difficulty in keeping our feet as we felt for the sludgy ridges to avoid sinking into the bottomless centres. On one occasion, with a deep groan from the wounded man, we flopped thigh deep into a hole and as we were fast sinking deeper we laid down the stretcher, as gently as possible, and struggled to the side, from where we reached out and, with the greatest difficulty, dragged the stretcher and its recumbent burden to safety. By the time we got our man out and deposited at the dressing station it was mid-day and we were dead-beat. We had eaten nothing since the evening before, so it was with grateful

thanks we accepted the cup of cocoa and biscuit kindly handed out to us by a Red Cross orderly. As we were not capable of making another trip through that morass, we staggered off and flung ourselves into our various 'bivvies' and, wet through and muddy as we were, slept the afternoon away. On waking we had the Devil's own job trying to get rid of the mud which we endeavoured to scrape from our putties and trousers with our jack-knives. What was left hardened the cloth to cardboard. One of the new draft that joined our Company a few days back was killed last night as he lay asleep in his bivvie. I was one of the burial party and we buried him this evening in a shallow grave just as he was, with the exception of removing his personal effects from his pockets to send back to his people. Poor chap, the War was a short one for him.

PRIVATE N.M. INGRAM, 3RD WELLINGTON REGIMENT, NEW ZEALAND EXPEDITIONARY FORCE

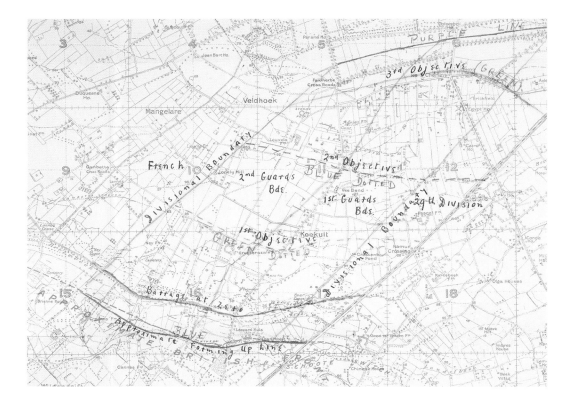

Above
Guards Division objectives in the last encounter before First Passchendaele on the northern flank of the battlefield. The third objective was achieved, creating the only bright spot for 9 October.

The New Zealanders had been particularly badly mauled during 'First Passchendaele'. In their sector, Gravenstafel, there was no surprise, the wire was dense and uncut, and British guns had been able to offer the most minimal of assistance. A minimally unmolested enemy almost wiped out the entire attacking force. It must have been a difficult battle title to contrive, for nowhere did gains exceed 400 metres. Sir Douglas Haig had informed the press that on 9 October 'it was simply the mud that defeated us', his troops were 'practically through the enemy's defences' and that the ground ahead contained no more pillboxes. It was rhetoric, but the pressmen were unlikely to be able to decide that for themselves by viewing the actual situation.

Haig's statements may have been pure public relations, but the state of the battleground and deplorable lack of artillery support was certainly acknowledged by GHQ. At a conference of army commanders and senior staff officers on 13 October at Cassel, it was agreed that attacks should not be further pressed until the conditions improved. Now the battlefield itself demanded special treatment, for they had been forced to accept that the once-assured delineation of opposing trenches was entirely – and possibly forever – gone. During September it had become expedient to have sappers follow up in the immediate wake of attacks, not as fighting support but on an orienteering mission. After consolidation the captured ground was immediately surveyed by specialists. Without this action it was found that units often had no idea where they were situated in the landscape, on a trench map, or in relation to others; they were therefore totally unable to report their true position either to HQ or the guns.

The gallant but silly old man who commanded our Brigade had been impressed by the danger that everyone underwent when going up the slope to the observation post or coming down it again, and he arrived at the crazy idea that the thing would be to dig a communication trench up the slope. Now, digging a communication trench in a bog requires tons and tons of revetting material, and can only be done at the rate of a few feet an hour. Any attempt just to dig a trench up the slope would simply result in the mud falling in as fast you dug it out. However, I was sent to Brigade Headquarters and instructed to take thirty men with spades and picks, drawn from all the batteries in the Brigade, and dig the trench during the night. Obediently I started out, but only with half the thirty men, the remainder having been slightly wounded by a small shell near them. I went on with the survivors through the dark and rain – it was of course raining. The two infantry runners who had been sent to guide us were quite excusably lost, and so were we, and could only tell the direction to go in by aiming at the Very lights which the infantry of both sides were putting up in the front line. Presently I found us coming upon what had obviously been a farmhouse and was now a ruin. Now one thing I did know from my previous visits was that on our part of the front there was no ruined farmhouse within our line, though there was a ruined farmhouse within the German line. The inference was only too clear. We must have got, in the rain and the darkness, through not only our own but also the German front line posts, and were now several hundred yards inside the German line. In a hoarse whisper, I commanded my faithful companions to turn around, and each man hold the belt of the man in front of him. I put myself at the head of this ignominious crocodile, and we set out away from the Very lights, towards what we hoped was home. Suddenly there was shout from the darkness in front of us, an electric torch was turned on, and we found ourselves staring into the muzzle of a field gun. Fortunately the officer in charge reacted very quickly and stopped the firing, with the result that we were not, as would probably have happened otherwise, blown off the face of the earth by the blast. At dawn I

Below
FOOs observing and reporting.

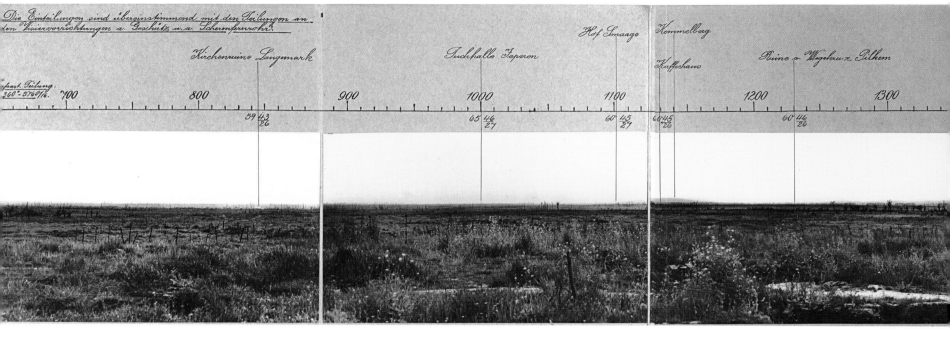

Die Einteilungen sind übereinstimmend mit den Teilungen an den Visiervorrichtungen u. Geschütz u. a. Scherenfernrohr.

Kirchenruine Langemark

Tuchhalle Jeperen

Hof Smaage *Kemmelberg*

Kaffeehaus *Ruine u. Wegekreuz Pilkem*

apart. Teilung 360°=5760/16. 700 800 900 1000 1100 1200 1300

59 43/26   65 46/27   60 45/27   60 45/26   60 46/26

took the party back to Brigade Headquarters and received the expected severe rocket for my failure to accomplish my mission. Another subaltern was sent for and given the order to dig the communication trench the next night. Now he was a much more experienced soldier than I was, and before nightfall he reconnoitred the area, located a deserted German pillbox hundreds of yards within our line, and when the time came set out towards it with his party of men with shovels and picks. He put them immediately into the pillbox where he and they spent a dry, reasonably comfortable night, until dawn next day. When they returned to Brigade Headquarters and he reported that he too had failed, he also received a severe rocket but, to everyone's relief, the Colonel dropped the scheme, and a bit later was transferred elsewhere, to be replaced by the commander of one of the batteries in our Brigade.

Lieutenant Cyril Dennys, 212th Siege Battery, Royal Garrison Artillery

An incorrect report of one's whereabouts – very easy to make in a featureless landscape – could lead not only to reliefs appearing in the wrong place, but barrages falling on one's own position. A forest of signboards therefore appeared (an average of 23,000 per month were produced by the RE during the war) as soon as ground was consolidated. Map references marked important or well-known points and intersections, directional signs indicated where duckboard or cross-country tracks terminated (both ends), every farm ruin, blockhouse and pillbox sported a large white board with black letters clearly naming the spot. Signage to wells was especially clear. The boards were erected whether a structure still stood or had been pulverised out of existence. They served to bring men faster towards their fate.

Above
A sobering German panorama taken in June 1918 showing the once wooded landscape of the Veldhoek. Although recovering fast, it has been swept clean of man-made features as far as Ypres and beyond.

Rundbild
n der Feld-Art.-Beob. „Griff" (Veldhoek?)
Linker Teil.
Schloss Vlamertingen

Die Bezeichnung ⁶⁴⁵/₆₄₀₀ besagt, daß der Punkt in der Karte im Quadrat 51 liegt u. d. Pkt. Nummer 26 im Quadrat hat.

Kirchturm Poperingen
Kirchturm Woesten

Hierzu eine Karte mit den photogrammetrisch festgelegten Punkten.

1400 1500 16000 1700 1800 1900 2000

64 51/26

On this chill, grey, 13 October day, Lieutenant General Arthur Currie received Sir Douglas Haig's first request to bring his troops north to Flanders from the Gohelle and Vimy sectors. They departed First Army to join Plumer's Second. After the severe casualties the Canadians had suffered under Gough in Picardy in 1916 it was thought best not to put them again in the ranks of Fifth Army – they did not 'work kindly under the latter', noted Haig. The Canadians had already enjoyed the taste of recent successes. First there had been the magnificent triumph at Vimy Ridge in April, then between 15 and 20 August, ironically in a diversionary attack to assist Gough's labours at Ypres, they had decisively captured Hill 70 near Lens. Despite twenty-one counter-attacks and losses of over 20,000 the Germans never retook the position. Haig held the Corps in high esteem; they were now rested, up to establishment and fit. With all hope of coastal attacks now lost in the mists of autumn, Currie was aware that the C-in-C's sole desire was to gain the high ground, and that this time his assignment was to be no diversion but one of the most critical actions of the war. Westroosebeke and Passchendaele were hardly a stone's throw from the present British line; if only they could be taken, Haig told his staff, the rest of the Stadenberg ridge would certainly follow, regardless of the weather because the high ground would be so much drier. So just a few decent days – 'a fair prospect of fine weather,' as he said – could at least leave the troops in a dominating and relatively dry position for the winter. He was now fully aware of the shocking battlefield conditions, for reports were hourly coming in of horses, mules and men drowned, guns, wagons and even railways sinking in the mud, and the all-important forward roads chewed up by the weight of traffic required to feed the front.

OCTOBER 13TH 1917.

Heavy shelling all day. The Royal West Kent's left during the afternoon, our Battalion taking over their front in addition to our own. We Signallers took over their Signal Station, which consisted of a single telephone line to Forward Brigade Headquarters, which was at Pheasant Farm. This line was twice cut by shells during the night. The first time, the two Signallers (Dick Morris and Porky) went out to find and repair the 'break', heard cries for help, and after a search found two of the Royal West Kent's stuck in the mud. They were not wounded in any way, but were unable to get out of their own accord. The Signallers 'tapped in' on the line, and phoned us for stretcher-bearers – the men could not walk, even after they had been extricated. Had our phone wire not run past the spot, those two men might have remained there, fast in the mud, until they died of starvation or exhaustion. It will never be known how many died in that way at Ypres. A small party of us went to a 'tramway head' which was, apparently, about three miles away, for rations. We had some job finding it – it was too dark to see far and we had to walk across miles of mud and shell holes before we found the tramway or light railway. We struck it about half a mile below the 'head' but once having found it, it was an easy matter to follow the rails to the end. Here we found men from the 'Stores' with the rations and with the latter in the usual petrol-cans. We secured these and distributed them as equally as possible among the carriers, and started back. We dare not go 'across country' in the darkness as we would certainly have missed our way in the (literally) trackless waste, so we retraced our steps, back along the light railway, then along a road till we struck a duckboard track which we knew led to Pheasant Farm.

PRIVATE S.T. FULLER, 8TH SUFFOLK REGIMENT

Charteris had recently informed Haig that certain German units were so equally demoralized by the conditions that some had 'refused to attack'. Curiously, just a few days earlier War Office Intelligence reported no anxiety within German High Command concerning morale. The truth? The Germans were certainly suffering from exactly the same battlefield conditions, overwork, fear, stress and privations as everyone else, but they were as equally determined to hold the ridge as the British were to take it. Even *alleged* mutinous enemy behaviour was music to Haig's ears at this sombre time. As far as he was concerned the offensive must continue, and future prospects mainly balanced upon how Currie would react to his Passchendaele proposals. As the Canadians arrived, so a lucky few sprinted off for a respite – leave.

TUESDAY 16TH OCTOBER

My 'leave' application form arrived this morning and I am off tomorrow!! Ye gods, what a place to go on leave from!! Hynes turned up to relieve me this afternoon, poor devil and I got off at once. It was a nasty walk – that 2 kilometres to Spoil Bank – I expected every minute to feel a shell in my back: and I was in a devil of a hurry to get away from the cursed spot. By gum I am thankful to be away from that area – my only regret being that it was Hynes and not Burton who relieved me. However I am away now for 12 days at least from it all and lots of things may happen before that is over.

MAJOR A. G. P. HARDWICK MC, 59TH FIELD AMBULANCE, 19TH (WESTERN) DIVISION

By the time Major Hardwick returned to the Salient, conditions had deteriorated further, into the unmitigated squalor that the word Passchendaele now instantaneously conjures.

Right
The squalour of the Houthulst Forest. It is hardly surprising that no army commanders relished the possibility of being ordered to attack it. Despite the conditions, it was strongly garrisoned by German troops.

Above

Second Army pan 130 reveals the view from the Broodseinde Ridge (300 metres east of the crossroads) in late October 1917 – and the same prospect today. Beyond the shattered foreground, the 1917 view would have looked just as verdant.

CHAPTER FOURTEEN
Into the Mire

The 39th Division arrived in the YPRES salient on 19th November 1916 and has been in the line throughout the winter 1916/17 except for 5 days, and since that date it has, in addition to holding the line for practically the whole period, fought several battles, e.g., St Julien, Bulgar Wood, Tower Hamlets. It was nominally at rest from September 28th to October 16th 1917, but during that period a Brigade was employed on work in the forward area north of the Menin Road. It will be easily realised from the above sketch that this Division has now got down to bed-rock and the high sick wastage at present is indicative of every measure that foresight and experience could suggest has not yielded to treatment. Since the Division arrived in France the casualties in killed and wounded are as follows up to 31 October 1917.

Officers: killed 183, wounded 587; other ranks killed 2,283, wounded 15,706.

Add this to the wastage from sickness and you have a graphic picture of the demands of modern warfare. Personally I am of the opinion that the great factor at present obtaining in production of sick wastage in this Division is the mental outlook, which in all ranks is one of war weariness, and thereby the resistive power to disease is greatly diminished. A reasonable period of rest, with the hope of a change of scene from the YPRES salient at its termination, would in my opinion restore the vim and morale of this Division to that high standard with which it has in the past achieved its well-earned reputation of a first-class fighting Division.

REPORT FROM COLONEL G.W. BRAZIER CREAGH,
ASSISTANT DIRECTOR MEDICAL SERVICES, 39TH DIVISION,
TO X CORPS HQ

Below
German prisoners and wounded being escorted back by Canadian troops; working parties taking forward yet more ubiquitous duckboards make way for the injured.

Although these words were written on 22 November, they illustrate the problem now faced by GHQ. The Army in Flanders was practically worn out. Men had seen action several times, been employed as beasts of burden when not in the line, and had become mentally and physically depleted. Part of Haig's design in bringing in the Canadians was to introduce fresh troops who had not been subjected to the pressures and conditions of the 1917 Salient. Alongside other selected and rested British divisions he looked to Lieutenant General Sir Arthur Currie's men to spearhead the attacks that would deliver the last prize that the encroaching winter allowed: the Passchendaele-Staden Ridge.

The prospect was not a pleasing one for Currie and upon first meeting he had been immediately reluctant. But Haig was canny. He *enquired* whether the Canadians might wish to accept the challenge – no order was issued. Having led 2 Brigade of the 1st Canadian Division at Second Ypres, Currie had got to know, like and respect Plumer with whom, if the

Flanders task was accepted, his men would work. Plumer was doubtful he would rise to Haig's bait, but Passchendaele proved too tempting. The Canadians would do it – subject to certain conditions. Haig remained shrewd, immediately visiting Currie's HQ to deliver the following persuasive address:

Gentlemen, it has become apparent that Passchendaele must be taken, and I have come here to ask the Canadian Corps to do it. General Currie is strongly opposed to doing so, but I have succeeded in overcoming his scruples. Some day I hope to be able to tell you why this must be done, but in the meantime I ask you to take my word for it. I may say that General Currie has demanded an unprecedented amount of artillery to protect his Canadians and I have been forced to acquiesce.

On arrival in the Salient in mid-October Currie went forward with his staff to survey the prospective battlefront. The ground was a shambles and littered not only with the shattered detritus of battle, but countless human corpses – to bring them in, even at night, would not only be perilous

but consume labour that was essentially required elsewhere. The conditions shocked everyone, but Currie still came to the conclusion that with careful planning – and overwhelmingly heavy gunfire – the ridge could be conquered.

21ST OCTOBER, SUNDAY

Went to Ypres and made several pictures of the Cloth Hall. A great number of Canadian troops are now passing through to take over the section held by the Australians and New Zealanders. As the town is under balloon observation by the Boche, it received a heavy shelling, especially the Poperinghe Gate. Here he dropped shells throughout the afternoon and killed some 40 men as well as holding up the traffic. On my way home I had to motor by this way, and raced the car through the shell fire. Fortunately there was room around the shell craters and no other traffic. It was a few minutes of great excitement as the shells *lobbed on both sides and spattered us with debris and splinters. At the top of the road stood a cheering crowd of Anzacs. I thoroughly enjoyed the run, but it rather unnerved the driver and my timid and always scared camera bearer.*
CAPTAIN FRANK HURLEY, OFFICIAL PHOTOGRAPHER,
AUSTRALIAN IMPERIAL FORCE

As the Canadians streamed through Ypres and into the Salient to join the Second Army for their own baptism of mud and fire, support work behind the lines became more frantic than ever. Throughout August and September the ribbon of tortured earth that formed the combat zone had gradually widened making the task of reconstruction and traversal a colossal enterprise. For thousands of men it appeared not only hopeless, but endless.

Left
Westhoek, 27 October. An ammunition column transporting 18-pounder shells to the advanced guns passes the remains of a battery knocked out in earlier actions.

Below
St Julien, October. A working party armed with specially designed mud scoops makes its way back to rest.

As the weeks slipped by, and one looked at the mass of shell craters filled with poisonous coloured liquid, the narrow trench board tracks straggling eastward, and considered the astounding loss of life in this most barren region of the world, a feeling of futility lurked in the background. For the first time I heard open expressions of doubt. Was it worth it? Human nature was being strained to the limit. Divisions came, and half or less divisions returned. The endless tide of men went on. Looking over that vast plain of mud I heard one man say: 'If they want it, why don't we let them have it?' A young officer laboriously making his way through the sticky morass told me he had transferred into the air force. 'Better the air than this mud.' A corporal of mine started a discussion among the men as to why we were fighting and what for. No one seemed to know. If they ever did know it was all so long ago, and they had forgotten. Exiles. To most men who look back through their war years there are many bright lights, shining out through the darkness. It may be some lucky billet they had, the charms of one or more pretty faces, a good dinner with their pals, or even trivial incidents which they cherish to themselves alone. But the Salient. Here was nothing, except abomination and desolation. Certainly 'Pop' struggles to be one of the bright lights. It may have been to some. To me an air of desperation hung about the place, as if it knew it was all sham and tinsel. There was something forced in its gaiety behind closed doors. It didn't ring true. And not far away, where there were no roads, men were fighting against men, and even, it seemed, against the Gods themselves. The struggle went on – a few yards at a time, ceaselessly, pitilessly. And later when the storming had died down a soft wind would blow over the battlefield tainted with the message of death.

LIEUTENANT F. HOWKINS, 253RD TUNNELLING COMPANY, ROYAL ENGINEERS

Like the tunnellers, temporarily helping with roads and bridges, there were now as many 'unarmed' troops installing and maintaining infrastructure around Ypres and in the old battle areas as armed men in the front lines. Comparison of casualty rates between these 'front and rear' troops had reached parity; nowhere in the Salient could be considered safe.

My Battalion was engaged on 'Working Parties' outside the Menin Gate at Ypres. The Boche were at the time sending over time-bombs, i.e. bombs which did not explode immediately upon impact but which were 'timed' to go off at unexpected intervals afterwards. On this particular occasion one of our lads – only a boy – was in a temporary latrine when one of these bombs exploded and blew both him and the latrine to pieces. Some time later I saw one of the Sergeants coming towards me carrying a sand bag. 'This is all we could find, Sir, of Private …..' he said. 'Never mind, Sergeant, we'll give him a Christian burial.' So a small grave was dug, the sand bag reverently laid in it and the Committal words spoken. Afterward I wrote to the lad's mother and told her that her boy had been given a Christian burial, and later received a most grateful letter in a rather large hand thanking me and adding 'I'm so glad my dear boy was buried 'comfortable'!' It was pathetic.

REVEREND E.V. TANNER MC AND BAR, ATTACHED 2ND WORCESTERSHIRE REGIMENT

Such burials so far from the battlefront were far from uncommon. Labour on supply, roads, tracks, trams, rail, cables and trenches was round the clock; water tanks were being mounted as far forward as possible, captured pillboxes and dugouts cleaned out, gas-proofed and converted for use as relay posts for stretcher bearers, field ambulance posts, cab stands, dressing stations, foot preparation rooms (to treat trench foot), soup kitchens, collecting posts, and brigade, battalion and company HQs and communication centres – one example captured by 49th (West Riding) Division somehow became a chapel. For those near the communication arteries, the roads (mainly timber now), hardstanding for cars, trucks, ambulances and horse watering-points were created from the bricks of smashed buildings. And every night critical cable buries were pushed forward another few hundred metres.

The most essential part of the enterprise was feeding the troops up front – with a hot meal wherever possible – dispensing their little portion of the 3.25 million tons of foodstuffs delivered to France and Belgium during the war. It was almost impossible to cook in the line for fear of smoke drawing hostile fire. As everywhere else, in the Salient food was delivered by parties drawn from units in reserve.

After we had done our bit at Poelcappelle they put us on carrying parties. We only worked at night and during the day lived in Ypres at the old Belgian infantry barracks. Later we spent all day in dugouts – never saw any daylight at all for about a month. They had us start moving up before dusk to load up with whatever we were carrying forward that night. It could be ammunition, trench stores, but often it was food. We picked up from the field kitchens. It had been put into sort of backpacks [Yukon packs], a big heavy thing with straps that you put on your back. It was like a Thermos and was meant to keep the food hot – well, warm at least – and it was a Godsend in the winter. They were much better than dixies which needed two men to carry them. A bit of warm stew was wonderful when you'd sat there shivering all day with nothing to do. They were awkward things in a trench, catching on everything, but at Broodseinde – which is where we usually delivered our stuff to – you could get right up to the posts on the tracks without going into the trenches – you could do that anywhere in the Salient at night. It was not a bad job because the men were delighted when you rolled up, especially if you were a bit late in coming and the stew was still warm. You'd had to wait often enough yourself, so you knew

what it meant to others, and we did what we could to get there on time. You always thought, if the rations were late, 'Oh, they've cocked it up again', no hot food tonight, but very often a party might have got a shell to themselves – the Germans had the tracks taped, and there were spots where you had to rush over in pairs – try to time the shells coming and rush along the track between them. Some of us would have these haversack things, others would take a couple of sandbags with bread, cheese, tea, jam, tins of butter and bully. It was never any good though, because we always moaned about the food generally no matter what it tasted like – it was traditional to bait the cooks. You moaned about everything, but actually the food was very often

Left
Drinking water tank at the foot of the Passchendaele Ridge. Water was piped here (and elsewhere around the Salient) either overland or in trenches in several stages.

Below
Plank road construction.

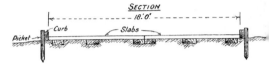

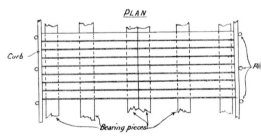

Left
A plank road being laid. The truck is delivering more beech timber.

Right
This little house near Kansas Cross is almost entirely built from wartime materials and was one of the first to be erected after the war. The walls are of beech planks salvaged from the timber 'Panet' road, which ran past the gates in the foreground.

Above
Squeegees and brooms being employed to clear liquid mud from a plank road.

Right
Australian cooks (2nd Infantry Battalion) preparing meat to make bully beef rissoles for an evening meal.

better than I would have got at home, and there was a lot more of it. Mind you, it often tasted of something else – whatever they'd used the cauldron for before. 'Why doesn't my tea taste of onions, Private,' was the old joke. Or petrol.

PRIVATE BERT FEARNS, 2/6TH LANCASHIRE FUSILIERS

Cooking, or rather warming food in the trenches, was possible, but only with the right kind of fuel. Smokeless varieties such as coke and charcoal were sometimes available, especially in winter for braziers, but what was needed was something that could be used by small groups or even indi-

viduals. The favoured material was solidified alcohol which gave off no smoky fumes. With winter approaching the challenge grew greater by the day.

OCTOBER 18TH.
Your letter of the 13th came today. I haven't a scrap of news for you. I went out to the Dump this morning and rode along in hot sunshine under a blue sky. Since then I've been very busy with the problem of rations and how to get them to the battalion so that they may have as appetising a meal as possible. All cooking has to be done down here and I have to invent all kinds

of ways for giving them a hot drink. The latest is cold tea and some jam tins with a flannelette wick half filled with fat rendered down and paraffin mixed. The question of clothing too is very acute at present owing to our many moves. But it is settling itself all right now.

LIEUTENANT A.O. TERRY, [TRANSPORT OFFICER] 23RD NORTHUMBERLAND FUSILIERS (4TH TYNESIDE SCOTTISH)

Thursday, 18 October was the first clear, warm day for ages, the mercury soaring to a welcome 60 degrees Fahrenheit (15.5° C). It began to dry both mud and man, lifting spirits, and also allowing the airmen to do their critical work. But this was Flanders in late October: on Friday the thermometer plunged 10 degrees and rain and cloud returned. The 3,574 calories per man per day that the military dieticians recommended was grossly insufficient given the season, conditions on the battlefield and the interminable, inescapable nervous tension. The window for the kind of Indian summer that Sir Douglas Haig yearned for, even a brief one, was now closing fast. Crown Prince Rupprecht, meanwhile, made a note in his diary: 'Most gratifying – rain. Our most effective ally.'

As the date for Currie's first foray approached, and despite objectives being the same as those for 9 October, the Canadian's left-hand neighbour, Sir Ivor Maxse, regarded the conditions on his XVIII Corps front astride Poelcappelle as bleak. In recent actions his men had gained but yards and it was he who had pleaded most vehemently for the delay granted on 13 October. Postponement did not apply to the guns. Whilst more were dragged forward in an effort to supply proper co-operation, those already within range began preliminary bombardments, targeting pillboxes and cutting wire, making it crystal clear to all – on both sides of no man's land – that the campaign was far from being closed down.

'NOT YET IMPOSSIBLE' – THE CANADIANS TAKE THE FIELD

All the tanks had left the theatre, and were now en route for Picardy to take part in another offensive near Cambrai, to be prosecuted by General Sir Julian Byng's Third Army. Strategy in Flanders had now become three-pronged: not only were the troops required to attain the ridge, but in so doing Sir Douglas Haig hoped to deter enemy support transferring to Cambrai, and an imminent French venture in Champagne. More than aware of the wretched and desolate state of the battlefield and his troops, he demanded preparations, as hard and as fast as possible, for a restart at the first window of climatic opportunity. In all three theatres, every day counted.

The dog-tired II Anzac Corps was relieved by the Canadians on 22 October. Having argued and won his case for more artillery with Major General Birch, Sir Arthur Currie acquired almost 600 guns, most of them of heavy calibre, 9-inch and upward, with many brand-new pieces. The state of the roads restricted not only artillery but all motorized or heavy traffic to a line Zonnebeke–Kansas Cross–Winnipeg; beyond this was solely the domain of man and mule. Not surprisingly, only light ordnance was able to be employed here, but as the Salient elongated northwards and the enemy were pushed back, all but long-range guns were beginning to reach their extreme operational range. And much

British artillery was also suffering from wear. This could be somewhat ameliorated by adjustment, but whether a gun was brand new, recalibrated or tired out, a solid platform was critical. In favourable ground it took a good two days to create a really durable gun-pit. Now foundations were so sloppy and mobile that guns had to be relaid almost after every round fired. If not, the recoil plunged the trail ever further backwards and downwards, lifting the elevation which in turn caused shells to fall short – on Canadian, Australian and British positions. This was a serious problem, for troops had now learned to follow the creeping barrage so closely that many Germans believed their enemy advanced amongst the bursting shells – it was often true, but never by design. As for the problem of range, it could be extended by using a heavier charge, but this increased wear on the barrel which in turn blighted accuracy, and amplified the disruptive effects of recoil, which often led to the breaking of platforms. Above all, batteries in a landscape without a scrap of cover were horribly visible and vulnerable. Before they were installed

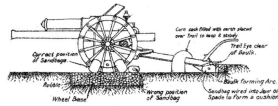

Above left
The 2nd Australian Division returns to the Salient on 26 October after a period of rest following the Menin Road and Poelcappelle actions.

Above
The model 18-pounder gun platform using rubble instead of timber. Every artillery weapon demanded different treatment, but these ideals were seldom met during the later stages of the battle.

Below
24 October. 18-pounders dug in to good pits during the welcome dry interlude near the end of the month.

TRAIL-SUPPORT SHOWING FIXED SUPPORT. AT "A" AND CUSHION AT "B"

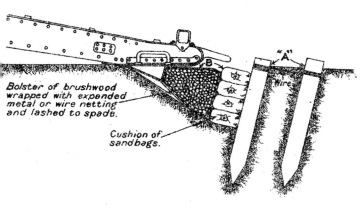

Bolster of brushwood wrapped with expanded metal or wire netting and lashed to spade.

Cushion of sandbags.

ALTERNATIVE DESIGN WITHOUT BOLSTER

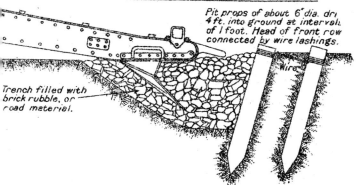

Pit props of about 6" dia. dri 4 ft. into ground at intervals of 1 foot. Head of front row connected by wire lashings.

Trench filled with brick rubble, or road material.

Above
Alternative trail supports for an 18-pounder.

in position showers of mustard gas and high-explosive arrived; such hostility could be expected to be incessant until the offending enemy guns were neutralized by counter-battery work, now of course severely truncated. Across the entire Salient gas was probably the most serious problem for the British. As soon as masks had to be applied, every action slowed to a crawl. It was a question of dissipation: in the cool early winter conditions, not all the lethal oily liquid spat out of the shell was able to vapourize instantly into gas; it lay in pools and droplets awaiting victims.

I am properly knocked up with that wretched mustard gas, it took days for the effect to come out, but my system must have got poisoned as I stuck up twice as long as any of the others, this time it was due chiefly to a gas infected dugout where I lived for a fortnight. When we went into action here, the officers' dugout had received a gas shell right on the door, killing 3 of the 4 of our predecessors and the place stank like a chemical works, however, it was that or a waterlogged shellhole in the rain, so I got fires going, nearly burnt the place down, and practically erased most of the apparent gas, but the three of us up there first got affected. C was very bad and I had to pack him off. The other subaltern T has been speechless for a week, shows how the stuff lingers. What! I've lit upon plenty of tough corners one way and another the last three years, make a sort of speciality of it in fact, but it's here the record is beaten for

all-round unpleasantness. To start with we have not exactly had a restful time all the summer, and had been promised and were looking forward to a quiet time, so this show hardly found us at the top of our stride. Then the conditions under which one lives are so impossible, the accommodation, the continual wet and mud, with no prospect or hope of betterment in front of us, but rather the certainty that for every whip that now afflicts us, the future will provide half a hundred scorpions to twist an ancient metaphor. The fighting brings us no tangible results from the artillery point of view, a few more acres of brown slime and a few battered pill boxes It is a strain you know, under these conditions and the continual expectation of a messy end at any moment, plus the responsibility immeasurably greater. Everything is vague, however I expect there'll be a big balance somewhere.

As to foodstuff; a cake occasionally and more and more of that delicious shortbread and any odds and ends in the way of soups, etc.

MAJOR C.E.L. LYNE, 119 BRIGADE, ROYAL FIELD ARTILLERY.

Should it be present on clothes, tools etc. when a man entered a shelter or dugout – environments where the temperature was several degrees warmer than the ambient due the presence of human bodies – the oil vapourized into gas (at around 60° Fahrenheit, 15.5° C), often with tragic consequences. Even food could be a threat to life. One artilleryman's account mentions two gunners dying in agony after eating bread spattered with mustard oil, the blistering and bleeding taking place internally. There was no hope for such victims, only morphia could help them die without pain. Every road and track now passed through wide bands of gas-saturated ground, and nowhere in the Salient was it possible to live and work without taking the most careful precautions. It was at this time that the Germans took this insidious form of warfare one

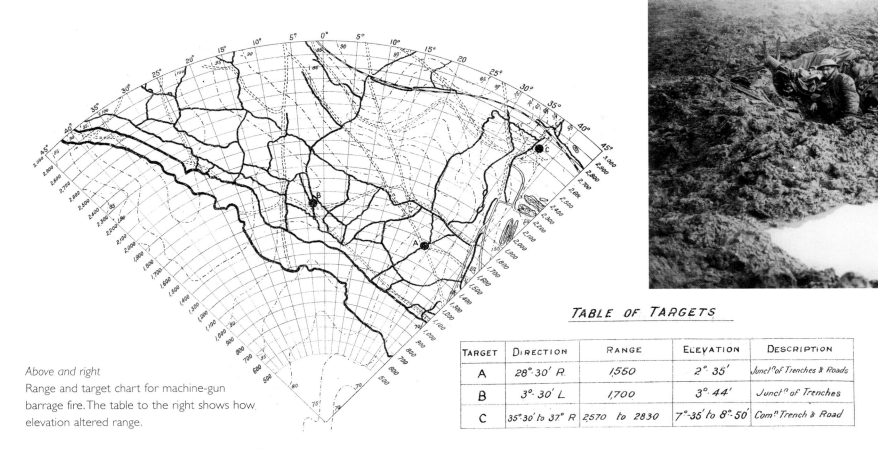

Above and right
Range and target chart for machine-gun barrage fire. The table to the right shows how elevation altered range.

TABLE OF TARGETS

TARGET	DIRECTION	RANGE	ELEVATION	DESCRIPTION
A	28°·30' R.	1,550	2°·35'	Junctⁿ of Trenches & Roads
B	3°·30' L	1,700	3°·44'	Junctⁿ of Trenches
C	35°·30' to 37° R	2570 to 2830	7°·35' to 8°·50'	Comⁿ Trench & Road

clever step further by carrying out a preliminary attack with sneezing gas (known as Blue Cross) before launching a barrage of mustard (Yellow Cross). The Blue Cross had been deliberately formulated to penetrate British box respirator gas masks causing troops to remove them from time to time to sneeze, thereby becoming vulnerable to its lethal chemical cousin, Yellow Cross.

For some time we had seen walking wounded passing us, some men almost staggering along. The latter had been affected by gas, because they had removed their box respirators from time to time

so that they could see better to follow the men in front of them. During theses interludes the gas had done its deadly work, though some hours elapsed before the damage was realised. Mustard gas was really lethal and it had a burning effect on the lungs, eyes and skins. As long as the respirator was being worn eyes and lungs were safe, but not the skin. Pip realised that his back was hurting him and when he squatted down and rested it against a trench side it pained him very much. He opened his tunic and slid his hand under his shirt. Under his arm he felt a huge blister. Further probing made him realise that he had many such blisters, especially under the other arm and at the tops of his thighs; the weak, tender parts of his skin. His tunic and trousers showed no

Above
Canadian machine-gunners in support positions. The pickets holding the barrel in a fixed position guns reveal they are employing long-range harrassing fire, probably at night.

Right
Instructions on how to modify a shell hole for use. The troops above appear to have followed Sketch C to the letter, fitting the parapet with a crescent-shaped rubberized sheet.

signs of anything being abnormal, Pip had been closer to the gas shells than I had been and I had kept my gas helmet on longer. Many men were affected by still more and their eyes became matted with a kind of sticky matter, some developed a racking cough. George Bramley, with whom I had enlisted, was very unfortunate that a gas shell dropped straight in front of him and very close. He collapsed and remembered nothing till he came round in a hospital in Hastings.

RIFLEMAN GERALD V. DENNIS, 21ST KING'S ROYAL RIFLE CORPS (THE YEOMAN RIFLES)

A minor whiff caused nausea and tiredness. Some areas were so drenched that work was forced to cease. The further the troops advanced towards the ridge, the more vulnerable they became – indeed, General Birdwood suggested that it was the debilitation and exhaustion caused by constant subjection to gas that had prevented his Anzacs from taking the Passchendaele–Staden Ridge by October. The toxic burden had but one advantage: as a rat killer. The British, although not yet employing mustard, were also keen to hit the enemy with chemicals, but unlike the Germans they faced delivery problems.

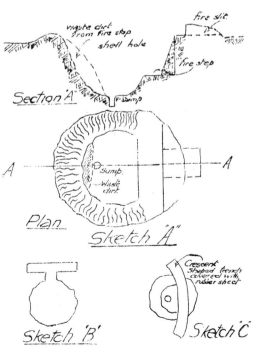

The next night Langdon and I had to take a carrying party of 100 men up the line. We reported to the R.E. officer at the dump and there each man was given a 60 lb gas shell. The 100 men were divided into parties of 33 each and Langdon went with the first party, a sergeant was put in charge of the second party and I brought up the rear with the third party. There was also a guide for each party. The night was pitch-dark and it was no easy job carrying these heavy shells along shelled duck-boards. This was the worst carrying party I have ever been on, a great many men felt tired and did their best to dump their shell, others got very scared when a shell exploded near them, and it was only by bullying them that I could make them get on with the job. I must say of all line work except an attack, working and carrying parties were the worst. Walking up duck-boards is not the best employment as there isn't enough cover for a rabbit if the enemy shells or machine-guns. Just before we arrived at Alouette Farm, I met Langdon with the first party going back having taken the shells to the dump. The dump was a little distance beyond Alouette Farm and as the rear of the third party reached the farm, the enemy commenced to shell a spot on the duck-boards about 100 yards from the farm. The front men came running back and all the men got in an awful state of panic. Two or three had got shell-shock and were gibbering about people being killed in large numbers up front. I got all the men into shelters behind the farm and then asked for two volunteers to go out with me and find the wounded. I then went up the duck-board track with these two stretcher-bearers and found one man terribly mangled by a shell. He died in my arms and then we took his identity discs and belongings and went further up where we found one man badly wounded in the leg. We got him onto the stretcher and after finding no other men we returned. The enemy were still shelling heavily but we got back to Alouette Farm without mishap. When I got to the farm I found to my astonishment that the R.E. man had cleared off and so here I was in the middle of nowhere with 30 men and a stretcher case and not knowing the road back. It was impossible for me to take the rest of the shells to the dump. As soon as the shelling had stopped, I sent my only NCO back with the men to the shelters, and six volunteers and I started the slow journey back with the stretcher case. The next afternoon I was sent with a sergeant from each platoon to find the way back as we were to be relieved. That night we got out in good time, and we fairly sped down the duck-boards. We found our way quite easily to Redan Camp at Dawson's Corner. I got the men into the farm nearby, saw that they got tea and their rum ration, and then went to find my own tent. My servant had got a canvas bed all ready and had put out my things. There was a pile of letters and a parcel of kit. The first night after being in the line was one of the best times in France, getting into pyjamas and a warm valise

Fifth Army Panorama 128 - Winchester Farm
22 October 1917
From: Sheet 28 D 2 a 50.58
70 degrees, 42 - 112

Westroosebeke

Mallet Wood

Valuation House

Goudberg Copse

Virile Farm

Virtue Farm

V

after a period in the line was much appreciated, added to which the pile of letters that had collected was very welcome.
SECOND LIEUTENANT GEORGE MCMURTRIE,
7TH SOMERSET LIGHT INFANTRY

With the poor flying weather Royal Artillery counter-battery fire dwindled almost to nothing, a fact gleefully noted in German artillery histories. Still invisible behind the ridge, and enjoying the benefit of relatively dry and carefully sited, moveable guns, they took full advantage.

Currie was furious and frustrated with the serious impairment to his preparations, but there was little to be done: his gunners, fully aware of the consequences of failure, were doing their level best. The sloppy ground around every target did not help. Shells simply buried themselves in the mire, losing explosive potency, merely producing fountains of mud. Targeting pillboxes, even with the assiduous guidance of Forward Observation Officers became a lottery. Canadian machine gunners were having better luck with their barrage fire. During the four nights leading up to 22 October they fired hundreds of thou-

Top
The Winchester Farm sector looking towards Westroosebeke (left) and Passchendaele (right). The modern photograph shows that the clutch of German pillboxes were replaced by a single British construction in early 1918. The photograph was taken on the very day and in the very sector of the last Chinese attack of the Third Ypres campaign. Private V.R. Magill and his colleagues are therefore hiding somewhere within this frame.

Valour Farm | Mosselmarkt | Remains of Institute | Passchendaele Church | Duck Lodge?

Above
The same view today, with the churches of Westroosebeke and Passchendaele visible at left and right.

sands of rounds upon predetermined boxed targets behind the German line, delaying reliefs, further tiring the harassed enemy, and disrupting supplies of food and materiel.

A minor 'line straightening' action on 22 October also saw a typical alternative strategy employed by XVIII Corps' imaginative commander Ivor Maxse: a 'dummy-stunt'. Millboard soldiers (12,000 were made during the war) were produced in ten different 'attitudes' of attack, from kneeling and shooting to charging. Each was a full-sized representation with features painted (by women in factories) to look like a determined enemy. During the hours of darkness 300 figures were carried up and arranged in no man's land on a frontage of about 1,500 metres in the Winchester–Wellington sub-sector just south of Poelcappelle. After being firmly pegged in place, wires, springs, ropes and pulleys were attached enabling some figures to be raised and dropped at will by a two-man team from the shelter of a trench or shell hole some 200 metres away, whilst others were spring loaded, leaping to their 'feet' when a small charge broke a restraining cord.

'Attacks' took place under the cover of a smoke barrage as soon as the light was good enough for the 'troops' to be clearly discernible. If successful it caused the enemy to man parapets, betray troop numbers, weapon types and quantities, and lay themselves open to shellfire. On this occasion it was designed as a feint assault to distract German attention from the 8th Norfolks' attack on Poelcappelle brewery. The wooden troops that took part in the 'attack' were carried forward under cover of darkness – and under shellfire. The following account, however, describes a similar attack made by the same unit on 14/15 September 1917.

Why did they pick on a night like this for such a stunt? With an aching back with rifle and equipment and the dummy figures slung round it, and a craving thirst through those choking cordite fumes which filled the air, little wonder that men cursed and swore. To hear men wish they had never been born and blasting the war was a common thing. Pushing on, or rather stumbling on, we came to a road. In the light of the gun flashes limbers and wagons could be seen lying smashed with dead horses by their side. We turned our faces towards the rockets which could be seen quite distinctly now, perhaps only a mile away. Out of the darkness would loom a captured German pillbox, here and there the ghost-like remains of a farmhouse. A tank, battered and useless with nose high in the air stood out here and there prominent in the gun flashes. By this time we were practically through our artillery zone. Only the field batteries on our front remained, their ear-piercing 'crack' being easily discernible from the dull 'boom' of the heavy guns now in our rear. In the light of their fire, the gun teams of these our most forward batteries could be seen feverishly feeding the guns stripped of their tunics. Here come some more of those blasted five-nines. Down we went into a prone position. They were bursting right in front of us. 'Keep moving there! What the hell

are you stopping for?' 'Stretcher bearers!' came the cry from the front party, 'Forward the remainder'. We discovered men of Scotland held the line [51st (Highland) Division]. It was not a trench as was usually known, no square cut six foot six affair, but merely linked up shell-holes.
PRIVATE V.R. MAGILL, CYCLIST BATTALION,
18TH (EASTERN) DIVISION, XVIII CORPS

Protective parties of Highlanders crept out into no man's land and the cyclists followed, each carrying two dummies per man. Their first task was to negotiate perhaps 100 metres of ground before trying to find a piece of level and firm earth upon which to fix their plywood 'colleagues'. The work was awkward and nerve-wracking, for not only were the men semi-blinded by Very lights and starshells, but enemy machine guns regularly swept the ground at knee-height, searching for patrols and working parties.

For a moment I stood upright just as there was a 'pop' and then a flood of light burst overhead. Standing still for the few seconds it lasted I could plainly see the enemies' lines on the fringe of a ruined village I took to be Poelcappelle. Crouching low we very soon had those dummies in position. When laid on the ground face downwards, two staples held it firm at the foot end, which was on a swivel. A thin wire would then be attached at the back and led to a trench or shell-hole in the rear. At a given time the wire would be pulled, up would come the dummy in an upright position looking from a distance as though men were going over the top. When hundreds of these things were used they were very realistic. One man in a shell-hole could operate four or five of these soldiers which would be thirty or forty yards in front of him.
PRIVATE V.R. MAGILL, CYCLIST BATTALION,
18TH (EASTERN) DIVISION, XVIII CORPS

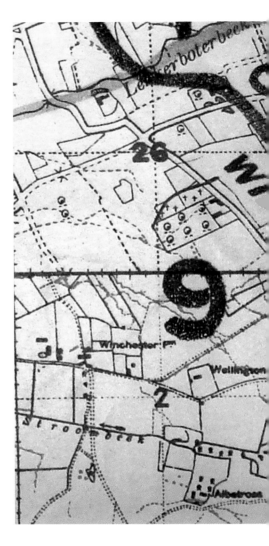

Above
Segment of XVIII Corps map marked with the Chinese attack front. Note Winchester Farm to left.

Having completed stage one, the fixing, it was a question of waiting for dawn to arrive – zero hour. In the half-light the 'attack' started under cover of a smoke screen. The effect was immediate, forcing the Germans to stand to, at which point they were subjected to a storm of pre-registered British artillery fire. As this crashed into the lines up went the German SOS rockets and down came their own counter-barrage on no man's land, beginning what had long been the customary tit-for-tat mutual bludgeoning.

Death and destruction on every hand. Trenches blown in and their defenders buried beneath them. In the meantime those figures that appeared from the opposite lines have not got any nearer. Hurrah! We have beaten them back. They have not even reached our trenches! Yes, they have given it up. The English swine barrage ceases. The 'Chinese attack' is over. The figures the Germans saw were dummy ones manipulated by XVIII Corps Cyclist Battalion from shell holes in no man's land while the troops holding the line kept under cover as far as possible, as the enemy would pound our front trenches in their efforts to smash the 'attack', inflicting some casualties amongst the wire pullers and infantry in the line, but chiefly on the poor dummies. I wonder to this day what the German GHQ thought when they discovered how their leg had been pulled, that is if ever they did.
Private V.R. Magill, Cyclist Battalion,
18th (Eastern) Division, XVIII Corps

The men working the wires were able to sense the slow 'death' of their charges, for as the wooden soldier was slowly torn to pieces by shrapnel and bullet, they became ever lighter to manipulate. Eventually, no more resistance could be felt and the dummy was 'dead'. The cyclists knew the stunt was over when the British barrage ceased, soon followed by that of

the Germans. Now, sharing the plight of all men caught in no man's land after daybreak, Magill and his colleague Noaks were expected to survive the day in their chosen shell holes until nightfall.

We had already been six long hours cramped up in this position, already my legs felt useless, how I ached to get up and stretch them. After recovering ourselves a little we had a look around to see if we could improve matters. It was a great temptation to have a peep over the top of the shell-hole, in fact it was nearly a fascination. I realised though, that was certain death as enemy snipers were busy, an occasional 'ping' told us of their alertness. The stench we smelt during the night was now more noticeable as the sun was slowly getting stronger. It was sickening and seemed to be right under our noses. Noaks suddenly wondered whether anything was at the bottom of the crater which our hole was on. He peered over the side, and then turned to me and said, 'There's a body there. Have a look.' I reached over and looked down. Yes, there it was. Some poor devil – one of our own too. What an end to come to. Rotting there in a muddy shell-hole, just as he had fallen. Some mother's son, God knows how many like him were lying about too. Noaks had taken a packet of cigarettes from his pocket, 'Have one,' he said. We were puffing away our smokes when I happened to glance up at the top of our shellhole, which we had built up during the night. What the hell was that object stuck up as a lump of clay? Was it clay though? It has features surely? Looking closer, to my horror I could see it was a human head. It was mud splashed and clay stuck to it in places. We must have taken it for a chunk of earth and put it up there during the early morning. What a sight. What are we going to find next? I should have liked to move it out of sight. Noaks advised we left it alone as we should have had to expose ourselves to the enemy in doing so. We let the head stay where it was. As the time was about nine ack emma, I suggested having some food as we had not eaten since before 'coming up'. Taking out our

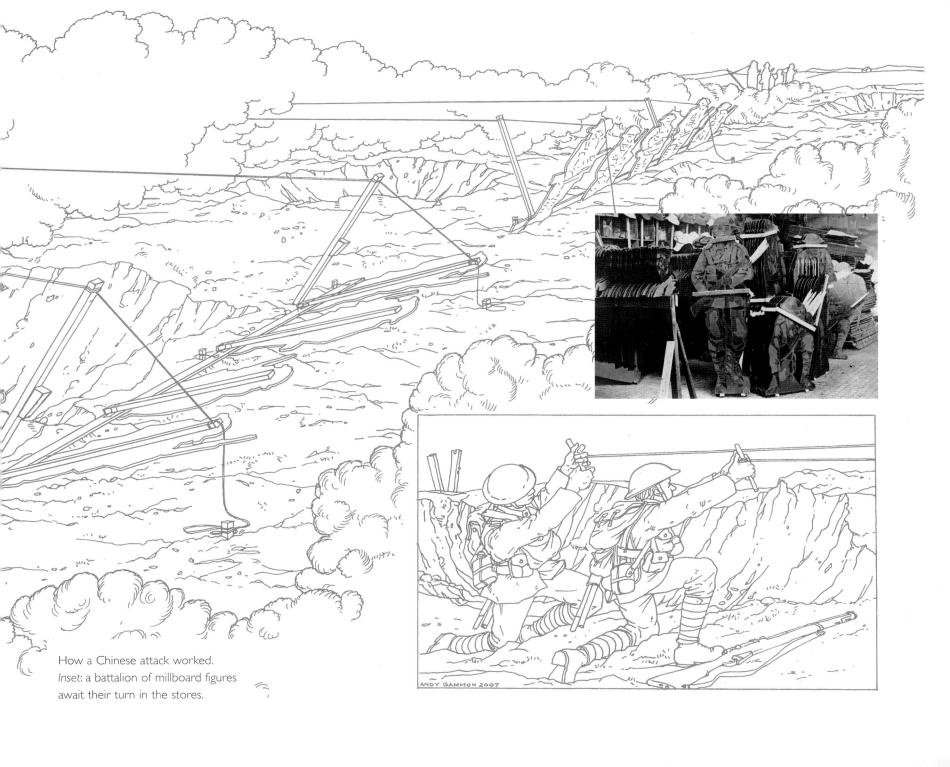

How a Chinese attack worked.
Inset: a battalion of millboard figures await their turn in the stores.

ANDY GAMMON 2007

rations which consisted of 'Bully' and a piece of bread, we ate in silence which was only broken by the crack of snipers rifles or the occasional burst of a shell.

PRIVATE V.R. MAGILL, CYCLIST BATTALION, 18TH (EASTERN) DIVISION, XVIII CORPS

Throughout the day the two men trembled as enemy aircraft scudded over, shells crashed, snipers' bullets cracked, and fear of counter-attack flowed and ebbed. As soon as night fell they stumbled back to the front line and retraced their steps through the gun lines to Ypres, reaching camp just as dawn was breaking the following morning. They had not fired a shot in anger.

In Maxse's attack of 22 October the same Corps cyclists had again been the sham. Their diversionary efforts helped Poelcappelle brewery to fall at long last into 53 Brigade (18th Division) hands and then the entire village. On their left 101 and 102 Brigades of the 34th Division pushed the line forward too, the dual effort producing a fair jumping-off point for the big assault of the 26th. The most appealing characteristic of the Chinese attacks, and one that made the troops smile even when working the wires whilst stuck between two barrages and under a mutual hail of machine-gun fire: until destroyed (which they ultimately were) the figures could be made to

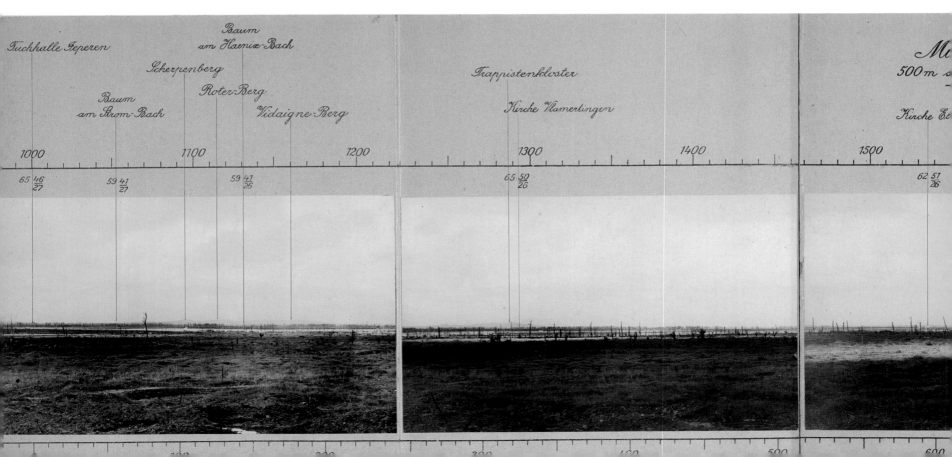

expire and 'rise again from the dead' as the operator wished. The first such attack associated with Third Ypres had taken place on 28 July, three days before the offensive opened. In order to rile the enemy, on this occasion the 'surviving dummies' were left standing afterwards! At least four subsequent XVIII Corps attacks took place between July and November, all perpetrated by Maxse's cyclists.

If, perhaps, Chinese attacks on a grand scale could have been organized to support every subsequent assault in the battle for Passchendaele, results may have been different. As it was, only flesh and blood could accomplish the task, and the human frame was suffering under the strain, for in the great offensive scheme, if such a thing could be still said to exist, 'success' was still meagre. Few had the energy and optimism to look upon such tiny advances with anything but vacant symbolism.

On 22nd the stunt comes off, and in pouring rain at that, perhaps this weather is what the Staff has been waiting for, or else they have just begun to realise that if they are going to wait for the weather, it is a hopeless proposition. At 7.20am, the first message was through to the effect that after 8 hours intense bombardment, 53rd and 54th Brigades, with help of Queens, go over, and the brewery is ours for the asking. Casualties are

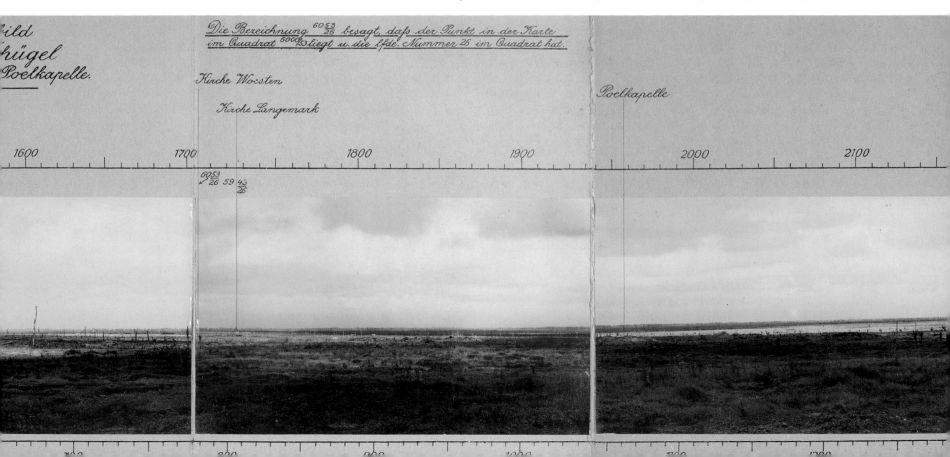

very light, and the right and left flanks are also up waiting to go forward for final objectives. I hope that they are successful and that in event of a counter-attack they will maintain the ground that has cost so much to gain. This will mean relief, I think. We are terribly cut up, and will need a new Division almost to bring us up to strength again. Immediately upon arrival, we have a Kit inspection, and in no uncertain voice, we cuss him up and down – not in his hearing. What an Officer, another shoe-black pre-war. An inspection immediately upon arrival, is a thing unheard of, even in the Battalions. He is probably out after a decoration, which we all hope he will get. Of one thing one and all here are in accord, and that is that he is not a man but a half bred dog.

PRIVATE ROBERT CUDE MM, 7TH EAST KENT REGIMENT
(THE BUFFS)

The following day Robert Cude would know that this bizarre minor action was indeed being looked upon as successful, albeit at the price of another 1,000 casualties.

Sir Douglas Haig, never by doubt diverted, now began to rely more and more upon Canadian flesh and blood. Technology – the tanks – could no longer help the troops, and German gunners and airmen made every part of the preparation period a trial – within and even behind the Salient.

On October 24th I went to the rear B.H.Q. at Huddersfield Dugouts. They were in the northern bank of the Yser Canal about half a mile south of Boesinghe. The front was approached by means of several long duck-board tracks, in places more like wooden bridges than the ordinary trench footboards. In the morning I did my best to investigate where these tracks started, not altogether an easy matter in an entirely strange country. In the afternoon I was asked by the Staff-Captain to see that the hot food and tea and rum for the use of the troops next morning were ready

for delivery to the carrying-parties, and that the O.C. carrying-party knew exactly what to do. I found that the food etc. was ready packed up in the hot food containers by the four transport officers, but I had great difficulty in finding the officer in charge of the carrying parties. After waiting about for over two hours I did get in touch with him. And by nightfall I had the satisfaction of seeing the hot food set off with this carrying-party up one of the tracks leading to the front. We obtained guides for this party from the 50th Divisional Signals, who gave us every assistance in their power.

CAPTAIN FRANCIS BUCKLEY, 7TH NORTHUMBERLAND
FUSILIERS

As the 'big' day for the Canadians approached – 26 October – it appeared that Mother Nature was at last smiling upon Plumer and Currie's plans. Not only was the weather improved, the Salient itself appeared calmer.

24TH OCTOBER

Left Steenvoorde 8 a.m. and with good weather favouring took the car to Birr Cross Roads. The shelling of a few days past has all been repaired and the roads though suffering from the rains are in reasonably good condition. Ypres is fairly quiet. At Birr Cross Roads we left the car, and walked over the duck-boards right out to Zonnebeke. The shell craters are filled with water and the battlefield is a vast quagmire. One of the most pitiful and heroic sights is to see the ammunition pack horses bringing up shells and charges – their drivers leading and often going up to the thigh in slimy mud; the horses stumble through, sometimes falling into shell craters from which they have to be hauled. Oh, it is a wicked, agonising sight. Here and there lay dead half buried in mud, horses and broken wagons all cogently telling some tragedy and horror, but one is immune to all these and passes by as unperturbed as though they were just pieces of rock. Colonel Shellshear called during the evening and is going to spend the evening with us. Outside it is blowing a

Above
The atrocious ground conditions endured in the Salient in late autumn were caused mainly by the unceasing traffic of foot, wheel and hoof.

Right
Part of a British map showing potential locations of Eingreif troop formations and probable German counter-attacks in the sector straddling Passchendaele.

gale and pelting rain. The distant sky shimmers with the reflection of the artillery, which is in action day and night. My pity is for the poor wretches in the trenches, who are freezing and soaked to the skin.

25TH OCTOBER

Visitors are a confounded nuisance. Colonel Shellshear stayed the night, and though perfectly welcome, delayed an early start. My results suffered, as the days are now short and today was one of rare sunshine. The 58th [battalion] are moving up into line this evening to take part in a push which is to come off tomorrow. Fortunately today has been fine and windy, so that the frightful mud has dried up sufficiently to prevent one sinking in deeply. The Canadians have taken over the line immediately behind Passchendaele, and this place is the objective.

Captain Frank Hurley, Official Photographer,
Australian Imperial Force

If Plumer's bite-and-hold endeavours had been seen as limited advances, Currie had yet more truncated territorial objectives. The capture of just 500 metres of ground was his ambition, and on a narrower front than ever before, 2.5 kilometres. On the left four divisions of Gough's Fifth Army were to attempt to force a passage into the Houthulst Forest and up the Goudberg Spur, whilst on the right flank I Anzac Corps, still in theatre, were to hold firm on to Broodseinde Ridge. The 25th of October was a good day too – clear, bright, dry and cool. The guns appeared to be wire-cutting productively, and throughout the hours of daylight shells could be seen falling around every visible pillbox. Spirits rose again. At midnight the rains returned. Gough called

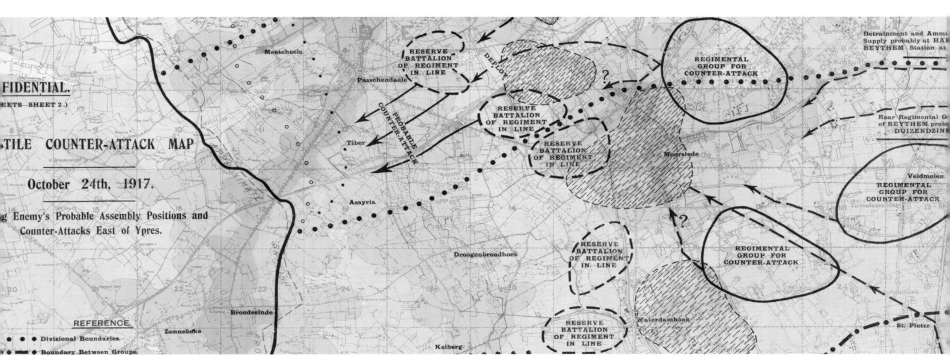

Harington to ask Plumer to postpone. When told of this, Plumer did not speak to Gough but asked Currie and Morland (X Corps) for their opinions. Both agreed that with the attack due to begin in less than five hours it was too late to cancel the operation orders. When Gough's telephone next rang he was to hear Plumer wish him good luck, at the same time accepting full responsibility for the outcome.

SECOND PASSCHENDAELE

26TH OCTOBER

Fiendish weather, heavy rain all day. Captain Castle (the Canadian photographer) and his assistant Lieutenant Ryder stayed with us last night and we all made for the Menin Road just after breakfast. The Australian 2nd Division were moving up in a vast concourse of motor lorries and omnibuses, so that the roads were choked with transports and men. Mud splashed in a continual spurt from thousands of wheels, whilst soaked and weary men heartily cursed the weather, the war and even their existence. It's terrible that these poor soaked wretches have to go up into the front trenches this evening, and there be subject to the wretched weather and hellish shelling. The misery of it all is too terrible and appalling for words.
CAPTAIN FRANK HURLEY, OFFICIAL PHOTOGRAPHER, AUSTRALIAN IMPERIAL FORCE

Misery was indeed the *mot juste* for 50th (Northumbrian) and 57th (West Lancashire) Divisions (Fifth Army) on this day, and the results indicative of what was to come. At 5.40 a.m. their advance towards Westroosebeke began, with a brigade from each division attacking across the fields north of Poelcappelle. They were faced with possibly the worst conditions of the battle to date – the ground was almost impossible

to traverse. The barrage, although far from inadequate, again drifted into the distance, and the attacks gained literally a matter of metres before the exhausted troops sank into shell holes for cover. Even *a metre per minute* was more than they could manage.

I went over the top at Passchendaele, yes. I couldn't tell you where we were except that it was flat and wet – just muck as far as you could see. We were not in trenches but shellholes and short ditches, half-full of water. Our officers knew the conditions before the attack because they were there with us. It made no difference – orders is orders. We were up in the line the day before, and it poured all that night and all the next day, and it was bitter cold. From the start – early morning, I think, we couldn't keep up with the barrage [about 10 metres per minute]. You couldn't keep your boots on, the mud just sucked them off your feet if they weren't laced tight, tight. It felt like your legs were coming out of the sockets, you couldn't stand up straight, couldn't keep your balance – you certainly couldn't shoot because everything was wet through and

Above
Another Frank Hurley masterpiece. This image of Australian troops and German dead at Garter Point encapsulates how men came to accept daily the most ghastly conditions and sights. The pillbox pictured was regarded as a safe haven, being warm and dry.

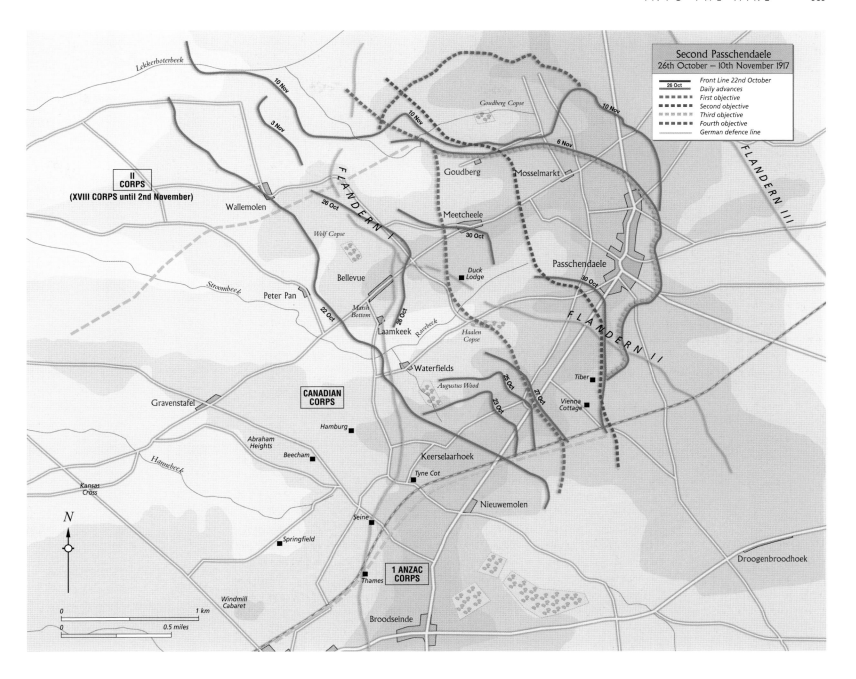

Second Passchendaele
26th October – 10th November 1917

26 Oct	Front Line 22nd October
	Daily advances
	First objective
	Second objective
	Third objective
	Fourth objective
	German defence line

Lekkerboterbeek

10 Nov

3 Nov

Goudberg Copse

10 Nov

6 Nov

10 Nov

FLANDERN III

II CORPS
(XVIII CORPS until 2nd November)

Goudberg   Mosselmarkt

Wallemolen

26 Oct

Meetcheele

30 Oct

FLANDERN I

Wolf Copse

Bellevue

Duck Lodge

Passchendaele

30 Oct

Stroombeek

Peter Pan

22 Oct

Marsh Bottom

26 Oct

FLANDERN II

Laamkeek   *Raveebeek*

Haalen Copse

Waterfields

Augustus Wood

25 Oct

Tiber

27 Oct

Vienna Cottage

Gravenstafel

28 Oct

CANADIAN CORPS

Hamburg

Abraham Heights

Beecham

Keerselaarhoek

Hannebeek

Tyne Cot

Kansas Cross

Nieuwemolen

N

Seine

Springfield

Droogenbroodhoek

1 ANZAC CORPS

Thames

Windmill Cabaret

0		1 km
0	0.5 miles	

Broodseinde

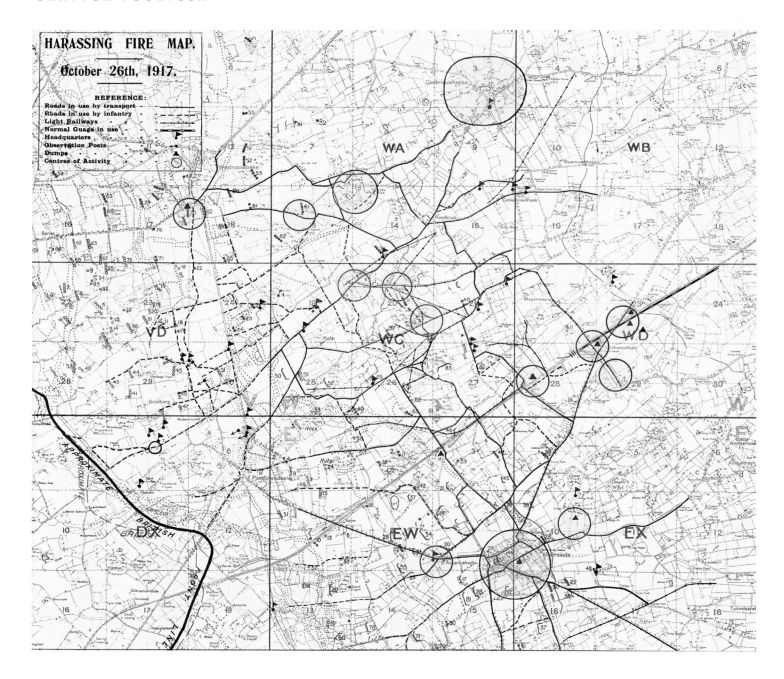

Left
Map identifying important German positions behind Passchendaele Ridge which would be subjected, day and night, to intense combined artillery and machine-gun fire.

clarted up with mud if you took off your cover. Twenty yards and you were done up. Eventually, a man couldn't move, you were too tired or too stuck. I was lucky to get under good cover – a fresh shellhole, that wasn't yet full of water. I'd had no idea what our target was, I just followed everyone else. We never got anywhere, never got near any Germans as far as I know, never saw one. You build yourself up for something like that; you want to do well, you know. But all that training only for men to be sent to die in that muck. It was wicked, but you said nothing because it was the same for everyone. No point moaning. Most of us came back without a rifle because we had used them to try to push ourselves out of the mud and lost them.

PRIVATE JACK HAYES, 2/5TH KING'S OWN
(ROYAL LANCASTER REGIMENT)

In pillboxes and shattered woods the enemy were now practically invisible. The phrases 'rushing a position' and 'fire and movement' had disappeared from the military lexicon. Those able to find cover or pull back to the starting position were fortunate; hundreds of men, stuck fast in the mud and in the open, fell prey to shrapnel and snipers. Although German counter-attacks were still failing to regain lost ground, and suffering heavily in the process (seven had been repulsed on the 23rd), British assaults were being brought to a standstill by mere handfuls of troops.

Taking one signaller with me I set out. There was a pill-box in front of us about half a mile away. Garnett had not been there, but it was certain to be a headquarters of some kind. I should find someone there who could give me information. That was where I should go. Inside our pill-box I had forgotten my super-stitious fears of the previous day, but they returned as soon as I came out and began to move across the dreadful and deserted waste. It was deserted, there was no living creature within sight.

Between ourselves and the low concrete rectangular block I was aiming for there was nothing to be seen except mud, shell-holes and water. We floundered through the mud, slipping, stumbling, trying to avoid the bigger holes and deeper pools, and with every step safety was receding, danger coming closer. All the trees at the edge of the Houthulst Forest had been destroyed, they were no more than gaunt stumps. No enemy could be hiding behind them but, beyond the stumps, the forest was darker. I just saw a dark mass. That was where the Eyes were, the Watching Eyes. All the time we were moving nearer to them, nearer, nearer. But it was the quiet time of day. Some of our own guns behind us were fir-ing. I heard the sound of their shells passing overhead; and a few German shells burst within sight, but none fell near us.

Bending low to make myself a smaller target, looking down for the best place to fall if I heard a near one coming, I began to hope. We were closer now to the grey block than we had been when we started. I could count on four or five seconds' warning, time enough to fall.

Four or five seconds! I got no warning at all. We were halfway across when it happened. I saw a hole opening between my feet, water and mud leaping away. I heard the scream of the oncoming shell and the blast of its detonation in the same instant. We were blown to the ground, muddy water splashed down on us from every side, but the swamp saved our lives, it smothered the shell's explosion, we were not hit. We got up and staggered on, neither of us speaking. I stopped under the wall of the pill-box and opened my mouth to speak, but no words came out, only meaningless sounds. There was a flask half full of neat whisky in my hip pocket. I took it out and swallowed a mouth-ful then passed it to my signaller who did the same.

SECOND LIEUTENANT P.J. CAMPBELL, 150 BRIGADE,
ROYAL FIELD ARTILLERY

So bad were the conditions here that with the action of constant heavy shellfire, pillboxes were sinking in the mud and canting over at strange angles, but were still operational. The key to any hope of success lay solely in being able to fight across and out of the swampy valleys and onto the sandy, better-drained ridge spurs – a fact that was implicit to German tactics.

In front of Passchendaele village Currie's Canadians advanced upon the traditional three sequential targets, the Red, Blue and Green lines, behind a creeping barrage that to suit the conditions had been slowed to 100 yards per eight minutes. It again proved too rapid, for the preceding days and nights of bombardment had ploughed the earth into a rolling sea of rust-coloured filth. There was no longer any good ground anywhere. Because of difficulties with stability, some field guns were firing short, further slowing the troops who again found alignment with flanking units awkward. No recognizable trenches existed. And it poured with rain again. The Canadians, however, were on slightly higher and drier ground than their neighbours and faced fewer pillboxes; they fought continuously for forty-eight hours, slowly pushing towards the objectives and fending off ever-weakening counter-attacks. The result was a remarkable 400-metre advance, with the 4th Canadians capturing objectives astride the Broodseinde–Passchendaele road. The 3rd Division, avoiding the slough of the Ravebeek, tackled the Bellevue Spur. It was considerably wetter ground but by tremendous courage and dash, almost certainly assisted by being fresh to the Salient, they scrambled to a position halfway to the objective. On the southern flank the British were again attempting to claw a little further onto the Gheluvelt Plateau. Again the target was the Reutel: the battered, blighted, cursed and surely God-forsaken sector with Polderhoek Chateau at its heart.

A matter that had exercised our minds in these conditions was how to keep the rifles and Lewis guns free from this all-pervading mud. We had received an issue of a very useful gadget which clipped on to the muzzle of the rifle with a spring flap which dropped over the bore, but there were not enough to go round, and in my own Company the men who were not provided with these protectors tied sacking round the muzzles and also round the bolts. Two days later, when we attacked, there was not a rifle that was not in a fit state to be fired.

I was holding the whole Battalion front with 'C', 'A' being in trenches behind in the neighbourhood of the Battalion Headquarters 'pill box', and 'B' and 'D' farther to the rear, and in these positions we quietly spent the day following the relief. To our front lay the wood surrounding the Chateau, to our left the low-lying marshy valley of the Reutelbeek, which, by reason of the impassable nature of the ground, constituted an effective protection for that flank, and on our right were the 14th Warwicks. For the attack the Reutelbeek formed our left boundary, and our right was a line excluding the Chateau itself by about fifty yards – the 14th Warwicks being detailed to take it. Our final objective lay about three hundred yards beyond the Chateau. 'C' Company was to lead off, and at a point where the front widened out the barrage was to halt for fifteen minutes to allow 'A' to come up on my left, with 'D' and 'B' following up in waves.

Colonel Miller scrambled up to us through the mud during the afternoon to wish us 'astonishing luck', and to check our watches. These were to have been synchronized with a watch sent up by Brigade to Battalion Headquarters. On arrival there the official watch was found to be twenty minutes different from that of everybody else, so it was decided to ignore it. A few minutes later the watch stopped altogether! Brigade had only forgotten to wind it up!

At night I got a tape out across my front to ensure an accurate jumping-off line in the dark next morning, and 'A', 'D' and 'B' Companies reported up to me and took up their assembly positions in depth.

The position we were up against had, as I have said,

Right
26 October attack map for 3rd and 4th Canadian Divisions, with the British 63rd Division on their left.

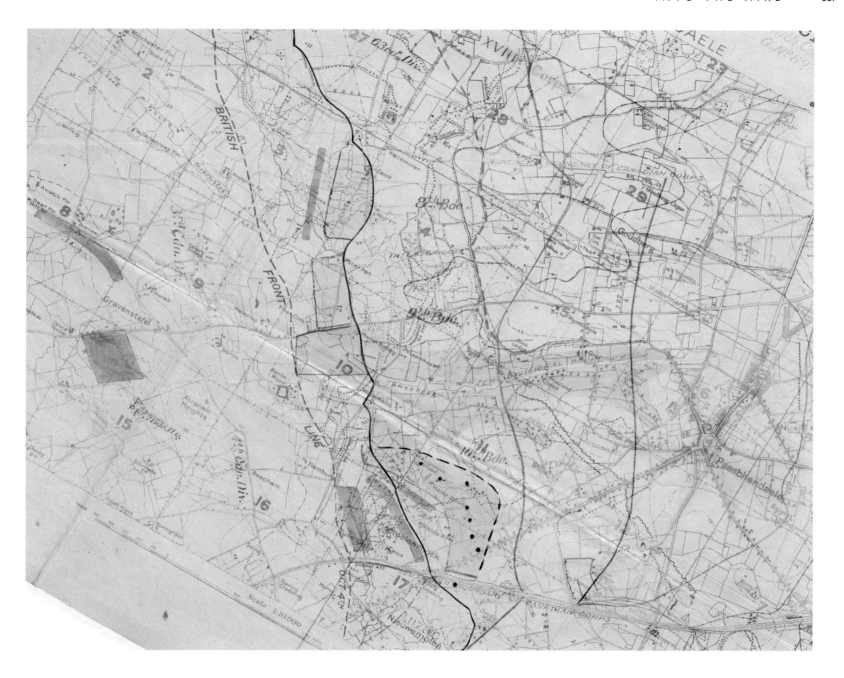

already resisted two attacks. The pill boxes dotted here and there and garrisoned by machine-guns were practically impervious to shell-fire, being built of reinforced concrete three feet or more thick and loop-holed, and the Chateau itself, situated on commanding ground, had been strengthened with concrete and turned into a veritable fortress, and numerous machine-guns were posted around in pits in the ground covered over with a bit of iron or timber.

It was just after midnight on the morning of October 26th when all Companies were reported in their assembly areas, and at 5.20 a.m. the attack started, and the long lines of men who had been tensely waiting moved forward in the dark. No word was said, no order given, the sudden opening of our barrage being sufficient indication that zero hour had at last come. There could be no mistaking it, for the barrage was magnificent both in accuracy and volume.

Major C.A. Bill, 15th Royal Warwickshire Regiment
(2nd Birmingham Pals)

Casualties everywhere were heavy. Major Bill was one such, suffering a shattered thigh by a bullet from the chateau. His description of the rest of the day epitomizes the efforts made and risks run by stretcher bearers.

My Company stretcher-bearers, having tied my legs together in rough splints, got me on a stretcher, and one of our batmen who had stayed with me took my revolver and brought along half a dozen prisoners, of the many we had taken, to carry me out of the fight. He had to go back a bit to find these fellows and it required considerable determination on his part, coupled with the persuasive power of the little gun, to get them to come back into the unhealthy, reeking wood. They got me up shoulder high, my faithful batman bringing up the rear, and we started off at about 6.30 for a thoroughly thrilling day, my own condition being such that I could only lie patiently and hope for the best, expecting every moment to be upset by my swaying, slithering bearers and landed in the mud. We missed our way for a start, and instead

of passing through our support lines near Battalion Head-quarters, we fetched up by a pill-box alongside the Menin Road in the neighbouring sector. Here we had to pass through an intense barrage which the German guns were putting down. Two of the German bearers were killed by shell splinters while they had me on their shoulders. I was sorry for them, but even more sorry for myself, as I fell with a crash on my broken thigh. Here my remaining bearers were made up into a batch with other prisoners and sent on down the line under escort and under almost as heavy a fire from their own guns as they had previously experienced from ours. The pill box was being used as a first-aid post and was already crowded with wounded, with numbers of other stretcher cases lying around outside. Rumours came along that the enemy was heavily counter-attacking in front, and every available man in khaki grabbed a rifle and 'stood to', even the Red-Cross men stripping off their armlets ready to fight if the Germans came through. For an hour or more this hell went on, and I made up my mind that it would be quite impossible to get through alive. Those of you who do not know war cannot conceive the torment of mind and body which hundreds of thousands of men suffered while lying maimed and helpless on the battlefield incapable of that action which so often alone preserved men's sanity. Pray God you never may know it. The threatened attack, however, did not materialize, and attention was again concentrated on the job of getting the wounded away. A whole battalion was engaged in this area as stretcher-bearers. I remember they were all very young – boys of eighteen to twenty they seemed, and I marvelled at the wonderful courage and devotion to duty they showed. Their job was to carry from the first-aid posts down to the field ambulances, and magnificently they did their splendid work, through hellish barrages and suffering casualties all the time. We made up a convoy and started down the Menin Road. That sounds a simple matter until you realize that not one vestige of the original surface of this main highway could be seen. Every inch had been shell-shot as well as the ground on both sides, until the whole was nothing but a broad strip of interlocked shell craters, half-full of mud and water. And to this confusion must be added

Above
More of the same daily activity. Whilst German prisoners carry back Canadian casualties, pioneers bring forward yet more duckboards; these have been fitted with specially designed anti-slip wire.

the fallen trees which had originally made of it an avenue as is usual in the French and Belgian main roads.

To indicate the most navigable route through this track of devastation a broad white tape had been laid down wandering hither and thither, over and round – and along this our bearers slowly wended their way. Added to this there was continual shell-fire, and as I watched the shells bursting perhaps fifty, perhaps a hundred yards ahead of us, I wondered whether we should get safely past that spot before that particular gun fired again, or whether we should be just in time to stop one. After a mile or so of this we left the road and took to a duck-board track on the left which wandered down the valley through Dumbarton Lakes, behind what was left of Inverness Copse. And here again we were in trouble, for flying low, backwards and forwards, on a figure-of-eight course, was a German aeroplane, machine-gunning the stretcher parties as they came down. We were on a down track only – there was no up traffic at all, so that even the excuse that the stretchers might have looked like machine-guns could not be made, and to their everlasting discredit the German airmen must be convicted of deliberately firing on wounded troops being evacuated from the battle. Two of the lads carrying the stretcher in front of me were struck down and my bearers stepped over their dead bodies lying on the duck-board track. At 6 o'clock that night – nearly twelve hours from the time we started down – I reached the Clearing Station and was operated on. In the ward near me was one of my own men who had survived the fight until the afternoon, and from him I learned the heartbreaking news that after getting right through to its final objective and also taking the Chateau with numerous prisoners and stores, which was more than it had been asked to do, the Battalion had come back, under pressure, to its original jumping-off line. I'm not ashamed to say that I very nearly wept.

MAJOR C.A. BILL, 15TH ROYAL WARWICKSHIRE REGIMENT (2ND BIRMINGHAM PALS)

The Canadians provided the only bright spot in a disappointing encounter. For the British, persistent failure was beginning to tell. The troops were not sentimentalists, but day after day, week after week, and now month after month, they had lived with the biological and psychological effects of suffering and death. The war and its means and ends may have been bitterly and colourfully condemned at every opportunity, but grousing and cursing in such conditions were worthless, for it appeared that, like the French and their mutiny, no one outside the battalion 'family' cared a damn for their lives. Every action in the last month had followed a similar pattern: poorly fed and tired men going into a dawn attack behind an unfavourable barrage, with the state of the ground making it impossible to 'storm' the enemy. And the mud. Armed with trustworthy intelligence regarding dates and locations, the Germans could rely upon this stubborn repetition and prepare accordingly. The lack of tactical alternatives was glaringly obvious to all, and it was crushing to the spirit. Now it was almost November, and there was no end in sight.

I met two officers, both in command of different units. One must have been a padre by nature, the other was an elephant hunter. We discussed God; and all the Gods, openly and shamelessly.
'If there is a God, why all this war?'
'For our sins.'
'But I didn't bring it on.'
'We're all responsible.'
'How could I stop it when I was in Africa?' said the elephant hunter.
'When I say our sins, I didn't mean only our own shortcomings, but those who preceded us.'
'But they're not here,' I chipped in.
'Speak no ill of the dead,' said the elephant hunter.
Then we struck another approach to an old subject.
'We're all part of a scheme worked out by God.'

'Then we're not to blame,' one of us said.

'What about the Germans? Are they to blame?' we asked.

'It will all be apportioned,' was the answer.

'Apportionment, why you look upon God as a chartered accountant.'

'No, I don't.'

'Well, what is He?'

'The one who knows all.'

'Then why doesn't He stop it?'

'We don't know the purpose. There's a reason for it.'

'What is it?'

'I don't know,' and so on for hours. We discussed the Bible, alien faiths, history, everything connected with religion we could think of, and the result – nil. And yet in each of us was a faith that somehow the world was not chaos. Of proof there was none.

LIEUTENANT F. HOWKINS, 253RD TUNNELLING COMPANY, ROYAL ENGINEERS

Leave was practically non-existent: twice a year for an officer, for other ranks perhaps ten days every two years. Teenagers with two years of service under their belts resembled middle-aged men, both physically and mentally; at the same time the likelihood of peace was more than just remote, and the familiarity *with* peace was dissipating fast. The troops began to feel like exiles, doomed to separation from families until they were no longer capable of fighting, and no longer capable of thinking and conversing outside the military milieu.

Young officers went home on leave, put up in town, saw everything worth seeing and many things that were not, and returned with gramophone records of the latest revue and lurid tales of their meetings with Kitty or Dolly. They got their satisfaction in their own way, and who could blame them? A short life and a merry one. Contrast this with another type.

'I'm due for leave tomorrow,' someone said.

'Good luck, old man, where are you putting up?'

'In town I suppose,' as if it didn't matter where he stayed.

'At the Regent,' someone chipped in. The youngest got an angry stare.

'Good God, no – I want somewhere quiet, where there's no band, and where I can be alone.'

An improvised committee meeting was hastily held, which unanimously recommended the Langham Hotel. The place was described in detail. It seemed just what he wanted.

'Thanks very much. I'll try it.'

But not one of us had ever set foot inside the place.

LIEUTENANT F. HOWKINS, 253RD TUNNELLING COMPANY, ROYAL ENGINEERS

The politicians too were not acting to end things by diplomacy – they still wanted a military resolution. But could anyone ever win this war? What commanders were now having to contend with was a disillusionment so profound that it was far beyond their talents as man managers to control. Fortunately, the military were able to rely upon things which no one, not even the Regimental Sergeant Major, could instil: humour (of the blackest kind), pride and the profoundest camaraderie.

On October 27th the poor shattered remnants of my battalion passed B.H.Q., very weary and very few in numbers. Besides the Battalion H.Q. Company there were just enough men to make one decent-sized company. Lieutenant Colonel G. Scott Jackson stopped to speak to me, and the tears trickled down his weather-beaten face, as he said 'Buckley, this has fairly done me.' Only those who have had a fine battalion cut to pieces can realise the feelings of their commander at such a moment. I set to work with my observers packing a wall of sandbags round the wooden huts, as a protection against bomb splinters. It was not possible to pro-

tect the roof, but these sandbags were effective against anything but a direct hit.

I have never known German night bombing more persistent or more heavy than it was in the Salient just at this time. And although we never got a bomb in the same field as our camp they dropped close enough to be disturbing. A camp with some of the Divisional details was struck some little way from us, and the same night D.H.Q. at Elverdinghe Château were bombed, several motor-lorries being set on fire.

CAPTAIN FRANCIS BUCKLEY, 7TH NORTHUMBERLAND FUSILIERS

On 27 October even the thrusting Gough suggested waiting for frost before pressing on further. Although recommending that commanders solicit the opinions of their men on the matter of adjournment, in his own mind Haig dismissed the notion, for he believed 'today's operations at the most decisive point [Passchendaele] have been adequately successful.' Without some period of dry weather the prospects for the troops, however, were ghastly, and those for wounded colleagues simply evil. Many units had now served several tours of duty and were desperately in need of rest. Their reservoir of courage was being rapidly and daily drained.

Ypres was dreaded by all our troops and we were disappointed to leave the Scarpe at the end of September to go into this offensive. The country was flat with a long slope up to a ridge at Passchendaele and the ground had been churned up by shell fire as we had advanced a few yards at a time. Even today the names Langemark, Poelcappelle, Houthulst Forest, Broombeck and Passchendaele make me shudder. One approached the front along a duck-walk across and between brimming shell holes for several miles. The troops who had been relieved were generally heavily shelled as they struggled out along the duck-walks. Many men

were drowned in the shell holes – too tired or unable through wounds to struggle out. We made two of these trips in October across the Broombeek.

Desertion was fairly common and we provided a firing party to execute some poor wretch in another Brigade. Our Morale generally was low and one of our men – whose name I shall not disclose – walked off when the orders came to go up again. He was a little weak minded, or he would have given himself a self inflicted wound – shot his foot through a sandbag or blown a finger off – and so got home. Of course, he was picked up by the Military Police in the rear areas and tried by Court Martial, after a long delay while the papers passed to Brigade, Division, Corps, Army, General HQ and back again, we were paraded and the sentence of death was read out. Another unit in the Division, the 7th East Yorks, carried out the execution. The prisoner was strapped to a post, and blindfolded and a foolscap envelope doubled and fastened over his heart with a safety pin. The firing squad had previously been marched up and grounded their rifles and marched away. The M.P. then loaded the rifles, using one blank and the remainder live. The firing party were told this, but no one knew which rifle had the blank – at any rate no one knew until they fired – and afterwards everyone claimed his had been the rifle with the blank.

PRIVATE ERIC HARLOW MM, 10TH SHERWOOD FORESTERS

Although the death penalty was thought by many to be a splendid deterrent and was liberally applied (but in nine cases out of ten commuted), the rates of self-inflicted woundings and desertions remained stable throughout the war. The Australians refused to be subject to British rule on this point saying that no man who had volunteered to come and fight halfway around the world 'for the old country', was going to be shot by anyone except the enemy. One British soldier was sentenced to death three times for three separate acts of 'cowardice' before finally suffering the ultimate penalty. It appears that the only people deterred were the victims of the firing squad themselves. There were simply limits to everyone's fortitude.

Tonight a bombshell drops, for the East Surreys move off back to line, followed by West Kents. Both are on Army Fatigues. God knows that this is a wicked imposition upon the part of someone to whom they are of no more consequence than pawns in the game. It helps us to realise what cannon-fodder really is. No wonder at men deserting the line, they are not the men of funk or terror, but in a good number of cases are men of spirit to whom this constant chasing in and out of the line, and the unsympathetic attitude adopted by the General Staff toward the rank and file of the Infantry has become unbearable. They are not afraid of death, for the punishment for desertion is death, or some punishment almost equally as bad. I suppose it is punishment for the Brigade's inability to take the Brewery at the first time of asking. If this is so, I ask why should we be pulled up and punished. Rather give credit to Fritz for his magnificent system of defence.
PRIVATE ROBERT CUDE MM, 7TH EAST KENT REGIMENT
(THE BUFFS)

Sir Douglas Haig's optimism received another dent on the evening of 26 October. Not only were there almost 12,000 casualties on the day, 3,400 of which were Canadian, but a directive from Lloyd George arrived instructing the immediate despatch of two infantry divisions plus guns and aircraft to support Italian troops that in the previous two days had been routed at Caporetto by the Germans and Austro-Hungarians. There was no choice but to comply. Worse still, GHQ was informed it was only a 'preliminary measure' – yet before the battle ended another three divisions would disappear southwards. And Haig needed to tighten his Flanders bootstraps further

on account of events in the Eastern theatre. After the Tsar abdicated the Russian throne in March 1917, a provisional government had been formed. They had done their best to remain faithful to the Triple Entente by placing the sympathetic General Brusilov in command of an offensive against the German Southern Army in Galicia. The attacks were initially successful before Generals Hoffmann and Hutier stopped the rot by counter-attacking – brutally. The ensuing Russian withdrawal became retreat, retreat became rout and as the army began to disintegrate open civil war swept across the country. It was plain to see that before long the Eastern Front would be a thing of the past and a pack of German divisions would be soon released for service in the West. Haig's window of opportunity in Flanders was becoming an arrow-slit. His vision of a great victory had already dissolved long ago, and with the repercussions of events in Russia and Italy to consider, the taking and holding of Passchendaele Ridge was simply essential. Retirement to the higher ground at Frezenberg, the old German front line where Third Ypres had commenced, was an option and was discussed, but still none would dare perform the deed, for the fields of Flanders were drenched with the blood of half a generation. Pragmatism, not plaudit was the watchword now. Haig, as ever, still exuded optimism and fierce determination, bolstering the fortitude of others at GHQ. But with divisions being drawn away, and talk of offensives elsewhere, there was a growing feeling that the Ypres campaign, in which so much hope and so many lives had been invested, was itself in danger of becoming a diversion. There was a growing sense of inescapable futility and any

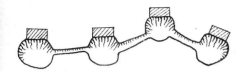

FROM SKETCH CAPTURED BY SECOND ARMY. 30. 9. 17.

'*Shell holes with funkholes for two men*'

'*Shell hole with funkhole covered with boards; sheets of galvanised iron are also good*'

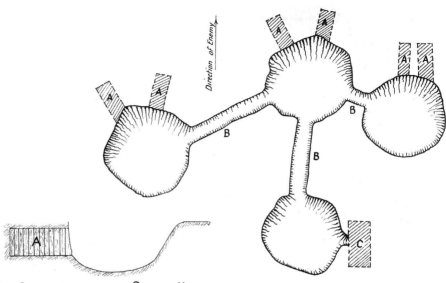

Direction of Enemy

SECTION THROUGH SHELL HOLE.

Above
Captured German sketches from September 1917 showed how German tactics incorporated instructions on how to improve shell-hole positions for defence. The defenders would be practically invisible in such fieldworks.

Opposite page
Top: Eingreif troops await the call. Middle and bottom: two-man German shelters in the Passchendaele wasteland. Note grenades ready for use.

opportunity of distraction, even for few hours, was tantamount to a vacation.

25TH OCTOBER

A party of us sent in a lorry about 10 miles behind the line for a gun piece but it hadn't arrived so we had a ride round and a good dinner of eggs, chips and custard. First civilians we had seen for over four months, we were like a party of school children let loose for a day. We returned at 6 p.m. after eight hours riding back to the reality of war.

26TH OCTOBER

On duty again, our boys are trying to take more ground and a terrible time they are having. As for us we are not out of it, we are carrying our shells knee deep in mud with Fritz sending plenty of shells over all night. When finished duty we could not lay down to rest in the dugout, for the mud.

27TH OCTOBER

Stayed up on the gun on fatigues, Fritz dropped a bomb about

20 yards from where we were working and blew some bodies from a pit where they had been buried together. The stench was terrible. I helped to bury some of the poor chaps (Germans they were). All bits of legs and arms etc., had to wear my gas mask. We are suffering from wet and cold feet. It is really wonderful what the human frame can stand, week after week. What a terrible thing is War, living in mud and the scenery composed of stumps of trees and heaps of bricks that once were peaceful dwellings of people.
GUNNER E.J. DRANE, 197TH SIEGE BATTERY, ROYAL GARRISON ARTILLERY

On 28 October the 23rd and 41st Divisions left for Italy. There had been an improvement in the weather, and with only a smattering shower here and there roads and tracks recovered a little. There was no appreciable improvement for those living in the shell-hole sea, for although rain-free it was becoming distinctly wintry. The mud, churned and re-churned like butter, grew stickier.

If you leave a bar of soap in a basin of water overnight, that's what it was like in Flanders [mud]. It wasn't like soil from the garden; there was no grit in it; it was a sort of yellowish-orange colour, but dried white on your clothes. You were covered in it, your body was covered. It got in your pores. You couldn't get it off your uniform by wiping it, that just spread it about like butter, but it would bash off in clouds of dust when it dried, which wasn't too often! You just had to go over your ankle to make it difficult to move . . . it just sucked at your feet, and this is what made having to go anywhere off duckboard tracks so tiring. Trying to pull out one foot got the other one deeper in. You needed help, and the lads would hold out their rifles to you and tug. Of course, wherever you went you were always carrying something, usually heavy. You never went anywhere without fetching or carrying. A bundle of pickets maybe, a bag of nails, a lump of timber, a couple of sandbags of rations, and the extra weight helped to shove you deeper in. Everything but rifle ammunition was bloody awkward; the boxes had rope loops for handles; a two-man job. That was the worst thing: when something needed more than one man to carry it, like a big piece of timber or corrugated tin; then you were at the mercy of the other blokes. If they lost their footing you could end in a hell of a mess. You couldn't see them because all this was done at night, you know, but sometimes their cursing would just give you a split-second to brace yourself for whatever was coming. If a bloke dropped a big lump of wood at his end it could pull your shoulder out, but it was always a hell of a jolt – a shock. The worst stuff to carry up was tin [corrugated-iron sheets]; a bit of wind and they were like a kite, they'd have you off the track in a flash. You got so done up with the carrying parties, a lot of the stuff never reached its destination. It was, 'Sorry Sarge, a shell blew it out of our hands.' But we'd just chucked the stuff in a shellhole, a ditch, anywhere. The trouble was, they knew, you see. So they'd give you something to carry back – three or four rifles for repair or something, a tripod, shell cases to the dump. And they'd check to see if you'd fetched them back too. The only thing we never dumped was food.

PRIVATE BERT FEARNS, 2/6TH LANCASHIRE FUSILIERS

Between major operations patrols were still required to creep out to reconnoitre ground, attempt to find out where their enemy lay and establish forward posts ready for the next step. There were many small, isolated, nocturnal skirmishes to capture a section of trench here, a pillbox there, but most activity apart from the ubiquitous mutual shelling was aerial, with planes and balloons taking advantage of clearer skies to steer the guns onto almost 120 hostile batteries that still had key British positions and routes nicely taped. The Royal Flying Corps were by no means dominant in the air, however, and to the troops on the ground hostile aircraft seemed to be having far too much their own way.

27 OCTOBER – SATURDAY

Early move at 8 a.m. and arrived at Ypres 9.30 a.m. The road much congested with traffic, and muddy. The Boche is now settling down to winter positions, and as we can no longer push forward on account of the frightful mud, he has had time to register his artillery. This has had the effect of jeopardising all points where traffic is busy and also traffic routes and salient places. Ypres is still being harassed and last night was bombarded with his long-range guns and Gothas.

We took the car to the head of the Menin Road and I decided to leave it there on account of the shelling. We were locked in congestion of traffic and unable to move anyway, when a large fleet of 16 Gothas came over and fairly put the wind up us. We opened fire with 'Archie', but without effect and we fully expected to be bombed. They hovered over our observation balloons and the observers not being able to be hauled down quick

Below
Even as the Allies pushed the line forward, German observation remained superior. Corduroy roads such as this one leading from Bellewaerde over Westhoek Ridge were prime targets.

Right
Chateau Wood near Hooge then and now. Today it is a well-known amusement park.

enough jumped out in parachutes. Why the balloons were not set on fire is beyond me, for the Boche had it all his own way. One of our machines within range of this formidable fleet made a magnificent nose-dive of about 500 feet and escaped disaster. The Gotha fleet gave a fine demonstration, but apparently were only bent on prying into our doings and photographing.

I went with Joyce and Wilkins on an ambulance to Hooge, and had a considerable excitement on account of the Boche shelling the road. Afterwards we went through the infamous Chateau Wood and up the enfiladed road to Westhoek Ridge. This region always suffers heavy shelling and we passed through nearly a mile of straffed limbers and wagons and dead horses. I have not seen a more terrible scene of desolation, waste and destruction than hereabouts on the Westhoek. The Boche observation on this area is superb, and the least congestion invariably brings shelling. We returned over the duckboards by a safer route to Hellfire Corner, and thence to Ypres. A fine sunset beautified the solemn ruins, that awakened feelings of awe and made one sorrow for the things which war has done. Took 18 plates.

CAPTAIN FRANK HURLEY, OFFICIAL PHOTOGRAPHER, AUSTRALIAN IMPERIAL FORCE

Sunday, 28 October was a day of reliefs and final preparations – again under persistent shellfire. Nothing the British guns could do seemed to diminish the force of the daily and nightly hostile battering. Train after train of pack mules toiled to feed the guns, and each day dozens of animals were lost to shellfire and gas, drowned in the mire, or despatched through the merciful application of a bullet through the brain. Frank Hurley prepared to capture yet another stage of the Flanders saga.

29 OCTOBER 1917

My premonitions of a windy day were amply fulfilled. To start with, my driver who has a holy fear of shell fire, is absolutely

regardless of reckless driving, gave me qualms on the way to Ypres. The traffic was congested and the road sticky. Rushing for narrow openings and scraping the wheels of the up and down traffic made me more windy than actually being in a barrage. Anyhow, we got to the head of the Menin Road in safety and left the car; then we walked the length of the road up to Hooge, an occasional shell lobbing none too far away. The day was foggy so the Boche balloon observation was bad. Under these conditions he shells on registered and favourite points and also does a considerable amount of area firing. We succeeded in reaching the infamous Chateau Wood. It must have been a glorious spot with its lake on one side and heavily foliaged timber. It is now so lonely and desolate that one feels as if death alone dwelt there. The trees are smashed and splintered and only stumps; the ground is heaved into wavelike ridges with shelling and here and there along the lonely duckboard track lies a stricken soldier. One does not linger more than necessary in this place over which hangs the pall of gloom and death. Guns boom all around, yet everyone dodges the awful loneliness and hazards of Chateau Wood.

Just in front of Chateau Wood I came across a 9.2 howitzer battery: three guns had been knocked out before they were set up in position. Westhoek Ridge was fairly quiet for the moment, till I got near the crest. Then the fun began. I took shelter in a thin sandbag dugout, and had the cinema trained on bursting shells of which there was an ample sufficiency. They screamed overhead like a flight of rockets. One fell a little short and threw mud over the dugout and fell but a yard away. I owe my life to it being a dud. The position became so unhealthy that with Joyce I decided to run the gauntlet and get out of the barrage if possible, as it seemed fatal to stay in our position. We therefore dodged from dugout to dugout, having the excitement of our lives. We were puffed, and sheltered for a few minutes behind Kit and Kat [pillboxes]. Wizsh-sh-sh-sh-sh-sh and a shell lobbed so close that had we been a few paces out we must have been a direct hit. This shell also was a dud! Of all the scores that whizzed over our heads I counted but four that failed to explode. Three times today my life has been miraculously spared. We returned with all speed out of the shelled area, but it was not before we left Ypres that we felt safe. It was a Boche day.

CAPTAIN FRANK HURLEY, OFFICIAL PHOTOGRAPHER, AUSTRALIAN IMPERIAL FORCE

Sir Douglas Haig and Sir Arthur Currie determined that the next step would belong to Briton and Canadian. Fire and movement was still the order of the day, but this time Currie modified the tactics so as not to advertise his intentions. Every night machine guns deluged German positions with millions of rounds from their Vickers, whilst the artillery dropped short sharp barrages on key points. Like other troops the Canadians too had studied models of the areas to be attacked (at this advanced season constructed under cover in an aircraft hangar) and discussed tactical alternatives. Speaking to experienced British colleagues the Canadians came to the conclusion that it was going to be impossible to 'run' the battle even from the most forward HQ dugout; a battalion commander's power was limited simply to pre-assault organization and ensuring supplies. Communication and control beyond the parapet interface was not going to be just difficult, it was recognized as being impossible, so more responsibility was invested in NCOs, who of course would be in the maelstrom of attack with their sections.

Because the projected territorial gain was so limited the traditional leapfrogging of first wave by second, and so on, was abandoned. The first wave was to advance against the *final* objective – the Green line – whilst the second acted as moppers-up and consolidators. In this way attacking momentum might, with luck, be maintained. As a result of these revisions the Canadians saw it necessary to send the men into battle with extra kit: more iron rations (enough for three days), extra small-arms ammunition (an additional 170 rounds), a shovel (GS Bulldog), a bundle of sandbags and a flare to

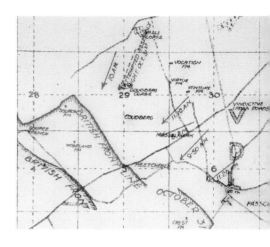

Above
German counter-attacks on the Goudberg Spur launched on 31 October.

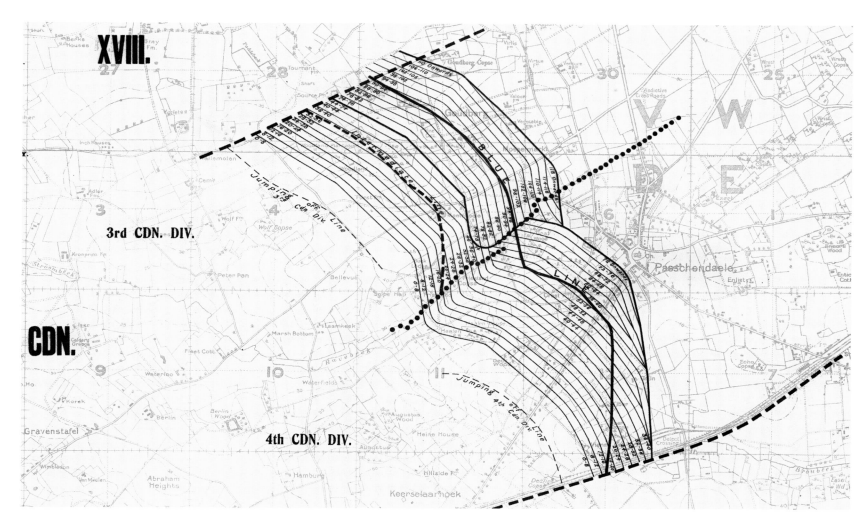

Above
The creeping barrage plan for the Canadian attacks of 30 October, which spawned the counter-attacks opposite.

signal positions to spotter aircraft plotting the battle's progress and directing guns. The creeping barrage was to be at the same rate as before – 100 metres per eight minutes – and because of the proximity of the German 'lines' (pillboxes and fortified shell holes) the Canadians were to reproduce British tactics at Poelcappelle by withdrawing before the barrage began, allowing the guns to fire freely without worrying about 'shorts', now a ubiquitous problem.

The attack began in a grey, chill, windy dawn at 5.50 a.m. The temperature had dropped to 44° Fahrenheit (8° C) but at least the day only promised to be showery. Under cover of a 420-

gun barrage two brigades of the 3rd Canadian Division advanced astride the Bellevue Spur. On the highest ground, 7 Brigade came close to reaching its objective, eventually digging in along a surprisingly straight line from shell holes in front of Vapour Farm to Meetchele crossroads. The word surprisingly is used advisedly, for such was the condition of the battlefield that few men knew exactly where they were located upon a trench map – there were no trenches and precious few other features. Nor were the troops aware of precisely what constituted the target – or where the enemy were located until they opened fire. 12 Brigade of the 4th Canadian Division took their line beyond the Crest Farm strongpoint (which put up an exceptional defence until outflanked) to the very outskirts of Passchendaele village. En route, so many intact machine guns were captured that they were able to use them against their former owners. Eyewitnesses remarked upon the extraordinary concentration of machine guns on the ridge, with some pillboxes holding no less than four crews. Although objectives were largely being achieved and counter-attacks staved off, a curious gap, imposed by the impossibly wet Ravebeek valley existed between the two divisions. But it was not seen as a problem because the Germans were unlikely to wish to plug it.

To the north at Wallemolen the 63rd (Royal Naval) Division attempted to cover the Canadian left flank.

We are to go over from tapes laid by the Engineers. The whole thing must be done with mathematical precision, for we are to follow a creeping barrage which is to play for four minutes only a hundred yards in front of the first 'ripple' of our first 'wave'.

I am in the second 'ripple' fifty yards behind the first. The first 'ripple' is to go over in extended order, four paces apart, the second 'ripple' is to start in artillery formation – sections in single file at a given distance apart – changing to extended order after having covered two hundred yards. It is of the utmost importance that we should keep as close as possible to our own barrage and even risk becoming casualties from it. Well, if we know our own gunners we haven't much doubt about the risk! At midnight we move up to the tapes amid heavy shell-fire. Each section digs for itself a little pit in which to crouch. It is called intensive digging. Each man in turn digs like fury until he is fagged out and flops, the others meanwhile lying on their bellies and waiting their turn to seize the spade. In this way quite a big hole, like a small section of a trench, can be dug in a very few minutes. All the while shells are screaming over our heads, throwing up great geysers of mud all around us and further mutilating the ruined landscape. Our better 'ole is about big enough to accommodate us when there is a cry for help. The section which includes Dave Barney has been buried by a shell. Dave has given up stretcher-bearing for the time being, and is a rifleman or bomber – I forget which. We dig them out again, swear at them heartily, and get back to our own slot in the ground. Ten minutes later they are all blown up and buried again, with worse results than before. Dave is the only one of them left alive, and he is entirely unscathed but badly shaken, and inclined to think that war is an overrated pastime. I want some rest, and beg him not to make a hobby of getting himself buried. One could always say light-hearted and stupid things even when one was frightened to death. We went back to our little slot in the wet earth, and I crouched down and proceeded to sleep like a hog. It would have been rather amusing if everybody had slept as I did, for there wouldn't have been any attack.
PRIVATE ALFRED BURRAGE, 28TH LONDON REGIMENT
(ARTISTS RIFLES)

190 Brigade, within which Alfred Burrage's Artists Rifles served, was to suffer some of the heaviest losses on 30 October, almost half their

Above
Low-level German aerial photograph showing Canadian troops packed in newly captured positions. The men were required to disperse into smaller shell-hole based parties as soon as was practicable.

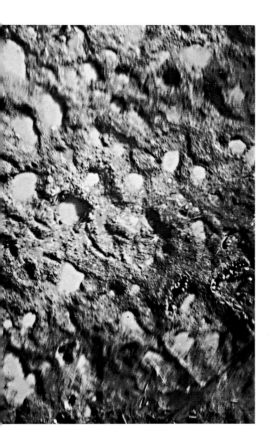

fighting establishment. Although the air was alive with planes, most were concentrating on ground attack rather than observing for the guns; British counter-battery work was again difficult due to poor flying conditions during the previous few days, but by contrast, German barrage work across the battlefront was perfectly timed, perfectly located and heavy, catching the British struggling through the deep mud of the valleys.

We had already seen what had happened to the first 'ripple'. They had all made for that spot of higher and drier ground, and the Germans, having retired over it, knew exactly what must happen, and the sky rained shells upon it. Shrapnel was bursting not much more than face high, and the liquid mud from ground shells was going up in clouds and coming down in rain. The first 'ripple' was blotted out. The dead and wounded were piled on each other's backs, and the second wave, coming up behind and being compelled to cluster like a flock of sheep, were knocked over in their tracks and lay in heaving mounds. The wounded tried to mark their places, so as to be found by stretcher-bearers, by sticking their bayonets into the ground, thus leaving their rifles upright with the butts pointing at the sky. There was a forest of rifles until they were uprooted by shell-bursts or knocked down by bullets like so many skittles. The wounded who couldn't crawl into the dubious shelter of shell-holes were all doomed. They had to lie where they were until a stray bullet found them or they were blown to pieces. Their heart-rending cries pierced the incessant din of explosions. The stretcher-bearers, such as still survived, could do nothing as yet.
PRIVATE ALFRED BURRAGE, 28TH LONDON REGIMENT (ARTISTS RIFLES)

Although the Artists believed they had advanced, the troops had in fact only succeeded in reaching the jumping-off point of the first wave, which had been cut down the moment they had moved.

How my section had so far remained intact is a mystery which I shall never solve in this world. After a minute or two of stupor we discovered that we were all as thickly coated with mud from the shell-bursts as the icing on a Christmas cake. Our rifles were all clogged, and directly we tried to clean them more mud descended. If the Germans had counter-attacked we had nothing but our bayonets. In the whole battalion only one Lewis gun was got into action, and I don't think that more than half a dozen men in the three attacking companies were able to use their rifles during the first few hours. We saw Germans rise out of the ground and bolt like rabbits, and we had to let them bolt. They had been able to keep their rifles covered and clean, but we had bayonets on ours. Moreover, their artillery knew just where we were, and our own gunners were now firing speculatively. We were getting the shells and the rain of mud and the German wasn't. Good soldier that he was, he soon took advantage of this, and we began to suffer from the most hellish sniping.

The mud which was our enemy was also our friend. But for the mud none of us could have survived. A shell burrowed some way before it exploded, and that considerably decreased its killing power.
PRIVATE ALFRED BURRAGE, 28TH LONDON REGIMENT (ARTISTS RIFLES)

A single brigade of 58th (London) Division advanced on the left shoulder of the Naval Division. A report later stated that if the barrage had been as slow as 100 yards in half an hour, their troops could still not have kept up with it. Exposed, they still persevered, reaching a point close to the Spriet road. As long as the Germans thought the British might advance again, the hostile barrage continued.

There was still a tornado of shells raging around us, and one must have landed in the same shell-hole with me. I didn't hear it come and I didn't hear it burst, but I suddenly found myself in

the air, all arms and legs. It seemed to me that I rose to about the height of St. Paul's Cathedral, but probably I only went up about a couple of feet. The experience was not in the least rough, and I can't understand why it disturbed me so little. I think that by this time I was so mentally numb that even fear was atrophied. It was like being lifted by an unexpected wave when one

is swimming in the sea. I landed on all fours in the shell-hole which Edmonds had told me to leave, sprawling across the backs of the rest of the section.

'And now,' I said firmly, 'I'm going to stop.'

Edmonds didn't demur, and I asked him what about some rum. The Nonconformist conscience prevailed, and he said that

Above
British pan 129 illustrating the final line reached in this sector in 1917. The village of Westroosebeke can be seen at left at the end of the tree-lined road, with Passchendaele Ridge to the right.

we might need it presently.

Merciful heavens, didn't I need it now! We lit cigarettes and I began trying to think. I wondered if I could smile, and, still having control of my face muscles, found that I could. After all, I was not very much afraid in that shell-hole, but I knew that I daren't move out of it. I dared not go out and try to do

anything for the wounded – coward and hound that I was. After all I wasn't a stretcher-bearer. A damned good excuse! Nothing had stood up and lived on the space of ground between ourselves and the pill box a hundred and fifty yards away. I saw a stretcher-bearer, his face a mask of blood, bending over a living corpse. He shouted to somebody and beckoned, and in that instant he crumpled and fell and went to meet his God. To do the enemy justice, I don't suppose for one moment that the man was recognized as a stretcher-bearer. Another man, obviously off his head, wandered aimlessly for perhaps ninety seconds. Then his tin hat was tossed into the air like a spun coin, and down he went. You could always tell when a man was shot dead. A wounded man always tried to break his own fall. A dead man generally fell forward, his balance tending in that direction and he bent simultaneously at the knees, waist, neck and ankles. Several of our men, most of whom had first been wounded, were drowned in the mud and water. One very religious lad, with pale blue watery eyes, died the most appalling death. He was shot through the lower entrails, tumbled into the water of a deep shell-hole, and drowned by inches, while the coldness of the water

added further torture to his wound. Thank God I didn't see him. But our C. of E. chaplain – who went over the top with us – was killed while trying to haul him out.

Private Alfred Burrage, 28th London Regiment
(Artists Rifles)

Finally, the troops realized that going forward was no longer an option. If they were not all to perish, cover must be found.

[Second Lieutenant] Edmonds and I held a sort of council of war. If we were counter-attacked in our present circumstances we hadn't the chance of mice against cats. My theory was that we ought to make a bolt for the pill box behind us, clean our rifles

Below
The Westroosebeke sector just fifteen months earlier.

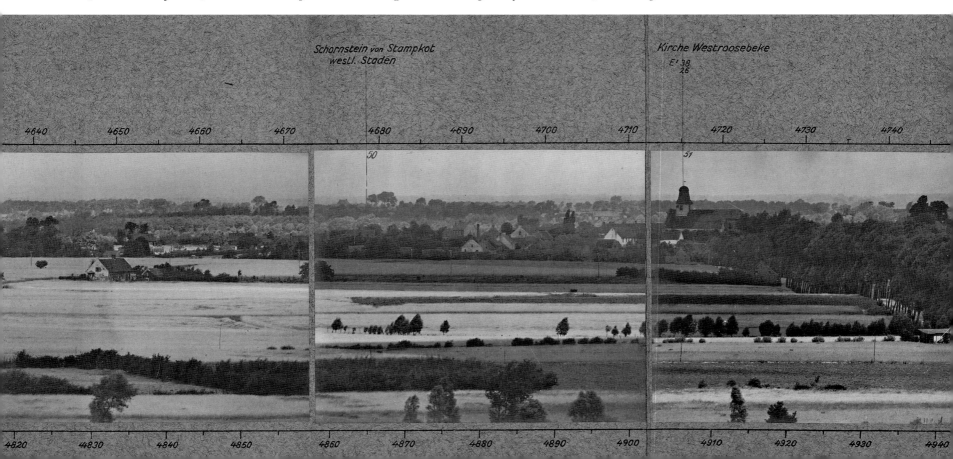

Schornstein von Stampkot westl. Staden

Kirche Westroosebeke

E' 38
26

4640   4650   4660   4670   4680   4690   4700   4710   4720   4730   4740

50

51

4820   4830   4840   4850   4860   4870   4880   4890   4900   4910   4920   4930   4940

once we were inside, and thus have a defensive position and a chance to fight for our lives if Jerry decided that the bit of ground we had won was worth retaking. Edmonds agreed with me, but was loath to retire. I dare say he thought that an extra hundred yards or so of mud was going to make a material difference to the result of the war. If he had had a Union Jack with him I think he would have stuck it in the ground as a kind of announcement that we were there. He wouldn't go back on his own initiative, and at last told me to go and find company headquarters and get an order from Captain Medville. Company headquarters was any shell hole that Captain Medville might be in if he happened to be still alive. I didn't want to wander about in an area in which nobody had been seen to stand up for much more than a minute, so I told Edmonds I didn't know where to look. He saw by my eyes that I was afraid to go, and before I could summon a little more resolution and stop him he went himself. By a miracle or an accident he found Medville, who seemed to have agreed with my suggestion. Edmonds came lumbering back and waved us towards the pill box, himself starting in that direction. But he hadn't gone ten yards before he rolled over, clutching at one of his thighs. I saw him crawl into a shell-hole, and I am glad to be able to say that eventually he got back to safety. That left me in command of the section.

Private Alfred Burrage, 28th London Regiment (Artists Rifles)

The casualty count for 30 October was a devastating 50 per cent. The Canadians had made it to

the southern shoulder of the ridge and were now able to gaze straight into the ruins that had once been Passchendaele, the remains of the church being just 330 metres ahead. It was not over yet. Now the task was to clear the village and push out the line east and north, capturing a little of the rear slope and annexing as much of the high ground towards Staden as possible. On 31 October reliefs took place.

Around nine o'clock orders came for us to put our equipment on, ready to move. There was still a slight drizzle as we waded over to the duckwalk. We proceeded slowly as we were continually meeting men, some walking wounded cases, going back. One dared not yield too much right of way, because to step from the wooden bath mats might mean immersion to the waist. On and on we went, with the occasional halt as we waited for guides or runners. At noon we reached an area dotted with rusting derelict tanks and stood there, sideways on, as the remnants of a relieved battalion edged by us, men who looked like grisly discards of the battlefield, long unburied, who had risen and were in search of graves. Not one of them spoke, nor did we. Three sausage balloons had gone up above Ypres as the rain had stopped. A German airman came over, flying deliberately, swooped down and sprayed bullets into the nearest blimp. There were forked flames, billowing smoke, a meteor of fiery fabric, charred fragments, and two swaying figures attached to parachutes. They dangled a moment and sank from sight as two of our planes appeared. The German had spotted them and went away. The other two balloons remained aloft. After standing around an hour amid much going back and forth of runners, we were told we had to stay in the place and make any shelter possible. There would be no chore for us until after dark. Some of the men managed to get into the derelict tanks and slept there. Tommy and Baillie and I went to one and could tip it with our weight. But there was water in it, and water around it. As we rocked the monster, a head squeezed out of the muck, a face without eyes, the skin peeled as though from lard, a corpse long dead and frightful.

We left the tanks and wandered about, being lucky enough to find a mound of solid mud, enough to make our bed, and there we stayed between sandbagged walls, with a roof of salvaged corrugated iron. Nearby was an old trench revetted with German stick work, blocked at one part with broken wire and the black dead of forgotten fights. About dark we wriggled outside to make room enough to set up our Tommy cookers, and hot tea put life into us.

PRIVATE WILL BIRD, 42ND BATTALION (ROYAL HIGHLANDERS), CANADIAN EXPEDITIONARY FORCE

Hostile shelling hampered and harassed reliefs. At the recently captured Vapour Farm, however, it was a single 'friendly' gun that was causing men to curse. It had dropped shells upon the farm ruins since before their capture, and was still doing so. Signals were clearly not reaching the battery. Archie Irving and Bill Blaney, two Canadian pals, sheltered amongst the blasted bricks.

Dear Friend

There is no doubt that you will have received the sad news by the time you get this letter, but I thought you would like to hear from me seeing I was in the same Company as Bill. Well, I was near him just as we went over the top and I can tell you it was not the Germans that killed Corporal Blaney but, of course, as you will understand, I am not allowed to put much in about him, but if I am spared to have my leave I shall give you all I know. At present all I can say is that he was killed by a shell. My address is Cpl. Irving A, 760734, A Coy, 2nd Canadian Mounted Rifles, B.E.F. France, so let me know if you get this letter as I can tell you the day we went over the top was just as if Hell was let loose, in fact I never thought that any man could stand such terrible endurance, and I got a good belly full of gas which nearly put me out.

Above

The embankment of the Langemarck–Staden railway, used as an artery for supplies. A fine daily and nightly target for German guns, close scrutiny will reveal three British casualties in this picture.

Well you will have to excuse me and hope to be able to see you again.

I remain your old friend,

Archie

[Lance Corporal Bill Blaney, 2nd Canadian Mounted Rifles (British Columbia Regiment) was killed on 31 October 1917 and is commemorated on the Menin Gate. The author of the letter, Lance Sergeant Archie Irving, was killed on 10 August 1918 and is buried in Bouchoir New British Cemetery]

The permanent stress of living a hair's breadth from eternity took its toll. Commanders recognized the fact and made sure that every unit went out for a proper few days' rest after action. Bombs there may have been, but in the camps there were at least no fatigues, plenty of hot food and opportunities to visit estaminets. Much more infrequent respite was possible for those toiling on battlefield infrastructure, supply and communication. Few suffered more than the signallers. Whereas infantry and artillery were able to 'go to ground' for cover (in varying degrees), signal stations and offices had to be constantly manned, and breaks constantly mended. The SOS rocket (used by both sides, of course) served its purpose admirably for immediate retaliatory action, and stationery targets such as batteries, railheads, dumps etc., could be effectively set upon with minimal if any telephonic interaction; but for information regarding mobile threats, such as a battery being shifted or more especially the formation of hostile counter-attacks, the gunners were absolutely reliant upon swift and unbroken contact if they were to produce satisfactory results. The speed and accuracy of response could mean the difference between life and death for scores, even thousands, of men. On the first day of the Passchendaele battles (12 October) and despite the narrowness of the attacking front, over 1,000 urgent messages were passed via divisional lines. From this statistic alone one may extrapolate the significance a prolonged communication breakdown might have.

NOVEMBER

As November 1917 loomed the promise of a decisive conclusion to the war in a year – or two, five, ten – was more of a chimera than ever. A sense of interminable inevitability gripped everyone.

The utter misery of the conditions at this time are indescribable. Soaked to the skin by the incessant rain, weighed down by equipment, tools, and the duckboard or what not for use on the work in hand, stumbling and dragging along the slippery slats on the narrow ridges between the shellholes, meandering sloughs hardly recognisable as paths, or digging, mauling, building in squalor and sludge, it was one long struggle of horror. Add to this the physical effort, the psychological effect of the dismal outlook, the waste of treeless, houseless, greenless landscape, destruction incarnate, the all-pervading smell of stagnant shellholes, with their frequently dreadful contents, and the ever-present expectation of a sudden 'area shoot', a storm of high explosive and shrapnel breaking out at a moment's notice; and one marvels that any human being could live through such conditions and keep sane.

Major R.L. Bond DSO MC, 23rd Field Company, Royal Engineers

Men were indeed suffering from the miseries of their exile, and being pushed beyond their powers of endurance. Sir Douglas Haig brought the Fifth Army's suffering to an end by closing down most of the northernmost sectors. At long last Maxse's XVIII Corps was relieved. Sir Claud Jacob's II Corps shuffled across from Polderhoek to guard the Canadian left flank for the next push against Passchendaele. Haig now knew there were no grounds for greater gains beyond the capture of that portion of the Passchendaele Ridge incorporating the sprawling village. Westroosebeke, barely 1,000 metres from his present front line, was out of reach; Staden, at the end of the ridge and a potential target for Day One all those weeks and months and lives ago, may as well have been on another planet. The fighting – or rather the guns and the Flemish climate –had truly created a hell on earth, just as it had so many times before down the ages.

31 OCTOBER

The mist lifted a trifle during the afternoon and I made another balloon ascent to 3,500 feet. From this altitude I had a superb view of Ypres, the fragmentary walls looking like innumerable tombstones. In fact Ypres viewed from that height looks like a vast Necropolis. The view over the battlefield was inexpressibly wondrous and grand. It is just as one's imagination would compare it. Although the visibility was bad, the misty atmosphere enhanced the terrible desolation and reality of this artificial hell, whereon thousands of lives are being expended and the resources of the world thrown. Imagine one's feelings suspended in a tiny rocking cradle, with the ruins of Ypres 3,500 feet below, in front a vast stretch of smoky misty flat desolation, criss-crossed with familiar tracks, and scintillating with innumerable red flashes. Looking back was a wondrous bird's eye over more peaceful landscapes, but peppered with little round white dots and almost equal-sized circular pools of water. The little white dots were an army in bivouac, and the pools, shell craters brimming with the recent rains.

Scarcely had we been in the air more than half an hour, when a fleet of Gothas (Boche planes) came over. They came down from the north and were heavily laden with bombs. When about two miles off they began releasing them on battery positions and roadways. We had a wonderful view of the results. As they flew over the landscape they left a trail of bursting bombs behind them. The ground rose in vast columns and resembled the effect produced by dropping huge stones in a calm pool. The whole fleet came directly over us, and as we could not see them on account of our gas bag, we had a few minutes of anxiety. Expecting to be shot down or ignited by tracer bullets, we stood on the rim of the basket ready to leap into space in a moment. Why they did not shoot us down is more than I can tell, but I felt a trifle sorry, even though they were the enemy, that such a good target should have escaped. We remained up a couple of hours, spotting on the fire of one of our batteries and telephoning down the results and giving them direction. At 4 p.m. the mist came over in a heavy veil and blocked further observation. The other balloons were being hauled down and we also followed. A cup of hot tea warmed us up immensely.

Captain Frank Hurley, Official Photographer, Australian Imperial Force

Far away beyond the front lines Hurley's scintillating red flashes signalled the product of an order issued this day by Sir Herbert Plumer, who demanded maximum British counter-battery fire. The balloons were slowly reeled down in turn; as the last one reached the ground, on the battlefield night was beginning to fall. There was no hot tea. In fact there was no line.

There was no front line; just an irregular chain of shell holes seldom in touch with one another, each occupied by men whose faces were blue with cold and whose teeth chattered and hands shook. All were wet to the skin and crouching in mud and water sometimes up to their waist, not daring to raise their heads for fear of enemy snipers. Here and there, lying behind mud heaps, lay our own snipers, watching for a glimpse of the enemy. A feeling of intense misery pervaded the area – and always that smell of decaying flesh which one could not ignore or forget. Curiously enough, the most poignant memory of the front line is just a tiny piece of army biscuit. In a large shell hole there was a machine gun and its team. It was sandbagged one side and water had to be baled out continuously. On the sandbagged side, a rubber groundsheet was hanging down. The sergeant asked in a hopeless way: 'Can anything be done about this man?' He lifted up the groundsheet which was covering a niche in the wall in which lay a soldier. His face was waxen and his eyes were closed. His tunic was covered with bloodstained mud and he was breathing very faintly. He had been hit four days before and there had been no possibility of evacuating him in any way. The machine gun crew had done all they could, bandaging him and rubbing his limbs to stop them becoming frostbitten. It was obvious that the wounded man was nearly dead, and when spoken to made no reply; but on his half-opened lips were little bits of army biscuit. That was all his fellow machine gunners had had to offer a mortally stricken man.

At that time there were a number of wounded men lying about on the knee-deep muddy battlefield and conditions were so impossible that no stretcher-bearers or carrying-party of any kind could rescue them. They lay dying in icy shell holes or in the open. It was so bitterly cold that they did not mercifully bleed to death but just lay there in hopeless misery. For six days one of our men, shot through both legs, lay out in No Man's Land which was periodically swept by rain, hail, snow, machine gun fire, and shrapnel from both sides. Each night Germans from a nearby shell hole crept out to give him a warm drink, every drop of which they must have longed for themselves as their plight was as bad as that of the British.
MAJOR GEORGE WADE, 172ND MACHINE GUN COMPANY

In June, Sir Herbert Plumer had started the Flanders campaign with a siege, brilliantly prosecuted that resulted in a leap over the Messines Ridge in a matter of hours – a great platform for great things. Having taken over the reins in front of Ypres in late-August his progress became a walk; eight weeks later it was a crawl. What was required at this point was another dozen Messines-like mines planted beneath the Passchendaele Ridge. No such assistance was possible.

THE TIMES, SATURDAY, 27 OCTOBER 1917

PASSCHENDAELE HIGH GROUND WON
PROGRESS ALONG THE SPURS

THE FOLLOWING TELEGRAPHIC DESPATCHES WERE YESTERDAY RECEIVED FROM GENERAL HEADQUARTERS IN FRANCE:

11.19 A.M. – At 5:45 a.m. this morning, attacks were launched by the British and French Armies east, northeast, and north of Ypres.

The Allied troops are reported to be making satisfactory progress. Rain fell heavily during the latter part of the night, and is still continuing.

10.05 P.M. – Operations with limited objectives were undertaken by the British and French Armies early this morning on the Ypres battle-front.

After a fine day yesterday, with a fine drying wind, which gave the promise of improved conditions, the weather changed suddenly during the night. Heavy rain has fallen almost without break since a very early hour this morning.

Notwithstanding the great difficulties with which the Allied troops had to contend, considerable progress has been made and valuable positions have been won on the greater part of the fronts attacked.

EVENING

In Belgium there was no reaction by the enemy against our new positions. The number of prisoners taken by us during the operations this morning exceeds 200.

GERMAN REPORT:

FRONT OF CROWN PRINCE RUPPRECHT. – *The artillery duel was lively along the whole front in Flanders yesterday and during the night. Specially violent was the fire from Houthulst Wood as far as Hollebeke, where it increased in the morning to drumfire.*

Nocturnal local attacks by French and English failed everywhere before our lines.

According to reports at present to hand, enemy attacks have taken place at several points of the front since dawn.

EVENING – *Today's combats in Flanders developed into a great battle.*

Strong French and English attacks from Bixschoote to the Roulers-Ypres Railway, and on both sides of the Menin-Ypres road, broke down with heavy losses in our defensive zone, in spite of the enemy's repeated assaults.

Left
The November landscape of battle. Canadian pioneers take advantage of the early morning mist to carry out essential maintenance work.

There are some days which sort of lay themselves out to take the biscuit, such a one was today. To start with I have a wretched cough and throat, due to gas and also to our subaqueous mode of living. The Colonel asked me if I would like to go on leave now, but I should like December 20. But my word Christmas seems a long way off when you strike a show like this, and one feels tempted to take leave when offered. However, I expect it will be worth waiting for. It has rained in torrents all day, we were fighting at 3.30 this morning in a perfect deluge, until I was soaked and coated in mud. The mud which was horrible before became absolutely impassable. I had to get two guns into new places, one stuck muzzle deep in mud, and for hours defeated our most frenzied efforts. Finally the Hun strafed blue hell out of us unceasingly throughout the day. Time after time he blew the candles out in our cubby holes, which means close shooting. There were crumps here and crumps there, oh we had a jolly old time. Our cubby hole got flooded out, our cook abandoned us. I had sent my servant down to the wagon line for a spell. Finally, just as it got dark and I was changing my sodden garments, one of the dugouts got blown in with a direct hit, and out we went in the mud and dark to excavate the survivors. The place was absolutely wrecked; the wonder was that a single occupant was left alive. Horrible groans from inside and with great difficulty we at last extracted some battered looking figures and hurried them off on stretchers to the dressing station during which process, we all, including the wounded man, fell repeatedly into shell holes full of water, cost me five casualties which makes a great difference as I am only keeping two or three men per gun up in this savoury spot. We returned to our shelter and found it, alas, submerged, torrents of rain . . . awful life.
MAJOR C.E.L. LYNE, 119 BRIGADE, ROYAL FIELD ARTILLERY.

By November the battlefield was entirely untraversable other than by constructed routes. There was no shelter other than captured pillboxes and elephant shelters. Such was the case everywhere forward of a line drawn between Zonnebeke and Langemarck. Even relief was no guarantee of freedom from strife.

3 NOVEMBER 1917.

The boys have come out of the trenches and I have been very busy since as I have now six officers and six servants to look after. Fritz came over again last night, five raids, the moon was out for 7 hours and it was as light as day. He did not do much damage but he dropped them a bit too close for my liking. We lay here and hear him overhead and there are generally about 20 of them. There is no cover anywhere and I shake like a jelly, laying down under a ground sheet which is the only cover to stop the bits of bomb. Not very comforting and we all get the wind up. Our guns seem to be fed up with these raids and they do not trouble to fire at them much. Our boys are having a terrible time in the trenches. They are up to the waist in mud and water, each side of the roads there are dead horses and men, carts, motor lorries etc in the hundreds. Our transport have managed to get the rations up to the boys and have only lost two horses and one man up to now. This Menin Road is a cobbled road, or was before the shells smashed it up. I have only had to go up there once and I do not want to go again but I may have to go to-morrow morning. The Somme was bad enough but this is a thousand times worse. The censor, if he reads his letters, may say that I am chancing my arm for sending this news. All I can say to him is let the papers publish what the troops out here are really doing, also the torture they are going through, then perhaps the public will realise that a man out here in the fighting forces deserves better treatment than he gets. There are men now in the trenches fast dying of cold, they go sick, see the doctor, go back and try and stick it until they get relieved. I am not running our doctor down, he is a good man but he has his orders from others. When the men do get relieved some of them find that they are too ill to walk all the way back to where the regiment is going and they have to stop for a rest on the road where no one wants to stop but only run, and while resting on the road they might get hit by a piece of shell and then they may be taken on a stretcher to the dressing station, that is if we

have any brave stretcher bearers who are willing to risk their lives.
PRIVATE D.J. SWEENEY, 1ST LINCOLNSHIRE REGIMENT

The Salient was an all-consuming monster. The three field companies looking after communications in the newly arrived 1st Division sector on the northern flank, for instance (occupying the Yser Canal–Langemarck–Poelcappelle corridor), were amongst many other tasks presented with the maintenance of 35,000 yards of duckboard track. The work required a daily supply of 1,000 boards just to keep up with extensions and damage. Owing to transport difficulties and shelling, the positions of major RE dumps, where such material was stored in quantity, had to be fixed far behind the line. Working parties thus frequently covered 15 miles moving to and from work, always carrying tools, boards and other ungainly materiel on the forward journey. Hence the vast numbers of disgruntled infantry required even when ostensibly out of the line 'on rest'. The message that this tedious and dangerous work was ultimately for their own benefit was constantly repeated. Gradually the tracks snaked their way further up the slopes of the Passchendaele Ridge, where on 4 November the 3rd Canadian Division was relieved by the 1st.

We went forward up there over the old duck walks. We could see a plank road that had been built of nothing else but planks and the guns were moving up there, and ammunition, but we had nothing else to do but just walk the little duck walk which was just like a lumber sidewalk about two feet wide and probably eight feet long, in sections. Every once in a while we'd come to one (and I came to one of them) that wasn't there and step off of it. I had a Lewis gun on my back. We had been told to keep two paces apart in our walking. If it was convenient, of course, we'd be able to do it, on account of the shelling, you know. I happened to fall off with my gun. A young officer was behind me and he started to try to drag me out. There was another little incident there that I could never forget. The officer was trying to pull me out. I created an obstruction and the men were bunching up. Some kind friend at the back, I won't use his expression, but he did say, 'Leave the son of a gun there.' That's what he should have said if he was going to be polite. It was better to lose one man than a dozen. They got me out anyway and we carried on up into Passchendaele. We got out from there quite late in the evening and we were told to dig in. It was a case of every man for himself because the gunfire was so heavy. I think our battalion headquarters was in a big German pill box, one of these concrete creations, and if my memory serves me correctly, I may be wrong here, we lost our regimental sergeant major that night due to the fact that a shell exploded just about in front of the door of headquarters. I think his name was Thatcher. They hammered the daylights out of us all night long. We were trying to dig, and as fast as we dug one shovelful of mud out two rolled in, but we did eventually establish ourselves and then at daybreak we got the word, 'You're in the wrong place. Advance two hundred yards.' We advanced the two hundred yards losing quite a few men. We went in to take a nice trench in gravel and got out of the mud for a while. It was a little higher, I guess.*
PRIVATE W.E. CURTIS, 10TH BATTALION,
CANADIAN EXPEDITIONARY FORCE

Private Curtis' testimony illustrates what the commanders wished to achieve – organized jumping-off positions on higher and drier contours, for from here not only would the ground be easier to negotiate in attack, but a known line made the artillery's job simpler – and much safer for the assaulting troops. 'Line', however, was entirely the wrong word. It was simply a series of shell holes, some connected, all brimming with water and mud.

Above
Repairing smashed duckboard tracks.

Right
As the campaign extended into the winter months, the evacuation of wounded became ever slower and more exhausting. Canadian stretcher bearers struggle through the mire.

On the ridge the Germans knew not how long their enemy was prepared to keep attacking. It did not matter. The High Command was fully aware of conditions and losses, but, like Sir Douglas Haig, they too simply had no choice. Just as the British had to keep pushing to gain the heights, so the Germans must deny them. The situation was most worrying for Haig because for weeks there had been no sign of defences crumbling – like the Somme every metre of ground was fought for, every raid echoed, and enemy artillery still almost as effective as at any time in the entire battle. It was a question of time: how long would or could Haig, Plumer and Currie keep battering at Ludendorff's 'Iron Wall'? The entire army was exhausted with the effort, not just through fighting but in simply suffering the unrelenting stress of the Salient. At this time, Second Army was employing the equivalent of 2 battalions of attached infantry, plus 10 Field Companies, 7 Pioneer battalions, 7 Tunnelling Companies, 4 Army Troops Companies and 2 Labour Companies – *on roads alone*. It was an effort without which the offensive simply could not be continued. The tracery of tracks and roads was mirrored in the work of the Signals who strove night and day to keep communications open and extend new lines over captured ground to new battery positions. It is seldom noted just how difficult and dangerous a task this was. Overwhelming shellfire still remained the sole foundation of success. Artillery communication networks had already long outgrown those of the infantry, but seldom at Third Ypres, particularly in the latter stages, did signallers know how many advanced (1-2 kilometres behind the front line) field-gun batteries were to be installed for each attack. Naturally, infantry commanders

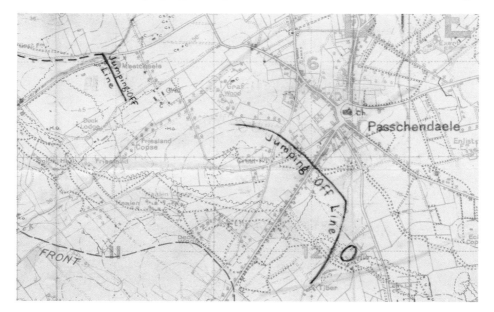

Left
The attack that finally captured Passchendaele village. The jumping-off lines for the 1st Canadian Division (top) and 2nd Canadian Division (bottom) separated by the impassable ground of the Ravebeek valley.

required the maximum number that ground and transport conditions would allow, and to be efficient each and every battery *had* to be made a part of the delicate signals system, for innumerable lives depended upon it. Where cables had been buried to maximum depth the signals officer could almost rest easy (such breaks in these lines were nightmarish to repair), but there were 'forward limits' as well as geological restrictions for deep buries, and the vast majority of lines serving the most advanced positions were simply laid on the surface, usually alongside the infantry and mule tracks. They too consumed hundreds of men in maintenance. And still none of this industry could yet be hidden from enemy eyes. By their accuracy, German gunners had long made it all too clear they could easily delineate between track, battery, road, waterline and cable work, and select preferred targets both at will and at times most inconvenient for the British. Not only were lines made obvious by the strings of personnel laying and repairing them, but locations of forward relay stations and signal offices were often confined to the one single form of cover the battlefield now possessed: captured German pillboxes and blockhouses. Cables were regularly broken as soon as laid and the shell-torn, flooded, gas saturated ground claimed the lives of linesmen every day – men who never had the opportunity of shooting back. Signallers spent hours slithering in and out of shell holes repairing lines and were almost permanently soaked. Now, as the thermometer refused to venture above the 50-degree mark and wind chill made conditions yet more miserable, all human life on the surface was simply becoming untenable.

I had to go to ---------- yesterday and I saw some terrible sights. I saw motor lorries sunk in the mud right over the wheels, horses with part of their heads showing above the swamps, two tanks were buried and the men who were in them will never be able to tell the tale of the fight they had, but they were heroes. I have never seen so many dead before and they were mostly Germans, we are burying them as quickly as possible but the weather has been so bad that we have been unable to get to some of them and a lot have been buried in the bogs and that accounts for so many men who are missing. I should have liked you to have seen my overcoat two days ago. It was four times its weight with mud and water and my puttees and trousers were mud up to my waist and boots full of mud. If you put a pair of dry socks on they are the same in about ten minutes. It is impossible to sleep as it is getting so cold now and it is not too good lying on a muddy floor with a wet water sheet.
PRIVATE D.J. SWEENEY, 1ST LINCOLNSHIRE REGIMENT

RESUMPTION

The next step to annexe Passchendaele village and much of the rest of the crest to the north was rescheduled a little later than originally intended in order to make sure that forward roads and tracks had been progressed far enough to both deliver and feed the necessary guns. The chosen day was Tuesday, 6 November. The sectors guarding the ridge crest contained a lesser concentration of pillboxes than those of earlier actions; without the mutually supporting crossfire they were proving somewhat easier to overcome, but a clutch of strong points were potentially treacherous. A host of small localized assaults were made before the 6th, principally by elements of the 63rd (Royal Naval) Division and 3rd Canadians. Some simply required the capture of a single pillbox to straighten an awkward kink.

Above
Pillboxes – the only safe and relatively dry accommodation on the battlefield.

One such venture was against Graf House, a single pillbox perched on the margin of quagmire and ridge. The experiences of the unit designated to eliminate it – at night – can be extrapolated to illustrate the bewildering battlefield conditions that everyone now faced.

Every man sitting or squatting in that trench knew two things. First, that McIntyre had no sure idea of where the pillbox was. Second, that he had had too much rum. He told us it was not far to the pillbox, that the main attack was to be on a strong point called Graf House, that one party was to be on the bank of the Gravenstafel-Mosselmarkt Road to protect our advance. There would not be any barrage. We were to work up a road as quietly as possible and to reach our objective at two a.m. The Stokes guns were moving into position and would send over salvos if they received a signal. When he had finished talking, McIntyre climbed out of the trench and had another session with Clark. Then he called to me. 'You are to follow close to me all the way,' he said. 'When we have our objective I want you to take the message back to company headquarters. I can't trust it to a runner.'

'How far is it up the road to the pillbox?' I asked.

McIntyre said it was about one hundred and fifty yards. Clark said it was twice that far, and to the right of the road. McIntyre said he was wrong. He had seen the map. It was left of the road. Never through the war was I more sickened and discouraged than at that moment. The whole affair was cock-eyed. We were new in the sector. None knew the terrain. None knew what defences the German had or his strength. The place after dark was a swampy wilderness without anything to use as a guide. Half the men had never been in an attack, and that included the officers. Furthermore, in those few minutes I discovered that Clark had also had too much rum.

Word came to get ready. Every man was to have two Mills bombs to throw if need be. Baillie came and shook hands with me, a long hard clasp without a word spoken. Then I was amazed when Ira Black came and whispered he was glad we were on our way. The waiting was deadly and now we would have action and get from the hateful swamp when it was over. Then a sergeant came with a jug of rum and every man who would take it had a stiff jolt. At least we found the road. It wasn't much. Shell fire had almost erased it in spots. We started in four little parties, McIntyre leading on the left. I was crawling directly behind him and told him if I saw anything of the enemy I would pull his foot.

There was quite a drop of bank on our left. McIntyre did not look left or right but kept scrambling along as fast as possible. I peered over the bank from time to time and suddenly saw three or four Germans raise their heads no more than twenty yards from us. I seized McIntyre's foot to signal him. He yanked it away and spoke angrily. The Germans fired instantly. A bullet creased the top of Lugar's head, slicing his scalp and causing him to be temporarily insane. Hale and I had to hold him down by main force, as had he raised he would have been shot. In our struggle Hale raised up higher than he thought and was likewise creased with a bullet. Now it was Stewart, the stretcher bearer, and I holding Lugar, but he began to quiet and the moment I could let go of him I threw my grenades over the bank. Both exploded as they went down, and the Hun shooting stopped at once.

The next thing was to get Lugar's bombs to replace mine, which I did. McIntyre had never stopped and was quite a distance ahead. Clark's party kept up with him. Brown had crawled forward and now he and I left the group and ran to catch up with McIntyre. Machine-guns opened up on all sides. The night was an uproar. We dove into the mud and saw the signal go up for the Stokes support. The German Maxim stopped firing and we jumped and started running again. There was a flaming white-hot instant – and oblivion!

When I recovered consciousness my head was splitting with pain and a terrible nausea had seized my stomach. The Stokes shell had dropped beside us, throwing me bodily across the road and knocking Brown down. He was rolled over on his back, feeling for wounds, as I saw him. All around us was a clamour of machine-guns, bombs and rifles. I heard McIntyre shouting

'Five rounds rapid!' Then his voice shut off abruptly. I discovered my nose had been bleeding, and when I tried to get up I collapsed again with dizziness.

The burst of shooting stilled. There were no more bomb explosions. But far on our left another eruption of shooting began to dominate the night. Brown had tried to stand and had just slumped down again when we heard plunging noises in the mud and two dim figures came toward us, puffing and blowing, carrying something and grunting in conversation. They were Germans, big men, and had a machine-gun on a tripod. They went past us, apparently thinking us dead, and set up their weapon about thirty feet from us. One man yanked at a long cartridge belt, while the other grunted something. I pulled the pin from one of my grenades, held it for a count of two, then hurled it at the Germans and flattened myself in the mud.

The bomb burst between the two gunners. Not a bit of metal touched Brown or myself. One German never moved but lay on his back, dead. The other pawed at his side feebly for a time, then was still.

PRIVATE WILL BIRD, 42ND BATTALION (ROYAL
HIGHLANDERS), CANADIAN EXPEDITIONARY FORCE

Graf House was conquered, then snatched back by the enemy. Later that same morning, at 5.30 a.m., two fortified farmhouses, Vanity and Vine Cottages, received similar treatment, the latter also proving too difficult to hold. All these 'minor' actions took place with the intermittent accompaniment of the heaviest preliminary bombardment and fiercest counter-battery exchange that Allied guns could furnish. To the surprise (and delight) of probably every man in the Salient, the five days prior to the second battle were practically rainless. It was November, however, and the mud declined to dry, instead becoming more glue-like. But the unexpected window at least offered the gunners

a singularly generous period in which to establish adequate pits and platforms, and lay and register their weapons ready to torture another narrow ribbon of Flanders. The Germans knew what was coming. As their artillery ceaselessly searched roads and tracks, still the stretcher bearers were struggling to find and clear wounded from earlier actions.

They were magnificent. You would see them slowly picking their way down the duckboard tracks in the midst of an inferno – never ducking, or laying down their precious burden. Then they would disappear altogether in a cloud of smoke as some big shell dropped close, and when it disappeared on they came at their slow walk. On this duck-board the normal ran as hard as he could, flinging himself down in the mud every few yards at the shriek of an oncoming shell – but nothing moved the bearers. Of course, their casualties were very heavy and many, many wounded were hit again, or killed when on the stretchers along with their bearers. The ordinary public at home seem to think that the R.A.M.C. personnel do this work – they do not, never working in front of the advanced dressing stations, it is the regimental bearers who have the hellish time of slowly walking with the wounded through an inferno of shell fire.

LIEUTENANT DOUGLAS WIMBERLEY,
232ND MACHINE GUN COMPANY

Strangely, whilst the troops waded through the mire before the ridge, much of the ground obliterated during the August attacks, now some 5 kilometres behind the line, had greened over under the reclaiming hand of nature. Many of the old trenches had been backfilled to facilitate road and rail links and precious timber was being salvaged from dugouts for reuse in the rash of new subterranean accommodation now being installed in the re-expanded Salient. Hosts of

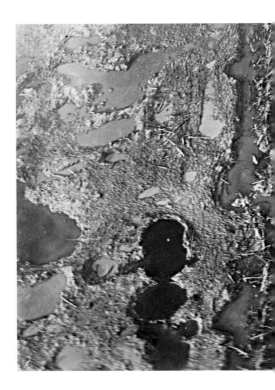

bridges of all shapes and sizes traversed the Yser Canal, and although well within range of German guns, hutted and tented camps were established in areas that had once lain immediately behind the British lines of 31 July.

The central thrust for 6 November was to be delivered by 1st and 2nd Canadian Infantry Divisions, all fresh troops. They had had the benefit of being able to practise the attack before moving into the line, a dubious rehearsal that took place under cover in aircraft hangars. Although I Anzac, IX and VIII Corps were in attendance on Passchendaele's immediate right, they were directed to feign attacks along the Broodseinde Ridge. On their right a small diversionary assault on the hated Polderhoek sector was handed to the unlucky troops of 95 Brigade, 5th Division (X Corps). Apart from his own guns, Sir Arthur Currie also had the use of all II Corps' artillery, Sir Claud Jacob's troops now being installed on the northern boundary.

Sir Douglas Haig had precious little time left to make a closing impression in Flanders. He was actively engaged in planning the tactically complex tank-based Cambrai offensive, and fighting the politico-military fires started by Lloyd George's decision to send more and more units from every arm of the services to Italy. The two men met in Paris on Sunday, 4 November. Haig's diary notes: 'gave LG a good talking to on several of the questions raised, and felt I got the best of the arguments'. He appears at this time to be satisfied with the way things were going in Flanders and especially with the lack of interference from the politicians. No more had been heard from the War Cabinet in Whitehall since the October meetings. Yes, they had met, talked, demanded

casualty figures, sucked their teeth, but again done nothing. Lacking the support of major military figures willing to put their money where their mouth was, and decry not only Sir Douglas Haig but many other respected senior commanders into the bargain, the Cabinet was still unwilling to act. The casualties for October had been deplorable, the worst of the campaign: more than 110,000 losses, with 22,777 on the 19th of the month alone – statistics that almost demanded comparability with the first day on the Somme. And the French had recently provided an extra lever, requesting British takeover of additional sectors of the Western Front. There was no finer opportunity for the Cabinet to act. Nothing again transpired. At the meeting of 2 November, however, they too could see just how close to taking Passchendaele the troops were. In fact, it was actually too late to make any difference. By not acting earlier the politicians had allowed the offensive to reach the delicate and dangerous point whereby the village and the ridge *must* now be taken, simply for future security. The responsibility for past, present and forthcoming loss in Flanders was therefore a shared one between political and military leadership.

Three months of campaigning was closing with a strategic whimper, but certainly not a tactical or symbolic one. When added to the ocean that swilled in the shell holes of the Salient, the fresh blood that was soon to be shed wrenching an extra few hundred metres of Flemish mud from German claws assured that the words Third Ypres would echo down the decades as an overwhelming tragedy. An end to the agony was in sight, but there would be no titanic climax to 1917. That was being hoped for elsewhere.

AN EXPEDIENT ATTACK

Sir Douglas Haig was satisfied and indeed excited by the preparations for the Cambrai venture. Why, given the season and the conditions at Ypres, was he investing so much hope in this fresh offensive – and in winter? The people of the British Empire desperately needed some kind of triumph to offset more than three months of grinding carnage and despair. Despite the glorified misinformation daily plastered across the press, via casualty lists, testimonies of the countless wounded, the disturbing ramblings of the shell-shocked and the opinions of those home on leave, civilian populations were beginning to realize certain truths about operations in Flanders.

I never got any leave whilst I was in France. That's over two years, but I was a prisoner for quite a bit of that time, of course. I never felt I'd earned it anyway, so I didn't feel envious of the blokes who got home. It often didn't do them a lot of good, you know. Some men would come back and say there was no point in going home because you couldn't talk to anyone. Where would you start? You couldn't make people understand. It was a different world, so they said nothing. What you read in the papers wasn't what was happening – we got them in the trenches too, so I know that's right. We laughed about it, I don't know why, because we should have been concerned, shouldn't we? One or two said they'd get home and couldn't socialise at all, just spent the time waiting for the day they had to come back. We had no money to go out on the town and that, like some of the officers. Others said they tried to tell it like it was – but people either didn't believe them or didn't want to hear. I can understand that, I had it myself for years and years after the war. How do you put that lot into words for people who have never seen it – and don't want to hear it anyway? It just can't be imagined. I can't do it today, and I've had seventy years to think about it. I think if I'd had had leave after our attacks at Passchendaele I think I wouldn't have wanted to talk about it either for fear of worrying folk about the way things were going and being done. Looking back, it was disorganised, but I didn't think that then: I had faith in everyone who was my senior. We had pride as well, you know, and that's a very big thing. I did what I was told without asking questions, like we all did. I suppose you could say I knew my place. That's the military way; it wouldn't work any other way. I did notice when I got home in 1919 no one wanted to hear the truth. It was a funny world in the days just after the war. I'd been knocked about a bit in March [1918] and my face was scarred. I tried to hide it because I felt ashamed, to this day I don't know why, but kids never stopped teasing you and calling you names. If you weren't there, you see, you could have no idea of what people had to do, what they saw, what they had to live with. It's the same with all wars – they're all fought by kids, and the memories can never leave you.

PRIVATE BERT FEARNS, 2/6TH LANCASHIRE FUSILIERS

Cambrai was a distraction. Another prime reason the attacks were contemplated at all, however, was because the ground in the region had never been fought over, and being chalk based was free draining and dry. With luck, the gently rolling hills would provide good going for man and especially machine. A greater contrast with Ypres could hardly be found. The tactics were specially devised to benefit the massed assault of 380 tanks, the first in history. They included no preliminary barrage that would chew the terrain into porage. Sir Douglas Haig had faith in tanks, having always been a devotee. He knew too that when Passchendaele was at last over it would never be trumpeted as a victory, for all were tragically aware the village had been tentatively earmarked for conquest on Day One of the Third Ypres offensive – more than ninety days

Above

Hussar Camp was situated near Frezenberg Ridge, just behind the lines from which the original attacks commenced in July.

earlier. Now, to combat gloomy public mood and an inevitable onslaught of Lloyd George's powerful rhetoric, he was prepared to take a chance to end 1917 on a high note, and that note could only be sounded at Cambrai. First, though, business in Flanders must be concluded.

6TH NOVEMBER

Practice barrage at 4 a.m. then all quiet. At 5.45 a real barrage started and over went the boys to take Passchendaele which we have been after for so long. Big preparations being made in Artillery. What a bombardment, Fritz replying very quickly. Relieved at 8 a.m. and stayed at fatigues all day, it was the hottest place I have been in, we were not allowed to leave the guns. We lost four men wounded during the day and very lucky to escape so lightly. The boys took all their objectives by midday but it made Fritz very angry by the stuff he sent back.
GUNNER E.J. DRANE, 197TH SIEGE BATTERY, ROYAL GARRISON ARTILLERY

Zero hour on 6 November was fixed for 6 a.m., the troops moving into the line on the night of the 4th. Across no man's land German reliefs had taken place, the exhausted 39th Reserve Infantry Regiment sidling out to be replaced by a newly arrived 11th (from Champagne). Their task was simply to protect the high ground until the weather finally beat the enemy. Like the Lancashire Fusiliers on the 9th and the Australians on 12 October, Canadian patrols had actually entered Passchendaele village on the night of the 30th, returning to report a German withdrawal. They had actually observed reliefs taking place. No action was taken because everyone was too aware that the enemy attached quite as much importance to the ridge as Currie, Plumer and Haig. If proof were needed, it was

falling incessantly from the sky in the form of high explosive, gas and shrapnel.

Another growing concern was the increased attention of hostile aircraft. As the weeks had passed, more and more attacks had been made on troops occupying ever more exposed positions from which they dare not move during daylight. From dawn to dusk the troops had been bombed and machine-gunned by German scouts and latterly the Gothas had appeared, dropping a new form of frightfulness upon dispersed but vulnerable troops: clusters of small charges. There was nowhere to go and nothing to be done but cringe beneath one's groundsheet, for to uncover a Lewis gun or rifle in retaliation put them at risk of becoming hopelessly mud-caked in moments. The troops therefore elected to stay quiet, grit their teeth and save the weapons for the battle ahead.

Everything once more depended upon the guns, most of which were now firing at extreme range and with maximum charge. Some enemy batteries were out of reach. Tactically, the infantry had few alternatives left in the box. Against the pillbox threat, fire and movement was still effective and the troops were undoubtedly good at it – but now there was the mud. Fire was possible, but movement? Creeping closer by slopping from shell hole to shell hole not only caked everything in filth, it put the troops at risk of becoming mired, or even drowned. So how was one to negotiate the perils of the crater-field and reach a position from which the close-combat phase might begin? Currie chose to try something unexpected but highly dangerous. He issued orders that before zero his men should form up in no man's land under cover of darkness. The attack too, was to take place almost an hour before dawn.

Had the enemy caught wind of the plan, carnage might have followed (as with the German Guards at Broodseinde), but given the dire conditions they probably looked upon the idea as unlikely. Although suffering from random shellfire, the Canadians managed largely to avoid the attentions of two hostile barrages, one at 4.30 a.m. and a second just after zero, each dropping relatively harmlessly to the rear. Fortunately their own protective screen of shells and mortars was considerably better deployed than most barrages of the previous week. First, in front of Passchendaele the German front line was deluged with drumfire and it included another surprise: the deluge lasted just two minutes before moving on. The unsuspected speed and surprise of the infantry attack from advanced positions caused the line to fall quickly with little resistance; then the Canadians, on better ground now, swept into the village on the very heels of their barrage, so close that enemy SOS shellfire again fell behind them.

The shock effect was telling, and numbers of German troops were seen to bolt rearwards only to be caught by their own counter-barrage and defence-in-depth machine guns, the gunners naturally believing anyone emerging through the smoke and fumes to be British or Canadian. Almost 800 metres of ground was seized, with consolidation of the village completed by 9.00 a.m. In the left sector of the attack, two battalions (1st and 2nd) of the 1st Canadian Division reached the shoulder of the plateau by again advancing up the only negotiable piece of ground, the narrow ridge spur separating the Ravebeek and the Lekerboterbeek. It presented an attacking front only 350 metres wide, but the troops annexed the hamlets of Mosselmarkt and Goudberg, and

drove on, surrounding and rooting entire garrisons from every pillbox before coming to rest at their own objective at 7.45 a.m. To the left, the customary story of every flank attack of the campaign unfolded once more. The British II Corps was taking part with artillery only, leaving just one battalion of Canadians, the 3rd, to move across the torn and sodden pasture and woodland in front of Vapour Farm and Vine Cottages, and on up the slope ahead towards the 50-metre contour – the top of the ridge. They made poor progress

Left
German troops forced to find rest in the most primitive of cover.

Right
60-pounder guns in action in precarious and unstable positions near Langemarck.

and lost heavily, advancing only by linking with more successful neighbouring units. Once more, it left a sharp bend in the final Allied line.

On the Anzac-held southern flank south of Passchendaele, furious artillery activity fooled the Germans into thinking a major assault was imminent on a front stretching from Broodseinde to Zandvoorde. The ploy was useful for several hours, until revealed to be a hoax when no infantry assault transpired. By then the village was in tight Canadian grasp. Afterwards the German guns turned their attentions on lost ground but with little profit and through the afternoon a series of counter-attacks was easily driven off. By about 7.30 p.m. calm began to descend. Over 700 Canadians lay dead. The sole British endeavour of the day, a fifth attempt to straighten the line in the Polderhoek sector, was yet again a costly washout. Whilst mopping up was still progress on the chaotic battlefield, night fell and the stretcher bearers moved in once more.

We went up after dark and when we went up we got up to the front line and they had quite a few wounded up around in there. But the four of us brought out one wounded man and we had an awful job getting him out. You see everything was pitch black and there was still lots of Jerries around in those shell holes and that, you see, that had been missed and they were taking potshots at you from the shell holes.

You could only go about twenty feet and you had to put the stretcher down and take a rest. You see the mud was knee deep up at Ypres: first one guy would slip into a shell-hole and somebody else would go, it's a wonder the man ever stayed on the stretcher. Of course he hung on on both sides of the stretcher, he was wounded in the leg, but that man really stuck it. I don't know who he was or what his name was; I might have known at the time. He had a hard job hanging on to the stretcher because there was one or the other of us slipping into a shell hole, and it took us — I don't know now what time it was — but we got him out by day-

light. By the time we got down to the dressing station on the plank road there it was daylight and we started up about eight o'clock at night. It took so long to get up in there and the tapes [to show where they were] had been blown away, when you come to the end of the tape well you had to go and find the other end. Somebody had to get out and scout around and find out where the other end of it was. It took us a long time to get up there but we got there.
PRIVATE WALLACE CARROLL, 15TH BATTALION (48TH HIGHLANDERS), CANADIAN EXPEDITIONARY FORCE

The attacks had taken the front line well onto the ridge-top plateau, but not quite far enough to offer security. Broodseinde Ridge was firmly consolidated all the way to the village; now a few acres of extra ground to the north were required. For three days consolidation and preparation took place. The great Cambrai tank experiment was just ten days away, so it was decided that the next attack must conclude the Third Battle – it had to succeed. During these few days Sir Herbert Plumer ended his long association with Second Army and the Ypres and Messines salients; the great tactician was off to Italy to command five British divisions in the fallout following Caporetto. On 19 November he was replaced by Sir Henry Rawlinson who had spent the summer and autumn kicking his heels waiting to command the aborted venture on the Belgian coast.

For the final movement of the deadly ballet in the mud, the Canadians (elements of 1st and 2nd Divisions once more) were to be assisted on the left by the British 1st Division. Now shifted to Ypres from the coast and fresh to the contest, they were allotted the dubious honour of holding the dreaded left flank. As usual, all three units formed up on an irregular line of short trenches and shell holes. It was pouring with rain, as it had done all night.

10TH NOVEMBER

At the guns again before daybreak to carry in shells (bye the bye this phrase 'carry in shells' means to carry shells from the lorry from the nearest point they can get to the guns, sometimes the roads are dotted with shell holes and it is a very long carry, each shell weighing 100 lbs). We took over the gun at 6 a.m. and learned the boys are going over again. We finished the barrage at 8 o'clock, standing in the gunpit talking to our pals and Fritz was shelling a road nearby when a Silent Percy* burst in our gunpit, killed poor Hartley, Yeldham and Skellon and wounded 6 others, me included. I shall never forget the sight. Sergeant Arthur was the only one left and the strangest thing was that while walking from our billet that morning to take over, I told Sergeant Arthur I had a feeling I should not return to that billet.
GUNNER E.J. DRANE, 197TH SIEGE BATTERY,
ROYAL GARRISON ARTILLERY
[ACTING BOMBARDIER ERNEST HARTLEY, GUNNER A.E.
YELDHAM AND GUNNER S. SKELLON ARE BURIED
SIDE BY SIDE IN WHITE HOUSE CEMETERY]

With the British and Canadian artillery under severe pressure from counter-battery fire, the attacks went in at 6.45 a.m. On the left the 1st Division got well on to the ridge, then in the confusion contrived to split their two leading battalions, the 1st South Wales Borderers veering right, the 2nd Royal Munster Fusiliers, left. The Germans counter-attacked into the gap, cutting off the Munsters, of whom more than 400 were killed, wounded or missing, and clawing back the top of the spur around Goudberg Copse. British gains were again minimal, measured in mere yards. The Borderers, with only marginally fewer casualties, came under such pressure from the

* Silent Percy, Silent Susie or Rubber-heeled Percy:
German 4.5-inch high-velocity shell, practically inaudible
in flight.

Above
British prisoners are marched back
towards Roulers (Roeselare).

Left
The results of British harassing fire in the
German rear areas: a transport team
suffers at the hands of the guns.

now exposed left flank and were forced to retire to their original starting point. The result can clearly be seen by the curious shape of the 10 November line on the map. On the Borderers' right, astride the Passchendaele–Westroosebeke road, 2 and 4 Canadian Brigades again achieved their objectives – another advance of almost 500 metres, gaining a further jumble of pulverized ruins. And that was where the battle for Passchendaele and the Third Battle of Ypres officially closed.

We arrived at Poperinghe that night at six o'clock. It was dark, a drizzling rain was falling, and the mud was thick. We could hear the big guns firing, and the men were coming and going in all directions. We took a hasty farewell of one another and then parted. No one we met cared whether we had come from Italy or were going to Jericho. The men did not know where their headquarters were, and I was particularly anxious not to find mine. I went over to the Officers' Club and secured a shakedown in the garret, but, as I heard that our Division had made an attack that day, I determined to go up to the line. I started off after dinner in an ambulance to the old mill at Vlamertinghe, where there was a repetition of the sights and sounds which I had experienced there on two previous occasions. Later on, I went forward in another ambulance through Ypres to an advanced dressing station. Then I started to walk up the terrible muddy roads till I came to the different German pill-boxes which had been converted into headquarters for the battalions. Finally, after wading through water and mud nearly up to my knees, I found myself the next afternoon wandering through the mud and by the shell holes and miserable trenches near Goudberg Copse, with a clear view of the ruins of Passchendaele, which was held by another division on our right. The whole region was unspeakably horrible. Rain was falling, the dreary waste of shell-ploughed mud, yellow and clinging, stretched off into the distance as far as the eye could see. Bearer parties, tired and pale, were carrying out the wounded on stretchers, making a journey of several miles in doing so. The

bodies of dead men lay here and there where they had fallen in the advance. I came across one poor boy who had been killed that morning. His body was covered with a shiny coating of yellow mud, and looked like a statue made of bronze. He had a beautiful face, with finely shaped head covered with close curling hair, and looked more like some work of art than a human being. The huge shell holes were half full of water often reddened with human blood and many of the wounded had rolled down into the pools and been drowned. As I went on, someone I met told me that there was a wounded man in the trenches ahead of me. I made my way in the direction indicated and shouted out asking if anybody was there. Suddenly I heard a faint voice replying, and I hurried to the place from which the sound came. There I found sitting up in the mud of the trench, his legs almost covered with water, a lad who told me that he had been there for many hours. I never saw anything like the wonderful expression on his face. He was smiling most cheerfully, and made no complaint about what he had suffered. I told him I would get a stretcher, so I went to some trenches not far away and got a bearer party and a stretcher and went over to rescue him. The men jumped down into the trench and moved him very gently, but his legs were so numb that although they were hit he felt no pain. One of the men asked him if he was only hit in the legs. He said, 'Yes,' but the man looked up at me and pulling up the boy's tunic showed me a hideous wound in his back. They carried him off happy and cheerful. Whether he ever recovered or I do not know. That was our last attack at Passchendaele. Our Division had taken its final objective. The next morning, the infantry were to come out of the line, so in the late afternoon I returned with some stretcher bearers. Several times shells came near enough to splatter us with mud, and here and there I turned aside to bury those for whom graves had just been prepared. At the front that day, a runner and I had joined in a brief burial service over the body of a gallant young officer lying where he fell on the side of a large shell-hole. As I uttered the words, 'I am the Resurrection and the Life, saith the Lord,' it seemed to me that the lonely wind bore them over that region of gloom and death as if it longed to carry the message of

From Primus Dugout OP
Passchendaele Ridge
March 1918
Sheet 28 D 12 c 2.6

Tiber

Vienna Cott

Ypres - Roulers railway

Ypres-Roulers railway

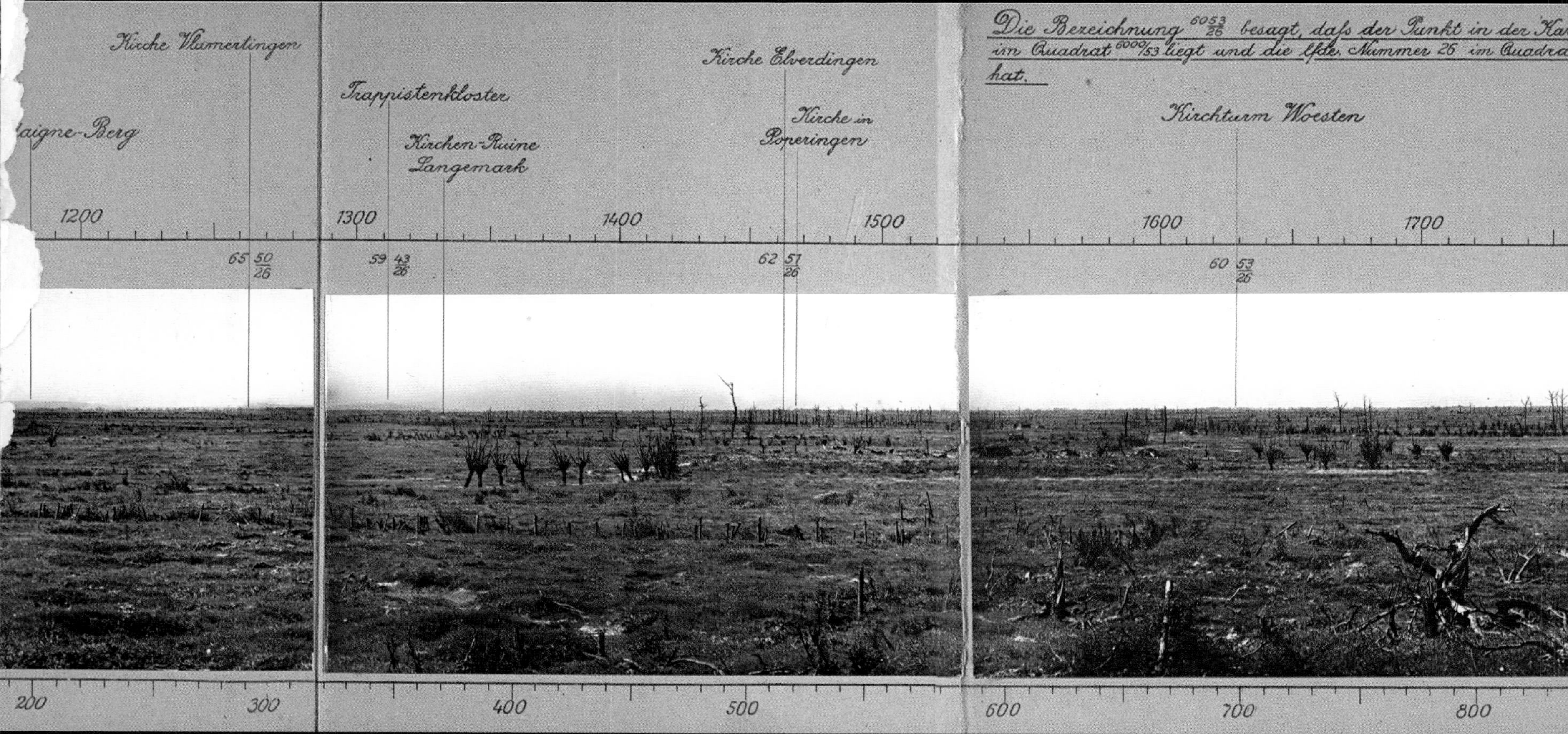

Die Bezeichnung 6053/26 besagt, dafs der Punkt in der Ka
im Quadrat 6000/53 liegt und die lfde. Nummer 26 im Quadra
hat.
Kirche Vlamertingen
aigne-Berg
Trappistenkloster
Kirchen-Ruine Langemark
Kirche Elverdingen
Kirche in Poperingen
Kirchturm Woesten
1200
1300
1400
1500
1600
1700
65 50/26
59 43/26
62 57/26
60 53/26
200
300
400
500
600
700
800

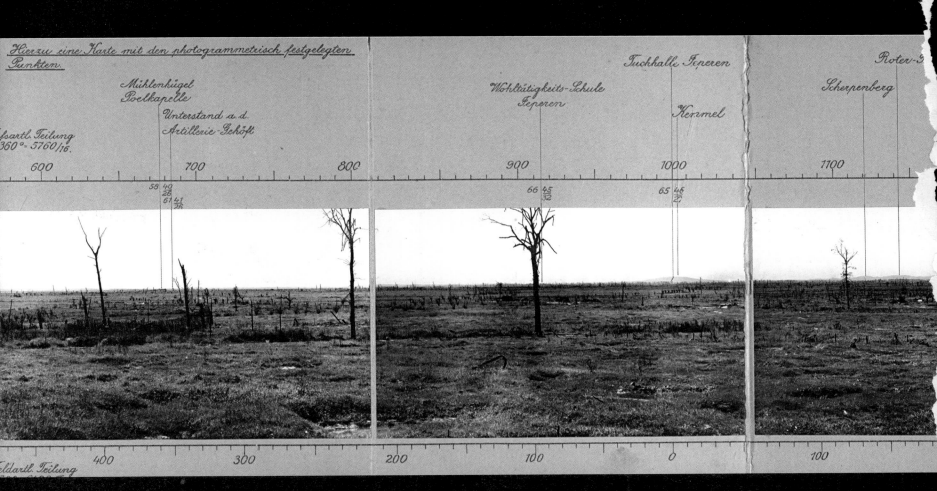

Hierzu eine Karte mit den photogrammetrisch festgelegten Punkten.

Tuchhalle Jeperen

Roter-

Mühlenhügel
Poelkapelle

Wohltätigkeits-Schule
Jeperen

Scherpenberg

Unterstand a. d.
Artillerie-Gehöft

Kemmel

...sartl. Teilung
360° = 5760/16.

600   700   800   900   1000   1100

58 40   66 45   65 46
28   32   27
61 41
26

400   300   200   100   0   100

...ldartl. Teilung

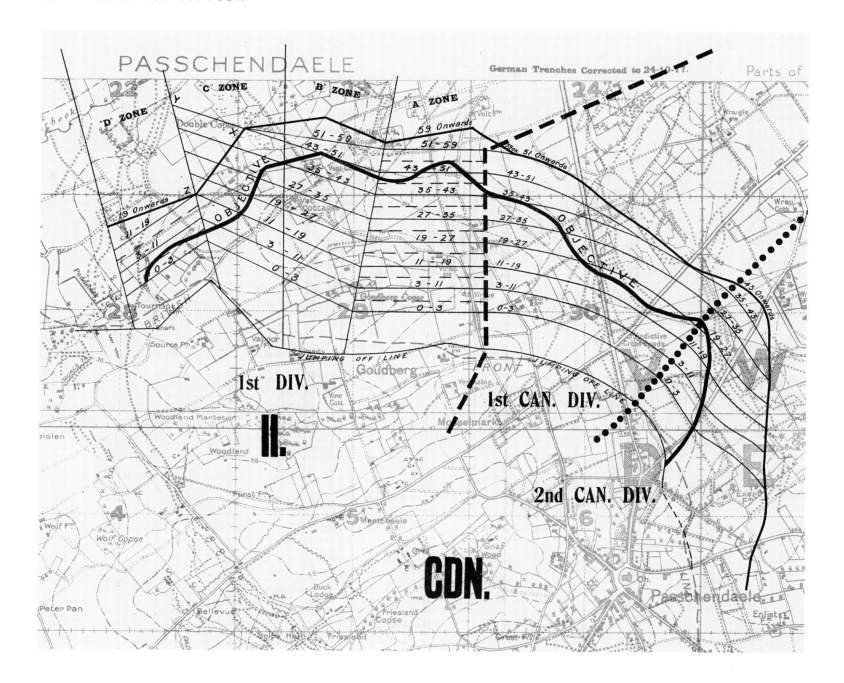

Previous pages
The promised land?
Panorama 131 taken through
a slit in an observation hood
in Primus, a British dugout
tunnelled beneath the crest
of the ridge.

Left
The final barrage of the battle
was designed for 10
November attacks by 1st
Division (British II Corps) and
1st and 2nd Canadian
Divisions.

Right
The mortal remains of
Passchendaele village after its
capture, showing Siegfried
shelters.

Below
The final line attained on the
day after the campaign came
ostensibly to an end. The first
things to be marked on new
maps were, as always, the
sites of potable water
supplies.

Inside pages
The German view from
Schaap Balie mill in June
1918. The entire May
1915–July 1917 salient is once
again their property.

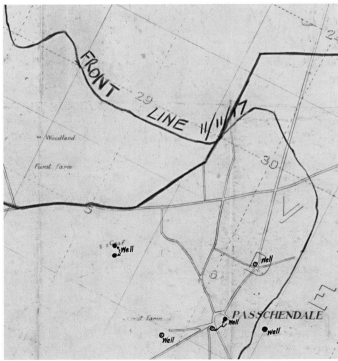

hope far away to the many sad hearts in Canada whose loved ones will lie, until the end, in unknown graves at Passchendaele.
Canon F.G. Scott DSO, Senior Chaplain to
1st Canadian Division

The result of the final two weeks of bloody endeavour was an elongated salient with a protruding bulbous nose – a nose the Germans would find all too easy to tweak. Whilst newspapers across the entire English-speaking world trumpeted a glorious victory, hundreds of thousands of families felt the cost.

Then we came to a ruin where a man sat on a fragment of wall. I went to him and asked if he could spare a drink of water. He did not answer. He was not wounded, but absolutely everything in his mind was dead. I took his water bottle from his equipment, took it to Mickey and Hughes in turn, then took it back and replaced it.

We went on down the road and there came a salvo of 'whizz-bangs'. As the last soul-tearing smash crashed in my ears I saw Mickey spin and fall. I let go of Hughes and jumped to him. He had been hit in several places and could not live ten minutes.

'Mickey . . . Mickey!' I called his name and raised him up and he nestled to me like a child.

'I'm through,' he said. 'I don't want to kill people anyway. Tell my mother . . .'
Private Will Bird, 42nd Battalion (Royal Highlanders), Canadian Expeditionary Force

The Canadians were not doomed to spend Christmas at Passchendaele. By 14 November the Corps had already returned to the Lens front. They left behind a legacy of 15,500 casualties; almost exactly the number estimated by Sir Arthur Currie when he had accepted Sir Douglas

Houthulster Wald

Strassenkreuzung

Die Einteilungen sind übereinstimmend mit den Teilungen
an den Visiervorrichtungen am Geschütz u. am Scherenfernrohr.

2400   2500   2600   2700   2800   2900

1600   1700   1800   1900   2000   2100

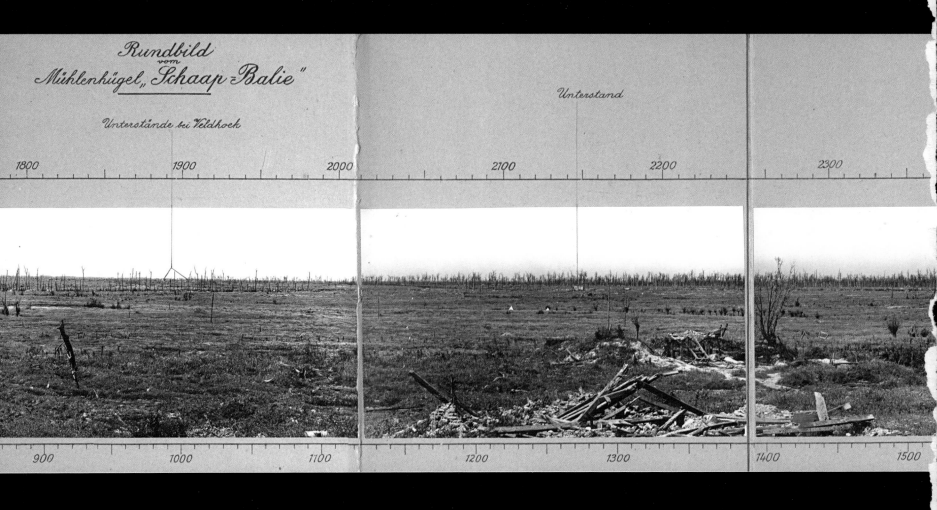

Rundbild
vom
Mühlenhügel "Schaap-Balie"

Unterstände bei Veldhoek

Unterstand

1800 1900 2000 2100 2200 2300

900 1000 1100 1200 1300 1400 1500

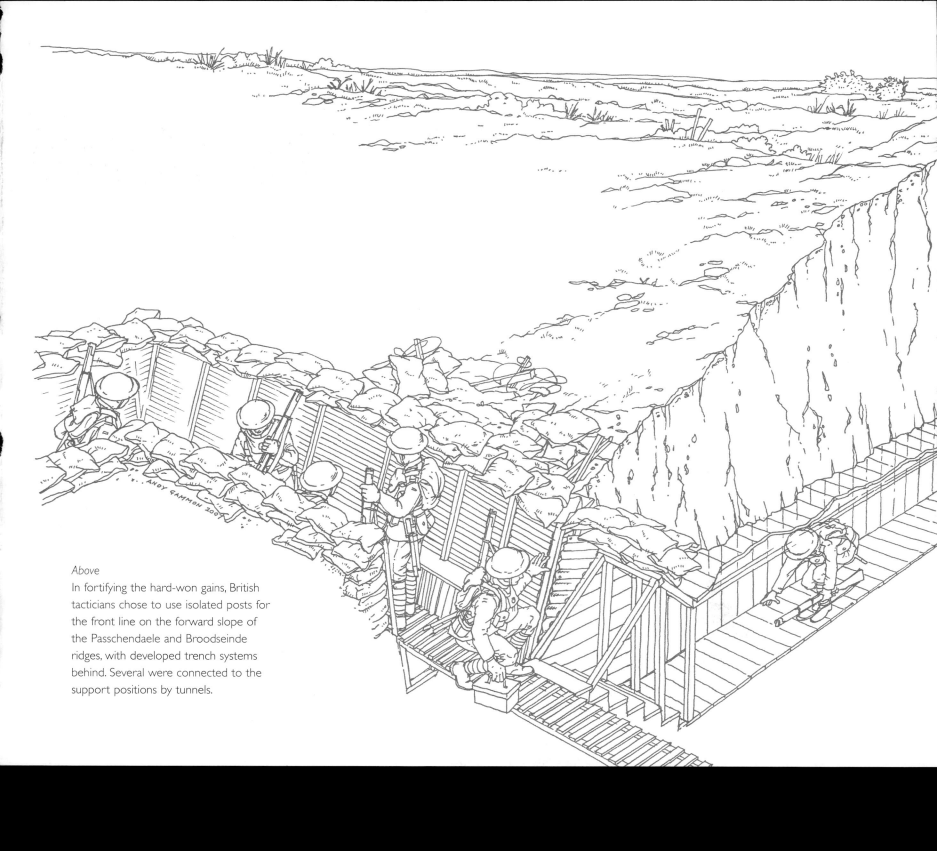

Above
In fortifying the hard-won gains, British tacticians chose to use isolated posts for the front line on the forward slope of the Passchendaele and Broodseinde ridges, with developed trench systems behind. Several were connected to the support positions by tunnels.

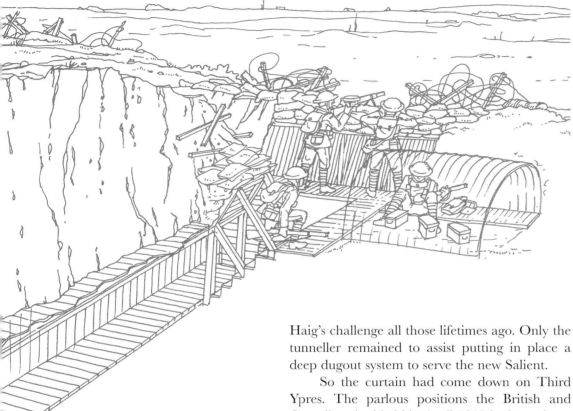

Haig's challenge all those lifetimes ago. Only the tunneller remained to assist putting in place a deep dugout system to serve the new Salient.

So the curtain had come down on Third Ypres. The parlous positions the British and Canadians had held in April 1915 had now been not only replicated, but by courtesy of the final few pushes, made yet more exposed and perilous. As soon as Rawlinson assumed responsibility he let it be known that the line was a nightmare. As was his custom, the day the offensive closed Sir Douglas Haig displayed immense initial satisfaction, meeting with staff to impress upon them the importance of planning for the spring – look again at the Belgian coast, was the message. Haig's diary entry regarding the final 10 November operation noted: 'our troops have improved their position on the Passchendaele

ridge very greatly.' It was as if he were only trying to persuade himself, however, for the buoyancy was short-lived. Within days he was already concurring with Rawlinson. The nose of the new Salient would be almost sure to implode under the kind of heavy attacks that the Germans, now freed from the burdens of the Eastern Front, were likely to be able to throw at it in the spring – possibly sooner according to Charteris, for enemy battalions were already reported to be streaming westwards. It was far from what GHQ had envisaged even at the beginning of November 1917.

Sporadic fighting and violent shelling continued after 10 November (and would do so throughout the winter of 1917/18). Sir Henry Rawlinson began laying plans for continued attacks, hoping to further extend British lines northwards from Passchendaele, thereby making the Salient less vulnerable. Haig ordered him to plan away, but do nothing until the outcome at Cambrai was clear. Although histories record Second Passchendaele as ending on the 10th, the Third Ypres campaign continued until officially closed down by the Commander-in-Chief on 20 November 1917. Omnipresent shudders of hostile shellfire took no heed of the date – it went on …and on.

We left the 'Hell' trenches on the night of the 12th. November. We do not get any mail sent up there as it is one hundred to one that it would be blown up before it reaches us and we cannot send any letters from there. I managed to send a field card by one of our men who happened to go out a couple of days before us. We have had a terrible five days of it up there and it was raining most of the time and we have been up to our thighs in mud and water – my feet are not too good but I have not got frostbite as yet. We had a terrible time going up to relieve another regiment. Going up Fritz dropped two shells right on top of my company. How any of us got out of it alive I cannot say, thank God I was one of the lucky ones. It was a black night and we could not see the men in front of us and we were just leaving the road to start on the trench boards when the two shells came killing twelve men and wounding thirty. The officer I refused to cook for was in front and he was wounded but after getting the wound dressed and on the way to Hospital he was killed by another shell – Hard Luck. The few of us that were left went as fast as we could but we had to be so careful for if we missed the board we would go into the mud. Try and picture it on the boards and Fritz dropping shells, you dare not turn back, you might run into a shell so you just go forward as there is no place to take cover at all. I have thanked God for sparing me. When we were relieved and started to come out of the trenches Fritz did not shell much but when we were half way across the boards he started sending gas shells – it was bad enough trying to see the way but when you have to put on a gas mask as well you can guess what it was like and we were in a valley and the gas clung to the low ground. When we got on the road we were able to take our gas helmets off and went on as quickly as we could but that was not as quick as I should have liked owing to the weight we had to carry and having nothing to eat for two days. They tried to get food up to us as much as possible but a lot of poor chaps got killed in the attempt. When we were up there I had a piece of shrapnel tear the sleeve of my overcoat. It would have torn into my wrist if it had been an inch lower but God was watching over me and I am now not so bad after the time we had. We are still in a place where his shells hit a bit but tomorrow we go away in motor buses a bit further back, then the next day we go for a train ride and a well earned rest. It will be a rest this time as we are so smashed up, not that it will be impossible for them to send us up the line again until we get strongly reinforced. The papers say that the German soldiers are all nerves, but what about us? Yes, you can see the fear in all of us as we go up to these trenches. Brave men we did have once but most of them we have now, including officers, are the men who have been slacking in England until they were fetched and more than half of them are not worth a few of 'The Contemptible Little Army of 1914'.

<small>PRIVATE D.J. SWEENEY, 1ST LINCOLNSHIRE REGIMENT.</small>

For a few brief moments it appeared that Cambrai might achieve more than just a political and public relations coup for Sir Douglas Haig. On 20 November 380 tanks rolled forward alongside six infantry divisions. No pre-battle barrage signalled Sir Julian Byng's Third Army attack, complete surprise was achieved, and three lines – a depth of almost 7 kilometres – of enemy trenches were soon overrun until only a semi-constructed, lightly garrisoned rear section of the Hindenburg Line separated the British from open country. It was a tremendous achievement and a great potential victory beckoned. Church bells triumphantly rang out the length and breadth of Britain. But the tanks, against the advice of their Corps leaders, had been sent in wholesale, leaving no fresh machines and crews to exploit the unoccupied gap that had been made to open up. It hung in the balance for several hours. But those tanks already on the battlefield could do no more, many had been knocked out, while many had ditched or broken down, and the crews of the remaining machines were exhausted. Conditions appeared perfect for cavalry and into action they galloped only to find they were no more bullet-proof than ever, being promptly baulked by a handful of machine guns. Sir Douglas Haig, who after the first day of battle had declined further assistance by an entire French army corps placed at his disposal, sent in fresh British infantry divisions. But it was too late – the breach had been plugged. Two more days

Right
The fighting goes on through the winter. A British machine gunner keeps up the harassment of enemy working parties or patrols.

of attacks left Haig with another unpleasant salient to defend. Rumours of a heavy German counter-stroke then abounded, but Commanders took little notice, and failed to strengthen the line. On 30 November, with two lightning flank attacks, the Germans retook almost all the ground the tanks had earlier helped secure. In December, a report drawn up by Lieutenant Colonel Wetzell, head of the German Operations Section, noted: 'What a difficult situation should we not have found ourselves in if this blow [Cambrai] had taken place simultaneously with the great Flanders attack.'

For the Allies the year could hardly have ended more dismally.

At the moment of midnight, December 31, 1917, I stood with some acquaintances in a camp finely overlooking the whole Ypres battlefield. It was bitterly cold, and the deep snow all round lay frozen. We drank healths, and stared across the snowy miles to the line of casual flares, still rising and floating and dropping. Their writing on the night was as the earliest scribbling of children, meaningless; they answered none of the questions with which a watcher's eyes were painfully wide. Midnight; successions of coloured lights from one point, of white ones from another, bullying salutes of guns in brief bombardment, crackling of machine-guns on the tingling air; but the sole answer to unspoken but importunate questions was the line of lights in the same relation to Flanders as at midnight a year before.
LIEUTENANT EDMUND BLUNDEN MC,
11TH ROYAL SUSSEX REGIMENT

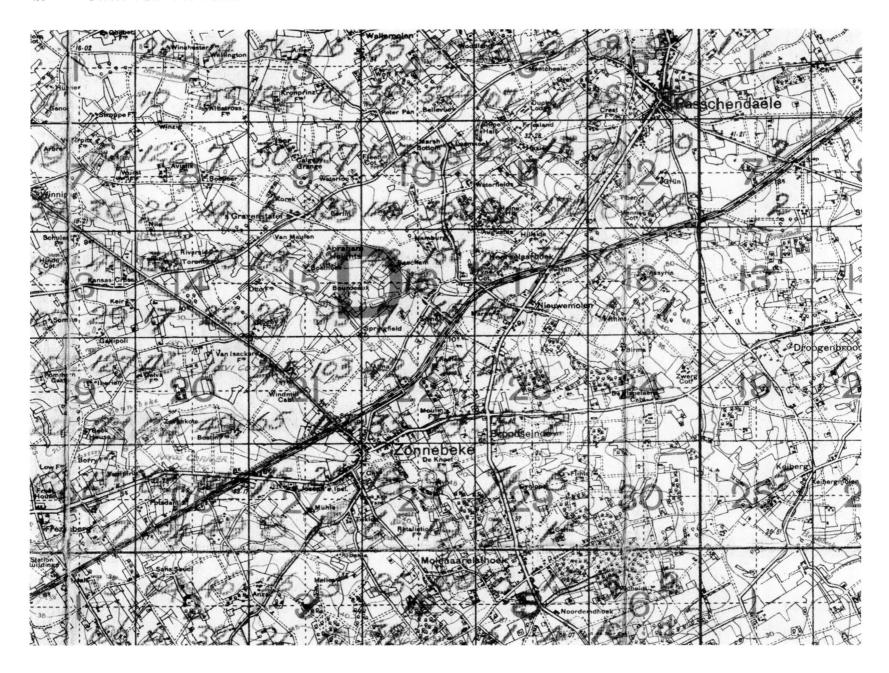

Left
Segment of an Imperial War Museum casualty map showing the Zonnebeke and Passchendaele sectors. The annotation denotes the number of bodies found in each map square on the first sweep of the battlefields by specialist recovery companies after the war.

Above
The true texture of the later stages of the Passchendaele campaign. The German caption for this 4 November aerial photograph is 'Englisches Totenfeld' – English field of death. It needs no further elaboration.

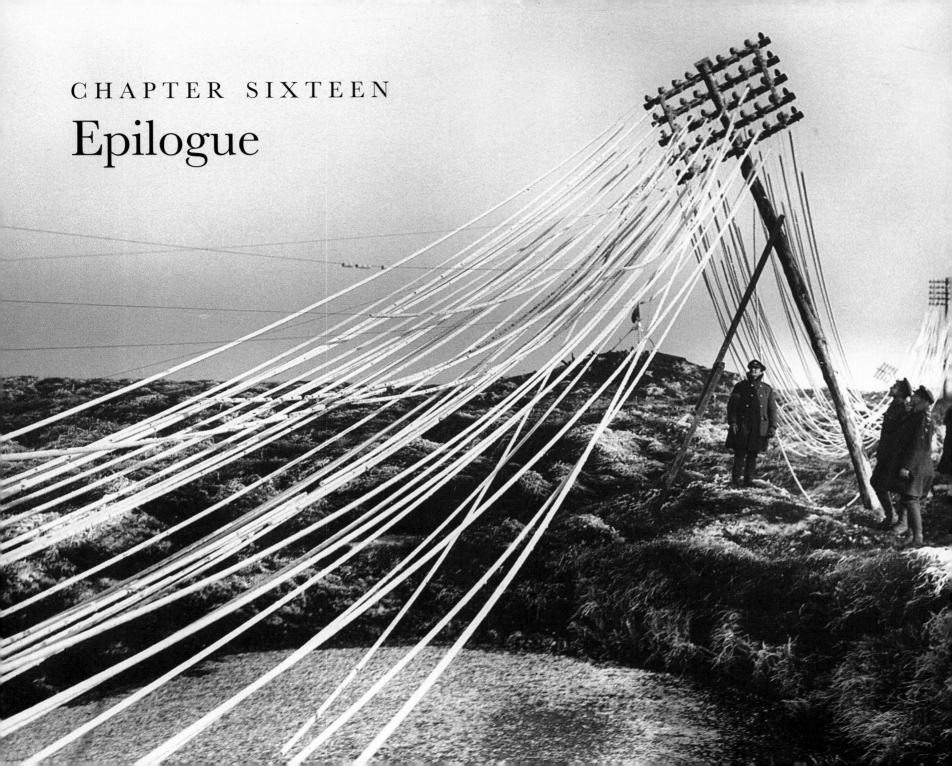

Epilogue

Well, we were in and out of the front line trenches and in reserve. Winter would soon be coming, which we all dreaded – mud, water, cold, frost, ice, snow, shells, machine gun, rifle bullets and chats thrown in. We had leather jackets to wear as well as our overcoats. Some of the soldiers could not stand it – trench feet and other ills – so they went sick. This was my fourth winter out here in action in France and Belgium. Passchendaele was an awful place to spend the winter. 1917 was the coldest winter out here for me. The shell holes were full of mud and water, and then there was the frost. I opened a tin of milk and it was a block of ice. I was under an old piece of galvanised sheeting to keep me warm. Once, when coming out of the front line, we were sitting on our tin helmets waiting for the light engine and trucks to take us back in reserve, and I could not get up. I wasn't the only one either. So the other soldiers had to lift us up and put us in the truck. We were all glad to leave Passchendaele.
PRIVATE F.D. COOPER, 5TH OXFORDSHIRE AND
BUCKINGHAMSHIRE LIGHT INFANTRY

In mid-November 1917 and despite the campaigning season being long waned by normal standards, the fighting in the Salient was far from over. Throughout the winter the attrition was perpetuated, mainly by the guns. At the same time defences were feverishly repaired, prepared and built anew, for come spring both sides planned to attack again. The energy expended by the British to make the 'new' Salient defensible during the four months following the Second Battle was prodigious. Sheltered within the arc of the lee side of the ridge scores of every kind of deep dugout were installed, some housing over 2,000 men; the ridge itself was organized with posts on the forward slope (no connected front line), trenches on the rear (each connected underground), and tunnelled observation, signals and accommodation positions. A panoply of Royal Artillery weaponry was re-diffused across the Salient and the whole enterprise connected to a labyrinthine system of telephonic communications. Much of the underground work was drained, lit and ventilated by electric power. Every sector enjoyed mains water fed close up to the front lines, and the road and rail system was no less than a marvel. But the efforts of the hundreds of thousands of troops who installed this extraordinary infrastructure were to come to nothing.

Sir Douglas Haig has long been criticized for not bringing Third Ypres to a swifter close, but could and should he have done so? Since the Somme the war had become yet more complex. Britain was still the junior coalition partner. Given her standing in the world, it was a burden which carried its own pressures in relation to personal and national pride. During the course of the campaign Haig was presented with a host of dramatic stumbling blocks: the crumbling of the Eastern Front; the Italian debacle at Caporetto; increasing enemy attacks upon the UK mainland; unrestricted submarine warfare and loss of allied shipping; unreliable intelligence; mutiny in the French army; plus a Prime Minister, Lloyd George, who was fighting his own campaign against the Commander-in-Chief and General Staff in an effort (ultimately unsuccessful) to disconnect them from military policy-making. In civil life no one was more determined than Lloyd George to see the war through to a decisive end. Haig was ultimately proved correct in his belief that it could only be won on the Western Front; indeed, this occurred – quite remarkably – exactly a year and a day after Passchendaele came to an end. But the chief reason behind his vilification appears to be a propensity for inflexibility in the hope of creating conditions suitable for cavalry. Herein perhaps lies the key, for cavalry had long been an insignificant force in a conflict which had quickly come to be ruled by artillery. Such firm, undeviating determination may have been a great asset in open warfare, but in Flanders, a region where failure even without the intervention of carpet shellfire had been almost ritualistic for centuries, and where defence in depth was at its most developed, mounted

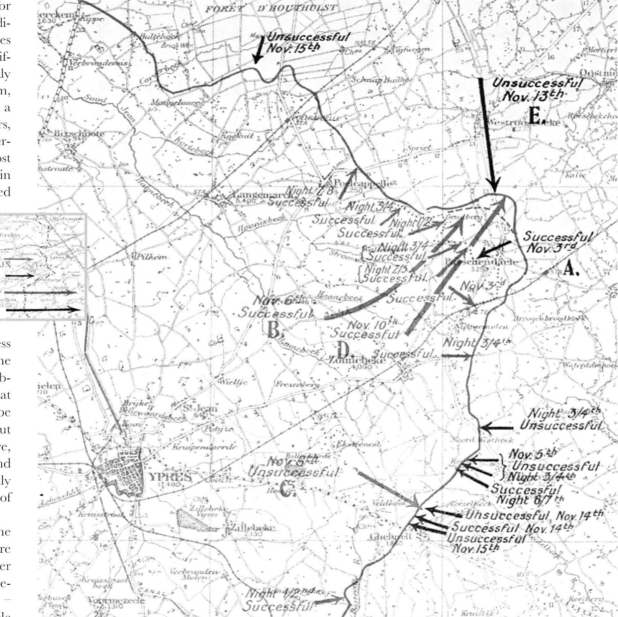

troops should have been seen as valueless long before June 1917. In later years he defended his inflexibility by simply describing the First World War as a single great offensive – which, of course, it cannot be denied that he played a part in winning. But for the peoples of the British Empire, Passchendaele was something else. First and foremost, like the Somme, it was a brilliantly flexible defensive endeavour on the part of the Germans.

Was it futile? Certainly, none of the original Anglo-French strategic goals were achieved. The problem was that the longer the battle went on, the longer events elsewhere decreed it must continue, not – although occupation of the Passchendaele

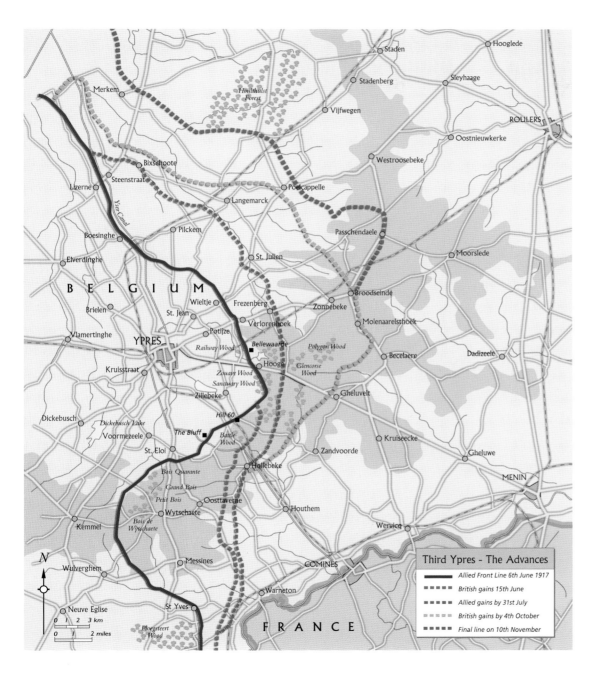

Third Ypres - The Advances

━━━━ Allied Front Line 6th June 1917

▪▪▪▪▪ British gains 15th June

▪▪▪▪▪ Allied gains by 31st July

▪▪▪▪▪ British gains by 4th October

▪▪▪▪▪ Final line on 10th November

Ridge was undoubtedly desirable – to attain a valuable territorial objective, but as a facilitator for other actions. The troops would have had no inkling of this. It is hard to come to any conclusion except that the enemy was hit hard and the German war effort was again deeply injured by Third Ypres. Was Haig to blame for the carnage? We cannot know how the nature and duration of the war might have been altered by earlier cessation in 1917, nor, in the light of the appalling number of casualties in 1918, say that fewer lives would ultimately have been lost. Perhaps the complexion may have been different without the lengthy delay following Messines, or perhaps not. What we do know is that command and control of the battle was most definitely a multi-handed affair, with advice being sought and freely offered from numbers of high-ranking sources, many of whom had reputations for sensitivity and caution. Much of this advice helped to prolong the carnage. But, almost alone, it is Sir Douglas Haig's name that has come to be synonymous with attrition, suffering and loss.

FINAL SPRING

On 21 March 1918 the German armies launched a sequence of grand attacks in an attempt to snatch victory before the intervention of the Americans. They began in Picardy. Since November 1917 and the collapse of the Russian front, fifty-two extra German divisions had become available for redeployment in the West, twenty more than the Allies had calculated. The total was now an alarming 235 divisions with an establishment of 4,600,000 troops. At the same time the British had taken over an extra 90 kilo-

Left and inset
The formidable German defensive lines beyond the ridges showing fields of fire of machine guns. Inset: British concrete shelter constructed at Winchester Farm during the winter.

Below
The entire British defensive infrastructure of the Salient was reconstructed between December 1917 and April 1918.

metres of front. They were thinly spread, were still protecting the Channel ports and had less room than the French for potential retirement. The first German thrust – Operation Michael – drove 65 kilometres over the old Somme battlegrounds, the intention being to break in here and roll northwards. A stout defence and supply shortages forced a halt by 5 April. The Germans sat facing Amiens. On 9 April the Battle of the Lys began, the 'St George' attacks (later Georgette) created another wide but shallow bulge in the British line between Béthune and Armentières. Subsequent blows occurred northwards, directed at Messines, Wytschaete and then Ypres. On 26 April Kemmel village and parts of Kemmel Hill, that talisman of British resistance at this time defended by French troops, fell, the resulting 16-kilometre enemy advance making the Passchendaele pocket yet more vulnerable. The *Flandern* lines guarding Roulers and Menin had been immensely bolstered, and by 9 May continuing pressure in the sectors south of Ypres made the ridge no longer viable; the entire area over which an ocean of blood had been spilled the previous summer and autumn was sacrificed in the name of security. Plumer, returned from Italy only on 17 March, twice railed against the decision to withdraw, describing the orders as 'heartrending'; but he too knew that without this gloomy act Ypres itself might succumb, and possibly far worse. The British line had to be quickly shortened to release troops for action elsewhere. Although distressing and disheartening, it was just another scene in the Flanders act of the great strategic play that was the wider war, a war that was becoming more complex to wage, command and control every month.

Coastwards beyond Ypres the inundation and canal defences were still secure; it was on the southern flank of the town between Kemmel and Dickebusch that the greatest peril lay, so the British dropped back to pre-prepared positions *behind* those held between May 1915 and July 1917, before the Third Battle of Ypres. German troops took up residence as far forward as Hellfire Corner, a mere kilometre from the Menin Gate.

Now a race against time began. Since 21 March the German Army had everywhere struck where their enemy had been weak, but despite the heavy influx of troops from the East the disposition of their own manpower upon such a wide front, and with such huge attacks, was limited. In addition, they still had no tanks to deploy in the ideal spring conditions; although requested, blockade-stricken German industry was simply incapable of substantial production. The offensives went on and on, with the Allies always leaving little of use to the enemy in their wake, and always falling back upon reserves, whilst the German line of communication grew ever longer and supplies ever thinner. At the end of May the French collapsed on the Chemin des Dames. Resistance was crushed with the help of 3,700 German guns, and almost 50,000 French troops were taken prisoner. The attacks had been suspected, but no preventive action could be taken. Long-range artillery had already begun the bombardment of Paris. Throughout the summer of 1918 the Allies were to face the potential nightmare of total defeat. An indication of the ferocity of this period can be found in the casualty rates, which incredibly outstripped those of Third Ypres by almost 75 per cent. But it was in Ludendorff's decision to push on into

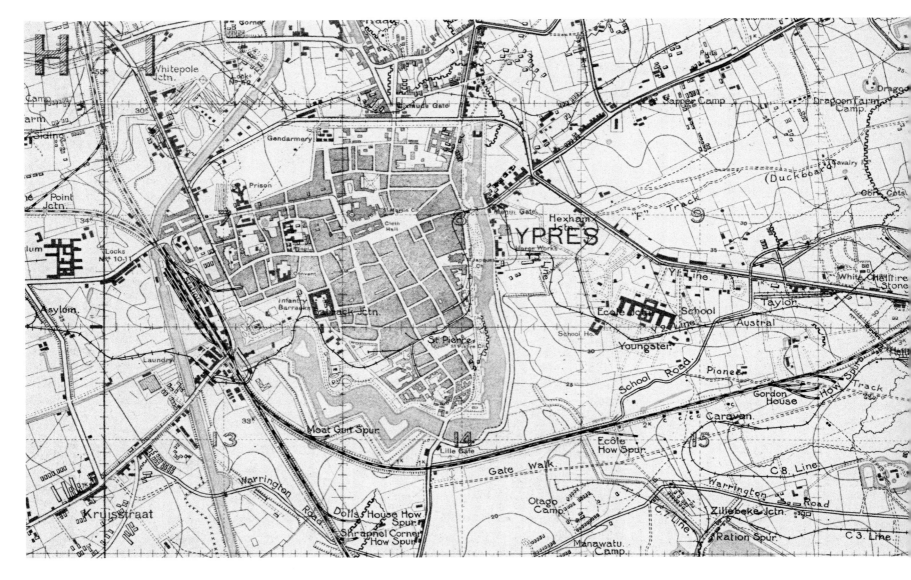

Champagne following the Chemin des Dames victory that the seeds were sown that signalled a change of Allied fortune, for liquid enticement in the newly subjugated wine region between Rheims and Soissons was too ubiquitous and too tempting. German progress slowed again. By mid-June many breaches still existed in the Allied line, but none had been further widened or deepened. General Henri Philippe Pétain, the commander of French forces, felt confident enough to state, 'If we can hold on until the end of June, our situation will be excellent. In July we

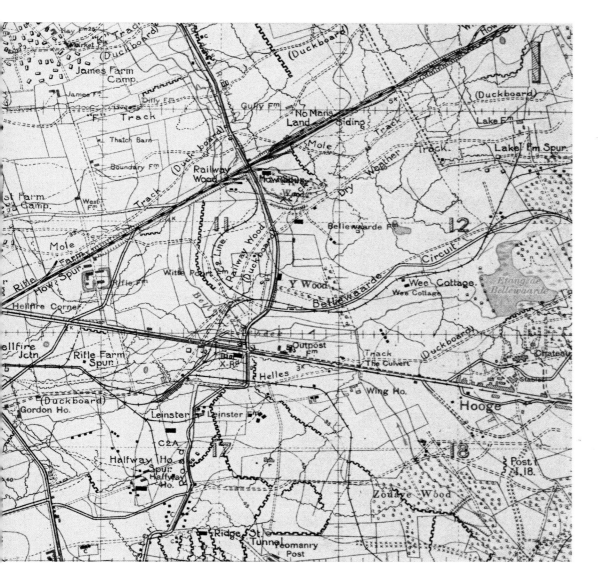

tramways laid, deep dugouts installed by the score, camps established, water pipes dug in, and hundreds of kilometres of electricity and communication cables laid. The majority of the creation was forcibly abandoned in May 1918.

can resume the offensive; after that victory will be ours.' The Allies awaited the exhaustion of the German Army – as Sir Douglas Haig had done the previous year. By the end of June two further onslaughts fell upon the French east of Paris. This time both were absorbed.

British and Dominion resistance was as dogged in defence as it had been in attack at Third Ypres, and the French not unnaturally fought for every square metre of their precious soil. Although Ludendorff took more than 80,000 further prisoners, his tactics constantly interrupted momentum, which served to drain resources and left many a window for Allied counter-attacks. Nocturnal air raids were amplified, further hampering German supply efforts, but the greatest influence on the future complexion of battle was the economic stranglehold imposed upon Germany by the shipping blockade. Now, soldiers heard tales of acute privation at home, with defenceless families suffering greater distress than those on the field of battle. Then supplies to the front began to dwindle too, food quality and quantity fell, health suffered, divisional establishments waned, and morale plummeted; it now dawned upon the ordinary German soldier that they had been receiving the best their country had to offer – the longer the military struggle continued, the greater would be the hardships at home.

And by now the Americans were arriving in numbers that far exceeded expectation. On 21 March there had been 300,000 AEF troops training in France; by June that same number was arriving every month.

It was the influence of hunger that finally turned the tide. On 8 August a local offensive by 456 tanks and thirteen divisions spearheaded by Australians and Canadians in front of Amiens swept across a weak defence, easily throwing the Germans back 12 kilometres. Although the Battle of Amiens was not pressed further, Ludendorff felt the shock profoundly. In plain language he reported to his sovereign, dubbing it the 'Black

Day' of the German Army. The Kaiser's personal verdict was simple and immediate: 'I see that we must strike a balance. We are at the end of our reserves. The war must be ended.' He decreed that peace negotiations be instigated before the situation put the country at risk of total humiliating defeat. But delays ensued, for after months of promises of victory, combined with outstanding efforts and sacrifices by their troops, a proud German High Command could as yet find no stomach and no words to break such catastrophic news.

END

The final strokes were played out by all the Allies, but by no means in the expected quick time. It was to be September before Flanders was at last liberated by a joint Belgian-British force that swept over the Third Ypres battlefields in a little less than two days. The momentum might have taken them all the way to Brussels if it had not been for heavy rain and mud. Now fighting in unison with the Americans, intense pressure on all fronts was sustained throughout September and October until realization and indeed revolution finally struck Germany. On 30 September, Ludendorff himself appeared to accept the impossibility of victory, advocating an appeal for an armistice. Although the reaction was only temporary, his deep anxiety was widely reported in the press. Hindenburg too concurred, suggesting to his colleagues that the ceasefire should be immediate to save their army from annihilation. The German government could now do no more than avoid losing the war

Above
The Allied advance begins. Lille suffers under British artillery fire.

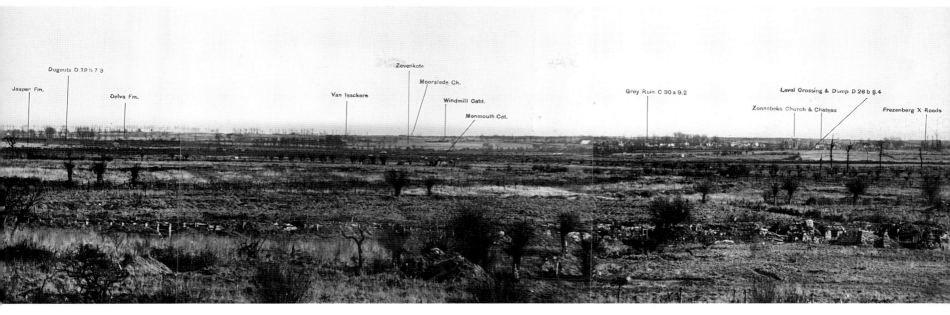

Dugouts D.19 h 7 3

Zevenkote

Moorslede Ch.

Jasper Fm.

Delva Fm.

Van Isackere

Windmill Cabt.

Monmouth Cot.

Grey Ruin C 30 a 9.2

Level Crossing & Dump D 26 b 8.4

Zonnebeke Church & Chateau

Frezenberg X Roads

Above
A final glance at where it all started. In September 1918 all the ground pictured in this panorama was overrun in less than twenty-four hours.

Right
A backward glance towards lost opportunities. A German soldier leaves Flanders for the last time.

outright – total defeat – and on 3 October a plea for immediate cessation was delivered. Meanwhile, the Turks had collapsed in Palestine, and Bulgaria was forced into seeking an armistice in Salonika. It was the continuing action in other theatres and a certain calming of the Western Front that encouraged Ludendorff to believe that perhaps all was not lost, and a fighting withdrawal might be made to the German border, thus avoiding total defeat and humiliation. But at home the earlier sentiments of his own and others had entered the soul of the German people; as the days had passed, so had hope. There was no civil will for more conflict, just an overwhelming desire to end the misery. It could only happen by accepting the Allies' crippling peace terms. This was done, and on 11 November 1918 the guns fell silent. The German

military were left with the dubious honour of being *unbesiegt im Feld* – undefeated in the field.

RETURN

In the Ypres and Messines Salients it was now up to the peoples of West Flanders to rebuild their tortured pastures and broken lives. Hundreds of thousands had dispersed to Holland, France and Britain. A great many came back. Some, surveying the devastation, believed the land beyond repair, and returned to their erstwhile refugee homes to rebuild a fresh future. With help of German prisoners of war and Labour Corps personnel, those who chose to stay began the task of clearing the ribbon of death and detritus that was the Salient. With 3,200,000 shells per week fired by the British alone during the summer and autumn of 1917, the challenge was colossal, claiming many more lives in the clearance of munitions, as indeed it still does to this day. The restoration years deserve a book of their own, but to conclude it is worth describing just one extraordinary activity arising as a consequence of the greatest mutual siege the world had ever known. In Passchendaele, Zonnebeke, St Julien – indeed in every blighted village of the region – amongst the multitudes of hazards on the surrounding post-conflict battlefield was their own share of the three million miles of barbed wire believed to have been spread about the Western Front during the war. Clearance was obligatory, for agriculture could not recommence otherwise. How did the local populace deal with the problem? Every village drew together the able-bodied and supplied each with a stout, wooden, lidless box and a heavy steel hand stamp. The wire, cut

into manageable thickets, was dragged from the battlefield to form mountains of rusty thorns. It was then painstakingly reduced to 30-centimetre lengths with wire cutters; these were laid in the boxes, layer upon layer, and gradually beaten with the stamp into solid blocks. The result was a sort of 'brick' of compressed barbed wire. For month after month, wagons carted them away for burial or recycling at furnaces. It was just one of many monumental endeavours made to clear the battlefields. Eventually, Flanders was largely freed from the visible memories of the First World War, and by the hand of man and nature her pastures slowly healed. Scars remained, but they became harder and harder to find.

LOOKING BACK

Belgium and the Ypres Salient was behind us. One striking feature about that Salient is that you can walk for three hours and reach its deepest point and in so doing cover the areas of all those famous struggles from '14 to '18. Attack and counter-attack surged back and forth in that big Salient wheel on such a scale that it gave rise to many stories regarding the capture of certain points. One such story is of a disgruntled Tommy loading his lorry with brick from a heap of ruins. When asked what he was doing he explained: 'We're moving this lot over the ruddy hill so that them Staff gents can say we've made an advance. It's one of these 'ere Belgian villages.'

Standing at Bellevue Spur one gets a wonderful view of the Salient. It is a great saucer of green dotted with red and banded with grey roads. Stand there and you realise the immense superiority of the German positions, and the compete observation he had of every move that we made. No person could move above ground without being seen, and where the high netting and camouflage was strung, a puff of dust was enough to betray traffic. German observers could sit snugly on these ridges, marking maps,

Above

The Bellevue spur in 1919.

Above and right

A pilgrimage by an officer and his family to the St Julien sector, 1919.

Below
Meetchele pillbox and graves, 1919.

talking to gunners over the telephone wires, and register on every crossroad battery, duckboard track, or working; could define every foot of every parapet and take its measure accurately. That men survived in these places will always be an incredible thing to the veteran from other fronts, and that the enemy, with such an advantage, could not conquer, proves that those who held Ypres had something stronger than the science of war, something beyond the measure of the enemy's calculations.
WILL BIRD, THIRTEEN YEARS AFTER

The First World War, fought largely by civilians and chronicled more extensively than any previous conflict, left behind a vast mass of evidential material, official and otherwise. It is still being uncovered in great quantity across the world. To follow an individual's footsteps day to day, month to month, year to year, especially around the Western Front, is far from difficult, and can be extraordinarily rewarding. Many today wish to visit sites where their forebears served, suffered or died, to stand a little closer to a fascinating conflict that not only changed the world so profoundly, but one that affected and moulded the actions, relationships, attitudes and collective memories of their own families – indeed, by received wisdom quite possibly their own thoughts, opinions and lives. The healing process following such cataclysms is a slow one. Four out of five sufferers from shell shock, for instance, were never able to return to duty. Even in the mid-1960s, there still existed hospitals entirely filled by men who had not recovered from their own personal darknesses. The last such First World War 'casualty', David Ireland of the Black Watch, died in June 2001. Unable to rejoin society he had spent more than eighty years in care.

Interviews reveal that, as in all wars, people

continue to carry various degrees of trauma, guilt and fear, none of which can ever be entirely comprehensible to those who did not share the experience. Most curious is the inexplicable feeling of shame that almost every veteran seems to have regarding some aspect or moment of his contribution. But with just a handful of veterans still alive, it is too late now to explore such cases and support the sufferers. The First World War still retains an almost unique relevance and resonance, not only for those directly affected by events, but with 'disconnected' later generations. Because the troops were fixed upon this tiny tortured ribbon of Flanders for so many years, Ypres not unnaturally holds a significant place in the collective psyche of a dozen countries worldwide. Unhappily, for many the Third Battle and especially its final stages at Passchendaele have come to epitomize the entire campaign in Flanders; a matter that only education can resolve. In the process of research and writing, one is constantly reminded that the learning process is something that never ceases, and in drawing to a close this account it is worthwhile considering a single example of the author's 'further education'. It concerns what one might call latent personal repercussion, and can at once be considered both representative (given the required bizarre combination of circumstances) and unique. We must return now to July 1917.

The La Brique sector north-west of Wieltje was held by Sir Ivor Maxse's meticulously trained XVIII Corps, consisting of the 51st (Highland) and 39th Divisions. The latter included the 6th Battalion of the Cheshire Regiment.

The battalion had arrived in the Salient from the Somme the previous November, and had soon fallen into their individual cadence of trench life: at this time a week in the line, a week in reserve and a week's rest. On the night of 4/5 July 1917, in preparation for the forthcoming battle, elements of the battalion carried out a vital raid against Caliban Trench, close to Mouse Trap Farm (see map and photo on pages 128 and 129). Considerably smaller but similar to the attack on The Ravine described in detail in Chapter 5, it was carefully planned, well rehearsed and determinedly carried out. Whilst a party of RE attended to the general destruction of dugouts with mobile charges, the infantry hunted down prisoners. Seven were snaffled, only two of whom arrived back in the British trenches alive. The Cheshires had seven men wounded, with one officer missing believed killed, but much useful information was gathered as to the nature of the enemy defences and their garrison. On 20 July 1917 Sir Douglas Haig himself decorated the leading raiders, one of whom, Sergeant William Rhodes, received the Distinguished Conduct Medal, an award for gallantry second only to the Victoria Cross.

A well-liked and well-respected family man from Stalybridge near Manchester, William, and his wife Annie, had two young children, Harold and Mary. A Territorial since 1908, he had mobilized with the Cheshires on 14 August 1914, fought at Messines in December that year, taken part in the Christmas Truce, served in the front line throughout 1915, fought at Givenchy in 1916, and subsequently on the Somme at Fricourt, Thiepval and in the final November flourish on the Ancre. He was especially noted (in both civilian and army life) for a splendid, deep, rich bass voice, with which he entertained his battalion on many occasions. The next time William Rhodes was to lead his section out of these same trenches was against troops of III Bavarian Corps on 31 July 1917.

It was not uncommon for operation orders to alter several times before an action, and those of the Cheshires were amended on 9, 13, 17 and 25 July; even then the date and hour for Zero had not yet been finally decided, for late-arriving guns were still being hauled onto platforms.

Above
Sergeant William Rhodes.

Below
The trenches along Admiral's Road as seen from Crossroads Farm. Second Army pan 4, June 1915.

Above
Photograph given to William Rhodes by a German soldier during the truce of Christmas 1914.

Right
Cheshire Regiment Territorials on pre-war exercises. William Rhodes is seated at centre with cap.

After Sir Douglas Haig had sanctioned Sir Hubert Gough and General Francois Anthoine's request for a three-day deferral, Z-day was finally fixed for 31 July. Many a commander was in fact somewhat thankful for the extra time to complete the immensely complex arrangements, for with all the adjustments and ever-changing dates it was essential that officers and NCOs unambiguously understood what was required of them. Arrangements on the eve of battle were as efficient as those at Messines, each unit knew its time and position of assembly, hour of attack and objective, and arrived in the line rested and fed. As their sector allocation had not altered, the Cheshires' attack was to take place from the very same trenches along Admiral's Road from which they had made their earlier raid.

The assembly was completed in accordance with orders by 1.50 a.m. with but few casualties, and a meal of hot coffee and sausages was issued to all ranks of the attacking Infantry Brigades. During the assembly the enemy shelled communication trenches with gas and other shells but units approached their positions across country [i.e. deliberately avoiding the trenches].
REPORT ON OPERATIONS OF 31 JULY 1917, 39TH DIVISION

The leading wave climbed over the parapet and strode forward within 35 metres of the creeping barrage. With the help of twenty-four tanks they quickly broke the enemy front line and moved on, entering St Julien. After a short hiatus when 'our

Panorama No. 130 made on 28·5·18 from C 22 b. 8. 3.   Sh. 28 N.W.

ncluding a field of view of 50° from about N.E. to S.E.

(Approximate Scale of Degrees (1 degree equals 1·07 inches).)

artillery shelling and ourselves got somewhat mixed up', men started crossing the all-important Steenbeek. The wire was well cut in most places, but during the advance it was noted with surprise that many concrete emplacements had been 'practically undamaged' by British shellfire; machine-gun nests lurking in them and in fortified shell holes were cleared by the 'employment of rifle grenades and Lewis guns under the cover of which the infantry were enabled to work around the flanks and then rush the emplacement' – the fire-and-movement drill so extensively and repeatedly practised prior to battle. Momentum was good and the tanks were momentarily left behind until the first planned stoppage (see barrage map on page 148). The halt had been written in to the plan to allow fresh supports to arrive and leapfrog the first waves. Amongst these second-wave troops were 118 Brigade, including the 6th Cheshires, who had advanced in artillery formation (a chequerboard pattern rather than a wave) from Admiral's Road.

They reached the new firing line beyond St Julien at about 7.00 a.m., and moved into the attack at 8.00 a.m. alongside the 1st Hertfordshire Regiment and 4/5th Black Watch. The tanks were now once more in attendance.

Heavier fire was soon encountered and the Division forced to set up forward aid posts in shell holes, which the war diary enchantingly records as being 'plentiful'. Progress was excellent, however, not least because the tricky Steenbeek barrier had been crossed on the entire 39th Division front. But because so many battles within battles were taking place to eliminate pillboxes and strong points, the attack now started to become disjointed. The Cheshires and the Hertfordshires, still moving forward but subject to increased hostile attention, crossed the Winnipeg–Springfield road and arrived at Wurst Farm. Here, they expected to meet the 2/5th Lancashire Fusiliers (55th Division), but the Lancastrians' advance had gone far less smoothly.

Above
British 1918 panorama taken from near Mousetrap Farm showing Wurst Farm where the 1/6th Cheshires met a small party of Lancashire Fusiliers during the attack of 31 July 1917.

Below

The Rhodes family before the outbreak of war. Their firstborn, Harold, poses on his rocking horse.

The field was strewn with wreckage, with the mangled remains of men and horses lying all over in a most ghastly fashion – just like any other battlefield I suppose. Many brave Scottish soldiers were to be seen dead in kneeling positions, killed just as they were firing on the enemy. Some German trenches were lined with German dead in that position. It was hell and slaughter. On we went. About a hundred yards on my right, slightly in front, I saw Colonel Best-Dunkley complacently advancing, with a walking stick in his hand, as calmly as if he were walking across a parade ground. I afterwards heard that when all C Company officers were knocked out he took command in person of that Company in the extreme forward line. He was still going strong last I heard of him. We passed through the 166th Brigade. We left St. Julien close on our left. Suddenly we were rained with bullets from rifles and machine-guns. We extended. Men were being hit everywhere. My servant, Critchley, was the first in my platoon to be hit. We lay down flat for a while, as it was impossible for anyone to survive standing up. Then I determined to go forward. It was no use sticking here for ever, and we would be wanted further on; so we might as well try and dash through it. 'Come along – advance!' I shouted, and leapt forward. I was just stepping over some barbed wire defences – I think it must have been in front of Schuler Farm

(though we had studied the map so thoroughly beforehand, it was impossible to recognize anything in this chaos) when the inevitable happened. I felt a sharp sting through my leg. I was hit by a bullet. So I dashed to the nearest shell-hole which, fortunately, was a very large one, and got my first field dressing on. Some one helped me with it. Then they went on, as they were, to their great regret, not hit! My platoon seemed to have vanished just before I was hit. Whether they were in shell-holes or whether they were all hit, or whether they had found some passage through the wire, I cannot say. I only know that, with the exception of Corporal Hopkinson and one or two Lewis Gunners who went forward soon after, they had all vanished.

SECOND LIEUTENANT THOMAS HOPE FLOYD,
2/5TH LANCASHIRE FUSILIERS

Instead of a whole company, only one officer and three men of the 2/5th Lancashire Fusiliers appeared at Wurst Farm. Heavily shelled and machine-gunned from both flanks, the mixed group decided to push on, occupying their allotted portion of the Langemarck system. Three lines had now been attained, an advance of almost 5 kilometres. Pushing out a support-seeking patrol to the north-west, the Cheshires occupied von Tirpitz Farm and there joined a party of Black Watch. A defensive flank was thrown out from nearby Triangle Farm to the Steenbeek. In so doing, the two units inadvertently created their own dangerous mini salient. The Black Watch operations report later commented on how little damaged were the fortified farmhouses and outbuildings in the region, and how impossible it had been to silence machine guns secreted within.

It was now early afternoon. The barrage was as violent as ever, but few men followed on its heels. No one was sure of where the enemy lay, and there was still a disconcerting paucity of visible British troops on either flank. Two hostile counter-attacks then developed, one from due north, the other from The Cockcroft, both unchecked by British gunfire. It encouraged several Germans who had already surrendered to pick up discarded rifles and start to shoot down the British. Still with no support on the right flank, the mixed group of Cheshires, Black Watch and Hertfordshires were now almost enveloped on three sides. At 3.00 p.m. it began to rain. A British counter-attack some way to the left momentarily changed the bleak complexion, but the respite was brief. Divisional HQ ordered a withdrawal to the Steenbeek, but it was too late for the group – the German noose had closed upon them. By 5.00 p.m. a consolidated 39th Division line had been established that ran from St Julien along the east bank of the stream, connecting with 55th Division troops at The Culvert. Most of the 6th Cheshires were not there to assist.

Almost 1,000 prisoners were taken by the

39th Division on 31 July, and many weapons captured. The casualty count was 145 officers and 3,716 men. Of the all the units to take part, the 6th Cheshires suffered the greatest, recording a total of 486 casualties out of around 790. One name on the register was Sergeant William Rhodes DCM, who was listed as missing, believed killed. Like all families, the Rhodes's harboured a faint hope that he had been captured. On 14 March the following year, however, the dreaded letter arrived, confirming his death on 31 July 1917. William Rhodes's body had lain where it had fallen, until discovered just a few days before the authorities contacted the family. The envelope also enclosed his identity disc and DCM ribbon, both soiled with Flanders mud. A survivor of the attack later stated that he had seen Sergeant Rhodes badly wounded and lying

Opposite and below
The consecration of Tyne Cot Cemetery in the summer of 1927. The Rhodes family are all present.

Above right
The grave of Sergeant William Rhodes DCM today

Right
The family's inscription at the foot of the headstone.

in a shell hole near Aviatik Farm – at the apex of Sir Hubert Gough's 31 July attack. On 14 October 1921 William Rhodes's body was exhumed from the small burial ground near Gravenstafel where it had been temporarily interred, and was transferred to the great Tyne Cot concentration cemetery where it lies today in grave IX.E.6. The story illustrates many another, of course, and the ghastly plight of countless families during the First World War, but in one aspect it may well be unique. In December 1916, William Rhodes had fallen ill. Having served since the early days of the war he was allowed home to recuperate. Whilst there enjoying an unexpected Christmas in Blighty, Annie conceived their third child. Irene Rhodes – now

Irene Smith – was born on 18 September 1917 ... six weeks after her father's death.

During the summer of 2004 in connection with investigatory work on the projected extension of the A19 motorway across the Pilckem battlefields (since re-routed), Belgian archaeologists led by Marc Dewilde were carrying out an excavation on a section of British trenches at La Brique to assess the historical and archaeological significance of the threatened area. During this period the author, who was researching on behalf of the archaeologists, happened to be guiding a Genesta Battlefield Club tour; Irene Smith was a member of the party. She had regularly visited the Salient since 1927 when her mother Annie and all three children had attended the consecration of Tyne Cot Cemetery. In later life brother Harold and sister Mary forged close personal bonds in Flanders, and in the years following their deaths Irene continued to visit the Salient on an annual pilgrimage with the Genesta Battlefield Club. Following my explanatory talk about the dig, and the actions witnessed by this 70-metre section of front line between 1915 and 1918, Irene recounted a little of her father's story, saying that she seemed vaguely to recall mention of La Brique amongst the various papers in her possession. Subsequent research showed that it was from those very excavated trenches that her father had raided Caliban Trench to win his DCM, *and* from which the 6th Cheshires

advanced on 31 July 1917 (see aerial photographs on pages 115 and 129). Irene returned to Flanders with the author soon afterwards (during a suitably appalling spell of wet weather) and was thus able to walk in her father's last footsteps in the very trenches in which he served throughout July 1917. It was, she said, 'the closest I have ever been to him'. But, she firmly emphasized, she was 'only one of thousands, possibly millions' to suffer in such a way during the war; indeed, she said, Stalybridge seemed to be permanently in mourning. Her greatest regret? Never hearing her father sing.

Irene Smith has not yet cleaned the boots she wore that day, and nor shall she. Still caked with the same mud that her father walked through on the last day of his life, they are packed neatly in a box to be passed on to future generations. Although her father's medals, identity disc and ribbons have survived, a more apt inheritance is difficult to imagine.

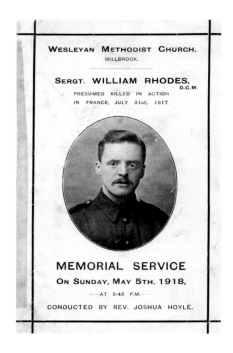

WESLEYAN METHODIST CHURCH,
MILLBROOK.

SERGT. WILLIAM RHODES,
D.C.M.

PRESUMED KILLED IN ACTION
IN FRANCE, JULY 31st, 1917

MEMORIAL SERVICE
ON SUNDAY, MAY 5TH, 1918,
—AT 2·45 P.M.—
CONDUCTED BY REV. JOSHUA HOYLE.

Right
2005. Irene Smith stands in the very trenches her father walked through eighty-eight years before.

Inset
The child the father never knew.

Above
Irene Smith – 'not upset, just amazed' – at the
excavation site.

Further Reading

Anon. Variously titled volumes on *The Work of the Royal Engineers in the European War, 1914-1919*. RE Institute, Chatham, 1922 (Military Mining, Geological Work, Water Supply, Supply of Engineer Stores, Experimental Work, Work under the Director of Works, Bridging, The Signal Service)

Anon. Unpublished reference material: *Fieldworks Designs, Fieldworks Plates, German Fieldworks, Mining Notes.*

Anon. *Report on the Survey of the Western Front 1914-1918, Appendix VIII*, HMSO, London, 1924

Anon. *The Wipers Times*, Eveleigh, Nash & Grayson, London, 1930

Anon. *History of the Corps of Royal Engineers, Volume V.* Institution of Royal Engineers, Chatham, 1952

Barton, Peter, *The Battlefields of the First World War*, Constable, 2005

Barton, Peter, Doyle, Peter, Vandewalle, Johan, *Beneath Flanders Fields*, Spellmount, Staplehurst, 2004.

Beaverbrook, Lord, *Politicians and the War*, Butterworth, 1928

Blunden, Edmund, *Undertones of War*, Cobden-Sanderson, 1930

Brice, Beatrice, *The Battle Book of Ypres*, John Murray, London, 1927

Carmichael, Jane, *First World War Photographers*, Routledge, London, 1989

Carrington, Charles, *Soldier from the Wars Returning*, Hutchinson, London, 1965

Cave, Nigel, *Ypres - Passchendaele, the Fight for the Village*, Leo Cooper, Barnsley, 1997

Chapman, Guy, *A Passionate Prodigality*, Ivor Nicholson and Watson, London, 1933

Chapman, Guy, *Vain Glory*, Cassell, London, 1937

Charteris, John, *Field-Marshal Earl Haig*, Cassell, 1929.

Chasseaud, Peter, *Topography of Armageddon, A British Trench Map Atlas of the Western Front*, Mapbooks, Lewes, 1991

Edmonds, Brigadier-General Sir James, *History of the Great War, Military Operations, France & Belgium, 1918.* HMSO, London

Edmonds, Charles, *A Subaltern's War*, Peter Davies, London, 1929

Evans, Martin Marix, *Passchendaele and the Battles of Ypres 1914-1918*, Pen and Sword, Barnsley, 2005

Fletcher, David, *Landships – British Tanks in the First World War*, HMSO, London 1984

Fletcher, David (Ed.), *Tanks and Trenches*, Sutton, 1994

Giles, John, *Flanders Then and Now: the Ypres Salient and Passchendaele*, Battle of Britain Prints, London, 1987

Gough, Hubert, *Soldiering On*, Arthur Barker, 1954.

Grant Grieve, W and Newman, Bernard, *Tunnellers*, Herbert Jenkins, London, 1936

Griffith, Paddy, *Battle Tactics of the Western Front*, Yale University Press, London, 1994

Groom, WHA – *Poor Bloody Infantry: The Truth Untold*, William Kimber & Co. Ltd, London, 1976

Holmes, Richard, *The Western Front*, BBC Worldwide Ltd, London, 1999

Holmes, Richard, *Tommy: the British Soldier on the Western Front 1914-1918*, HarperCollins, 2004

Holt, Major and Mrs, *Major and Mrs Holt's Battlefield Guide to the Ypres Salient*, Leo Cooper, 1997

Jackson, John – *Private 12768: Memoir of a Tommy*, Tempus Publishing Ltd, Stroud, 2005

Liddell Hart, Basil, *The War in Outline*, Faber 1936

Ludendorff, Erich, *Ludendorff's Own Story*, Hutchinson, 1919

Macdonald, Lyn, *They Called It Passchendaele*, Penguin Books, London, 1993

McCarthy, Chris, *Passchendaele, The Day-by-Day Account*, Arms and Armour, London, 1995

Messenger, Charles, *Call to Arms: The British Army 1914-1918*, Weidenfeld & Nicolson, London, 2005

Prior, Robin & Wilson, Trevor, *Passchendaele: The Untold Story*, Yale University Press

Quigley, Hugh, *Passchendaele and the Somme*, Methuen, 1928

Reed, Paul, *Walking the Salient*, Leo Cooper, Barnsley, 1999

Robbins, Simon, *British Generalship on the Western Front 1914-18: Defeat into Victory*, Frank Cass, London, 2005

Steel, Nigel & Hart, Peter, *Passchendaele: The Sacrificial Ground*, Cassell & Co., London, 2000

Terraine, John, *The Road to Passchendaele: the Flanders Offensive of 1917: A Study in Inevitability*, Leo Cooper, Barnsley, 1977

Van Emden, Richard, *Britain's Last Tommies*, Pen and Sword, Barnsley, 2005

Von Hindenburg, Paul, *Out of My Life*, Cassell, 1920

Warner, Phillip, *Passchendaele*, Sidgwick and Jackson, London, 1987

Williamson, Henry, *The Wet Flanders Plain*, Beaumont, 1929

Wolff, Leon, *In Flanders Fields*, Readers Union, 1958

Acknowledgements

Primary thanks must go to Maggie Lindsay Roxburgh and Clair Banning for marvellous support at times of great change in both their lives. On the historical side I would like to express my gratitude to Simon Jones, Nick Fear, Nigel Steel, Jack Sheldon, Brian Philp, Johan Vandewalle, Kristof Jacobs, Peter Doyle, Peter Chasseaud, Luc Salomez, and Laurie Milner. And of course to my friend and colleague Jeremy Banning, without whom this book would have taken five times as long to produce.

Thanks also to Tom Barton for his forcibly truncated research effort on this volume, Bex Barton for unfailing encouragement, to Mark Banning for supplying material unknown to the author, Margaret Banning for her kind transcription service, and to my agent Anne Dewe of Andrew Mann. I am very grateful to Dr Claudia Condry for invaluable assistance with translations and for navigating me around German archives, to Giles Guthrie and the Staff of the Maidstone Museum (Royal West Kent Regiment), to Mr Peter Stevens of the Faversham Archives, Richard & Anna van Emden for the usual host of reasons, and to Johan Vanbeselaere of the Poelcapelle 1917 Association for help regarding tank movements. Thanks once again to the Clinch family for a thousand kindnesses, to Bob Alexander and Judith Lappin of the Machine Gun Corps History Project, to Hugh Alexander at the National Archives, Kew, to Laurence Martin for the use of the diary of his grandfather, Sapper Albert Martin, and to Wilf Schofield for Archie Irving's letter describing the death of Bill Blaney. And to Malte Znaniecki for permission to use photographs from his extraordinary website www.1914-18.info.

I am indebted to E Lindholt for the use of the papers of Lt Alan May, Duncan Symington for the papers of Private Laurence Symington, Ann Evans for Private HL Chase MM, Caroline Walker for Lieutenant J T P Jeyes, Susan Ashton for Private Robert Cude MM, Tim Hardwick for Major AGP Hardwick MC, Mrs J Nesfield for Lieutenant Gerald Brunskill, Carol Ashburner for Private Frank Pope. Mr B Rudge for Private Walter Hoskyn, Mrs Audrey Deal for Private ST Fuller, Sheila Halliwell for Lieutenant Jack Walthew, Sir Sydney Giffard KCMG for the papers of Captain Edmund Giffard, Arthur Littlewood for Major Martin Littlewood, Mrs Doris Gerrard for Private James Gerrard DCM MM, Marjorie Cliff for Captain Donald Coutts, Brian Prichard for Captain NP Pritchard MC, and to J.O Trundle for the papers of Captain Edwin Trundle. And finally, my profound thanks to Irene Smith for her extraordinary story, and for braving a Flanders winter to re-visit the trenches that witnessed her father's last footsteps, before the site was closed up forever.

Sources

Every effort has been made to obtain permissions to use testimony and illustrations in this book. Where this has not been possible the author would be happy to hear from copyright holders.

Imperial War Museum

I am very grateful indeed to the staff of the Department of Documents, the Department of Printed Books, and, at the All Saints Annexe, the staff of the Sound Archive, Film Archive, Photograph Archive and Photographic Unit. Also to the Western Front Association volunteers carrying out the formidable and valuable task of scanning previously unpublished IWM maps and plans.

Department of Documents:

AG May – 88/46/1; L Symington - 05/54/1; HL Chase MM - 06/54/1; Lieutenant JTP Jeyes - 73/195/1; R Cude MM - PP/MCR/C48; AGP Hardwick MC - 98/14/1; Gerald Brunskill - 03/6/7; Frank Pope - 06/55/1; Walter Hoskyn - P253; ST Fuller - 86/32/1; Lieutenant JS Walthew - 84/34/1; MW Littlewood - 98/33/1; James Gerrard DCM MM – DS/MISC/78; Major DD Coutts DSO – 96/51/1; NP Pritchard MC - 03/17/1; Edwin Trundle - PP/MCR/403; Captain WS Ferrie – 03/19/1; Captain JE March MC – 89/2/1; Lieutenant HA Blundell – 79/51/1; GT Marwood – 97/10/1; Lieutenant TE Rogers – 79/2/1; DJ Sweeney – 76/226/1 Lieutenant FH Ennor – 86/28/2; VR Magill – P163; EC Allfree – 77/14/1; Lieutenant J T Capron – 87/33/1; Lieutenant Colonel CEL Lyne – 80/14/1; EJ Drane – 99/36/1; FD Cooper – 82/16/1; EH Giffard - 06/55/1 N.B. The wartime diaries of all three Giffard brothers have been published as *GUNS, KITES AND HORSES: THREE DIARIES FROM THE WESTERN FRONT*, edited by Sydney Giffard, (Radcliffe Press, 2004)

Sound Archive

Norman Macmillan – AC 4173

Leslie Briggs - AC 5

The Liddle Archive, University of Leeds Special Collections

Leeds University Library, University of Leeds, Leeds LS2 9JT. www.leeds.ac.uk

Papers of:

JR Bellerby – GS 0117

ECP Thomas – ANZAC (AUST)

DN Wimberley – GS 1771

GV Dennis – GS 0447

Ronald Wilson – GS 1766

Charles Birnstingl – GS 0143

Cyril Dennys – GS 0450

George Wade – GS 1660

GA Brett – GS 0194

Nottinghamshire Archives, Record Office, County House, Castle Meadow Road, Nottingham, NG2 1AG   www.nottinghamshire.gov.uk
Letters of JG Morris

Australian War Memorial, Canberra. www.awm.gov.au
Extracts from the diary of Captain Frank Hurley, Official Photographer, Australian Imperial Force. Ref: PR85 - 291

Trustees of the Army Medical Services Museum and the Wellcome Library
Thanks to Captain Pete Starling (Curator of Army Medical Services Museum) and Lesley Hall (Wellcome Library). Army Medical Services Museum, Keogh Barracks, Ash Vale, Aldershot GU12 5RQ
www.ams-museum.org.uk   Papers are held in the Royal Army Medical Corps Muniment Collection at the Wellcome Library, 210 Euston Road, London NW1 2BE
http://library.wellcome.ac.uk/
Personal experiences of an N.C.O. in charge of stretcher squads, by Sergeant Norman Fermor, RAMC. Ref: RAMC 1781

The Royal Green Jackets Museum, Peninsula Barracks, Romsey Road, Winchester, Hampshire SO23 8TS. www.royalgreenjackets.co.uk
Thanks to Major (Retd) Ken Gray.
Diary of Lt-Colonel RT Fellowes, 1st Rifle Brigade, Ref: 7A-0617

The Royal Hampshire Regiment Museum, Serle's House, Southgate Street, Winchester, Hampshire SO23 9EG. www.royalhampshireregimentmuseum.co.uk.
With thanks to Rachel Holmes and Captain (Retd.) Michael Stephens.
Written material:
Papers of Private B Hutchings, 1st Hampshire Regiment - Ref: M.1457
Pictures:
Page 52. Le Gheer barricade from M.1494, Plugstreet 1914-15 album
Page 56. Soldier pumping from M.1488 album

Regimental Museum of the Royal Welsh (formerly South Wales Borderers & Monmouthshire Regimental Museum), The Barracks, Watton, Brecon, Powys LD3 7EB. www.rrw.org.uk   With thanks to Martin Everett and Celia Green.
War Diary of C.S.M Cornelius Love DCM, 2nd Monmouthshire Regiment, Ref: 1999.147
Unpublished Diary, July 1913 – March 1919 of Private C.P. Heare, 1/2nd Monmouthshire Regiment, Ref: 1997.139
Captain Quarter Master Ernest Kirkland Laman MBE MC, 2nd South Wales Borderers, Ref: 2005.70
Pictures: all from file: 1988.82
MBA 2961 (Page 201)
MBA 2963 (184)
MBA 2964 (142)
MBA 2969 (52)

The Fusiliers Museum of Northumberland, The Abbott's Tower, Alnwick Castle, Alnwick, Northumberland NE66 1NG   www.northumberlandfusiliers.org.uk
Thanks to Lesley Frater and staff.
Diary & Letters of A. O. Terry, 23rd Bn, NF (4th Tyneside Scottish) January 1916 - July 1918 [34th Division]

The King's Own Royal Border Regiment Museum, Queen Mary's Tower, The Castle, Carlisle, Cumbria CA3 8UR   www.kingsownbordermuseum.btik.com
Many thanks to Stuart Eastwood and Tony Goddard
Captain Walter Ewbank MC & Bar taken from 'The War Letters of Leonard and Walter Ewbank, 1915 - 1917', Ref: 30/C/030/61A
Private William Graham taken from 'Memories of the Border Regiment in the First World War', edited by Walter F Ewbank

The Tank Museum, Bovington, Bovington Camp, Bovington, Dorset BH20 6JG
www.tankmuseum.co.uk   Thanks to Janice Tait and David Fletcher.
Testimony of William Taylor Dawson – Ref: WW1/DAWSONWT
The Brewery, Poelcappelle, October 1917 – Ref: E1975.20

Museum of Army Chaplaincy, Amport House, Amport, Hampshire SP11 8BG
www.army.mod.uk/chaps   Thanks to David Blake.
An Army Chaplain's Work in Wartime by The Reverend E.V. Tanner MC - A talk given at Weymouth College in the 1920s in abridged form.

The Sherwood Foresters Regimental Archives, RHQ WFR, Foresters House, Chetwynd Barracks, Chilwell, NG9 5HA. With thanks to Major (Retd.) J.O.M. Hackett and Mr I.E. Edwards (Eddie Edwards)
Private Eric Harlow MM – Ref: 2004-6521

The Royal Engineers Museum and Library, Brompton Barracks, Prince Arthur Road, Gillingham, Kent ME4 4UG. www.remuseum.org.uk
As always, my profound gratitude to Rebecca Cheney and her staff for their marvellous service and kindness.

The National Archives (formerly Public Record Office), Kew.
Material has been sourced from a wide selection of original documents, written both during the war (e.g. war diaries, reports, despatches, maps and plans) and afterwards (queries made by various parties during the compilation of the Official History). The page numbers and NA class and piece numbers for the maps are:
83 - WO153/909
94/95 - WO153/1146
102 and 104 - WO153/909
120/121 - WO157/532
131 - WO95/865
135 - WO157/532
148 and 181 - WO95/951

182/183 - WO95/927
204 – WO95/643
209 and 210 - WO95/951
237 - WO153/1147
239 -WO153/973
247, 255 and 265 - WO95/643
258 - WO153/1146
290 - WO153/973
326 - WO95/3383
329 and 331 - WO153/269
333 - WO95/3141
354 - WO95/1222
374/375 - WO95/951
381 - WO153/270
384 - WO153/494
387 - WO95/1051
396 - WO157/120
397 - WO153/269
413 – WO95/1051
424 - WO153/269
440 - WO157/120
444/445 - WO297/690

Haupstaatsarchiv, Stuttgart. Konrad-Adenauer Strasse 4, 70170 Stuttgart. My thanks to Fr. Judith Bolsinger and Herr Cadauli. Material is referenced under 'HS' prefix.
Bayerisches Hauptstaatsarchiv, Munich. Schonfeldstrasse 5-11, 80539 Munchen. My deep appreciation to Dr Lothar Saupe and his staff. Referenced under 'HM' prefix.

Secondary Sources

The quotes of WE Curtis and Walter Carroll are taken from CBC's radio broadcast entitled *In Flanders Fields*, a series of interviews with veterans of the Canadian Expeditionary Force, which aired from November 11, 1964 to March 7, 1965. Extracts can be found on the www.collectionscanada.ca website.

Anonymous account by NRP of the 12th Glosters taken from *'Bristol's Own at Home and Abroad'*, part of a booklet issued by *The Western Daily Press*.

The writings of Lt WG Fisher are reproduced from:
Chapman, Guy (Ed.), *Vain Glory*, Cassell, London, 1937

The writings of George McChlery, Lt Gardner and John Allden are reproduced from:
Fletcher, David (Ed.), *Tanks and Trenches*, Alan Sutton, Stroud, 1994

The following quotes were taken from *The Great War …. I Was There! – Undying Memories of 1914-1918*, edited by Sir John Hammerton and published by The Amalgamated Press, 1939. Some derived from works previously published. Where known, these are listed. The writings of HV Drinkwater were specially commissioned for *'The Great War…I Was There!'* Others used from this publication are:

Bill, CA, *The 15th Battalion Royal Warwickshire Regiment in the Great War*, Cornish Brothers, Birmingham, 1932
Burrage, AM, *War is War' by EX-PRIVATE X (pseudonym)*, Gollancz, London, 1930
Lambert, Arthur, *Over the Top – A PBI in the HAC*, John Long, London, 1930
Lucy, John F., *There's a Devil in the Drum*, Faber and Faber, London, 1938
Maze, Paul Lucien, *A Frenchman in Khaki*, Heinemann, London, 1934
Wade, Aubrey, *The War of the Guns*, Batsford, London, 1936

Other written sources:
Binding, Rudolph – *A Fatalist at War*, Allan and Unwin, London, 1929
Bird, Will R. – *Ghosts Have Warm Hands*, Clark, Irwin & Company, Toronto, 1968
Bird, Will R. – *Thirteen Years After*, Maclean Publishing Company, Toronto, 1932
Blunden, Edmund – *Undertones of War*, Cobden-Sanderson, London, 1929
Buckley, Francis – *Q6A and Other Places*, Spottiswoode, Ballantyne & Co. Ltd, London, 1920
Campbell, PJ – *In the Cannon's Mouth*, Hamish Hamilton, London, 1979
Chapman, Guy – *A Passionate Prodigality*, Ivor Nicholson and Watson, London, 1933
Floyd, Thomas Hope – *At Ypres With Best-Dunkley*, John Lane, London, 1920
Ingram, NM – *Anzac Diary: A Nonentity in Khaki*, Treharne Publishers, Christchurch, n.d.
Jones, Paul – *War Letters of a Public-School Boy*, Cassell & Company Ltd, London, 1918
Scott, Canon FG – *The Great War As I Saw It*, F.D. Goodchild, Toronto, 1922

Picture Credits

All photographs with a Q (British official), E (Australian) or CO (Canadian) prefix are copyright the Imperial War Museum. Plans and drawings are from Royal Engineer manuals' journals and publications in the author's collection.

AC: Author's Collection
CWGC: Commonwealth War Graves Commission
HM: Bayerisches Haupstaatsarchiv, Munich
HS: Haupstaatsarchiv, Stuttgart
JV: Johan Vandewalle
LS: Luc Salomez
MZ: Malte Znaniecki
NA: National Archives (Formerly Public Record Office)
PC: Private collection
REM: Royal Engineers Museum or Library
RH: Royal Hampshire Regiment Museum
RRW: Regimental Museum of Royal Welsh

Page 2 – IWM CO 2157
13 – E(Aus)1111
14 – LS
22 above – HS, M704-178-1, below – HS, M705/1-13
23 above – HS, M705/1 68, right – IWM Q70235
24 above – AC
25 above – HS, Rundbild 44; below – AC; above right – Q2951
26 above – HS M706 Mappe 15 501; right – AC
29, above – Q5788
31, left – Q60708, below – HS, M705/1 Bd.2a 178
32, above – MZ; below – Q60737
33, above – Q60693
34/35, below – RE
36, below – RE
37, right – Q 49104
38, above – RE
41, left – Q55560, below – IWM
42, JV
43, MZ
44/45, IWM
49, left – HM, 17912, below, IWM
50/51 – HM, Rundbild from Doktor Haus, Wytschaete

52 above – RRW 1988.82, below – RH M1494, right – PC
54/55 above – HM, Rundbild IV/1, right – HS, M 705/1 Bd.1
56 above – RH M1488
57 (clockwise from bottom left) – Peter Doyle, CO 282, HU 72865, Q 49387, CO 272, CO 713, AC.
58, top – HM, BS-N13-68, above – HS, M705/1 Bd.1
60 inset – AC
62 above – HM, BSN 10/1 365, below left – PC
63 below – RE
64 above – PC, below – JV
65 above – HM, BSN 63/4A 111
67 top – CWGC 21580(17), above – AC
71 above – HS, M 705/1 Bd.2, left – JV, right Q23642
72 background – IWM
73 above – HS, M 705/1 Bd.1, left – HS, M 705/1 Bd.3
76 right and left – RE, below – Q 60479
80 above – Q45545
81 left – HS, M704 Bd.166 IV
82 below – HM, Rundbild Hohe 60
85 left and right – HS, M 704 166 V
86 right – AC, below – HM, Rundbild von Kapelle Wytschaete
88 above – HM, Rundbild Box II/17
89 left – E(Aus)632
90/91 – IWM
92/93 insets – JV
97 above – Q 2295
98 above – JV, right – E(Aus)1269
100 inset – Q 3092
101 above – HS, M201-125
103 below – Q 6221
106 above – IWM, right – HM, BSN 10/2 620
110/111 above – HM, Rundbild M706 Mappe 14 – 481
113 left and below – HM, BSN 63/4A 87 and 88
115 left and below – IWM
116 below – IWM
120 above left – E(Aus)2093, above right Q 2894
121 above – Q 45947
123 to 126 – IWM, inset – AC
127 left – IWM, above – NA, WO 157-532
129 above – E(Aus)1144, below – MZ,

right – IWM
130 background – Q 5706, below left – Q 2907, below – Q 6010
132 above – Q 8447, right Q 34088, Q34091, Q4808
134 below – AC
136 right – HM, III K11 76r, 17650
138/139 – HS, M706 Mappe 15 – 486
140 above – IWM, right – Q 1426
142 right – CO 995, below – RRW, 1988.82 – MBA 2964
144 above – LS
146/147 above – IWM panorama, left – AC
150 above – Q 2738
152 above – IWM
153 below – Q 5988
154 above – IWM, right – JV
157 above – JV, below – IWM
158/159 – IWM, inset – CO 995
160 below – IWM and AC
162 below – AC
163 above – JV
164/165 above and below – IWM
167 above – LS
170 above – IWM, below – AC
174/175 above – IWM, below – AC
176 right – AC, below – E(Aus)1411
178/179 – IWM
180 above – PC
182 right – Q 1338
184 above – RRW, 1988.82 MBA 2963
185 below – Q 2631
186 above – Q 5730
188 below – Q 2639
190 above – Q 3007
191 below – IWM
192 full page – Q 8428
194 above right – AC
197 right – HS, M704 Nr 135a, below – E(Aus) 4677
199 right – Q 5889, left – AC
200 above – Q 5859
201 above – RE, right – RRW, 1988.82 MBA 2961
206 left – HS, M704 Nr 135a
207 full page plus top inset – HS, M704 Nr 135a, inset below – MZ
211 above – HS, M704 166-1

212 above – IWM
213 below – HM, 7420
214 below – HS 06/5/17
216 above – AC, right – E(Aus)1141
218 right – E(Aus)968, inset – Q 7914, below – HS, M 704 Nr 135a
220 right – HS, M 704 Nr 135a
225 above – Courtesy of Sherwood Foresters Museum
228 right – E(Aus)661
231 above – Q 7818, left – Q 23775
232/233 – HS, M706 M14 Nr 493/4
234 above – E(Aus) 871
235 below left – E(Aus) 813, below – AC
236 above – E(Aus) 846
238 below – E(Aus) 922
239 inset – MZ
241 above – Q 3086, left – AC
243 above – Q 5723
244 above – IWM, right – E(Aus) 1919
246 RE Museum
249 Q 2861, inset – CO 3758
251 above – E(Aus) 2327
253 left – Q 11684, below – IWM and AC
255 left – E(Aus)2321, right – RE, below left – E(Aus)714
256 above – IWM, right – Q 5968, inset – Q 5970
259 above – AC
260/261 above – IWM
262 above – HS, M 704 Nr 135a, right – Q 2627
264 above – HM, 17341
267 left – E(Aus)1127, below – E(Aus)858
269 left – E(Aus)818
271 left and below – JV
272 background – AC
273 below – E(Aus)689, bottom – E(Aus)4516
274 above – MZ, right – HS, M 704 Nr 135a
276/277 – AC
278 above – E(Aus)4653, below – AC
280 left – AC, below – Q 11657
281 top – Q 10491, above – Q 3005, right – HS, M704 XIII 135i
283 above – E(Aus)916, left – E(Aus)1249, right – Q 2990
284 above – E(Aus) 825, right – LS, inset – LS
286 – IWM and AC
287 right – Q 3028

Index

Page numbers in *italic* denote an illustration.